Cybercrime and Digital Forensics

The emergence of the World Wide Web, smartphones, and computer-mediated communications profoundly affect the way in which people interact online and offline. Individuals who engage in socially unacceptable or outright criminal acts increasingly utilize technology to connect with one another in ways that are not otherwise possible in the real world due to shame, social stigma, or risk of detection. As a consequence, there are now myriad opportunities for wrongdoing and abuse through technology.

This book offers a comprehensive and integrative introduction to cybercrime. It is the first to connect the disparate literature on the various types of cybercrime, the investigation and detection of cybercrime and the role of digital information, and the wider role of technology as a facilitator for social relationships between deviants and criminals. It includes coverage of:

- key theoretical and methodological perspectives;
- computer hacking and digital piracy;
- economic crime and online fraud;
- pornography and online sex crime;
- cyberbullying and cyberstalking;
- cyberterrorism and extremism;
- digital forensic investigation and its legal context;
- cybercrime policy.

This book includes lively and engaging features, such as discussion questions, boxed examples of unique events and key figures in offending, quotes from interviews with active offenders, and a full glossary of terms. It is supplemented by a companion website that includes further exercises for students and resources for instructors. This text is essential reading for courses on cybercrime, cyberdeviancy, digital forensics, cybercrime investigation, and the sociology of technology.

Thomas J. Holt is an Associate Professor in the School of Criminal Justice at Michigan State University who received his Ph.D. in criminology and criminal justice from the University of Missouri-St. Louis in 2005. His work has been published in various journals including *Crime & Delinquency*, *Deviant Behavior*, *Journal of Criminal Justice*, and *Youth & Society*.

Adam M. Bossler is an Associate Professor of Criminal Justice and Criminology at Georgia Southern University. He earned his doctorate in criminology and criminal justice from the University of Missouri-St. Louis. His most recent publications can be found in *Crime & Delinquency*, *Youth & Society*, *Policing*, and *Journal of Criminal Justice*.

Kathryn C. Seigfried-Spellar is an Assistant Professor in the Department of Criminal Justice at The University of Alabama. She received her Ph.D. in cyberforensics from Purdue University in 2011. Her publications focus on personality characteristics associated with computer deviance and digital forensic investigations involving child pornography.

"There is little doubt that digital technology will continue its dramatic growth for years to come. These developments will have profound effects on social relations, often for the better. Unfortunately, digital technology will also present unprecedented opportunities for criminal exploitation. Individuals, governments, and businesses will be challenged as a result. *Cybercrime and Digital Forensics* is the most thorough and comprehensive introduction to cybercrime and its control that I have come across to date. It is, without doubt, the best of its kind. Exceptionally readable and richly documented, this contribution by Holt, Bossler, and Seigfried-Spellar is an ideal undergraduate text for courses on cybercrime and its control. Not only will it engage students, but the book's broad coverage also makes it a valuable resource for scholars and lay readers."

Peter Grabosky, Professor Emeritus, Australian National University, Australia

"The authors have produced an excellent book in *Cybercrime and Digital Forensics* – clear, accessible, up to date, and thorough in its coverage of all issues related to cybercrime and its investigation. This is an invaluable resource for all students and instructors in criminology and criminal justice who are interested in cybercrime."

Majid Yar, Professor of Sociology, University of Hull, UK

"The initial chapters of the book do an excellent job of establishing the conceptual and empirical foundation of the analysis presented in later chapters: they clearly and comprehensively explain the interaction between cybercrime and technology, which is an essential foundation for understanding the issues the book goes on to address; they also outline the nature and origins of hackers and hacking and the law that applies to such activity, as well as providing a similar, detailed introduction into other areas of cybercrime. The book is unusual, and unusually valuable, in that it does not just confine its focus to cybercrime, but also addresses cyberterrorism and cyberwarfare, an essential element given that it can be difficult to distinguish crime, war, and terrorism in cyberspace. And, finally, the final chapters provide an insightful, detailed description, and analysis of the conceptual, legal, and technical issues involved in the use of digital forensics in investigating any or all of the three types of cyberthreats."

Susan Brenner, Professor and Samuel A. McCray Chair in Law, University of Dayton, USA

"This book occupies an important position in the field by helping readers to understand the nuances of cybercrime and digital forensics. I highly recommend this book to both students and those experienced in cybercrime and digital forensics."

George E. Higgins, Ph.D., Professor, Department of Justice Administration, University of Louisville, USA

Cybercrime and Digital Forensics

An introduction

Thomas J. Holt, Adam M. Bossler, and Kathryn C. Seigfried-Spellar

Routledge
Taylor & Francis Group

LONDON AND NEW YORK

First published 2015
by Routledge
2 Park Square, Milton Park, Abingdon, Oxon OX14 4RN

and by Routledge
711 Third Avenue, New York, NY 10017

Routledge is an imprint of the Taylor & Francis Group, an informa business

British Library Cataloguing in Publication Data
A catalogue record for this book is available from the British Library

Library of Congress Cataloguing in Publication data
Holt, Thomas J.
  Cybercrime and digital forensics: an introduction / Thomas J. Holt,
  Adam M. Bossler, Kathryn C. Seigfried-Spellar.
    pages cm
  1. Computer crimes. 2. Forensic sciences. I. Bossler, Adam M.
  II. Seigfried-Spellar, Kathryn C. III. Title.
  HV6773.H648 2015
  363.25'968–dc23
  2014028368

ISBN: 978-1-138-02129-7 (hbk)
ISBN: 978-1-138-02130-3 (pbk)
ISBN: 978-1-315-77787-0 (ebk)

Typeset in Sabon
by Out of House Publishing

Thomas J. Holt
This book is dedicated to my wife Karen and our beautiful
daughter, Scarlett.

Adam M. Bossler
For my amazing wife Jordan and our two wonderful children Kate
and Bennett.

Kathryn C. Seigfried-Spellar
I would like to dedicate this book to Dr. Marcus K. Rogers, my
mentor and friend, for his continued support and encouragement
at every stage of my career.

Contents

Figures

Text Boxes

Images

Acknowledgments

There are a number of people who we must thank for their assistance in making this work possible. First and foremost, we would like to thank Tom Sutton, Heidi Lee, and the production staff at Routledge for their dedication to this book. Their assistance and oversight at all stages of the process were greatly appreciated. Second, we would like to thank the various anonymous reviewers who provided feedback on our work. Their comments and suggestions were much appreciated and improved the quality of this text. Third, we would like to thank Lt Dennis McMillian, of the University of Alabama Police Department, and Mr Eric Katz, Instructor and Law Enforcement Coordinator at Purdue University's Cyber Forensics Laboratory, for helping us procure screenshots and images of a variety of digital forensics software and tools. Fourth and finally, we would like to thank our families for their understanding and support during the hours it took to develop this book.

chapter 1

Technology and cybercrime

Chapter goals

- Explain how technology has affected human behavior
- Identify the difference between digital natives and digital immigrants
- Discuss the three ways that technology can be abused by individuals
- Recognize a subculture and their role in offending behaviors
- Identify the differences between cyberdeviance, cybercrime, and cyberterror
- Understand how computers and technology produce digital evidence and its value in criminal investigation
- Explain the factors that make cybercrimes attractive to certain people
- Explore the various forms of cybercrime that occur across the world

Introduction

The Internet, computers, and mobile technologies have dramatically reshaped modern society. Though it is difficult to comprehend, less than two decades ago most individuals did not own a cell phone and personal computers were still somewhat expensive pieces of equipment. Individuals could not text, and email was uncommon. Internet connectivity was possible through dial-up modems or Ethernet cabling, and people paid by the hour for access to the web. Video game systems used 16-bit graphics and did not connect to other devices. Global Positioning Systems (GPS) were largely used in military applications only.

Today, most of the world now depends on computers, the Internet, and cellular technology. Individuals now own laptops that are connected via Wi-Fi, cell phones that may also connect to the Internet, and one or more video game systems that may be networked. In addition, people have multiple email accounts for personal and business use, as well as social networking profiles in multiple platforms. Cell phones have become a pre-ferred method of communication for most people, especially text messages. In fact, individuals under the age of 20 regularly send more texts than any other age group, and prefer to send texts rather than make phone calls (Zickuhr, 2011). Individuals also frequently purchase goods online and are increasingly using e-readers for books and newspapers rather than trad-itional print media.

It is amazing to consider that the world and human behavior have changed so quickly through the use of technology. In fact, there are now 2.1 billion Internet users worldwide, and 245 million of those individuals reside within the US (Central Intelligence Agency, 2011). The United States has the second largest population of Internet users worldwide behind China. By contrast, the United Kingdom had 36 million Internet users as of 2013 (Office for National Statistics, 2013).

The proliferation of technology has led to distinct changes in how individ-uals engage with the world around them. People now shop, communicate, and share information in digital formats, which was previously impossible. Additional changes in behavior are likely to continue in the face of techno-logical innovations as they are developed and implemented. In fact, the soci-ologist Howard Odum referred to this process as **technicways**, recognizing the ways that behavior patterns change in response to, or as consequence of, technological innovations (Odum, 1937; Parker, 1943; Vance, 1972). From Odum's perspective, technicways replace existing behavior patterns and force institutional changes in society (Vance, 1972). For instance, if an individual 30 years ago wanted to communicate with other people, he/she might call them, see them in person if possible, or more likely send a letter through postal mail. Now, however, that person would send a text, write an email, instant message, or poke them through Facebook rather than write a letter through "snail mail."

The impacts of technicways are evident across all demographic groups in modern society. For instance, in 2011, 71 percent of Americans used video sharing sites, particularly African American and Hispanic users, which many attribute to the increased access to broadband Internet connectivity and increased use of smartphones and mobile devices (Moore, 2011). In the UK, 42 percent of households in 2013 had fiber optic or cable broadband Internet connections, meaning that high-speed connectivity is somewhat common (Office for National Statistics, 2013). In 2011, over 80 percent of adults in the US owned a cell phone, and approximately one-third of those adults owned a smartphone that can be used to check their email or connect

technology and cybercrime

to the Internet (Smith, 2011); 61 percent of individuals in the UK in 2013 owned a smartphone that could connect to the Internet (Office for National Statistics, 2013).

In much the same way, technology has had a massive impact on youth populations who have never experienced life without the Internet and **computer-mediated communications (CMCs)** like email and texting. Today, youth in the US acquire their first cell phones when they are between the ages of 12 and 13 (Lenhart, 2010). In addition, a recent study using a nationally representative sample of US youth suggested that 75 percent of youth own either a laptop or desktop computer, and 15 percent own both devices (Lenhart, Madden, and Hitlin, 2005). Likewise, 93 percent of American youths between the ages of 12 and 17 use the Internet, meaning that almost *all* youth have some presence on the Internet. Furthermore, not only do youth have a presence, it is a frequent presence – 88 percent of children who go online do so at least once a week (Lenhart and Madden, 2007). A similar national study found that 49 percent of children are online for five to seven days each week on average (Wolak, Mitchell, and Finkelhor, 2006).

> **For more information on statistics of social media and technology use, go online to: 1)** www.pewinternet.org/ **and 2)** www.huffingtonpost.com/april-rudin/life-on-a-social-media-is_b_4600429.html

Technology has not simply shifted the behaviors of youth, but has actually shaped and molded their behavior and worldview from the start. Most people born in the mid to late 1980s have never lived without computers, the Internet, or cell phones. As a consequence, they do not know a world without these devices and what life was like without these resources. Thus, Prensky (2001) argued that these youth are **digital natives,** in that they were brought into a world that was already digital, spend large amounts of time in digital environments, and utilize technological resources in their day-to-day lives. For instance, individuals between the ages of 18 and 34 now own the most technological resources and are among the heaviest Internet users in the US (Lenhart, Purcell, Smith, and Zickuhr, 2010). In fact, 87 percent of US teens use the Internet, relative to 66 percent of adults (Zickuhr, 2011). This roughly translates to 18 million youth online every day and using CMCs in various ways, including 89 percent of youths who send or read email while online, and 81 percent who play online games (Lenhart *et al.*, 2010). Similarly, 94 percent of individuals between the ages of 16 and 24 in the UK use a mobile phone (Office for National Statistics, 2013). In addition, individuals between the ages of 18 and 34 comprise 49 percent of the entire population of Facebook users in the United States (Socialbakers, 2011).

By contrast, **digital immigrants** are those who were born before the creation of the Internet and digital technologies (Prenksy, 2001). These individuals quite often need to adapt to the digital environment, which changes much more rapidly than they may be prepared for otherwise. This is especially true for many older individuals who were born decades before the creation and advent of these technologies. As a consequence, they may be less willing to immediately adopt these resources or utilize them in diverse ways. For instance, only 45 percent of adults in the US over the age of 65 own either a laptop or desktop (Zickuhr, 2011). In addition, some resources may be more difficult for digital immigrants to understand, such as Facebook, which requires users to regularly talk about themselves and their interests and give up some degree of privacy in order to communicate with others. In fact, people aged 55 and older constitute only 13 percent of the entire population of Facebook users in the US (Socialbakers, 2011). In the US, individuals aged 45 and older receive an average of no more than 14 texts per day, while those aged 18–24 receive an average of 109.5 messages daily (Zickuhr, 2011). Similarly, only 17 percent of individuals aged 65 or older use a mobile phone in the UK (Office for National Statistics, 2013). Thus, digital immigrants have a much different pattern of adoption and use of technologies relative to digital natives.

The proliferation of technology in modern society has had a massive impact on human behavior. The world is being restructured around the use of CMCs, affecting the way that we interact with governments, businesses, and one another. In addition, technology use is also creating a divide between generations based on the way individuals use technology in their day-to-day lives. In turn, individuals are adapting their behavior in ways that subvert the original beneficial design and application of computers and the Internet.

Technology as a landscape for crime

The continuing evolution of human behavior as a result of technological innovations has created unparalleled opportunities for crime and misuse. Over the last three decades, there has been a substantive increase in the use of technology by street criminals and novel applications of technology to create new forms of crime that did not previously exist. The World Wide Web and the Internet also provide a venue for individuals who engage in crime and deviance to communicate and share information, which is not otherwise possible in the real world. As a result, it is vital that we begin to understand how these changes are occurring, and what this means for offending in the twenty-first century. There are three key ways that computer and cellular technologies may be abused or subverted by offenders:

(1) as a medium for communication and the development of subcultures online;
(2) as a mechanism to target sensitive resources and engage in crime and deviance;
(3) as an incidental device to facilitate the offense and provide evidence of criminal activity both online and offline.

Technology as a communications medium

The Internet, telephony, and digital media can be used as a means for communication between individuals in a rapid and decentralized fashion across the globe. Computers, cell phones, and technological equipment can be obtained at minimal cost and used with a high degree of anonymity. For instance, major retailers and convenience stores sell phones that can be used without a contract through a carrier like Sprint or Verizon. The ability to use the phone depends on the number of minutes purchased and it can be disposed of after use.

In turn, criminals can use these devices to connect with others and share information that may be of interest. For example, the customers of prostitutes use web forums and chatrooms to discuss where sex workers are located, services provided, pricing, and the police presence in a given area (Holt and Blevins, 2007; Holt, Blevins, and Kuhns, 2008; Sharpe and Earle, 2003). This exchange of first-hand information is difficult to conduct in the real world, as there are no outward signs to otherwise suggest that someone is interested in or has visited a prostitute. In addition, there is a high degree of social stigma and shame surrounding paying for sex, so it is unlikely that someone would admit this behavior to another person in public (McKeganey and Barnard, 1996; O'Connell Davidson, 1998). The faceless, anonymous nature of the Internet, however, allows people to talk about such actions with little risk of harm or reprisal.

The distributed nature of the Internet and CMCs enable individuals to connect to other people and groups that share similar likes, dislikes, behaviors, opinions, and values. As a result, technology facilitates the creation of subcultures between individuals based on common behaviors and ideals regardless of geographic or social isolation. From a sociological and criminological perspective, **subcultures** are groups that have their own values, norms, traditions, and rituals which set them apart from the dominant culture (Kornblum, 1997; Brake, 1980).

Participants in subcultures generate their own codes of conduct to structure the ways they interact with other members of the subculture and different groups in society (Foster, 1990). In addition, membership in a subculture influences individual behavior by providing beliefs, goals, and values that approve of and justify activity (Herbert, 1998). For instance, a subculture may emphasize the development of skills and abilities that may find less value in the general culture, like an ability to use multiple programming languages and manipulate hardware and software among computer hackers (Holt, 2007; Jordan and Taylor, 1998; Taylor, 1999). Members of a subculture also have their own argot or slang to communicate with others and protect their discussions from outsiders (Maurer, 1981). The use of this language can serve as a practical demonstration of membership in any subculture. Thus, subcultures provide members with a way to gauge their reputation, status, and adherence to the values and beliefs of the group.

There are myriad subcultures in modern society, many involving both online and offline experiences. However, not all subcultures are deviant, and you can also be a member of several subcultures at once. For instance, you may belong to a subculture of sports team fans (whether football, basketball, or any athletics) if you: (1) enjoy watching their games, (2) know the statistics for your favorite players, (3) know the historic events in your team's previous seasons, and (4) you debate others over who may be the best players in certain positions. Similar subcultures exist for gardening, fashion, cars, movies, and other behaviors. Finding others who share your interests can be beneficial as it allows for social connectivity and a way to channel your interests in positive ways.

> **For more on the changing nature of subcultures since the advent of the web, go online to:** www.theguardian.com/culture/2014/mar/20/youth-subcultures-where-have-they-gone

In much the same way, subcultures can emerge on and offline for those with an interest in certain forms of crime and deviance (Quinn and Forsyth, 2005). Technology allows individuals to connect to others without fear of reprisal or social rejection, and even enables individuals who are curious about a behavior or activity to learn more in an online environment without fear of detection (Blevins and Holt, 2009; Holt, 2007; Quinn & Forsyth, 2005). New technologies also enable the formation of and participation in multiple subcultures with greater ease than is otherwise possible offline. In fact, individuals can readily communicate subcultural knowledge through email and other CMCs, such as techniques of offending that may reduce their risk of detection from victims and law enforcement (Holt *et al.*, 2008; Holt and Copes, 2010). Because of the prominence of technology as a means to communicate with others, this book will focus extensively on the role of online subcultures to facilitate crime and deviance in virtual and real-world environments.

For more info on the current state of online subcultures, go online to: http://fusion.net/culture/entertainment/story/subcultures-strong-online-presence-7735

Technology as a target of or means to engage in crime

The second way that technology can be misused is much more insidious – as a resource for individuals to attack and to cause harm to individuals, businesses, and governments both online and offline. Many devices in our daily lives have the capability to connect to the Internet, from mp3 players to desktop computers. These technologies contain sensitive bits of information, ranging from our shopping habits to usernames and passwords for bank and email accounts. Since these devices can communicate with one another, individuals can potentially gain access to this information through various methods of computer hacking (see Chapter 2 for more detail).

While hacking is often thought to involve highly skilled individuals with a significant understanding of technology, the simple act of guessing someone's email or computer password could be defined as a hack (Bossler and Burruss, 2011; Skinner and Fream, 1997). Gaining unauthorized access to personal information online is often key to definitions of hacking, as an individual is attempting to gain entry into protected systems or data (see Schell and Dodge, 2002; Wall, 2001). In turn, that information, such as who a person talks to or which financial institution they choose for banking purposes, can be used to cause additional harm. In fact, research on college students suggests that between 10 and 25 percent of undergraduates have tried to guess someone else's password (Holt, Burruss, and Bossler 2010; Rogers, Smoak, and Liu, 2006; Skinner and Fream, 1997). Thus, the information that can be assembled about our activities online can be compromised and used by others to cause financial or emotional harm.

For more information on creating passwords, go online to: http://passwordsgenerator.net/

Similarly, some hackers target websites and resources in order to cause harm or express a political or ideological message. Often, the hacker and activist community use **web defacement** in order to spread a message and cause harm at the same time (Brenner, 2008; Denning, 2001, 2011; Kilger, 2011). Web defacements are an act of online vandalism wherein an individual replaces the existing HTML code for a web page with an image and message that they create. For example, a person might try to deface the website for the White House (www.whitehouse.gov) and replace the content with a message that they want others to see. Although this is an inconvenience and embarrassment to the site owner, it may be more malicious if the defacer chooses to delete the original content entirely.

Defacements have become a regular tool for politically motivated hackers and actors to express their opinions, and have been used around many hot-button social events. For instance, the Turkish hacker community began a widespread campaign of web defacements after the publication of a cartoon featuring an image of the prophet Mohammed with a bomb in his turban (Holt, 2009; Ward, 2006). Many Muslims were deeply offended by this image, and Turkish hackers began to deface websites owned by the Danish newspaper that published the cartoon, along with any other site that reposted the image. The defacements were conducted in support of the Islamic religion and to express outrage over the way their faith was being portrayed in the popular media (Holt, 2009; Ward, 2006). Thus, motivated actors who want to cause harm or express an opinion may view various resources online as a target.

> For more on web defacements and images of such content, go online to: www.zone-h.org

Defining computer misuse and abuse

Since technology can be used both as a communications medium and target for attacks against digital targets and infrastructure, it is vital to delineate what constitutes the abuse and misuse of technology. For instance, the term **deviance** is used to refer to a behavior that may not be illegal, though it is outside of the formal and informal norms or beliefs of the prevailing culture. There are many forms of deviance, depending on societal norms and societal contexts. For instance, texting and using Facebook while in class may not be illegal, but it is disruptive and generally frowned upon by faculty and administrators. The same is true in movie theaters and other public settings. Therefore, texting and using Facebook could be viewed as deviant in the context of certain situations and locations, but may not be illegal otherwise. The fact that this activity is engendered by technology may allow it to be referred to as **cyberdeviance**.

A more pertinent example of cyberdeviance is evident in the creation and use of pornography. The Internet has made it exceedingly easy for individuals to view pornographic images and videos, as well as make these materials through the use of webcams, cell phone cameras, and digital photography. It is legal for anyone over the age of 18 to either access pornographic images or star in these films and media. If the larger community shares the view that pornography is morally wrong, then viewing these materials may be considered deviant in that area. Therefore, it is not illegal to engage in this activity; rather it simply violates local norms and belief systems, making it a deviant behavior.

Activities that violate codified legal statutes move from deviance to criminal acts. In the context of pornography, if an individual is under the age of 18 in the US, they are not legally allowed to either create or view pornographic images. Therefore, such an act is considered a **crime** because it carries legal sanctions. The criminal statutes in the United States at both the state and federal level recognize a variety of offenses in the real world. The rapid adoption and use of technology in order to facilitate criminal activity, however, have led to the creation of several terms in order to properly classify these behaviors. Specifically, cybercrime and computer crime emerged a few decades ago to refer to the unique way that technology is used to facilitate criminal activity. **Cybercrime** refers to crimes "in which the perpetrator uses special knowledge of cyberspace," while **computer crimes** occur because "the perpetrator uses special knowledge about computer technology" (Furnell, 2002: 21; Wall, 2001). In the early days of computing, the difference between these terms was useful to clarify how technology was incorporated into the offense. The fact that almost every computer is now connected to the Internet in some way has diminished the need to segment these two acts (Wall, 2007). In addition, they have become nearly synonymous in both academic circles and popular media. As a result, this book will use the term "cybercrime" due to the range of crimes that can occur through the use of online environments and the massive number of computers and mobile devices that are connected to the Internet.

The borderless nature of the Internet complicates the criminal justice response to crime and deviance since the ways that nations define an act do not generally hinder individuals from accessing content. Using the example of pornography, it is legal to produce and access this content in the United States and most other parts of the globe. Islamic majority nations like Iran and Saudi Arabia, however, have banned and made it illegal to access pornography due to their religious beliefs (Wall, 2001, 2007). Other countries like Sweden, however, place minimal restrictions on the production of pornographic content, including images of animals or "bestiality." Although it is illegal to create or view this content in the United States and most other nations, individuals can access bestiality, violent, or unusual pornographic material from across the globe, regardless of their nation's laws, due to the connectivity afforded by the Internet (Brenner, 2008; Wall, 2007). Thus, it is difficult to restrict or enforce local laws on individual conduct because of the ability to access content globally.

The intersection of cybercrime and cyberdeviance is also related to the emerging problem of **cyberterrorism** (see Figure 1.1 for detail). This term emerged in the mid-1990s as technology began to play an increasingly significant role in all aspects of society (Denning, 2001; Britz, 2010). There is no single accepted definition for cyberterrorism, though many recognize

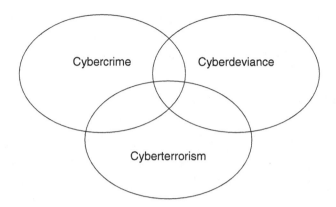

Figure 1.1 Venn diagram of cybercrime, cyberterrorism, and cyberdeviance

this behavior as the use of digital technology or computer mediated communications to cause harm and force social change based on ideological or political beliefs (Brenner, 2008; Britz, 2010). Though there are few known incidents of cyberterrorism that have occurred over the last two decades, the ubiquity of technology could allow extremist groups like Al Qaeda to target military systems containing sensitive information, financial service systems that engender commerce, power grids, switching stations, and other critical infrastructure necessary to maintain basic services. Criminals may also attack these targets using similar tactics, making it difficult to separate acts of cyberterror from cybercrime (Brenner, 2008).

For more information on the technologies supporting power grids, go online to: www.tofinosecurity.com/blog/scada-cyber-security-international-issue

In order to classify these phenomena, it is necessary to consider both the motive of the attacker and the scope of harm caused. For instance, criminal acts often target single individuals and may be motivated by economic or other objectives, whereas terrorist attacks are often driven by a political motive and are designed to not only hurt or kill innocents but also to strike fear into the larger population (Brenner, 2008; Britz, 2010). In addition, the communications capability afforded by the Internet creates an interesting intersection between cyberdeviance and cyberterror. For example, members of extremist and hate groups increasingly depend on web forums and blogs to post their views to audiences across the globe. The laws of a given country may not allow such language, as in Germany where it is illegal to post Nazi-related content (Wall, 2001). In the United States, though, such speech is protected under the First Amendment of the Constitution; therefore, the

technology and cybercrime

act of using online forums to express an opinion largely unsupported by society is deviant, rather than illegal, behavior. Thus, cybercrime, terror, and deviance are all interrelated and share common elements due to the nature of online environments.

What makes cybercrime and deviance attractive?

The rise of cyberdeviance, cybercrime, and cyberterror has led many to question why some people choose to engage in wrongdoing in virtual environments. There are several unique factors that may account for offending online, most especially the availability of technology in the modern world. First and foremost, the ubiquity of technology makes it easy for individuals to gain access to the tools necessary to offend with relative ease. The prices of laptop and desktop computers have dropped substantially over the last decade, making it easy to acquire this equipment. For instance, the price of laptop PCs decreased from an average of $1,640 in 2001 to $1,000 in 2005 (Associated Press, 2005). The price has continued to drop, and now these devices compete with even smaller portable computers, like the iPad and smartphones, that can connect to the Internet through cellular technology. As a result, offenders can readily acquire and access information from anywhere through these resources. If a person cannot afford to buy these devices on their own, they can always use computers in Internet cafes and public libraries for free or a small cost. Thus, there are minimal barriers to computer technology globally.

In addition, there is a wide range of cybercrimes that can be performed dependent upon the individual's technical skill. Some forms of cybercrime require a good deal of skill and proficiency, though simple offenses can be performed with minimal investment on the part of the offender. For instance, anyone can download pirated music or movies from online environments or post an ad for sexual encounters on craigslist or another website. Technology also acts as a force multiplier in that computers and CMCs allow a single person to engage in crimes that otherwise involve multiple people or complex schemes in order to target victims (Brenner, 2008; Taylor, Fritsch, Liederbach, and Holt, 2010). For instance, if a criminal attempted to rob a person in the real world, they must often target single individuals due to the difficulty in intimidating and managing groups of people. The offender must also try to determine in advance if the individual he is attempting to rob has money, jewelry, or other goods that are of value.

In online environments, offenders can target thousands of victims at a time, worldwide, within seconds. For example, individuals regularly send out unsolicited emails, called **spam**, to thousands of victims using addresses harvested from information posted on public websites (Holt and Graves, 2007; King and Thomas, 2009; Wall, 2004). For instance, public universities often post the addresses of professors, faculty, and staff on their websites. In turn, individuals can copy and collate these addresses into lists and use them to send a variety of different spam messages. In fact, one of the most common forms of spam message appears to originate in part from Nigeria, where the sender claims to be foreign royalty, bankers, or attorneys who need assistance in moving large sums of money (Holt and Graves 2007; King and Thomas, 2009; Wall, 2004). They request information from the email recipients like names, addresses, phone numbers, and bank account details so that they can reuse the information to commit identity theft or bank fraud. Since few people fall for this sort of scheme, sending out thousands of messages increases the likelihood that a victim may respond. Thus, fraudsters increase the likelihood of success by targeting thousands of victims at once.

> **For more information on the rate of spam distribution, go online to:** www.zdnet.com/worldwide-spam-rate-falls-2-5-percent-but-new-tactics-emerge-7000025517/

The risk of detection from law enforcement is much lower in online environments than in the real world. Offenders in the real world must take several steps to reduce the likelihood that their actual identity can be determined. For example, robbers may wear a mask or baggy clothing to conceal their face and build (Miller, 1998; Wright and Decker, 1997). They may also try to disguise their voice by speaking in a higher or lower tone. Victims may be able to recall information about the offender and video cameras may capture the incident on film, making it harder to hide the offense from police.

These issues are largely absent in online environments, as it is easier for offenders to conceal their real identity (Wall, 2001). The faceless nature of the Internet makes it easy for individuals to hide their gender, age, or race in various ways. A profile in a social networking site like Facebook or email account can be created using false information through Google, Yahoo, or Hotmail. This false account can be used to send threatening or harassing messages to others to help conceal their true identity (Bocij, 2004). Similarly, various technological resources are designed to hide a person's location from others. For example, **proxy servers** can be used to hide a computer's location by acting as an intermediary between a computer and the servers and systems it connects to through the Internet. If, for instance, we try to access Google from a PC using a proxy, the command will be routed through a service that will make the request on our behalf and send the information back to us. In turn, the servers at Google will not register our computer as the one making the request, but rather associate it with the proxy server. Some offenders are even able to route their web and email traffic through other people's computers in order to minimize the likelihood that they are caught (see Chapter 3 for more detail).

For more on proxy servers, go online to: 1) www.publicproxyservers. **com, and 2)** http://proxy4free.com

Cybercrimes are also attractive for some actors based on the laws of their nation. Since individuals can target victims across the world, local laws make a significant difference to whom and what an offender targets. Many industrialized nations have laws against cybercrimes, increasing the risk of prosecution and investigation for offenders if caught (Brenner, 2008). Therefore, attacking people within that country may increase the likelihood of being prosecuted. If, however, a country does not allow their citizens to be extradited to another country to face prosecution for crimes, then the actor cannot be successfully investigated (Brenner, 2008). For instance, there is no treaty allowing Russian citizens who engage in attacks against US citizens to be brought to the United States for prosecution. Russian criminals cannot be extradited for these offenses and may generally receive no punishment for their actions (see Text Box 1.1 for an example). In turn, it is extremely difficult to deter or sanction cybercriminals in foreign countries and may encourage attacks against certain countries with no consequences.

Text Box 1.1: Getting around Russian extradition laws

www.nbcnews.com/id/3078784/ns/news-internet_underground/t/fbi-agent-charged-hacking/#.U3rXvihLqt8

FBI agent charged with hacking

Russia alleges agent broke law by downloading evidence

In a first in the rapidly evolving field of cyberspace law, Russia's counterintelligence service on Thursday filed criminal charges against an FBI agent it says lured two Russian hackers to the United States, then illegally seized evidence against them by downloading data from their computers in Chelyabinsk, Russia.

This article provides interesting insights into the challenges posed by cybercrime investigations that cross national boundaries.

By contrast, some developing nations may not have laws against computer misuse. If there are no laws, then the nation serves as a sort of "safe haven" for actors where they can operate with minimal risk of legal sanctions (Brenner, 2008; Holt, 2003). This was exemplified in the creation of the ILOVEYOU virus that spread around the world in 2000. This form of malware attacked millions of computers and spread through infected email attachments, effectively crippling the Internet at the time (Poulsen, 2010). The program started in the Philippines on May 4, 2000 and spread across the world in a single day. It is thought to have been created by a Filipino college student named Onel de Guzman, based on the start of the program from Manila and his interest in hacking (Poulsen, 2010). At the time, there were no laws against writing malware in the Philippines, making prosecutors unable to pursue de Guzman. Thus, the absence of laws can make it extremely difficult to combat cybercrimes internationally.

Taken as a whole, the global reach of the Internet has created substantial difficulties for law enforcement agencies at home and abroad to enforce cybercrime laws globally. The structure of policing, especially in the United States, establishes guidelines for the investigation of crimes at the local, state, and federal level. Offenses that occur within a single jurisdictional boundary are often the responsibility of local municipal police departments or sheriffs' departments, while those that cross state or national boundaries are handled by state or federal agencies. Many cybercriminals may not live within the same region as their victim (Holt, 2003; Wall, 1998), though even if they were in the same region, a victim may have no idea where the offender actually resides. This creates significant confusion as to the appropriate agency to contact, and diminishes the amount of cybercrime reported to law enforcement (Goodman, 1997; Wall, 1998). In fact, this under-counting is referred to as "the dark figure" of cybercrime, in that the true number of offenses is unknown.

One reason for the lack of reporting is the inherent difficulty in recognizing when illegal activities have taken place. Individuals may be completely unaware that they have been the victim of cybercrime until it is too late. For example, failures in computer hardware and software may be either the result of an error in the equipment, or a direct result of criminal activities designed to hide their occurrence. Many in the general public do not have the skills necessary to discern the root cause, making it hard to know when some sort of compromise has taken place. Since cybercriminals attempt to target as many victims as possible, it is also difficult to identify any patterns for risky behavior online (Bossler and Holt, 2009). Finally, protective software programs designed to reduce individual risk of victimization do not always work. Approximately 25 percent of personal computers around the world that use a variety of security solutions have malicious software, such as a virus, loaded into their memory (PandaLabs, 2007).

The embarrassment, shame, or harm that may come from reporting cybercrime victimization also reduces the likelihood of contacting law enforcement. For instance, Nigerian email scams often target naïve individuals who believe that an unlikely claim may be valid. Reporting that they have been defrauded may be substantially embarrassing and thereby diminish the likelihood of reporting. Within corporate and government computing environments, there are several issues that may reduce the likelihood of

technology and cybercrime

reporting when a cybercrime has occurred. For instance, a company may lose customers or overall stock value if they report that their systems have been compromised. Embarrassment over the loss of sensitive information may engender cover-ups or diminished reporting in order to reduce the loss of business.

Taken as a whole, technology affords multiple unique advantages for offenders that are not necessarily present in the real world. Technology is readily available across the globe, providing offenders widespread access to resources. The number of people online provides a wealth of prospective victims that can be affected with greater ease than is possible in the real world. Technology also offers people the ability to hide their actual identity behind a variety of false names and locations, making it difficult to determine who is responsible for a criminal incident. Finally, the different legal structures and cooperative agreements in place across the globe make it difficult to successfully prosecute cybercrimes. As a result, individuals who engage in cybercrime and deviance face a much lower risk of detection and arrest and may experience greater monetary or emotional rewards from cybercrime.

> **For more information on the challenges of prosecuting cybercrimes, go online to:** www.justice.gov/criminal/cybercrime/docs/ccmanual.pdf

Technology as evidence

The third and final way that technology may be used in the course of an offense is through its **incidental** role or involvement in a crime. In this case, the computer may either be involved in the commission of a crime or is being used merely as a storage device (Maras, 2012). For instance, the presence of child pornography on a laptop or cell phone suggests that it is incidental to the offence. This information, wherever it is stored, constitutes **digital evidence**, defined as information that is either transferred or stored in a binary form (Casey, 2011). Digital evidence can be anything from the browser history of an individual to the emails, chat logs, and photos present on mobile phones, GPS devices, and cameras of both victim and offenders (see Chapter 11). Computers, in the traditional sense, are no longer the only devices capable of sending emails, chatting, and browsing the Internet. Tablets, music players, and various other devices can be connected to the Internet and provide some evidence of an individual's behaviors.

There are several valuable examples that help clarify what is digital evidence and when it may be pertinent for various forms of crime both online and offline (Clifford, 2006; Maras, 2012). For example, BTK (Bind, Torture, Kill) was a serial killer in Kansas (USA) from 1974 until 2005 when he was arrested and convicted of ten homicides (Williams and Landwehr, 2006). The killer murdered ten people in Kansas between 1974 and 1991 and then went dormant, though he constantly wrote letters to the media and police describing his exploits. The investigation went cold, though the BTK Killer indicated that he had committed another murder that had not been attributed to him (Williams and Landwehr, 2006).

Police then began communicating directly with BTK, when the killer asked if it was possible to trace his identity on the basis of data on floppy disks. The agency erroneously said that they could not, and BTK sent them a disk with a document discussing his behaviors (Williams and Landwehr, 2006). Using specialized computer forensic software to help process the data and evidence located on the disk, investigators determined the location of the computer where the disk had been opened, as well as the person who created the document (Williams and Landwehr, 2006). In turn, they were able to develop detailed information about the killer and gather enough circumstantial evidence to suggest a prospective identity, which turned out to be a man named Dennis Rader. He was subsequently arrested and pled guilty to the murders, receiving ten consecutive life sentences, one for each murder (Williams and Landwehr, 2006).

Digital evidence can also be derived from online sources that may be present on websites and social media. In fact, digital evidence collected from social media sites, such as Facebook and Twitter, has also been influential in law enforcement over the last few years. Following the Vancouver Canucks' loss to the Boston Bruins in the Stanley Cup finals in 2011, a massive riot broke out in Vancouver with fans setting vehicles on fire, breaking windows, looting stores, and dancing atop overturned cars (CBC News, 2011). Within hours of the riot, police received over 3,500 emails that included videos, photos, and web links to various social media sites. In addition, a "Vancouver Riot Pics" Facebook page was created to identify those individuals involved in the riots by allowing the public to "tag" the pictures and videos (Leger, 2011). More than 100 people were arrested through the assistance of social media.

With virtually every crime incorporating some form of digital evidence, it is up to law enforcement to be able to identify the possible sources of information and the locations where such information may be found. Various peripheral devices like flash drives, CDs, DVDs, and even gaming systems may contain digital evidence that can be collected. Some companies even produce removable storage media that are easily disguised, such as a pair of sunglasses or a wristband that contains a flash drive. With digital devices increasingly being used to target, act as a tool, or provide support for criminal activities, law enforcement and investigators must understand the nature of the digital crime scene.

For more on hidden media devices, go online to: www.trendhunter.com/slideshow/disguised-usb-drives

Law enforcement response to cybercrime

Given the challenges posed by cybercrime and technology-enabled offenses, it is vital that individuals understand who to contact in the event that they are victimized and which agencies are assigned responsibility to protect us. Policing and law enforcement agencies, however, are complex bureaucracies with roles that are bound by jurisdiction. In many cases, these jurisdictional issues, coupled with the complexity of many forms of cybercrime, make most cybercrimes the purview of national or federal law enforcement agencies rather than local law enforcement.

Just as with traditional forms of crime, most individuals may think that the first entity to contact in helping with a cybercrime is their local law enforcement agency. Local law enforcement is responsible for responding to a wide variety of calls, helping citizens, investigating crimes, arresting offenders, preventing crime, increasing public feelings of safety, and generally responding to a wide range of citizen requests within their limited jurisdiction. There is, however, a substantial degree of variation in the size and response capabilities of local law enforcement. In the United States, the majority of law enforcement agencies serve small populations in rural or suburban communities with populations under 50,000 (LEMAS, 2010). As of 2008, about half of all local agencies had less than ten sworn officers; 75 percent of these agencies served less than 10,000 citizens in total (LEMAS, 2010). In the UK, territorial police forces are responsible for policing a specific jurisdictional region and comprise the majority of police agencies generally (Yar, 2013). In Canada, major urban centers, such as Toronto or Montreal, also have their own police forces which serve the local population.

Local law enforcement agencies in most countries, including the United States, do not currently have a large role in preventing and investigating many forms of cybercrimes. They are responsible, however, for investigating crimes in which a victim and offender reside within their jurisdiction. For example, local law enforcement is primarily responsible for investigating most cases of online harassment or stalking (see Chapter 7). Person-based cybercrime cases such as the creation and consumption of child porn (Jenkins, 2001), as well as sexual solicitation and prostitution cases in the US, may also be investigated by local police agencies (Cunningham and Kendall, 2010) – see Chapter 6.

Over the last decade, both scholars and police administrators have created lists of reasons why cybercrime poses significant challenges for local law enforcement and why they are not more heavily involved (Burns, Whitworth, and Thompson, 2004; Goodman, 1997; Holt, Bossler, and Fitzgerald, 2010; Senjo, 2004; Stambaugh *et al.*, 2001). As one can see from the list below, some of the challenges can be addressed by placing more priority (i.e. funding) on these offenses. Others are not so easily addressable. The list includes but is not limited to:

- jurisdictional issues caused by the victim and offender not living in the same municipality or county;
- lack of a standard definition for cybercrime;
- little public outcry in comparison to traditional crime, particularly violent crime;
- difficulty in investigating an invisible crime;
- difficulty in acquiring and maintaining the technologies required to investigate these resources (see Chapters 10–12);
- difficulty in training and retaining trained officers;
- lack of managerial and police support for the investigation of cybercrimes.

Although the above list of reasons why local law enforcement has been challenged by cybercrime appears to be insurmountable to some, scholars and police administrators have still argued that local law enforcement must play a larger role in investigating cybercrimes (e.g. Bossler and Holt, 2012; Goodman, 1997; Stambaugh *et al.*, 2001). Some have argued for the development of more local cybercrime investigation units that could directly respond to crimes involving digital evidence in order to decrease assistance from state and national/federal levels (Hinduja, 2007; Marcum, Higgins, Freiburger, and Ricketts, 2010). Insufficient funding, however, has led to few specialized cybercrime units at the local level in the United States.

> For more information on the challenges cybercrimes pose to local law enforcement, go online to: https://www.ncjrs.gov/pdffiles1/nij/186276.pdf

Other scholars and commentators have focused on the need for improvement of patrol officers in acting as first responders to crime scenes with computers or digital evidence (Holt, Bossler, and Fitzgerald, 2010; National Institute of Justice, 2008; Stambaugh *et al.*, 2001). Almost no data exists on how often patrol officers actually respond to cybercrime calls, although it seems quite rare (Bossler and Holt, 2012; Holt, Bossler, and Fitzgerald, 2010). Nevertheless, government documents and training manuals indicate that government officials expect this not to be the case in the future. For example, in the United States, the National Institute of Justice (NIJ) published the second edition of *Electronic Crime Scene Investigations: A Guide for First Responders* in 2008. This guide was created primarily for patrol officers and provided both basic and more advanced information on how to properly respond to a digital crime scene, including how to recognize, seize, document, handle, package, and even transport digital evidence. In addition, scholars and police administrators similarly argue for more computer training for patrol officers since patrol officers in the United States are ill prepared to respond to digital evidence scenes (Hinduja, 2007; Holt, Bossler, and Fitzgerald, 2010; Stambaugh *et al.*, 2001). It would seem to be a necessity that patrol officers have minimal computer literacy in order to know what to secure and to understand the lexicon of witnesses.

Interestingly, however, it appears that police officers themselves do not view their future role in dealing with cybercrime the same way that scholars and police administrators do. Patrol officers know that local law enforcement agencies generally place low priority on most forms of cybercrime unless it is child pornography related (Hinduja, 2004; Holt and Bossler, 2012; Senjo, 2004; Stambaugh *et al.*, 2001). Local agencies may also be increasing their capabilities to investigate various forms of online economic crimes, but they focus little on computer intrusion offenses (Holt, Bossler, and Fitzgerald, 2010). In addition, they feel that police management, and prosecutors for that matter, have little knowledge of cybercrime and do not have the appropriate resources to adequately investigate and prosecute most forms of cybercrime (Burns *et al.*, 2004; Holt, Bossler, and Fitzgerald, 2010; Stambaugh *et al.*, 2001). They therefore do not believe that local law enforcement should be primarily responsible for dealing with cybercrime (Bossler and Holt, 2012; Burns *et al.*, 2004). They place less emphasis than police administrators on the importance of creating local cybercrime investigative units and implementing additional computer training (Bossler and Holt, 2012). Instead, they believe that the best strategies for dealing with cybercrime would be for citizens to be more careful online and for changes to the legal system. It would seem that they would not prefer any substantial changes to their roles of primarily dealing with traditional forms of crime and order maintenance.

The next level of law enforcement that currently has any substantial responsibility in addressing cybercrime is state (US, Australia) and provincial (e.g. Canada) police agencies. In the United States, state agencies can focus on highway traffic control, state law enforcement, or provide laboratory services to smaller agencies depending on the state's Constitution and the mission of the state agency. In general, many states have a state law enforcement agency that can investigate crimes where a jurisdictional conflict exists or limited resources prevent a smaller agency from investigating the crime adequately. They may also simply provide forensic laboratory needs, including digital, for state and local agencies and manage repositories of data through fusion centers to develop crime and terror intelligence. In many cases, the procedures and resources discussed in Chapters 10–12 of this text are not available to local law enforcement and instead are conducted by state and federal labs. Thus, state agencies and resources are a crucial resource to investigate cybercrimes that do not cross state boundaries.

The highest levels of law enforcement in the US and Australia operate at the federal level. They are often the entities most frequently engaged in the investigation of cybercrimes due to the transnational nature of these offenses. In many cases, the victim and offender may live in different states or even different countries. In addition, many types of cybercrime are quite complex and require highly technical investigations. Nations have generally provided more resources for federal or national law enforcement agencies to investigate these offenses rather than state or local agencies. Federal agencies may also play a large role in addressing crimes or managing catastrophic incidents which require cooperation among many agencies across several jurisdictions affecting large populations.

The first federal law enforcement agency in the United States was the Coast Guard, which began in 1790 in order to prevent smuggling and to properly collect import taxes and duties from incoming ships (Bowling and Sheptycki, 2012). Over time, additional agencies were added due to the expansion of the nation and changes in the responsibilities of the government. Students will read in the upcoming chapters about the prominent roles that federal or national law enforcement agencies have with dealing with a wide variety of cybercrime. Many of these agencies serve multiple roles ranging from the prevention, investigation, and apprehension of cyber offenders to intelligence gathering and sharing. Readers of this volume will discover the Federal Bureau of Investigation's (FBI) role in investigating computer intrusion (Chapter 2), piracy and intellectual theft (Chapter 4), economic crimes (Chapter 5), child pornography (Chapter 6), serious forms of stalking that cross state boundaries (Chapter 7), and cyberterror (Chapter 8). Readers will also see that there is considerable jurisdictional overlap at the federal level, considering that several agencies are responsible for investigating the same categories of cybercrime. For example, the United States Secret Service also investigates computer intrusions (Chapter 2) and economic crimes (Chapter 5), the Bureau of Customs and Border Patrol (CBP) may play a role in investigations of intellectual theft (Chapter 4) and economic crimes (Chapter 5), while Immigration and Customs Enforcement (ICE) may also be involved with intellectual theft (Chapter 4), economic crime (Chapter 5), and child pornography (Chapter 6) cases. When problems escalate to the level of national safety, non-law-enforcement agencies may become involved in addition to the abovementioned agencies. For example, the Department of Defense's US Cyber Command and the National Security Agency (NSA) are involved in cases of cyber terror and warfare.

The highest levels of law enforcement in nations such as Canada, South Korea, and the UK are national police forces, though they serve the same function as federal law enforcement in the US. The UK operates multiple "special police forces" that serve across multiple jurisdictions, such as the National Domestic Extremism and Disorder Intelligence Unit which serves to respond to incidents of extremist activity within the UK and the National Crime Agency which contains multiple commands including Border Policing and the National Cyber Crime Unit (National Crime Agency, 2014). In Canada, the Royal Canadian Mounted Police (RCMP) serve as both the national police force and as local police patrols for seven of the ten provinces and three territories within the nation. The RCMP operates in a similar fashion to the US FBI or Australian Federal Police and is responsible for the investigation of both traditional and cybercrimes (Bowling and Sheptycki, 2012).

A typology of cybercrime

In light of the various ways that technology engenders crime and deviance as well as fosters unique tactics for offending, it is necessary to understand the wide range of behaviors that constitute cybercrime. David Wall (2001) created one of the most recognized typologies of cybercrime, which encapsulates behavior into one of four categories: (1) cyber-trespass; (2) cyber-deception and theft; (3) cyber-porn and obscenity; and (4) cyber-violence. These categories reference the wide range of deviant, criminal, and terrorist behaviors that have emerged utilizing technology, as well as the subcultures supporting offenders throughout the world.

Cyber-trespass

The first category is **cyber-trespass**, referring to the act of crossing boundaries of ownership in online environments. This may seem confusing at first. If you go to a coffee shop or restaurant, you may notice they offer free Wi-Fi. Their network probably has a name that they chose which identifies their network and indicates who manages and is responsible for that space. In order to use the service, you must join their network and accept the terms of service that may come up when you open your web browser. In this instance, the coffee shop owns and manages this wireless network, but allows others to use the connectivity. By contrast, if the shop did not offer connectivity to customers, but you attempt to join and use their Wi-Fi anyway, you are trespassing because you are trying to break into the network that they own without the company's permission.

The issue of ownership is critical in instances of trespass; especially for computer hackers who often attempt to access computer systems, email accounts, or protected systems that they do not own (Furnell, 2002; Jordan and Taylor, 1998). Many in the general public recognize hackers for their involvement in criminal acts of trespassing sensitive boundaries of ownership, contributing to the belief that hackers cause significant harm to citizens, industry, and government alike. Though not all hackers engage in crime, those who do cost individuals and corporations a great deal of money each year. For example, the Government Accounting Office (2007) estimates that various forms of computer crime cost the US economy over $100 billion annually. Additionally, the Internet Crime Complaint Center (2009) found that the total dollar losses attributed to computer crime complaints was $559 million in 2009, with an average dollar loss per respondent of $575. Individuals who are interested in computer hacking operate within a large online subculture with participants from across the globe. They often come together online to discuss various techniques of hacking and their attitudes toward hacking with or without permission from system owners. Because not all hackers engage in crime, there is a rift within the subculture based on an individual's willingness to engage in acts of cyber-trespass in support of hacking (see Chapter 2 for more detail).

Cyber-deception/theft

The second category within Wall's (2001) typology is **cyber-deception and theft,** which can extend from hacking and other forms of cyber-trespass. This category includes all the ways that individuals may illegally acquire information or resources online and often goes hand in hand with trespass. For instance, criminals can use email messages to acquire bank account information from victims through the use of **phishing** messages (James, 2005). In this case, a criminal sends a message claiming to be from a bank or financial institution which needs the prospective consumer to validate their account information by clicking on a web link provided in the message. The individuals are then sent to a fraudulent website that resembles the actual financial institution and are asked to enter in their bank account username, login, and other sensitive information (James, 2005). This data is then stored and used by the criminal to engage in fraud, or resold to others through an online black market for stolen data. These crimes are particularly costly for consumers and businesses, as the Gartner Group estimates that phishing victims in the US lost $3 billion in 2007 alone (Rogers, 2007).

The problem of digital piracy is also included in cyber-theft, encompassing the illegal copying of digital media, such as computer software, digital sound recordings, and digital video recordings, without the explicit permission of the copyright holder (Gopal, Saunders, Bhattacharjee, Agrawal, and Wagner, 2004). The financial losses stemming from digital piracy are quite high. For instance, one company estimates that the US recording industry loses over 12 billion dollars each year from piracy (Siwek, 2007). This is because piracy is an extremely common activity, as evidenced by one study which found that between 50 and 90 percent of all broadband Internet traffic involved the transfer of pirated media (Siwek, 2007). In addition, studies of college students in the US find that between 40 and 60 percent of respondents have engaged in piracy within the last year (Gunter, 2009; Higgins, 2005; Hinduja, 2003; Skinner and Fream, 1997).

For more information on the problem of software piracy, go online to: www.huffingtonpost.com/2012/06/01/software-piracy-study-bsa_n_1563006.html

The problem of piracy appears to be facilitated in large part by the sub-culture of pirates operating online. The participants in this subculture help break copyright protections on DVDs, Blu-ray disks, and software and distribute these materials online. In fact, individuals can access pirated media and software through various outlets including file sharing services, torrents, and web sites (Cooper and Harrison, 2001; Holt and Copes, 2010). Participants in this subculture also encourage piracy by sharing their attitudes toward copyright law and minimizing the harm caused by pirating media (see Chapter 4 for detail). Many young people believe piracy is an acceptable behavior that has little impact on artists or private industry (Hinduja, 2003; Ingram and Hinduja, 2008). Thus, cyber-deception and theft involves multiple activities that cause significant financial harm.

Cyber-porn/obscenity

The third category in Wall's typology of cybercrime is **cyber-porn** and obscenity, representing the range of sexually expressive content online. As noted earlier, sexually explicit content is defined differently based on location. Thus, porn and obscenity may be deviant or criminal based on local laws. The relatively legal nature of adult pornography has enabled the development of an extremely lucrative industry, thanks in part to the availability of streaming web content and high-speed connectivity (Edelman, 2009; Lane, 2000). In addition, amateurs are increasingly active in the porn industry due to the ease with which individuals can produce professional quality images and media through HD digital cameras, web enabled cameras, and other equipment (Lane, 2000). While viewing pornographic content is not illegal for individuals over the age of 18, accessing certain content, such as violent or animal-related material, may be criminal depending on local laws.

The ability to access pornographic content has also enabled the development of online subcultures focused on various deviant sexual activities. Individuals with niche sexual fetishes can identify multiple outlets to discuss their interests with others in web forums, email lists, and online groups that engender the exchange of information in near real time (DiMarco, 2003). In turn, these spaces help to make people feel they are part of a larger group that validates their beliefs and attitudes. Sexual subcultures can also move into criminal activity when the actors victimize children and adults either online or offline. For instance, prostitutes increasingly utilize the Internet to advertise their services and keep in touch with clients (Cunningham and Kendall, 2010). The customers of sex workers also utilize this technology in order to discuss their experiences, provide detailed accounts of their interactions, and warn others about police activities in a given area (Holt and Blevins, 2007; Sharpe and Earle, 2003). Similarly, pedophiles who seek out sexual relationships with children frequently use CMCs in order to identify and share pornographic and sexual images (Jenkins, 2001; Quayle and Taylor 2002). They may also use forums and instant messaging to connect with children in an attempt to move into offline relationships (Wolak, Finkelhor, and Mitchell, 2004; Wolak, Mitchell, and Finkelhor, 2003).

Cyber-violence

The final form within Wall's typology is **cyber-violence**, referring to the ability to send or access injurious, hurtful, or dangerous materials online. This may encompass emotional harm such as embarrassment or shame, and in limited circumstances physical harm through suicidal ideation (Hinduja and Patchin, 2009). For example, the volume of information available through social networking sites, coupled with frequent use of CMCs, has increased the likelihood that individuals will be bullied, harassed, or stalked online (Finkelhor, Mitchell, and Wolak, 2000; Finn, 2004; Hinduja and Patchin, 2009; Holt and Bossler, 2009). Individuals from various age groups are increasingly receiving threatening or sexual messages via email, instant message, or texts (Bocij, 2004; Finn, 2004). People can also use CMCs to post embarrassing video, images, and text about another person for the public to see. In fact, technology has greatly increased the likelihood of emotional or psychological harm resulting from these messages (Finkelhor et al., 2000; Wolak et al., 2004).

Political and social movements also utilize CMCs in order to spread information about their causes or beliefs, as well as to engage in attacks against different targets on and offline (Brenner, 2008; Cere, 2003; Denning, 2011). For instance, riots in England and Arab states across the Middle East have organized through the use of social media, like Twitter and Facebook (Stepanova, 2011). In fact, CMCs can be used to form **flash mobs**, or mass organizations of people, to organize quickly and move rapidly through the use of online media without alerting local citizens or law enforcement (Taylor et al., 2010). Various extremist groups with their own subcultural norms and values utilize the Internet in order to promote their beliefs and connect interested parties together (see Chapter 8 for details). To that end, white supremacist groups use web forums and media sites to promote their message of hate to a wide audience (Taylor et al., 2010). Resistance Records operates a website where individuals can purchase CDs and merchandise for hard rock and heavy metal bands that promote hatred of other races and religions (Resistance Records, 2011). Individuals can also donate directly to this cause through the website, though it is primarily designed to spread their ideology to others through a socially acceptable format, like music.

In addition, extremist groups have utilized the Internet in order to engage in attacks against governmental targets worldwide. The hacker group Anonymous has engaged in a variety of **Distributed denial of service (DDoS)** attacks against governments, the recording industry, and private businesses (Correll, 2010; Poulsen, 2011). In a DDoS attack, individuals send multiple requests to servers that house online content to the point where these servers become overloaded and are unable to be used by others. As a consequence, these attacks can completely knock a service offline, causing companies to lose money and, potentially, customer confidence. The group Anonymous uses these attacks as a protest against attempts to reduce the distribution of pirated media online. Anonymous believes intellectual property laws are unfair, that governments are stifling the activities of consumers, so the group wishes to elicit a direct response from the general public to stand up against this supposed tyranny (Correll, 2010; Poulsen, 2011). Thus, the use of technology has expanded the capability of extremist groups to affect populations and targets well beyond their overall capacity in the real world.

This text

Given the range of criminal and deviant acts that are enabled by the Internet and CMCs, it is critical that we understand as much about these phenomena as possible. Thus, this book will explore the spectrum of cybercrimes in detail, considering how real-world crimes have incorporated technology, as well as the unique forms of offending that have emerged as a direct result of technology. In addition, each chapter will consider the unique subcultures that have emerged in online environments around either a form of deviance, crime, or a specific ideology. The subcultural norms of each group will be explored in order to understand how involvement in this subculture affects behavior both on and offline, as well as its influence on attitudes toward crime and deviance. Finally, statutes in the US and abroad that have been created to address these issues will be covered, along with the local, state, national, and international law enforcement agencies that have responsibilities to investigate and enforce those laws.

Chapter 2: *Computer hackers and hacking* explores computer hacking in depth, including its role in attacks against individuals and corporations alike. Chapter 3: *Malware and automated computer attacks* explores the problem of malicious software and its evolution over time. Chapter 4: *Digital piracy and intellectual property theft* considers the issue of digital piracy, including the theft and release of software, music, movies, television, and other digital content. More serious forms of fraud and theft are explored in Chapter 5: *Economic crimes and online fraud*, including the use of email scams in order to acquire financial information from unsuspecting victims.

Chapter 6: *Pornography, prostitution, and sex crimes* covers a wide variety of online sexual behavior, including pornography, how the Internet has affected traditional prostitution, and how the criminal justice system has attempted to evolve to address these issues. Sexual crimes against children, including child pornography and child molestation, are also discussed in this chapter, emphasizing the ways that these offenses are uniquely engendered by technology. Chapter 7: *Cyberbullying, online harassment, and cyberstalking* investigates the problem of online harassment, bullying, and stalking, while Chapter 8: *Online extremism, cyberterror, and cyber warfare* explores the use of technology to spread hate speech and extremism across the globe.

Chapter 9: *Cybercrime and criminological theories* will provide the reader with an in-depth examination of whether traditional criminological theories can help us understand why individuals commit the wide range of behaviors that is encompassed in cybercrime. It will also explore the idea of whether new cybercrime theories are needed or whether our current stock of criminological theories is adequate in explaining these "new" forms of crime.

Chapter 10: *Evolution of digital forensics* will elaborate the concept of digital forensics and the process of seizing evidence from various devices. Chapter 11: *Acquisition and examination of forensic evidence* details the various tools used in the process of evidence analysis, as well as the techniques involved in data recovery and investigation generally. Chapter 12: *Legal challenges in digital forensic investigations* focuses on the process of evidence presentation in court, and the laws that affect what is admissible and when by an analyst. Finally, Chapter 13: *The future of cybercrime, terror, and policy* considers the future of cybercrime with a discussion of the ways that the global nature of technology hinders our ability to effectively regulate these offenses.

Key terms

Computer crime
Computer-mediated communications (CMCs)
Cybercrime
Cyber-deception
Cyberdeviance
Cyber-porn
Cyberterrorism
Cyber-trespass
Cyber-violence
Deviance
Digital evidence
Digital immigrant
Digital native
Distributed denial of service attack
Flash mob
Incidental

Phishing

Proxy server

Spam

Subculture

Technicways

Web defacement

Discussion questions

1) Think carefully about your current access to technology. How many laptops, desktops, tablets, and mobile devices do you own? How much time do you spend online? How would you compare your use of technology to your peers'?

2) Take a few moments to think critically about the way in which you share information with the world through online environments. Do you cautiously share personal information? How much detail do you place about yourself into Facebook and other social networking sites? Do you use the same credit card for all online purchases? How often do you pirate music and media? Keeping this in mind, detail the various ways in which you could become a victim of as many forms of cybercrime as is possible.

3) Do you belong to any subcultures, on or offline? What are they, and how do you think they affect your activities and attitudes toward the world around you?

4) How much overlap do you see between real-world crimes and cybercrimes? Should we have distinct terms to recognize crime or deviance in online environments, or should all offenses just be classified as crimes, regardless of where and how they occur?

References

Associated Press. (2005). *Average price of laptops drops to $1,000*. [Online] Available at: www.msnbc.msn.com/id/9157036/ns/technology_and_science-tech_and_gadgets/t/average-price-laptops-drops/

Blevins, K., & Holt, T. J. (2009). Examining the virtual subculture of johns. *Journal of Contemporary Ethnography*, 38, 619–648.

Bocij, P. (2004). *Cyberstalking: Harassment in the Internet Age and How to Protect your Family*. Westport, CT: Praeger.

Bossler, A. M., & Burruss, G. W. (2011). The General theory of Crime and Computer Hacking: Low Self-Control Hackers? In T. J. Holt & B. H. Schell (eds), *Corporate Hacking and Technology-Driven Crime: Social Dynamics and Implications* (pp. 38–67). Hershey, PA: IGI Global.

Bossler, A. M., & Holt, T. J. (2009). On-line activities, guardianship, and malware infection: An examination of routine activities theory. *International Journal of Cyber Criminology*, 3, 400–420.

Bossler, A. M., & Holt, T. J. (2012). Patrol officers' perceived role in responding to cybercrime. *Policing: An International Journal of Police Strategies & Management*, 35, 165–181.

Bowling, B., & Sheptycki, J. (2012). *Global Policing*. Thousand Oaks, CA: SAGE.

Brake, M. (1980). *The Sociology of Youth Cultures and Youth Subcultures*. London: Routledge and Kegan Paul.

Brenner, S. W. (2008). *Cyberthreats: The Emerging Fault Lines of the Nation State*. New York: Oxford University Press.

Britz, M. T. (2010). Terrorism and Technology: Operationalizing Cyberterrorism and Identifying Concepts. In T. J. Holt (ed.), *Crime On-Line: Correlates, Causes, and Context* (pp. 193–220). Raleigh, NC: Carolina Academic Press, 2010.

Burns, R. G., Whitworth, K. H., & Thompson, C. Y. (2004). Assessing law enforcement preparedness to address Internet fraud. *Journal of Criminal Justice*, 32, 477–493.

Casey, E. (2011). *Digital Evidence and Computer Crime: Forensic Science, Computers, and the Internet* (3rd ed.). Waltham, MA: Academic Press.

CBC News. (2011, June 16). Vancouver police arrest more than 100 in riot. CBC News. Retrieved from www.cbc.ca

Cere, R. (2003). Digital Counter-Cultures and the Nature of Electronic Social and Political Movements. In Y. Jewkes (ed.), *Dot.cons: Crime, Deviance and Identity on the Internet* (pp. 147–163). Portland, OR: Willan Publishing.

Central Intelligence Agency. (2011). *The World Factbook 2011*. Washington, DC: Central Intelligence Agency. [Online] Available at: https://www.cia.gov/library/publications/the-world-factbook/index.html

Clifford, R. D. (ed.) (2006). *Cybercrime: The Investigation, Prosecution, and Defense of a Computer-Related Crime* (2nd ed.). Durham, NC: Carolina Academic Press.

Cooper, J., & Harrison, D. M. (2001). The social organization of audio piracy on the Internet. *Media, Culture, and Society*, 23, 71–89.

Correll, S. P. (2010). *An interview with Anonymous*. PandaLabs Blog. [Online] Available at: http://pandalabs.pandasecurity.com/an-interview-with-anonymous/

Cunningham, S., & Kendall, T. (2010). Sex for Sale: Online Commerce in the World's Oldest Profession. In T. J. Holt (ed.), *Crime On-Line: Correlates, Causes, and Context* (pp. 40–75). Raleigh, NC: Carolina Academic Press.

Denning, D. E. (2001). Activism, Hacktivism, and Cyberterrorism: The Internet as a Tool for Influencing Foreign Policy. In J. Arquilla & D. F. Ronfeldt (eds), *Networks and Netwars: The Future of Terror, Crime, and Militancy* (pp. 239–288). Santa Monica, CA: Rand.

Denning, D. E. (2011). Cyber-Conflict as an Emergent Social Problem. In T. J. Holt & B. Schell (eds), *Corporate Hacking and Technology-Driven Crime: Social Dynamics and Implications* (pp. 170–186). Hershey, PA: IGI-Global.

DiMarco, H. (2003). The Electronic Cloak: Secret Sexual Deviance in Cybersociety. In Y. Jewkes (ed.), *Dot.cons: Crime, Deviance, and Identity on the Internet* (pp. 53–67). Portland, OR: Willan Publishing.

Edleman, B. (2009). Red light states: Who buys online adult entertainment? *Journal of Economic Perspectives*, 23, 209–220.

Finkelhor, D., Mitchell, K. J., & Wolak, J. (2000). *Online Victimization: A Report on the Nation's Youth*. Washington DC: National Center for Missing and Exploited Children.

Finn, J. (2004). A survey of online harassment at a university campus. *Journal of Interpersonal Violence*, 19, 468–483.

Foster, J. (1990). *Villains: Crime and Community in the Inner City*. London: Routledge.

Furnell, S. (2002). *Cybercrime: Vandalizing the Information Society*. London: Addison-Wesley.

Goodman, M. D. (1997). Why the police don't care about computer crime. *Harvard Journal of Law and Technology*, 10, 465–494.

Gopal, R., Sanders, G. L., Bhattacharjee, S., Agrawal, M. K., & Wagner, S. C. (2004). A behavioral model of digital music piracy. *Journal of Organizational Computing & Electronic Commerce*, 14, 89–105.

Government Accounting Office. (2007). *Cybercrime: Public and Private Entities Face Challenges in Addressing Cyber Threats*. United States Government Accountability Office Report to Congressional Requesters. [Online] Available at: www.gao.gov/new.items/d07705.pdf

Gunter, W. D. (2009). Internet scallywags: A comparative analysis of multiple forms and measurements of digital piracy. *Western Criminology Review*, 10, 15–28.

Herbert, S. (1998). Police subculture reconsidered. *Criminology*, 36, 343–369.

Higgins, G. E. (2005). Can low self-control help with the understanding of the software piracy problem? *Deviant Behavior*, 26, 1–24.

Hinduja, S. (2003). Trends and patterns among software pirates. *Ethics and Information Technology*, 5, 49–61.

Hinduja, S. (2004). Perceptions of local and state law enforcement concerning the role of computer crime investigative teams. *Policing: An International Journal of Police Strategies & Management*, 27, 341–357.

Hinduja, S. (2007). Computer crime investigations in the United States: Leveraging knowledge from the past to address the future. *International Journal of Cyber Criminology*, 1, 1–26.

Hinduja, S., & Patchin, J. W. (2009). *Bullying Beyond the Schoolyard: Preventing and Responding to Cyberbullying*. New York: Corwin Press.

Holt, T. J. (2003). Examining a transnational problem: An analysis of computer crime victimization in eight countries from 1999 to 2001. *International Journal of Comparative and Applied Criminal Justice*, 27, 199–220.

Holt, T. J. (2007). Subcultural evolution? Examining the influence of on- and off-line experiences on deviant subcultures. *Deviant Behavior*, 28, 171–198.

Holt, T. J. (2009). The Attack Dynamics of Political and Religiously Motivated Hackers. In T. Saadawi & L. Jordan (eds) *Cyber Infrastructure Protection* (pp. 161–182). New York: Strategic Studies Institute.

Holt, T. J., & Blevins, K. R. (2007). Examining sex work from the client's perspective: Assessing johns using online data. *Deviant Behavior*, 28, 333–354.

Holt, T. J., Blevins, K. R., & Kuhns, J. B. (2008). Examining the displacement practices of johns with on-line data. *Journal of Criminal Justice*, 36, 522–528.

Holt, T. J., & Bossler, A. M. (2009). Examining the applicability of lifestyle-routine activities theory for cybercrime victimization. *Deviant Behavior*, 30, 1–25.

Holt, T. J., & Bossler, A. M. (2012). Police perceptions of computer crimes in two southeastern cities: An examination from the viewpoint of patrol officers. *American Journal of Criminal Justice*, 37, 396–412.

Holt, T. J., Bossler, A. M., & Fitzgerald, S. (2010). Examining state and local law enforcement perceptions of computer crime. In T. J. Holt (ed.), *Crime On-Line: Correlates, Causes, and Context* (pp. 221–246). Raleigh: Carolina Academic.

Holt, T. J., Burruss, G. W., & Bossler, A. M. (2010). Social learning and cyber deviance: Examining the importance of a full social learning model in the virtual world. *Journal of Crime and Justice*, 33: 15–30.

Holt, T. J., & Copes, H. (2010). Transferring subcultural knowledge online: Practices and beliefs of persistent digital pirates. *Deviant Behavior*, 31, 625–654.

Holt, T. J., & Graves, D. C. (2007). A qualitative analysis of advanced fee fraud schemes. *The International Journal of Cyber-Criminology*, 1, 137–154.

Ingram, J. R., & Hinduja, S. (2008). Neutralizing music piracy: An empirical examination. *Deviant Behavior*, 29, 334–366.

Internet Crime Complaint Center. (2008). *IC3 2008 Internet Crime Report*. [Online] Available at: www.ic3.gov/media/annualreport/2008_IC3Report.pdf.

James, L. (2005). *Phishing Exposed*. Rockland: Syngress.

Jenkins, P. (2001). *Beyond Tolerance: Child Pornography on the Internet*. New York: New York University Press.

Jordan, T., & Taylor, P. (1998). A sociology of hackers. *The Sociological Review*, 46, 757–780.

Kilger, M. (2011). Social Dynamics and the Future of Technology-Driven Crime. In T. J. Holt & B. Schell (eds), *Corporate Hacking and Technology-Driven Crime: Social Dynamics and Implications* (pp. 205–227). Hershey, PA: IGI-Global.

King, A., & Thomas, J. (2009). You Can't Cheat an Honest Man: Making ($$$s and) Sense of the Nigerian E-mail Scams. In F. Schmalleger & M. Pittaro (eds) *Crime of the Internet* (pp. 206–224). Saddle River, NJ: Prentice Hall.

Kornblum, W. (1997). *Sociology in a Changing World* (4th ed.). Fort Worth, TX: Harcourt Brace and Company.

Lane, F. S. (2000). *Obscene Profits: The Entrepreneurs of Pornography in the Cyber Age*. New York: Routledge.

Leger, D. L. (2011, June 23). Social media aid Vancouver police in identifying rioters. *USA Today*. Retrieved from www.usatoday.com

LEMAS. (2010). *Law Enforcement Management and Administrative Statistics 2010*. Washington DC: United States Department of Justice, Office of Justice Statistics.

Lenhart, A. (2010). *Is the age at which teens get cell phones getting younger?* Pew Internet and American Life Project. [Online] Available at: http://pewinternet. org/Commentary/2010/December/Is-the-age-at-which-kids-get-cell-phones-get ting-younger.aspx

Lenhart, A., Madden, M., & Hitlin, P. (2005). *Teens and Technology*. Pew Internet and American Life Project. [Online] Available at: www.pewinternet.org/~/media/ Files/Reports/2005/PIP_Teens_Tech_July2005web.pdf.pdf

Lenhart, A., & Madden, M. (2007). *Teens, Privacy, and Online Social Networks*. Pew Internet and American Life Project. [Online] Available at: www.pewinternet. org/Reports/2007/Teens-Privacy-and-Online-Social-Networks.aspx

Lenhart, A., Purcell, K., Smith, A., & Zickuhr, K. (2010). *Social Media and Young Adults*. Pew Internet and American Life Project. [Online] Available at: www.pewinternet.org/Reports/2010/Social-Media-and-Young-Adults.aspx

Maras, M. (2012). *Computer Forensics: Cybercriminals, Laws, and Evidence*. Sudbury, MA: Jones and Bartlett Learning.

Marcum, C., Higgins, G. E., Freiburger, T. L., & Ricketts, M. L. (2010). Policing possession of child pornography online: Investigating the training and resources dedicated to the investigation of cyber crime. *International Journal of Police Science & Management*, 12, 516–525.

Maurer, D. W. (1981). *Language of the Underworld*. Louisville, KY: University of Kentucky Press.

McKeganey, N. P., & Barnard, M. (1996). *Sex Work on the Streets: Prostitutes and their Clients*. Buckingham: Open University Press.

Miller, J. (1998). Up it up: Gender and the accomplishment of street robbery. *Criminology*, 36, 37–66.

Moore, K. (2011). *71% of online adults now use video-sharing sites*. Pew Internet and American Life Project. [Online] Available at: http://pewinternet.org/Reports/2011/Video-sharing-sites.aspx

National Crime Agency. (2014). *About us*. [Online] Available at: www.nationalcrimeagency.gov.uk/about-us

National Institute of Justice (2008), *Electronic Crime Scene Investigations: A Guide for First Responders* (2nd ed.), NCJ 219941, Washington, DC.

O'Connell Davidson, J. (1998). *Power, Prostitution, and Freedom*. Ann Arbor, MI: University of Michigan Press.

Odum, H. (1937). Notes on technicways in contemporary society. *American Sociological Review*, 2, 336–346.

Office for National Statistics. (2013). *Internet Access – Households and Individuals, 2013*. [Online] Available at: www.ons.gov.uk/ons/dcp171778_322713.pdf

PandaLabs (2007). *Malware infections in protected systems*. Panda Labs Blog. [Online] Available at: http://research.pandasecurity.com/blogs/images/wp_pb_malware_infections_in_protectedsystems.pdf

Parker, F. B. (1943). Social control and the technicways. *Social Forces*, 22, 163–168.

Poulsen, K. (2010). *This Day In Tech: May 3, 2010: Tainted 'Love' Infects Computers*. Wired This Day In Tech. [Online] Available at: www.wired.com/2010/05/0504i-love-you-virus/

Poulsen, K. (2011). *In 'Anonymous' Raids, Feds Work From List of Top 1,000 protesters*. Wired Threat Level. [Online] Available at: www.wired.com/threatlevel/2011/07/op_payback/

Prensky, M. (2001). Digital natives, digital immigrants. *On the Horizon, October 2001*, 9(5). Lincoln: NCB University Press. [Online] Available at: www.marcprensky.com/writing/Prensky%20-%20Digital%20Natives,%20Digital%20Immigrants%20-%20Part1.pdf

Quayle, E., & Taylor, M. (2002). Child pornography and the Internet: Perpetuating a cycle of abuse. *Deviant Behavior*, 23, 331–361.

Quinn, J. F., & Forsyth, C. J. (2005). Describing sexual behavior in the era of the internet: A typology for empirical research. *Deviant Behavior*, 26, 191–207.

Resistance Records. (2011). *What's New Here?* [Online] Available at: http://resistance.com/catalog/

Rogers, J. (2007). *Gartner: Victims of online phishing up nearly 40 percent in 2007.* SC Magazine. [Online] Available at: www.scmagazineus.com/Gartner-Victims-of-online-phishing-up-nearly-40-percent-in-2007/article/99768/

Rogers, M., Smoak, N. D., & Liu, J. (2006). Self-reported deviant computer behavior: A big-5, moral choice, and manipulative exploitive behavior analysis. *Deviant Behavior, 27*, 245–268.

Schell, B. H., & Dodge, J. L. (2002). *The Hacking of America: Who's Doing it, Why, and How.* Westport, CT: Quorum Books.

Senjo, S. R. (2004). An analysis of computer-related crime: Comparing police officer perceptions with empirical data. *Security Journal, 17*, 55–71.

Sharp, K., & Earle, S. (2003). Cyberpunters and Cyberwhores: Prostitution on the Internet. In Y. Jewkes, (ed.), *Dot.cons: Crime, Deviance and Identity on the Internet* (pp. 36–52). Portland, OR: Willan Publishing.

Siwek, S. E. (2007). *The true cost of sound recording piracy to the U.S. economy.* [Online] Available at: www.ipi.org/ipi/IPIPublications.nsf/PublicationLookupFul lText/5C2EE3D2107A4C228625733E0053A1F4

Skinner, W. F., & Fream, A. F. (1997). A social learning theory analysis of computer crime among college students. *Journal of Research in Crime and Delinquency, 34*, 495–518.

Smith, A. (2011). *Smartphone Adoption and Usage.* Pew Internet and American Life Project. 2011. [Online] Available at: http://pewinternet.org/Reports/2011/ Smartphones.aspx

Socialbakers. (2011). *United States Facebook Statistics.* [Online] Available at: www. socialbakers.com/facebook-statistics/united-states

Stambaugh, H., Beaupre, D. S., Icove, D. J., Baker, R., Cassady, W., & Williams, W. P. (2001). *Electronic Crime Needs Assessment for State and Local Law Enforcement.* Washington, DC: National Institute of Justice, U.S. Department of Justice.

Stepanova, E. (2011). *The role of information communications technology in the "Arab Spring": Implications beyond the region.* PONARS Eurasia Policy Memo No. 159. [Online] Available at: www.gwu.edu/~ieresgwu/assets/docs/ponars/ pepm_159.pdf

Taylor, P. (1999). *Hackers: Crime in the Digital Sublime.* London: Routledge.

Taylor, R. W., Fritsch, E. J., Liederbach, J., & Holt, T. J. (2010). *Digital Crime and Digital Terrorism* (2nd ed.). Upper Saddle River, NJ: Pearson Prentice Hall.

Vance, R. B. (1972). Howard Odum's technicways: A neglected lead in American sociology. *Social Forces, 50*, 456–461.

Wall, D. S. (1998). Catching cybercriminals: Policing the Internet. *International review of Law, Computers & Technology, 12*, 201–218.

Wall, D. S. (2001). Cybercrimes and the Internet. In D. S. Wall (ed.), *Crime and the Internet* (pp. 1–17). New York: Routledge.

Wall, D. S. (2004). Digital realism and the governance of spam as cybercrime. *European Journal on Criminal Policy and Research, 10*, 309–335.

Wall, D. S. (2007). *Cybercrime: The Transformation of Crime in the Information Age.* Cambridge: Polity Press.

Ward, M. (2006). *Anti-cartoon protests go online.* BBC News, February 8, 2006. [Online] Available at: http://news.bbc.co.uk/2/hi/technology/4691518.stm

Williams, N. D. & Landwehr, K. (2006, December). Bind, Torture, Kill: The BTK Investigation. *The Police Chief, 73*(12).

Wolak, J., Finkelhor, D., & Mitchell, K. (2004). Internet-initiated sex crimes against minors: Implications for prevention based on findings from a national study. *Journal of Adolescent Health*, 35, 424.

Wolak, J., Mitchell, K., & Finkelhor, D. (2003). *Internet Sex Crimes Against Minors: The Response of Law Enforcement*. Washington, DC: Office of Juvenile Justice and Delinquency Prevention.

Wolak, J., Mitchell, K., & Finkelhor, D. (2006). *Online Victimization of Youth: Five Years Later*. Washington, DC: National Center for Missing & Exploited Children.

Wright, R. T., & Decker, S. H. (1997). *Armed Robbers In Action: Stickups and Street Culture*. Boston, MA: Northeastern University Press.

Yar, M. (2013). *Cybercrime and Society* (2nd ed.). Thousand Oaks, CA: SAGE.

Zickuhr, K. (2011). *Generations Online in 2010*. Pew Internet and American Life Project. [Online] Available at: www.pewinternet.org/Reports/2010/Generations-2010/Overview.aspx

chapter 2

Computer hackers and hacking

Chapter goals

- Define what is a "hack" and "hacker"
- Identify the way that both people and technology can be compromised by hackers
- Differentiate between nation-state and non-nation-state hackers
- Explain the key norms and values of the hacker subculture
- Identify the various terms used to define and differentiate hackers
- Consider the evolution of hacking in tandem with technology over the last 60 years
- Assess the legal frameworks used to prosecute hackers and the ability of law enforcement agencies to address computer hacking

Introduction

Many in the general public conceive of hackers as skilled technological wizards who break into the Department of Defense, financial institutions, and other protected networks with the intent to do harm. The notion of a hacker may also conjure up images of various characters from television and movies, such as Neo and Morpheus from the Matrix Trilogy, who had the ability to "see" in programming language code and bend "virtual" reality around them. These stories and representations have become the dominant model for hackers in popular media and news organizations (Furnell, 2002). Although there are a number of hackers who engage in malicious activities, and some who are amazingly sophisticated technology users, they do not accurately represent the entire population of hackers. Instead, hackers operate to defend computer networks and expand the utility of technology. In addition, an increasing proportion of the hacker community has a relatively low level of technological sophistication; only a small group has expert-level knowledge of computer hardware and software. The global hacker community is also driven by a wide range of motivations which leads them to engage in both legal and illegal hacks.

This chapter is designed to present the subculture of hackers in a realistic light devoid of the glitz and flash of what may be portrayed in films. By the end of this chapter, you will be able to understand the variations in the legal and ethical perspectives of hackers, as well as the norms and values of the hacker subculture. The history of hacking over the last 60 years will also be explored to ground your understanding of the actions of hackers over time, including the way that individual motives for hacking have changed with the explosion in computer technology. In turn, you will be able to consider the activities of hackers from their point of view rather than from stereotypes and media hype. Finally, we will explore the various legal frameworks that have been created to address illegal computer hacking and the abilities of law enforcement agencies to actually make an impact.

Defining computer hacking

While many in the general public equate computer hacking with criminal activity, it is actually a skill that can be applied in a variety of ways depending on the ethical perspective of the actor. A **hack** involves the modification or alteration of computer hardware or software to enable technology to be used in a new way, whether for legitimate or illegitimate purposes (Holt, 2007; Levy, 2001; Schell and Dodge, 2002; Turkle, 1984). There are myriad applications of hacking for beneficial uses that are not necessarily illegal. For instance, iPhones and iPods are designed to only run Apple approved software and applications. Any "app," ringtone, or wallpaper design that the company has deemed unacceptable due to risqué or inappropriate content will not work on their devices (Kravets, 2010). If you want to use these resources, or even change the appearance of the icons and applications on your Apple device, you must find a way to work around these limitations. Thus, programmers have created "jailbreaking" programs that enable users to install third party designers' programs to be used on an iPhone or other Apple product. The use of jailbreaking programs constitutes a hack, as they enable actors to use their devices in ways that were not initially allowed by the designer. The use of these programs is not illegal, though they can void the product warranty, making the user accountable for their use of hacking programs (Kravets, 2010).

The use of hacking for practical applications like jailbreaks is actually common, although many in the general public and law enforcement simply perceive hacking to be a crime (Furnell, 2002; Schell and Dodge, 2002). Hacks that modify programs and subvert security protocols can be used to obtain information or gain access to computer systems and protected resources in

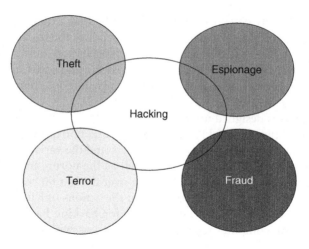

Figure 2.1 Venn diagram of computer hacking

furtherance of illegal acts ranging from stealing credit cards to acts of terror (Brenner, 2008; Chu, Holt, and Ahn, 2010; Kilger, 2010; see Figure 2.1 for details). In addition, hackers utilize very basic non-technical strategies to obtain information. For instance, individuals can steal someone's passwords for email accounts or access to a system by looking over their shoulder and watching their keystrokes. This act, called **shoulder surfing**, is simple and can be performed by anyone in order to obtain sensitive information (Mitnick and Simon, 2002; Wall, 2007). Similarly, hackers can employ **social engineering** tactics to try to fool or convince people to provide them with information that can be used to access different resources (Furnell, 2002; Huang and Brockman, 2010; Mitnick and Simon, 2002). These attacks often involve making simple requests and acting clueless in order to prey upon people's willingness to help others (Mitnick and Simon, 2002). These sorts of non-technical attacks are invaluable to attackers because it is extremely difficult to protect individuals from being compromised, unlike computer systems and physical buildings (Huang and Brockman, 2010; Mitnick and Simon, 2002). In fact, more than half of all investigated data breaches in a sample of businesses and universities were completed through the use of techniques that required little or no skill (Computer Security Institute, 2008).

For more on social engineering, go online to: www.csoonline.com/article/2123756/fraud-prevention/9-dirty-tricks–social-engineers–favorite-pick-up-lines.html

The information victims provide in non-technical attacks frequently includes usernames and passwords for different resources like email. In turn,

computer hackers and hacking

the attacker can gain access to personal or corporate information sources that they may not own or have permission to access. The issue of ownership and access is why Wall (2001) conceived of computer hacking as an act of cyber-trespass in keeping with burglary in the real world. A hacker must cross network boundaries without approval from the owner or operator in much the same way as a burglar enters a dwelling without permission. In order to compromise a computer system or network, the hacker must utilize **vulnerabilities,** or flaws, in computer software or hardware, or people in the case of social engineering (Furnell, 2002; Taylor, 1999). There are hundreds of vulnerabilities that have been identified in all manner of software, from the Microsoft operating system Windows, to the web browsers you use every day (Wang, 2006). In much the same way that burglars in the real world attempt to identify weaknesses in the design of homes, entrances, exits, and residents' behaviors and activities in order to find ways to get inside a location (e.g. Wright and Decker, 1994), hackers' first steps in developing a hack using technical means is identifying these vulnerabilities.

> **For more information on vulnerabilities, go online to:** http://nvd.nist. gov/

Once a vulnerability has been identified in a piece of technology, a hacker can then develop an **exploit,** a program that can take advantage of vulnerabilities to give the attacker deeper access to a system or network (Furnell, 2002; Taylor, 1999; Wang, 2006). There are myriad tools available online for hackers to use in order to exploit existing vulnerabilities in computer software (Chu *et al.*, 2010; Wang, 2006), and various forms of malicious software, which can be acquired for free from web forums or purchased from vendors in online black markets (see Chapter 3 for details; Chu *et al.*, 2010). Similarly, burglars can use tools, such as crowbars and keys, to gain access into a residence through vulnerable points of entry (Wright and Decker, 1994).

In the context of hacking, vulnerabilities and their attendant exploits can be used by anyone regardless of their ethical beliefs. For instance, there are vulnerability scanning tools available online like Nessus, which allows individuals to easily determine all the vulnerabilities present on a computer system (Wang, 2006). This tool can be used by hackers working on "red teams" or "tiger teams" hired by corporations to identify and penetrate their networks in order to better secure their resources. Red teams are authorized by system owners to engage in these acts; thus they are not violating the law. The same scanner could be used as a first step in an attack to identify vulnerabilities on a system to determine what exploits should be used to compromise the system. Running such a scan without permission from the system owners would be viewed as an illegal form of hacking (Wall, 2001).

Victims of hacking

Despite misconceptions over who and what is a hacker, it is clear that the use of hacking for malicious purposes can have severe economic and social consequences for computer users. The most common targets for attack by malicious hackers are individual computer users, private industry, and governments (Brenner, 2008). In fact, the general public present an excellent target for the majority of hackers since they may have sensitive information stored on their computer and can serve as a launch point for subsequent attacks against different targets (discussed in Chapter 3). A malicious hack can often affect multiple groups at the same time, and may be performed by individuals acting alone, in small groups, or in conjunction with a foreign military or government. When individuals act without any sort of state backing, they are referred to as **non-nation-state actors** because they have no immediate affiliation to an organization (Brenner, 2008; Denning, 2010).

> **For more information on cyberthreats at the nation-state level, go online to:** www.europeaninstitute.org/EA-November-2011/main-cyber-threats-now-coming-from-governments-as-state-actors.html

Non-nation-state actors who engage in hacking frequently target individuals and institutions in order to steal sensitive information that can be resold or used in some fashion for a profit (Franklin, Paxson, Perrig, and Savage, 2007; Holt and Lampke, 2010; Peretti, 2009). For instance, credit and debit card numbers are a regular target for hackers, as this information can be used by the hacker to obtain funds or sold to others to facilitate fraud (Franklin *et al.*, 2007; Holt and Lampke, 2010; Thomas and Martin, 2006). These attacks negatively affect both the cardholders and the financial institutions who manage customer accounts (Peretti, 2009). One of the most extreme examples of this sort of compromise took place in January 2009 against the Heartland Payment Systems company (Vijayan, 2010). This company processed credit card transactions for over 250,000 companies across the United States and was compromised by a piece of malicious software planted inside the company's network in order to record payment data as it was sent by retail clients (Krebs, 2009). As a consequence, hackers were able to acquire information from 130 million credit and debit cards processed by 100,000 businesses (Vijayan, 2010). The economic impact of such theft from hacking can be staggering. Based on some of the most recent available data, individual consumers lose an average of $223 through credit card fraud (Internet Crime Complaint Center, 2008) and companies lose $268,000 from the loss of customer information or employee personal data (Computer Security Institute, 2008).

By contrast, hackers who engage in attacks at the behest of or in cooperation with a government or military entity can be referred to as **nation-state actors** (Brenner, 2008; Denning, 2010). Though it is unclear how many nation-state hackers there are internationally, they are most likely a small number relative to the larger population of non-nation-state actors. The targets of nation-state actors' attacks differ substantially. They frequently target governments and corporations using hacks to engage in both espionage and theft of intellectual property (Brenner, 2008). For example, Chinese hackers with government ties were thought to be responsible for a series of attacks against multiple high profile businesses, including Google, Adobe, Juniper Networks, Yahoo, Symantec, Northrop Grumman, and Dow Chemical through the use of innovative and never before identified attack tools (Zetter, 2010). The attackers initially sent targeted phishing emails to individuals within corporations in order to compromise their machines and harvest intellectual property within these companies to gain corporate or political advantage (Markoff and Barboza, 2010; Zetter, 2010).

Over the last two decades, there have been an increasing number of attacks performed by non-nation-state actors against government and industry targets due to social conflicts both online and offline (Brenner, 2008; Denning, 2010; Kilger, 2010). This was exemplified by the recent international conflict between Russia and Estonia over the removal of a Russian war monument from a national memorial garden in Estonia in April 2006 (Brenner, 2008; Jaffe, 2006; Landler and Markoff, 2008). This action enraged Russian citizens living in Estonia and elsewhere, leading to protests and violence in the streets of both nations. Hackers soon began to target government and private resources in both nations, and co-opted actors outside of the hacker community to participate in their attacks (Brenner, 2008; Jaffe, 2006). The attacks became so severe that portions of the Estonian government and financial service sector were completely shut down, causing substantive economic harm (Brenner, 2008; Landler and Markoff, 2008).

> **For more information on the Russia/Estonia cyber conflict, go online to:**
> www.youtube.com/watch?v=fzFc1HH6Z_k

The human aspects of the hacker subculture

In light of the various targets affected by hacks, it is necessary to understand the individuals responsible for these attacks (see Text Box 2.1 for details). Individuals who utilize hacks may be referred to as **hackers**, though this term has different meanings to different groups (Jordan and Taylor, 1998; Schell and Dodge, 2002; Taylor, 1999; Turkle, 1984). Individuals within the hacker community may argue that a person can only be a hacker dependent on their level of skill or interest in technology (Holt, 2007; Jordan and Taylor, 1998). Individuals in the general public might often define a hacker, however, as a young, anti-social nerd who can only relate to others via their computer (Furnell, 2002; Schell and Dodge, 2002). They may also be viewed as misfits who are involved in criminal or illicit activities, or perhaps computer technicians within corporations or at electronics retailers (Furnell, 2002; Schell and Dodge, 2002).

Text Box 2.1: The Jargon File definition of hacking

http://catb.org/jargon/html/H/hacker.html

> 1. A person who enjoys exploring the details of programmable systems and how to stretch their capabilities, as opposed to most users, who prefer to learn only the minimum necessary.

The Jargon File provides a very distinct and well-accepted set of definitions for what constitutes a hacker. The definition also recognizes the differences between a hacker who is motivated by curiosity and intellect relative to malicious intent.

These conceptions are not necessarily accurate based on the findings of empirical studies of the hacker community. Research suggests that hackers are predominantly males under the age of 30, but that there are older hackers working in the security community as well (Bachmann, 2010; Gilboa, 1996; Jordan and Taylor, 1998; Schell and Dodge, 2002). Younger people may be attracted to hacking because they have greater access and exposure to technology, as well as the time to explore technology at deep levels. Older hackers appear to be gainfully employed, working primarily in the computer security industry (Bachmann, 2010; Schell and Dodge, 2002). Younger hackers may or may not be employed; some may be students in high school or universities. In fact, hackers tend to have a mix of both formal education and knowledge acquired on their own through reading and experiential learning (Bachmann, 2010; Holt, 2007). Limited evidence suggests that a proportion of skilled actors may have at least a community college education, while a small number have degrees from four-year institutions (Bachmann 2010; Holt, Soles, and Leslie, 2008; Holt, Kilger, Strumsky, and Smirnova, 2009; Schell and Dodge, 2002). Hackers also appear to be predominantly male, though it is unknown what constitutes the true gender composition of the subculture (Gilboa, 1996; Jordan and Taylor, 1998; Schell and Dodge, 2002; Taylor, 1999). This is because most hackers conceal their identities from others online and are especially resistant to being interviewed or participating in research studies (Gilboa, 1996; Holt, 2007).

computer hackers and hacking

Thus, it is difficult to identify the overall composition of the hacker community at any given point in time.

There is also substantive evidence that hackers have a number of social relationships that influence their willingness to engage in different forms of behavior over time (Bossler and Burruss, 2011; Holt, Bossler, and May, 2012; Skinner and Fream, 1997). Peer relationships often emerge online through involvement in forums, IRC channels, and other forms of computer-mediated communication (Holt, 2009a; Jordan and Taylor, 1998; Skinner and Fream, 1997), though a portion may involve social relationships cultivated in the real world. These associations are invaluable as friends and relatives can provide models to imitate hacks (Morris and Blackburn, 2009), positive encouragement and praise for unique hacks, and justifications for behavior, including excuses and beliefs about the utility of malicious hacks (Bossler and Burruss, 2011; Morris, 2011; Skinner and Fream, 1997). In fact, many hackers deny any harm resulted from their actions (Gordon and Ma, 2003), or blame their victims for having inadequate computer skills or systems to prevent victimization (Jordan and Taylor, 1998).

Hacking history

1950s – The origins

In order to understand the hacker community, it is important to explain its historical evolution in the context of computing technology since its infancy in the late 1950s (see Figure 2.2 for details). Some researchers argue that the term "hacking" emerged from engineering students at the Massachusetts Institute of Technology (MIT) in the 1950s (Levy, 2001). This phrase was used by students to refer to playful, but skilled, tinkering with electronics and was largely synonymous with "goofing off" or "fooling around." In fact, the MIT model railroad club (TMRC) used the term to describe their work on the club's railroad systems (Levy, 2001). They perceived hacking as a way to solve problems in spite of conventional techniques for engineering and electronics.

The emergence of computing in the 1950s in university settings like MIT, Cornell, and Harvard also facilitated the emergence of hacking. At the time, computing mainframes were massive systems encompassing whole climate-controlled rooms with relatively limited memory and overall processing power (Levy, 2001; see Text Box 2.2 for details). These devices were not linked together in any networked fashion as is the case with current computers, and individuals working with these systems had to develop their own unique solutions to problems experienced by programmers and users. Computer programmers who managed the systems of the time were often pressed to find ways to speed up the otherwise slow processing of their mainframe computers. The elegant and innovative solutions to these problems were referred to as "hacks," and the programmers responsible were

Timeline of computer hacking

1965	The first computer hackers emerge at MIT. Members try their hand in rigging the new mainframe computing systems being studied and developed on campus.
1968	The UNIX operating system is developed by Dennis Ritchie and Keith Thompson.
1971	Phone hackers or phreaks break into regional and international phone networks to make free calls. John Draper discovers that a toy whistle found inside a Cap'n Crunch cereal box generates a 2600 Hz tone. By building a "blue box" using the toy whistle, resulting in free calls, John Draper and other phreaks land feature story in Esquire Magazine entitled "Secrets of the Little Blue Box."
	The first email program is created by Ray Tomlinson.
1975	Microsoft is created by Bill Gates and Paul Allen.
1976	The Apple Computer is created by Steve Jobs, Stephen Wozniak, and Ron Wayne.
1980–1982	Phone phreaks move into computer hacking, and message boards are created called electronic bulletin board systems (BBSs) to exchange information and tactics with other phreaks. Emergence of many hacking groups, including Legion of Doom and The Warelords in the United States, and the Chaos Computer Club in Germany.
1981	Ian Murphy becomes the first hacker to be tried and convicted as a felon for computer hacking.
1983	"War Games" sheds light on the capabilities that hackers could have. Generates fear among the public.
	"414" gang arrested for allegedly breaking into 60 computer systems from Los Angeles to Manhattan, As a result the story gets mass coverage and the US House of Representatives holds hearings to discuss cyber security.
1984	The Hacker Magazine or Hagazine called "2600," and the online 'zine Phrack a year later, are created to give tips to upcoming hackers and phone phreaks.
	The comprehensive crime control act is passed, giving the Secret Service jurisdiction over computer fraud.
1985	The first PC virus, called the brain, is created. The virus used stealth techniques for the first time and originated in Pakistan.
1986	As a result of numerous break-ins on government and corporate computer systems Congress passes the Computer Fraud and Abuse Act, which makes it a crime to break into computer systems; this law did not apply to juveniles.
1988	The Morris Worm incident is caused by Robert T. Morris, the son of a Chief Scientist of a division of the National Security Agency, and a graduate student at Cornell University. Morris plants a self-replicating worm on the government's Arpanet in order to test what effect it would have on the UNIX system. The worm spread and clogged 6,000 networked computers belonging to the government and the university. As a result, Morris was expelled from Cornell, given probation, and fined $10,000.
	The Computer Emergency Response Team (CERT) is created by DARPA (Defense Advanced Research Projects Agency), an agency of the United States Department of Defense responsible for the development of new technologies for use by the military. DARPA would address network security.
1989	The Hacker's Manifesto is published by "The Mentor," and the Cuckoo's Egg is published by Clifford Stoll.
	Herbert Zinn becomes the first juvenile to be convicted under the Computer Fraud Act.
1990	The Electronic Frontier Foundation is founded in order to protect and defend the rights of those investigated for computer hacking.

Figure 2.2 A timeline of notable events in the history of hacking

	Operation Sundevil commences, a prolonged sting operation where Secret Service agents arrested prominent members of the BBSs in 14 US cities during early-morning raids and arrests. The arrests were aimed at cracking down on credit card theft and telephone and wire fraud. This resulted in the breakdown in the hacking community, whereby members were informing on each other in exchange for immunity.
1991	A federal ban to bar business from the Internet is lifted.
1993	DefCon hacking conference held in Las Vegas to say goodbye to BBSs. Popularity of event resulted in a meeting every year thereafter.
1994–2000	Emergence of the World Wide Web. Hackers adapt and transfer all information to web sites; as a result the face of hacking changes.
1994	Russian crackers siphon $10 million from Citibank and transfer money to bank accounts around the world, led by Vladimir Levin who transferred funds to accounts in Finland and Israel using his laptop. Levin was sentenced to three years in prison. All but $400,000 was recovered.
1995	Kevin Mitnik is charged with illegally accessing computers belonging to numerous computer software and computer operating system manufacturers, cellular telephone manufacturers, Internet service providers, and educational institutions. Mitnik was also responsible for the theft, copying, and misappropriation of proprietary computer software from Motorola, Fujitsu, Nokia, Sun, Novell, and NEC. Mitnick was also in possession of 20,000 credit card numbers once captured.
	Chris Pile becomes the first person to be jailed for writing and distributing a computer virus.
1994/1997	AOHell, a freeware application that allows unskilled script kiddies to wreak havoc on America Online or AOL is released, resulting in hundreds of thousands of mailboxes being flooded with email bombs and spam.
1996	Hackers alter the websites of the United States Department of Justice, the CIA, and the US Air Force. Reports by the General Accounting Office state that hackers attempted to break into Defense Department computer files approximately 250,000 times, 65 percent of which were successful.
1998	NASA, the US Navy, and universities across the country are targeted by denial of service attacks on computers running Microsoft Windows NT and Windows 95.
	Carl Fredrik Neikter, the leader of The Cult of Dead Cow, releases the Trojan Horse program "Black Orifice," which allows hackers remote access to computers once installed.
1999	Napster is created by Shawn Fanning and Sean Parker, attracting millions of users before being shut down in July of 2001.
	The first series of mainstream security software is released for use on personal computers.
	Bill Clinton announces a billion-dollar initiative to improve computer security and the establishment of a network of intrusion detection monitors for certain federal agencies.
	The Melissa virus is released causing the most costly malware outbreak to date.
	The Cult of the Dead Cow releases an updated version of Black Orifice.
2000	DOSO hackers launch attacks, shutting down Yahoo, Buy.com, Amazon, eBay, and CNN.
2001	The Department of Energy's computer system at Sandia National Laboratories in Albuquerque is compromised.
	Microsoft's main server is hacked by DDoS attacks.
2002	January: Internal training and quality control campaign started by Bill Gates in order to insure the security of Microsoft.
	June: George W. Bush's administration submits a bill that would create the Department of Homeland Security, which would have, as one of its many roles, the responsibility of protecting the nation's critical information technology (IT) infrastructure.

Figure 2.2 (cont.)

The CIA warns of an impending launch of cyber-attacks on US computer networks by Chinese hackers funded by the Chinese government.

August: "Shatter Attacks" is published by Chris Paget, showing how the Windows messaging system could be used to take control of a machine and questioning the security of the Windows system itself.

2003	Anonymous is formed. The United States Department of Commerce allows hacker groups to export encrypted software.
2004	Myron Tereshchuk is taken into police custody for an attempt to extort millions from Micropatent. North Korea claims to attempt to break into South Korea's computer systems.
2005	Rafael Nunez, member of "World of Hell," is taken into custody for cracking into the Defense Information Systems Agency. Cameron Lacroix is convicted for hacking into T-Mobile's USA network. Jeanson James Ancheta, member of "Botmaster Underground," is arrested by FBI.
2006	Kama Sutra, a worm specializing in destruction of data, is discovered and found to replicate itself through email contacts, disrupting documents and folders. The threat turned out to be minimal. Jeanson James Ancheta convicted for his role in hacking systems of the Naval Air Warfare Center and the Defense Information Systems Agency, sentenced to prison, and ordered to pay damages in addition to handing over his property. Iskorpitx hacks more than 20,000 websites. Robert Moore and Edwin Pena, hackers featured on *America's Most Wanted*, are convicted, and ordered to pay restitution. FairUse4WM is released by Viodentia, removing DRM from music service websites.
2007	Estonia recovers from DDoS attacks. During Operation "Bot Roast," the FBI locates over a million botnet victims; the second botnet operation uncovers a million infected computers, results in a loss of millions of dollars, and several indictments. Office of Secretary of Defense undergoes a spear-phishing scheme, resulting in the loss of US Defense information as well as causing communication and identification systems to be altered. The United Nations website is hacked.
2008	Project Chanology occurs on a Scientology website by Anonymous resulting in the loss and release of confidential information.
2009	The Conficker worm hacks into the computer networks of personal computers and government.
2010	"Operation Aurora": Google admits to attacks on its infrastructure from China resulting in the loss of intellectual property. Stuxnet worm discovered by VirusBlockAda, deemed to be a cyber attack on the nuclear facilities of Iran. MALCON conference held in India, founded by Rajshekhar Murthy. Event gives an opportunity to display the techniques of malware coders from around the world.
2011	The website of Bank of America is hacked by Jeopardy, who is accused of stealing credit card information by the FBI. The PlayStation Network is compromised revealing personal information of its consumers, recognized as one of the largest data breaches to date. Youtube channel of Sesame Street hacked. Palestinian Territories' internet networks and phone lines hacked from multiple locations around the world.
2012	Hundreds of thousands of credit card numbers from Israel released by Saudi hacker named 0xOmar. As a result Israel releases hundreds of credit card numbers from Saudi Arabia.

Figure 2.2 (cont.)

computer hackers and hacking

Team Appunity, a Norwegian hacker group, is taken into custody for releasing the user database for the largest prostitution ring in Norway.

Foxconn is hacked by Swagg Security, compromising information.

WHMCS and MyBB are hacked by UGNazi due to the use of its software.

Government sites including Farmers Insurance, MasterCard, and others are hacked by Swagg Security resulting in the release of personal information.

2013   Burger King twitter account is hacked by McDonald's.

The above information was accessed from:
1. http://steel.lcc.gatech.edu/~mcordell/lcc6316/Hacker%20Group%20Project%20FINAL.pdf
2. http://en.wikipedia.org/wiki/Timeline_of_computer_security_hacker_history
3. http://edition.cnn.com/2001/TECH/internet/11/19/hack.history.idg/index.html
4. www.symantec.com/about/news/resources/press_kits/securityintelligence/media/SSR-Timeline.pdf

identified as "hackers" in keeping with the original concept as generated among the student body at MIT (Levy, 2001).

Text Box 2.2: Mainframe computing systems

http://now.uiowa.edu/2013/03/hello-maui-goodnight-mainframe

What's a mainframe? Sometimes called "big iron," a mainframe is a large-scale computer that can support thousands of users simultaneously and run vital operations reliably and securely. The mainframe probably got its name from massive metal frames that once housed it, often occupying thousands of square feet.

This article describes the early phases of mainframe computing and the eventual transition from these room-sized devices to the laptops of today.

For more information on the history of hacking at MIT, go online to: http://tmrc.mit.edu/hackers-ref.html

---

1960s and 1970s – The hacker ethic

The perception of the hacker as a skilled programmer and tinkerer continued through the 1960s. The social upheaval and civil unrest experienced during this decade, however, would affect the ways that hackers viewed their relationship to technology and the larger world. As computer technology moved from universities into military applications, the number of programmers and "hackers" began to expand. As a consequence, a culture of programmers emerged based on a series of ideas called the **hacker ethic** by Steven Levy (2001):

1. Access to computers – and anything that might teach you something about the way the world works – should be unlimited and total.
2. All information should be free.
3. Mistrust authority – promote decentralization.
4. Hackers should be judged by their hacking, not bogus criteria such as degrees, age, race, or position.
5. You can create art and beauty on a computer.
6. Computers can change your life for the better.

Though these six ideas are interrelated, the core belief within the hacker ethic is that information should be open and free to all so that individuals can understand how things work and identify ways that they could be improved (Thomas, 2002).

The importance of transparency through technology became even more salient in the 1970s with the introduction of two activities: phreaking and homebrew computing. The emergence of phone phreaking, or tampering with phone technology to understand and control telephone systems, was espoused by elements of the 1960s and 70s counterculture movement (Landreth, 1985; Wang, 2006). Individuals like Abbie Hoffman, an activist and protestor who wrote *Steal This Book*, advised people to engage in phreaking as a way to strike out against telephone companies for profiteering from a wonderful service. Hoffman and other groups wanted people to phreak because they could make free calls to anyone in the world by controlling telephone system switches through various devices and tones. The novel application and manipulation of telephony through phreaking led this activity to be the first form of hacking to gain a broader audience outside of traditional computing.

The act of phreaking gained national attention in the mainstream media through an article published in *Esquire* magazine on John Draper and various other "phreaks" in 1971 (Wang, 2006). Subsequently, law enforcement and telephone security began collaborative crackdowns to eliminate phreaks from penetrating telephony. The absence of laws pertaining to the exploration and manipulation of computers and telephony made it difficult for police agencies until the late 1970s, when the first legal statutes were developed (Wang, 2006). In fact, one of the first computer crime laws in the United States was passed in Florida in 1978 making all unauthorized access to computer systems a third degree felony (Hollinger and Lanza-Kaduce, 1988).

> **For more information on blue boxes and phreaking, go online to:** www. youtube.com/watch?v=fF2NuFXVJS8

The 1970s also saw the emergence of hobbyist groups focused on the development of computer hardware and software. These groups operated through informal meetings run in garages and other settings to facilitate conversations on the design and construction of personal computers (PCs). These hobbyists often used a combination of commercial computer kits sold through magazines, as well as their own innovative designs and "hacks" of existing resources. Their practices helped to advance the state of personal computing, though they did not typically refer to themselves or their activities as hacking (Ceruzzi, 1998).

1980s – PCs, entertainment, and The Hacker Manifesto

The adoption of PC technology was initially slow, and did not take hold until the early 1980s when middle income families began to purchase computers. The concurrent explosion of video games and home electronic entertainment systems exposed young people to technology as never before. Young people, particularly males, were increasingly attracted to these devices and began to explore and use computers beyond their advertised value as learning tools. Similarly, modem technology, which connects computers to other computers and networks via telephone lines, improved and became accessible to the common home user. Individuals who had never before had access to computer technology could now identify and explore connected computer networks (Furnell, 2002). This led to the rise of the bulletin board systems (BBS) culture where local groups and hackers across the country could connect and share information with others (Slattala and Quittner, 1995). At the same time, a growing underground media began to publish homemade magazines on computers, hacking, and phreaking, such as *Phrack* and *2600*. These publications helped to propel individual interests in hacking and connect the burgeoning computer-using community together.

The increasing popularity of technology in the general public led to increased media attention around computers and youth. This was due, in part, to the theatrical release of the movie *WarGames*, which featured a teenage hacker played by Matthew Broderick who unsuspectingly gains access to military computer systems and nearly causes a nuclear holocaust (Schneider, 2008). The film piqued the curiosity of some youth and increased interest in hacking and computer use in general (see Text Box 2.3 for details). Media outlets quickly published stories on malicious hacker groups in order to capitalize on the public interest in computer misuse stemming from the film (Marbach, 1983a, b). For instance, the FBI began raiding and filing suits against the members of a local group of hackers known as the "414s" based on their Milwaukee area code (Krance, Murphy, and Elmer-Dewitt, 1983). The teen boys compromised protected networks but did not cause harm to systems or data (Hollinger and Lanza-Kaduce, 1988). Their acts drew attention from both federal law enforcement and the media to the growing perceived use of hacking for criminal purposes.

Thus, this marked a distinct divergence in the concept of hacking and hackers from the notion in the 1950s and 60s of ethical computer tinkerers to a more criminal orientation.

For more information on 1980s hacker groups, go online to: http://archive.wired.com/wired/archive/2.12/hacker_pr.html

---

Text Box 2.3: A hacker talks about *WarGames* (interview conducted with Mac Diesel by Thomas J. Holt)

When *WarGames* came out, that was probably the biggest boon to the modern hacker that there ever was. Because right after that war dialers came out ... programs that you could download to your computer that were all over the BBS that you could download that would call up people's computers and just look for modem tones. And then, they'd record the greetings that the computers gave. Everybody was friendly back then so when you dialed into a computer, it gave you the identification of who the computer was and uh, if it was governmental or something like that. Uhm, it would either tell you, you know this is so and so's computer or simply would not tell you anything and that would be a flag that hey, this is, you know, is something worth looking at. If it's just asked you for your username and password, then maybe I need to go in here. Most of 'em didn't even ask for usernames. They just wanted passwords ... So you start doing things and when I got my first modem uhm, *WarGames* came out as a movie and I saw all these dialers and I thought you know, this is cool. And so you download one of the dialers and you run it. You check every phone number in your neighborhood and after it had checked for five days and like come up with four numbers or whatever and you would take those numbers and call 'em and you would get the greeting protocols. And from that point in time you'd bring in your second program which was just, it would dial up, connect, and then it would randomly generate a password. Try to get through and it would keep doing it ... so you would take this wardialer and you would tell it, ok I'm going to dial every phone number in there looking for a modem and hang up. And you know if I don't get a modem in so much time, hang up, go to the next one. So the people think they get a hang-up phone call, it's annoying, but that's it. When you finally do get one, it sends across its I-identification which was usually a welcome greeting if, you know, you know, "welcome to blah-blah blah-blah-blah" and, uh, it would record that and then you'd go through at the end of, you know, after you'd let it sit for however long it took to go through that exchange and for the ten thousand numbers in the exchange it might take eight hours. You'd come back at the end of eight hours you'd look at all your greetings and see if any of 'em were what you were looking for. Once you knew they were what you were looking for then it was a matter of brute forcing the passwords.

The criminalization of hacking and the growing schism in the hacker community was exacerbated by the publication of a brief text called *The Conscience of a Hacker*, or **The Hacker Manifesto** (Furnell, 2002). The document was written by "The Mentor" in 1986, and first published in the magazine *Phrack*. The Mentor railed against adults, law enforcement, and schools, arguing that hackers seek knowledge even if that means breaking into or gaining access to protected computer systems. These activities do not make hackers criminals according to the Mentor, but rather misunderstood and unappreciated by adults who have no conception of the value of technology. He also encouraged hackers to engage in phreaking because telephone companies were "run by profiteering gluttons." This document supported some of the criminal aspects of hacking that were in opposition to the 1960s conception of hacking and the broader hacker ethic. As a consequence, a rift began to form between hackers based on their support of either the *Manifesto* or the hacker ethic, as well as their perception of malicious and exploratory hacks.

In fact, there are two terms that are used by some to attempt to differentiate between hackers who seek to harm or destroy systems and those who do not. The term **crack** emerged within the hacker subculture to recognize and separate malicious hacks from those acts supported by the hacker ethic (Furnell, 2002; Holt, 2010). Those who engage in deviant or criminal applications of hacking could be labeled as **crackers** since true hackers consider destructive hackers to be "a lower form of life" (Furnell, 2002). Thus, the act of cracking is thought to be different from hacking based on the outcome of the attack and not the techniques applied by the actor.

For the full text of the *Hacker Manifesto*, go online to: www.phrack.org/issues/7/3.html#article

The criminalization of hacking continued through the creation of the federal Counterfeit Access Device and Computer Fraud and Abuse Act of 1984, and its subsequent revision in 1986. The 1984 law initially focused on the use and abuse of credit card information and established that any criminal incident involving $5,000 of loss or more was a federal offense to be handled by the Secret Service (Hollinger and Lanza-Kaduce, 1988). The 1986 revision of this act, however, expanded legal protections to all computerized information maintained by banks and financial institutions. Furthermore, the law added three new violations: (1) unauthorized access to computer systems with the intent to defraud; (2) unauthorized access with intent to cause malicious damage; and (3) the trafficking of computer passwords with the intent to defraud (Taylor, Fritsch, Lieberbach, and Holt, 2010). These laws not only codified criminal applications of hacking, but also afforded police agencies with better tools to prosecute the activities of hackers across the country (Hollinger and Lanza-Kaduce, 1988; Sterling, 1992; Taylor *et al.*, 2010). In turn, multiple high profile law enforcement investigations developed during the late 1980s and early 1990s, such as the pursuit of Kevin Mitnick (Shimomura and Markoff, 1996; see Text Box 2.4 for details) and Kevin Poulsen (Littman, 1997).

Text Box 2.4: The criminal exploits of Kevin Mitnick

Mitnick's own words about his 'hacking' – forbes.com interview 5/99

www.forbes.com/1999/04/05/feat.html

FORBES.COM [F]: How would you characterize the media coverage of you?

MITNICK [M]: When I read about myself in the media even I don't recognize me. The myth of Kevin Mitnick is much more interesting than the reality of Kevin Mitnick. If they told the reality, no one would care …

In this article, Kevin Mitnick discusses his hacks and his life during incarceration for violations of the Computer Fraud and Abuse Act. He also discusses his thoughts on the post-release conditions he would have to live with once he completed his prison sentence.

As technology became increasingly user friendly and affordable in the early 1990s, the hacker population continued to expand. The hacker subculture became more segmented based on the use of perceived unethical hacking techniques by the increasing number of young hackers (Taylor, 1999). For instance, modern hackers would typically attempt to gather internal documents after accessing a system, both for bragging rights and to allow for the free exchange of information through the hacker network. This desire to spread information and discuss attack techniques afforded a mechanism for law enforcement to gather evidence of illegal activities (Holt, 2007). As a consequence, the free exchange of information within the hacker community began to evolve into trying to diminish the likelihood of detection and prosecution (Kilger, 2010; Taylor, 1999). Local hacker groups began to support conferences on the topic of hacking in the United States, including DefCon, Hackers On Planet Earth (HOPE), and PumpCon (see Figure 2.3 for details). Similar conferences have been held since the mid 1980s in

computer hackers and hacking

Germany, such as the **Chaos Communication Congress (CCC)**, which began in 1984 in Hamburg, then moved to Berlin in 1998 (Kinkade, Bachmann, and Bachmann, 2013). These meetings afforded the opportunity to connect in the real world and gave the hacker population an air of respectability in the face of increasing criminal prosecutions of hacker groups (Holt, 2007).

Timeline of computer hacking conferences

1984   Chaos Communication Congress, Europe's largest hacker conference, began in Berlin and was held by the Chaos Computer Club. There are four sections of the event including: the Conference, the HackCenter, Art and Beauty, and the Phone Operation Center. The main topic categories of the event include: Hacking, Science, Community, Society, and Culture.

1987   SummerCon, one of the oldest conventions in the US, began and was run by Phrack in St. Louis, Missouri until 1995. The SummerCon conference influenced the HOPE and DefCon conferences. The Legion of Doom took over in 1995 and moved the conference to Atlanta, Georgia. After this, the conference was held in numerous locations such as Washington, DC, Pittsburgh, Pennsylvania, and Austin, Texas.

1990   HoHoCon Conference began in Houston, Texas during Christmas from 1990–1994. The event was sponsored by Drunkfux, Dead Cow, and Phrack. The conference, being one of the largest and most influential gatherings, influenced the DefCon and HOPE conferences.

1993   DefCon, held initially in Las Vegas, Nevada, began; it is the world's largest annual hacker convention to this day. Conference participants include average citizens, interest groups, federal employees, and hackers. The conference focuses on a variety of topics from computers to social events and contests. The conference is usually held in the summer from June to August.

1994   HOPE (Hackers On Planet Earth) conference began. The event is sponsored by hacker magazine *2600: The Hacker Quarterly*, and like DefCon continues to this day. The conference is also diverse in who attends. The individuals range from hackers and phreaks to net activists and government spooks. The conference is held for three days, usually during the summer, at the Hotel Pennsylvania in New York City. The HOPE conferences invest in social and political agendas advocating hacker activity.

PumpCon conference held in Philadelphia, PA from mid-90s to now. The conference is held in October before Halloween.

1997   Black Hat Briefings was started in 1997 by Jeff Moss. The company sought to provide education to security professionals in global corporations and the federal government. The event is held in Las Vegas, Nevada and Washington, DC, as well as internationally in locations such as Tokyo and Singapore. The training also includes hands-on experience with recent security threats and countermeasures.

PhreakNIC was created by the Nashville 2600 organization. The conference is held annually in Nashville, Tennessee and focuses on technical presentations. Popular culture is also a focus in the conference. The conference attracts individuals from all around the United States as well as regional states including Washington, DC, Georgia, Kentucky, Alabama, Missouri, and Ohio.

1999   ToorCon started by 2600 user group but founded by Ben Greenberg and David Hulton. The hacker conference is held annually in September and focuses on topics of hacking and security.

2003   Notacon (Northern Ohio Technological Advancement Conference) was created by "FTS Conventures" to fill the void left by the Detroit, Michigan Rubi-Con. The conference focuses on the art of hacking as a technique and how to apply the idea to art and music. "Community through Technology" is a main focus of the event. The conference was last held in April of 2009 in Cleveland, Ohio.

Figure 2.3 A timeline of hacker cons

2004	T2 infosec conference began. The conference is held annually in Helsinki, Finland, focusing on information security research and topics from security and defense to auditing.
2005	CarolinaCon conference began and is held annually in North Carolina. The conference is dedicated to sharing information about technology, security, and information rights. It also seeks to create local and international awareness about technology issues and developments.

2005 (cont.)

SchmooCon conference was created. The conference is held annually on the east coast in Washington, DC for three days. The conference focuses on technology exploitation and inventive software and hardware solutions, and has open discussions about critical infosec issues.

Ekoparty was created by Juan Pablo Daniel Borgna, Leonardo Pigner, Federico Kirschbaum, Jerónimo Basaldúa, and Francisco Amato. The security conference is held annually in Argentina and focuses on information security.

2007	Kiwicon began in Wellington, New Zealand. The conference is open to all ages and focuses on a variety of subjects including modern exploit techniques, security philosophy, and New Zealand law.
2009	AthCon conference was created by Cyberdefend Limited. AthCon is an annual IT security conference held in Athens, Greece. The conference focuses on giving technical insight.
2010	Malcon was created by Rajshekhar Murthy. The international technology security conference is held in India, bringing together malware and information security researchers.

THOTCON was created by Nicholas J. Percoco, Zack Fasel, Matt Jakubowski, Jonathan Tomek, and other DefCon volunteers in Chicago, Illinois. The conference focuses on information security and hacking.

2011	DerbyCon conference began in Louisville, Kentucky. The conference invites security professionals from around the world to share ideas.

INFILTRATE was founded. The security conference is hosted by Immunity, Inc annually in Miami, Florida. The conference focuses on offensive technical issues.

2012	SkyDogCon (New) was founded by a group of volunteers with a wealth of conference participation experience in Nashville, Tennessee. The event was created by hackers for hackers to share knowledge and facilitate learning.

HackInTheBox security conference held annually in the Netherlands and Malaysia. The conference provides hands-on technical training.

The Hackers Conference is held annually in New Delhi, and is one of India's biggest hacker conventions. The conference focuses on addressing the most topical issues of the Internet security space.

GrrCon is a midwestern information security conference held in Grand Rapids, Michigan. The conference is an information hub for sharing ideas and building relationships.

Hackers 2 Hackers Conference is a security research event held in Latin America.

Hactivity is an informal information security conference held annually in Budapest, Hungary.

Hackfest is a bilingual conference held annually in Quebec, Canada that focuses on hacking games.

Nuit Du Hack is a hacker conference held in Paris, France during the month of June.

ROOTCON is a premier hacker conference, held annually in the Philippines between the months of September and October.

QUAHOGON is a hacker conference that is held annually in Providence, Rhode Island at the end of April.

The above information was accessed from:

www.cse.wustl.edu/~jain/cse571-07/ftp/hacking_orgs.pdf
http://en.wikipedia.org/wiki/Computer_security_conference
http://carolinacon.org/#About

computer hackers and hacking

www.shmoocon.org/shmoocon
http://hackercons.org/index.html
http://en.wikipedia.org/wiki/Notacon
http://en.wikipedia.org/wiki/PhreakNIC
https://www.derbycon.com/
http://blog.pumpcon.org/
www.athcon.org/about.php
www.thehackersconference.com/about.html
http://grrcon.org/

1990s – Affordable technology, the computer security community, and financial gain

At the same time, the computer security community began to emerge in the 1990s with the incorporation of skilled hackers who understood the process of identifying and securing vulnerable software and hardware. This created a new tension within the hacker community between supposedly ethical hackers who worked for private industry and unethical hackers who used the same techniques to explore and exploit systems (Jordan and Taylor, 1998; Taylor, 1999). Some felt this was an important transition back to the origins of the hacker ethic, while others viewed the change from hacker to security professional as a process of selling out and betraying the very nature of open exchange within the hacker community (Taylor, 1999).

The prosecution and detention of Kevin Mitnick exacerbated this issue in the mid 1990s. Mitnick was viewed as a hero by the hacker community because of his substantial skill and the overly harsh treatment at the hands of law enforcement and prosecutors (Taylor *et al.*, 2010). In fact, federal prosecutors barred Mitnick from using a computer or Internet-connected device for several years after his release from a federal prison due to fears that he might cause substantial harm to telephony or private industry (Painter, 2001). Many hackers donated to Mitnick's legal defense fund and felt that he was a scapegoat of fearmongering by legislators and law enforcement (Taylor *et al.*, 2010). Shortly after his release from prison, Mitnick began a computer security consulting business and angered those in the subculture who viewed this as a betrayal of the basic principles of the hacker community. As a result, he lost a good deal of respect but provided a model for others to transition from known criminal to security insider in an increasingly technologically driven society.

For more information on Mitnick's prison experience, go online to:
www.youtube.com/watch?v=IJFCbrhLojA

By the late 1990s, the World Wide Web and PC had radically altered the nature of business and communications. The global expansion of connectivity afforded by the Internet led to the digitization of sensitive financial and government information and massive databases accessible online. Financial service providers and business platforms moved to online environments to offer services directly to home computer users, offering convenient modes of communication and shopping. As a consequence, the landscape and dynamics of computer hacking and the computer security industry changed.

The motives for hacking also shifted during this period from acquiring status and acceptance from the social groups that dominated hacking in the 1980s and 90s, toward economic gain (Chu *et al.*, 2010; Kilger, 2010; Holt and Lampke, 2010). The complexity of the tools used by hackers increased, and their functionality changed from infecting and degrading global networks to attacking and stealing sensitive information surreptitiously. In fact, the problem of **phishing**, where consumers are tricked into transmitting financial information into fraudulent websites where the information is housed for later fraud, grew in the late 1990s and early 2000s (James, 2005; Wall, 2007). These crimes are particularly costly for both the individual victim and financial institutions alike, as the Gartner Group estimates that phishing victims in the US lost $3 billion in 2007 alone (Rogers, 2007). The scope of phishing attacks is tremendous, with at least 72,758 phishing attacks reported in virtually all nations around the world during the first three months of 2013 alone (Anti-Phishing Working Group, 2013). Many of these attacks were facilitated by maliciously registered domain names for websites, many of which appear to stem from the activities of Chinese phishers (Anti-Phishing Working Group, 2013).

During this time, individuals began to apply hacking techniques and skills in attacks based on political and social agendas against government and private industry targets. For instance, members of the hacker collective the "Electronic Disturbance Theater" created and released an attack tool called FloodNet (Denning, 2010; Jordan and Taylor, 2004). This program was designed as a standalone tool to enable unskilled actors to engage in **denial of service** attacks against various government services as a form of "civil disobedience" (Cere, 2003; Schell and Dodge, 2002). Such an attack keeps individuals from being able to use communications services, thereby rendering them useless. This tool was first employed in an attack against the Mexican government because of their treatment of Zapatista separatists who were fighting against what they perceived to be governmental repression (Denning, 2010).

Similarly, hackers in India and Pakistan engaged in a series of defacement attacks over a four-year period from 1998 to 2001 due to the use of nuclear weapons testing and development in India (Denning, 2010). Web defacements allow an actor to replace the original web page with content of their own design, including text and images. Such an attack is an ideal mechanism for politically motivated attackers to express their attitudes and

computer hackers and hacking

beliefs to the larger world. Thus, the number of defacements dramatically increased during this period as more countries became connected to the Internet and saw this environment as a means to express their political and religious ideologies (Denning, 2010). To understand how hacking is used as a method for both legitimate and malicious activities that affect individuals and governments around the world, it is necessary to examine the modern hacker subculture and its influence on structuring the hacker identity.

> For more information on web defacements, go online to: www.zone-h. org/

The modern hacker subculture

The activities of hackers are driven, in large part, by the values and beliefs of the modern hacker subculture. Three primary norms within the hacker community have been identified across multiple studies: (1) technology; (2) knowledge; and (3) secrecy (Holt, 2007; Jordan and Taylor, 1998; Meyer, 1989; Taylor, 1999; Thomas, 2002). These norms structure the activities and interests of hackers *regardless* of their involvement in ethical or malicious hacks; they are highly interconnected and important in understanding the overall hacker subculture.

Technology

The act of hacking has been directly and intimately tied to technology since the development of the term "hack" in the 1950s (Holt, 2007; Jordan and Taylor, 1998; Meyer, 1989; Taylor, 1999; Thomas, 2002). The interests and activities of hackers center on computer software and hardware, as well as associated devices like electronics, video games, and cell phones (Holt, 2007; Jordan and Taylor, 1998; Turkle, 1984). These interests are interrelated, as understanding of hardware can improve an individual's understanding of software and vice versa. Thus, an individual's connection to technology increases their ability to hack (Holt, 2007; Jordan and Taylor, 1998; Taylor, 1999; Thomas, 2002).

To generate such a connection, hackers must develop a deep appreciation of computers and be willing to explore and apply their knowledge in new ways (Jordan and Taylor, 1998). Hackers must be curious and explore technology often through creative play with devices, hardware, and software. For instance, one of the most well-known hackers is John Draper, also known as Cap'n Crunch. He was very active in the 1970s and 1980s in the hacker community and is known for having blown a giveaway whistle found in a box of Cap'n Crunch cereal into his phone receiver (Furnell, 2002; Wang, 2006). The whistle created the perfect 2600 Hz tone that was necessary to enable an individual to connect to long distance lines at that time. Such an act of hacking the telephone system is known as **phreaking**, combining the notion of "phone" and "hacking" together (Furnell, 2002; Holt, 2010; Wang, 2006). Draper's unique application of phreaking knowledge through the use of a simple children's toy garnered a great deal of respect and attention from the phreaking community and popular media. In turn, this act demonstrates the importance of exploration and creativity in the hacker community.

The importance of technology for hackers often emerges early in youth. Many who become involved in the hacker community report developing an interest in technology at an early age. Many hackers report gaining access to computers in their early teens or even younger (Bachmann, 2010; Holt, 2007). Simply utilizing computers in public cafes and schools can also help pique a hacker's interest in technology (Holt, 2010). Identifying peers who share their affinity for technology on or offline is also extremely valuable because it helps to maintain their interests. Hackers maintain loose peer associations with individuals in online environments that may be useful in the development of their skill and ability (Holt, 2009a, b; Holt and Kilger, 2008; Meyer, 1989; Schell and Dodge, 2002; Taylor, 1999).

There are myriad communities operating via CMCs across the globe for hackers at every skill level to identify others who share their interests. In fact, there are hacker-related discussions in social groups via Internet Relay Chat (IRC), forums, blogs, and other online environments (Holt, 2007, 2009a, b). Hackers have operated in **bulletin board systems** (BBSs) since the late 1970s and early 1980s to provide information, tools, and techniques on hacking (Meyer, 1989; Scott, 2005). The content was posted in plain text and occasionally featured images and art made from ASCII text, in keeping with the limitations of the technology at the time (see www.asciiworld.com for examples). These sites allowed asynchronous communications between users, meaning that they could post a message and respond to others. In addition, individuals hosted downloadable content including text files and tutorials, though some also hosted pirated software and material, called **warez** (Meyer, 1989; for more on piracy, see Chapter 4). The BBS became an important resource for new hackers, since experienced technology users and budding hackers could share detailed information about systems they explored and discuss their exploits (Landreth, 1985).

The BBS allowed hackers to form groups with private networks based on password-protected boards intended to keep out the uninitiated and maintain privacy (Landreth, 1985; Meyer, 1989). Closed BBSs were initially local in nature based on telephone area codes, but changed with time as more individuals obtained computers and sought out others online. Local hacker groups grew to prominence as a result of BBSs based on their exploits and intrusions into sensitive computer systems, such as the Masters of Disaster and the Legion of Doom (Slatalla and Quittner, 1995). As a result, it is common for individuals to belong to multiple forums and websites in order to gain access to pivotal resources online.

> **For more information on what hacker BBSs looked like in the 1980s, go online to:** http://hackers.applearchives.com/pirate-BBSs.html

In addition to online relationships, hackers often report close peer associations with individuals in the real world who are interested in hacking (Holt, 2009a, b; Meyer, 1989; Schell and Dodge, 2002). These networks may form in schools or through casual associations in local clubs. There are also a substantial number of local affiliates of national and international hacker groups, like the 2600 and DefCon, or DC, groups (Holt, 2009a). For example, local 2600 groups began to form around the publication of the underground hacker/phreaker magazine of the same name in the early 1980s (2600, 2011). These chapters operate in order to bring interested individuals together to share their knowledge of computers and technology with others. Similarly, **hacker spaces** have emerged over the last decade as a way for individuals with knowledge of technology to come together in order to share what they know with others (Hackerspaces, 2011). There are now over 500 hacker spaces operating around the world, often in warehouses or large buildings rented by non-profit groups in order to give individuals a chance to play with various technologies in an open and encouraging environment (Hackerspaces, 2011). This stimulates interest in technology and expands individual social networks to relate to a larger number of people who share their interests.

> **For more information regarding hacker spaces, go online to:** www.hackerspaces.org/

There are also a number of regional and national conferences in the United States and Europe focusing on hacking and computer security. They range from regional **cons** organized by local groups, such as PhreakNIC in Nashville, Tennessee, and CarolinaCon in Raleigh, North Carolina, to high profile organized meetings arranged by for-profit industries like DefCon. In fact, **DefCon** has been held since 1993, and is now one of the preeminent computer security and hacking conferences in the world (DefCon, 2011). The conference draws in speakers and attendees from law enforcement, the intelligence community, computer security professionals, attorneys, and hackers of all skill levels for discussions on a range of topics covering hardware hacking, phreaking, cryptography, privacy laws, and the latest exploits and vulnerabilities in everything from ATMs to cell phone operating systems (Holt, 2007). Similar cons are held around the world, such as the Chaos Communication Congress (CCC), which is the oldest hacker conference in Europe. The CCC has been held since 1984 in various locations across Germany, with more than 9,000 attendees in 2013 (Kinkade *et al.*, 2013). Thus, cons play an important role in sharing information about technology and connecting hackers in the real world which might not otherwise happen in online environments.

Knowledge

The central importance of technology in this subculture drives individuals to have a deep knowledge and mastery of a variety of hardware and software (Meyer 1989, Holt, 2007; Thomas 2002). Hackers spend a significant amount of time learning about technology in order to understand how devices work at deep levels. The hacker community stresses that individuals need to learn on their own rather than ask others to teach them how to do things (Holt, 2007; Jordan and Taylor, 1998; Taylor, 1999). Though social connections provide access to information and accumulated knowledge, the idea of being a hacker is driven in part by experiential knowledge that can only be developed through personal experience.

An individual interested in hacking cannot ask others to teach them how to hack (Holt, 2007; Jordan and Taylor, 1998; Taylor, 1999). Such a request would lead to a person being ridiculed or mocked and embarrassed publicly by others. Instead, most hackers learn by spending hours every day reading manuals, tutorials, and forum posts in order to learn new things (Holt, 2007, 2009a; Jordan & Taylor, 1998; Taylor, 1999). Hackers also belong to multiple forums, mailing lists, and groups in order to gain access to resources and information (Holt, 2007, 2009a; Holt and Kilger, 2008; Meyer, 1989; Taylor, 1999). The increasing importance of video sharing sites has also enabled people to create tutorials that describe in explicit detail and demonstrate how to hack. For instance, Turkish hackers regularly post videos on YouTube and hacker forums that explain in detail how certain hacks work so that they can help others learn about technology (Holt, 2009b). Constant changes in technology also require hackers to stay on the cutting edge of innovations in computer hardware and software in order to improve their overall understanding of the field.

Individuals who can apply their knowledge of technology in a practical fashion often garner respect from others within the subculture. The hacker subculture is a meritocracy where individuals are judged on the basis of their knowledge of computer hardware and software. Those with the greatest skill have the most status, while those with little to no ability but a desire to hack receive the least respect from others. Hackers who create new tools, identify unknown exploits, and find novel applications of technology often generate media attention and respect from their peers in forums and blogs. Demonstrations of technological mastery provide cues that they are a hacker with some skill and ability. By contrast, individuals who engage in poorly executed hacks or have minimal skills but try to brag about their activities can be ostracized by others (Holt, 2007; Jordan and Taylor, 1998; Meyer, 1989).

One of the most salient demonstrations of mastery of technology can be seen at cons, where individuals can compete in hacking challenges and competitions. For example, DefCon and some regional cons hold **Capture the Flag** (CTF) competitions where hackers compete against each other individually or in teams to hack one another, while at the same time defending their resources from others (Holt, 2009a). This demonstrates the dual nature of hacking techniques for both attack and defense. Many cons also hold trivia competitions with questions about computer hardware, software, programming, video games, and the exploits of well-known hackers (Holt, 2009a). These games allow individuals to demonstrate their understanding and connection to the social history of hacking, as well as their technical knowledge. The winners of these competitions are usually recognized at the end of the con and are given prizes for their accomplishment (Holt, 2009a). Such recognition from the general public helps to validate an individual's knowledge and skill and demonstrate their mastery over social and technical challenges.

> **For more information on CTFs, go online to:** www.youtube.com/watch?v=-oUpNLJAl3Y

The importance of knowledge is also reflected in the way that hackers refer to individuals within the hacker subculture, as well as those who operate outside of it (Furnell, 2002; Holt, 2007, 2010; Jordan and Taylor, 1998; Taylor, 1999). There are a variety of terms that are used to describe hackers. Individuals who are new to hacking and have minimal knowledge of technology may be referred to as a **noob** or **newbie** (Holt, 2010). This may be used derogatorily in order to embarrass that person, although many simply identify themselves as noobs in order to clearly delineate the fact that they may not know much about technology. Regardless, those who are considered noobs generally have no status within the hacker community (Furnell, 2002; Holt, 2010).

As hackers learn and gain an understanding of computer software and hardware, they may attempt to apply their knowledge with limited success. One of the key ways that a person may hack early on involves the use of tools and kits found on hacker websites and forums (Bachmann, 2010; Furnell, 2002; Holt, 2010). The proliferation of hacker tools over the last two decades has made it relatively easy for individuals to engage in various hacks because these resources automate the use of exploits against known vulnerabilities. The ability to quickly and easily hack a target is enticing for individuals who are new to the subculture because they may feel such an act will garner status or respect from others (Furnell, 2002; Holt, 2007; Taylor, 1999). They do not, however, understand the way that these tools actually affect computer systems so their attacks often fail or cause greater harm than initially intended. As a consequence, many within the hacker subculture use the term **script kiddies** to refer to such individuals and their acts (Furnell, 2002; Holt, 2007, 2010; Taylor, 1999). This derogatory term is meant to shame individuals by recognizing their use of pre-made scripts or tools, their lack of skill, and the concurrent harm that they may cause. In addition, older members of the hacker community may also refer to noobs or script kiddies as **lamers** or **wannabees**, referencing their limited capacity and skills (Furnell, 2002).

Those hackers who spend a great deal of time developing a connection to technology and robust understanding of computers may be able to demonstrate that they are more than just a noob or script kiddie (see Holt, 2010). Eventually, they may be able to demonstrate enough capacity to be viewed as a hacker by others in the subculture. There is no single way, however, to determine when a person is "officially" considered a hacker (Holt, 2007). For instance, some people may not refer to themselves as hackers because they feel that being a hacker is something that others must apply to you, rather than something you can bestow upon yourself (Holt, 2007). Thus, they may simply allow others to call them a hacker rather than use the term on their own. Others argue becoming a hacker is based on experience, such that you are only a hacker after you can use various programming languages, repair your own computer, and create your own tools and scripts (Holt, 2007; Taylor, 1999).

Within the community of skilled hackers, some use the terms **white hat, black hat,** or **gray hat** to refer to an actor based on the way that they apply their knowledge (see Furnell, 2002; Holt, 2007, 2010; Thomas, 2002). White hats are thought to be "ethical" hackers who work to find errors in computer systems and programs to benefit general computer security (Furnell, 2002; Holt, 2007, 2010). Black-hat hackers use the same techniques and vulnerabilities in order to gain access to information or harm systems (Furnell, 2002; Holt, 2007, 2010). Thus, black hats may sometimes argue that they are no different from white hats; instead it is a perceptual difference among security professionals (Holt, 2007). Gray-hat hackers fall somewhere between these two camps, as their motives shift or change depending on the specific situation (Furnell, 2002; Holt, 2010). The ambiguous nature of hacker ethics, however, makes it difficult to clearly identify when someone is acting purely in a black or white context. The use of a term like gray hat is used to identify the ethical flexibility and lack of consistency in individual hackers' actions (Furnell, 2002; Holt, 2007, 2010; Jordan and Taylor, 1998). A gray-hat hacker may use their knowledge for beneficial purposes one day, while breaking into a computer system to steal information the next day. Thus, there is significant variation in the actions of skilled hackers.

Secrecy

The importance hackers place on demonstrations of knowledge and deep commitment to technology creates a unique tension within the hacker subculture: the need for secrecy (Jordan and Taylor, 1998; Taylor, 1999; Thomas, 2002). Since some forms of hacking are illegal, an individual who attempts to brag about their activities to others can place themselves at risk of arrest or legal sanctions (Kilger, 2010; Taylor, 1999). This does not stop hackers from talking about or engaging in illicit activities in relatively public arenas online. Instead, they use various techniques to reduce the likelihood that their real identity is compromised, such as **handles** or nicknames in online and offline environments in order to establish an identity separate from their real identity (see Furnell, 2002; Jordan and Taylor, 1998). Handles serve as a digital representation of self. They may be humorous or serious, depending on the individual. For example, one hacker adopted the handle TweetyFish under the assumption that no judge would ever take criminal hacks associated with that name seriously (Furnell, 2002). Others take names that are associated with scofflaws and villains, like the group the Legion of Doom in the 1980s, or represent violence and pillaging like Erik Bloodaxe (Furnell, 2002). Regardless of the handle an individual chooses, its use helps to create a persona that can be responsible for successful hacks and activities and diminish the likelihood of reprisals from law enforcement (Furnell, 2002; Jordan and Taylor, 1998; Taylor et al., 2010).

Some hackers also attempt to segment themselves and shield their activities from the general public through the use of closed web forums and private message boards. Requiring individuals to register with a website or forum helps to give some modicum of privacy for posters and diminishes the likelihood that anyone in the general public may stumble upon their conversations (Meyer, 1989). Law enforcement officers and computer security researchers can still gain access to these forums and generate information about serious hacks and attacks, though it is harder to identify these resources when they are closely kept secrets. In fact, some hacker groups keep their sites from appearing in search engine results like Google by turning off the feature "robots.txt" in the HTML coding (Chu et al., 2010). This keeps web spiders from logging the site and reduces the likelihood that outsiders may access their resources. Individuals within the hacker subculture can still identify and gain access to these resources. Hackers, therefore, tread a fine line between sharing information and keeping certain knowledge private (Jordan and Taylor, 1998).

The issue of secrecy has also affected the way that individuals engage with one another at conferences and in public settings. The substantive increase in law enforcement investigations of hackers and the concurrent incorporation of hackers into government and private industry to secure resources means that individual attendees may be surrounded by people who are focused on identifying malicious hackers (Holt, 2007, 2010; Schell and Dodge, 2002). Conferences like DefCon have actively attempted to single out when an individual is in such a position through their "Spot the Fed" contest (Holt, 2007). The game involves pulling an attendee out of the crowd who people perceive to be a federal agent and asking them a series of questions about their life and job. If the person is, in fact, a federal agent, both the fed and the spotter receive t-shirts to commemorate the experience (Holt, 2007).

> To see "Spot the Fed" in action, go online to: www.youtube.com/watch?v=oMHZ4qQuYyE

The Spot the Fed game was initially designed to draw attention to the presence of law enforcement at the con, and stress the need to carefully manage what is shared with strangers in the open. The game also helps demonstrate the boundaries between hackers and law enforcement and sheds light on the role of law enforcement in the hacker subculture. Over time, however, the game has become much more playful, and has occurred with less frequency as the conference has become a more established part of the computer security community. The presence of such a game still emphasizes the need for secrecy in managing how hackers interact with others on and off-line.

Legal frameworks to prosecute hacking

The federal government within the United States is the primary level of government that attempts to curtail computer hacking activities by passing and enforcing legislation through various agencies. At the federal level, the primary statutes used to prosecute hacking cases are referred to as the **Computer Fraud and Abuse Act** (CFAA; discussed previously). This act, listed as Section 1030 of Title 18 of the US Criminal Code, was first passed in 1986 and has been revised multiple times over the last three decades. These laws prosecute attacks against a "protected computer," which are defined as any computer used exclusively or non-exclusively by a financial institution or the federal government, as well as any computer used to engage in interstate or foreign commerce or communication generally (Brenner, 2011). This broad definition was adopted in 1996 in order to provide protection to virtually any computer connected to the Internet and to increase the efficacy of federal statutes to prosecute hacking crimes (Brenner, 2011).

computer hackers and hacking

The CFAA stipulates seven applications of hacking as violations of federal law, though we will focus on four of these statutes here (18 USC § 1030). The other three statutes are discussed in Chapter 3 because they pertain more to malicious software and certain attacks that may extend beyond or can be completed without the use of computer hacking. With that in mind, there are four offenses that immediately pertain to hacking as discussed thus far:

1) Knowingly accessing a computer without authorization or by exceeding authorized access and obtain information protected against disclosure which could be used to the disadvantage of the US or the advantage of a foreign nation and willfully deliver that information to another person not entitled to receive it or retain the information and refuse to deliver it to the person entitled to receive it (18 USC § 1030 Sect. (a)(1)).

2) Knowingly accessing a computer without authorization or by exceeding authorized access to:
   a) Obtain information contained in a financial record of a financial institution or of a card issuer or contained in a file of a consumer reporting agency on a consumer;
   b) Obtain information from any federal department or agency;
   c) Information from any protected computer (18 USC § 1030 Sect. (a)(2));

3) To intentionally and without authorization access any non-public computer of a US department or agency that is exclusively for the use of the government and affects the use of that computer (18 USC § 1030 Sect. (a)(3)).

4) To knowingly and with the intent to defraud access to a protected computer without authorization or by exceeding authorized access and thereby further the intended fraud and obtain anything of value (18 USC § 1030 Sect. (a)(4)).

These acts cover a wide range of offenses and are written broadly enough to prosecute hackers regardless of whether they are **internal** or **external attackers** (Brenner, 2008; Furnell, 2002). Specifically, an internal attacker is an individual who is authorized to use and has legitimate access to computers, networks, and certain data stored on these systems. For example, college students are typically allowed to use online registration systems, access course content hosted on Blackboard or other learning sites, and use computer systems on campus through a username and password sign-in system. They are not, however, allowed to enter in grades or use sensitive systems that are reserved for faculty and administrators. If a student wanted to change their grades electronically, they would have to exceed their authorized use by guessing a password or exploiting a system's vulnerability in order to gain access to grading systems. Thus, their use of existing internal resources makes them an **internal attacker**. Someone who attempts to change grades or access sensitive systems, but is not a student or an authorized user, would be defined as an **external attacker** (Brenner, 2008; Furnell, 2002). This is because they have no existing relationship with the network owners and are completely outside of the network.

The punishments for these acts vary based largely on the harm caused by the incident. For example, the minimum sentence for these crimes can be a 10 to 20 year sentence related to acts of trespass designed to obtain national security information (Sect. (a)(1)), while simply accessing a computer and obtaining information of value (Sect. (a)(2)) varies from one year in prison and/or a fine to up to ten years if the offender has either multiple charges brought against them or if they engaged in the offense for commercial or private gain (18 USC § 1030). Individuals who trespass in government controlled computers (Sect. (a)(3)) can receive both a fine and imprisonment for not more than one year, though if it is part of another offense then it can be up to ten years.

The greatest sentencing range involves attempts to access a computer in order to engage in fraud and obtain information (Sect. (a)(4)). If the object of the fraud and the thing obtained consists only of the use of the computer and the value of that use does not exceed $5,000 in any one-year period, then the maximum penalty is a fine and up to five years in prison. If the incident involves harm that exceeds $5,000, affects more than ten computers, affects medical data, causes physical injury to a person, poses a threat to public health or safety, or affects the US government's administration of justice, defense, or national security, then the punishments can start at ten years and/or a fine (18 USC § 1030). If the hack either attempts to cause or results in serious bodily injury, the actor can receive up to 20 years in prison, and he or she can be eligible for a life sentence if the hack either knowingly or recklessly caused death. These changes were a direct result of the Cyber Security Enhancement Act, which was a subsection of the Homeland Security Act of 2002 (Brenner, 2011; 18 USC § 1030; see also Chapter 10). This Act amended the punishments available to federal judges when dealing with cybercrime cases in order to more accurately reflect the severity of harm that may result from hackers' attacks against computer systems and data.

The CFAA also allows victims of hacking cases to pursue civil suits against the attacker (18 USC § 1030). Specifically, the statute allows any person who suffers either damage or losses due to a violation of the CFAA the opportunity to seek compensatory damages within two years of the date of the complaint or discovery of damages. It does not place limits on the amount of damages that an individual may seek, though the statute stipulates that computer software and hardware manufacturers cannot be held liable for negligent designs or manufacturing (Brenner, 2011). As a result, this essentially releases a vendor from any civil responsibility for the presence of vulnerabilities within their products. Instead, it is the attacker who is held liable for the identification and use of exploits against those vulnerabilities.

An additional federal statute pertaining to hacking is 18 USC § 1030 Sect. 2701(a), referencing unlawful access to stored communications. Given that so much personal information is now stored in email accounts hosted on web servers that are protected through limited security protocols, like passwords that can be easily hacked, there is a need to protect this information at all points. This statute makes it an offense to intentionally either (1) access without authorization a facility through which an electronic communication is provided; or (2) exceed an authorization to access such a facility and then obtain, alter, or prevent authorized access to a wire or electronic communication while it is in electronic storage. This law is designed to help secure personal communications and information, particularly against nation-state attackers who may attempt to use email or communications to better understand a target (Brenner, 2011).

Initially, the punishments for these offenses involved a fine and/or imprisonment for not more than one year for the first offense, and up to five years for a subsequent offense. This statute was amended by the Homeland Security Act of 2002 to increase the penalties if the offense was completed for "purposes of commercial advantage, malicious destruction or damage, or private commercial gain, or in furtherance of any criminal or tortuous act in violation of the Constitution or laws of the United States or any State" (Cybersecurity Enhancement Act, 2002). If the attacks occurred for these reasons, an actor may receive a fine and up to five years in prison for the first offense, and then up to ten years imprisonment for multiple offenses.

In addition to federal statutes, all states have laws against computer hacking in some shape or form (Brenner, 2011). Often this involves defining hacking in two ways:

1) the unauthorized access to computers or computer systems;
2) unauthorized access leading to the acquisition, theft, deletion or corruption of data.

There is some variation in how states define hacking in these contexts, ranging from "unauthorized access" to "computer trespass" to "computer tampering." In addition, some states place computer hacking laws under existing criminal statutes pertaining to burglary, theft, and robbery (Brenner, 2011). For instance, Missouri defines computer hacking as "tampering" with either computers or data and has placed these offenses under Chapter 569, that includes "Robbery, Burglary, and Related Offenses." Others, like North Carolina, place computer hacking and related cybercrimes under their own statutes in order to encapsulate the unique nature of cybercrimes (Brenner, 2011). Regardless of the term used, many states consider unauthorized access on its own as a misdemeanor, while access and manipulation of data is typically defined as a felony.

Similar legislation is present in countries around the world, though there are some variations in the way in which these statutes can be applied or the punishments associated with the offense. For instance, the **United Kingdom's Computer Misuse Act** of 1990 defines three behaviors as offenses:

1) unauthorized access to computer material (whether data or a program);
2) unauthorized access to a computer system with intent to commit or facilitate the commission of a serious crime;
3) unauthorized modification of computer material.

The structure of this Act recognizes variations in the way that hackers operate, such as the fact that only some hackers may attempt to gain access to systems, while others may attempt to maliciously use or modify data. Any individual found guilty of a violation of the first statute can face a maximum sentence of six months or a fine of £2,000, or both. Subsequent charges under the second and third statutes are associated with more severe sanctions, including up to five years in prison, a fine, or both.

Several researchers hold this legislation up as a model for other nations because of its applicability to various forms of hacking and compromise (see Brenner, 2011; Furnell, 2002). The law itself, however, emerged because of the absence of existing laws that could be used to prosecute the crimes performed by Robert Schifreen and Steven Gold in 1984 and 1985. Specifically, Schifreen noticed the username and password of a system engineer at the British Telecom firm, Prestel, and he and Gold used this information to access various parts of the network and gain access to sensitive account information (Furnell, 2002). The two were then caught by Prestel administrators and arrested, but there was no legislation against the activities they performed. Thus, prosecutors charged the pair under the Forgery and Counterfeiting Act of 1981, under the auspices that they "forged" the user credentials of others (Furnell, 2002).

Though both Schifreen and Gold were found guilty, they appealed their case claiming that they caused no actual harm and had been charged under inappropriate statutes (Furnell, 2002). The two were acquitted based on the conclusion that forgery laws were misapplied and their actions were not, in fact, a violation of existing criminal law. As a result, the English Law Commission recommended that new legislation be developed to criminalize various forms of hacking (Furnell, 2002). The law was introduced and passed in 1990, though subsequent revisions have been introduced over the last 25 years to increase sanctions, apply the law to offenses involving smartphones, and cover offenses involving malicious software (Brenner, 2011; Furnell, 2002).

The **Convention on Cybercrime (CoC)**, also known as the Budapest Convention on Cybercrime, is the first international treaty designed to address cybercrime and synchronize national laws on these offenses

(Weismann, 2011). This Convention was developed in conjunction with the Council of Europe, Canada, and Japan in 2001 and came into force in 2004. The language of the treaty specifically addresses a number of cybercrimes, with the intent to create common criminal policies and encourage international cooperation in the investigation and prosecution of these offenses. The CoC does not, however, encourage extradition, which limits its value in enforcement. Additionally, those states that sign and ratify the CoC are under no obligation to accept all parameters of the Convention. Instead they can select which provisions they choose to enforce, further limiting its utility. Some of the primary offenses detailed in the Convention include illegal access and illegal interception of data and communications, as well as data interference, system interference, and misuse of devices (Weismann, 2011). Thus, the CoC has inherent value for the development of consistent legal frameworks and definitions for hacking-related crimes in a global context (Weismann, 2011).

At present, 42 nations have ratified the treaty and entered its policies into force, with the majority being members of the Council of Europe and European Union generally, including Italy, Germany, Turkey, the Ukraine, and the United Kingdom. Several nations that are not members of the Council have also ratified the CoC, including Australia, Japan, and the United States (Weismann, 2011). In addition, 11 states have signed the CoC but not ratified its provisions, including Canada, Ireland, Poland, and South Africa. The acceptance of the CoC in these nations creates some standards for enforcement and investigation, though the absence of some nations, such as Russia, limits the value of the CoC (Weismann, 2011). The language of the CoC has served as a model for a number of nations' cybercrime laws, particularly in a number of South American and African nations (Riquert, 2013; Weismann, 2011). Thus, the Convention on Cybercrime may be invaluable in structuring consistent laws regarding cybercrime.

Enforcing and investigating hacker activity

It is important to note that federal agencies are responsible for cases where the victim and offender reside in different states or countries. We will focus our discussion on the primary federal agencies responsible for the investigation of computer hacking since there are few local law enforcement agencies investigating computer hacking. This appears to stem from the fact that these cases are often very technically complex. In addition, these crimes involve local victims compromised by offenders living in completely separate jurisdictions that cannot be affected by a police or sheriff's office (Holt, Bossler, and Fitzgerald, 2010; Senjo, 2004).

One of the most prominent federal law enforcement bodies involved in the investigation of hacking cases is the **United States Secret Service** (USSS). The Secret Service was initially part of the Department of the Treasury, dating back to its creation in 1865 in order to combat the production and use of counterfeit currency after the Civil War (USSS, 2013). Now, however, the Secret Service is housed under the Department of Homeland Security (DHS) (see Chapter 10 for more detail). The Secret Service was initially tasked with hacking cases through the CFAA because of their mandate to investigate crimes against financial institutions and counterfeit currency (18 USC § 1030). The growth of technology and Internet connectivity among banks and financial service providers made the Secret Service seem like an experienced agency, capable of investigating hacking and on-line fraud (USSS, 2013).

Today, the Secret Service operates the Financial Crimes Division with three primary investigative responsibilities concerning cybercrime (USSS, 2013). The first involves financial institution fraud (FIF) against banks, savings and loan institutions, and credit unions (see Chapter 5 for additional detail). The second includes access device fraud, such as the use of passwords in order to engage in fraud or hacks against various targets. The final responsibility involves acts of fraud that affect computers of "federal interest," that directly facilitate interstate or international commerce and government information transfers.

The other prominent agency involved in the investigation of hacking cases is the **Federal Bureau of Investigation** (FBI). Cybercrime is one of the FBI's top three investigative priorities, in part by legal mandate in the CFAA. The law stipulates that the FBI has the primary authority to investigate hacking cases that involve espionage, foreign nation-states, counter-intelligence, and classified sensitive data that affects national defense or foreign relations. To that end, the FBI operates Cyber Task Forces (CTFs) in all of its 56 field offices across the country in order to investigate cyber-security threats (FBI, 2013a). These task forces are focused on investigating attacks against critical infrastructure, hacks that target private industry or financial systems, and other cybercrimes. The CTFs in each region are also responsible for developing and maintaining relationships with public and private industry partners in order to improve their response capabilities (FBI, 2013a).

> **For more information on the FBI, go online to:** www.fbi.gov/about-us/investigate/cyber

The FBI also operates the National Cyber Investigative Joint Task Force (NCIJTF) in partnership with the **Department of Defense Cyber Crime Center** (DoD DC3), a specialized agency run by the Air Force to perform forensic analyses and training for attacks against DoD computers and defense contractors (DC3, 2013). The NCIJTF was created in 2008 by presidential mandate in order to serve as the coordinating response agency for all domestic cyberthreat investigations. This group is not focused on reducing vulnerabilities, but rather pursuing the actors responsible for various attacks (FBI, 2013b). In addition, their domestic focus does not mean they are centered only on US-based actors, but also any individual interested in attacking the nation's infrastructure. In fact, the NCIJTF coordinates with each CTF in order to provide investigative resources and assistance to facilitate their mission (FBI, 2013b).

The Bureau also operates Cyber Action Teams (CATs), which are highly trained small groups of agents, analysts, and forensic investigators who can respond to incidents around the world. These teams are designed to collect data and serve as rapid first responders to any incident, no matter where it occurs around the world. In addition, the FBI serves as the coordinating agency for the global Strategic Alliance Cyber Crime Working Group. This international partnership includes the Australian Federal Police, Royal Canadian Mounted Police (RCMP), New Zealand Police, and the UK's National Crime Agency. This five-way partnership is designed to facilitate investigations, share intelligence on threats, and synchronize laws in order to promote more successful partnerships against both organized criminal groups and cybercrimes. In fact, this partnership has led to a shared Internet portal that is designed to share information between these countries, joint international task forces, and shared training programs in order standardize investigative techniques and training (FBI, 2008).

To see the global scope of the FBI's Working Group, go online to: www. fbi.gov/news/stories/2008/march/cybergroup_031708

In addition, the FBI operates the **InfraGard** project, which is a non-profit public–private partnership designed to facilitate information sharing between academics, industry, and law enforcement (InfraGard, 2013). The group is designed to aid in collaborations in order to better protect critical infrastructure and reduce attacks against US resources. InfraGard operates in chapters across the US, which hold regular meetings to discuss issues of interest with members. In fact there are over 54,000 members of the group, all of whom must go through a vetting process in order to participate (InfraGard, 2013). In turn, members gain access to a secured web portal where intelligence on threats, vulnerabilities, and general information is shared. This partnership has been very successful, though members of the hacker group LulzSec attacked InfraGard chapter websites in order to embarrass the FBI (see Satter, 2011; Text Box 2.5 for more detail). This attack, however, appears to be an isolated incident in the otherwise positive partnerships afforded by InfraGard.

While the FBI and Secret Service focus on the investigation of cybercrimes,
they must work in close concert with the United States Attorney's Office,
which is a part of the **US Department of Justice** (DOJ) focused on the prosecution of federal criminal cases. Though the FBI is part of the DOJ, they
operate as an investigative arm, while the Attorney's Office represents the
federal government in court to prosecute suspects. In fact, the investigation
of cybercrimes is largely handled by the Criminal Division's **Computer Crime
and Intellectual Property Section** (CCIPS). Initially, violations of the CFAA
were prosecuted at the federal level through the Computer Crime Unit, first
established in 1991 (US DOJ, 2013a). The expansion of the Internet and the
resulting range of cybercrimes that became possible led to a restructuring of
the unit to a full Section with the enactment of the National Information and
Infrastructure Protection Act of 1996 (US DOJ, 2013a). The unit now deals
exclusively with the investigation and prosecution of cybercrime cases and
intellectual property crimes, through close collaboration with law enforcement agencies and private industry. The CCIPS division also provides support for prosecutors handling similar cases at the federal, state, and local
levels, and works with legislators to develop new policies and legal statutes
to deal with cybercrime generally (US DOJ, 2013a).

For more information on the Department of Justice, go online to: www.
justice.gov/criminal/cybercrime/

In addition, there is now a Computer Hacking and Intellectual Property (CHIP) Unit within DOJ which first appeared in the Northern District of California in 2000 (US DOJ, 2013b). The section was established in order to provide prosecutors to handle cybercrime cases related to the massive technology industries operating in Silicon Valley, California. This unit was almost immediately successful and involved in prosecutions related to economic espionage, piracy cases, spam, and other hacking cases. The success of this unit has led to its replication across the country with more than 260 prosecutors operating, including one in each of the 94 US attorney's offices (US DOJ, 2013b). In addition, there are 25 CHIP units across the country, with representation in most regions in the United States, though the majority are in California, Texas, Florida, Virginia, and most states on the northeastern seaboard.

Specialized law enforcement agencies operate around the world to investigate cybercrimes that may violate local or federal laws. For instance, the **Metropolitan Police Central e-crime Unit (PCeU)** in the United Kingdom operates to respond to serious forms of cybercrime affecting citizens (Metropolitan Police, 2013). They are specifically tasked with responses to computer intrusions, malware, and denial of service attacks that affect the UK, though they do not handle local cybercrimes or offenses involving children. Thus this unit serves a similar role to that of the US Secret Service or FBI in the response to serious cybercrimes (Metropolitan Police, 2013). The Australian Federal Police also operates a High Tech Crime Unit designed to enforce laws targeting cybercrimes that do not involve children (Australian Federal Police, 2013). Similar structures are present in the Korean National Police and the Royal Canadian Mounted Police through their Integrated Technological Crime Unit (Andress and Winterfeld, 2011).

Summary

The computer hacker subculture is distinctive and provides justifications for individuals to develop a deep understanding of technology and the ability to apply their knowledge in innovative ways. Some hackers use their skills for malicious purposes, while others use them to protect computer systems. Both ethical and malicious hackers may have to utilize the same skill sets to complete an activity. In fact, hackers judge one another on the basis of their skill, connection to technology, and depth of knowledge. Those with demonstrable skills garner more respect from their peers, while those with minimal skill may be derided by others.

The perception of hackers as malicious actors stems directly from the evolution of hacking and technology. The criminalization of hacking in the late 1970s and 1980s, coupled with the development of the personal computer, enabled a shift in the hacker subculture and the expansion of hacking to new populations. As technology became more user friendly, the hacker culture changed, creating significant variation in the skill and ability of hackers. These factors have produced the current population of skilled and semi-skilled hackers with various motives and ethical orientations. Thus, there is no single way to deal with hackers who use their skills for criminal gain. Instead, it is critical to understand that script kiddies and noobs present a different threat than those black-hat hackers who can successfully penetrate systems without detection.

Key terms

Black-hat hacker
Bulletin board system (BBS)
Capture the Flag
Chaos Communication Congress (CCC)
Computer Crime and Intellectual Property Section (CCIPS)
Computer Fraud and Abuse Act (CFAA)
Con
Convention on Cybercrime (CoC)
Crack
Cracker
DefCon
Denial of service
Department of Defense Cyber Crime Center
Exploit
Federal Bureau of Investigation (FBI)
Gray-hat hacker
Hack
Hacker
Hacker ethic
The Hacker Manifesto
Hacker Space
Handle
InfraGard
Lamer
Metropolitan Police Central e-crime Unit (PCeU)
Nation-state actor
Non-nation-state actor
Noob
Phishing

Phreak

Phreaking

Script kiddie

Shoulder surfing

Social engineering

UK Computer Misuse Act

United States Department of Justice (US DOJ)

United States Secret Service (USSS)

Vulnerability

Wannabe

Warez

White-hat hacker

Discussion questions

1) Think about the various ways that you have seen hackers portrayed in popular media over the last few years. Are they heroic characters or dangerous criminals? Do the representations conform to any of the realities of the hacker subculture, or do they simply further stereotypes about hackers as a whole?

2) If hacking is a skill or ability, does it share any similarities to other real-world activities that can be applied in malicious or ethical ways?

3) Compare the ideas expressed in the hacker ethic against the comments made by the Mentor in the *Hacker Manifesto*. Do they make similar points, or are they very different documents? If there are common themes, what do they suggest about hacking and the complexities of the hacker subculture?

4) Given the range of actors evident in the hacker subculture, is it possible that ethical and unethical hackers may share similar motives? If so, what might those motives be, and is it possible to identify an individual's ethical stance based solely on their motives?

5) What were the weaknesses of using "traditional" legislation to prosecute hackers? How did newer legislation address those problems?

References

18 USC § 1030.

2600. (2011). *2600: The Hacker Quarterly.* [Online] Available at: www.2600.com/

Andress, J., & Winterfeld, S. (2011). *Cyber Warfare: Techniques, Tactics, and Tools for Security Practitioners.* Waltham MA: Syngress.

Anti-Phishing Working Group. (2013). *Global Phishing Survey: Trends and Domain Name Use in 1H2013*. Anti-Phishing Working Group. [Online] Available online at http://docs.apwg.org/reports/APWG_GlobalPhishingSurvey_1H2013.pdf

Australian Federal Police. (2013). High tech crime. [Online] Available online at: www.afp.gov.au/policing/cybercrime/hightech-crime.aspx

Bachmann, M. (2010). The risk propensity and rationality of computer hackers. *The International Journal of Cyber Criminology*, 4, 643–656.

Bossler, A. M., & Burruss, G. W. (2011). The General Theory of Crime and Computer Hacking: Low Self-Control Hackers? In T. J. Holt & B. H. Schell (eds), *Corporate Hacking and Technology-Driven Crime: Social Dynamics and Implications* (pp. 38–67). ISI Global: Hershey, PA.

Brenner, S. W. (2008). *Cyberthreats: The Emerging Fault Lines of the Nation State*. New York: Oxford University Press.

Brenner, S. W. (2011). Defining Cybercrime: A Review of Federal and State Law. In R. D. Clifford (ed.), *Cybercrime: The Investigation, Prosecution, and Defense of a Computer-Related Crime*, 3rd edition (pp. 15–104). Raleigh, NC: Carolina Academic Press.

Cere, R. (2003). Digital Counter-Cultures and the Nature of Electronic Social and Political Movements. In Y. Jewkes (ed.), *Dot.cons: Crime, Deviance and Identity on the Internet* (pp. 147–163). Portland, OR: Willan Publishing.

Ceruzzi, P. (1998). *A History of Modern Computing*. Cambridge, MA: MIT Press.

Chu, B., Holt, T. J., & Ahn, G. J. (2010). *Examining the Creation, Distribution, and Function of Malware On-Line*. Washington, DC, National Institute of Justice. [Online] Available online at: www.ncjrs.gov/pdffiles1/nij/grants/230112.pdf

Computer Security Institute. (2008). *Computer Crime and Security Survey*. [Online] Available at: www.cybercrime.gov/FBI2008.pdf

DefCon. (2011). *What is Defcon?* [Online] Available at: http://defcon.org/html/links/dc-about.html

Denning, D. E. (2010). Cyber-Conflict as an Emergent Social Problem. In T. J. Holt & B. Schell (eds), *Corporate Hacking and Technology-Driven Crime: Social Dynamics and Implications* (pp. 170–186). Hershey, PA: IGI-Global.

Department of Defense Cyber Crime Center. (2013). *Fact Sheet: Department of the Air Force*. [Online] Available at: www.dc3.mil/data/uploads/dc3-fact-sheet-fy13-2013-12-24.pdf

Federal Bureau of Investigation. (2008). *Cyber Solidarity: Five Nations, One Mission*. [Online] Available at: www.fbi.gov/news/stories/2008/march/cybergroup_031708

Federal Bureau of Investigation. (2013a). *Cyber Task Forces*. [Online] Available at: www.fbi.gov/about-us/investigate/cyber/cyber-task-force-fact-sheet

Federal Bureau of Investigation. (2013b). *National Cyber Investigative Joint Task Force*. [Online] Available at: www.fbi.gov/about-us/investigate/cyber/ncijtf

Franklin, J., Paxson, V., Perrig, A., & Savage, S. (2007). An inquiry into the nature and cause of the wealth of internet miscreants. Paper presented at CCS07, October 29–November 2, in Alexandria, VA.

Furnell, S. (2002). *Cybercrime: Vandalizing the Information Society*. London: Addison-Wesley.

Gilboa, N. (1996). Elites, Lamers, Narcs, and Whores: Exploring the Computer Underground. In L. Cherny & E. R. Weise (eds) *Wired_Women* (pp. 98–113). Seattle: Seal Press.

Gordon, S., & Ma, Q. (2003). *Convergence of virus writers and hackers: Factor or fantasy.* Cupertino, CA: Symantec Security White Paper.

Hackerspaces. (2011). *About hackerspaces.* [Online] Available at: http://hackerspaces.org/wiki/Hackerspaces

Hollinger, R., & Lanza-Kaduce, L. (1988). The process of criminalization: The case of computer crime laws. *Criminology, 26,* 101–126.

Holt, T. J. (2007). Subcultural evolution? Examining the influence of on- and off-line experiences on deviant subcultures. *Deviant Behavior, 28,* 171–198.

Holt, T. J. (2009a). Lone Hacks or Group Cracks: Examining the Social Organization of Computer Hackers. In F. Schmalleger & M. Pittaro (eds), *Crimes of the Internet* (pp. 336–355). Upper Saddle River, NJ: Pearson Prentice Hall.

Holt, T. J. (2009b). The Attack Dynamics of Political and Religiously Motivated Hackers. In T. Saadawi & L. Jordan (eds) *Cyber Infrastructure Protection* (pp. 161–182). New York: Strategic Studies Institute.

Holt, T. J. (2010). Examining the role of technology in the formation of deviant subcultures. *Social Science Computer Review, 28,* 466–481.

Holt, T. J., Bossler, A. M., & Fitzgerald, S. (2010). Examining State and Local Law Enforcement Perceptions of Computer Crime. In T. J. Holt (ed.) *Crime Online: Correlates, Causes, and Context* (pp. 221–246). Raleigh, NC: Carolina Academic.

Holt, T. J., Bossler, A. M., & May, D. C. (2012). Low self-control, deviant peer associations, and juvenile cyberdeviance. *American Journal of Criminal Justice,* 37(3), 378–395.

Holt, T. J., & Kilger, M. (2008). *Techcrafters and makecrafters: A comparison of two populations of hackers.* 2008 WOMBAT Workshop on Information Security Threats Data Collection and Sharing (pp. 67–78).

Holt, T. J., Kilger, M., Strumsky, D., & Smirnova, O. (2009). *Identifying, Exploring, and Predicting Threats in the Russian Hacker Community.* Presented at the Defcon 17 Convention, Las Vegas, Nevada.

Holt, T. J., & Lampke, E. (2010). Exploring stolen data markets on-line: Products and market forces. *Criminal Justice Studies, 23,* 33–50.

Holt, T. J., Soles, J., & Leslie, L. (2008). *Characterizing malware writers and computer attackers in their own words.* Paper presented at the 3rd International Conference on Information Warfare and Security, April 24–25, in Omaha, Nebraska.

Huang, W., & Brockman, A. (2010). Social Engineering Exploitations in Online Communications: Examining Persuasions used in Fraudulent E-mails. In Holt, T. J. (ed.), *Crime On-line: Causes, Correlates, and Context* (pp. 87–112). Raleigh, NC: Carolina Academic Press.

InfraGard. (2013). *InfraGard in the News.* [Online] Available at: https://www.infragard.org/

Internet Crime Complaint Center. (2008). *IC3 2008 Internet Crime Report.* [Online] Available at: www.ic3.gov/media/annualreport/2008_IC3Report.pdf

Jaffe, G. (2006). Gates Urges NATO Ministers To Defend Against Cyber Attacks. *The Wall Street Journal On-line.* June 15, 2006. [Online] Available at: http://online.wsj.com/article/SB118190166163536578.html?mod=googlenews_wsj

James, L. (2005). *Phishing Exposed.* Rockland: Syngress.

Jordan, T., & Taylor, P. (1998). A sociology of hackers. *The Sociological Review, 46,* 757–780.

Jordan, T., & Taylor, P. (2004). *Hacktivism and Cyber Wars*. London: Routledge.

Kilger, M. (2010). Social Dynamics and the Future of Technology-Driven Crime. In T. J. Holt & B. Schell (eds), *Corporate Hacking and Technology-Driven Crime: Social Dynamics and Implications* (pp. 205–227). Hershey, PA: IGI-Global.

Kinkade, P. T., Bachmann, M., & Bachmann, B. S. (2013). Hacker Woodstock: Observations on an Off-line Cyber Culture at the Chaos Communication Camp 2011. In Holt, T. J. (ed.), *Crime On-line: Correlates, Causes, and Context*, 2nd edition (pp. 19–60). Raleigh, NC: Carolina Academic Press.

Krance, M., Murphy, J., & Elmer-Dewitt, P. (1983). The 414 Gang Strikes Again. *Time*. [Online] Available at: www.time.com/time/magazine/article/0,9171,949797,00.html

Kravets, D. (2010). U.S. declares iPhone jailbreaking legal, over Apple's objections. *Wired Threat Level*. [Online] Available at: www.wired.com/threatlevel/2010/07/feds-ok-iphone-jailbreaking/

Krebs, B. (2009). Payment Processor Breach May Be Largest Ever. *The Washington Post*. [Online] Available at: http://voices.washingtonpost.com/securityfix/2009/01/payment_processor_breach_may_b.html

Landler, M., & Markoff, J. (2008). Digital Fears Emerge After Data Siege in Estonia. *The New York Times*, May 24, 2007. [Online] Available at: www.nytimes.com/2007/05/29/technology/29estonia.html

Landreth, B. (1985). *Out of the Inner Circle*. Seattle, WA: Microsoft Press.

Levy, S. (2001). *Hackers: Heroes of the Computer Revolution*. New York: Penquin.

Littman, J. (1997). *The Watchman: The Twisted Life and Crimes of Serial Hacker Kevin Poulsen*. New York: Little Brown.

Marbach, W. (1983a). Beware: Hackers at Play. *Newsweek*, 42.

Marbach, W. (1983b). Cracking Down on Hackers. *Newsweek*, 34.

Markoff, J., & Barboza, D. (2010). Two China Schools Said to be Linked to Online Attacks. *The New York Times*. [Online] Available at: www.nytimes.com/2010/02/19/technology/19china.html

Metropolitan Police. (2013). PCeU Police Central e-crime Unit: What we do. [Online] Available at: http://content.met.police.uk/Article/What-we-do/1400015320495/pceu

Meyer, G. R. (1989). *The Social Organization of the Computer Underground*. Master's thesis, Northern Illinois University.

Mitnick, K. D., & Simon, W. L. (2002). *The Art of Deception: Controlling the Human Element of Security*. New York: Wiley Publishing.

Morris, R. G. (2011). Computer Hacking and the Techniques of Neutralization: An Empirical Assessment. In T. J. Holt & B. H. Schell (eds), *Corporate Hacking and Technology-Driven Crime: Social Dynamics and Implications* (pp. 1–17). ISI Global: Hershey, PA.

Morris, R. G., & Blackburn, A. G. (2009). Cracking the code: An empirical exploration of social learning theory and computer crime. *Journal of Crime and Justice*, 32, 1–32.

Painter, C. M. E. (2001). Supervised release and probation restrictions in hacker cases. *United States Attorneys' USA Bulletin*, 49. [Online] Available at: www.cybercrime.gov/usamarch2001_7.htm

Peretti, K. K. (2009). Data breaches: What the underground world of "carding" reveals. *Santa Clara Computer and High Technology Law Journal*, 25, 375–413.

computer hackers and hacking

Riquert, M. A. (2013). Rethinking how criminal law works in cyberspace. Paper presented at the Crimina Cybercrime Research Conference, October 14, 2013, Elche Spain.

Rogers, J. (2007). Gartner: Victims of online phishing up nearly 40 percent in 2007. *SC Magazine*. [Online] Available at: www.scmagazineus.com/Gartner-Victims-of-online-phishing-up-nearly-40-percent-in-2007/article/99768/

Satter, R. G. (2011). LulzSec hackers claim breach of FBI affiliate in Atlanta. *Huffington Post: Tech*. [Online] Available at: www.huffingtonpost.com/2011/06/05/lulzsec-hack-fbi-infragard-atlanta_n_871545.html?view=print&comm_ref=false

Schell, B. H., & Dodge, J. L. (2002). *The Hacking of America: Who's Doing it, Why, and How*. Westport, CT: Quorum Books.

Schneider, H. (2008). *Wargames*. United Artists.

Scott, J. (2005). *BBS: The Documentary*.

Senjo, S. R. (2004). An analysis of computer-related crime: Comparing police officer perceptions with empirical data. *Security Journal*, 17, 55–71.

Skinner, W. F., & Fream, A. M. (1997). A social learning theory analysis of computer crime among college students. *Journal of Research in Crime and Delinquency*, 34, 495–518.

Slatalla, M., & Quittner, J. (1995). *Masters of Deception: The Gang that Ruled Cyberspace*. New York: Harper Collins Publishers.

Shimomura, T., & Markoff, J. (1996). *Takedown: The Pursuit and Capture of Kevin Mitnick, America's Most Wanted Computer Outlaw—by the Man Who Did It*. New York: Hyperion.

Sterling, B. (1992). *The Hacker Crackdown: Law and Disorder on the Electronic Frontier*. New York: Bantam Books.

Taylor, P. (1999). *Hackers: Crime in the Digital Sublime*. London: Routledge.

Taylor, R. W., Fritsch, E. J., Liederbach, J., & Holt, T. J. (2010). *Digital Crime and Digital Terrorism*, 2nd edition. Upper Saddle River, NJ: Pearson Prentice Hall.

Thomas, D. (2002). *Hacker Culture*. Minneapolis, MN: University of Minnesota Press.

Thomas, R., & Martin, J. (2006). The underground economy: Priceless. *;login*, 31, 7–16.

Turkle, S. (1984). *The Second Self: Computers and the Human Spirit*. New York: Simon and Schuster.

United States Department of Justice. (2013a). *About CCIPS*. [Online] Available at: http://www.justice.gov/criminal/cybercrime/about/

United States Department of Justice. (2013b). *CHIP Units*. [Online] Available at: www.justice.gov/usao/briefing_room/cc/chip.html

United States Secret Service. (2013). *Frequently Asked Questions*. [Online] Available at: www.secretservice.gov/faq.shtml#faq1

Vijayan, J. (2010). Update: Heartland breach shows why compliance is not enough. *Computerworld*. [Online] Available at: www.computerworld.com/s/article/9143158/Update_Heartland_breach_shows_why_compliance_is_not_enough

Wall, D. S. (2001). Cybercrimes and the Internet. In D. S. Wall (ed.), *Crime and the Internet* (pp. 1–17). New York: Routledge.

Wall, D. S. (2007). *Cybercrime: The Transformation of Crime in the Information Age*. Cambridge: Polity Press.

Wang, W. (2006). *Steal This Computer Book 4.0: What They Won't Tell You About the Internet*. Boston, MA: No Starch Press.

Weismannn, M. F. (2011). International Cybercrime: Recent Developments in the Law. In R. D. Clifford (ed.), *Cybercrime: The Investigation, Prosecution, and Defense of a Computer-Related Crime*, 3rd edition (pp. 257–294). Raleigh, NC: Carolina Academic Press.

Wright, R. T., & Decker, S. H. (1994). *Burglars on the Job: Streetlife and Residential Break-Ins*. Boston: Northeastern University Press.

Zetter, K. (2010). 'Google' hackers had ability to alter source code. *Wired*. [Online] Available at: www.wired.com/threatlevel/2010/03/source-code-hacks/82

chapter 3

Malware and automated computer attacks

Chapter goals

- Define what is malware and the role of vulnerabilities and exploits in their activation
- Identify the differences between viruses, trojans, worms, and blended threats
- Understand why individuals write and distribute malicious software
- Identify the role of malware markets in facilitating attacks, and the norms of these market participants
- Assess the legal frameworks used to pursue cyberattacks facilitated by malicious software
- Recognize the role of law enforcement agencies and the security industry to mitigate malware in the wild

Introduction

Much like the threat posed by computer hackers explored in Chapter 2, there is a good deal of confusion and misunderstanding around the issue of malware or malicious software. Many in the general public may have heard the term virus or perhaps trojan in computing, though they may not understand what they do or how they operate. The lack of understanding is compounded by the number of security tools available to protect computer systems from malware. Although most laptops and desktop computers are sold with some form of antivirus software pre-installed, owners may not know how, when, or why to properly use these tools. Additionally, most mobile phones and tablet computers, such as iPads or Kindles, do not have this software even though they can be infected by malware.

Computer users who understand the value and necessity of antivirus software and security tools to minimize the likelihood of infections may not realize that they are still vulnerable to attacks from new code that has just been identified. Though that may seem like a relatively minor dilemma, consider that there were at least ten million new strains of malware identified in the first nine months of 2013 alone (F-Secure, 2013)! Additionally, the behavior of malware can often be so subtle that an individual may not know that they have been affected.

For examples of vulnerabilities and malware, go online to: www.fox-business.com/government/2013/08/07/cyber-hackers-on-course-for-one-million-malware-apps/

This chapter is designed to provide a basic understanding of malware, including the most common forms of malware that are active in the wild. Due to the substantive technical details involved in the classification and operation of malware, this chapter will provide descriptions of each form without going into overly technical explorations of their functionality. Instead, a summary description will be provided using minimal technical jargon in order to give readers a basic appreciation for the range of malware currently operating, its role in attacks, and any historical evolution of these tools in the hacker and computer security community generally. Visual examples of the user interfaces associated with malware will also be provided to demonstrate the ease with which some tools can be used. The legal frameworks used to prosecute malware-related cybercrimes and their relationship to hacking will also be discussed. Finally, we will consider the legal and computer security entities operating to protect users from malware threats.

The basics of malware

Malicious software, or **malware,** is largely an umbrella term used to encapsulate the range of destructive programs that can be used to harm computer systems, gain access to sensitive information, or engage in different forms of cybercrime. Malware can serve a countless number of different functions, but are generally designed to automate attacks against systems and simplify the process of hacking overall. Various forms of malware have increased in complexity in keeping with the evolution of technology over the last two decades (BitDefender, 2009; Symantec, 2014). Malware, however, exists in a nebulous legal space as there are no specific laws against the creation of malicious software (Brenner, 2011). It is simply computer code, which writers can argue is necessary in order to better understand the limits of computer and network security. The *use* of these tools in or to access computers without permission from the system owner is, however, illegal. Thus, individuals who write malicious code may have minimal legal culpability for the way that others use their creations so long as they are not the ones utilizing it on networks without authorization (Brenner, 2011).

Malicious software programs operate by exploiting **vulnerabilities**, or flaws, in computer software or hardware (Symantec, 2014). Every program has design flaws. There are literally thousands of vulnerabilities that have been identified in systems that individuals use every day, such as Microsoft Windows and popular web browsers. The presence of a vulnerability allows an attacker to understand and gain initial access to a target system in some way. Many security professionals attempt to identify vulnerabilities in order to help secure computer systems, though this information is typically released to the public through open forums or email lists like BugTraq (see Text Box 3.1; Taylor, 1999). As a result, attackers can immediately use information on vulnerabilities to their advantage.

Text Box 3.1: The debate over public or private vulnerability disclosures

http://web.archive.org/web/20100102144837/http://spirit.com/Network/net0800.html

Vulnerability disclosure debate

Today, there are appeals to put the genie back into the bottle. That is, to stop the publishing of new vulnerabilities. There is even a proposed law that would make some forms of vulnerability testing illegal in the US.

This article provides an interesting debate on the issue of vulnerability disclosures and the relationship between black-hat and white-hat hackers who identify and provide this information to the public for free, or to companies and security vendors for a profit. This work helps to give context to the difficult need to balance privacy and free information exchange in the security community.

Once a vulnerability is identified, malware writers then create an **exploit**, or a piece of code, that can take advantage of vulnerabilities to give the attacker deeper access to a system or network (Symantec, 2014). These exploits are often built into malware to compromise and influence the victim machine more efficiently. The changes that a piece of malware causes to a computer system are effected by what is commonly called its **payload**. When a piece of malware is activated and executes the program it contains, the resulting impact on the system can range from benign to highly destructive, depending primarily on the skills of the writer and their interests. In fact, early malware typically caused no actual harm to the system or its contents, but annoyed the victim by presenting them with messages or playing music at a high volume. Many variants of malware often delete or change system files, causing harm to the user's documents and files, or collect information that users input or store on their system, causing a loss of personally identifiable information. Some malware can even disrupt the basic functions of an operating system, thereby rendering a computer unusable.

Malware is generally used to disrupt email and network operations, access private files, steal sensitive information, delete or corrupt files, or generally damage computer software and hardware (Kaspersky, 2003; Nazario, 2003; Symantec, 2014). As a result, the dissemination of malware across computer networks can be costly for several reasons, including, but not limited to: (1) the loss of data and copyrighted information; (2) identity theft; (3) loss of revenue due to customer apprehension about the safety of a company's website; (4) time spent removing the programs; and (5) losses in personal productivity and system functions. The interconnected nature of modern computer networks also allows an infected system in one country to spread malicious software across the globe and cause even greater damage. Thus, malware infection poses a significant threat to Internet users around the globe.

Viruses, trojans, and worms

Malicious software is a problem that many individuals in the general public with minimal technical proficiency do not understand. Part of the confusion lies in identifying the diverse range of current malware. The most common forms of malware include computer viruses, worms, and trojan horse programs that alter functions within computer programs and files. These programs have some distinctive features that separate them from one another, though more recent forms of malware combine aspects of these programs together to create what are commonly called **blended threats**. We will explore the most common forms of malware here and differentiate them based on their unique features and utility in an attack.

Viruses

Viruses are perhaps the oldest form of malware, operating since the earliest days of computing (Szor, 2005). This form of malware cannot be activated nor execute its payload without some user intervention, such as opening a file or clicking on an attachment. The target must execute the code in some fashion so that the virus will be installed in either existing programs, data files, or the boot sector of a hard drive (Szor, 2005). In addition, many viruses may access sensitive data, corrupt files, steal space on the hard drive, or generally disrupt system processes.

malware and automated computer attacks

Viruses can install themselves in data files or existing programs and operate based on the parameters of a specific operating system, whether Windows, Linux, or Mac OS. These viruses will attempt to install themselves in any executable file so as to ensure their success. Some viruses can overwrite the contents of their target file with malicious code which renders the original file unusable (Szor, 2005). Such a tactic is, however, easy to identify because the error or failure that results may be immediately obvious to the user. Other viruses can insert their code into the file, but leave it operational so that it will not be identified by the user. Finally, some viruses can clone an existing file so that it runs instead of the original program (Szor, 2005).

Boot sector viruses operate by attempting to install their code into the boot sector of either a form of storage media like a flash drive or into the hard disk of the targeted computer (Szor, 2005). A **boot sector** is a region of any sort of storage media or the hard disk of a computer that can hold code which is loaded into memory by a computer's firmware. There are a range of boot sectors, but the operating system loader of most devices is stored starting in the first boot sector so that it is the first thing that the system loads (Szor, 2005). As a result, virus writers create boot sector viruses so that they can load the code of their virus into the Random Access Memory (RAM) of the computer. This ensures that the virus will always be present in the system from the start to finish of each session (Szor, 2005). In fact, boot viruses can gain control of the entire system by installing itself into a specific region and then changing the boot record so that the original code is no longer in control of the system. The malware then becomes extremely difficult to identify and eradicate and can severely impact the functionality of the system (Szor, 2005).

Some of the first viruses observed in the home PC market during the 1980s were boot sector viruses and those that spread to other machines via floppy disks. These viruses generally had limited functionality or malicious utility. For example, they might often play music or delete letters in documents. For instance, one of the first viruses observed in home computers was called **Elk Cloner** and was designed to infect Apple II computers via a floppy disk (Manjoo, 2007). The code was written as a prank by Rich Skrenta, a 15 year old who liked to play and share computer games. He wrote Elk Cloner in order to play a practical joke on his friends without clueing them in to the presence of the code (Manjoo, 2007). The virus was attached to a game which when played 50 times would display the following poem:

Elk Cloner: The program with a personality
It will get on all your disks
It will infiltrate your chips
Yes, it's Cloner!
It will stick to you like glue
It will modify RAM too
Send in the Cloner!

Though the program caused no actual harm, the code was difficult to remove and infected many people because the virus would install locally on any computer and then infect other floppy disks inserted into the infected system (Manjoo, 2007).

Macro viruses are also a popular way to infect systems by using a common weakness in a variety of popular programs like Excel, Word, and PDFs (Szor, 2005). Virus writers can write a program using the **macro programming languages** associated with specific applications and embed the code into the appropriate file, such as a PowerPoint presentation. Opening the file actually executes the virus, enabling the infection payload to be activated and subsequently embed the code into other documents of the same type so that any attempt to share a file will lead to other systems being infected (Szor, 2005). Macro viruses designed to target Microsoft Outlook can infect a user's computer by including infected files, or even by the user previewing an infected email.

In the early 1990s, virus writers began to employ encryption protocols in order to make the code more difficult to detect and remove (Szor, 2005). This novel tactic was further adapted through the development of **MuTation Engine (MtE)** in 1991, a polymorphic generator that not only encrypted the virus but randomized the routine used so that it varied with each replication (Szor, 2005). The term polymorphic references the ability to take multiple forms or go through various phases. In the context of malware, this term references the use of code to hide viruses from detection by changing their structure to not match existing signatures. Thus, the emergence of polymorphic engines led to an increase in the number of these viruses in the wild in 1993.

For a deeper explanation of polymorphic engines in malware, go online to: www.dailymotion.com/video/xcetxj_avg-tutorials-what-is-polymorphic-v_tech

During this period, the Microsoft Windows operating system emerged and became tremendously popular among home computer users for its easy use and various features. As a result, virus writers began to target Windows users and incorporated the use of macros in order to compromise the system. The first macro virus, called **Concept**, was found in 1995 (see Text Box 3.2 for more detail; Paquette, 2010). This code would only replicate itself and displayed the following message: "That's enough to prove my point." This was not necessarily malicious, but demonstrated that macros were a weakness that could be exploited. As a result, a number of macro-based viruses were released, affecting both Windows and Mac OS computers since both operating systems could run the Microsoft Office software suite (Paquette, 2010). This common business-based software includes Excel and

Word, which both could be easily affected by macro-based viruses as they support a macro programming language.

Text Box 3.2: F-Secure report on virus W32/Concept malware

www.f-secure.com/v-descs/concept.shtml

Virus:W32/Concept

> The virus gets executed every time an infected document is opened. It tries to infect Word's global document template, NORMAL.DOT (which is also capable of holding macros). If it finds either the macro "PayLoad" or "FileSaveAs" already on the template, it assumes that the template is already infected …

This technical brief provides an in-depth analysis of how a macro virus operates in a Windows system, including a breakdown of how it infects programs overall.

Around the same time, viruses began to spread through the Internet as the World Wide Web was becoming popular among home users, and more easily accessible through an increase in Internet service providers. In fact, one of the most prominent viruses of this period, the **Melissa virus**, which was first identified in 1999, spread through the web and utilized macros to infect users' computers (F-Secure, 2014). The Melissa virus was distributed through an online discussion group titled *alt.sex* by sending an infected file titled "List. DOC" that contained passwords for pornographic websites. Anyone who opened the file using Microsoft Word 97 or 2000 was infected. The macro code then attempted to email itself out to 50 people using the email client in Microsoft Outlook (F-Secure, 2014). Given that it would send 50 emails per infected system, the infection rate was quite substantial. Additionally, the code altered the Word program to infect any new document created.

The virus payload was not necessarily harmful in that it did not delete files or corrupt systems, but it clogged email servers because of its distribution pattern. In the end, it was estimated that approximately 1.2 million computers were infected in the US with $80 million in damages worldwide due to system outages and the costs to remove the malware (Szor, 2005). Based on the success of the Melissa virus and others, malware writers quickly began to adopt the web as a means to spread their code as widely and as easily as is possible. They not only targeted common OS products like Microsoft Office, but programming languages commonly used in web browsing software and tools such as Java.

Trojans

In addition to viruses, **trojans** are a prevalent form of malware. This form of malware is similar to viruses in that it cannot replicate on its own, but requires some user interaction in order to execute the code; it got its name from the Trojan horse of ancient Greece, which was a giant wooden horse concealing soldiers inside (Dunham, 2008). The horse was brought inside fortified city walls under the belief that it was a gift; this enabled the warriors to sack the city. Computer-based trojans share a similar structure in that they appear to be a downloadable file or attachment that people would be inclined to open, such as photos, video, or documents with misleading titles such as "XXX Porn" or "Receipt of Purchase" (Dunham, 2008). When the file is opened, it executes some portion of its code and delivers its payload on the system. Thus, trojan writers utilize social engineering principles in order to entice users to open their files (see Chapter 2 for more detail).

Trojans do not typically replicate themselves on the infected system or attempt to propagate across systems. Instead, trojans most often serve to establish backdoors that can be used to gain continuous unauthorized access to an infected system (Dunham, 2008). Specifically, the code can open ports and establish remote controls between the infected system and the operator's computer allowing them to invisibly execute commands on that system. This is achieved through the use of a client and server system, where the victim executes the trojan and establishes a server on their computer that can be remotely accessed by a client program on the attacker's computer (Dunham, 2008). The commands sent between the client and server are largely invisible to the infected user, though if the attacker utilizes too much of the available processing power it may slow down the infected system.

The benefit of trojan programs to an attacker are that they can configure the tool to perform a range of functions, including keystroke logging, access to sensitive files, use of the webcam or other system tools, use of the infected system as a launch point for attacks against other systems, and even send additional forms of malware to the system to engage in secondary infections (Dunham, 2008). Many trojans also allow the attacker to restart a computer remotely and manage its activities without the victim's knowledge. Some even give the attacker the power to uninstall or deactivate security tools and firewalls rendering the system unable to protect itself from harm (Dunham, 2008).

One of the more noteworthy trojans that combined all of these functions into a single tool was **Back Orifice 2000 (BO2K)**, a piece of malware written by members of the hacker group the **Cult of the Dead Cow (cDc)**. The tool takes its name from the then popular Microsoft BackOffice Server program and was designed to infect Microsoft systems (Messmer, 1999). BO2K was released at the DefCon 7 hacker conference on July 10, 1999, to much fanfare as the group threw copies of the code on compact discs, along with raw meat, into the crowd. This release was argued to be a remote administration tool rather than a form of malware because the functions were similar to those of legitimate security tools that help end users chat between the server and client (Messmer, 1999). The creators, however, noted that the victims were not supposed to know that the BO2K server had been installed on their system (Messmer, 1999). Some of the functions of the tool were also similar to malware, in that it could install a backdoor in the system, access the computer through security firewalls, remotely access files, control the keyboard, mouse, and webcam, and capture all keystrokes entered by the user (Sourceforge, 1999).

For more information on BO2K, go Online to: www.youtube.com/watch?v=Vvlr8nVVmlU

The utility of trojans has led them to become one of the most popular forms of malware available (BitDefender, 2009). In fact, one of the most dangerous and common trojans currently active today is commonly called **Zeus**. This malware targets Microsoft Windows systems, and is often sent through spam messages and phishing campaigns in which the sender either sends attachments or directs the recipient to a link that can infect the user (see Chapter 5 for more detail). Once installed, the trojan creates a backdoor in the system so it can be remotely controlled. It also affects the web browser in order to capture sensitive data entered by a user (Symantec, 2014). In addition, Zeus can collect passwords stored locally on the infected system and act as a traditional keylogging program.

To see Zeus malware distribution patterns, go online to: http://threat-info.trendmicro.com/vinfo/web_attacks/ZeuS_and_its_Continuing_Drive_Towards_Stealing_Online_Data.html

---

This trojan is extremely adaptable, and has been used as the basis for a range of malware used in attacks against various financial institutions across the globe. In fact, a form of Zeus has been identified that infects the Google Android operating systems common on smartphones and tablets (Leyden, 2012). This malware acts as a banking app that can be downloaded and installed on a phone in order to capture SMS messages sent to bank customers from financial institutions in order to authenticate transactions. The use of SMS messaging is common in European banking in order to authenticate account information and transactions made by a customer (Leyden, 2012). Obtaining this information allows attackers to engage in fraudulent transfers between accounts and verify that they are correct without the need for victim interaction. As a result, a group of cybercriminals was able to obtain 36 million Euros from over 30,000 customers in Italy, Germany, Spain, and Holland using this malware (Leyden, 2012).

A Zeus variant was also used in a series of attacks against hundreds of victims across the US leading to losses of over $70 million during 2009 (FBI, 2010). This campaign was operated by multiple individuals living in Eastern Europe, the US, and the UK. The ring of thieves was disrupted by a multi-national investigation spearheaded by the Federal Bureau of Investigation in 2010. There were over 100 arrests in this case. The majority of the arrests were in the US for violations of fraud and money laundering statutes (FBI, 2010).

Worms

Worms are a unique form of malware that can autonomously spread on their own, though they do not necessarily have a payload. Instead, they utilize system memory to spread, self-replicate, and deteriorate system functionality (Nazario, 2003). Worms are written as stand-alone programs in that they do not need to attach to existing system files or modify any code. Once it is activated, it copies itself into the system memory and attempts to spread to other systems through email address books or other mechanisms (Nazario, 2003). Should an unsuspecting recipient click on an attachment sent from a worm-infected system, the code will execute and infect that system, replicating the process.

As a result, worms can spread rapidly, and depending on their function-ality, cause massive network outages. For example, the **Code Red worm**, activated online on July 13, 2001, began infecting any web server using Microsoft's IIS web server software. The initial growth of the worm was small, but by July 19, it exploded and infected more than 359,000 computer systems worldwide within a 14-hour period (CAIDA, 2001). The infec-tion rate was so fast that it was infecting 2,000 hosts per minute during its peak spread that day. The sheer number of the worm's attempts at replica-tion caused a virtual denial of service attack across most of the industrial-ized world as the worm's traffic absorbed almost all available bandwitdth (CAIDA, 2001).

> **To see a video of the spread of the Code Red worm, go online to:** www. caida.org/research/security/code-red/coderedv2_analysis.xml

In addition to network degradation, some worms contain secondary payloads to affect computer systems or servers. For instance, the Code Red worm contained code to display the following message on any web page hosted on a server infected by the worm: "HELLO! Welcome to http://www.worm.com! Hacked by Chinese!" In addition, the worm contained a secondary payload to engage in denial of service attacks against various websites, including the White House. The infected systems, however, seemingly terminated all activities within 28 days, suggesting there may have been some code within the worm that triggered it to shut down independently (CAIDA, 2001).

Beyond payloads, it is critical to note that worms can cause tremendous harm on their own by crashing email servers, overloading networks with floods of requests, and severely diminishing the functionality of infected systems by forcing them to constantly scan and attempt to replicate the code to other systems (Nazario, 2003). The first example of a worm in the wild was created by Robert Tappan Morris and became known as the **Morris worm**. The worm went active on November 2, 1988 after being released by Morris through a computer at MIT. Morris, a student at Cornell University, claimed he designed the worm to assess the size of the Internet at the time by copying the worm code on each computer connected online at that time (Eisenberg, Gries, Hartmanis, Holcomb, Lynn, and Santoro, 1989). The code was improperly written and malfunctioned, establishing multiple copies of itself on each system which caused them to slow down dramatically due to the copies trying to replicate themselves and spread to other systems. Morris' errors caused an estimated 6,000 UNIX computer systems to be infected multiple times over and become effectively unusable (Eisenberg *et al.*, 1989).

> **For more information on the Morris worm, go online to:** www.youtube.com/watch?v=1kl2XgGEzms

Morris was prosecuted and convicted in federal court for violating the Computer Fraud and Abuse Act. Interestingly, Morris was the first person to be convicted under this law. He eventually received three years probation, 400 hours of community service, and a substantial fine (Markoff, 1990). The incident also demonstrated the need for a coordinated response to a large-scale online threat. Researchers at MIT, Berkeley, Purdue, and other institutions pooled their resources in order to determine the best solution to mitigate the worm (Eisenberg *et al.*, 1989). It was, however, a substantial investment of time and resources due to the distributed nature of the teams and the attack itself. Thus, DARPA, one of the founders of the Internet itself, sponsored the foundation of the first **Computer Emergency Response Team (CERT)** at Carnegie Mellon University in order to serve as a coordinating point for responses to major network emergencies (Eisenberg *et al.*, 1989). This CERT now serves a pivotal role in the dissemination of information related to serious cyberthreats and determining large-scale responses to vulnerabilities and security threats.

Blended threats and ancillary tools

In addition to these three forms of malware, there are now blended threats operating online that combine the distinct aspects of these codes into a single functional tool. A common blended threat is **botnet** malware, which combines aspects of trojan horse programs and viruses together in a single program. Botnet malware is often sent to a victim through an attachment or other mechanism (Bacher, Holz, Kotter, and Wicherski, 2005). Once the program is executed, it then installs a "bot" program, meaning that the computer can now receive commands and be controlled by another user through IRC channels or the web via HTTP protocols (Bacher *et al.*, 2005). The infected machine then surreptitiously contacts a pre-programmed IRC channel to wait for commands from the bot operator. Multiple machines that are infected with this malware will contact the channel, creating a "botnet," or network of zombie machines (see Image 3.1; Bacher *et al.*, 2005). This form of malware is often very easy to control through the use of sophisticated interfaces that make sending commands to the network quite easy to accomplish.

For more information on botnets, go online to: www.youtube.com/watch?v=Soe3b6sXuVl

The size of botnets enables their operators to engage in a wide range of cybercrimes, including the distribution of spam and other malware. Botnets can also be used to perform **distributed denial of service (DDoS) attacks**. In a DDoS attack, each computer in the network attempts to contact the same computer or server (Bacher *et al.*, 2005). The target system becomes flooded with requests and cannot handle the volume, resulting in a loss of services to users. This is an extremely costly form of cybercrime for companies, as they can lose millions of dollars in revenue if customers cannot access their services (Bacher *et al.*, 2005).

Botnets are now a common form of malware as indicated by active infections and operations around the world. In fact, the US FBI has engaged in two separate investigative crackdowns against botnet operators under the codename **"Operation: Bot Roast"** between 2005 and 2010 (Hedquist, 2008). The first operation led to charges being brought against four individuals who had infected over one million computers through botnet malware. One of these actors, Owen Walker, lived in New Zealand and was arrested for denial of service attacks against the University of Pennsylvania in the US (Hedquist, 2008). This investigation also led to the first individual ever to be prosecuted for the use of botnets in the US – Jeanson James Ancheta, who advertised his services as a bot-herder to others through malware markets (Goodin, 2007). He was 20 years old when arrested in 2005 as part of an undercover operation led by the FBI. Ancheta pled guilty to four felony

malware and automated computer attacks

Image 3.1 Botnet command and control distribution
http://commons.wikimedia.org/wiki/File:Botnet.svg

counts of violating the Computer Fraud and Abuse Act on May 9, 2006 (Goodin, 2007). As a result, he received a five-year sentence in a federal prison, a $15,000 fine, and forfeited his car and income from leasing his botnet infrastructure.

Similarly, malware writers have recently developed tools that can infect web browsers and thereby enable remote takeovers of computer systems. These programs are called **exploit packs** and must be installed on a web server in order to attack individuals visiting a website. There have been more than a dozen variations of exploit packs operating in the wild at different points in time due to the substantive popularity of these tools to straightforwardly attack a range of users (Symantec, 2009). The exploit pack malware contains multiple common vulnerabilities for the most prevalent web browsers, and its associated exploits. The program then detects the type and version of browser software that an individual is using to go to that website, and cycles through these vulnerabilities and exploits until it can infect the user (Symantec, 2009).

This type of attack exponentially increases the ease of infection by operating surreptitiously and without the need for true user interaction to activate the malicious code (see Text Box 3.3 for an interview with the creator of the exploit pack MPack; Symantec, 2009). An individual must (unknowingly) direct their web browser to a site hosted on a server with the toolkit in order to begin the process of infection, which is much simpler than trying to get someone to open an attachment or file. This is why such attacks are commonly known as "drive-by downloads" in that a victim need only visit the site without clicking on anything in order to be infected (Symantec, 2009). In addition, web browsers often store sensitive information about a user such as passwords and common sites visited, thereby increasing the risk of identity theft, data loss, and computer misuse (Symantec, 2009). Once the infection payload is executed, the attacker can then send additional malware to the system, including rootkits and trojans to gain further control over the system (Symantec, 2009).

Text Box 3.3: Interview with MPack creator

www.theregister.co.uk/2007/07/23/mpack_developer_interview

MPack developer on automated infection kit

> In late June, SecurityFocus answered an online advertisement for the MPack infection kit, sending an ICQ message to the identifier listed in the ad. A few days later, a person contacted SecurityFocus through ICQ ... What follows is the result of two weeks of interviews that took place ...

This article provides an interview with one of the developers of the well-known and highly profitable exploit pack called MPack. This interview provides insights into the nature of malware creation, distribution, and the individuals responsible for their development.

An additional blended threat that has gained a great deal of popularity over the last decade is called **ransomware** or **scareware**. These threats demand that the operator of the infected system pay in order to have their system's functionality restored (Russinovich, 2013). Ransomware is similar to a trojan in that it spreads through downloadable files or through websites. Once the prospective target executes the file, it will then deploy its payload which either encrypts files on the user's hard drive or may modify the boot record of the system (similar to a virus) to restrict what the user can access (Russinovich, 2013). The payload also includes messages that are displayed to the victim indicating that their computer has been used for illegal activities like child pornography and has been shut down by law enforcement. Some also indicate that the operating system of the infected computer has been corrupted or is counterfeit and will not work until the user pays a fee (Russinovich, 2013). These messages require the user to pay so that the functionality or files will be restored. Once payment is received, the victim receives a program to decrypt the file or unlock the affected portions of the system.

There have been several notable examples of ransomware, including the recent **Cryptolocker** program which was first identified in September 2013 (Ferguson, 2013). The program spreads via attachments in emails or as downloadable malware online and targets Microsoft Windows systems. Once it is executed, the code encrypts data on any hard drives attached to the infected system using a very strong encryption protocol (Ferguson, 2013). The key to decrypt the file is sent to a command-and-control structure (similar to a botnet) and the victim is told that they have to pay a $300 fee or the key will be deleted within three days (Ferguson, 2013). Though the malware itself can be removed with some ease, the encrypted files cannot be readily repaired, which makes this a very challenging threat for computer users.

> **For more detail on Cryptolocker in action, go online to:** www.youtube.com/watch?v=Gz2kmmsMpMI

The global impact of malware

Computer security experts continue to express alarm about the current number of malicious software programs and the increases they expect to see in the future. In a 2011 quarterly report, Panda Security (2011) stated that "[t]he title of Guns N' Roses hit 'Welcome to the Jungle' perfectly sums up the events that have taken place in the computer security world during Q2 2011" (p. 1). Unfortunately, the statistics over the last several years have not improved. Before providing additional statistics and insights, it should be pointed out that these companies profit by selling computer security services to individuals and corporations. Thus it behooves them to discuss this issue as a crisis, though all available statistics appear to support their concerns.

The number of new malicious software programs introduced into the wild each year is tremendous. Panda Security reported in their 2013 annual report that 30 million variations of malware were released into the wild in 2013 alone, making an average of 82,000 identified each day (Panda Security, 2013). These additional 30 million strains bring their total database of malware to approximately 145 million! This also means that 20 percent of all malware that has ever existed was actually created in 2013 alone. Examining the types of malware also helps to demonstrate the changing nature of the software used. More than seven out of every ten (71.11 percent) new malware strains released in 2013 were trojans (Panda Security, 2013). This is an increase from 55.9 percent back in 2010 (Panda Security,

2010). In addition, 78.97 percent of new infections were caused by trojans (Panda Security, 2013). Viruses were the second most common form of malware released (13.30 percent; Panda Security, 2013), down from 22 percent in 2010 (Panda Security, 2010).

Statistics on the percentage of infected computers around the world clearly illustrate that malware infection is a global problem. Panda Security (2013) estimated that 31.53 percent of all computers around the world were infected in 2013. This estimate might be high considering that their sample consists of individuals using their free online scanning program. Many of the individuals who used this free scan may have done so out of fears that their computer was infected. Asian and Latin American nations compose the highest proportion of nations with infected systems based on the use of this free scanning tool: (1) China (54.03 percent); (2) Turkey (42.15 percent); (3) Ecuador (40.35 percent); (4) Peru (39.85 percent); (5) Argentina (38.18 percent); (6) Russia (38.01 percent); (7) Taiwan (37.97 percent); (8) Guatemala (36.38 percent); (9) Poland (35.01 percent); and (10) Brazil (34.99 percent; Panda Security, 2013). Besides Japan, the top ten countries with the smallest percentage of computers infected are all in Europe: (1) Sweden (20.28 percent); (2) Norway (21.13 percent); (3) Finland (21.22 percent); (4) UK (22.14 percent); (5) Germany (22.68 percent); (6) Switzerland (23.05 percent); (7) the Netherlands (23.64 percent); (8) Japan (24.84 percent); (9) Denmark (25.34 percent); and (10) Belgium (25.40 percent). Note that the country with the least percentage of computers infected (Sweden) still has one out of every five computers infected with malware. Three other countries of interest to our readers all had infection rates below the international rate: Australia (26.84 percent); Canada (27.82 percent); and the US (28.96 percent).

A review of US-CERT weekly vulnerability summaries, released by a governmental agency and part of the National Cyber Alert System, illustrates that the identification of vulnerabilities is a constant challenge. Each Cyber Security Bulletin provides a summary of the new vulnerabilities recorded during the past week by the National Institute of Standards and Technology (NIST) National Vulnerability Database (NVD). This database is sponsored by the Department of Homeland Security (DHS) National Cybersecurity and Communications Integration Center (NCCIC)/United States Computer Emergency Readiness Team (US-CERT). The vulnerabilities are categorized by severity (high, medium, and low) based on the Common Vulnerability Scoring System (CVSS) standard. For example, a vulnerability will be categorized as high if its CVSS score is between 7.0 and 10.0, medium if between 4.0 to 6.9, and low if between 0.0 and 3.9. This information is made more informative by organizations and US-CERT providing additional information, including identifying information, values, definitions, related links, and patches if available.

Any examination of two of these weekly vulnerability reports shows how many serious vulnerabilities are identified and reported on a weekly basis.

In Cyber Security Bulletin SB14-077 (US-CERT, 2013a), which covers the week of March 10, 2014, there were 68 high-threat vulnerabilities, including reports of problems in popular items such as Apple iOS, Google Chrome, and Microsoft Internet Explorer. In addition, there were 141 medium vulnerabilities and 19 low vulnerabilities. For the week of March 17, 2014, reported in Cyber Security Bulletin SB14-083 (US-CERT, 2013b), there were 56 high vulnerabilities, 131 medium, and 20 low.

Although this chapter primarily focuses on computer systems and their users, scholars and security experts also warn about the vulnerabilities of smartphones, particularly Android operating systems, and personal digital assistants (PDAs). Though mobile attacks are still less common relative to PC attacks, there is an expectation that mobile attacks will increase substantially in the near future (Panda Security, 2013; Ruggiero and Foote, 2011). Panda Security (2013) reported that there were over two million strains of malware for Android released in 2013 alone. This is because smartphones and PDAs have some of the same advanced computing abilities as traditional computer systems. They give the user access to the Internet and email, have address books, and have GPS navigation. They also allow people to purchase items using wireless networks, access bank accounts, set alarms on houses, and make purchases through various online retailers.

The issue that separates mobile devices from computers is their use of security protections. Smartphones and PDAs have lax or poor security as they do not come pre-installed with firewalls or antivirus programs. These tools are available for purchase, though it is unclear how many individuals actually install antivirus protection on their mobile devices. In addition, operating systems for mobile phones are updated less frequently than those for computers, creating greater opportunities for attackers to exploit known vulnerabilities. This problem is compounded by the fact that smartphone and mobile device users are generally unaware of these problems but believe that their devices are just as secure as their computers. Thus, many computer security experts believe that as smartphones become more prevalent and have more of the same capabilities and data files as PCs, they will become a more lucrative venture for malware writers.

It is difficult to create even rough estimates on the amounts that hackers and malicious programs have cost citizens, organizations, government agencies, and the global economy. When considering the financial costs, one has to not only count the actual direct damage of the malware, such as having to replace a computer, but also the amount of time, money, and manpower spent trying to prevent an infection and then fix the problem if an infection occurs. Malware can disrupt network operations, delete, steal, or manipulate files, allow access to confidential files, and generally damage computer systems and hardware. In addition, there are the indirect costs to businesses that arise from consumer lack of confidence in online purchases or credit card usage. If consumers lose confidence in the security and privacy of their online purchases, they will be less likely to spend money online in general and with specific companies that had reported particular problems. On the other end, vendors themselves might also fear online transactions if they are unsure that the person on the other side is really who they say they are. In order to address these problems, companies and financial institutions spend billions of dollars on verification and other computer security programs to ensure safety. In the end, these costs increase the cost of doing business, which is handed down to the consumer.

Over the last decade, various experts and companies have estimated that hack attacks cost the world economy over $1 trillion per year. Considering that (1) more malicious software is created each year; (2) the number of specialized hacks occurring throughout the world has increased; (3) more individuals around the world are connected to the Internet; (4) more companies conduct online business transactions; and (5) more companies and governments spend additional funds on computer security to address these problems, it is safe to say that the cost of malware must be higher than what is otherwise spent to mitigate and prevent malicious software infections and hacks. Other estimates, however, are much lower. One estimate placed the global effect of malware and spam at $100 billion globally in 2007 (International Telecommunications Union, 2008). According to a recent issue of *Consumer Reports* (2011), one-third of households that completed a survey were infected with malware, costing consumers $2.3 billion, while 1.3 million PCs had to be replaced because of an infection.

While the estimates of the impact of malware and hacking on the US economy are obviously lower than for the global economy, they are just as varied considering that different experts and agencies estimate the costs differently. The Bureau of Justice Statistics (BJS) reported that two-thirds of businesses experienced some form of cybercrime, totaling $867 million in 2007 (Rantala, 2008). Malicious software was the most common form of cybercrime affecting these businesses (Rantala, 2008).

The costs of hacking and malware infection, however, are not only financial. There are also potential emotional consequences for victims, though there is little criminological research on the way that victims of malware infection and hacking incidents feel afterward. For many people, malware infection is nothing more than a minor nuisance that can be fixed easily. Some, however, may feel that their personal space was violated and personal privacy forever lost. Victims may not be able to identify the source of the infection, whether from a website, bad attachment, or other medium. As a result, some may change their online habits in order to reduce their perceived risk of future infections.

In addition, some victims may feel that they are to blame for their victimization experience. Since computer security principles currently revolve around self-protection practices, like the use of protective software, hard passwords, and careful online behavior, victims may see themselves as the source of their financial and emotional harm resulting from an infection.

Hackers and malware writers

Although hackers are often associated with the use of malware, not all hackers have the ability to create these programs. It takes some degree of skill and knowledge of programming languages, vulnerabilities, and exploits in order to create effective malware. There is a good demand for malicious code among hackers of all types as they can make an attack much easier to complete. As a result, the demand for malware can far surpass the capacities present in the current hacker community.

The very limited body of research considering the activities and interests of malware writers suggests that they generally operate within and share the norms and values of the larger hacker subculture (see Chapter 2 for details). Malware writers have a deep interest in technology, which is an absolute necessity in order to identify distinct vulnerabilities in software or hardware and find innovative ways to exploit them. Writing malicious code can therefore be an exercise in creativity, as the individuals must challenge themselves and their understanding of the limits of an operating system and their own coding capabilities. For instance, the Elk Cloner virus mentioned earlier is an excellent example of creative malware coding as the author liked to play pranks and creatively apply his knowledge to computer systems.

They may also be motivated by the desire to cause harm or get revenge against someone who they perceive to have wronged them (Bissett and Shipton, 2000; Gordon, 2000). For instance, a system administrator named Andy Lin was sentenced to 30 months in a US federal prison in 2008 for planting a form of malicious code called a "logic bomb" on the servers of Medco Health Solutions where he worked for some time (Noyes, 2008). Lin installed a program in 2003 that would execute its payload and wipe out all data stored on over 70 servers in the company's network in the event he was laid off. When it appeared possible that he would lose his job, he set the code to activate on April 23, 2004 (Noyes, 2008). The program, however, was unsuccessful. He therefore kept it in place and reset the deployment date to April 2005. A system administrator within the company found the bomb code in the system and was able to neutralize the code (Noyes, 2008). While this scheme was unsuccessful, it demonstrates the inherent danger that malware can cause in the hands of the right actor.

Writers may also develop a piece of malware because they believe they may garner fame or notoriety in the hacker community (Bisset and Shipton, 2000; Gordon, 2000; Holt and Kilger, 2012). In the late 1990s and early 2000s, the preponderance of worms and viruses led their creators to generate worldwide attention because of the harm they could cause to the majority of computer users around the world. That kind of attention could easily serve as an individual's calling card and help them to demonstrate their level of skill in order to gain a legitimate job in the security industry (Taylor, 1999). Alternatively, the author may simply be able to show everyone what they are capable of doing with enough careful planning and execution.

As patterns of technology use have changed and individuals are increasingly using technology in all facets of everyday life, malware writers have begun to target these users to set up stable attack platforms based on networks of infected computers (Holt and Kilger, 2012). Virus writers and creators now recognize that not everyone has the ability to write such code, but if the actor is proficient enough as a hacker they will understand how to leverage a tool to their own benefit. As a result, malware writers are increasingly motivated by economic gain through sales of tools and code to others in the community (Holt, 2013; Holt and Kilger, 2012). Typically, tools are advertised through forums and IRC channels and then direct negotiations occur between buyers and sellers. Direct sales of programs to others can generate a relatively healthy income that exceeds what may otherwise be available as a salary through existing jobs (see Text Box 3.4 for details). Thus, malware writers share some common ideas with the larger hacker community, though the skill and sophistication involved in the creation of malware differentiates them from the larger population of unskilled or semi-skilled hackers.

Text Box 3.4: Interview with the malware writer Corpse

http://computersweden.idg.se/2.2683/1.93344

Meeting the Swedish bank hacker

> For the price of 3,000 dollars, our reporter was offered his personal bank Trojan. In an interview with Computer Sweden, the hacker behind the recent Internet frauds against Sweden's Nordea bank claims responsibility for more intrusions. "99 percent of all bank intrusions are kept secret," he insists.

This in-depth interview with Corpse, the creator of a well-known trojan, describes why he made it. The account demonstrates that some hackers are clearly aware of how their programs have malicious application and will harm individuals on a global scale.

The market for malicious software

The range of currently active malware is staggering and appears to increase every year. Even new devices and platforms, such as tablet computers and mobile phones, are being targeted by malware writers. The continuing evolution of malware raises a fundamental question about the true capability of malware users and creators: Are malware users primarily writing these codes on their own or gaining access to these resources through others? There is sufficient evidence that the skills needed to identify vulnerabilities and devise malware around that weakness is limited in the hacker community (see Chapter 2 for details). Unskilled hackers, therefore, must acquire malware for their personal use from other sources.

In the 1990s, hackers would share their resources for free through direct downloads hosted on forums and file-sharing sites (Taylor, 1999). The global proliferation of the Internet and computer technology expanded the number of available targets for compromise. As personal information became more prevalent in online spaces, the use of attacks to gain monetary advantage also increased (Holt, 2013). As a result, some hackers recognized the monetary value of their attack tools and resources and began to sell them to others through online markets operating in forums and IRC. The emergence of botnets was a critical factor in the facilitation of cybercrime markets, as bot owners and operators realized that they could lease out their infrastructure to others who were unable to develop similar resources on their own (Bacher *et al.*, 2005). Since botnets could be used for DDoS attacks, spam distribution, and as a mechanism to route attack traffic through victim systems, the operators began to offer these services to others at a relatively low price. This is why some in the cybersecurity community refer to botnets as "**crimeware**" in that it can be used as a stable platform for cybercrime (Bacher *et al.*, 2005).

For more information on the market for malware, go online to: www. youtube.com/watch?v=bVo5ihJoQek

In order to understand the normative orders that shape cybercrime markets, it is necessary to first consider the structure of the market as a whole. Forums and IRC channels constitute an interconnected marketplace where sellers advertise products openly for others to buy, or alternatively describe the products they are seeking from other vendors (see Chu, Holt, and Ahn, 2010; Holt, 2013; Motoyama, McCoy, Levchenko, Savage, and Voelker, 2011). Both buyers and sellers provide as thorough a description of their products or tools as possible, including the costs and preferred payment mechanisms and their contact information. For example, the following is an ad posted by a botnet operator who would lease out his infrastructure to others:

Lease of bot networks!, $100 a month (volume 6.9k online from 300 [nodes])

I'm leasing the admin console of a bot network! – there are ~9,000 bots in the network (200–1,500 online regularly) – Countries: **RU,U S,TR,UE,KI,TH,RO,CZ,IN,SK,UA**(upon request countries can be added!) – OS: **winXP/NT** functionality: [+] list of bot socks [known proxies] type: **ip:port** time (when it appeared the last time) Country|City [allows you to] load ... files on the [infected] bot machines (trojans/ grabbers ...) [the] admin console quite simple, convenient and functional, even a school kid can figure it out. Today 1,000 more (mix) bots were added with good speed indicators + every 3,4 days 2k fresh machines are added (the person who works with the reports receives a unique service with unique and constantly new machines) Super price-**100wmz [Web Money in US currency]** a month! all questions to **icq:** [number removed] Spammers are in shock over such an offer (: ps: we also make networks for individual **requests/orders**

This post illustrates the functionality of the malware, the global spread of this botnet with infected systems throughout the world, and the costs to lease their services. It also indicates the user prefers to be paid though the online currency system Web Money (Holt, 2013). The preference for electronic payment systems is driven in part by the fact that they allow relatively immediate payments between buyers and sellers with no need for face-to-face interactions. This provides a modicum of privacy and anonymity for the participants and rapid dissemination of the goods (Holt, 2013). At the same time, however, buyers are disadvantaged because a seller may not deliver the goods for which they provided payment. In addition, individuals could advertise their products directly to others with little regulation or constraint. Thus, buyers must carefully consider who they purchase goods and services from and in what quantities, to reduce their risk of loss.

Social forces within cybercrime markets

The forums that support the market for malware provide a unique interactive experience that is driven by exchanges between buyers and sellers. The behavior of participants is, however, structured by the needs and risks that they face. Research by Holt (2013) suggests that there are three factors that affect the practices of market actors: (1) price; (2) customer service; and (3) trust.

The cost of goods and services played an important role in the vetting of goods and services within the market. Price may be one of the most pertinent factors in cybercrime markets to draw in potential customers because they may have limited funds or seek the greatest value for their investments (Holt, 2013; Motoyama *et al.*, 2011). Individuals who offered a service or form of malware were subject to scrutiny based on the price for a product, particularly if it was perceived to be too high or low. The active questioning of costs helped to clarify the acceptable price for a given product and reduce the likelihood that individuals would pay exorbitant fees for specific services (Holt, 2013).

The importance of price in the decision-making process led some advertisers to offer discounts and deals to attract prospective customers. One of the

malware and automated computer attacks

most common techniques involved offering bulk discounts to sell products in large quantities (Holt, 2013). For example, individuals who operated botnets would lease their infrastructure for DDoS attack services to knock websites and individual users offline. For instance, a DDoS service provider used the following language in one of their ads: "When ordering the DDoS service for 3–6 days, discount is 10%, with a DDoS service of more than 7 days, discount is 20%, and with a DDoS service for 3 sites, gives a free service for the 4th site." The pricing and discount structures suggest that the prices of goods and services are variable, but those making large purchases received the greatest overall value (Holt, 2013). In addition, price serves as an important first step in establishing a relationship between buyers and sellers.

The second and interrelated factor affecting market actors was customer service. Though competitive pricing may help to entice prospective customers, individuals also sought the most satisfactory experience possible. The outcome of a purchase was significantly influenced by the ways that sellers cater to their customers, particularly those individuals without substantive technological skills (Holt, 2013; Motoyama et al., 2011). Since the market allows less-proficient hackers to acquire goods and services that increases their overall attack efficacy, individual sellers took steps to ensure that all buyers would be satisfied with their products and services.

One of the most critical indicators of customer services lies in the speed with which sellers respond to requests from potential buyers. Sellers who were regularly online and could be easily contacted were more likely to generate positive reviews and feedback from customers (Holt, 2013). Those who did not quickly respond to messages from prospective buyers or were difficult to reach received negative comments from forum users.

The quality of the product or service a seller offered was also critical for their prospective buyers. This was exemplified in a post from the malware installer cryptor, who noted "our price may look to you not so adequate, but the quality will cancel this out, do not forget, that the cheap one pays twice." If a tool was ineffective or data was insufficient, a buyer may post bad reviews or not recommend that provider. The importance of quality was particularly evident in posts from DDoS vendors who regularly noted that they would give customers a free ten-minute test to measure the efficacy of their services against a particular target (Holt, 2013).

The final factor affecting participant relations in the market for malware was trust between participants. Buyers sought out commodities that they valued and were required to pay for goods without actually interacting with a seller in person (Holt, 2013; Motoyama et al., 2011). As a result, they may not receive the goods they paid for or may receive bogus products with no value. In addition, most data and services sold were either illegally acquired or a violation of law. Buyers therefore could not pursue civil or criminal claims against a less than reputable seller. As a result, three informal mechanisms emerged within the market to ensure a degree of trust between participants and reduce the likelihood of loss.

The first mechanism available to validate a seller's claims was the use of checks or tests by the forum administration as a means to validate the quality of a product sold in the forum. For instance, one forum described its checking process through this simple description: "[The] Administration [of the forum] has the right to ask any seller to present his/her product for check. You present the product in the form that it is being sold, so that it can be checked for a test. No videos, audio, screens." Going through a checking process demonstrates that a vendor is willing to demonstrate that his services are reliable and trustworthy. In turn, prospective clients can feel comfortable with an assessment of the individual's level of trust based on their product or services (Holt, 2013).

The second method employed in malware markets to build trust was the use of guarantor programs (Holt, 2013). Given that the majority of the products and services offered in these markets are illegal or can be used to break the law, participants have little legal recourse if they are slighted at some point in their exchange. Guarantors served as a specialized payment mechanism that can be used to deal with individuals who may or may not be trustworthy. The following quote is from a well-known market's description of their guarantor service process:

> The seller and the buyer get in touch with one of the representatives of the guarantor service by icq and they come to agreement on the **EXACT** terms of the transaction. When agreement has been reached, the buyer gives the guarantor the amount of the transaction (or as it was shown in the contract) … The Seller gives the goods to the buyer, after examining the quality of the goods, the buyer advises that the seller can give the money, and the guarantor gives the money. Commission is not charged by the guarantor.

This post demonstrates the value of guarantors to minimize the potential risk of loss that an individual may incur. The use of guarantors is not consistent across the various markets operating, but those who operate such a service may be better organized and more sophisticated than others (Holt, 2013).

The third way that individuals could gain or demonstrate trust within the forums was through customer feedback. Feedback was directly impacted by fair pricing and strong customer service (Holt, 2013). Individuals who purchased a product or service could provide detailed comments about their experience with a seller for other users so that they may understand how that person operates. Posts that gave favorable reviews or positive comments demonstrated that an individual is trustworthy. Such information helps to build a solid and trustworthy reputation for a seller and may potentially increase their market share and customer base over time (Holt, 2013). At the same time, individuals who provided bad services or were untrustworthy received negative feedback. As a whole, the market for malicious software and attack services provides unique insights into the process of acquiring the resources needed to engage in cybercrime.

Legal challenges in dealing with malware

Despite the substantial harm that malware can cause, many nations have not criminalized its creation. The process of creating malware is an exercise in creative thinking and innovation, which can be inherently valuable to the computer security community to better secure systems. Instead, most nations choose to prosecute malware use under existing statutes regarding computer hacking. The direct connection between malware use and hacking outcomes, such as data loss or manipulation, makes intuitive sense and creates a more streamlined criminal code without the addition of statutes that may not otherwise exist.

A few nations have, however, specifically defined malware in their criminal codes. The **US Computer Fraud and Abuse Act** includes malware-related offenses in addition to specific hacking-related offenses. The fifth statue of this act (18 USC § 1030(a)5) involves the use of malware, making it illegal to:

1) knowingly cause the transmission or a program, information, code, or command and thereby intentionally cause damage to a protected computer,
2) intentionally access a protected computer without authorization and thereby recklessly cause damage,
3) intentionally access a protected computer without authorization and thereby cause damage or loss.

The first portion of this statute recognizes the distribution of malware, though that term is not used in favor of the terms program, information, or code, as it provides greater latitude in the identification of viruses, worms, and forms of software. The remaining two items involve ways that malware can be used in the course of either reckless or intentional damage. If an individual is found guilty of violating this act, they may receive a fine and a prison sentence of two years to life depending on the severity of their actions (see also Chapter 2). For instance, if the use of malware leads to the death of another human being, they may be eligible for a life sentence. Though the likelihood of such an outcome is low, the recognition by legislators that malware may be used – intentionally or unintentionally – to cause harm in a real-world context is a clear step forward for federal prosecutors to fully pursue justice for the actions of cybercriminals.

Since malware may be used to acquire sensitive passwords and other data, the CFAA now includes language criminalizing the sale or exchange of user information. Specifically, 18 USC § 1030(a)6 makes it illegal to knowingly sell, buy, or trade passwords or other information used to access a computer with the intent to defraud the victims. For instance, if an individual used a keylogging trojan to gather passwords and then sold that information to others, he may be prosecuted under this statute. Importantly, the computers harmed must be either: (1) involved in interstate or foreign commerce, or (2) operated by or for the federal government. This language is quite broad and may be interpreted to include a wide range of computers connected to the Internet owned or operated by civilians (Brenner, 2011). Currently, any individual found guilty of this crime may be fined and imprisoned for one to five years depending on whether the offender gained commercial or financial gain for their actions or if the value of the data exceeds $5,000. If, however, the individual is found guilty on multiple counts, they are eligible for up to ten years in prison (Brenner, 2011).

In addition to these statutes at the federal level, there are currently 29 states in the United States that have outlawed the creation or distribution of malware. It is important to note that these statutes do not typically use the term virus or malware, but "**computer contaminants**" designed to damage, destroy, or transmit information within a system without the permission of the owner (Brenner, 2011). The use of malware may constitute either a misdemeanor or felony depending on the harm caused and the individual's access to sensitive data or information of a monetary value.

Many other nations share similar legal frameworks regarding malware in that existing statutes concerning hacking can also be used to pursue malicious software cases. Few nations specifically criminalize the use of malware but rather apply existing laws regarding hacking in these incidents. Canada and Australia are two examples of this strategy. In the UK, the **Computer Misuse Act 1990** has some utility to account for malware-related offenses as it criminalized unauthorized access to computer material and unauthorized modification of computer material (see Chapter 2). This is a direct outcome of the use of malware, though the law did not allow for direct cases against malware writers. As a result, the **Police and Justice Act 2006** extended and revised this section of law to account for malware distribution. The Act added three offenses related to "making, supplying, or obtaining articles for use in computer misuse offenses," including:

1) Making, adapting, supplying, or offering to supply any article intending it to be used to commit, or to assist in the commission of, an offence under the Computer Misuse Act.
2) Supplying or offering to supply any article believing that it is likely to be used in the commission of offenses under the Computer Misuse Act.
3) Obtaining any article with a view to its being supplied for use to commit or assist in the commission of offenses under the Computer Misuse Act.

These offenses carry a maximum sentence of two years and a fine, though it has drawn criticism for its potential use to prosecute professionals and legitimate security tool developers (Brenner, 2011).

malware and automated computer attacks

The Council of Europe's Convention on Cybercrime does not specifically include language on malware in order to avoid the use of terms that may become dated or irrelevant over time (Council of Europe, 2013). Instead, the existing articles of the convention can be applied in some way to malware used in the course of cybercrime. The most relevant language is currently included in Article 6 regarding misuse of devices. Specifically, this article makes it a violation of law to produce, sell, or otherwise make available a program or device designed to access computer systems, intercept or harm data, and interfere with computer systems generally (Council of Europe, 2013). This article is not designed for use in prosecuting cases where individuals have penetration-testing tools or codes designed to protect computer systems. Additionally, this article allows flexibility for each nation to decide whether they want to include this language in their own criminal codes (Council of Europe, 2013). However, the use of malware can be criminally prosecuted under laws designed to pursue illegal access of systems.

Coordination and management in addressing malware

Since malware is prosecuted using similar legislation to computer hacking, many of the same agencies are responsible for the investigation of these offenses (see Chapter 2). The Federal Bureau of Investigation in the US, Metropolitan Police Central e-crime Unit (PCeU) in the UK, and other agencies all investigate these crimes. There is, however, a much larger body of private agencies and commercial entities involved in the detection and mitigation of malicious software.

One of the most prominent resources available for industry and businesses to help mitigate the threat of malware and insulate them from future attack are computer emergency response teams (CERTs). As noted earlier, the first CERT was born out of the Morris Worm, which demonstrated the need to develop a coordinated response to cyberthreats. As malware became more prevalent and damaging to the rapidly expanding population of Internet users in the mid 1990s, the need for coordinated responses to threats increased substantially.

For more information on CERTs, go online to: www.cert.org

There are now 292 publicly identified response teams in 64 nations around the world (FIRST, 2014). They may go by different names depending on location. Some nations or locations may use the term CERTs while others use the name **Computer Security Incident Response Teams (CSIRT)**, but they serve generally similar purposes. There are 65 CERT or CSIRT groups in the US alone. Some of these are housed in financial institutions like Bank of America and Yahoo, while others are located in government agencies such as the National Aeronautics and Space Administration (NASA). The primary CERT within the US (US CERT-Coordination Center) is housed at Carnegie Mellon University. It provides reporting mechanisms for vulnerabilities and threats to systems, as well as security tools to help patch and protect systems from attack (US-CERT, 2013c). The CERT can also serve to analyze and track threats as they evolve for virtually any branch of government and civilian networks, including threats for both home users and businesses. They act as a focal point for the coordination of information concerning cyberattacks that threaten civilian infrastructure (US-CERT, 2013c).

At a global level, there are now CERTs or CSIRTs on every continent. The greatest representation of units are within industrialized nations. Given the wide distribution of teams and threats based on the resources within a given nation, there is a need for a unifying body to help connect all these groups together. The global **Forum for Incident Response and Security Teams (FIRST)** serves to coordinate information sharing and connections between all teams worldwide (FIRST, 2014). FIRST offers security courses, annual conferences for incident responses, best practice documents for all forms of incident response, and a full reference library of security research and materials from across the globe. The Forum also creates working groups based on common interests or specific needs, such as their **Special Interest Group for Vendors (SIG Vendors)** which links respondents with software, hardware, and security vendors in order to handle emergent threats and mitigation techniques. Similarly, there is a working group for **Law Enforcement and CSIRT Cooperation (LECC-BoF)** which is designed to provide a venue for police and response teams to work together in the event of a large-scale incident and create trusted relationships between these communities (FIRST, 2014). There is even an arm of FIRST that is connected to the International Standards Organization (ISO) in order to help inform policies and standards for cybersecurity incident management, evidence handling, and vulnerability disclosure in the field (FIRST, 2014).

Perhaps the most identifiable entities involved in the response to malware and hacking incidents are members of the antivirus and cybersecurity industry. There are dozens of companies offering security tools to protect desktop, laptop, tablet, and mobile computer systems either for a fee or at no cost to the user to secure various operating systems, whether Mac OS, Windows, Linux, or mobile OSs. You may know some of the more prominent companies in the field, and use some of their products, including BitDefender, Kaspersky, McAfee, Symantec, and Trend Micro. Most of these companies offer some type of antivirus software which protects the user by checking incoming files and data requests to protect against active infection attempts in real time and/or scanning existing files to detect and remove malware that may already be installed. Antivirus software works through the use of heuristics, or signature-based detection, where all system files on a computer are compared against known signatures or definitions of malware to determine whether an infection has taken place. Similarly, any attempted download is compared against known definitions of malware in order to eliminate the likelihood of being actively infected.

The benefit of antivirus software is that it can help to reduce the risk of malware being able to actively infect a protected system. The use of heuristic detection systems is, however, limited by their available knowledge. The definitions that the software has on file run the risk of being outdated every day, as new variants of malicious code are being produced all the time. Antivirus vendors have to create signatures for any new malware variant identified, thus they are constantly updating definitions. In addition, there is no necessary agreement between security companies as to the name or classification for a specific form of malware. Some vendors may tag something as a trojan, while another labels it a virus, making it difficult to standardize the identification of malware generally. If users do not have an up-to-date definitions file for their antivirus software before it starts to scan for infections, the risk of infection from new malware is increased (Symantec, 2013). If an individual never updates this information, then his or her antivirus software can do very little to protect the system from new threats. As a result, the value of protective software is severely limited by the knowledge and skills of both the end user operating the software and the continual advancements in malware in the wild.

For more information on antivirus vendors, go online to: 1) www. norton.com, **2)** www.sophos.com, **and 3)** www.avg.com

---

In light of the limitations of antivirus software and the challenges posed by malware generally, a non-profit organization called the **Anti-Malware Testing Standards Organization (AMTSO)** was formed in 2008 (AMTSO, 2014). The organization exists to provide a forum to improve the process of malware identification and product testing, the design of software and methodologies for analysis, and to identify standards and practices that can be implemented across the security industry. In fact, they have published a range of documents describing testing guidelines and standards for the analysis of malware and testing of security products. The AMTSO is comprised primarily of major security vendors, which is sensible given they have a vested interest in developing sound products. Some have questioned whether this is a good thing, as the vendors may have little interest in truly assessing the quality of their products or revealing the limits of what their tools can do (Townsend, 2010). Thus, the AMTSO is one of the few entities that attempts to police the antivirus industry, though there are limits to its capabilities.

Summary

The threat of malware is diverse and ever-changing, affecting virtually all forms of computer technology. Malicious software takes many forms, though the use of programs that blend various attack techniques into a single platform are increasingly common. The creation of malware is, however, a skill that only a few have and can implement in the wild. As a result, some have taken to selling their resources in open markets operating online, which increases the capability of less-skilled attackers while enriching talented programmers. The criminal laws available to prosecute malware users are substantive, though there are no necessary laws against actually writing malware. Thus, law enforcement agencies are not necessarily able to mitigate the threat of malware. Instead the computer security industry has become the pertinent resource to minimize the threat of malware for the general public, governments, and industry generally.

Key terms

Anti-Malware Testing Standards Organization (AMTSO)

Back Orifice 2000 (BO2K)

Blended threat

Boot sector

Boot sector virus

Botnet

Code Red worm

Computer contaminants

Computer Emergency Response Team (CERT)

Computer Misuse Act 1990

Computer Security Incident Response Teams (CSIRT)

Concept virus

Crimeware

Cryptolocker

Cult of the Dead Cow (cDc)

Distributed denial of service (DDoS) attack

Elk Cloner

Exploit

Exploit packs

Forum for Incident Response and Security Teams (FIRST)

Law Enforcement and CSIRT Cooperation (LECC-BoF)

Macro programming language

Macro virus

Melissa virus

Morris worm

MuTation Engine (MtE)

Operation: Bot Roast

Payload

Police and Justice Act 2006

Ransomware/scareware

Special Interest Group for Vendors (SIG Vendors)

Trojan

US Computer Fraud and Abuse Act

Worms

Virus

Vulnerability

Zeus trojan

Discussion questions

1) Since malware writers tend to target popular software and resources, what do you think will be the likely targets for infection over the next five years? Please explain why you think a certain target may be selected over another.

2) If malware markets are making it easy to obtain malware and engage in sophisticated attacks, what impact will this have on the hacker subculture over time? How can we protect networks in light of these changes?

3) Why do you think nations have not criminalized the creation of malicious software generally? Should the legal code be amended to reflect this activity? Why?

4) If the antivirus software industry has grown since the 1990s, but malware continues to evolve and expand, is it reasonable to say that they are effective in reducing infections? If vendors are not technically stopping infections, then how can we assess their real value?

References

AMTSO, (2014). *FAQs*. [Online] Available at: www.amtso.org/amtso---faqs.html

Bacher, P., Holz, T., Kotter, M., & Wicherski, G. (2005). *Tracking botnets: Using honeynets to learn more about bots.* The Honeynet Project and Research Alliance. Retrieved July 23, 2006 from www.honeynet.org/papers/bots/

Bissett, A., & Shipton, G. (2000). Some human dimensions of computer virus creation and infection. *International Journal of Human-Computer Studies, 52,* 899–913.

BitDefender. (2009). *Trojans continue to dominate BitDefender's top ten e-threats. BitDefender.* [Online] Available at: www.bitdefender.com/news/trojans-continue-to-dominate-bitdefender%E2%96%93s-top-ten-e-threats-for-october-1208.html

Brenner, S. W. (2011). Defining Cybercrime: A Review of Federal and State Law. In R. D. Clifford (ed.), *Cybercrime: The Investigation, Prosecution, and Defense of a Computer-Related Crime,* 3rd edition, (pp. 15–104). Raleigh, NC: Carolina Academic Press.

CAIDA. (2001). *CAIDA Analysis of Code-Red.* [Online] Available at: www.caida.org/research/security/code-red/

Chu, B., Holt, T. J., & Ahn, G. J. (2010). *Examining the Creation, Distribution, and Function of Malware On-Line.* Washington, DC, National Institute of Justice. [Online] Available at: www.ncjrs.gov/pdffiles1/nij/grants/230112.pdf

Consumer Reports. (2011, June). *Online exposure: Social networks, mobile phones, and scams can threaten your security.* [Online] Available at: www.consumerreports.org/cro/magazine-archive/2011/june/electronics-computers/state-of-the-net/online-exposure/index.htm

Council of Europe, (2013). *T-CY Guidance Note #7: New forms of Malware.* www.coe.int/t/dghl/cooperation/economiccrime/Source/Cybercrime/TCY/TCY%20 2013/T-CY%282013%2912rev_GN7_Malware_V4adopted.pdf

Dunham, K. (2008). *Mobile Malware Attacks and Defense.* Burlington, MA: Syngress.

Eisenberg, T., Gries, D., Hartmanis, J., Holcomb, D., Lynn, M. S., & Santoro, T. (1989). The Cornell Commission: On Morris and the Worm. *Communications of the ACM, 32,* 706–709.

Federal Bureau of Investigation. (2010). Cyber banking fraud: Global partnerships lead to major arrests. [Online] Available at: www.fbi.gov/news/stories/2010/october/cyber-banking-fraud

Ferguson, D. (2013). CryptoLocker attacks that hold your computer to ransom. *The Guardian,* October 18, 2013. [Online] Available at: www.theguardian.com/money/2013/oct/19/cryptolocker-attacks-computer-ransomeware

FIRST, (2014). *Global Initiatives.* [Online] Available at: www.first.org/global

F-Secure. (2013). *Mobile Threat Report, July–September 2013.* [Online] Available at: www.f-secure.com/documents/996508/1030743/ Mobile_Threat_Report_Q3_2013.pdf

F-Secure. (2014). *Virus: W32/Melissa.* [Online] Available at: www.f-secure.com/v-descs/melissa.shtml

Goodin, D. (2007). FBI logs its millionth zombie address. *The Register,* June 13, 2007. [Online] Available at: www.theregister.co.uk/2007/06/13/millionth_botnet_address/

Gordon, S. (2000). *Virus Writers: The End of the Innocence?* Accessed June 1, 2007, from http://vxheaven.org/lib/asg12.html

Hedquist, U. (2008). Akill pleads guilty to all charges. *Computer World, 31,* March, 2008. [Online] Available at: www.computerworld.co.nz/article/495751/akill_pleads_guilty_all_charges/

Holt, T. J. (2013). Examining the forces shaping cybercrime markets online. *Social Science Computer Review, 31,* 165–177.

Holt, T. J., & Kilger, M. (2012). Examining willingness to attack critical infrastructure on and off-line. *Crime and Delinquency*, 58(5), 798–822.

International Telecommunications Union. (2008). *ITU Study on the Financial Aspects of Network Security: Malware and Spam*. ICT Applications and Cybersecurity Division, Policies and Strategies Department, ITU Telecommunication Development Sector. [Online] Available at: www.itu.int/ITU-D/cyb/cybersecurity/docs/itu-study-financial-aspects-of-malware-and-spam.pdf

Kaspersky, E. V. (2003). The classification of computer viruses. Metropolitan Network BBS Inc., Bern, Switzerland. [Online] Available www.avp.ch/avpve/classes/classes.stm (last accessed June 3, 2004).

Leyden, J. (2012). Major £30m cyberheist pulled off using MOBILE malware. *The Register*, 7 December 2012. [Online] Available at: www.theregister.co.uk/2012/12/07/eurograbber_mobile_malware_scam/

Manjoo, F. (2007). The computer virus turns 25. *Salon*, July 21, 2007. [Online] Available at: www.salon.com/2007/07/12/virus_birthday/

Markoff, J. (1990). Computer intruder is put on probation and fined $10,000. *New York Times*, May 5, 1990. [Online] Available at: www.nytimes.com/1990/05/05/us/computer-intruder-is-put-on-probation-and-fined-10000.html

Messmer, E. (1999). Bad rap for Back Orifice 2000? *CNN.com*, July 21, 1999. [Online] Available at: www.cnn.com/TECH/computing/9907/21/badrap.idg/

Motoyama, M., McCoy, D., Levchenko, K., Savage, S., & Voelker, G. M. (2011). An analysis of underground forums. In Proceedings of the 2011 ACM SIGCOMM Internet Measurement Conference, 71–79.

Nazario, J. (2003). *Defense and Detection Strategies against Internet Worms*. Artech House.

Noyes, K. (2008). Logic bomb dud sends medco sysadmin to jail. *TechNewsWorld*, January 9, 2008. www.technewsworld.com/story/61126.html

Panda Security. (2010). *Annual Report PandaLabs 2010*. [Online] Available at: http://press.pandasecurity.com/wp-content/uploads/2010/05/PandaLabs-Annual-Report-2010.pdf

Panda Security. (2011). *Quarterly Report PandaLabs April–June 2011*. [Online] Available at: http://press.pandasecurity.com/wp-content/uploads/2011/07/PandaLabs-Report-Q2-2011.pdf

Panda Security. (2013). *Annual Report Pandalabs 2013 Summary*. [Online] Available at: http://press.pandasecurity.com/wp-content/uploads/2010/05/Annual-Report-PandaLabs-2013.pdf

Paquette, J. 2010. *A History of Viruses*. Symantec. [Online] Available at: www.symantec.com/connect/articles/history-viruses

Rantala, R. R. (2008). *Cybercrime against businesses, 2005* (NCJ 221943). Bureau of Justice Statistics. [Online] Available at: www.bjs.gov/content/pub/pdf/cb05.pdf

Ruggiero, P., & Foote, J. (2011). *Cyber Threats to Mobile Phones*. [Online] Available at: www.us-cert.gov/reading_room/cyber_threats_to_mobile_phones.pdf

Russinovich, M. (2013). Hunting down and killing ransomware (scareware). *Microsoft TechNet Blog*. [Online] Available at: http://blogs.technet.com/b/markrussinovich/archive/2013/01/07/3543763.aspx

Sourceforge. (1999). *Basic BO2K setup tutorial*. [Online] Available at: http://bo2k.sourceforge.net/docs/bo2k_1_1_5/BasicTutorial.html

Symantec. (2009). *Fragus Exploit Kit Changes the Business Model.* [Online] Available at: www.symantec.com/connect/blogs/fragus-exploit-kit-changes-business-model

Symantec. (2013). *Internet Security Threat Report. 2012 Trends, Vol. 18.* April 2013. [Online] Available at: www.symantec.com/content/en/us/enterprise/other_resources/b-istr_main_report_v18_2012_21291018.en-us.pdf

Symantec. (2014). *Trojan.Zbot.* [Online] Available at: www.symantec.com/security_response/writeup.jsp?docid=2010-011016-3514-99

Szor, P. (2005). *The Art of Computer Virus Research and Defense.* New York: Addison-Wesley.

Taylor, P. (1999). *Hackers: Crime in the Digital Sublime.* London: Routledge.

Townsend, K. (2010). *AMTSO: A serious attempt to clean up anti-malware testing or just a great big con?* [Online] Available at: http://kevtownsend.wordpress.com/2010/06/15/amtso-a-serious-attempt-to-clean-up-anti-malware-testing-or-just-a-great-big-con/

US-CERT. (2013a, March 10). *Cyber Bulletin SB14-077.* [Online] Available at: www.us-cert.gov/ncas/bulletins/SB14-077

US-CERT. (2013b, March 17). *Cyber Bulletin SB14-083.* [Online] Available at: www.us-cert.gov/ncas/bulletins/SB14-083

US-CERT. (2013c). *About Us.* [Online] Available at: https://www.us-cert.gov/about-us

chapter 4

Digital piracy and intellectual property theft

Chapter goals

- Understand what intellectual property is and how piracy affects property owners
- Identify the ways that piracy has changed over time
- Understand the ways that pirates justify their theft of intellectual property
- Know the legal protections afforded to intellectual property and the legislation designed to protect digital media
- Recognize the methods employed by property owners to deter or sanction pirates

Introduction

Over the last two decades, high-speed Internet connectivity and the World Wide Web have transformed the way in which individuals access music, movies, television, and other forms of entertainment content. The ability to stream traditional terrestrial radio stations online allows individuals to access content from anywhere around the world. At the same time, streaming-music services like Pandora and Spotify allow individuals to listen to only the content they most prefer and to share with friends. Netflix, Hulu, YouTube and other streaming-video services allow individuals to watch television, movies, and clips on demand. Even e-reader devices like the Kindle and Nook tablets provide wireless access to digital copies of books and magazines, allowing a virtual library to be transported and enjoyed anywhere. All of this content can even be enjoyed via smartphone applications, meaning you are no longer tethered to a television in order to view certain content.

The technologies that sustain the media-saturated environment we now live in provide unparalleled access to any and all forms of entertainment. At the same time, they can be readily subverted in order to acquire, copy, and unlawfully distribute media that was illegally obtained. These activities are commonly referred to as **digital piracy,** a form of cybercrime encompassing the illegal copying of digital media such as computer software, digital sound recordings, and digital video recordings without the explicit permission of the copyright holder. Digital piracy is a common form of cybercrime, so much so that between 10 and 40 percent of college students appear to have engaged in some form of piracy (Gunter, 2009; Higgins, 2006; Higgins, Wolfe, and Ricketts, 2009; Hinduja, 2003; Skinner and Fream, 1997). In fact, one of the most unusual examples of the prevalence of pirated materials occurred in 2009 with the release of the film *X-Men Origins: Wolverine* (see Text Box 4.1). This sci-fi action film was set to be released in the early summer in the hopes that it would be a blockbuster hit. One film critic, Roger Friedman, decided to publish a review of a pirated version of the film that was available online prior to its cinematic release. The version was incomplete, missing many computer-generated elements that had yet to be completed, though Friedman felt that he could gain advantage over his peers by publishing this early review. As a consequence, he was fired and roundly criticized by the press for his efforts.

Text Box 4.1: Friedman *Wolverine* review

Fox fired up over "Wolverine" review

> Friedman came under fire for posting a review of a pirated version of 20th Century Fox's "X-Men Origins: Wolverine." Friedman posted a review of the film Thursday, one day after an incomplete version of the tentpole was leaked on the Internet ...

This article provides an interesting discussion of the controversy surrounding a professional film critic's review of a pirated version of the film *X-Men Origins: Wolverine* prior to its actual box office release. This incident highlights the problem of digital piracy and the ethical dilemmas created by the availability of pirated material.
www.variety.com/article/VR1118002128

Though this is an odd occurrence, Friedman's behaviors conform to many of the arguments made by individuals who frequently pirate materials. Many suggest that downloading a movie, song, or piece of software does not cause any substantive harm because the economic loss should be relatively small by comparison to the millions or billions of dollars that are otherwise made. In fact, the superhero film *The Avengers* made over $600 million while in theaters, despite the fact that several high quality pirated versions of the film were available online within days of its theatrical release. Additionally, piracy is especially high in low income countries where the ability to acquire media is limited relative to its cost. For instance, evidence from the Business Software Alliance (BSA) suggests that piracy is highest and remains high in Central and Eastern Europe, Latin America, and Asia relative to Canada, Europe, and the United States.

> For more information on the rates of piracy, go online to: http://globalstudy.bsa.org/2011/

As such, some have begun to question the value of pursuing piracy as a criminal act. If copyright holders still profit from their efforts despite individuals being able to access ideas and media for free, can any harm truly result from piracy? In fact, would the ability to access any and all information improve the open nature of society and stimulate creativity as a whole? The recently formed political group Pirate Parties International believes that reforming copyright laws to favor more open distribution would be a boon to society and foster transparency in governments across the world. This group has found success throughout the Americas, Europe, and Asia, and may have far-reaching consequences for society over the next decade.

> For more information on Pirate Parties International, go online to: www.youtube.com/watch?v=QeJ_1kwrkTg

In order to understand the current climate toward piracy, it is important to identify the changes in technology, the law, and societal perceptions of media. This chapter will provide a focused discussion of intellectual property and the evolution of piracy techniques over the last 30 years. Additionally, the laws and tactics used to pursue pirates internationally will be explored so that readers understand the challenges posed by this offense in a globally connected world.

What is intellectual property?

Before discussing piracy, it is important to understand how ideas and intellectual works are legally protected. For instance, this book has value because it is useful to readers as an assembled document with information synthesized from works, ideas, and information that already exist. Similarly, music, movies, art, and creative endeavors all have value to their developer, as well as prospective economic value. When an original idea that involves some creative expression is put into a fixed medium, such as being written down on paper or drafted on canvas using paint, it can be defined as **intellectual property**. Ideas become "property" because they are physically tangible works that can be viewed by others. Thus, any work of art, novel, design, blueprint, invention, or song can be intellectual property.

To protect an idea or work from being stolen, and to ensure that an individual receives appropriate credit for a creation, many people try to **copyright, trademark**, or **patent** an idea. These are all forms of legal protection for intellectual property that provide exclusive use of an idea or design to a specific person or company, the right to control how it may be used, and legal entitlement to payment for its use for a limited period of time. For instance, the logos and branding for a product like Coca-Cola or Apple are important symbols that link a product to a company and have been trademarked to ensure that they are not misused by other companies or individuals for their own gain. Similarly, copyright protections are automatically granted to an individual who creates a literary, musical, or artistic work of some type from the moment it is created in a fixed format like a recording or a typed and printed medium (Yar, 2013).

It is important to note that while copyright protections are available in a cross-national context, there is a distinction with regard to US law. Individuals are given copyright protections from the time a work is created, though they must register their copyright with the government to ensure that they are given all necessary protection under the law. Specifically, an individual can only pursue criminal or civil actions through the state *if* the content creator has acquired a registered copyright or other legal protection. As a result, legal protection for intellectual property requires some forethought on the part of the creators to secure their ideas in the US.

For more information on copyright laws, go online to: 1) www. copyright.gov, 2) www.ipo.gov.uk/types/copy.htm

The ability to maintain and enforce copyrights and legal protections over intellectual property in the Digital Age is, however, extremely difficult due to the transitory nature of an idea and the ability to access information from anywhere at any given point in time. This is where the problem of intellectual property theft, or piracy, has emerged as a substantive economic threat to artists and copyright holders. Our ability to access any work, be it cinematic, musical, or literary, through the Web, television, or streaming media has made it much easier to reproduce works without notifying the original creator of our intentions. This means that copyright holders do not receive appropriate reimbursement and must find ways to ensure that their rights are upheld. As a result, **copyright laws** have evolved substantially in the last 30 years to ensure that individuals and corporations with legal rights to a piece of intellectual property are given their appropriate due. Additionally, those who wish to circumvent legal protections continuously change their behaviors in order to reduce the likelihood of detection and risk of arrest. The evolution of both piracy and legislation to protect intellectual property will be explored in detail to contextualize the current state of this problem.

The evolution of piracy over time

The theft of music and video recordings existed prior to the emergence of the Internet. The development of affordable audio and video recording equipment in the 1970s and 1980s enabled individuals to easily record music or videos during live concerts as well as radio and television broadcasts. For example, the audiotape allowed individuals to record songs and programming on the radio while it played live. This allowed individuals to create "mix tapes" with content that was aired for free. Similarly, the VHS tape and home video cassette recorder (VCR) allowed individuals to record content from their televisions and replay it at a time of their choosing. In turn, those with multiple VCRs could connect them together in order to create "bootleg" tapes by playing content on their television while recording it on another VCR at the same time. This method could be applied in order to obtain free copies of films which were still prohibitively expensive for purchase, but inexpensive to rent from various retail outlets.

Moving into the 1990s, the emergence of the compact disc (CD) helped usher in a change in the way in which media was recorded, formatted, and handled. Vinyl records and cassette tapes were the standard media format of choice for many; these were analog formats, meaning that the sound waves produced by musicians, while playing, are reproduced in an analogous electrical signal that is then reproduced into variations in the recording medium, such as the grooves on a record. The CD, however, was a digital medium, whereby sound waves were converted into a sequence of numbers that were then stored electronically. This format was thought to be of superior quality to traditional analog recordings and had the potential to be much less expensive than other formats to produce. As a result, media companies could obtain a higher rate of return on investments for their intellectual property.

In 1996, the Motion Picture Experts Group (MPEG) was actively working with the ISO to develop a mechanism to compress large audio and media files into a smaller size for distribution over the Internet. Since most users at this time used dial-up Internet connectivity, the connection speeds and volume of data that could be downloaded were relatively small. Thus, they developed the **MP3 format** in order to compress audio files, which became the industry standard for compression and media formatting.

For more information on the evolution of MP3, go online to: www.npr.org/blogs/therecord/2011/03/23/134622940/the-mp3-a-history-of-innovation-and-betrayal

The release of the MP3 format led to the creation of MP3 players, like Winamp, for desktop computers. These programs became extremely popular and the first portable MP3 player was produced and marketed just three years later, in 1999. In turn, individuals were able to use this compression standard to their advantage in order to pirate media and share it with others through various services. In fact, the production of desktop computers with CD drives that could both read and write onto CDs made it tremendously easy to duplicate and pirate materials with immediate gratification and minimal risk.

The same can be said for DVDs and BluRay media, which provide high quality image and sound in a format that can now be readily cracked and shared. There are now various "ripping" software programs that allow users to remove Digital Rights Management (DRM) protection from media in order to copy content to a storage device. In fact, the company 321 Studios in the US developed a software product called DVD X Copy that allowed users to copy any DVD movie to a blank DVD (Karagiannis et al., 2004). This program required no technical knowledge, rather the user simply installed the software and followed the prompts in order to copy the media. An injunction was brought against the company that forced them to shut the service down in 2004, but various programs are available that provide the same facilities. Thus, the evolution of media presentation and recording technology is innately tied to the problem of piracy.

The changing methods of pirates

The availability of pirated materials has been intimately tied to the evolution of technology and the role of computer hackers who develop tools to enable piracy. Media and software companies have always utilized tools to minimize the likelihood of their intellectual property being copied. In fact, hackers in the early 1980s began to subvert protections on software in order to share programs with others. The individuals who posted and shared programs were commonly referred to as **warez doodz,** which is a combination of the words "software" and "dudes." Their **warez,** or pirated files, were initially distributed through password-protected BBSs, and individuals could gain status by providing access to new or hard-to-find files. Thus, warez doodz were important players in the early days of the hacker scene.

For more information on the early days of piracy, go online to: http://arstechnica.com/gadgets/2014/01/modems-warez-and-ansi-art-remembering-bbs-life-at-2400bps/

As technology became more user friendly, and the cost of Internet connectivity decreased, warez creation and sharing became more prominent. The techniques to share files, however, began to change with innovations in the technology and creative computer engineering. For instance, the risk associated with sharing cracked or pirated files through single servers or web-based repositories increased because a law enforcement agency could take out that one server and eliminate all access to the files. Thus, the development of various **peer-to-peer (P2P) file-sharing protocols** in the late 1990s enabled **file sharing** directly between users, which dramatically reduced the likelihood of detection. For instance, the development of IRC channels in 1998 allowed users to connect and communicate with others in literally thousands of chat rooms established and run by various individuals. This was, and still is, a communications vehicle for technologically savvy users and was initially populated by those involved in the hacking and warez scenes.

The social nature of IRC coupled with its global reach led many to use it as a means to engage in direct file sharing, particularly for software and music (Cooper and Harrison, 2001). Typically, individuals would enter a chatroom and specify what they were looking for, and a user with those materials would negotiate with that person in order to get some files in return (Cooper and Harrison, 2001). The reciprocal relationships that developed in IRC fostered the formation of a piracy subculture where individuals were judged on their ability to find and access programs or files and share them with others (Cooper and Harrison, 2001).

While the technical nature of IRC limited its use as a file sharing service to more technically literate populations, the larger population of Internet users was able to engage in piracy through the development of the program **Napster** in 1999. This freely available specialized software was developed by Shawn Fanning and others in order to provide an easy-to-use program to share MP3-encoded music files between computer systems. Specifically, a user needed to download the Napster program, which would connect that computer to the larger network of user systems that also had the program installed. Users would then select a folder or folders that they wanted to share with others, which would then be indexed onto servers maintained by the Napster Corporation. This allowed users within the network to quickly identify media that they wanted and be directly connected to the appropriate computer to complete the download.

Napster became an extremely popular file-sharing service in a short amount of time. In fact, over 2.7 billion music files were traded between

Napster users in February 2001. The development and adoption of high speed Internet connectivity for home users also stimulated involvement in piracy. Individuals could download several complete songs in the time it took to obtain one file through traditional dial-up connectivity. Thus, Napster played a pivotal role in the growth of the piracy problem.

For more information on the government debates over Napster, go online to: www.c-span.org/video/?159534-1/records-v-napster

The popularity of Napster was, however, stymied by lawsuits brought against the corporation by the heavy metal band Metallica and A&M Records in 2001. These suits argued that the service was facilitating piracy and negatively impacting the financial well-being of artists and recording companies (McCourt and Burkart, 2003). These lawsuits forced Napster to become a paid service, which quickly declined in popularity. Several other P2P services quickly took its place, such as LimeWire and Kazaa, which utilized similar protocols in order to connect users and distribute media.

Shortly after the decline of Napster, a new file-sharing protocol called Bit Torrent emerged that became extremely popular. The use of **torrent** sharing software allows concurrent uploads and downloads of media through multiple sources. Specifically, users must download a torrent client, which connects them to the larger network of users. From there, a person can search for a piece of media he/she wants to download through various indexing services. Once they find that movie or music, they then begin to download the file by connecting to a series of user computers who have that file, referred to as "seeders." The torrent protocol links the downloader to an indexed list of all seeders and captures bits of the full file from multiple users at once. This process makes downloading much faster and decentralized in order to make it more difficult to disrupt the network of file sharing. As a result, the torrent protocol is a true P2P mechanism because of the ability to access the required file directly from dozens of users at once.

For more information on torrents, go online to: www.bittorrent.com/_

Torrent clients became extremely popular in the mid 2000s and were thought to have accounted for over half of all pirated materials online by 2004 (Pouwelse, Garbacki, Epema, and Sips, 2005). In fact, one of the most popular resources in the torrent community is **The Pirate Bay** (TPB), which maintains indexed torrent files for music, software, video games, and new-release movies. The group operates out of Sweden and has been in existence for years despite being raided by police and having three of its key operators convicted of copyright law violations requiring one year in jail and millions of dollars in fines (Nhan, 2013). As a result, torrents appear to be the latest file-sharing mechanism available to pirates (see Text Box 4.2 for details on the most common files shared), though this may change in the next few years with innovations in technology as a whole.

Text Box 4.2: Top ten most pirated movies of all time

http://torrentfreak.com/top-10-most-pirated-movies-of-all-time-111012/

> Netflix recently published a list of the ten most rented movies of all time. This got us thinking; what are the most downloaded movies on BitTorrent? Today we present the full chart of the top ten most pirated movies transferred via the now ubiquitous protocol, a list headed by Avatar ...

This article provides an overview of the most pirated movies on BitTorrent relative to their actual box office profits. The results are surprising as the evidence suggests these films made substantial profits despite their rate of piracy.

The subculture of piracy

Due to the global spread of the Internet and the diverse nature of digital media and formats, there are now multiple piracy subcultures that may be present, consisting of: (1) persistent downloaders who obtain large quantities of pirated materials, and (2) those who have the capacity to create, distribute, and share pirated materials. Research on persistent pirates suggests they place significant value on high speed Internet connectivity and the ability to host significant amounts of data (see Hinduja, 2001). This is due to the main goal of piracy – to rapidly disseminate electronic media in large quantities to people around the globe (Cooper and Harrison, 2001). At the same time, individuals who occasionally engage in piracy find it easier to access files when they can do so through high speed connections (Downing, 2011; Holt and Copes, 2010). Furthermore, persistent pirates appear to develop large collections of media or content in order to have complete discographies or works by an artist or television show (Cooper and Harrison, 2001; Downing, 2011). As a result, those pirates who can share unusual or exotic materials with others are able to generate status within the subculture. Their ability to distribute these materials allows them to develop a reputation for file sharing that leads to respect from both casual and persistent pirates (Cooper and Harrison, 2001; Downing, 2011). Thus, there are some commonalities between the beliefs of persistent and casual pirates.

Within the existing research on piracy, there are a few specific justifications that pirates use to support their behaviors, regardless of the materials they acquire. Specifically, the benefits of piracy are quite high as a person can obtain what they want with no cost and minimal risk of detection. The immediate material benefits also facilitate larger individual interests in certain artists, genres, or gaming systems. For instance, persistent media pirates reported that they might download a single episode of a television show or piece of music to determine if they might enjoy the product (Holt and Copes, 2010). If they find it entertaining, then they may actually buy the full season of that show or pay for other music by an artist so that they can enjoy the product in a better format. Similarly, individuals who pirate older video games indicate that their downloading helps to maintain their interest in older consoles and gaming systems (Downing, 2011). In fact, Downing (2011) argues that video game piracy may be a consequence of the general success and popularity of video games rather than a source of market failures.

At the same time, there are certain risks that arise as a consequence of engaging in piracy that cannot be ignored. There are clear legal risks that may come from violating copyright laws, such as fines or potential arrests depending on the depth of one's involvement in piracy. The decision-making processes of pirates do not, however, appear to be impacted by the deterrent influence of legal sanctions (Al-Rafee and Cronan, 2006; Gillespie, 2006; Holt and Copes, 2010). Similarly, a persistent pirate noted: "I think the govt/companies pick people to make an example out of them ... I think they take someone who they know cannot pay for it or is a regular person and try to make an example out of them to scare people" (Holt and Copes, 2010: 638). In fact, most individuals are able to justify their piracy based on the notion that they do not otherwise shoplift or steal CDs, software, and games from bricks-and-mortar stores. For instance, one individual involved in gaming piracy suggested, "Piracy is not Theft. It's piracy" (Downing, 2011: 765). Thus, the subculture of piracy appears to support and justify these behaviors in a variety of ways.

The evolution of legislation to deal with piracy

Though digital piracy is a recent phenomenon, the larger issue of protection for intellectual property is quite old. In fact, there have been laws pertaining to copyright in existence in England since the mid 1600s. These laws were primarily designed to restrict the ability to reproduce materials at a time when printed type and the ability to read were still highly restricted to the wealthy classes. As technologies related to printing, recording, and photography evolved, so too did laws pertaining to the ownership and management of intellectual property.

The recognition of a need for consistent international protections for intellectual property came to the fore in the late 1800s. At that time, copyright protections were only afforded in the nation where they were published. A book published in France could be copied and sold in other countries with no concern for the existing copyright or the author. Thus, nations became concerned about the ways that intellectual property would be handled and protected internationally. These concerns led to the formation of the United International Bureaux for the Protection of Intellectual Property in 1893 in Berne, Switzerland, to develop protections and frameworks for intellectual property. This became the **World Intellectual Property Organization (WIPO)** in 1967 and was integrated as an organization in the United Nations in 1975 (WIPO, 2012).

The most salient outcome of the WIPO is the development of the **Berne Convention for the Protection of Literary and Artistic Works**, created in 1986 to provide a common framework for intellectual property rights (WIPO, 2012). This convention was developed by the WIPO and signed by member nations, called members of the Berne Union. The purpose of this convention is to ensure that copyright laws of one nation are recognized and applied in other places (WIPO, 2012). The copyright is based on the country of origin of a work, determined by the publication of an idea or work in a given nation or by residents of that place; so long as either: (1) that country is a signatory nation, or has signed the convention and is a member of the Union; or (2) the author is a citizen of a signatory nation, then these protections apply (WIPO, 2012). As a result, individuals living in the European Union or the UK who obtain a copyright for a piece of music or other intellectual property in their nation consistently receive this protection everywhere, including the United States.

While this law is useful for the protection of copyrighted works internationally, the Convention clearly states the copyright laws of the country where it is claimed apply first. This is meant to ensure that a copyrighted work is not given a longer period of protection internationally and is referred to as "the rule of the shorter term" (WIPO, 2012). With that in mind, the copyright term afforded to most published works by the Berne Convention is for the lifetime of the author plus at least 50 years after their death, though this can be extended depending on the existing laws of a nation. The protections are different for photos, which is 25 years after the creation of the photo, and cinematic works, afforded a minimum of 50 years after the first showing or its creation (WIPO, 2012).

This legislation does not, however, consistently apply to US citizens based on standards within the US Copyright Office. Although the US is a member of the Union, citizens who create a work that they want to be protected in US courts have to obtain a copyright within the US to ensure they receive equal protection under the law. For instance, if a US citizen or organization develops intellectual property and feels that their idea has been infringed upon, they cannot legally file suit unless they have received a copyright there (Brenner, 2011). This is due to existing copyright laws in the US, which are harsher than other nations.

The United States has had criminal penalties for the infringement of protected intellectual property since 1909 (Copyright Act of 1909). Interestingly, the United States also removed the power to prosecute copyright infringement cases from state courts in 1976 with the introduction of the revised **Copyright Act of 1976**, which introduced new criminal sanctions under Titles 17 and 18 of the US Criminal Code (Brenner, 2011). Currently, the most stringent legal statutes in the US pertaining to copyright infringement are contained under Title 17 of the US Criminal Code (506), which make it a federal crime for someone to willfully infringe an existing copyright for either commercial advantage, private gain, or by reproducing or distributing one or more copies of a copyrighted work with a value of more than $1,000 in a 180-day period (Brenner, 2011). In fact, distributing or reproducing one or more copyrighted works with a value of at least $1,000 in a 180-day period can lead to misdemeanor charges. A felony charge requires that a person reproduce or distribute at least ten copies of one or more copyrighted works with a total value of more than $2,500 within 180 days (Brenner, 2011). As such, persistent pirates would be more likely prosecuted with felony charges, such as the members of The Pirate Bay.

This statute is commonly used to prosecute software piracy due to the high costs associated with certain forms of commercial software. For instance, a single copy of the popular media manipulation software Photoshop can cost $599 off the shelf. Thus, an individual who makes two copies of this program could easily be charged with a misdemeanor under this law. The low cost of music and movies makes it much more difficult to successfully prosecute an individual under these statutes due to the massive volume of materials they would have to reproduce.

Media conglomerates began to pressure the US Congress in the 1990s to change existing copyright laws and increase protections for intellectual property. Their efforts led to the creation of several laws including the **No Electronic Theft (NET) Act of 1997**, which increased the penalties for the duplication of copyrighted materials (Brenner, 2011). Specifically, this law revised the language of the copyright act to recognize infringement when an individual receives or expects to receive a copyrighted work, including through electronic means, regardless of whether they receive commercial or private financial gain. Until this point, criminal infringement had to involve some sort of economic advantage. Thus, the expected receipt of uploaded and/or downloaded copyrighted materials online was made illegal, making it possible to pursue individuals who acquired pirated materials through file sharing rather than paying for these items (Brenner, 2011). Additionally, these revisions introduced sanctions for the reproduction or distribution of one or more copies of "phonorecords," making it possible to legally pursue music piracy. Finally, the act increased the penalties for piracy to up to five years in prison and $250,000 in fines, and increased the statutory damages that copyright holders could receive.

Shortly after the adoption of the NET act, the US Congress also approved the **Digital Millennium Copyright Act (DMCA)** in 1998 (Brenner, 2011). This law was designed to directly affect media piracy online through further revisions to the Copyright Act. Specifically, this law extended protection to various music and performances that have been recorded in some fashion. The second section under this title added section 1201 to the Copyright Act, making it illegal to circumvent any protective technologies placed on copyrighted works, and section 1202 making it illegal to tamper with copyright management software or protections (Brenner, 2011). While this law was intended to apply to computer software, it can be extended to DVDs and music with protections on the disc that provide a modicum of protection from infringement or copy. Criminal sanctions for these behaviors were also added under section 1204 of the Copyright Act.

Title II of the DMCA is titled the *Online Copyright Infringement Liability Limitation Act*, which gives extended protections to ISPs against copyright infringement liability (Brenner, 2011). In order to qualify for these protections, ISPs must block access to infringing materials or remove them from their systems once a complaint is received from a copyright holder or their agent. This Title also enables copyright holders to subpoena ISPs for the IP addresses, names, and home addresses of customers who have engaged in the distribution of copyrighted materials (Brenner, 2011). These changes enabled copyright holders to pursue civil or criminal suits against those sharing pirated materials with others, rather than the services making it possible to engage in file sharing overall.

While US laws may seem particularly punitive, European legislation is equally punitive in some cases. For instance, the European Union also has a series of directives designed to protect intellectual property in various forms. **Directive 91/250/EEC/2009/24/EC** provides legal protection for computer programs and harmonized copyright protection across the EU. This Directive was first implemented in 1991 and afforded copyright protection to computer programs in the same way as literary works, like books or poems. The Directive also gives the copyright owner the right to temporary or permanent copying of the program, any translations of the program, or the right to distribute it by any means. The life of the copyright extends for the lifetime of the software creator plus 50 years, though it has been extended to 70 years through a subsequent directive in 2009. This Directive also provides the person purchasing software the right to back up the software for their personal use, though they must have a license for the program itself. Similar protections are also afforded to databases of distinct information under Directive 96/9/EC.

Additionally, **Directive 2001/29/EC**, or the Copyright Directive, establishes guidelines concerning the adequate legal protection of copyrighted materials through technological means. This Directive defines rights to copyright holders, including the right to reproduce their materials, and make them available to the public through publication and transmission of products over the Internet, including music, media, and software. This Directive also requires all Member States to provide legal protections against attempts to circumvent technologies that prevent copying of intellectual property and databases. Additionally, Member States must provide protection against products and services designed to circumvent protective measures on intellectual property for illegal purposes or limited commercial goals. As a result of this language, this Directive is more stringent than the US DMCA.

The law enforcement and industry response

Though there are myriad laws designed to protect intellectual property, there are relatively few law enforcement agencies that pursue cases against those who pirate materials. For instance, the US removed the power to prosecute copyright infringement cases from state courts in 1976 with the introduction of the revised **Copyright Act of 1976** (Brenner, 2011). As a result, the **Federal Bureau of Investigation (FBI)** tends to prosecute active investigations against piracy groups (Haberman, 2010). Additionally, the **Bureaus of Customs and Border Patrol (CBP)** and **Immigration and Customs Enforcement (ICE)** investigate and seize imported goods that infringe upon existing intellectual property rights. This includes digital transfers of pirated goods, as individuals who attempt to bring these materials from outside servers onto their home computer are technically importing pirated goods (Haberman, 2010). These three agencies have operated in concert to take down various groups and individuals involved in the distribution of pirated materials, for example in Operation Buccaneer in 2001. This investigation affected 62 people involved in software piracy in six countries as part of the piracy ring DrinkorDie (Nhan, 2013).

Similarly, the City of London Police has launched **Police Intellectual Property Crime Unit (PIPCU)** in order to investigate and handle various forms of piracy (City of London, 2013). This unit works as an independent group designed to handle serious forms of intellectual property crime including counterfeit products and pirated materials on and offline. Its goal is to integrate with various international enforcement and industry agencies and become a hub for investigations to disrupt organized piracy and fraud, as well as develop strategies to deter and reduce piracy generally (City of London, 2013).

One of the greatest challenges law enforcement agencies face in dealing with intellectual property laws is the fact that it is exceedingly difficult for intellectual property owners to identify when and how their materials are shared illegally. Copyright holders must scour sites across the globe in order to locate distribution networks and participants. As a consequence, industry groups play a more prominent role in the enforcement of intellectual property rights. They manage and promote the interests of major corporations and copyright holders within their country, and internationally as well. For instance, the **Recording Industry Association of America (RIAA)** is a trade organization that supports the recording industry and those businesses that create, manufacture, or distribute legally sold and recorded music within the US. The group was founded in 1952, helped define standards related to music production, and is a broker for the collective rights management of sound recordings. In fact, its stated goals are to: (1) protect intellectual property rights and the First Amendment rights of artists; (2) perform research about the music industry; and (3) monitor and review relevant laws, regulations, and policies. Currently the RIAA represents over 1,600 recording companies and other industries, such as Sony Music Entertainment and Warner Music Group (Brenner, 2011).

> For more information on the industry bodies protecting intellectual property, go online to: 1) www.riaa.com, 2) www.iprcenter.gov

There are many other groups, such as the **Motion Picture Association of America (MPAA)**, that operate to protect the intellectual property of their artists and creative producers. In the UK, the **Federation Against Copyright Theft (FACT)** is the primary trade organization dedicated to the protection and management of intellectual property, notably those of film and television producers. The group was established in 1983 and is actively engaged with law enforcement to combat piracy. For instance, FACT regularly works with the UK police to take down piracy websites and sue groups engaged in the distribution or facilitation of digital piracy (FACT, 2013). They also work in conjunction with the **Australian Federation Against Copyright Theft (AFACT)**, which targets pirates in the Australia and Oceania generally (AFACT, 2013).

All of these entities work in concert to pursue and protect their economic and intellectual interests. This is a substantive challenge in the current international landscape as the laws of one country governing intellectual property may be entirely different than those of another nation. Consider TPB, the aforementioned group central in the distribution of torrent files, which was founded in Sweden in 2003. Though the members assumed they would be safe from law enforcement efforts, several of their homes were raided and they were prosecuted by Swedish and US law enforcement for facilitating the distribution of pirated materials. In an attempt to avoid future incidents, the group attempted to purchase Sealand, a micro-island off the coast of England. The group raised $25,000 in donations to facilitate this endeavor, operating under the assumption that they could turn the island into a safe haven for pirated materials. This attempt was unsuccessful, as the government of Sealand felt that the group was only going to violate international laws. Their efforts, however, demonstrate the extent to which piracy groups are organizing and attempting to avoid legal efforts.

The recording industry also pursues civil suits against various individuals and businesses for their role in the facilitation of piracy. For instance, the music industry sued the file-sharing service Napster over their role in the distribution of pirated materials, which led to an out of court settlement and the shuttering of Napster as a free service. The recording industry also began to sue individual pirates for their downloading behaviors, which often involved hundreds of thousands of dollars in fines against the pirates. This tactic has, however, been largely abandoned in favor of tracking file-sharing programs to detect torrent seeders. In turn, they work with ISPs to send cease and desist letters in order to help slow down the volume of pirated materials traded online. In fact, the RIAA and FACT began to distribute letters to Internet users who were thought to have engaged in illegal file sharing to demand payment in settlement for their copyright violations (Nhan, 2013). This tactic was thought to be a way to directly reduce the legal costs these entities incurred as a result of pursuing settlements against file sharing.

Recently, the recording and media industries have begun to take unique extra-legal attempts to affect piracy networks. For instance, some private companies have been hired to disrupt file-sharing processes by "poisoning" torrent files to either corrupt content, identify the downloaders, or disrupt P2P networks generally (Kresten, 2012). Some of the more common methods involve attempting to share a corrupted version of a piece of music or media to deter users from downloading the file or making it more difficult to identify the actual content (Kresten, 2012). Alternatively, some companies such as MediaDefender will attempt to share a file that attempts to download content from non-existent peers or false sites in order to deter offenders (Kresten, 2012).

More extreme measures have been employed by the MPAA in order to disrupt P2P sharing groups. In 2010, the MPAA hired the company Aiplex Software to engage in DDoS attacks against websites like The Pirate Bay that would not respond to takedown notices to remove pirated materials (Whitney, 2010). These tactics were largely ineffectual at disrupting piracy networks and actually led to a backlash by members of both the piracy and hacker subculture (Whitney, 2010). Members of the group Anonymous engaged in a number of Denial of Service attacks against recording artists, companies, and the RIAA website in order to protest their efforts to stop piracy (Whitney, 2010). The attack, referred to as Operation Payback, effectively knocked critical websites offline and slowed email traffic, making it difficult for these groups to engage in regular commerce (Nhan, 2013). As a result, there has been a reduction in the use of these extra-legal methods by the recording industry to avoid further embarrassment.

Summary

Taken as a whole, the problem of piracy is extremely complicated. Individuals interested in obtaining copyright-protected materials without paying for them have had a variety of ways to acquire these goods, though it has become increasingly easy to acquire pirated materials over the last two decades. The emergence of the Internet and digital media have made it easy for individuals to share media, though pirates have subverted these technologies to share copyrighted files. As a consequence, it is extremely challenging to affect the rates of piracy through traditional measures such as lawsuits or arrests. In fact, as copyright holders continuously adapt legal strategies to deter pirates, the piracy subculture is increasingly vocal about their right to have access to digital media of all sorts. This tension cannot be easily solved, especially as technologies that increasingly provide access to digital materials, such as the Kindle, rise in popularity. Therefore, the criminal justice response to piracy will continue to evolve over the next decade.

Key terms

Australian Federation Against Copyright Theft (AFACT)
Berne Convention for the Protection of Literary and Artistic Works
Bureau of Customs and Border Patrol (CBP)
Copyright
Copyright Act of 1976
Copyright laws
Digital Millennium Copyright Act (DMCA)
Digital piracy
European Union Directive 91/250/EEC/2009/24/EC
European Union Directive 2001/29/EC
Federation Against Copyright Theft (FACT)
Federal Bureau of Investigation (FBI)
File sharing
Immigration and Customs Enforcement (ICE)
Intellectual property
Motion Picture Association of America (MPAA)
MP3 format
Napster
No Electronic Theft (NET) Act of 1997
Patent
Peer-to-peer (P2P) file-sharing protocols
The Pirate Bay
Police Intellectual Property Crime Unit (PIPCU)
Recording Industry Association of America (RIAA)

Torrent

Trademark

Warez

Warez doodz

World Intellectual Property Organization (WIPO)

Discussion questions

1) What are your thoughts on digital piracy? Do you think there is a victim involved in intellectual property theft?

2) Consider how the evolution in technology has influenced how you watch movies and listen to music. Think about how it must have been to listen to music on vinyl records or watch movies on tapes. Would holding a physical object, such as a record or cassette tape, affect your views on digital piracy?

3) How different is digital piracy from traditional theft?

4) Considering that digital pirates are always one step ahead of the movie and music industries, how should private companies attempt to protect their intellectual property?

References

Al-Rafee, S. & Cronan, T. P. (2006). Digital piracy: Factors that influence attitude toward behavior. *Journal of Business Ethics, 63*, 237–259.

Australian Federation Against Copyright Theft. (2013). *Resources.* www.screenassociation.com.au/resources.php

Brenner, S. W. (2011). Defining Cybercrime: A Review of Federal and State Law. In R. D. Clifford (ed.), *Cybercrime: The Investigation, Prosecution, and Defense of a Computer-Related Crime*, 3rd edition (pp. 15–104). Raleigh, NC: Carolina Academic Press.

City of London. (2013). *Police Intellectual Property Crime Unit (PIPCU).* www.cityoflondon.police.uk/advice-and-support/fraud-and-economic-crime/pipcu/Pages/default.aspx

Cooper, J., & Harrison, D. M. (2001). The social organization of audio piracy on the Internet. *Media, Culture, and Society, 23*, 71–89.

Downing, S. (2011). Retro gaming subculture and the social construction of a piracy ethic. *International Journal of Cyber Criminology, 5*(1), 749–771.

Federation Against Copyright Theft. (2013). *About FACT.* www.fact-uk.org.uk/about/

Gillespie, T. (2006). Designed to "effectively frustrate": Copyright, technology, and the agency of users. *New Media and Society, 8*(4), 651–669.

Gunter, W. D. (2009). Internet scallywags: A comparative analysis of multiple forms and measurements of digital piracy. *Western Criminology Review*, 10(1), 15–28.

Haberman, A. (2010). Policing the information super highway: Custom's Role in Digital Piracy. *American University Intellectual Property Brief*, Summer 2010, 17–25.

Higgins, G. E. (2006). Gender differences in software piracy: The mediating roles of self-control theory and social learning theory. *Journal of Economic Crime Management*, 4, 1–30.

Higgins, G. E., Wolfe, S. E., & Ricketts, M. L. (2009). Digital piracy: A latent class analysis. *Social Science Computer Review*, 27, 24–40.

Hinduja, S. (2001). Correlates of Internet software piracy. *Journal of Contemporary Criminal Justice*, 17, 369–382.

Hinduja, S. (2003). Trends and patterns among online software pirates. *Ethics and Information Technology*, 5, 49–61

Holt, T. J., & Copes, H. (2010). Transferring subcultural knowledge online: Practices and beliefs of persistent digital pirates. *Deviant Behavior*, 31, 625–654.

Karagiannis, T., Briodo, A., Brownlee, N., Broido, A., Claffy, K. C., & Faloutsos, M. (2004). Is P2P dying or just hiding? *IEEE Globecom Global Internet and Next Generation Networks*. Retrieved from http://alumni.cs.ucr.edu/~tkarag/papers/gi04.pdf

Kresten, P. V. (2012). *Torrent Poisoning*. New York: VolutPress.

McCourt, T., & Burkart, P. (2003). When creators, corporations and consumers collide: Napster and the development of on-line music distribution. *Media, Culture & Society*, 25, 333–350.

Nhan, J. (2013). The Evolution of Online Piracy: Challenge and Response. In Holt, T. J. (ed.). *Crime On-line: Causes, Correlates, and Context*, pp. 61–80. Raleigh, NC: Carolina Academic Press.

Pouwelse, J., Garbacki, P., Epema, D., & Sips, H. (2005, February). *The bit torrent P2P file-sharing system: Measurements and analysis*. 4th International Workshop on Peer-to-Peer Systems (IPTPS'05). Available at: http://iptps05.cs.cornell.edu/PDFs/CameraReady_202.pdf

Skinner, W. F., & Fream, A. M. (1997). A social learning theory analysis of computer crime among college students. *Journal of Research in Crime and Delinquency*, 34, 495–518.

Whitney, L. (2010, September 20). 4chan takes down RIAA, MPAA sites. *CNET*. Retrieved from www.cnet.com/news/4chan-takes-down-riaa-mpaa-sites/

World Intellectual Property Organization. (2012). *Berne Convention for the Protection of Literary and Artistic Works*. Available at: www.wipo.int

Yar, M. (2013). *Cybercrime and Society*, 2nd edition. London, Sage Publications.

Economic crimes and online fraud

Introduction

When many people discuss the benefits of computer technology and the Internet, they may identify the ease with which these resources allow us to shop and manage our personal finances. Consumers can now acquire virtually any item from anywhere in the world through major online retailers, like Amazon, or directly from other consumers via eBay and craigslist. In fact, 60 percent of US consumers purchase goods online at least once per fiscal quarter (Anderson, 2010). This figure skyrockets during the holiday season: US consumers spent approximately $46.5 billion online between November 1 and December 31, 2013 (comScore, 2014). Similarly, it was estimated that consumers in the UK would spend £40.3 billion during this period (Maidment, 2013). Much of this expansion stems from the belief that consumers can save money and actively research products and price points by purchasing goods through online retailers (Wilson, 2011). Thus, there has been a significant increase in the use of websites and online auction houses to identify goods and services at lower price points than are otherwise available in bricks-and-mortar stores.

> **For more information on consumer shopping trends, go online to:** www. internetretailer.com/trends/consumers/

Consumers also feel a great deal of trust in the safety and security of online retailers to manage their financial data. Services like Amazon and iTunes store credit or debit card information on file so that customers can pay for an item through a single click in order to minimize the processing time required to pay for a product. Others use third-party payment systems like PayPal to send and receive payments for services rendered. As a result, web-based financial transactions have become commonplace in the modern world.

The ability to access and buy goods anywhere at any time represents a revolution in commerce. The benefits of these technological achievements, however, are balanced by the increasing ease with which our personal information can be compromised. The paperless nature of many transactions means that we must now put our trust in companies to maintain the confidential nature of our financial data from hackers and data thieves. At the same time, consumers have to be vigilant against deceptive advertisements for products that are either too inexpensive or lucrative to miss.

In fact, one of the most commonly reported forms of cybercrime are forms of cyber-deception and theft, otherwise known as **fraud**. Though there are many definitions for fraud, one of the most commonly accepted involves the criminal acquisition of money or property from victims through the use of deception or cheating (e.g. Baker and Faulkner, 2003). Various forms of fraud existed prior to the Internet and required some interaction between the victim and the offender, either through face-to-face meetings (Kitchens, 1993; Knutson, 1996) or telephone-based exchanges (Stevenson, 1998). As technology, such as email and web pages, became more popular, fraudsters began to adapt their schemes to suit online environments where less direct interaction with victims was necessary to draw in prospective targets. In fact, some forms of fraud require virtually no interaction with a victim, as criminals can now compromise databases of sensitive information in order to steal identities and transfer funds.

The near ubiquity of technology has now afforded fraudsters multiple opportunities to obtain money or information from victims for various purposes. Fraudsters can utilize email, texts, instant messaging systems, Facebook, Twitter, and online retailing sites to capitalize on unsuspecting victims. Some offenders have even begun to track the behavior of naïve individuals to obtain sensitive information. For instance, teens and young adults have begun a dangerous habit of posting pictures of new drivers' licenses, passports, and credit/debit cards online to brag to friends (see Text Box 5.1 for details). In this case, the victims are providing their personally identifiable information to others freely, which can be used to engage in identity crimes with some ease. As a result, this presents an immediate and simple resource for fraud based solely on the poor personal security habits of users.

Text Box 5.1: Follow Friday: Where debit card numbers get stolen

Who tweets their debit card number?
www.slate.com/blogs/browbeat/2012/07/06/debit_card_pictures_on_twitter_the_hilarious_new_twitter_account_that_shames_people_for_posting_their_debit_cards_.html

> Enter @NeedADebitCard, a new Twitter account that's either a service for sense-deprived people, a boon for identity thieves, or sadistic public shaming, depending on your point of view. "Please quit posting pictures of your debit cards, people," its bio implores …

This article summarizes a unique and unusual phenomenon: individuals posting their personal details for others to see via social media. The cultural imperative to post information and the potential harm that may result are discussed.

This chapter will provide an overview of the most common forms of fraud employed online, most notably those sent via email to wide audiences. The utility of e-commerce sites for the sale of counterfeit goods and the theft of sensitive personal information for identity crimes will also be considered in detail. We will also consider the difficulty law enforcement agencies face in attempting to combat these crimes, due in part to their international scope.

Fraud and computer-mediated communications

When discussing online fraud, it is important to note that email is a critical resource for fraudsters. Prior to the World Wide Web and CMCs, scammers had to depend on their ability to craft convincing stories, whether in person or through either phone-based or print scams in magazines and newspapers. These efforts required some degree of investment on the part of the scammer, as they had to develop and pay for an ad to be created or pay for bulk mail. In fact, some of the most well-known email scams today were previously run through handwritten letters in postal mail or faxes in the 1980s (United States Department of State, 1997).

The creation and proliferation of email was a boon to scammers, as they could use this medium in order to access millions of prospective victims simultaneously for virtually no cost (Wall, 2004). The use of email is ubiquitous; many people have multiple accounts at their disposal for different purposes. Email is extremely simple to use, requires virtually no cost for users or senders, and allows the distribution of images, text, web links, and attachments. This enables a scammer to create convincing messages using branded, well-known images that can fool even the most careful of users. For instance, if individuals wanted to create an email that appeared to come from a bank, they could visit that institution's website to download the official logos and language posted in order to craft a more realistic message. They can also utilize HTML redirects that would not otherwise be noticed by a casual web user in order to make a more believable message.

In much the same way, fraudsters have begun to sell counterfeit clothing or pharmaceuticals to unsuspecting victims via spam email (Holt and Graves, 2007; King and Thomas, 2009; Taylor, Fritsch, Liederbach, and Holt, 2010; Wall, 2004; Wood, 2004). Spammers can create ads for online retail spaces or post ads on craigslist and eBay selling high-value consumer items, such as Coach® purses, Cartier® watches, and prescription pharmaceutical drugs like Viagra, at a dramatically reduced price (Balsmeier, Bergiel, and Viosca Jr., 2004). Victims of these spam emails are sent what looks like a legitimate advertisement for the desired product, including legitimate branding logos and images. The virtual nature of online retail makes it nearly impossible for the consumer to determine the validity of a claim because they cannot see the packaging or inspect the quality of an item in person. Consumers who purchase items may receive a fraudulent product, as with purses or jewelry, or adulterated products in the case of pharmaceuticals which may contain few, if any, active ingredients (Balsmeier *et al.*, 2004; Wall and Large, 2010). In fact, the Organisation for Economic Co-operation and Development (OECD) reported that an estimated $200 billion was produced from the sale and distribution of counterfeit products in 2005, with additional billions when including Internet retailers (OECD, 2008).

For more information on fraud statistics, go online to: www. telegraph.co.uk/motoring/news/10869408/Online-fraud-costs-car-buyers-17.8million-a-year.html

Identity theft

In addition to economic losses stemming from fraud, there is a tremendous threat posed by the loss of sensitive, **personally identifiable information (PII)**, or the unique identifiers individuals use in their daily lives (Krebs,

2011). A range of personal details are considered PII, including names and birthdates, as well as government identification numbers assigned to you, like social security numbers, passport numbers, and drivers' license numbers. This information is inherently valuable since it serves as the basis for obtaining credit cards, mortgages, loans, and government assistance (Federal Trade Commission, 2013). Criminals who obtain this information can use it to fraudulently apply for such services. Additionally, they may use this information to create fraudulent identification in order to conceal their identities or evade law enforcement.

For more information on the value of your PII, go online to: www.ft.com/cms/s/2/927ca86e-d29b-11e2-88ed-00144feab7de. html#axzz33UytNvd7

The use of PII to engage in fraud or impersonation has led to a unique set of terms in the legal and academic fields: identity theft and fraud. These terms are often used interchangeably, though their use varies by place. In addition, there is no single definition for either term (Copes and Vieraitis, 2009). There are, however, some consistencies in their meaning. One of the most widely recognized and accepted definitions of **identity theft** in the US involves the unlawful use or possession of a means of identification of another person with the intent to commit, aid, or abet illegal activity (Allison, Schuck, and Learsch, 2005; Copes and Vieraitis, 2009). In the UK and Australia, the term **identity fraud** is more commonly used to reference when someone else's personal information is used by another individual in order to obtain money, credit, goods, or services, and can be used to enable other forms of fraud, such as mortgage fraud (National Fraud Authority, 2013). In fact, this creates an interesting dichotomy: possession of PII without authorization from those persons is not illegal in the UK, though it is in the US.

Over the last decade, evidence suggests identity crimes are increasing exponentially and cause substantive economic harm. In fact, the most recent evidence from the United States suggests there were 369,132 reported complaints of identity theft in 2012 alone (Federal Trade Commission, 2013). The majority of these complaints involved misuse of government documents or attempts to obtain government benefits, as well as individuals attempting to create new bank accounts (Federal Trade Commission, 2013). In addition, the costs of identity theft to victims, industry, and the government in the US totaled $24.7 billion in 2012 (Harrell and Langton, 2013). Similarly, estimates from the UK suggest that 8.8 percent of a nationally representative sample of citizens had been a victim of identity fraud in 2012. They lost an average of £1,203 each, which is the equivalent of £3.3 billion at the national level (National Fraud Authority, 2013).

Given the scope of identity theft and fraud, it is important to note that criminals can obtain PII in two ways: *low-tech* and *high-tech* methods. Low-tech identity theft can involve simple techniques such as taking personal information out of mailboxes and trash cans or during the commission of a robbery or burglary (Allison *et al.*, 2005; Copes and Vieraitis, 2009). Offenders may also use high-tech methods via computers and/or the Internet to obtain personal information that is seemingly unprotected by the victim (Chu, Holt, and Ahn, 2010; Holt and Lampke, 2010; Newman and Clarke, 2003; Wall, 2007).

It is not clear how many identity crimes stem from low- or high-tech means due to the fact that victims may not be able to identify when or how their identity was stolen. Also, law enforcement and trade agencies are only beginning to measure the scope of identity crimes and capture this information effectively (Federal Trade Commission, 2013; Harrell and Langton, 2013; National Fraud Authority, 2013). It is possible that there may be an increase in the number of identity theft and fraud incidents stemming from high-tech means due to the ease with which individual offenders can compromise the PII of thousands of victims at once. For instance, businesses and financial institutions store sensitive customer information in massive electronic databases that can be accessed and compromised by hackers (Chu *et al.*, 2010; Holt and Lampke, 2010; Newman and Clarke, 2003; Wall, 2007).

The extent of hacks affecting consumer PII was demonstrated when the US company Heartland Payment Systems announced that their system security had been compromised during 2008 by a small group of hackers. The company processes over 11 million credit and debit card transactions for over 250,000 businesses across the US on a daily basis (Verini, 2010). Thus, hackers targeted their systems and were able to infiltrate and install malware that would capture sensitive data in transit without triggering system security (Krebs, 2011). In turn, they were able to acquire information from 130 million credit and debit cards processed by 100,000 businesses (Verini, 2010). These sorts of mass breaches are increasingly common, as evidenced by the compromise of the US retail giants Target and Neiman Marcus in late 2013. More than 40 million credit and debit card accounts were thought to have been lost through these two institutions, with prospective losses for consumers estimated to be in the millions (Higgins, 2014).

While financial data is a tremendously attractive target for thieves and fraudsters, there is also evidence that health-care data breaches are increasing. The amount of sensitive PII that could be acquired through an error or weakness in health-care data storage is tremendous (Carr, 2013). The information stored by health-care providers in the US frequently includes social security information and other bits of identifying information that can be used for traditional identity fraud, but could also provide information to assist in medical and insurance fraud in the US. In fact, the company Experian in the US reported working on remediating damages and repairing systems involved in over 2,200 health-care breaches in 2013 alone (Carr, 2013). The sheer number of accounts cannot be matched through low-tech means. We will explore the impact of such incidents later in this chapter.

Email-based scams

In the context of online fraud, some of the most common schemes are perpetrated based on initial contact via email. The interactive nature of email content coupled with the ability to access hundreds of thousands, if not millions, of users makes this an ideal medium for fraudsters. There are several fraud schemes that are sent to prospective victims every day. In the following sections, we discuss some of the most prevalent forms. This is not meant to be an exhaustive list. Instead, our purpose is to expose you to the most common types of schemes you may encounter on a consistent basis.

Nigerian email schemes

In the realm of online fraud schemes, one of the most common and costly types is the **advance fee email scheme**. These are so named because the sender requests a small amount of money up front from the recipient in order to share a larger sum of money later (see Text Box 5.2 for an example). These messages are more commonly referred to as "Nigerian" scams because the emails often come from individuals who claim to reside in a foreign country, particularly Nigeria or other African nations (see Smith, Holmes, and Kaufmann, 1999). Some also call them **419 scams** as a reference to the Nigerian legal statutes that are used to prosecute fraud (Edelson, 2003; Holt and Graves, 2007).

Text Box 5.2: Nigerian email text (personal correspondence)

Re:Re:Transfer of: $USD4,500,000 to you Ref No:KCB/00Y/2014

Beneficiary of email id.

I wish to notify to you through this medium that your outstanding transaction has been perfected and the fund release application as earlier made in your favor has been approved. The approval was granted this morning by the appropriate department.

Meanwhile, due to the bureaucratic bottleneck that has militated against the completion of the direct transfer of this fund to your account in past, an arrangement has this morning been concluded with our affiliate bank in Kenya to carry out the transfer.

---

economic crimes and online fraud

We resorted to this arrangement in order to avoid some bureau-cratic challenges which emanates when an international transfer has been unnecessarily delayed.

In a nutshell.

your detail information has been forwarded to the bank, and you shall be contacted in due course for further directive on how you should receive the fund. However, you should remain advised to cooperate with them as to facilitate swift transfer of this fund.

Finally, to hasten up the transaction, state below is the detail information of the affiliate bank for you to contact the bank and then remind them of your fund with them.

KENYA COMMERCIAL BANK LTD

Address:P. O. Box 48400–00100, Nairobi Kenya Tele:: +254-707-032-620, Fax: +254-20-22164055 Payment director::Mr. Daniel Alex info@kenya.ncommercialbnk.com

Kindly furnish your details as stated below.

Full name:::

Home address::

Phone numbers::

Country/City::

Occupation::

Bank credential::

Once more I wish to commend your mutual cooperation on this transaction and do be in touch with me as you deal with the Kenya Commercial bank.

Regards

Jose Anita

There are several variations of this scam used on a regular basis to defraud individuals. One of the most common messages involves the sender making a claim that they are a wealthy heir to a deceased person who needs help moving inherited funds out of the country. In turn, they will give the recipient a portion of the sum in exchange for financial and legal assistance (Edelson, 2003; Holt and Graves, 2007). Another popular variation of the message involves the sender posing as a public official who has been able to skim funds from a business or government contract (Edelson, 2003). They are seeking a contact to help get the money they illegally obtained out of the account. A similar scheme takes the form of a banker or attorney trying to close a dead customer's account using the potential victim as the deceased's next of kin (Edelson, 2003). Other adaptations have been identified, includ-ing the sender being in legal trouble or involved in some form of illegal behavior. Thus, the sender attempts to ensnare the recipient in an illicit, yet ultimately false, transaction.

Potential victims who receive and respond to one of these messages are defrauded through the use of two techniques. First, and most often, the respondent will contact the sender, and the sender will then ask for a small donation to get an account or fund out of a holding process. The sender will then continue to receive small payments from the victim because of complications in obtaining their account or additional legal fees that are needed to move the account (Smith *et al.*, 1999). The process continues until the victim is no longer willing or is too embarrassed to pay additional money, which can cause a significant dollar loss for the victim.

An additional proportion of scammers will avoid the long-term process in favor of more immediate fraud. They achieve this by requesting the recipient provide personal information, such as their name, address, employer, and bank account information. The sender may make this request under the guise of ensuring that the recipient is a sound and trustworthy associate (Edelson, 2003; King and Thomas, 2009). The information is, however, surreptitiously used to engage in identity theft and drain the victim's accounts.

Due to the millions of spam messages that are sent every day, it is unknown how many respondents are victimized each year. Some may not report their experience to law enforcement agencies out of fear they will be prosecuted for their involvement in the potentially illegal fund transfers described in the initial message they received (Buchanan and Grant, 2001). They may also feel too embarrassed that they lost substantial money because they responded to an email or were swindled by an otherwise implausible scam (Buchanan and Grant, 2001).

As a result, advance fee fraud victims constitute a substantial dark figure of cybercrime. It is clear, however, that victims of advanced fee fraud email scams lose massive amounts of money each year. For instance, the average victim lost $1,500 due to these scams in 2009 alone according to the Internet Crime Complaint Center (2009). While this may seem small, if an individual is able to victimize several recipients over the course of a few weeks, the scammer can accumulate a substantial amount of money. Thus, it is to a scammer's advantage to send out as many messages as possible in order to increase the likelihood of a response.

For more information on advance fee frauds, go online to: https://www. onlinebanktours.com/banks/moneyBasics/preview.php?id=83

Phishing emails

The use of **phishing** messages is another insidious form of fraud perpetrated in part by email in which individuals attempt to obtain sensitive financial information from victims to engage in identity theft and fraud (James, 2005; Wall, 2007). These messages often mimic legitimate communications from financial institutions and service providers, such as PayPal or eBay. The message usually contains some of the branding and language commonly used by that institution in an attempt to convince the recipient that the message is legitimate (see Text Box 5.3 for an example). The message usually suggests that a person's account has been compromised, needs to be updated, or has some problem that must be corrected as soon as possible. The time-sensitive nature of the problem is commonly stressed to confuse or worry the prospective victim in order to ensure a rapid response.

Text Box 5.3: Phishing example (personal correspondence)

From: service@amazon.com
Subject: Update your Amazon.com account information
Dear Customer,

You have received this email because we have strong reason to believe that your Amazon account had been recently compromised. In order to prevent any fraudulent activity from occurring we are required to open an investigation into this matter.

Your account is not suspended, but if in 36 hours after you receive this message your account is not confirmed we reserve the right to terminate your Amazon subscription.

If you received this notice and you are not an authorized Amazon account holder, please be aware that it is in violation of Amazon policy to represent oneself as an Amazon user. Such action may also be in violation of local, national, and/or international law.

Amazon is committed to assist law enforcement with any inquires related to attempts to misappropriate personal information with the intent to commit fraud or theft.

Information will be provided at the request of law enforcement agencies to ensure that perpetrators are prosecuted to the full extent of the law.

To confirm your identity with us click the link bellow:
http://www.amazon.com/exec/obidos/sign-in.html
[this link actually leads to http://ysgrous.com/www.amazon.com/]

We apologize in advance for any inconvenience this may cause you and we would like to thank you for your cooperation as we review this matter.

The email will also include web links that appear to connect to the appropriate website so that the victim can immediately enter their login information for the affected account. Generally, however, the link redirects the user to a different site controlled by the scammer that utilizes collection tools to capture user data. Better fraudulent sites will also feature branding or logos from the institution to help further promote the legitimacy of the phishing email. Upon arriving at the site, individuals are prompted to enter sensitive information, such as their bank account number, username, password, or even in some cases **Personal Identification Numbers** (PINs) to validate their account. Upon entering the data, it is captured by the scammer for later use and may either redirect the victim back to the original website for the company or provide a page thanking them for their information.

This type of fraud is actually quite old, dating back to the 1990s when ISPs billed users by the hour for access. Skilled hackers would try to capture the usernames and passwords of unsuspecting victims by posing as an ISP, especially America Online (AOL) due to its scope and penetration in the market. Fraudsters would harvest known AOL email addresses and send messages claiming to need account updates or validation of user profiles. The mass mailing strategy was like fishing, in that they were hoping to hook victims through deceptive bait. The term "phishing" emerged as a corruption of the term akin to that of phreaking within the general argot of the hacker community. Unsuspecting victims who thought these messages to be legitimate would forward their information to the sender in the hopes of correcting their account. The fraudsters, however, would keep the accounts for their own use or trade the information with others for pirated software or other information.

The success of phishing techniques led some to begin to target e-commerce and online banking sites as they became popular with larger segments of the population in the early 2000s. Hackers began to recognize the value in targeting these institutions, and some began to create sophisticated phishing kits that came pre-loaded with the images and branding of the most prominent global banks. These kits, combined with spam email lists, enabled hackers to readily steal financial data from thousands of unsuspecting users around the world. In fact, the problem of phishing has become so commonplace that over 38,000 unique phishing websites were identified in June of 2013 alone (Anti-Phishing Working Group, 2013). These sites were hosted primarily in the United States due in part to the substantive proportion of hosting resources available to hackers, along with Germany, Canada, France, and the United Kingdom (Anti-Phishing Working Group, 2013). Thus, phishing is a global problem that cannot be understated, though the prevalence of phishing victimization in the general population is largely unknown.

Work-at-home schemes

The use of the Internet as a medium for job solicitation and advertisements enabled scammers to adapt existing schemes to virtual spaces. Specifically, some send out ads for so-called **"work-at-home" schemes** where they promise recipients substantial earnings for just a few hours of work per day (see Text Box 5.4 for an example; Turner, Copes, Kerley, and Warner, 2013). These jobs can all be performed in the home, whether online or through simple physical tasks, such as reviewing store performances, stuffing envelopes, selling various products, data processing, or repackaging and shipping goods for companies. Typically the recipient also requires no training or advanced degrees to complete the job (Turner *et al.*, 2013). Regardless of the form of work, the scammers typically make money by requiring prospective employees to pay fees for training materials, access to databases for work, or products and packaging materials. However, the scammer may not send these materials or may provide information that is of no actual value to the victim (Turner *et al.*, 2013). Alternatively, victims may be roped into cashing fraudulent checks or buying goods and services on another person's behalf.

Text Box 5.4: Work-at-home scheme (personal correspondence)

Dear candidates!
Work at home online around your schedule – Part time or Full time. We offer a simplistic High Tech approach to working at home!
If we could show you how to earn an extra $1,300 every month and could go up to $5,000, by working at home, part time around your full time schedule, would you be interested?
With our Home-Based Marketing program on the Internet we actually helped hundreds of people start making money from the comfort of their own homes by using their bank accounts. The Only Home-Based Marketing Group On The Internet That Has Actually Helped Thousands Of People
Your dream of working part-time and earning serious money will come true as soon as you get the job of an representative (assistant, agent, helper, helpmeet) in our company.
Our partners are huge Internet auctions, which have been cooperating with us for many years.
We do not hide our business connections, which makes us absolutely honest to our clients.
NOTICE: IF YOU ARE INTERESTED ABOUT THIS POSITION, EMAIL US AT:
Joe.Blow@hotmail.com
Best regards.

An extremely common form of work-at-home scheme is called a "**secret shopper**" **scheme**. Though there are legitimate companies that hire individuals to engage in shopping activities or review products, many disreputable or criminal groups utilize online ads to draw in unaware victims. In these schemes, the sender or fake company indicates that they are seeking people to shop at specific retailers to review the store's procedures and customer service (Turner *et al.*, 2013). The recipient is "hired," given a check or money order by mail to use at the retailer to purchase certain goods and is allowed to keep a portion of the check for compensation. The "employee" of the secret shopper company buys the specified items, writes up their experience, and then ships the items to a specified location (Turner *et al.*, 2013). This practice actually serves as a money laundering technique by cashing fraudulent checks or money acquired through various forms of fraud and providing scammers with goods. In addition, the prospective employees can be arrested or charged with criminal activity because of their unwitting role in the scheme (Internet Crime Complaint Center, 2009).

Pump and dump stock schemes

Over the last two decades, the Internet has become an ideal medium for small investors to trade stocks. The information-gathering and analytical capabilities afforded by technology allow investors to micromanage their accounts without the need to engage brokers and firms with their own conceptions of good or sound investments (Tillman and Indergaard, 2005). Instead, consumers can use firms that allow the individual to buy and sell stocks based on their own hunches and information. To that end, scammers have begun to leverage email as a means to advertise stocks with generally low value to the larger public (Tillman and Indergaard, 2005). Often, this is performed through the use of spam emails called **pump and dump messages** (see Text Box 5.5 for an example). The text of the message indicates that a small company with a low stock price is on the cusp of becoming a hot commodity due to the development of a product or idea with substantive growth potential. These companies may not be traded in larger markets such as the New York Stock Exchange (NYSE) because of the lack of publicly available information on the product, but are rather sold in smaller "over-the-counter" markets (Tillman and Indergaard, 2005). This makes it difficult for investors to determine the validity of claims or actively research a product. Some may take the advice that they see and, because of its generally low price, invest in the hopes of turning a profit.

Text Box 5.5: Pump and dump message (personal correspondence)

Subject: NEWS WAS RELEASED AFTER THE MARKET CLOSE ON FRIDAY! WATCH SBRX LIKE A HAWK MONDAY!! THE ALERT IS ON!!!
TRADING ALERT!
Date: Monday, May 1, 2006
Stonebridge Resources Exploration, Ltd.
Acquisition and Development of Oil and Gas Assets
Symbol: SBRX
Price: $1.13
IS THERE A HOTTER SECTOR TO TRADE?!! IS SBRX ON THE VERGE OF A "MONSTER MOVE?" LOOK AT FRIDAY'S ACTION IN THE STOCK? DID IT BREAK OUT?
THE NEWS: Go to Your Favorite Financial Website and Read The Full Story Right Now!!

Stonebridge Closes First M.O.U.!!!

Stonebridge Resources Exploration, Ltd. (Other OTC: SBRX.PK- News) has executed its first Memorandum of Understanding (MOU) with Christian Operating Company for the acquisition of 50% of Christian's No. 4 Port Arthur asset. The MOU with Christian Operating is the first of several acquisitions undertaken by Stonebridge in an effort to attain revenue producing oil and gas assets.

As part of the first MOU Stonebridge acquired the No. 4 gas well in Port Arthur, Texas, with 4 billion cubic ft. of natural gas.

RADAR IT FOR MONDAY'S OPEN NOW! GO SBRX!!!!

The scammers, however, are attempting to artificially "pump up" the price by enticing individuals to purchase the stock. This concurrently increases the stock price within the larger market, inspiring further investor confidence which may further increase its value. The individuals behind the scheme will then "dump," or sell, their shares when they feel it has reached a critical mass. By selling, the stock price will begin to drop, causing remaining shareholders to lose substantially as the price declines (Tillman and Indergaard, 2005). Thus, these schemes are worthwhile only to those insiders who can pump the stocks and dump them at the artificially inflated rate.

While this sort of scam may appear to be specialized and affect only those with substantial incomes, it is important to note that these spam messages may constitute as much as 15 percent of all spam email in a given year (Bohme and Holz, 2006). These messages are also different from other scams in that they do not require the sender to directly interact with the victims. Instead, the spam generators purchase the stocks in advance of their email campaigns and will track the rise of the stock they advertise (Hanke and Hauser, 2006). Often, the spammers will sell their stock within a few days of the initial message distribution, as the price of the stock will reach an inflated peak price. Selling at this time ensures the greatest possible rate of return on their investment. In fact, Frieder and Zittrain (2007) suggest that spammers can generate a four percent rate of return on their initial investment, while victims lose at least five percent within a two-day period.

The fact that the stocks affected are commonly traded through smaller investment markets makes them difficult to track and even harder to disrupt, as the spammers and investors cannot be readily identified. There have been several noteworthy arrests of pump and dump scammers, such as the recent indictment of seven individuals in the US for their roles in perpetrating a massive scheme via spam and false posts on social media sites (US Attorney's Office, 2013). The scope of this scheme was massive; it is estimated that the perpetrators gained more than $120 million in fraudulent stock sales, affecting victims in 35 countries (US Attorney's Office, 2013). The perpetrators were caught due to collaborative investigations by the FBI, RCMP, and agencies in the UK and China, particularly through the use of

intercepts of electronic communications and phone calls between participants (US Attorney's Office, 2013). Thus, pump and dump schemes require
a substantial investigative effort in order to detect and disrupt these scams.

E-commerce sites

The increased use of the Internet by consumers to identify and purchase
goods has also enabled fraudsters to find ways to distribute counterfeit goods
through online outlets due to the large return on investment and low risk of
detection (Wall and Large, 2010). The sale of counterfeit goods is actually
a form of intellectual property theft (see Chapter 4) in that individuals
create, distribute, and sell products that closely replicate or blatantly copy
the original designs of a privately owned product. The counterfeit product
is, however, of a lower quality despite utilizing similar branding and designs
to entice buyers, while none of the profits are returned to the original
copyright holder (Wall and Large, 2010). As a result, counterfeiting can
harm the economic health and reputation of a company due to the sale of
poor quality products utilizing stolen designs and intellectual property.

Spam email is a particularly practical way to advertise counterfeit products because the creator can use language that suggests their prices are very
low for high quality items that otherwise make a social statement or help
the buyer gain social position (Wall and Large, 2010). The lack of regulation
in online markets also allows sellers to offer counterfeit products, which
may look like the authentic product, directly to consumers (Wall and Large,
2010). Online spaces do not allow consumers to properly inspect an item,
forcing them to rely on the images and descriptions of products. As a result,
counterfeiters can use images including legitimate brand logos and photos
of the actual product to create advertisements that speak to the value and
low cost of their merchandise (Balsmeier *et al.*, 2004; Wall and Large, 2010;
see Text Box 5.6 for an example). In turn, consumers are only able to evaluate the advertisement and may not realize they have been swindled until a
poor quality forgery or fake arrives in place of the original item.

Text Box 5.6: Counterfeit luxury goods message (personal correspondence)

From: Prestigious Gift Shop
Subject: Christmas Sale, Thousands of Luxury Goods For Under $100
Dunhill, Mont Blanc, Yves Sant Laurent Shoes, Omega Watches,
The good price for new collections of prestigious accessories, fash-
ionable shoes and smart bags. Autumn-Winter 2011... On sale for a
reduced price
Tempting offers on fabulous replica watches abound

Spam email is a key resource for counterfeiters to advertise and lure in unsuspecting consumers, as fraudsters can drive traffic to online markets that they manage. Alternatively, they may use existing markets, like online auction sites, where they can artificially manipulate indicators of trust and reputation to appear more legitimate (Dolan, 2004). For instance, an existing eBay seller profile that has been inactive can be stolen and hijacked by a fraudster in order to sell counterfeit products while appearing to be a reputable seller in good standing (Chua, Wareham, and Robey, 2007; Gregg and Scott, 2006). Sellers can also create accounts using fake names or addresses, making it difficult to locate the identity of the person responsible for the sale of fraudulent goods (Gregg and Scott, 2006).

Limited research suggests that consumers who buy counterfeit goods wish to conform to current fashion norms and be part of the "it-crowd." They want to position themselves within the social elite who own authentic versions of a counterfeit product (Wall and Large, 2010). Thus, counterfeit luxury goods allow sellers to "trade upon the perception of and desire for exclusivity and to extract its high value by deceiving consumers into buying non-authentic and often low-quality products" (Wall and Large, 2010: 1099). Evidence suggests that the most popular brands sought after by consumers seeking counterfeit products are high-end luxury labels, including Louis Vuitton®, Gucci®, Burberry®, Tiffany®, Prada®, Hermes®, Chanel®, Dior®, Yves Saint Laurent®, and Cartier® (Ledbury Research, 2007). The majority of counterfeit products purchased through email-based ads are clothes (55 percent), shoes (32 percent), leather goods (24 percent), jewelry (20 percent) and watches (26 percent) (Ledbury Research, 2007).

Those consumers who are defrauded through eBay often have limited recourse to deal with the problem (Dolan, 2004). Currently, eBay does not offer monetary compensation to victims of fraud; the company will only log the complaint and mark the seller's profile. PayPal and payment providers may absorb fraudulent charges, though this does not guarantee victims will be fully compensated. As a result, many victims of auction fraud do not know where to turn to file a complaint. Those who do complain to some agency often report dissatisfaction with the process (Dolan, 2004). However, their experiences do not keep them from engaging in online commerce, as more than 75 percent of victims go on to buy goods via auctions and e-commerce sites (Dolan, 2004).

In addition to counterfeit luxury goods, spammers frequently target prescription drugs and supplements through email advertising. Almost one-quarter of all spam is advertising pharmaceutical products (Grow, Elgin, and Weintraub, 2006; see Text Box 5.7 for an example). According to the Pew Internet American Life survey, 63 percent of Internet users have received spam emails advertising sexual health medications, 55 percent received spam in regards to prescription drugs, and 40 percent received emails about an over-the-counter drug (Fox, 2004). MarkMonitor, a company that analyzes online pharmaceutical brands, found that consumers are possibly spending $4 billion annually on prescription medications from online websites linked to spam emails (Paul, 2004).

> **For more on the dangers of counterfeit pharmaceuticals, go online to:**
> www.youtube.com/watch?v=Yyatw3rxSMc

Text Box 5.7: Counterfeit pharmaceutical message (personal correspondence)

Diet Pill Breakthrough!!!
What if you could actually shed 10, 15 or even 25 pounds quickly and safely in less then [sic] 30 days?
NOW YOU CAN...
Click below to learn more about Hoodia:
http://051.mellemellepoa.com

The substantial volume of pharmaceutical spam is directly related to the increased use of prescription drugs in the general population across the globe (Finley, 2009). Many individuals legitimately use prescription drugs for assorted pains and ailments, and a small proportion of the population are addicted to prescription pain medications (Crowley, 2004). Regardless, the cost of pharmaceuticals rose substantially over the last decade, making it difficult for some to acquire necessary medications (Crowley, 2004).

The creation of Internet pharmacies over the last ten years has enabled individuals to access legitimate and illegitimate needs at a low cost and, in some cases, without prescriptions (Finley, 2009). In fact, online sales of prescription drugs from pharmacies hosted in Canada increased from $59 million in 2000 to $800 million in 2003 (Crowley, 2004). By 2005, the online prescription drugs market was estimated to be worth anywhere from $23 million to $1 billion (BuySafeDrugs.info, 2005). This increase is due in part to the ease with which consumers are able to obtain such prescription drugs without an actual prescription. The United Nations' International Narcotics Control Board (INCB) found that approximately 90 percent of all pharmaceutical sales made online are made without a prescription (Finley, 2009). Sullivan (2004) found 495 websites selling prescription drugs in a single week of analysis, and only approximately 6 percent of these sites required any evidence of an actual prescription. Similarly, the US General Accounting Office (2004) found that only 5 of the 29 pharmacies based in the United States required validation of a prescription before distributing drugs. Many online pharmacies hosted in foreign countries relied on medical questionnaires, or required no information at all from the consumer in order to acquire a prescription (Finley, 2009).

As a consequence, it is difficult to distinguish legitimate online pharmacies from those designed expressly to sell counterfeit products to unsuspecting consumers. In fact, there is a distinct threat to consumer safety posed by the sale of prescription drugs online (Grow *et al.*, 2006; Herper, 2005; Phillips, 2005; Stoppler, 2005; Tinnin, 2005). Unlike luxury goods counterfeiting, the consumers who buy from online pharmacies may not be cognizant of the potential for adulteration or outright useless ingredients included in these products. Stoppler (2005) reported that drugs purchased from illegal online pharmacies have the potential to: 1) be outdated or expired, 2) be manufactured in sub-par facilities, 3) contain dangerous ingredients, 4) be too strong or weak, 5) contain the wrong drug, or 6) be complete fakes. In fact, the US Food and Drug Association reported that approximately 90 percent of all prescription drugs coming into the United States purchased through email or postal mail are dangerous and include minimal active ingredients (Tinnin, 2005).

An additional concern lies in the difficulty of regulating or deterring illegal online pharmacies. This is a consequence of the anonymity afforded by the Internet and computer technologies. Offenders can quickly create a pharmacy, sell products, and either move their website to a different address or completely disappear before law enforcement can begin a proper investigation. In addition, the website creators can set up their web address to appear to be hosted in any country and utilize branding and imagery that would make the site appear to be legitimate. For instance, LegitScript and KnujOn conducted an investigation of "rogue" Internet pharmacies, designed to "sell or facilitate the sale of prescription drugs in violation of federal or state laws and accepted drug safety standards" through the search engine bing.com (LegitScript and KnujOn, 2009). The authors were able to identify ten rogue pharmacies advertising on the search engine, though they were all removed within days of their initial investigation. The authors were, however, able to obtain a prescription drug without an actual prescription through another rogue pharmacy advertising on bing.com (LegitScript and KnujOn, 2009). Thus, the problem of counterfeit pharmaceuticals poses a potentially serious risk to vulnerable populations, which may make this more difficult to combat than other forms of online fraud.

The problem of carding and stolen data markets

The range of fraud schemes discussed above suggests that anyone can be a target for online fraud and identity theft. Many of these schemes are too good to be true, such as the 419 emails that indicate a person can make millions of dollars if they are willing to pay a few hundred dollars up front. Other scams are more difficult to assess, such as phishing emails that mirror the originating website and company as closely as possible and prey on victims' fears of compromise. Each of these fraud types, however, requires the victim to engage an offender in some way.

The need for victim–offender interaction in order to facilitate fraud has decreased over the last decade with the growth of large-scale repositories of consumer data, such as bank records, personal information, and other electronic files (see Allison *et al.*, 2005; Furnell, 2002; Newman and Clarke, 2003; Wall, 2001, 2007). As discussed earlier, hackers can now simply compromise large databases of information to capture victim data without the need for any interaction with others. The success of such compromises is evident in the fact that offenders regularly target institutions for mass exploitation. In fact, members of the group that breached Heartland Payment Systems were also responsible for a similar attack against the Marshalls department stores and its parent company, TJX, in 2006 (see Text Box 5.8 for details on one of the hackers responsible for these breaches). That compromise led to the loss of 45 million credit card records and over $1 billion in customer damages (Roberts, 2007).

For more on data breach rates go online to: www.verizonenterprise.com/DBIR/2014/

Text Box 5.8: Albert Gonzales

In Surprise Appeal, TJX Hacker Claims US Authorized His Crimes
www.wired.com/2011/04/gonzalez-plea-withdrawal/

> Albert Gonzalez, the hacker who masterminded the largest credit card heists in U.S. history, is asking a federal judge to throw out his earlier guilty pleas and lift his record-breaking 20-year prison sentence, on allegations that the government authorized his years-long crime spree.

This story details the claims made by Albert Gonzales, an individual who admitted to engaging in some of the largest data breaches in the last decade, targeting TJX, Heartland Payment Systems, and national retail chains. He claimed these crimes were committed as a result of his role as an undercover informant for the US Secret Service, and that he should not be sanctioned for his involvement.

These instances demonstrate the amount of information that fraudsters can acquire in a short amount of time. This is not the only way that mass data can be acquired. For instance, phishing campaigns may generate a few hundred respondents who provide sensitive data in minutes (James, 2005). However, this begs the question of what offenders can do with hundreds, thousands, or millions of credit and debit card accounts. This is too much information for any one person to use, given the short window a scammer may have before fraudulent transactions are noticed. At the same time, these data have a tangible value that can be exploited in the right hands.

In order to garner the greatest possible return from stolen data, individuals have begun to sell the information they obtain via open markets operating online. This practice is sometimes referred to as **carding**, which involves the use and abuse of a credit card number or the identity associated with that account. This practice dates back to the mid 1990s when hackers would utilize statistical programs to randomly generate credit card numbers (Moore, 2010). They would then check to see if these generated numbers were actually active. If so, they would utilize the cards to engage in fraud. As access to credit card data increased through the use of phishing and other techniques, the use of these programs decreased in favor of purchasing information on the open market.

Several studies demonstrate that hackers advertise data they have stolen in a variety of ways through advertisements in IRC channels or web forums (Holt and Lampke, 2010; Franklin, Paxson, Perrig, and Savage, 2007; Motoyama, McCoy, Levchenko, Savage, and Voelker, 2011; Thomas and Martin, 2006). These markets appear to be hosted and operated primarily out of Russia and Eastern Europe, though a small proportion exist in the US and parts of Western Europe (Dunn, 2012; Symantec Corporation, 2012). Individuals commonly sell credit card and debit card accounts, PIN numbers, and supporting customer information from around the world in bulk lots (Holt and Lampke, 2010; Franklin *et al.*, 2007; Motoyama *et al.*, 2011). Some also offer "cash out" services to obtain physical money from electronic accounts by hijacking these accounts to engage in electronic fund transfers established by a hacker (Holt and Lampke, 2010; Franklin *et al.*, 2007; Motoyama *et al.*, 2011; Thomas and Martin, 2006). Others offer "drops services," whereby individuals purchase electronics and other goods electronically using stolen cards, have them shipped to intermediaries who pawn the items, and then wire the cash to interested parties (Holt and Lampke, 2010). A limited number of sellers also offer spam lists and malicious software tools that can be used to engage in fraud (Holt and Lampke, 2010).

The emergence of online **carding markets** enables individuals to efficiently engage in credit card fraud and identity theft with minimal effort and limited technical knowledge or skill (Franklin *et al.*, 2007; Holt and Lampke, 2010; Motoyama *et al.*, 2011). These markets allow skilled hackers to garner a profit through the sale of information they acquire to other criminals, while those who use the accounts can make money for a small initial investment (Honeynet Research Alliance, 2003; Franklin *et al.*, 2007; Holt and Lampke, 2010; Thomas and Martin, 2006). Furthermore, individuals around the world may be victimized multiple times, removing the ability to control where and how individuals have access to sensitive personal information.

Carding markets constitute a unique subculture driven by individual interests in the sale and trade of sensitive information. The social nature of sales requires that individuals actively engage one another in order to conduct business. The virtual nature of these markets, however, makes it difficult for actors to truly trust others because they are unable to physically inspect goods and merchandise prior to making a purchase (Franklin *et al.*, 2007; Holt and Lampke, 2010; Motoyama *et al.*, 2011). In the following section, we discuss the structure of the market in detail and the social forces that shape relationships between buyers and sellers. Though there are variations in the markets currently operating online, we discuss the most common structures observed across multiple studies.

Carding market processes, actors, and relationships

The process of buying and selling goods in carding markets begins with an individual posting an advertisement in a forum or IRC channel describing the goods and services they have available or which they need to complete a project (Franklin *et al.*, 2007; Holt and Lampke, 2010; Motoyama *et al.*, 2011). The level of information provided may vary, though the more detailed a post is, the more likely an individual may be to receive a response from interested parties. For instance, the following is an ad from a forum where an individual was selling credit card numbers along with the CVV2, or Credit Verification Value number. This three-digit number appears on the back of credit and debit cards in the signature line as a means to ensure the customer has the card on their person at the point of sale, particularly for electronic purchases. The seller has gone to great lengths to describe his products and their utility in fraud:

Hi everyone,

I'm just a newcomer here and I offer you a great service with cheapest prices. I sell mainly CC/Cvv2 US and UK. I also sell International Cvv2 if you want. Before I get Verified here, I sold Cvv2 in many forums. Some members in this forum know me. Hope I can serve you all long time.

Service details:

My CC/Cvv2 comes with these infos:
Name:
Address:
City:
State:
Zip:

Phone:
Email:
CC number:
Exp day:
CVN: (come with Cvv2, not with CC)

Basic prices for each CC/Cvv2:

++CC (without Cvv2 number) :
US: 0.5$ each
UK: 1$ each
++Cvv2:
US: 1$ each
Uk: 2.5$ each
*** Cvv2 UK with DOB: 10$ each ***
*** Cvv2 US with DOB: 3$ each ***
*** US Visa Business/Purchasing: 4$ each ***
*** US Amex/Discover : 3$ each ***

Add-on Prices:

+Special Card Type: +$1
+Special Gender: +$1
+Special City or State: +$1
+Special Card BIN: +$1.5
+Special Zip Code: +$1

Term of service:

- Payment must be done before CC/Cvv2 are sent.
- Order over 100 CC/Cvv2 get 10% discount.
- Order over 500 CC/Cvv2 get 15% discount.
- Order over 1000 CC/Cvv2 get 20% discount.
*** I do replace new cards if any invalid. ***

Contact details:

+PM me in the forum.
+Email me as [removed]
+Yahoo ID: [removed]
+ICQ: [removed]
^^ Have a good carding day and good luck ^^

As noted above, the seller will specify their terms of service and the degree of service they offer to customers who need assistance. This varies based on the individual and their overall reputation within the market. In addition, sellers or buyers will include their preferred payment mechanism, which is usually an electronic medium, such as Web Money (WM) or Yandex (Franklin *et al.*, 2007; Holt and Lampke, 2010; Motoyama *et al.*, 2011). A proportion also indicate that they will accept payments via Western Union, a wire transfer service that sends currency between individuals. Electronic payments are generally preferred because they can be anonymized to reduce the risk of detection or tracking by law enforcement (Franklin *et al.*, 2007; Holt and Lampke, 2010; Motoyama *et al.*, 2011). Wire transfers, like Western Union, require individuals to show identification in order to receive funds, which can increase the likelihood of arrest.

Sellers also provide their preferred method of contact, since the sales and negotiation process occurs outside of the forum or IRC channel. Most individuals use the instant messaging protocol ICQ, which is currently owned and operated out of Russia (Franklin *et al.*, 2007; Holt and Lampke, 2010; Motoyama *et al.*, 2011). A proportion of sellers also provide email addresses, or will accept private messages through forum communications venues. This helps to protect the details of a conversation from the general public, though it also makes it difficult for individuals to lodge a complaint if they feel they have been cheated or swindled.

In order to provide participants with some degree of information about the sellers in carding markets, some sites utilize a naming system in order to identify a person's status and reputation (Franklin *et al.*, 2007; Holt and Lampke, 2010; Motoyama *et al.*, 2011). An individual is given a title by the moderators or operators of a forum or IRC channel based on feedback from participants and the use of testers who can validate a seller's claims. Many markets use the term **unverified seller** to identify someone who is new and therefore unable to be fully trusted. Individuals who choose to do business with that person do so at their own risk (Franklin *et al.*, 2007; Holt and Lampke, 2010; Motoyama *et al.*, 2011).

An individual may become a **verified seller** by providing a sample of data to a forum moderator or administrator, or alternatively offering malware or other services to be reviewed. Those forums who offer validation services will typically write and post reviews of the seller as a means of vetting an individual (Franklin *et al.*, 2007; Holt and Lampke, 2010; Motoyama *et al.*, 2011). Reviewers describe the quality of a service or data source, problems they may have in using the data, and any support offered by the seller. Those sellers and service providers who meet the standards of the forum may then be given verified status (Franklin *et al.*, 2007; Holt and Lampke, 2010; Motoyama *et al.*, 2011).

Some markets do not utilize naming conventions to identify sellers, so the participants will often provide feedback within the forum or channel to provide a measure of reputation and reliability. Positive feedback helps to demonstrate the quality of a seller's data or services and may increase the overall reputation of a seller within the site (Franklin *et al.*, 2007; Holt and Lampke, 2010; Motoyama *et al.*, 2011). Negative feedback, however, can harm a seller's business and push customers toward other vendors with generally favorable reviews. A seller who does not provide data after being paid, is slow to respond to customers, or sells bad data and does not offer to replace their products may be called a **ripper**, or rip-off artist (Franklin *et al.*, 2007; Holt and Lampke, 2010; Motoyama *et al.*, 2011). This is a pejorative term in carding markets that, if left unanswered, may lead an individual to be banned from the site entirely.

The use of customer feedback and specialized terms to identify participants are the only real mechanisms available to participants in the event that they are dissatisfied with a transaction (Franklin *et al.*, 2007; Holt and Lampke, 2010; Motoyama *et al.*, 2011). Since the sale and distribution of stolen financial and personal data is illegal, participants cannot contact police or other customer protection services if they are cheated. Additionally, the virtual nature of the market makes it difficult for participants to confront someone in person (Franklin *et al.*, 2007; Holt and Lampke, 2010; Motoyama *et al.*, 2011). The use of informal sanctions is the only real way that markets can be regulated to ensure successful outcomes and general customer satisfaction.

Social forces within carding markets

The interactive nature of carding markets creates a unique series of social forces that shape the relationships between participants. In fact, research by Holt and Lampke (2010) indicates that there are four key forces that affect the interactions and behaviors of buyers and sellers. These include (1) communications, (2) price, (3) product quality, and (4) customer service. The first issue, communications, is vital to ensure the efficient and rapid creation and completion of deals (Holt and Lampke, 2010). Since data breaches and information theft may be detected by consumers and financial institutions, carders have a limited timeframe for data to remain valid and active. Those sellers who immediately respond to customer requests are more likely to receive praise and positive feedback. Individuals taking hours or days to respond to customer requests, or delaying the delivery of purchased product, would receive negative feedback (Holt and Lampke, 2010). This suggests that customer contact has a substantial influence on the behavior of sellers in order to garner trust and establish a reputation.

Price points also affect the way in which customers select the services of sellers. There is some demonstrable competition between sellers to provide the lowest cost for their services. Customer feedback often notes that low prices spur the decision to buy from a specific actor within the market (Holt and Lampke, 2010). To help maintain customer bases over time, some sellers offer bulk discounts to regular clients or free gifts with large purchases. This is helpful to increase the amount of data a seller is able to offload and maximize their profit. At the same time, customers view this as a beneficial mechanism to build trust and as a show of service (Holt and Lampke, 2010).

At the same time, the quality of a seller's products is vital to ensure customers return and buy from them over the long term. Those who offer bad data at low prices will receive generally unfavorable reviews because customers want to get the greatest return on their investments (Holt and Lampke, 2010). Thus, they will seek out sellers who have reasonable prices with a greater likelihood of active accounts with some value in order to exploit those funds.

The final aspect of the market is customer service, which is an important tool to help drive a seller's reputation and placate buyers who feel they have been cheated (Holt and Lampke, 2010). For instance, some sellers offer free replacements for inactive or dead accounts to ensure that their buyers are satisfied with a purchase. A number of reputable sellers also operate 24–7 customer support lines via ICQ to ensure that any technical questions or assistance can be immediately handled (Holt and Lampke, 2010). Such resources are an important mechanism to demonstrate a seller's reputation and willingness to aid clients. This helps to minimize the likelihood of customers being ripped off and promotes smooth transactions that satisfy market demands.

Taken as a whole, carding markets are a unique criminal subculture that mirrors elements of legitimate businesses. Their existence also engenders phishing, hacking, and other means of data theft in order to continually turn a profit through sales in the open market. As a result, there is a need for ongoing research to document the scope of this form of crime and identify enforcement mechanisms to disrupt their operation.

Identity theft and fraud laws

In light of the myriad forms of fraud that can be perpetrated online, it is critical that the criminal justice system have various mechanisms that can be employed to pursue these offenders. There are several legislative mechanisms that have emerged, primarily at the federal level, to punish fraud. The most pertinent laws in the US are listed under the **Identity Theft and Assumption Deterrence Act of 1998**, which makes it a federal crime to possess, transfer, or use a means of identification of another person without authorization with the intent to commit or aid in the commission of illegal activity at the local, state, or federal level (Brenner, 2011). This includes a variety of specific acts outlined in Title 18 of the US Legal Code (section 1028) including:

a. Knowingly, and without authority, produce an identification document or supporting materials for identification documents, such as holograms or other images
b. Knowingly transfer an identification document or materials with the knowledge that the item was stolen or produced without authority
c. Knowingly possess with the intent to use or transfer, five or more identification documents or materials

d. Knowingly possess an identification document or materials with the intent to use the item to defraud
e. Knowingly produce, transfer, or possess a document-making implement or authentication feature that will be used in the creation of a false identity document
f. Knowingly possess an identification document or supporting materials of the United States that is stolen or produced without lawful authority
g. Knowingly transfer, possess, or use a means of identification of another person without authorization with intent to engage in unlawful activity
h. Knowingly traffic in false authentication materials for use in the creation of false identification.

These activities could affect interstate or foreign commerce, as well as any materials that are sent through the mail, such as personal identifications or passports. The punishments for identity crimes range from 5 to 15 years in prison, as well as fines and prospective forfeiture of goods and materials obtained while using an identity (Brenner, 2011).

Under this law, an **identification document** is defined as "a document made or issued by or under the authority of the United States government ... with information concerning a particular individual, is of a type of intended, or commonly accepted for the purpose of identification of individuals" (USC 1028 d). This law also specifically outlaws the use of means of identification, which includes names, social security numbers, date of birth, drivers' license or identification numbers, passport information, employer identification numbers, biometric data (such as fingerprints), unique electronic identification numbers, addresses, bank routing numbers, or even the telecommunications identifying information of an access device, such as the IP address of a computer system (Brenner, 2011). Finally, this legislation made the Federal Trade Commission (FTC) a clearinghouse for consumer information on identity-related crimes.

The **Identity Theft Penalty Enhancement Act of 2003** added two years to any prison sentence for individuals convicted of a felony who knowingly possessed, used, or transferred identity documents of another person (Brenner, 2011). This act also added five years to the sentence received for identity theft convictions connected to acts of terrorism. This specific enhancement is designed to further punish actors who may develop or create fictitious identities in support of acts of terror.

In addition, the **Identity Theft Enforcement and Restitution Act of 2008** is important because of its impact on sentencing and the pursuit of identity crimes (Brenner, 2011). Specifically, this act allows offenders to be ordered to pay restitution as a penalty to victims of identity theft. This statute also enables more effective mechanisms to prosecute offenses unrelated to computer fraud that could otherwise be prosecuted under the Computer Fraud and Abuse Act (Brenner, 2011). Additionally, it expands the ability for agencies to pursue computer fraud actors engaging in interstate or international offenses. Finally, this act imposes criminal and civil forfeitures of property used in the commission of computer fraud behaviors.

A final piece of federal legislation to note is the **Fair and Accurate Credit Transactions Act of 2003**. This law provided multiple protections to help reduce the risk of identity theft and assist victims in repairing their credit in the event of identity theft (Brenner, 2011). This includes requiring businesses to remove customer credit card information (except the last four digits) from receipts to reduce the risk of victimization. The law also allowed consumers to obtain a free credit report every year from the major credit monitoring services to assist in the identification of fraudulent transactions or potential identity theft (Brenner, 2011). Finally, the act provided mechanisms for consumers to place and receive alerts on their credit file to reduce the risk of fraudulent transactions. These steps are integral to protecting consumers from harm.

Many states have outlawed acts of computer-based fraud and theft. Some choose to prosecute these offenses under existing computer hacking statutes, while others include separate language pertaining to computer fraud (Arkansas, Hawaii). A number of states have also outlawed computer theft, which may include forms of piracy or computer hardware theft (Colorado, Georgia, Idaho, Iowa, Minnesota, New Jersey, Pennsylvania, Rhode Island, Vermont, Virginia). Several states have also established statutes related to identity crimes, typically featuring language that makes it illegal for an individual to knowingly obtain, possess, use, or transfer identity documents, personal identification numbers, or other sensitive information relating to an individual with the intent to defraud that person for economic gain (Brenner, 2011). These states include Alabama, California, Connecticut, Delaware, Georgia, Iowa, Massachusetts, Mississippi, Oklahoma, and Pennsylvania.

In addition to laws pertaining to fraud and theft, a small number of states have developed legislation related to large-scale **data breaches**, like the Heartland Bank or TJX compromises (National Conference of State Legislatures, 2012). Breaches can affect hundreds of thousands of victims through no fault of their own, creating a substantive need to ensure that consumers are protected. California was the first state to develop such a law in 2003, titled the California Security Breach Notification Act (Cal. Civil Code). This legislation required California residents to be notified of a breach whenever a database compromise leads to the loss of an individual's first and last name along with any of the following information: (a) social security number, (b) driver's license number or California State ID card number, (c) an account, debit, or credit card number in combination with any security information that could be used to authorize a transaction, such as the three-digit security code on the card.

This law was designed to serve as a safeguard for consumers in the event that a breach led to the loss of sensitive information. Additionally, this legislation validated the idea that companies and organizations are obliged to protect consumer data from harm. The nearly unanimous passing of this legislation led other states to develop their own language pertaining to breach notifications. Currently, there are breach notification requirements mandated by law in 46 states, the District of Columbia, Guam, Puerto Rico, and the Virgin Islands (National Conference of State Legislatures, 2012). This will no doubt continue to evolve as the threats to large databases of information change and increase with time.

Many nations around the world have also criminalized identity crimes in some fashion, though their statutes may not actually include this phrase. For instance, India utilizes the phrase "identity theft" in their criminal code under Section 66C, making the fraudulent or dishonest use of passwords or unique identity information punishable by up to three years in prison and fines (Brenner, 2011). Australia does not use this phrasing in its Criminal Code Amendment Act 2000 in section 135.1, but this new code recognizes general dishonesty where a person is guilty if they do anything with the intention of dishonesty, causing a loss to another person, and that person is a Commonwealth entity (Brenner, 2011).

Canada's federal Criminal Code also has multiple sections related to identity crimes. Under section 402.2, anyone who knowingly obtains or possesses another person's identity information, such that the data can be used to commit some form of fraud or deceit, can be subject to up to five years in prison (Holt and Schell, 2013). Additionally, Section 403 criminalizes the fraudulent use of another person's identity information to 1) gain advantage for themselves or others, 2) obtain or gain interest in property, 3) cause disadvantage to the person being impersonated or others, or 4) avoid arrest or prosecution (Holt and Schell, 2013). Any violation of this statute can be punished with a prison sentence of up to ten years in total.

The UK utilizes similar language regarding fraudulent or dishonest use in order to gain advantage or cause another person to lose in some fashion in its Fraud Act of 2006. This statute applies specifically to England, Wales, and Northern Ireland, and also identifies three forms of fraud, including false representation of facts or laws, failure to disclose information when legally mandated, and fraud based on abuses of individual power to safeguard or protect personal or financial information (Holt and Schell, 2013).

The EU Convention on Cybercrime (CoC) also includes two articles pertaining to computer forgery and fraud, though it does not use the phrase identity fraud or theft (Brenner, 2011). The CoC requires nations to adopt legislation criminalizing access, input, deletion, or suppression of data that leads it to be considered as inauthentic or fraudulent, even though it would otherwise be treated as though it were authentic data (Brenner, 2011). Additionally, the CoC criminalizes the input or alteration of data and/or interference with computer systems with the intent to defraud or procure economic gain and cause the loss of property of another person. This language directly applies to various forms of online fraud and data theft, making it a valuable component for the development of cybercrime law globally.

Regulating fraud globally

The myriad forms of fraud that can be perpetrated, coupled with the potential for fraudsters to victimize individuals around the world, makes this a difficult form of crime to investigate. In the US, local law enforcement agencies may serve as a primary point of contact for a victim, as do the offices of state Attorneys General, who typically act as information clearinghouses for consumer fraud cases. Additionally, states' Attorneys General offices can accept complaints on behalf of fraud victims and can help to direct individuals to the correct agency to facilitate investigations when appropriate. It is important to note that federal agencies will be responsible for cases where the victim and offender reside in different states or countries. We will focus our discussion on the primary federal agencies in various nations who are responsible for the investigation of online fraud due to the fact that the majority of online fraud cases involve victims living in a separate jurisdiction from their offender (Internet Crime Complaint Center, 2009).

The **United States Secret Service** is one of the most prominent federal law enforcement bodies involved in the investigation of online fraud in the United States. The Secret Service was initially part of the treasury department and had a substantive role in investigating the production of counterfeit currency and attempts to defraud financial payment systems (Moore, 2010). As banks and financial industries came to depend on technology in the 1980s and 1990s, the Secret Service increasingly investigated Internet-based forms of fraud. In fact, the Secret Service operates a Financial Crimes Division which has three primary responsibilities concerning cybercrime. The first is the investigation of financial institution fraud (FIF), including banks, savings and loan institutions, and credit unions (Moore, 2010). These offenses typically involve the use of counterfeit currency created in part by computers and sophisticated printing devices, as well as checks and other protected financial products.

The second priority involves access-device fraud, whereby an individual utilizes credit card numbers, PINs, passwords, and related account information to engage in acts of fraud. The practices of carders are of particular interest to the Secret Service, as the sale and use of dumps and other financial information constitute acts of access-device fraud. The final area of interest involves the investigation of general acts of fraud involving computers and systems of "federal interest," such that they play a role in, or directly facilitate, interstate or international commerce and government information transfers (Moore, 2010). This is a very broad area of investigation, including hacking offenses and the use of computers as storage devices to hold stolen information or produce fraudulent financial materials. As a result, the Secret Service has been given the power to investigate a wide range of cybercrimes.

To help ensure successful detection, investigation, and prosecution of these crimes, the Financial Crimes Division operates the Electronic Crimes Branch which provides technical support for special agents investigating cybercrimes (United States Secret Service, 2014). This branch includes specialized forensic and technological resources designed to properly seize, store, and analyze computer-based evidence of these crimes. Additionally, this branch also operates the Electronic Crimes Task Force (ECTF), which meets quarterly to bring together law enforcement, prosecutors, private industry, and academia to discuss trends and developments in various financial crimes. There are now 25 active ECTFs across the country in many major cities and financial hubs in order to help support and investigate electronic crimes (United States Secret Service, 2014).

In addition to the Secret Service, the Federal Bureau of Investigation plays a prominent role in the investigation of online fraud. In fact, cybercrime is their third highest investigative priority, with internet fraud and identity theft as top crimes of interest (Federal Bureau of Investigation, 2014). This is a change for the Bureau, which had a focus on traditional forms of white collar crime and fraud in the real world until the early 2000s, when Internet use became nearly ubiquitous across the industrialized world. The expansion of FBI investigative responsibilities into online fraud is in keeping with their general role in the investigation of cyberattacks against national infrastructure and security (Federal Bureau of Investigation, 2014). Criminal entities, terrorist groups, and even nation-states may have a vested interest in identity theft in order to fund various illicit activities and generally harm the economic safety of the nation and its citizens. Thus, both the Secret Service and the FBI now play a role in the investigation of online fraud. This creates potential investigative challenges as investigators across agencies must find ways to coordinate operations in order to avoid the duplication of effort and de-conflict which criminal actors may be working with law enforcement (see Text Box 5.9 for details).

Text Box 5.9: The overlapping role of the Secret Service and Federal Bureau of Investigation

Crime Boards Come Crashing Down
   http://archive.wired.com/science/discoveries/news/2007/02/72585?currentPage=2

> While Thomas had been working on the West Coast for the FBI, the Secret Service's New Jersey office had infiltrated Shadowcrew separately, with the help of a confidential informant, and begun gathering evidence against carders on that site.

This article provides an overview of the relationships between the FBI and Secret Service in the investigation and takedown of the group "the Shadowcrew" and subsequent investigations of other hacker groups..

The **Internet Crime Complaint Center (IC3)** is a collaborative effort of the National White Collar Crime Center (NW3C) and the FBI operating for crime victims, consumers, and researchers to understand the scope of various forms of online fraud. Victims can contact the agency through an online reporting mechanism that accepts complaints for a range of offenses, though the most common contacts involve auction fraud, advance fee fraud victimization, and other forms of online fraud driven via spam (Internet Crime Complaint Center, 2009). In turn, victims may be directed to the appropriate investigative resources to further handle complaints.

The US **Immigration and Customs Enforcement (ICE)** and **Customs and Border Patrol (CBP)** agencies also have an investigative responsibility regarding financial crimes, fraud, and counterfeiting (Immigration and Customs Enforcement, 2014). Given that CBP agents monitor border crossings and ports, they serve a pivotal role in the identification of attempts to smuggle in cash and currency, as well as use or transfer fraudulent documents. In fact, ICE operates the cybercrime section which investigates identity crimes, fraud, and smuggling practices in general (Immigration and Customs Enforcement, 2014).

In the UK, the primary agency responsible for managing fraud is the **National Fraud Authority (NFA)**, which was formed in 2008 in order to increase cooperation between both the public and private sector (National Fraud Authority, 2014). The NFA acts as a clearinghouse for information on various forms of fraud and reports on the scope of fraud in any given year through the publication of the Annual Fraud Indicator report. Through assessments of threats to the public and not-for-profit sectors, this report attempts to estimate the total costs of fraud to UK residents each year (National Fraud Authority, 2014). The NFA also supports the Action Fraud reporting service, enabling citizens to file reports of fraud online or via phone and obtain information about how to better protect themselves from being victimized. In fact, the **Action Fraud** service is similar to that of the US IC3, in that any victim complaint is forwarded to law enforcement (National Fraud Authority, 2014). In this case, Action Fraud reports are sent on to the **National Fraud Intelligence Bureau (NFIB)**, operated by the City of London police, for further investigation (National Fraud Intelligence Bureau, 2014). The NFIB collects information on various forms of fraud and aggregates this data along with reports from business and industry sources into a large database called the NFIB Know Fraud system. Analysts can query this database to generate intelligence reports on the credibility of fraud reports and develop information that can be used to pursue criminal charges or other operations to disrupt fraudsters (National Fraud Intelligence Bureau, 2014).

> **For more on reporting fraud in the UK, go online to:** www.actionfraud.police.uk/report_fraud

Canada also utilizes a similar fraud reporting structure called the **Canadian Anti-Fraud Centre (CAFC)**, which is a joint effort of the RCMP, Ontario Provincial Police, and the Competition Bureau that collects reports on various forms of fraud that take place on and offline (Canadian Anti-Fraud Centre, 2014). The CAFC accepts complaints over the phone and online and has become a critical investigative resource for law enforcement agencies. The complaints received are also aggregated and developed into intelligence products for law enforcement around the world by the CAFC's Criminal Intelligence Analysis Unit (Canadian Anti-Fraud Centre, 2014). In addition, the CACF provides fraud alerts and information for the public to help reduce the incidence of fraud.

There are also a number of non-governmental organizations and groups that offer assistance in dealing with fraud. For instance, the **Anti-Phishing Working Group (APWG)** is a not-for-profit global consortium of researchers, computer security professionals, financial industry members, and law enforcement designed to document the scope of phishing attacks and provide policy recommendations to government and industry groups worldwide (Anti-Phishing Working Group, 2013). The APWG has members from over 2,000 institutions around the world, including financial institutions and treaty organizations, such as the Council of Europe and the United Nations Office of Drugs and Crime (UNODC). The group collects statistics on active phishing attacks provided by victims and researchers to provide information on the most likely targets for phishing attacks and shares this information with interested parties to help combat these crimes. Furthermore, the APWG operates various conferences designed to improve the detection, defense, and cessation of phishing and fraud victimization.

The **Federal Trade Commission (FTC)** is a key resource for consumers and victims of fraud, particularly after the passing of the Identity Theft Assumption and Deterrence Act of 1998. The FTC is an independent watchdog agency within the federal government responsible for consumer protection and monitoring the business community to prevent monopolies and regulate fair practice statutes. There are three separate bureaus within the FTC. The Bureau of Consumer Protection is tasked with the enforcement of laws related to consumer safety, fraud, and privacy protection. This Bureau is staffed with attorneys who have the power to pursue cases against various forms of fraud and identity crimes. In particular, the FTC serves as a key reporting resource for consumer complaints of identity crimes though both an online and telephone-based reporting mechanism. It is important to note that the FTC does not pursue individual claims to any resolution. Instead, the aggregation of reporting information is used to determine when and how federal lawsuits may be brought against specific groups or to develop legislation to protect consumers. The FTC also operates a spam-reporting database to help track the various scams that are used by fraudsters over time. Finally, they offer a variety of consumer-focused publications that discuss the risks for identity theft and ways to protect credit scores, bank accounts, and other sensitive information.

> **For more information on the FTC, go online to:** www.consumer.ftc.gov/features/feature-0014-identity-theft

The FTC is also increasingly involved in the regulation and monitoring of online advertising campaigns. As consumers increasingly utilize e-commerce sites in the course of their shopping, it is vital that their rights and personal information are safeguarded from deceptive advertising practices or unfair tracking policies. For instance, the FTC filed a complaint against Sears Holdings Management Corporation, the owner of the Sears and K-Mart retail chains, in 2009. The suit alleged that the websites for both stores engaged in a campaign titled "My SHC Community" that would allow users to provide their opinion about their shopping practices and preferences. Individuals who accepted the invitation were then asked to download a program that would confidentially track online browsing habits. Consumers would also be given $10 for leaving the application running for at least one month.

The user agreement did not, however, explain the full behavior of the tracking program up front, which had the potential to capture consumer information, including usernames, passwords, credit and bank account information, and other sensitive data that the company had no need to obtain. As a result, the FTC pursued its case against the corporation until such time as they agreed to clearly disclose the processes of the application on a secondary screen from the license agreement and contact all existing users to let them know of the potential for harm, as well as allow them to remove the program. Finally, the corporation was to destroy all data obtained from consumers prior to the filing of the suit.

There are similar entities for data protection across the world, such as the UK's Information Commissioner's Office (whose main purpose is to protect the public's information rights and privacy), the Australian Information Commissioner (OAIC), and Spain's Agencia Espanola de Proteccion de Datos (AEPD) (Federal Trade Commission, 2005). These agencies provide detailed information on governmental regulations, the protections that should be in place for personal data, and what individuals should do in the event that they are victimized in some fashion. Additionally, these agencies may work together to share information and investigate some forms of offending. For instance, these nations all have a collaborative working agreement with the FTC to collect data on spam and other consumer threats (Federal Trade Commission, 2005).

economic crimes and online fraud

Summary

As a society, we have increasingly come to depend on the Internet and computer technology to manage most every aspect of our financial lives. This has unparalleled benefits in that we can track expenses and monitor our purchases in near real time. Our ability to connect to others and to pay for purchases has also increased the opportunities for fraudsters to take advantage of vulnerable populations. The use of email-based scams allows individuals to create convincing replicas of messages from legitimate service providers and vendors. Consumers must now be extremely cautious about accepting what they see in online messages at face value. The amount of sensitive information about our financial and personal lives that is now outside of our regulation has also created opportunities for fraud that are beyond our control. Carders and data thieves can now victimize hundreds of thousands of people in a short amount of time and gain a substantial profit from the sale of this data.

The response from the criminal justice and financial sector to these crimes has improved greatly over the last decade. There are still great challenges involved in the detection, investigation, and successful prosecution of these cases due to the jurisdictional challenges that may exist. Since offenders and victims can be hundreds, if not thousands, of miles away from one another, it is difficult to arrest responsible parties or even make victims whole through restitution. Thus, we must continually improve consumer awareness of fraud to reduce the likelihood of victimization and simultaneously expand the powers of law enforcement to respond to these crimes.

Key terms

419 scams

Action Fraud

Advance fee email schemes

Anti-Phishing Working Group (APWG)

Canadian Anti-Fraud Centre (CAFC)

Carding

Carding markets

Customs and Border Patrol (CBP)

Data breaches

Fair and Accurate Credit Transactions Act of 2003

Federal Trade Commission (FTC)

Fraud

Identification document

Identity fraud

Identity theft

Identity Theft and Assumption Deterrence Act of 1998

Identity Theft Enforcement and Restitution Act of 2008

Identity Theft Penalty Enhancement Act of 2003

Immigration and Customs Enforcement (ICE)

Internet Crime Complaint Center (IC3)

National Fraud Authority (NFA)

National Fraud Intelligence Bureau (NFIB)

Pump and dump messages

Ripper

Personal identification number (PIN)

Personally identifiable information (PII)

Phishing

"Secret shopper" scheme

United States Secret Service

Unverified seller

Verified seller

"Work-at-home" schemes

Discussion questions

1) As we continue to adopt new technologies to communicate, how will scammers utilize these spaces? For instance, how might a scammer use FaceTime or Skype to lure in prospective victims?

2) What demographic groups seem most susceptible to email-based fraud schemes, like 419 scams? Why do you think this might be the case?

3) What steps and techniques can individuals use to reduce their risk of victimization via carding or other non-interactive forms of fraud?

4) How can nations work together better to address fraud? What is a nation supposed to do if its citizens are routinely victimized online by citizens of another nation which refuses to do anything about it?

References

Allison, S. F. H., Schuck, A. M., and Learsch, K. M. (2005). Exploring the crime of identity theft: Prevalence, clearance rates, and victim/offender characteristics, *Journal of Criminal Justice*, 33, 19–29.

economic crimes and online fraud

Anderson, J. (2010). *Understanding the changing needs of the US online consumer, 2010. An empowered report: How online and mobile behaviors are changing.* Forrester Research. Retrieved August 15, 2011 from www.forrester.com/rb/ Research/understanding_changing_needs_of_us_online_consumer%2C/q/ id/57861/t/2

Anti-Phishing Working Group. (2013). *Phishing Activity Trends Report, 2nd Quarter 2013.* [Online] Available at: http://docs.apwg.org/reports/apwg_trends_ report_q2_2013.pdf

Baker, W. E., and Faulkner, R. R. (2003). Diffusion of fraud: Intermediate economic crime and investor dynamics. *Criminology,* 41(4), 1173–1206.

Balsmeier, P., Bergiel, B. J., & Viosca Jr., R. C. (2004). Internet fraud: A global perspective. *Journal of E-Business,* 4(1), 1–12.

Bohme, R., & Holz, T. (2006). The effect of stock spam on financial markets. [Online] Available at: http://ssrn.com/abstract=897431 or http://dx.doi.org/10.2139/ ssrn.897431

Brenner, S. W. (2011). Defining Cybercrime: A Review of Federal and State Law. In R. D. Clifford (ed.), *Cybercrime: The Investigation, Prosecution, and Defense of a Computer-Related Crime,* 3rd Edition (pp. 15–104). Raleigh, NC: Carolina Academic Press.

Buchanan, J., & Grant, A. J. (2001). Investigating and prosecuting Nigerian fraud. *United States Attorneys' Bulletin,* November, 29–47.

BuySafeDrugs.info. (2005). *I-team investigation: The hidden dangers of online drugs.* [Online] Available at: www.buysafedrugs.info/reorts/nbsreport.html

Canadian Anti-Fraud Centre. (2014). *Mission of the Canadian Anti-Fraud Centre.* [Online] Available at: www.antifraudcentre-centreantifraude.ca/english/cafc_ aboutus.html

Carr, D. F. (2013). Healthcare data breaches to surge in 2014. *Information Week,* December 26, 2013. [Online] Available at: www.informationweek.com/healthcare/ policy-and-regulation/healthcare-data-breaches-to-surge-in-2014/d/d-id/1113259

Chu, B., Holt, T. J., & Ahn, G. J. (2010). *Examining the Creation, Distribution, and Function of Malware On-Line.* Washington, DC, National Institute of Justice. [Online] Available at: www.ncjrs.gov/pdffiles1/nij/grants/230112.pdf

Chua, C. E. H., Wareham, J., & Robey, D. (2007). The role of online trading communities in managing Internet auction fraud. *MIS Quarterly,* 31, 750–781.

comScore. (2014). 2013 holiday season U.S. desktop e-commerce spending reaches record $46.5 billion, up 10 percent vs. year ago. [Online] Available at: www. comscore.com/Insights/Press_Releases/2014/1/2013_Holiday_Season_US_ Desktop_ECommerce_Spending_Reaches_Record_465_Billion_Up_10_Percent_ vs_Year_Ago

Copes, H., & Vieraitis, L. M. (2009). Bounded rationality of identity thieves: Using offender-based research to inform policy. *Criminology & Public Policy,* 8(2), 237–262.

Crowley, B. (2004). *Lower prescription drug costs don't tell the whole story.* [Online] Available at: www.aims.ca/en/home/library/details.aspx/1081

Dolan, K. M. (2004). Internet Auction Fraud: The Silent Victims. *Journal of Economic Crime Management,* 2, 1–22.

Dunn, J. E. (2012). Russia cybercrime market doubles in 2011, says report. *IT World Today.* [Online] Available at: www.itworld.com/security/272448/ russia-cybercrime-market-doubles-2011-says-report

Edelson, E. (2003). The 419 scam: Information warfare on the spam front and a proposal for local filtering. *Computers and Security*, 22(5), 392–401.

Federal Bureau of Investigation. (2014). *What we investigate*. [Online] Available at www.fbi.gov/about-us/investigate

Federal Trade Commission. (2005). *FTC, Spanish Data Protection Agency Working Together to Fight Illegal Spam*. February 24, 2005. [Online] Available at: www.ftc.gov/news-events/press-releases/2005/02/ftc-spanish-data-protection-agency-working-together-fight-illegal

Federal Trade Commission. (2013). *Consumer Sentinel Network Data Book for January-December 2012*. [Online] Available at: www.ftc.gov/sites/default/files/documents/reports_annual/sentinel-cy-2012/sentinel-cy2012.pdf

Finley, L. L. (2009). Online Pharmaceutical Sales and the Challenge for Law Enforcement. In *Crime of the Internet*, ed. F. Schmalleger & M. Pittaro, 101–128. Saddle River, NJ: Prentice Hall.

Fox, S. (2004). *Prescription drugs online*. Pew Internet & American Life Project. [Online] Available at: www.pewinternet.org/2004/10/10/prescription-drugs-online/

Franklin, J., Paxson, V., Perrig, A., & Savage, S. (2007). An inquiry into the nature and cause of the wealth of internet miscreants. Paper presented at *CCS07*, October 29–November 2, in Alexandria, VA, 2007.

Frieder, L., & Zittrain, J. (2007). Spam works: Evidence from stock touts and corresponding market activity. Berkman Center Research Publication No. 2006–11; Harvard Public Law Working Paper No. 135; Oxford Legal Studies Research Paper No. 43/2006. [Online] Available at: http://ssrn.com/abstract=920553 or http://dx.doi.org/10.2139/ssrn.920553

Furnell, S. (2002). *Cybercrime: Vandalizing the Information Society*. Boston: Addison-Wesley.

Gregg, D. G., & Scott, J. E. (2006). The role of reputation systems in reducing on-line auction fraud. *International Journal of Electronic Commerce*, 10, 95–120.

Grow, B., Elgin, B., & Weintraub, A. (2006). Bitter pills: More and more people are buying prescription drugs from shady online marketers. That could be hazardous to their health. *BusinessWeek* [Online] Available at: www.businessweek.com/stories/2006-12-17/bitter-pills.

Hanke, M., & Hauser, F. (2006). On the effects of stock spam emails. *Journal of Financial Markets*, 11, 57–83.

Harrell, E., & Langton, L. (2013). *Victims of Identity Theft, 2012*. US Department of Justice Bulletin NCJ 243779. [Online] Available at: www.bjs.gov/content/pub/pdf/vit12.pdf

Herper, M. (2005). Bad medicine. *Forbes* [Online] Available at: www.forbes.com/forbes/2005/0523/202.html

Higgins, K. J. (2014). Target, Neiman Marcus Data Breaches Tip of the Iceberg. *Dark Reading*, January 13, 2014. [Online] Available at: www.darkreading.com/attacks-breaches/target-neiman-marcus-data-breaches-tip-o/240165363

Holt, T. J., & Graves, D. C. (2007). A qualitative analysis of advanced fee fraud schemes. *The International Journal of Cyber-Criminology*, 1, 137–154.

Holt, T. J., & Lampke, E. (2010). Exploring stolen data markets on-line: Products and market forces. *Criminal Justice Studies*, 23, 33–50.

Holt, T. J., & Schell, B. (2013). *Hackers and Hacking: A Reference Handbook*. New York: ABC-CLIO.

Honeynet Research Alliance. (2003). *Profile: Automated Credit Card Fraud*. Know Your Enemy paper series. Retrieved July 20, 2008, from http://old.honeynet.org/papers/profiles/cc-fraud.pdf

Immigration and Customs Enforcement. (2014). *Cyber Crimes Center*. [Online] Available at www.ice.gov/cyber-crimes/

Internet Crime Complaint Center. (2009). *IC3 2009 Internet Crime Report*. [Online] Available at: www.ic3.gov/media/annualreport/2009_IC3Report.pdf

James, L. (2005). *Phishing Exposed*. Rockland: Syngress.

King, A., & Thomas, J. (2009). You Can't Cheat an Honest Man: Making ($$$s and) Sense of the Nigerian Email Scams. In F. Schmalleger & M. Pittaro (eds) *Crime of the Internet* (pp. 206–224). Saddle River, NJ: Prentice Hall.

Kitchens, T. L. (1993). The cash flow analysis method: Following the paper trail in Ponzi schemes. *FBI Law Enforcement Bulletin*, August, 10–13.

Knutson, M. C. (1996). *The Remarkable Criminal Financial Career of Charles K. Ponzi*. [Online] Available at: www.mark-knutson.com/blog/wp-content/uploads/2014/06/ponzi.pdf

Krebs, B. (2011). Are Megabreaches Out? E-thefts Downsized in 2010. *Krebs on Security*. [Online] Available at: http://krebsonsecurity.com/2011/04/are-megabreaches-out-e-thefts-downsized-in-2010/

Ledbury Research. (2007). *Counterfeiting Luxury: Exposing the Myths*. 2nd ed. London: Davenport Lyons. [Online] Summary available at: www.wipo.int/ip-outreach/en/tools/research/details.jsp?id=583

LegitScript & KnujOn. (2009). *No prescription required: Bing.com prescription drug ads: A second look at how rogue Internet pharmacies are compromising the integrity of Microsoft's online advertising program*. Supplemental Report. LegitScript.com: Online Pharmacy Verification.

Maidment, N. (2013). UK shoppers to spend 1.4 billion pounds more this Christmas. *Reuters*. [Online] Available at http://uk.reuters.com/article/2013/11/25/uk-britain-retail-spend-idUKLNE9AO00720131125

Moore, R. (2010). *Cybercrime: Investigating High-Technology Computer Crime*, 2nd edition. London, Routledge.

Motoyama, M., McCoy, D., Levchenko, K., Savage, S., & Voelker, G. M. (2011). An analysis of underground forums. In Proceedings of the 2011 ACM SIGCOMM Internet Measurement Conference, 71–79.

National Conference of State Legislatures. (2012). *State Security Breach Notification Laws*. [Online] Available at www.ncsl.org/issues-research/telecom/security-breach-notification-laws.aspx

National Fraud Authority. (2013). *Annual Fraud Indicator June 2013*. [Online] Available at https://www.gov.uk/government/uploads/system/uploads/attachment_data/file/206552/nfa-annual-fraud-indicator-2013.pdf

National Fraud Authority. (2014). *What we do*. [Online] Available at: https://www.gov.uk/government/organisations/national-fraud-authority/about

National Fraud Intelligence Bureau. (2014). *How it works*. [Online] Available at: www.cityoflondon.police.uk/advice-and-support/fraud-and-economic-crime/nfib/Pages/how-it-works.aspx

Newman, G., and Clarke, R. (2003). *Superhighway Robbery: Preventing E-commerce Crime*. Cullompton: Willan Press.

OECD. (2008). *The Economic Impact of Counterfeiting and Piracy*. Organisation for Economic Co-operation and Development.

Paul, R. (2004). *Illegal Internet Pharmacies Pose Growing Threat.* Drug Topics: Advanstar Publication.

Phillips, T. (2005). *Knockoff: The Deadly Trade in Counterfeit Goods.* Sterling, VA: Kogan Page Ltd.

Roberts, P. F. (2007). Retailer TJX reports massive data breach: Credit, debit data stolen. Extent of breach still unknown. *InfoWorld.* [Online] Available at www.infoworld.com/d/security-central/retailer-tjx-reports-massive-data-breach-953

Smith, R. G., Holmes, M. N., & Kaufmann, P. (1999). *Trends and issues in crime and criminal justice No. 121: Nigerian Advance Fee Fraud.* Australian Institute of Criminology. [Online] Available at http://www.aic.gov.au/documents/D/C/4/%7BDC45B071-70BC-4EB1-B92D-4EEBE31F6D9E%7Dti121.pdf

Stevenson, R. J. (1998). *The Boiler Room and Other Telephone Scams.* Champagne: University of Illinois Press.

Stoppler, M. (2005). *Buying prescription drugs online – are the risks worth it?* Retrieved June 26, 2006, from www.medicinenet.com/

Sullivan, M. (2004). Online drug sales targeted. *PC World.*

Symantec Corporation. (2012). *Symantec Internet security threat report, Volume 17.* [Online] Available at: www.symantec.com/threatreport/

Taylor, R. W., Fritsch, E. J., Liederbach, J., and Holt, T. J. (2010). *Digital Crime and Digital Terrorism,* 2nd edition. Upper Saddle River, NJ: Pearson Prentice Hall.

Thomas, R., & Martin, J. (2006). The underground economy: Priceless. *:login,* 31, 7–16.

Tillman, R. H., & Indergaard, M. L. (2005). *Pump and Dump: The Rancid Rules of the New Economy.* Newark: Rutgers University Press.

Tinnin, A. (2005). Online pharmacies are new vehicle for raising some old legal issues. *Kansas City Missouri Daily Record.*

Turner, S., Copes, H., Kerley, K. R., and Warner, G. (2013). Understanding Online Work-At-Home Scams through an Analysis of Electronic Mail and Websites. In T. J. Holt (ed.) *Crime On-line: Causes, Correlates, and Context,* 2nd Edition (pp. 81–108). Raleigh, NC: Carolina Academic Press.

United States Attorney's Office. (2013). *Nine individuals indicted in one of the largest international penny stock frauds and advance fee schemes in history.* Federal Bureau of Investigation [Online] Available at: www.fbi.gov/newyork/press-releases/2013/nine-individuals-indicted-in-one-of-the-largest-international-penny-stock-frauds-and-advance-fee-schemes-in-history

United States Department of State. (1997). *Nigerian Advance Fee Fraud.* Bureau of International Narcotics and Law Enforcement Affairs.

United States General Accounting Office. (2004). *Internet pharmacies: Some pose safety risks for consumers.* General Accounting Office Report to the Chairman, Permanent Subcommittee on Investigations, Committee on Governmental Affairs, US Senate, Washington DC [Online] Available at: www.gao.gov/new.items/d04820.pdf

United States Secret Service. (2014). *Electronic Crimes Task Forces and Working Groups.* [Online] Available at www.secretservice.gov/ectf.shtml

Verini, J. (2010). The Great Cyberheist. *The New York Times* November 14, 2010. [Online] Available at: www.nytimes.com/2010/11/14/magazine/14Hacker-t.html?_r=1

Wall, D. (2004). Digital realism and the governance of spam as cybercrime. *European Journal on Criminal Policy and Research,* 10, 309–335.

Wall, D. S. (2001). Cybercrimes and the Internet. In D. S. Wall (ed.) *Crime and the Internet*, pp. 1–17. New York: Routledge.

Wall, D. S. (2007). *Cybercrime: The Transformation of Crime in the Information Age*. Cambridge: Polity Press.

Wall, D. S., & Large, J. (2010). Locating the public interest in policing counterfeit luxury fashion goods. *British Journal of Criminology*, 50, 1094–1116.

Wilson, M. (2011). Accenture survey: Discounters continue to dominate back-to-school shopping. *Chain Store Age*. Retrieved August 15, 2011, from www.chainstoreage.com/article/accenture-survey-discounters-continue-dominate-back-school-shopping

Wood, P. A. (2004). *Spammer in the works: Everything you need to know about protecting yourself and your business from the rising tide of unsolicited "spam" email*. A Message Labs White Paper, April. [Online] Available at: www.construct-it.org.uk/pages/sources/A%20spammer%20in%20the%20works.pdf>

chapter 6

Pornography, prostitution, and sex crimes

Chapter goals

- Understand the range of sexual expression and activity online
- Identify the evolution of pornography in tandem with technology
- Define the terms *child pornography* and *child exploitation*
- Understand the role of the Internet in prostitution
- Know the laws pertaining to obscenity, child pornography, and sex work
- Recognize the agencies responsible for the investigation of child pornography and obscenity around the world

Introduction

As technologies have improved over the last two decades, the ability for humans to connect in real time has increased dramatically. In the early days of the web, BBSs and chatrooms gave people the ability to talk via text, though this lost some of the context of facial and emotional expression, such as laughter or anger. As camera and video technology evolved, so did its use online through the introduction of Skype and other video-chat programs. In fact, most laptops, tablets, and mobile phones have cameras installed to ensure that we can share our experiences in visual and audio formats.

As a result, an increasingly large number of people are using these technologies to enhance their romantic relationships or flirt with others, though this was not perhaps the intention of the developers. People can send photos or videos of themselves in provocative outfits or engage in sexually suggestive activities with great ease through text messaging. This activity, colloquially called **sexting**, has become popular as it is perceived as a way to attract or stimulate a prospective partner with a degree of security since it is directed toward only one recipient, rather than routed through an email client, which might make the content visible to others (Mitchell, Finkelhor, Jones, and Wolak, 2012). Estimates of the prevalence of sexting vary, though a recent nationally representative sample of youth between the ages of 10 and 17 found that only 2.5 percent sent pictures of themselves in a nude or nearly nude state to others, 7.1 percent had received nude or nearly nude images of others, and 5.9 percent reported receiving images of sexual activity (Mitchell *et al.*, 2012).

Regardless of the proportion of people who engage in sexting, it is important to note that the instant the photo or video is sent, it is no longer something that the sender can control. A recipient can easily circulate the content to others or repost the image on a social media site, like Facebook, to embarrass the sender (Mitchell *et al.*, 2012). Worse still, a number of websites have emerged specifically for individuals to post sexual images and videos they received or acquired for others to see. These sites are often referred to as **revenge porn**, as people often post content they received from an intimate partner after a relationship sours, or by hacking someone's phone or email account in order to acquire pictures and embarrass the sender (Halloran, 2014). This sort of site has become popular. For instance, the website IsAnyoneUp.com, which was subtitled "Pure Evil," was created by Hunter Moore in 2010 (Dodero, 2012). He began to post pictures of a woman who continuously sent him sexual images on a blog space and provided a link for others to submit photos to be posted. As content began to roll in – some from hackers, some from ex-girlfriends and boyfriends, and some from individuals just interested in seeing themselves online – Moore would link the photos to the Facebook or Twitter page of the individual featured (Dodero, 2012). The site became quite popular, though it drew substantial criticism from individuals who were unwittingly featured on the site (see Text Box 6.1 for details). As a result, Moore sold the site to an anti-bullying group in 2012, arguing that he was no longer able to support the site due to its expenses and the difficulties of reporting the submitted images of child pornography to law enforcement.

Text Box 6.1: Story regarding revenge porn

www.forbes.com/sites/kashmirhill/2011/07/06/revenge-porn-with-a-facebook-twist/
   Revenge Porn With A Facebook Twist

Many of the photos that wind up on the site are "revenge porn" – pornographic souvenirs from relationships gone sour. While lots of the photos come from angry ex-boyfriends and ex-girlfriends, some come from exhibitionists as well, says site founder Hunter Moore ...

This article provides a discussion of the issue of "revenge porn," or sexual images initially provided by individuals to others with whom they were romantically linked, which eventually wind up online because of the fallout from a failed relationship, or other incident. The problem of revenge porn is complex and one that has no real legal or legislative solution at this time.

There are still a number of revenge porn sites operating online. Scholars and the public have struggled with the moral and legal implications of the content of such websites. On one side, individuals argue that if a person creates the content herself or himself (but normally herself) and sends it to others, s/he loses ownership of those images and possibly deserves to have those images posted anywhere. Others argue that it is a violation of trust and that the lack of consent from the person who took the image should keep the content from being posted elsewhere. In fact, individuals have a right to sue a person for posting images without consent. A number of criminal cases are being brought against site creators in the US and other countries. For instance, Hunter Moore was indicted in January 2014 in federal court on 15 counts of violations of the Computer Fraud and Abuse Act on the premise that photos were acquired through the use of hacking techniques and identity theft (Liebelson, 2014).

For more on legislative initiatives to combat revenge porn in the US, go online to: www.slate.com/articles/double_x/doublex/2013/09/revenge_porn_legislation_a_new_bill_in_california_doesn_t_go_far_enough.single.html

Sexting and revenge porn are just more recent examples of the way in which technology has been used to produce and disseminate sexually explicit content. Technological innovation and sexuality have in fact been intertwined since the first human attempted to paint on cave walls (Lane, 2000). This relationship has been brought to the forefront as we now utilize devices that can record and transmit any and all of our activities to others. As a result, this chapter will consider the ways that humans use technology to engage in various forms of sexual expression, ranging from legally produced pornographic images and video to the illegal and socially condemned practice of child pornography and exploitation. We will also consider the impact of technology on paid sexual encounters, or prostitution, which has been in existence since the emergence of society. Finally, we will consider the

pornography, prostitution, and sex crimes

complex legal structures used to define obscenity, pornography, and child pornography, as well as the wide range of well-connected agencies that investigate these offenses.

The spectrum of sexuality online

Computer-mediated communications allow individuals to easily engage in sexually explicit discussions, view pornography (Lane, 2000), and participate in more serious acts, including creating, disseminating, downloading, and/or viewing pedophilia and child pornography (Durkin and Bryant, 1999; Quayle and Taylor, 2002). In addition, the Internet has engendered the formation of deviant subcultures that were otherwise unlikely or limited in the real world (see Quinn and Forsyth, 2005). Individuals can connect with others who share their interests to find social support and information sharing. Virtual environments provide an opportunity for deviants to connect and communicate without fear of reprisal or scorn, though their actions may often take place in the real world (Quinn and Forsyth, 2005).

As a result, the Internet now provides resources that cater to all individuals, regardless of sexual orientation or preferences. Additionally, these services can be arrayed along a spectrum from legal but deviant to highly illegal depending on the nature of the content and the laws of a given country (Quinn and Forsyth, 2005). For example, there are a number of service providers offering completely legal resources to connect individuals together, such as dating services like Match.com and plentyoffish.com. These sites allow individuals to make personal profiles noting their likes and dislikes, connect with others who share their interests, and potentially meet offline for a date or build a long-term relationship. Similar services, however, also exist that are designed to facilitate short-term sexual encounters, including extramarital affairs, based on personal profiles that connect interested parties together. Websites like AshleyMadison.com have become extremely popular, despite the fact that they encourage casual sex between people who are otherwise engaged in monogamous relationships (Bort, 2013).

In addition to content designed to facilitate relationships, there is also a great deal of **pornography**, defined broadly as the representation of sexual situations and content for the purposes of sexual arousal and stimulation (Lane, 2000), available online. These erotic writings, photos, video, and audio content, which are easily accessible, are largely legal, but may be viewed as deviant depending on the social norms and values within a community (Brenner, 2011). In the US and most Western nations, pornographic content is legal so long as the participants (or those depicted in the work) are over the age of 18 and the consumer is of legal age. Some content, such as sex between animals and humans, forcible rape or physical harm, and images featuring children and minors, are illegal (Quinn and Forsyth, 2013).

The lack of boundaries in online spaces, however, makes it hard to completely regulate or restrict individuals' access to this content.

> **For more on the legal status of pornography, go online to:** http://en.wikipedia.org/wiki/Pornography_by_region

The availability of pornography and erotica has enabled individuals to find content that appeals to any interest, no matter how unusual. In fact, there is now a wide range of online content providers that cater to specific **sexual fetishes**, where individuals experience sexual arousal or enhancement of a romantic encounter based on the integration of physical objects or certain situations (Quinn and Forsyth, 2013). Fetishes can include anything from wearing high heels or a certain type of clothing (e.g. nursing or police officer uniforms), to more extreme acts, including sex with animals (**bestiality**) or the dead (**necrophilia**). The range of subjects that are now featured in pornographic content online has led to the concept of "**Rule 34,**" which essentially states that "if it exists, there is pornographic content of it" (Olson, 2012).

The Internet also facilitates paid sexual services of all kinds which operate at varying degrees of legality. The development of high-speed Internet connectivity and live-streaming video feeds allow male and female performers to engage in sex shows on demand where they are paid for their time (Roberts and Hunt, 2012). Sites like LiveJasmin provide access to **cam whores,** or performers who engage in text-based conversations with individuals viewing them on streaming-video feeds and take requests for specific behaviors or sexual acts. In turn, the performer can be taken into a private session where the viewer pays by the minute to interact with and direct the performer to engage in various activities (Roberts and Hunt, 2012). Though these exchanges do not involve actual physical contact between the provider and client, making the encounters completely acceptable from a legal standpoint, the acceptance of payment makes this a form of sex work.

> **For more on sex work, go online to:** http://rabble.ca/books/reviews/2014/05/working-it-sex-work-labour

Technology also facilitates traditional prostitution in the real world, where individuals pay for sexual encounters with another person. For instance, clients of sex workers use forums and other CMCs to discuss the sexual services available in a location and the acts that sex workers will engage in (Holt and Blevins, 2007; Milrod and Monto, 2012; Weitzer, 2005). Sex workers use websites, blogs, and email in order to arrange meetings with

pornography, prostitution, and sex crimes

clients and vet them before they meet in the real world (Cunningham and Kendall, 2010). Though these communications are not illegal, laws pertaining to the act of prostitution vary from country to country (Weitzer, 2012). Some nations, such as the US, Russia, and China, have criminalized both the sale of and solicitation of sex. Other nations including Sweden and Norway have made it illegal to pay for sex as a client, though sex workers can legally engage in prostitution. Still other nations have legalized prostitution entirely, such as the UK and Canada, though they may have laws against certain activities such as soliciting sex in public places (Weitzer, 2012). For those nations that have criminalized both the solicitation and sale of sex, technology is making it easier for both clients and providers to reduce their risk of detection and arrest.

Throughout this chapter we will consider the range of sexual activities that are facilitated by technology using examples of each behavior, though this will not be an exhaustive description of all sexual services or preferences.

Pornography in the Digital Age

Prior to the Internet and consumer access to digital media, the production of sexual materials was primarily limited to professional production studios and artists. Amateurs were able to write their own erotic fiction and paint or sculpt images, though they may vary in quality.

The development of audio and visual recording equipment in the nineteenth century revolutionized the creation of sexual images. No longer were individuals limited to line drawings or other artistic representations of sexual images; instead, the human body could be represented as it was in real life (Yar, 2013). The first photographs featuring nudes were popularized by Louis Daguerre of France as a means to support the training of painters and other artists. Due to the process of photography at this time, it took between 3 and 15 minutes for an image to be captured, making it virtually impossible to present individuals engaged in actual sex acts (Lane, 2000). As photographic processing evolved in the 1840s and 50s, the cost of creating images decreased, allowing nudes and erotic photos to be sold at a cost the middle class could easily afford. Images of nudes were also printed on postcard stock and sent through the mail to others, becoming colloquially known as "French postcards" (Lane, 2000).

The development of motion picture films in Europe in 1895 were followed almost immediately by the creation of the first erotic films (Lane, 2000). In 1896, the film *Le Coucher de la Marie* was made by Eugene Pirou and showed a woman engaging in a striptease. Shortly thereafter, European and South American filmmakers produced films featuring actual sex between couples, such as *A L'Ecu d'Or ou la Bonne Auberge* from 1908 and *Am Abend* from 1910.

Producing erotic images or pornographic films during this period was extremely risky, as social mores regarding sex were very different from those of today. Until the Victorian era of the mid 1800s, there were few laws regarding possession or ownership of sexual images and objects. In fact, the world's first laws criminalizing pornographic content were created in the UK through the **Obscene Publications Act of 1857** (Yar, 2013). This act made it illegal to sell, possess, or publish obscene material, which was not clearly defined in the law. Law enforcement could also search, seize, and destroy any content found, which were tremendous extensions of police powers at the time (Lane, 2000). Shortly thereafter, similar legal structures began to emerge throughout Europe and the Americas in order to help minimize the perceived corrupting influence of such content on the masses.

As a way to skirt these laws, pornography producers began to market their materials as either art materials or celebrations of health or nature, such as nudist lifestyles. Gentlemen's magazines also included images and drawings of nudes. The development of *Playboy* magazine in the 1950s epitomized the attempt to combine tasteful nudity coupled with traditional content regarding fashion, fiction, and news stories (Lane, 2000). These works pushed conventional attitudes toward perceived obscene content in mass media, while underground publishers were producing images of sexual intercourse and fetish materials that were sold through direct mail and in less reputable stores (Lane, 2000). These materials often drew the attention of law enforcement, though social standards began to soften in the late 1960s and 70s toward erotica and pornography. As a result, magazines and films became more prevalent and could be purchased at news stands and some retailers, leading to a range of publications from *Hustler* to *Penthouse* (Lane, 2000).

Social attitudes toward obscene content evolved concurrently with technological innovations that became available to consumers in the 1970s through 1990s. In the 1970s, the development of the Polaroid instant camera and relatively affordable home video recording equipment made it easier for individuals to create their own pornographic media in the privacy of their own homes (Lane, 2000). The creation of the **video cassette** during the 1970s was also revolutionary, as consumers could record content using inexpensive recording cameras that put images onto blank tapes rather than film stock. Thus, individuals could film their own sexual experiences, and could then watch them using **video cassette recorders** (**VCRs**) in their own homes on demand. These affordable devices revolutionized the production of pornography, so much so that the pornographic film industry began to record using VHS tapes rather than actual film stock. As a result, the industry exploded and became extremely profitable due to low costs and high volume sales and rentals. Similarly, amateur content became increasingly possible as consumers owned the equipment needed to make their own sex tapes at home.

As technology continued to improve in the late 1990s with the expansion of the World Wide Web, individuals began to experiment with how they could use computers and media to create sexual images in their own homes without the need for major distribution through existing publishers (Yar, 2013). Digital cameras, web cams, and high-speed Internet connectivity

pornography, prostitution, and sex crimes

allowed individuals to develop materials to sell directly to interested parties, regardless of whether they worked with existing porn producers or on their own out of their own homes. One of the prime examples of such a story is that of Sandra and Kevin Otterson, or **Wifey and Hubby,** who have operated their own pornographic website selling content that they produce since 1998 (Cromer, 1998). The couple had no prior involvement in the porn or sex industry but were simply interested in sharing images of themselves. Kevin first posted scanned images of Polaroid pictures of his spouse on a Usenet group in 1997 and received extremely positive feedback from others (Cromer, 1998). They continued to post pictures and eventually started to sell the materials through direct mailing. Their website first came online in January 1998 and had a monthly fee of $9.95 in order to access pictures, videos, and additional content that could be purchased through the real world. At the time, the couple estimated that they had made a few hundred thousand dollars from the sale of their content (Cromer, 1998).

The popularity of the web and computer technology led to a massive explosion of adult content online. In fact, there were some questions as to the impact that immediate access to porn could have on society as a whole. A study which exacerbated this issue was published by an undergraduate student named Martin Rimm at Carnegie Mellon University in 1995, and attempted to document the scope of pornography online at the time (Godwin, 2003). His study, commonly referenced as the **Carnegie Mellon Report,** suggested that over 80 percent of images on the Internet involved sexually explicit content, which led to tremendous coverage in major news outlets, like *Time* magazine and *Nightline,* about the threat of cyberporn (Godwin, 2003). Policy-makers began to call for restrictions on pornographic content on the Internet, creating a small moral panic over how youth may be corrupted by the ability to see porn online. Shortly after this firestorm began, academics began to review the methods employed in his work and discredited its findings based on limited methods and questionable ethics (Godwin, 2003). Regardless, Rimm's work has had long-standing impact on the perceived availability of porn on the Internet and affected legislation to deal with obscene content.

> **For more on the fallout from the Carnegie Mellon Report, go online to:**
> www.columbia.edu/cu/21stC/issue-1.2/Cyber.htm

Even now, the evolution of applications, high-quality digital cameras in mobile phones and tablets, and online outlets are affecting the production of porn. For instance, it is believed that at least 11 percent of the blogs on the popular social media outlet Tumblr, which allows individuals to post pictures with brief notes, feature pornographic or erotic content (Perez, 2013). Additionally, the phenomenon of sexting is leading to changes in the ways that individuals create and share prospectively pornographic content (Mitchell *et al.*, 2012). New programs are also being developed for wearable technologies, like Google Glass, to record and share sexual acts that wearers engage in with others (Thomas, 2014). As a result, the landscape of porn will continue to evolve in tandem with our use of popular technologies.

Identifying child pornography and exploitation

The production of pornography featuring consenting adults has created controversy around the ease of access to lewd or obscene content. This discussion pales in comparison to the social panic surrounding the availability and distribution of pornographic content featuring children via the Web (Lynch, 2002; Quinn, Forsyth, and Mullen-Quinn, 2004). **Child pornography** is defined as the depicting of "the sexual or sexualized physical abuse of children under 16 years of age or who appear to be less than 16 that would offend a reasonable adult" (Krone, 2004: 1). While child pornography existed well before the creation of the Internet, it can safely be assumed that the Internet has not only fueled the demand for such product, but that it has also created an environment for a subculture that accepts and encourages the continuing production and trading of such material (Edwards, 2000; Holt, Blevins, and Burkert, 2010; Krone, 2004; Quayle and Taylor, 2002). More than 100,000 websites of pornographic nature offer illegal child pornography, which has generated nearly $3 billion annually (Bissette, 2004; Pittaro, 2008). An astounding 20,000 images of child pornography are posted on the Internet each week; this number is growing at a distressing rate (Pittaro, 2008; Rice-Hughes, 2005). In addition, it appears that child pornography is a worldwide problem that allows individuals in multiple nations to acquire content from anywhere (see Text Box 6.2 for details).

Text Box 6.2: Detail on Operation Delego

www.justice.gov/opa/pr/2011/August/11-ag-1001.html

> Attorney General Eric Holder ... announced today the unsealing of three indictments and one complaint charging a total of 72 individuals ... in an international criminal network dedicated to the sexual abuse of children and the creation and dissemination of graphic images and videos of child sexual abuse throughout the world.

This press release details a massive investigation of an international child pornography distribution network operating online. The scope of this group and the harm they caused is tremendous and demonstrates the need for law enforcement interventions of child exploitation crimes.

---

pornography, prostitution, and sex crimes

Computers are the preferred medium for those individuals who are sexually interested in children by allowing them almost complete anonymity without fear of social stigma or legal ramifications (Alexy, Burgess, and Baker, 2005; Durkin, 1997; Durkin and Hundersmarck, 2007; Holt *et al.*, 2010; Rosenmann and Safir, 2006). These deviant subcultures take part in a variety of computer crimes involving children, ranging from using the Internet as a way to reach out and develop emotional and sexual relationships with children (Jenkins, 2001), to the distribution, trading, and production of child pornography (Durkin, 1997; Jenkins, 2001; Quayle and Taylor, 2002; Taylor, Quayle, and Holland, 2001).

A number of researchers have developed typologies to classify individuals on the basis of their use of child pornography (Alexy *et al.*, 2005; Durkin, 1997; Quayle and Taylor, 2002; Rogers and Seigfried-Spellar, 2013; Taylor and Quayle, 2003). The general finding is that the viewing and collecting of such material can possibly lead to more serious offenses. Durkin (1997: 16) described a typology involving four ways in which those who have sexual attraction to children misuse the Internet: (1) trafficking child pornography (**traders**); (2) communicating and sharing ideas with like-minded persons (**networking**); (3) engaging in inappropriate communication with children (**grooming**); and (4) attempting to find children to molest (**travelers**). It is possible that an individual may start with just viewing or trading pornographic images, but these images may ignite further curiosity. That individual may move on to grooming a child over the Internet and eventually meeting the child in real life with the intent to molest. Alexy *et al.* (2005) also found a similar typology with their study, classifying their subjects as traders (59.1 percent), travelers (21.8 percent), or a combination of the two (19 percent). Again, individuals may begin just being traders but could progress to being a traveler or even a combination trader/traveler.

The development of these typologies is important when looking at the subculture of pedophiles and users of online support forums. While not every admitted pedophile may engage in child pornography, it can be assumed that at some point they will come across the material while engaging in this type of deviant behavior. The extent to which viewing child pornography can lead to more serious offenses is still relatively unknown, but there is evidence that viewing child pornography can facilitate an interest in engaging in physical sexual encounters with youth (Federal Bureau of Investigation, 2002; Klain, Davies and Hicks, 2001; Perrien, Hernandez, Gallop and Steinour, 2000; Quayle and Taylor, 2002; Seto, Cantor and Blanchard, 2006; Seto and Eke, 2005). The creation of child pornography is also dependent on individuals victimizing youth in the real world and then sharing those images with others, perpetuating abuse over time.

> **For more information on pedophiles' use of the Internet, go online to:**
> www.taasa.org/library/pdfs/TAASALibrary107.pdf

Individuals interested in relationships with children may be classified as **pedophiles** based on diagnostic criteria established by the American Psychological Association. In the *Diagnostic and Statistical Manual* (DSM, the handbook of diagnoses), pedophilia is diagnosed using the following criteria:

(A) Over a period of at least 6 months, recurrent, intense sexual arousing fantasies, sexual urges, or behaviors involving sexual activity with a pre-pubescent child or children (generally age 13 years or younger);
(B) The fantasies, sexual urges, or behaviors cause clinically significant distress or impairment in social, occupational or other important areas of functioning; and
(C) The person is at least age 16 years and at least five years older than the child or children in Criterion A. (American Psychiatric Association, 2000).

The individual must demonstrate all three criteria in order to be diagnosed as a pedophile in clinical settings. The DSM-IV also subdivides the pedophilia diagnosis into more specific categories: sexually attracted to males, females, or both sexes, exclusive (attracted only to children) or non-exclusive (attracted to both adults and children), or limited to incest (American Psychiatric Association, 2000; O'Donohue, Regev, and Hagstrom, 2000). Marshall (1997) and O'Donohue *et al.* (2000) found the diagnosis of pedophilia is often ignored by both practitioners and researchers but is, instead, replaced with a construct of child molester. This proves problematic when looking at diagnosing individuals who claim to have no desire to sexually molest children. The diagnostic criterion does not explicitly state actual contact with a child must occur for an individual to be labeled a pedophile, only "recurrent, intense sexually arousing fantasies, sexual urges or behaviors" (p. 96). Therefore, under the current DSM-IV definition, those who publicly share and express such fantasies, urges, and behaviors in these online support forums have the potential for being diagnosed as pedophiles.

Explorations of the pedophile subculture online

Individuals who engage in either sexual activities with or fantasize about children are considered to be among the most hated deviants in society (Durkin, 1997; Durkin and Bryant, 1999; Holt *et al.*, 2010; Jenkins, 2001; Rosenmann and Safir, 2006). Adults who show a strong sexual interest toward children are, therefore, stigmatized by society and retreat to the virtual world to express their true feelings since the Internet can offer almost complete anonymity. Those who share these taboo sexual feelings come together to form what is known as the "pedophile subculture" (Jenkins, 2001; Pittaro, 2008). It is here where members of the subculture feel they are part of a group that accepts them for their sexual orientation. In fact, they can gain validation for their sexual beliefs.

In his 2001 book *Beyond Tolerance: Child Pornography On the Internet*, Philip Jenkins examined a BBS where individuals exchanged images of child pornography and found a subculture where individuals shared beliefs about the value of child porn and the need to exchange these materials, and socialized individuals into this activity. Jenkins (2001) wrote, "Joining the subculture marks less an entry into new activities and interest than an escalation of pre-existing behaviors, supported by a new sense of community" (p. 106). It is unlikely that these individuals happened upon these discussion boards by accident. These are individuals seeking acceptance; the anonymous nature of the Internet offers this. Users expressed fears of being detected by law enforcement, political reviews, and even a shared language (Jenkins, 2001). Jenkins observed, "one is likely to acquire gradually the peculiar language, mores, and thought patterns of this world and thus be inducted subtly into the subculture" (p. 108). In order to keep up with the language and the rapid change of discussion, users must visit and participate regularly if they hope to benefit from participation in this subculture.

Support, justification, and/or rationalization are also common among pedophile subcultures (Durkin and Bryant, 1999; Holt *et al.*, 2010; Jenkins, 2001; Mayer, 1985). Mayer (1985) wrote, "One striking characteristic of the pedophile is the ability to minimize or rationalize his activities" (p. 21). Most individuals belonging to such subcultures see nothing wrong with relationships between adults and children; in fact, they see many positive benefits from these interactions, such as being a positive role model in a child's life (Jenkins, 2001). They often do not associate themselves with pedophiles or child molesters and even condemn these individuals themselves. These individuals justify this type of sexual orientation by using the term "**child love**" to describe what they perceive to be a perfectly normal relationship between adult and child, which does not always have to involve sexual activity (Holt *et al.*, 2010; Jenkins, 2001). Pedophiles will also use neutralization strategies in attempts to normalize their type of deviance. For example, they may attempt to deny whether a "victim" existed ("denial of the victim") by rationalizing that the children were asking for or wanted sex. They may also use a technique called "denial of injury," saying sexual encounters can be rewarding and even educational for children (Jenkins, 2001). Some groups have even gone so far as to compare themselves to the Jewish population being hunted down by the Nazis in Germany; they believe that sexual attraction to children is much more widespread than society cares to accept, and by persecuting them, society is preaching hypocrisy (Jenkins, 2001).

The idea that "child love" is different from being a pedophile in the eyes of these individuals is a topic that has more recently been examined by researchers (Holt *et al.*, 2010; Jenkins, 2001). Many members of the child pornography discussion boards examined by Jenkins (2001) did not see themselves as pedophiles. In one thread, a user identified as "Humbert Humbert" wrote, "Am not a pedo, just like the beauty of pre-pubescent/ adolescent girls. Therefore, I don't think I am a perv. Just rational minded" (p. 119). They believe that those who actually abuse children represent just a small minority of their community and that most users are just looking, not acting (Jenkins, 2001).

It is hard to determine which members of these communities are or have actually been physically (sexually) involved with children, since the majority of users are intelligent enough to know not to reveal any illegal behavior that may have occurred for fear of legal ramifications (Jenkins, 2001). However, the concept of sharing fantasies, urges, and non-sexual interactions with children is seen in most of the pedophile online communities (Holt *et al.*, 2010; Jenkins, 2001). While most research and investigations have focused on targeting those who possess/trade child pornography and/ or child molesters, few have considered the members of the online pedophile subculture, who do not consider themselves pedophiles or child molesters but "child lovers" (Holt *et al.*, 2010).

Prostitution and sex work

Though public outrage has centered around pedophiles and child pornography, there has been much less consideration given to the influence of technology on what is arguably the world's oldest trade – **prostitution**. The practice of paying for sex can be viewed as a sort of labor market where there is both a demand from clients or those who pay for the encounter and those suppliers who are paid for their services.

There is a range of providers currently engaged in the sale of sexual services, with prostitutes who work soliciting individuals on the street comprising the lowest rung of sex work (Lucas, 2005). Though studies estimate **street prostitutes** compose 10 to 20 percent of all sex workers, they are often racial minorities who receive very low wages and face significantly higher rates of arrest (Alexander, 1998; Cooper, 1989; Hampton, 1988; Levitt and Venkatesh, 2007; Rhode, 1989; West, 1998). The larger proportion of sex workers operates behind closed doors in homes, apartments, and businesses (such as **massage parlors** and strip clubs), where the risk of arrest is substantially lower. Finally, **escorts** and high-end call girls comprise the highest echelon of sex workers and are thought to make much higher wages than any other sex workers (Lucas, 2005; Moffatt, 2005; Weitzer, 2000, 2005).

Paid sexual encounters were traditionally driven by discrete face-to-face exchanges on the street or behind closed doors in the real world. The emergence of the Internet and CMCs has revolutionized the practice by enabling providers and clients to connect on a one-to-one basis at any time. For instance, individuals can text or email sex workers to determine their availability and set up meetings. In fact, many escorts now operate their own websites and blogs and advertise in various outlets online to attract customers.

For more on the role of the Internet in prostitution and human traffick-ing, go online to: http://kfor.com/2013/05/02/alleged-prostitution-ring-may-involve-human-trafficking/

Similarly, the customers of sex workers now use the web in order to com-municate with others in order to gain insights into the resources available in their area and review the services of various providers (Blevins and Holt, 2009; Cunningham and Kendall, 2010; Holt and Blevins, 2007; Hughes, 2003; O'Neill, 2001; Raymond and Hughes, 2001; Sharp and Earle, 2003; Soothill and Sanders, 2005). These exchanges often occur in web forums and review websites and focus on the customer experience, including detailed discussions of the services offered by all manner of sex workers, as well as the attitude and behavior of prostitutes before, during, and after sex acts (Cunningham and Kendall, 2010; Holt and Blevins, 2007; Sharp and Earle, 2003; Soothill and Sanders, 2005). There are now numerous websites where individuals can post reviews of their experiences with sex workers, with names like **BigDoggie** and **Punternet** (see Text Box 6.3 for details). In add-ition, these websites provide specific detail on the negotiation process with sex workers, final costs for various sex acts, and the use of condoms during encounters (Cunningham and Kendall, 2010; Holt and Blevins, 2007; Sharp and Earle, 2003; Soothill and Sanders, 2005).

Text Box 6.3: The role of escort review sites

Escort-review Web sites thrive after failed sting, but women remain wary

www.nbcnews.com/id/10896432/ns/us_news/t/several-comfortable-steps-ahead-law/

> The Hillsborough vice unit pioneered the technique of register-ing with escort sites and posting bogus profiles when it launched Operation Flea Collar in 2002, targeting Big Doggie, which is in its back yard. Vice officers started their own fake Web page in order to join Big Doggie ...

This article provides a unique exposé on the ways that local law enforce-ment in the US use escort-review websites as a means to investigate prostitution and sex crimes generally.

The volume of information available online provides substantive detail on the largely hidden processes of the negotiations between clients and sex workers operating in the streets, as well as behind closed doors (Holt, Blevins, and Kuhns, 2013). Additionally, these posts give the client's point of view, which is often under-examined but critical, since their demand for sexual services affects the supply available. Prospective clients of sex workers who access these forums can use the information posted to evade high-risk areas while identifying and acquiring the sexual services they desire. This may decrease the success of law enforcement efforts in those nations where prostitution is illegal and, simultaneously, increase the knowledge of prospective customers to negotiate with workers across various environments (Holt *et al.*, 2013; Scott and Dedel, 2006).

The clients of sex workers

The emergence of online communities that enable information sharing among the clients of sex workers has changed the process of soliciting sex workers. The development of online communities allowed individuals to discuss their preferences and experiences with no fear of rejection or embarrassment. In fact, research by Blevins and Holt (2009) found that there is now a subculture of clients in the US operating in a series of web forums that is guided by their preferences and interests. This subculture places significant value on the notion that paid sexual encounters are normal and non-deviant. In fact, those who visited sex workers placed significant value on their experiences and knowledge of the sex trade. As a result, they would not refer to themselves as "**johns**" or "**tricks**," as they are known in popular culture (Scott and Dedel, 2006). Instead, forum users avoided such derogatory terms in favor of terms like monger or hobbyist to recognize that they are interested in paid sexual encounters and enjoy the experience. Individuals who posted great detail about their experiences with sex workers were often viewed as senior members. As a result, those who were unfamiliar with the sex trade can ask for assistance from more senior or experienced members in the forum to gain information.

Additionally, the customers of prostitutes viewed sex and sex workers as a **commodity**, in that encounters cannot occur without payment. Thus, johns regularly referred to sex workers on the basis of where they worked, whether in streets, strip clubs, or advertised online using abbreviations such as **streetwalker** or **SW** to indicate the worker is a street-walking prostitute. Similarly, forum users would include terms to describe the build and appearance of sex workers that objectify them in some fashion. In particular, forum users typically discussed the **mileage** of a sex worker, referring to their appearance and how it had degraded over time in the sex trade. The notion of mileage is most often used in reference to cars, motorcycles, and vehicles, suggesting that customers of sex workers view the providers, first and foremost, as a commodity rather than a person. In addition, the participants in prostitution forums focused heavily on the costs associated with various sexual acts and the negotiation process between the client and provider.

Finally, the subculture of client-centered prostitution forums focuses on sexuality and the way that sex is experienced. Many of the posts in these forums were dedicated to depicting the types of sex acts and services that certain prostitutes would provide in very graphic detail. The users commonly discussed the acts that providers would offer and whether or not they used condoms. There was also some discussion of the quality of the experience, as prostitutes who could make the experience feel like a consensual relationship with no money involved were said to provide **girlfriend experience**, or **GFE** (Blevins and Holt, 2009; Milrod and Monto, 2012; Sharp and Earle 2003; Soothill and Sanders, 2005). Since there was no way to guarantee that the experience of one user would be consistent with others, some would use the term **your mileage may vary** (**YMMV**) in reference to the variation in encounters.

Dealing with obscenity and pornography online

Existing legislation

The way that obscenity is defined varies by place and is heavily dependent on prevailing social standards. In the US, legal definitions of **obscenity** have evolved over time through cases reviewed by the Supreme Court. In fact, the case of **Miller v. California** in 1973 established the definition of obscene content that is still in use today (US Department of Justice, 2014). A work can be deemed obscene, and therefore not protected by the First Amendment right to free speech, if it meets one of these three criteria:

1) an average person who is capable of applying contemporary adult community standards finds that material appeals to prurient interests, defined as "an erotic, lascivious, abnormal, unhealthy, degrading, shameful, or morbid interest in nudity, sex, or excretion";
2) an average person applying contemporary adult community standards determines that a work depicts or describes sexual conduct in a patently offensive way, defined as "ultimate sexual acts, normal or perverted, actual or simulated, masturbation, excretory functions, lewd exhibition of the genitals, or sado-masochistic sexual abuse"; and
3) lacks serious literary, artistic, political, or scientific value (US Department of Justice, 2014).

This decision provides each community and state with the flexibility necessary to define what constitutes indecent or obscene materials (Tuman, 2003). In addition, it identified that there are differences between minors and adults, which require youth to be protected from obscene content. Because the government has the responsibility to protect youth from harmful or obscene content, the standard for what constitutes obscenity for minors is lower than that for adults. The three-pronged Miller standard still applies, though in the context of standards for "minors," harmful materials constitute "any communication consisting of nudity, sex, or excretion" (US Department of Justice, 2014).

A number of federal statutes are present concerning obscene content. Under Title 18 U.S.C. 1460–1470, it is a crime to:

1) possess obscene material with the intent to distribute those materials on Federal property,
2) import or transport obscene materials across borders,
3) distribute or receive obscene material through a common carrier in interstate commerce, including postal mail, private carriers, or computer and Internet based services,
4) broadcast obscene, profane, or indecent language via television, radio, or cable and subscription television services,
5) knowingly produce, transport or engage in the sale of obscene, lewd, or filthy material through interstate commerce, and
6) transfer obscene materials to minors.

The punishments for these offenses vary based on the severity of the offense (US Department of Justice, 2014). Possession with intent to distribute obscene materials on federal property and broadcasting obscene content can lead to a fine and/or a two-year prison sentence. All other offenses, with the exception of transferring obscene content to minors, can be punishable by a five-year prison sentence, a fine, or both. Individuals who are found guilty of transferring obscene content to minors can receive a prison sentence of up to ten years and/or a fine (US Department of Justice, 2014).

In addition, the US criminalized the use of misleading domain names in order to draw Internet users to websites hosting sexually explicit or obscene content under the **Truth in Domain Names Act of 2003** (Brenner, 2011). One of the first individuals arrested under this law operated a range of websites using domain names that were misspelled versions of popular artists and intellectual property for kids. For instance, his site www.dinseyland. com featured hardcore pornography, and was a direct misspelling of the legitimate website www.disneyland.com (CNN, 2003). The operator of the site can be imprisoned for up to two years (or up to four if the domain name was selected to intentionally attract minors to the site) and may be fined up to $250,000.

To demonstrate the variation in what is defined as obscene, the **Obscene Publications Act (OPA) 1959** for England and Wales indicates any article may be obscene if its effect on the audience member who reads, views, or hears it is to "deprave and corrupt" (Crown Prosecution Service, 2014). The

pornography, prostitution, and sex crimes

decision regarding what is obscene is to be determined by a jury without the assistance of an expert, which to a certain degree mirrors the US concept of community standards in establishing obscenity (Crown Prosecution Service, 2014). The law does specify that most depictions of sexual intercourse or fetish activities that are consensual are unsuitable for consideration as obscene, though more serious depictions of rape, torture, bondage, degrading sexual acts such as the consumption of excretion, and sex with animals are appropriate for prosecution (Crown Prosecution Service, 2014). This includes video, audio, and photographic images in physical print, such as magazines and DVDs, as well as content distributed over the Internet.

Individuals who publish or sell obscene articles for economic gain and are found guilty of violating this act can be fined and imprisoned for between three and five years, as a result of a recent enhancement of sentences through the **Criminal Justice and Immigration Act 2008** (Crown Prosecution Service, 2014). This act also criminalized the possession of **extreme pornography**, defined as materials produced for the purpose of sexual arousal which depict acts that "threaten a person's life; acts which result in or are likely to result in serious injury to a person's anus, breasts or genitals; bestiality; or necrophilia" (Crown Prosecution Service, 2014). For instance, acts involving the insertion of sharp instruments (such as blades or needles) mutilation and cutting, choking, or serious blows to the head or body are all potentially illegal under this new law. This legislation also allows individuals who possess extreme pornography that threatens a person's life or leads to serious injury to be fined or imprisoned for up to three years, while all other images, such as bestiality, can lead to a maximum sentence of two years in prison (Crown Prosecution Service, 2014).

Despite the variation in what constitutes obscene content, there is some consistency in laws regarding child exploitation. In the US, there are multiple federal laws designed to protect youth from exploitation and punish individuals who share or create images of child pornography. In fact, the first law criminalizing child pornography in the US was enacted in 1977, called the **Protection of Children Against Sexual Exploitation Act**. This law made it illegal for anyone under the age of 16 to participate in the visual production of sexually explicit materials, though this definition was extended to the age of 18 in 1986 (Brenner, 2011). Later legislation, though, has had the greatest impact on child porn and exploitation through the implementation of the **Child Pornography Protection Act of 1996**. This Act extended the existing laws regarding child pornography by establishing a new definition for this term. Specifically, this Act amended the criminal code under Title 18 to define child porn as "any visual depiction, including any photograph, film, video, picture, or computer or computer-generated image or picture of sexually explicit conduct" (Brenner, 2011: 51). The law also recognizes that the image: 1) must have been produced involving an actual minor engaging in sexual acts, 2) involved or appeared to involve a minor, and/or 3) was created, adapted, or modified to appear that a minor is engaging in sexual acts. This definition was established in order to provide needed flexibility to prosecute child porn cases that may have been created using Photoshop or other computer programs and sent electronically.

This act also made it illegal to engage in multiple activities associated with the production of child pornography. It is now illegal for anyone to persuade, entice, induce, or transport minors in order to engage in sexual acts for the purpose of producing images and/or video of the acts, and if they will be transported in foreign or interstate commerce (Brenner, 2011). Similarly, it is illegal for anyone to entice a minor to engage in sexual acts outside of the US in order to produce visual depictions of the behavior. It is also illegal for anyone to print or publish advertisements associated with the sexual exploitation of children (Brenner, 2011). This law also makes it illegal to either conspire or attempt to commit any of these offenses.

The penalties for these offenses are rather harsh and include a federal prison sentence between 15 and 30 years and/or a fine. If the offender has a prior charge of sexual exploitation on their record at either the state or federal level, they can receive between 25 and 50 years. If they have two or more charges, then they are eligible to receive a life sentence in prison (Brenner, 2011). In the event that a child dies in the course of the offenses above, then the offender is eligible for the death penalty.

In addition to the production of child porn, this Act also criminalized:

1) the transportation of sexually explicit material featuring minors by any means, whether physically or electronically;
2) the receipt or distribution of such material;
3) selling or possessing materials with the intent to sell them;
4) possessing books, films, and other materials that contain such depictions; and
5) conspiring or attempting to engage in any of these activities.

Any violation of the first three activities, or conspiring to engage in these acts, is punishable by a federal prison sentence ranging between 5 and 20 years minimum and/or a fine. If an individual has any prior convictions for sexual exploitation, then they can be imprisoned between 15 and 40 years minimum. The fourth offense can lead to a fine and/or a prison sentence of no more than 10 years, though a prior conviction increases the sentence to between 10 and 20 years (Brenner, 2011).

Section 2252 of this same Act also made it illegal to knowingly:

1) mail, transport, or ship child pornography by any means, physically or electronically;
2) receive or distribute child porn or materials containing child pornography;
3) reproduce child porn for distribution through the mail or by computer;
4) sell or possess child porn with the intent to sell;

5) possess any "book, magazine, periodical, film, videotape, computer disk, or other material that contains an image of child porn" (Brenner, 2011: 54); and
6) distribute, offer, or send a visual depiction of a minor engaging in sexually explicit conduct to a minor.

The first, fourth, and sixth act can lead an individual to be imprisoned between 5 and 20 years minimum, though if they have a prior conviction for child pornography, then they can receive a prison sentence of between 15 and 40 years. The fifth activity, possessing child porn, can lead an individual to be fined and imprisoned for up to 10 years, though if they have a prior offense history, they can be imprisoned between 10 and 20 years (Brenner, 2011).

These statutes all apply to images of real children who have been victimized in some way. Some argued that the ability to create images of virtual children using computer software or line drawings does not create the same issue of victimization. As a result, these materials should not be treated as illicit material because of the protections afforded by the First Amendment right to free speech in the US (Brenner, 2011). This challenge was struck down through the creation of the **Prosecutorial Remedies and Other Tools to end the Exploitation of Children Today Act (or PROTECT Act)** of 2003. This law criminalized virtual child pornography and extended the legal definition to include "a digital image, computer image, or computer-generated image that is, or is indistinguishable from, that of a minor engaged in sexually explicit conduct" (Brenner, 2011: 57). Also, this Act included language criminalizing "obscene child pornography," which involves any visual depiction, whether a sculpture, painting, cartoon, or drawing of minors engaging in sexually explicit conduct or obscene acts; or involves a minor engaging in bestiality, sadism or masochistic abuse, sexual acts of any kind; and lacks serious literary, artistic, or scientific value (Brenner, 2011). The language related to the value of the image is critical because it is synonymous with that of the Miller test of obscene material in the Supreme Court. As a result, this helps to ensure that this standard is constitutional when applied to any criminal case.

An additional set of laws were passed and implemented in 2001, requiring the implementation of filtering and security protocols to protect youth. The **Children's Internet Protection Act (CIPA)**, which covers all schools that teach students from kindergarten through 12th grade, and the **Neighborhood Children's Internet Protection Act (NCIPA)**, which encompasses public libraries, require Internet filters in these locations that block young people from accessing harmful content, including pornographic and obscene materials (Federal Communications Commission, 2013). Also, the law requires that a "technology protection measure" must be implemented on every computer within the facility that is connected to the Internet, and each institution must adopt and implement an Internet safety policy addressing most forms of cybercrime (Federal Communications Commission, 2013). In the event that such filters are not put in place, the school or library may lose certain federal funding and grants.

At the US state level, virtually all states have laws pertaining to the use, creation, possession, and distribution of child pornography and the sexual solicitation and exploitation of minors (Brenner, 2011). These offenses are treated as felonies, though the range of sanctions varies in terms of years in prison based on the individual's prior record and the severity of the offense. Additionally, as of September 2013, ten states have established laws that require IT workers to report any child pornography that they identify in the course of their work (Brenner, 2011). These laws are not designed to require computer technicians to actively seek out or search for child porn content but, rather, to ensure that such content is reported in the event it is uncovered in the course of normal operations. Reporting any child porn identified provides the individual and their company with immunity from criminal or civil liability in most states (Brenner, 2011). In the event an individual does not report child porn to law enforcement at the state and/or federal level, the individual can be charged with a misdemeanor and/or fined.

International laws regarding child pornography vary based in part on local standards for obscene content and their sanctions for use or possession of pornography (ICMEC, 2010). In the UK, the **Protection of Children Act 1978 (PCA)** was the first attempt to legislate against this activity, making it illegal to obtain, make, distribute, or possess an indecent image of someone under the age of 18 (Crown Prosecution Service, 2013). The law was extended in 1994 through the **Criminal Justice and Public Order Act** to include images that appear to be photos, so called pseudo-photographs. Additional legislation in 2009 called the **Coroners and Justice Act** extended the law to include all sexual images depicting youth under the age of 18, whether real or created (Crown Prosecution Service, 2013). The current punishment structures enable an individual to be imprisoned between 5 and 10 years, depending on the offense and the nature of the content the individual either acquired or viewed. For instance, possession of child pornography can be a minimum of two to five years in prison, though it can extend beyond that, depending on the nature of the pornography that the individual acquired (Crown Prosecution Service, 2013).

Canada utilizes a similar definition to that of the US, though they also include audio recordings of the sexual exploitation of children and written depictions of persons under the age of 18 engaging in sexual activities or those that actively induce or encourage sex with minors. In fact, Canadian courts can mandate that such content be deleted from the Internet if the materials are available on a computer system within the Canadian borders. Their sanctions for child pornography are also similar to the US, in that the possession of child pornography is punishable by up to ten years in prison, while the production and/or distribution of child pornography can lead to a

20-year prison sentence (Seidman, 2013). Similarly, Australian law prohibits any sexual image, real or created, of children under the age of 18. Their sanctions regarding child pornography offenses are consistent regardless of the offense, whether the production or possession of child pornography, and include a fine of up to A$275,000 and up to ten years imprisonment (Krone, 2005). All of these nations also have laws that require ISPs to monitor and report the presence of child pornography on systems that they control. In the event that such materials are not reported, the ISP can be held liable for the distribution of this content and eligible for fines and other sanctions (Brenner, 2011).

The **Convention on Cybercrime** deals with child porn under Article 9, requiring member states to make it illegal to produce, distribute, offer, procure, or possess child pornography via computer or media storage device. The CoC encourages the use of a definition of child pornography that includes visual depictions of minors, people who appear to be minors, or realistic images of minors engaged in sexual acts (Brenner, 2011). Due to the complexity of national standards, the CoC also allows signatory nations to define minors as individuals under the age of 16 or 18, depending on their current standards, and may choose not to criminalize created images or those where participants only appear to be minors (Brenner, 2011).

Finally, it is important to note that many nations have laws pertaining to prostitution at both the local and federal level. The sale of sex has been criminalized, though the extent to which it is enforced is highly inconsistent. Several southeast Asian nations (e.g. Malaysia, the Philippines, and Thailand) do not strictly regulate prostitution, making them an ideal locale for individuals interested in sex tourism, particularly for sexual encounters with minors (Nair, 2008). Additionally, few nations have language in their criminal codes regarding the use of technology in order to acquire or solicit sexual services. As a result, Western nations have criminalized the act of sex tourism (Nair, 2008). For instance, the US federal criminal code (18 USC § 2423(c)) criminalizes the act of traveling to a foreign country to engage in paid sexual encounters with minors. This is true even if the activity is legal in the country where the act took place (Nair, 2008). Individuals found guilty under this statute can be fined and imprisoned for up to 30 years. Additionally, many Western nations have criminalized the act of paying for sex with minors in order to protect youth from commercial sexual exploitation (Brenner, 2011).

Self regulation by the pornography industry

Currently, pornography producers are encouraged but not legally mandated to avoid exposing individuals under the age of 18 to obscene content. Prior laws that were specifically designed to minimize the likelihood that minors could access porn have been overturned in the US due to concerns over their effect on free speech rights (Procida and Simon, 2003). As a result, there are a range of techniques that pornographic websites hosted in the US use to reduce the likelihood that young people access their content. In the 1990s and early 2000s, a number of websites worked with **Age Verification Services (AVS)**, which would, upon entry into the website, verify the age of an individual via a valid credit card or driver's license (Procida and Simon, 2003).

These services waned in popularity with changes in legislation and the increased availability of pornographic content via YouTube-style video sharing sites. Individuals no longer needed to pay to access pornographic content, as both users of content and producers began to see the popularity of video sharing sites that offered such media free of charge. Instead, many pornographic websites began to provide a warning page that pops up on screen prior to entering the actual website that requires individuals to certify that they are over the age of 18 and, therefore, legally able to access pornographic content and that they will not hold the site responsible for obscene content. There has been no legal ruling by federal courts as to whether this constitutes an acceptable attempt to keep minors from viewing porn. In addition, a number of adult websites will also provide links at the bottom of the pop-up page to various parental monitoring software programs in order to encourage safe surfing habits for youth.

A final development in the way in which adult content is hosted online is the development of the **.xxx domain** (Matyszczyk, 2012). The creation of this top level domain, similar to .com, .net, and .edu websites, provides a voluntary option for individuals to host pornographic content online. This domain was approved in March 2011 and implemented in April 2011 by the **Internet Corporation for Assigned Names and Numbers (ICANN)**, which is responsible for the coordination and stability of the Internet over time. It was thought that the use of a .xxx domain would enable parents and agencies to filter content with ease, though some were concerned that these sites could be blocked entirely, thereby limiting individuals' rights to free speech (Matyszczyk, 2012). The most recent statistics from 2012 suggest that there are 215,835 .xxx domains currently registered, though only 132,859 of these sites are actually adult oriented (Matyszczyk, 2012). A majority are also registered by businesses and industries who did not want their brand or product associated with a pornographic website. At present, it is not clear how this new domain space may be used or to what extent individuals are interested in actually visiting .xxx spaces relative to those in the .com or .net space (Matyszczyk, 2012). Thus, this technique used to affect access to obscene or pornographic content may change over time.

Non-profit organization efforts

In the UK, the **Internet Watch Foundation (IWF)** is a charitable organization that is focused on reducing the amount of child pornography and exploitation materials hosted worldwide and criminally obscene adult

pornography, prostitution, and sex crimes

content in the UK. The IWF receives financial support from ISPs, technology and financial service providers, and the European Union (Internet Watch Foundation, 2014). Beginning in 1996, the IWF was created to provide a hotline for the public and IT professionals to report criminal content found on the Internet. These reports are processed and used to distribute takedown notices to ISPs in the event that child porn is identified. In fact, over 400,000 web pages have been examined since their inception, and the amount of child porn hosted in the UK has decreased dramatically since 1996 (Internet Watch Foundation, 2014). In addition, the IWF provides a block list to ISPs and industry so that individuals are unable to access content hosted online. They also provide assistance to UK law enforcement agencies to pursue the distributors and consumers of harmful content.

> **For more on agencies dealing with child abuse and harm, go online to: 1)** https://www.iwf.org.uk/, **2)** www.missingkids.com/home, **and 3)** www.icmec.org/missingkids/servlet/PublicHomeServlet

The **National Center for Missing and Exploited Children (NCMEC)** is one of the key non-profit organizations in the US that deals with missing children and child exploitation. The Center began in 1984 under mandate from the US Congress and then-President Ronald Reagan as a clearinghouse for information and resources regarding these crimes (National Center for Missing and Exploited Children, 2014). Currently, the NCMEC is funded in part by the US Congress, as well as donations from the private sector and matching donors. As a result, the NCMEC is authorized by Congress under 42 USC 5773 and performs multiple roles to facilitate the investigation of crimes against children (National Center for Missing and Exploited Children, 2014). Specifically, the NCMEC operates a national toll free hotline (1-800-THE-LOST) to collect information on runaway children, and the **CyberTipline**, which provides an electronic resource for individuals to report suspected incidents of child abuse, child pornography, and sexual exploitation. In fact, the Tipline has processed over 2.2 million reports since it was launched in 1998 (National Center for Missing and Exploited Children, 2014).

The NCMEC offers training programs for youth and educators involving the threats children face online. The NCMEC also offers training and resources for law enforcement, including the **Child Victim Identification Program (CVIP)**, which culls through images of child pornography in order to determine the identity and location of child victims (National Center for Missing and Exploited Children, 2014). This program has processed more than 104 images of child porn since its implementation in 2002. In addition, they support a joint operation with the US Marshals service to track sex offenders who violate the terms and conditions of their sentences.

The success of the NCMEC, and the recognition of a need for similar entities around the world, led to the formation of the **International Centre for Missing and Exploited Children (ICMEC)** in 1999. The Centre is also a non-profit agency with a similar mission to the NCMEC, though it is focused on building partnerships in a global context to better investigate child exploitation cases and build the legal capacity of nations so that there is consistency in laws to prosecute these offenses (International Centre for Missing and Exploited Children, 2014). They not only focus on child abduction and harm, but also have a substantive set of resources to support the investigation of child pornography and exploitation cases. In particular, the ICMEC operates the **Financial Coalition Against Child Pornography (FCACP)**, which is comprised of 39 financial institutions and ISPs who are jointly operating to take complaints of child pornography and disrupt the businesses that are engaged in the sale of or profit generation from this content (International Center for Missing and Exploited Children, 2014). They also offer training and assistance to law enforcement agencies internationally, along with legal consultations in order to develop model child exploitation law and harmonize legislation internationally. The ICMEC has national operational centers in Belgium, Greece, Romania, South Africa, the US, and has new regional offices in Singapore and Latin America to better service the nations of southeast Asia and Central and South America, respectively (International Center for Missing and Exploited Children, 2014).

Dealing with sex offenses on and offline

At the federal level in the US, there are a number of agencies involved in the investigation of sexual offenses. The **Federal Bureau of Investigation's (FBI) Violent Crimes Against Children (VCAC)** program investigates a range of sexual offenses and criminal activities that affect youth, ranging from child pornography to sex trafficking to kidnapping (FBI, 2014b). This program became operational in October 2012 when two pre-existing programs, called the Innocent Images Initiative under the Cyber Division and the Crimes Against Children program, within the Criminal Investigative Division, were merged together. Each of these groups had a unique function: the Innocent Images program investigated child exploitation and pornography cases online, while the CAC program handled cases of child prostitution, abduction, and sex tourism (FBI, 2014b). Combining these programs enabled a more effective approach to the investigation of these related crimes and helped to reduce the burden of pursuing the tremendous number of investigations of child exploitation that were tasked to the Cyber division, which was already responsible for investigating hacking and fraud cases.

The VCAC program now falls under the FBI's Criminal Investigative Division and develops investigative leads, which are pursued by field agents in each of the 56 field offices the Bureau operates across the United States (FBI, 2014b). Some of these cases are investigated by specialized **Child**

Exploitation Task Forces (CETFs), which are joint operations of federal, state, and local law enforcement officers. This program is both reactive, in that it actively investigates leads and tips provided by the general public and reports collected by NCMEC, and proactive, based on undercover investigations initiated by agents in chatrooms, social networking sites, website, and file sharing communities (FBI, 2014b). This program also investigates cases of child sex tourism in southeast Asia and Latin America in order to develop practical evidence against US citizens who engage in such tourism so that they can be successfully prosecuted in the US. As of December 2013, there were more than 7,700 active investigations of child exploitation of any kind underway within the VCAC program as a whole (FBI, 2014b).

The FBI also spearheads the **Violent Crimes Against Children International Task Force (VCACITF)**, which began in 2004 and is now the largest global task force in the world that investigates child exploitation cases (FBI, 2014c). There are 40 nations that participate in this force, with 69 active members, all of whom share information in order to investigate child exploitation cases. The VCACITF also has an annual meeting and training session designed to promote best practices in the field and coordinate complex investigations.

Additionally, the FBI operates the **Endangered Child Alert Program (ECAP)**, which seeks to identify the adults featured in some child exploitation content so they may be brought to justice (FBI, 2014a). The faces and identifying characteristics of individuals are stripped from the media and published as Jane/John Does in order to obtain arrest warrants and actionable information about their real identities. This program has led to 21 investigations and 13 arrests since its creation in 2004 (FBI, 2014a). A similar program, dubbed **Operation Rescue Me**, has been in operation since 2008 and is designed to identify the victims of child exploitation. Analysts sift through newly posted images and video of child pornography in order to capture clues about the location and timeframe of when the media was made so that victim identities can be determined and saved. Thus far, the program has led to 41 youths being successfully identified from information available in these materials (FBI, 2014a).

The **Immigration and Customs Enforcement (ICE) Agency** also plays an important role in the investigation of child exploitation cases (ICE, 2014). Their role is often viewed in the context of managing the people and property that enter the US, making the importation or distribution of child pornography and obscene content through its borders, electronic or otherwise, an investigative priority for ICE agents. As a result, ICE manages a program called **Operation Predator** that is designed to facilitate the investigation of child exploitation, both in the US and abroad (ICE, 2014). Not only do agents actively investigate these crimes, but they also work with state and local law enforcement agencies to provide intelligence and investigative resources to identify offenders and victims. In fact, ICE recently developed a mobile phone app that provides alerts and information about suspected and wanted child predators so that the public can report these individuals to law enforcement if they are spotted (ICE, 2014). This agency is also the US representative to Interpol's working group on child sexual abuse online. Agents actively identify materials online and use these images and video as the basis for investigative leads around the world (see Text Box 6.4; ICE, 2014).

Text Box 6.4: Immigration and Customs Enforcement operations in action

29 arrested in international case involving live online webcam child abuse

www.ice.gov/news/releases/1401/140116london.htm

> An organized crime group that facilitated the live streaming of on-demand child sexual abuse in the Philippines has been dismantled after a joint investigation by the U.K.'s National Crime Agency (NCA), the Australian Federal Police (AFP) and U.S. Immigration and Customs Enforcement (ICE).

This article provides an overview of a recent case investigated by a joint operation including agents from the US Immigration and Customs Enforcement (ICE). The case spanned multiple nations, with victims across the globe.

The **US Postal Inspection Service** plays a role in the investigation of child exploitation cases as well, since child porn and obscene content was distributed directly via postal mail prior to the development of the Internet. The Postal Inspectors have investigated these offenses for more than 100 years as the law enforcement arm of the US Postal Service (USPIS, 2014). There are approximately 1,200 criminal investigators working within the office, as well as 1,000 armed uniformed officers. They often work hand in hand with other law enforcement agencies to investigate a range of offenses, including identity crimes and drug offenses (USPIS, 2014). This is particularly true for child pornography cases, as the Service investigates thousands of potential leads regarding the distribution of materials. In addition, they perform several hundred arrests for child pornography possession or distribution each year (see Text Box 6.7 for details; USPIS, 2008).

For more information on the Postal Service's investigative role, go online to: www.justice.gov/usao/co/news/2013/sept/9-18-13.html

---

There are myriad specialized policing units at the federal or national level to investigate child pornography and exploitation cases around the world. The UK's **Child Exploitation and Online Protection (CEOP) Command** is a part of the **National Crime Agency (NCA)**, which became operational in October 2013. The CEOP takes reports of exploitation, abuse, and missing youth and will directly investigate threats and coordinate responses, depending on the scope of harm across multiple areas (CEOP, 2014). The CEOP also serves as the point of contact for multinational investigations in order to coordinate responses within the UK while working in concert with other agencies around the world. In addition to enforcement and investigative responsibilities, the CEOP also operates the **ThinkUKnow** program, designed to educate children and adults about threats to youth safety (CEOP, 2014).

In Australia, the Federal Police has a special subgroup called the **Child Protections Operations (CPO) team** that investigates and coordinates the response to child exploitation cases both domestically and internationally (Australian Federal Police, 2014). The RCMP serve as a key investigative mechanism in Canada and offer training and investigative support for local agencies. They also serve as a key partner in the **Canadian National Child Exploitation Coordination Centre (NCECC)**, the focal point of contact for online exploitation cases that cross jurisdictional boundaries within Canada or internationally (RCMP, 2014). All of these agencies also take online reports and tips concerning child porn and exploitation to serve as a basis for investigation.

In the United States, **Internet Crimes Against Children (ICAC)** task forces provide a mechanism for coordination between local, state, and federal law enforcement, as well as prosecutors (ICAC, 2014). The ICAC program is currently comprised of 61 task forces, with a presence in every state. Some states with larger populations and geography have multiple ICACs, such as Florida, California, and Texas (ICAC, 2014). The program began in 1998 under mandate from the Office of Juvenile Justice and Delinquency Prevention (OJJDP) in order to improve the resources available to combat youth victimization at all levels of law enforcement, including investigative resources, forensic and technological assistance, and prosecutorial guidance. In fact, there is now a regular schedule of digital forensic and investigative training for ICAC investigators offered across the country, which are supported by various federal agencies (ICAC, 2014).

Though this may seem like a complex organizational hierarchy to understand, the response to child pornography and exploitation cases requires multiple points of coordination and response. A successful investigation requires that arrests and takedowns occur as close together as possible to avoid offenders realizing that they may be caught and attempting to flee or destroy evidence that may implicate them in criminal activity. Investigations that begin at the local level may also lead to evidence of criminal activity in other nations, which may increase the scope of agencies that may need to become involved in order for arrests and prosecutions to be both legal and successful. This is evident in the recent series of arrests that took place around the world as part of **Operation Spade** (Ha, 2014). This investigation began in Canada in 2010 and implicated a child pornographer operating out of Romania under the name Azov Films, who produced content that was generated by individuals living in the US, UK, and Australia, among other nations (Ha, 2014). Agencies within each country investigated domestic incidents, shared this information with their partner agencies abroad, and timed arrests and takedowns to occur in such a way as to have the widest possible impact on content generators and users. As a result, hundreds of people were arrested around the world in 2013 with more expected in the coming months.

> **For more information on Operation Spade, go online to:** www.daily-mail.co.uk/news/article-2507459/Global-child-porn-ring-busted-leading-rescue-nearly-400-children.html

Given that child exploitation cases can be international in scope, there is the **Virtual Global Taskforce (VGT)** in order to coordinate responses to multinational investigations. The VGT was established in 2003 and is an alliance of agencies and private industry that work together in order to identify, investigate, and respond to incidents of child exploitation (VGT, 2014). The team is comprised of federal law enforcement agencies in Australia, Canada, Italy, Indonesia, South Korea, the Netherlands, New Zealand, the United Arab Emirates, the UK, and the US, as well as Europol and Interpol (VGT, 2014). The VGT takes complaints of child exploitation, coordinates multinational investigations, and provides resources for children and adults to protect themselves online. They have been tremendously successful in investigating child pornography and abuse cases, leading to over 1,000 investigations and hundreds of arrests around the world (see Text Box 6.5 for a recent example).

Text Box 6.5: The Virtual Global Taskforce in action

www.virtualglobaltaskforce.com/2014/attack-on-online-child-sexual
-abuse-network-saves-children/
4 February 2014

Attack on online child sexual abuse network saves children

A New Zealand multi-agency operation targeting an online child sexual abuse network has caught six offenders, safeguarded four children and rescued a 6-year-old victim in the United Kingdom from the part-time care of her grandfather ...

pornography, prostitution, and sex crimes

This study provides an overview of a recent case investigated and pursued by members of the Virtual Global Taskforce to combat child exploitation cases.

Summary

Taken as a whole, it is clear that any new technology that is made available to the general public will be incorporated into the pursuit of sexual encounters in some way. The extent to which that activity will lead to legal troubles is variable, based on who is being affected and how. For instance, many nations may not take issue with the production of sexually explicit material featuring consenting adults, so long as it does not involve activities that push boundaries of taste or social standards. However, any attempt to harm children either online or offline is seriously punished and heavily investigated in most Western industrialized nations. In fact, some of the sanctions used for child sex offenses are more severe than those used for computer hackers and data thieves. This is also one of the few crimes that lead to substantive international investigations and cooperative working agreements between agencies. Given that technology changes so frequently and can be subverted by offenders in distinct ways, there will be a need for constant inquiry into the nature of sexual offenses in online and offline environments to improve and adapt the criminal code to new offenses. Likewise, law enforcement must understand offender behaviors so as to better collect evidence that can support the investigation and prosecution of sex offenders.

Key terms

.xxx domain
Age Verification Services (AVS)
Bestiality
BigDoggie
cam whores
Canadian National Child Exploitation Coordination Center (NCECC)
Carnegie Mellon Report
Child Exploitation and Online Protection (CEOP) Command
Child Exploitation Task Forces (CETF)
Child love
Child pornography
Child Pornography Protection Act of 1996

Discussion questions

1) How do you use your computer, tablet, and/or smartphone for dating and romantic assistance? Do you think that the use of technology makes it easier for people to meet others, or harder?

2) How could the development of the Internet and CMCs help reduce the risk of harm for individuals interested in the sex trade? In what ways does the ability to communicate about sex workers and review their services make it a less dangerous activity?

3) Why do you think we sanction individuals who possess or access child porn with more severity than we do hackers or data thieves? Why would there be such differential sanction use?

References

Alexander, P. (1998). Position: A Difficult Issue for Feminists. In F. Delacoste & P. Alexander (eds), *Sex Work: Writings by Women in the Sex Industry* 2nd ed. (pp. 184–230). San Francisco, CA: Cleis Press.

Alexy, E. M., Burgess, A. W., & Baker, T. (2005). Internet offenders: Traders, travelers, and combination trader-travelers. *Journal of Interpersonal Violence*, 20(7), 804–812.

American Psychiatric Association. (2000). *Diagnosis and Statistical Manual of Mental Disorders* (4th ed., text revision). Washington, DC: Author.

Australian Federal Police. (2014). *Online child sex exploitation.* [Online] Available at: www.afp.gov.au/policing/child-protection-operations/online-exploitation.aspx

Bissette, D. C. (2004). *Internet pornography statistics: 2003.* [Online] Available at: www.healthymind.com/porn-stats.pdf

Blevins, K., & Holt, T. J. (2009). Examining the virtual subculture of johns. *Journal of Contemporary Ethnography*, 38, 619–648.

Bort, J. (2013). I spent a month on infidelity dating site Ashley Madison and was pleasantly surprised by how nice it was. *Business Insider* December 17, 2013. [Online] Available at: www.businessinsider.com/how-to-use-cheating-site-ashley-madison-2013-12?op=1

Brenner, S. W. (2011). Defining Cybercrime: A Review of Federal and State Law. In R. D. Clifford (ed.), *Cybercrime: The Investigation, Prosecution, and Defense of a Computer-Related Crime*, 3rd Edition (pp. 15–104). Raleigh, NC: Carolina Academic Press.

CEOP. (2014). *About CEOP.* [Online] Available at: http://ceop.police.uk/About-Us/

CNN. (2003). Man accused of luring kids to porn sites. *CNN* September 3, 2003. [Online] Available at: www.cnn.com/2003/TECH/internet/09/03/trick.names/

Cooper, B. (1989). Prostitution: A feminist analysis. *Women's Rights Law Reporter*, 11, 98–119.

Cromer, M. (1998). Inside Wifey Inc. *Wired*, 9.02.98. [Online] Available at: http://archive.wired.com/techbiz/media/news/1998/09/14784

Crown Prosecution Service. (2013). *Indecent photographs of children.* Prosecution Policy and Guidance. [Online] Available at: www.cps.gov.uk/legal/h_to_k/indecent_photographs_of_children/index.html

Crown Prosecution Service (2014). *Extreme Pornography.* Prosecution Policy and Guidance. [Online] Available at: https://www.cps.gov.uk/legal/d_to_g/extreme_pornography/

Cunningham, S., & Kendall, T. (2010). Sex for Sale: Online Commerce in the World's Oldest Profession. In T. J. Holt, (ed.), *Crime Online: Correlates, Causes, and Context* (pp. 114–140). Raleigh, NC: Carolina Academic Press.

Dodero, C. (2012). Hunter Moore makes a living screwing you. *The Village Voice*, April 4, 2012. [Online] Available at: www.villagevoice.com/2012-04-04/news/revenge-porn-hunter-moore-is-anyone-up/

Durkin, K. F. (1997). Misuse of the Internet by pedophiles: Implications for law enforcement and probation practice. *Federal Probation*, 14, 14–18.

Durkin, K. F., & Bryant, C. D. (1999). Propagandizing pederasty: A thematic analysis of the online exculpatory accounts of unrepentant pedophiles. *Deviant Behavior*, 20, 103–127.

Durkin, K. F., & Hundersmarck, S. (2007). Pedophiles and Child Molesters. In E. Goode, D. A. Vail (eds), *Extreme Deviance* (pp. 144–150). London: Sage Publications Ltd.

Edwards, S. S. M. (2000). The failure of British obscenity law in the regulation of pornography. *The Journal of Sexual Aggression*, 6(1/2), 111–127.

Federal Bureau of Investigation. (2002, March 17). *Operation Candyman press release.* Retrieved December 13, 2011, from www.fbi.gov/news/pressrel/press-releases/operation-candyman

Federal Bureau of Investigation (2014a). *Endangered Child Alert Program.* [Online] Available at: www.fbi.gov/about-us/investigate/vc_majorthefts/cac/operation-rescue-me-ecap

Federal Bureau of Investigation. (2014b). *Overview and History of the Violent Crimes Against Children Program.* [Online] Available at: www.fbi.gov/about-us/investigate/vc_majorthefts/cac/overview-and-history

Federal Bureau of Investigation. (2014c). *The International Task Force.* [Online] Available at: www.fbi.gov/about-us/investigate/vc_majorthefts/cac/international-task-force

Federal Communications Commission. (2013). *Children's Internet Protection Act (CIPA).* Federal Communications Commission Consumer and Governmental Affairs Bureau. [Online] Available at: http://transition.fcc.gov/cgb/consumerfacts/cipa.pdf

Godwin, M. (2003). *Cyber Rights: Defending Free Speech in the Digital Age.* Boston, MA: MIT Press.

Ha, T. T. (2014). Toronto child-porn investigation leads to major political scandal in Germany. *The Globe and Mail* February 16, 2014. [Online] Available at: www.theglobeandmail.com/news/world/toronto-child-porn-investigation-leads-to-major-political-scandal-in-germany/article16914457/

Halloran, L. (2014). Race to stop "Revenge Porn" raises free speech worries. March 6, 2014. *National Public Radio.* [Online] Available at: www.npr.org/blogs/itsallpolitics/2014/03/06/286388840/race-to-stop-revenge-porn-raises-free-speech-worries

Hampton, L. (1988). Hookers with AIDS – The Search. In I. Rieder & P. Ruppelt (eds), *AIDS: The Women* (pp. 157–164). San Francisco: Cleis Press.

Holt, T. J., & Blevins, K. R. (2007). Examining sex work from the client's perspective: Assessing johns using online data. *Deviant Behavior*, 28, 333–354.

Holt, T. J., Blevins, K. R., & Burkert, N. (2010). Considering the pedophile subculture on-line. *Sexual Abuse: Journal of Research and Treatment*, 22, 3–24.

Holt, T. J., Blevins, K. R., & Kuhns, J. B. (2013). Examining diffusion and arrest practices among johns. *Crime and Delinquency*, 60, 261–283.

Hughes, D. M. (2003). Prostitution online. *Journal of Trauma Practice*, 2, 115–131.

Immigration & Customs Enforcement. (2014). *Child Exploitation/Operation Predator.* [Online] Available at: http://www.ice.gov/predator/

International Centre for Missing and Exploited Children. (2010). *Child Pornography: Model Legislation & Global Review.* [Online] Available at: www.icmec.org/en_X1/icmec_publications/English__6th_Edition_FINAL_.pdf

International Centre for Missing and Exploited Children. (2014). *About the InternationalCenter for Missing and Exploited Children.* [Online] Available at: www.icmec.org/missingkids/servlet/PageServlet?LanguageCountry=en_X1&PageId=1222

Internet Crimes Against Children. (2014). *Internet Crimes Against Children Task Force Program.* [Online] Available at: https://www.icactaskforce.org/Pages/ICACTFP.aspx

Internet Watch Foundation. (2014). *About Us.* [Online] Available at: https://www.iwf.org.uk/about-iwf

Jenkins, P. (2001). *Beyond Tolerance: Child Pornography on the Internet.* New York: New York University Press.

Klain, E. J., Davies, H. J., & Hicks, M. A. (2001). *Child pornography: The criminal-justice-system response* (Report No. NC81). Retrieved December 13, 2011, from https://www.ncjtc.org/NCJTC_Member_Resources/Public/Child%20Pornography%20Criminal%20Justice%20Response.pdf

Krone, T. (2004). A typology and online child pornography offending. *Trends & Issues in Crime and Criminal Justice, 279,* 2–6.

Krone, T. (2005). Does thinking make it so? Defining online child pornography possession offenses. *Trends & Issues in Crime and Criminal Justice, 299.* [Online] Available at: www.aic.gov.au/media_library/publications/tandi/tandi299.pdf

Lane, F. S. (2000). *Obscene Profits: The Entrepreneurs of Pornography in the Cyber Age.* New York: Routledge.

Levitt, S., & Venkatesh, S. A. (2007). *An empirical analysis of street-level prostitution.* [Online] Available at: http://economics.uchicago.edu/pdf/Prostitution%205.pdf

Liebelson, D. (2014). FBI arrests "The most hated man on the Internet," Revenge-porn king Hunter Moore. *Mother Jones* Jan. 23, 2014. [Online] Available at: www.motherjones.com/mojo/2014/01/fbi-arrests-revenge-porn-king-hunter-moore

Lucas, A. M. (2005). The work of sex work: Elite prostitutes' vocational orientations and experiences. *Deviant Behavior, 26,* 513–546.

Lynch, M. (2002). Pedophiles and cyber-predators as contaminating forces: The language of disgust, pollution, and boundary invasions in federal debates on sex offender legislation. *Law & Social Inquiry, 27,* 529–557.

Marshall. (1997). Pedophilia: Psychopathology and theory. In D. Laws and W. O'Donohue (eds) *Sexual Deviance* (pp. 152–174). New York: Guilford.

Matyszczyk, C. (2012). Is anyone actually going to .xxx domains? *Cnet,* May 2, 2012. [Online] Available at: http://news.cnet.com/8301-17852_3-57426462-71/is-anyone-actually-going-to-.xxx-domains/

Mayer, A. (1985). *Sexual Abuse: Causes, Consequences and Treatment of Incestuous and Pedophilic Acts.* Holmes Beach, FL: Learning.

Milrod, C., & Monto, M. A. (2012). The hobbyist and the Girlfriend Experience: Behaviors and preferences of male customers of Internet Sexual Service Providers. *Deviant Behaviors, 33*(10), 792–810.

Mitchell, K. J., Finkelhor, D., Jones, L. M., and Wolak, J. (2012). Prevalence and characteristics of youth sexting: A national study. *Pediatrics, 129,* 13–20.

Moffatt, P. (2005). Economics of Prostitution. In P. Moffatt (ed.), *Economics Uncut: A Complete Guide to Life, Death, and Misadventure* (pp. 193–228). London: Edward Elgar Publishing.

Nair, S. (2008). *Child Sex Tourism.* US Department of Justice. Retrieved 13 January, 2012 from www.justice.gov/criminal/ceos/sextour.html

National Center for Missing and Exploited Children. (2014). *FAQs.* [Online] Available at: www.missingkids.com/Missing/FAQ

O'Donohue, W., Regev, L. G., & Hagstrom, A. (2000). Problems with the DSM-IV diagnosis of pedophilia. *Sexual Abuse: A Journal of Research and Treatment*, 12, 95–105.

Olson, P. (2012). *We are Anonymous: Inside the Hacker World of LulzSec, Anonymous, and the Global Cyber Insurgency.* Hachette: New York.

O'Neill, M. (2001). *Prostitution and Feminism.* London: Polity Press.

Perez, S. (2013). Tumblr's adult fare accounts for 11.4% of site's top 200k domains, adult sites are leading category of referrals. *TechCrunch*, May 20, 2013. [Online] Available at: http://techcrunch.com/2013/05/20/tumblrs-adult-fare-accounts-for-11-4-of-sites-top-200k-domains-tumblrs-ad ult-fare-accounts-for-11-4-of-sites-top-200k-domains-adults-sit es-are-leading-category-of-referrals/

Perrien, M., Hernandez, A., Gallop, C., & Steinour, K. (2000). *Admissions of undetected contact sexual offenses by participants in the Federal Bureau of Prisons' sex offender treatment program.* Poster presented at the 19th Annual Conference of the Association for the Treatment of Sexual Abusers, San Diego, CA.

Pittaro, M. (2008). Sexual Addiction to the Internet: From Curiosity to Compulsive Behavior. In F. Schmalleger & M. Pittaro (eds) *Crimes of the Internet*, pp. 134–150. Upper Saddle River, NJ: Pearson Education Inc.

Procida, R. & Simon, R. J. (2003). *Global Perspectives on Social Issues: Pornography.* Lanham, MD: Lexington Books.

Quayle, E., & Taylor, M. (2002). Child pornography and the Internet: Perpetuating a cycle of abuse. *Deviant Behavior*, 23, 331–361.

Quinn, J. F., & Forsyth, C. J. (2005). Describing sexual behavior in the era of the Internet: A typology for empirical research. *Deviant Behavior*, 26, 191–207.

Quinn, J. F., & Forsyth, C. J. (2013). Red light districts on blue screens: A typology for understanding the evolution of deviant communities on the Internet. *Deviant Behavior*, 34, 579–585.

Quinn, J. F., Forsyth, C. J., & Mullen-Quinn, C. (2004). Societal reaction to sex offenders: A review of the origins and results of the myths surrounding their crimes and treatment amenability. *Deviant Behavior*, 25, 215–232.

Raymond, J. G., & Hughes, D. M. (2001). Sex trafficking of women in the United States: International and domestic trends. Washington, DC: U.S. Department of Justice. Retrieved June 10, 2008, from www.ncjrs.gov/pdffiles1/nij/grants/187774. pdf

Rhode, D. L. (1989). *Justice and Gender: Sex Discrimination and the Law.* Cambridge, MA: Harvard University Press.

Rice-Hughes, D. (2005). *Recent statistics on Internet dangers.* [Online] Available at: www.protectkids.com/dangers/stats.htm

Roberts, J. W., & Hunt, S. A. (2012). Social control in a sexually deviant cybercommunity: A cappers' code of conduct. *Deviant Behavior*, 33, 757–773.

Rogers, M., & Seigfried-Spellar, K. (2013). Internet Child Pornography: Legal Issues and Investigative Tactics. In Holt, T. J. (ed.) *Crime Online*, pp. 113–132. Raleigh, NC: Carolina Academic.

Rosenmann, A., & Safir, M. P. (2006). Forced online: Pushed factors of Internet sexuality. A preliminary study of paraphilic empowerment. *Journal of Homosexuality*, 51, 71–92.

Royal Canadian Mounted Police. (2014). *Online Child Sexual Exploitation.* [Online] Available at: www.rcmp-grc.gc.ca/ncecc-cncee/index-accueil-eng.htm

Scott, M. S., & Dedel, K. (2006). Street prostitution. *Problem Oriented Policing Guide Series (2).* Washington D.C.: Office of Community Oriented Policing Services, U.S. Department of Justice.

Seidman, K. (2013). Child pornography laws 'too harsh' to deal with minors sexting photos without consent, experts say. *National Post,* November 16, 2013. [Online] Available at: http://news.nationalpost.com/2013/11/16/child-pornography-laws-too-harsh-to-deal-with-minors-sexting-photos-without-consent-experts-say/

Seto, M. C., Cantor, J. M., & Blanchard, R. (2006). Child pornography offenses are a valid diagnostic indicator of pedophilia, *Journal of Abnormal Psychology,* 115(3), 610–615.

Seto, M. C., & Eke, A. W. (2005). The criminal histories and later offending of child pornography offenders. *Sexual Abuse: A Journal of Research and Treatment,* 17, 201–210.

Sharp, K., & Earle, S. (2003). Cyberpunters and Cyberwhores: Prostitution on the Internet. In Y. Jewkes (ed.), *Dot Cons. Crime, Deviance and Identity on the Internet* (pp. 33–89). Portland, OR: Willan Publishing.

Soothill, K., & Sanders, T. (2005). The geographical mobility, preferences and pleasures of prolific punters: A demonstration study of the activities of prostitutes' clients. *Sociological Research On-Line* 10. [Online] Available at: www.socresonline.org.uk/10/1/soothill.html

Taylor, M., & Quayle, E. (2003). *Child Pornography: An Internet Crime.* Hove: Brunner-Routledge.

Taylor, M., Quayle, E., & Holland, G. (2001). Child pornography, the Internet and offending. *Isuma,* 2, 9–100.

Thomas, E. (2014). Google glass sex app lets you watch, record yourself in the act. *The Huffington Post,* January 25, 2014. [Online] Available at: www.huffingtonpost.com/2014/01/21/google-glass-sex_n_4637741.html

Tuman, J. (2003). Miller v. California. In R. A. Parker (ed.) *Free Speech on Trial: Communication Perspectives on Landmark Supreme Court Decisions* (pp. 187–202). Tuscaloosa, AL: University of Alabama Press.

US Department of Justice. (2014). *Citizen's guide to US federal law on obscenity.* [Online] Available at: www.justice.gov/criminal/ceos/citizensguide/citizensguide_obscenity.html

US Postal Inspection Service. (2008). *A law enforcement guide to the US Postal Inspection Service.* [Online] Available at: https://www.hsdl.org/?view&did=34409

US Postal Inspection Service. (2014). *Child Exploitation.* [Online] Available at: https://postalinspectors.uspis.gov/investigations/MailFraud/fraudschemes/ce/CE.aspx

Virtual Global Task Force, (2014). *VGT Making a Difference.* [Online] Available at: www.virtualglobaltaskforce.com/what-we-do/

Weitzer, R. (2000). *Sex for Sale.* London: Routledge.

Weitzer, R. (2005). New directions in research on prostitution. *Crime, Law and Social Change,* 43, 211–35.

Weitzer, R. (2012). *Legalizing Prostitution: From Illicit Vice to Lawful Business.* New York: NYU Press.

West, R. (1998). U.S Prostitutes Collective. In F. Delacoste & P. Alexander (eds), *Sex Work: Writings by Women in the Sex Industry*, 2nd ed. (pp. 279–289). San Francisco, CA: Cleis Press.

Yar, M. (2013). *Cybercrime and Society*. Thousand Oaks, CA: SAGE.

chapter 7

Cyberbullying, online harassment, and cyberstalking

Online threats, bullying, and harassment

The development of email and other forms of CMC has completely changed the way in which we engage socially with others. Facebook, Twitter, and other social media platforms make it easy for us to tell friends and the whole world what we are up to, when, and with whom, around the clock. Social living sites like Foursquare allow users to check in to a location so that everyone can know where to find them at any time of day. The ability to post videos and photos allows us to share virtually every facet of our lives with whoever is interested.

The relatively open nature in which people can now lead their lives is unparalleled and limited only by an individual's willingness to share. While it may seem that technology engenders users to be truthful about themselves and their lives, there is increasing evidence that people are very willing to say and post whatever they can to either become popular or to connect with individuals with whom they are interested to meet. In fact, the creation and development of relationships through social media predicated on false information has gained prominent attention in the last few years. This act has been referred to as "**catfishing**" after the documentary movie and television show of the same name (Peterson, 2013). Both the film and show follow individuals as they attempt to disentangle and identify who is actually behind the social networking profile with whom they have built an emotional, though non-physical, relationship (see Text Box 7.1 for an example of catfishing).

Text Box 7.1: Catfishing in the news

www.bostonglobe.com/ideas/2013/01/27/catfish-how-manti-imaginary-romance-got-its-name/inqu9zV8RQ7j19BRGQkH7H/story.html

Catfish: How Manti Te'o's imaginary romance got its name

"Catfish" is the name of a 2010 documentary about an online romance that turned out to be predicated on a fictitious identity. The makers of the movie developed a spinoff reality show for MTV, also called "Catfish," devoted to the same theme of duplicity in virtual relationships.

This article provides an overview of catfishing and the ways that individuals are affected by people who prey on their emotions and hide behind the anonymity afforded by technology.

While catfishing is not illegal, individuals can be emotionally hurt as a result of discovering a relationship they developed is predicated on lies. In addition, catfishing is just one of many problematic behaviors that can emerge from the Internet and CMCs. When relationships dissolve and couples break up, there is some evidence that the individual who was dumped may turn to email, Facebook, or even YouTube in order to post comments about his or her ex that are disparaging or hurtful. The increasing ability that we have to take video and images and send them to others has led some to post intimate or candid materials in online public places in order to embarrass or shame their ex.

At the same time, young people are increasingly using technology as a means to send bullying or harassing emails to classmates or people that they do not like. Such messages may be readily ignored, but if the sender is persistent, or if others begin to "like" or repost the messages, it may lead the victim to feel ashamed, frightened, or sad. A number of youth have tragically committed suicide over their experiences, though this is an extreme outcome. The most notable of these incidents occurred in 2006 with the suicide of a young girl named **Megan Meier**. She befriended who she thought was a young boy about the same age named Josh Evans through the social networking site MySpace (Morphy, 2008). Their conversations became frequent, and eventually she became emotionally attached to him. That is, until he began to send her mean and hurtful messages and told her that the world would be a better place without her. Shortly thereafter, Megan hanged herself and was found by her parents. It was subsequently discovered that the boy she was talking with did not actually exist. The account was an early instance of catfishing; it was actually created by **Lori Drew**, the mother of one of Megan's former friends. The two younger girls had a falling out, and Drew opened the account to embarrass Megan. Though the outcome was not at all what Drew had intended (Morphy, 2008), it did not change the fact that Megan died.

For more on the Megan Meier story, go online to: www.youtube.com/watch?v=fGYVHFYop9E

The Megan Meier case quickly became a lightning rod, drawing national attention to the problem of cyberbullying. Unfortunately, multiple instances of suicides stemming from cyberbullying have occurred worldwide. For instance, a 14-year-old girl named Hannah Smith in Lancashire, England, killed herself after receiving hundreds of harassing comments on the website Last.FM (Fricker, 2013). Similarly, a 16-year-old girl in Singapore was thought to have committed suicide as a result of a former boyfriend posting mean and hurtful comments on Facebook and via email (Chen, 2011).

All of these instances demonstrate that the use of technology can cause real-world harm, which David Wall would classify as cyber-violence (see Chapter 1 for further discussion). What we know about these issues, however, is challenged by the overlapping definitions of bullying, harassment, and stalking, as well as our limited knowledge of the prevalence of victimization. This chapter will explore these issues in depth, beginning with the common definitions used for these offenses, estimates of both victimization and offending, and the impact that they have on victims in general. We will also discuss the inherent legal challenges that have developed and the existing statutes that can be used to prosecute these offenses. Finally, we will explore the agencies and groups involved in the investigation of these offenses. In turn, readers should be able to have a greatly expanded appreciation for the overlap of these events and the general threats these forms of online harm can pose to all Internet users.

Defining cyberbullying

One of the most prominent concerns of the last decade is the issue of bullying, particularly cyberbullying, due to the increasing prominence of technology and its use among young people. In the physical world, bullying is typically defined as the use of intentional and repeated use of aggressive or negative behaviors based on an imbalance of power between individuals, most typically a weaker victim (Klomek *et al.*, 2008; Nansel *et al.*, 2001; Olweus, 1993). Bullying may take multiple forms, ranging from verbal threats or insults (like name-calling or teasing) to more serious physical harm (such as being hit or kicked). These behaviors may produce negative emotional reactions from the victim due to embarrassment, shame, intimidation, anger, sadness, or frustration (Klomek *et al.*, 2008; Nansel *et al.*, 2001).

Many of these characteristics are evident when considering bullying in virtual environments as well. In fact, **cyberbullying** can be defined as any intentional, aggressive behavior performed through electronic means (Hinduja and Patchin, 2008). Though a bully cannot physically injure an individual through CMCs, they can cause emotional harm and social embarrassment by sending threatening, mean, or hurtful messages via instant messaging, email, posts on social media, and text messages via cell phones (Hinduja and Patchin, 2008).

> **For more on cyberbullying, go online to: 1)** www.cyberbullying.us, **and 2)** www.bullying.co.uk/cyberbullying/

Similar to traditional bullying, cyberbullying can also take multiple forms. Willard (2007) proposed an eight-category typology of cyberbullying to characterize the activities of bullies and the experience of victims:

1) **Flaming**: engaging in online fighting where users directly target one another with angry or irritated messages, often featuring vulgar language;
2) **Denigration**: making comments about individuals' characters or behaviors that are designed to harm their reputation, friendships, or social positions, such as saying that someone is a homosexual or making fun of that person;
3) **Impersonation**: falsely posting as other people to harm their reputation or social status by logging into their existing accounts to post messages or by creating fake accounts to masquerade as that person;
4) **Outing**: posting real personal information about individuals to embarrass them, such as sending images of them in states of undress, posting who they are attracted to, or information about homosexual preferences which may not be known to the general public;

5) **Trickery**: convincing individuals to provide personal information about themselves in what they think is a personal conversation, which is then revealed to the general public;

6) **Exclusion**: intentionally keeping others from joining an online group, such as a network on Facebook or some other site online;

7) **Harassment**: the repeated distribution of cruel or mean messages to a person in order to embarrass or annoy them;

8) **Stalking**: the use of repeated and intense harassing messages that involve threats or cause the recipient to feel fear for their personal safety.

The typology proposed by Willard (2007) recognizes the substantive variation in harm that can occur online. In addition, it recognizes that bullying does not require repeated harm. Posting personal information online that was shared in confidence *one time* is cyberbullying. Messages, however, can also be sent repeatedly and nearly instantaneously to a prospective victim throughout the day (Jones, Mitchell, and Finkelhor, 2012). The constant exposure to hurtful messages can cause persistent and pervasive emotional and psychological harm for a victim. In addition, a message can be posted in multiple environments, such as Facebook, Twitter, and YouTube, within a short amount of time. As a result, multiple individuals may engage in a bullying experience by reposting content or "liking" what someone posts. This can cause significant harm for a victim by making them feel as though the whole world is laughing at them and they cannot escape it. Thus, cyberbullying may be just as harmful for the victim as real-world bullying – sometimes more.

As a final point of concern, bullying could also be viewed as harassment or stalking. Many typically associate bullying, on or offline, with juvenile populations where power differentials are common. One researcher even went so far as to argue that cyberbullying can only occur between minors, whereas any other involvement with adults should be viewed as harassment or stalking (Aftab, 2006). Others have suggested that adults can be bullied, particularly in the workplace where there is greater potential for individuals to intimidate or otherwise affect those with less power (Kowalski, Limber, and Agatston, 2008). This has some salience in school environments, where students may attempt to harass their teachers online or make fun of them for certain activities. However, the degree to which teachers are harassed or bullied by students has been given relatively little focus. Most researchers instead focus only on the issue of bullying in juvenile populations (Bossler, Holt, and May, 2012; Klomek *et al.*, 2008; Marcum, 2010; Nansel *et al.*, 2001). As a result, we will only discuss the issue of bullying in juveniles and discuss potential age variations later in the chapter.

The prevalence of cyberbullying

Rates of cyberbullying vary substantially based on the group of youth sampled, the time the data were collected, and the way in which bullying was defined, or operationalized, by the authors. These issues make it quite difficult to accurately document the scope of cyberbullying within a single place over time, let alone cross-nationally. In general, the proportion of kids who have experienced cyberbullying is somewhat lower than that of traditional bullying in the real world. Several nationally representative samples of youth in the US indicate that the rate of bullying is between 11 (Nansel *et al.*, 2001) and 30 percent in a given year (Haynie *et al.*, 2001). Rates in the UK demonstrate that between 29 (Department for Children, Schools, and Families, 2010) and 46 percent of youth experience bullying at some point in their lives (Chamberlain, George, Golden, Walker, and Benton, 2010). Thus, this is a substantive global problem for youth generally.

Initial estimates of cyberbullying within the US varied in the early 2000s with rates between 6 percent (Thorp, 2004) and 7 percent in a 12-month period (Ybarra and Mitchell, 2004). Recent estimates from the US suggest that rates of cyberbullying have increased, which may be a reflection of greater access to technology at early ages. Kowalski and Limber (2007) found that 18 percent of a sample of middle school youth reported being cyberbullied over a 12-month period. Similarly, a recent study of 4,441 10 to 18 year olds by Hinduja and Patchin (2012) found 20.8 percent of their sample had experienced cyberbullying at some point in their life. These rates may, however, be a result of distinctive student samples, as results from the nationally representative **National Crime Victimization Survey-Supplemental Survey** on bullying and cyberbullying found that approximately 6 percent of students aged 12 to 18 were cyberbullied during the 2008–2009 academic year (DeVoe, Bauer, and Hill 2011).

For more information and statistics on cyberbullying, go online to:
http://cyberbullying.us/2010_charts/cyberbullying_victim_2010.jpg

It is also important to note that there is some consistency between cyberbullying victimization rates and those of youth engaging in cyberbullying behaviors. Ybarra and Mitchell (2004) found 18 percent of a sample of youth engaged in cyberbullying offending in a one-year period. A similar rate has been identified across multiple studies conducted by Hinduja and Patchin (2012). In fact, their first sample of 370 youth found that 20.1 percent of their sample engaged in some form of online bullying. In one of their most recent studies from 2010 with 4,441 youth, 19.4 percent of kids engaged in cyberbullying behaviors. When viewed as an average, however, the reported rate of bullying is 16.9 percent overall. Thus, there is some consistency between the rates of cyberbullying offending and victimization.

When examined internationally, the rates of cyberbullying victimization reported are also substantial and similar to those of the US. Recent research from a Canadian sample suggests that almost 25 percent of middle school students had been cyberbullied (Li, 2008). Estimates from the UK suggest that rates of cyberbullying vary between 8 percent and 38 percent of youth, depending on the form of victimization, time of data collection, and the population studied (Department for Education, 2011; Tarapdar and Kellett, 2011). A study of 276 Turkish youth, aged 14 to 18, indicated that 23.9 percent experienced cyberbullying, 15.9 percent engaged in cyberbullying, and 21.4 percent experienced cyberbullying as both victim and perpetrator (Erdur-Baker, 2010). Research on cyberbullying in a Chinese sample suggests the lifetime victimization rate can be quite high at 33 percent of a middle school population (Li, 2008). Data from a nationally representative sample of youth in Singapore suggests that while 67 percent of youth experience some form of physical bullying, only 18.9 percent experience cyberbullying, and 18 percent report some form of cyberbullying via a mobile device during a 12-month period (Holt, Chee, Ng, and Bossler, 2013).

Predictors of bullying on and offline

Taken as a whole, these statistics suggest cyberbullying is a problem that at least one out of every six youth may experience in his or her life. It is not clear if this will increase over the next decade as phone adoption and social networking use expands across the world. Despite the lack of clarity on this issue, there are specific factors that may increase the risk of cyberbullying victimization for youth.

First, females may be more likely to report cyberbullying victimization than males based on the way that females and males differ in their expression of aggression and harmful behaviors. Boys generally report higher levels of physical bullying and aggressive behavior; females appear to use more indirect tactics focused on causing emotional harm through behaviors like spreading gossip (Boulton and Underwood, 1992; Klomek et al., 2008; Nabuzoka, 2003). The evidence on sex differences for cyberbullying victimization, however, is mixed based on the sample population. Several studies have found no gender differences in cyberbullying (Hinduja and Patchin, 2008; Li, 2006), although a small number of researchers have found that girls are more likely to be targeted (Kowalski et al., 2008; Ybarra, Mitchell, Finkelhor, and Wolak, 2007; Ybarra and Mitchell, 2004).

Second, there is also a link between age and cyberbullying victimization. While most research suggests that younger children are more likely to experience bullying in the real world (Borg, 1999; Olweus, 1993), cyberbullying is more likely to be reported by older youth (Sbarbaro and Smith, 2011; Tokunaga, 2010). The age variations noted may stem from differential access to technology since the very young may have limited access to computer and mobile phone technology (Smith et al., 2008). As kids reach their early teens, they are more likely to receive access to and free use of computers and phones, thereby increasing their exposure to bullying.

cyberbullying, online harassment, cyberstalking

Third, in keeping with access to technology, the use of certain technologies may increase the risk of cyberbullying victimization. Spending time online in social networks, chat rooms, and email can increase one's risk of experiencing electronic bullying or harassment (Berson, Berson, and Ferron, 2002; Hinduja and Patchin, 2008; Holt and Bossler, 2009; Twyman, Saylor, Taylor, and Comeaux, 2010; Ybarra and Mitchell, 2004). Ybarra and Mitchell (2004), however, also found that increased use of the Internet generally may also increase the odds of online harassment victimization for females, but not for males.

Fourth, the methods through which individuals share information in online environments are also related to online harassment victimization because it decreases personal guardianship, or the ability to protect oneself from harm. Individuals who provide sensitive information about themselves in public places, like a social network profile, have an increased risk of bullying victimization (Mitchell, Finkelhor, and Becker-Blease, 2007). Posting school schedules, home addresses, or images and stories of themselves in compromising situations provides offenders fodder for attack (Hinduja and Patchin, 2009). As a consequence, individuals who do not carefully manage personal or sensitive information may increase their risk of victimization.

Fifth, being bullied in the real world is also unfortunately a strong predictor for being bullied in the virtual world as well. The relationship between bullying across both environments appears consistently, regardless of where the sample was generated (Erdur-Baker, 2010: Hinduja and Patchin, 2008; Kowalski and Limber, 2007; Ybarra and Mitchell, 2004). This may be due to the fact that being bullied in the real world could immediately make someone a target for bullying in virtual spaces. In addition, the difficulty in escaping the bullying experience when it operates both on and offline may have a greater impact on the victim, making them more likely to report negative psychological and emotional outcomes (Holt et al., 2013; Olweus, 1993; Tokunaga, 2010).

To understand the predictors of bullying, we must also examine it from the offender's point of view in order to provide insight into which youth are more likely to bully others. In general, these youth appear to have a temper and may be easily frustrated (Camodeca and Goossens, 2005; Holt, Bossler, and May, 2012). They are also more likely to report lower levels of self-control and display behaviors indicating that as well. For example, they report greater problem behaviors at school (Hinduja and Patchin, 2008). At the same time, they also have low compassion and empathy toward others, making it difficult for them to understand how their actions affect other people (Camodeca and Goossens, 2005).

Individuals who engage in cyberbullying also tend to engage in assaultive behaviors offline, including bullying behaviors (Hinduja and Patchin, 2008). Cyberbullies also appear to spend more time online and engage in various online activities ranging from checking email to spending time in social networking sites, which is sensible given the mechanisms needed in order to bully others online (Hinduja and Patchin, 2008). There are, however, few demographic correlates, as neither gender nor age appear to be clearly related to cyberbullying activities. Studies find that both males and females engage in cyberbullying, though females may do so with somewhat greater frequency. Similarly, studies have found mixed relationships between age and cyberbullying (Tokunaga, 2010). There is some limited evidence that African Americans report higher levels of cyberbullying behaviors (Wang, Iannotti, and Nansel, 2009), though this relationship is not consistent across multiple studies. As a result, it is important that we consider how the behavioral and attitudinal correlates of bullying may be used to better understand and intervene in bullying encounters to reduce the negative outcomes kids may experience.

The challenge of online harassment and stalking

As identified earlier, some categorize harassment and stalking under the definition of cyberbullying. These definitional issues make it difficult to truly differentiate harassment and stalking. In fact, Sinclair and Frieze (2000) argue that there is no way to identify what behaviors should be classified as harassment or stalking, and thus the terms should be used interchangeably. There are, however, a few salient points that could be used in order to identify when an incident may be defined as **online harassment** or as **cyberstalking**. While both behaviors involve the constant use of email, text, or some other form of CMC, the effects these messages have on the victim are pertinent. Instances of harassment may be viewed as bothersome, annoying, or unwanted by the recipient, but these communications do not necessarily portray a threat (Turmanis and Brown, 2006). By contrast, **cyberstalking** may lead a victim to feel fear for their personal safety and/ or experience emotional distress (Bocij, 2004). In both cases, the recipient should indicate to the sender that they want the messages to stop. Such an indication is important in order to help law enforcement pursue a criminal case against the sender.

It is also important to recognize that cyberstalking is related to, but not equivalent to, traditional stalking activities (Bocij, 2004; Bocij and McFarlane, 2002). In cases of real-world stalking, the actor may track his victim and show up unannounced and unwelcome in various places, which may intimidate or cause fear in the victim (Bocij, 2004). Cyberstalking may involve a variety of online activities that produce similar results, such as monitoring a person's online behaviors, gathering personal information about that individual through various outlets, and sending hostile or threatening messages that imply they will cause bodily harm to the victim or to their property (see Text Box 7.2 for an example; Bocij, 2004).

The range of cyberstalking does not simply end with virtual threats. A few cyberstalkers have sent malicious software, like keylogging programs, in order to monitor all aspects of their victims' behaviors (Bocij, 2004). Other cyberstalkers make false posts in various sites impersonating their victims in order to embarrass them or cause them physical harm (Bocij, 2004). For instance, a convicted cyberstalker in the US named Shawn Sayer posted sexually explicit videos of his ex-fiancée to porn sites under her actual name, along with a Facebook account that reposted the videos (Hoey, 2012). He would then contact individuals who liked the content and arranged meetings with the men at her home in order to have sex. The various men who showed up at the victim's home were then confused when she had no idea why they were there and made her fear that she would be raped or otherwise hurt (Hoey, 2012).

A cyberstalker, however, does not have to engage in real-world stalking and vice versa (Bocij, 2004). The anonymity afforded by the Internet coupled with the volume of information available about individuals via social network sites and other self-generated content allows people to engage in stalking behaviors with ease (Bocij, 2004). In addition, cyberstalkers need not know their victims, which is in contrast to real-world stalking (Bocij, 2004). Instead, a prospective stalker can identify any random target through Google searches or simple online interactions (Bocij, 2004). The threats posed by cyberstalkers can be just as serious as those in the real world and can produce the same response in victims as those found in traditional stalking activities offline (Bocij, 2004).

For an example of a stranger-driven case of cyberstalking, go online to: www.buffalonews.com/apps/pbcs.dll/article?AID=/20121117/CITYANDREGION/121119227/1003

Rates of harassment and stalking

In light of the challenges inherent in differentiating between harassment and stalking, it is important to attempt to identify the rates of these offenses in the general population. One of the best estimates of online harassment in the US comes from the **Youth Internet Safety Survey (YISS)** sponsored by the National Center for Missing and Exploited Children (Jones *et al.*, 2012). This study of youths aged 10 to 17 years old who regularly used the Internet was administered in three waves, the first in 2000, the second in 2005, and the third in 2010. There was an increase in online harassment victimization across the three time periods. First, the proportion of youth who reported online harassment, as defined by receiving threats or offensive comments either sent to them or posted about them online for others to see, grew from 6 percent in 2000 to 9 percent in 2005 to 11 percent in 2010 (Jones *et al.*, 2012). Within these samples, the number of youths who reported distress, as measured by fear or being upset because of the harassment, increased from 3 percent in 2000 and 2005 to 5 percent in 2010 (Jones *et al.*, 2012). In addition, the proportion of youths who experienced repeated harassment increased from 2 percent in 2000 to 4 percent in 2005 to 5 percent in 2010 (Jones *et al.*, 2012).

The YISS also captures youth engaging in harassment against other children. These figures showed an increase in the proportion of youth engaging in harassment within each wave (Jones *et al.*, 2012). Specifically, those kids making rude or nasty comments online increased from 14 percent in 2000 to 28 percent in 2005 to 40 percent in 2010. A similar increase was evident in youths who used online spaces to embarrass or harass someone out of anger or spite. This rate increased from 1 percent in 2000 to 9 percent in 2005 to 10 percent in 2010 (Jones *et al.*, 2012). These figures clearly illustrate that the prevalence of harassment has increased for modern youth.

Similar responses are noted in populations of college students using assessments of their experiences over a 12-month period, though it again depends largely on the population sampled. In a study of New Hampshire college students, Finn (2004) found that 10 to 15 percent of students reported receiving harassing messages via email or instant messaging, and more than half received unsolicited pornography. Similarly, Holt and Bossler (2009) found that 18.9 percent of a convenience sample of college students at a southeastern university received unwanted emails or instant messages. Also, in a random sample of students from a single university, Marcum, Ricketts, and Higgins (2010) found that harassment victimization ranged from 6.5 to 34.9 percent, depending on the type of harassment reported.

There are also a small number of sources available to understand the scope of cyberstalking. One of the few truly nationally representative studies assessing cyberstalking in the US comes from the **National Crime Victimization Survey-Supplemental Survey** (NCVS-SS; Catalano, 2012). Using a population of 65,270 people collected in 2008, the survey found that 26.1 percent of those who reported being stalked were sent emails that made them feel fear (Catalano, 2012). Similarly, Fisher, Cullen, and Turner (2000) developed a nationally representative sample of college students and found that 24.7 percent of those who were stalked received repeated emails that seemed obsessive or led them to feel fear. Spitzberg and Hoobler (2002) found some degree of variation in responses based on the type of stalking reported, ranging from 1 percent to 31 percent for more common activities.

For more on the NCVS study, go online to: www.bjs.gov/content/pub/pdf/svus_rev.pdf

In Canada, statistics suggest that 7 percent of all adults received threatening or aggressive emails and instant messages (Perrault, 2013). The majority of these messages come from strangers (46 percent of male victims; 34 percent of female victims), or acquaintances (21 percent of male victims; 15 percent of female victims; Perrault, 2013). A recent survey conducted by the **National Centre for Cyberstalking Research** (2011) in the UK found that approximately 75 percent of a sample of 353 people experienced some form of online harassment. The majority of messages were sent via social networking sites (62.1 percent males; 63.1 percent female) or through personal email accounts (55.8 percent males/56.4 percent females). There are, however, no current national statistics collected within the UK to assess arrest rates or victim reports of cyberstalking victimization (National Centre for Cyberstalking Research, 2011).

Understanding victims' experiences of cyber-violence

It is clear that many aggressive and hurtful comments can be sent through CMCs and that many people are victimized as a result. The responses that victims have to bullying, harassment, and stalking, however, are quite varied. A proportion of individuals are able to brush off their experience and move forward without taking the comments of their harasser or stalker to heart. However, some experience emotional or physical harm, and a very small proportion even go so far as to seriously contemplate suicide (Ybarra and Mitchell, 2004). To better understand the victim response, we will examine each form of cyber-violence in turn.

Cyberbullying produces different effects on the victim and perpetrator, often mirroring reactions to physical bullying. Victims of cyberbullying often exhibit symptoms of depression, stress, and anxiety (Ybarra and Mitchell, 2004). Social withdrawal and school failure can also occur. These responses are more likely if cyberbullying incidents occur in tandem with offline bullying. Young people may begin to skip school, or be **truant**, in order to try to avoid persistent or repeated victimization (Katzer, Fetchenhauer, and Belschak, 2009; Ybarra *et al.*, 2007). In fact, data from a nationally representative survey of youth suggests that 4 percent of kids who were cyberbullied skipped school, relative to the 0.04 percent of those who skipped school but were not victimized (Robers, Zhang, Truman, and Snyder, 2012). Truancy may also occur because the victim feels that school is no longer a safe place to be, particularly when they experience substantive bullying both online and offline (Varjas, Henrich, and Meyers, 2009).

Some youth may also skip school to avoid shame, embarrassment, and stigma associated with their bullying experiences on or offline. In fact, Kowalski *et al.* (2008) argue that the negative impact of cyberbullying can even be worse than physical bullying experiences, due to the persistent nature of their victimization. A youth may be shoved, hit, or called names in the hallways at school, but they can escape that experience once they leave the campus. In contrast, cyberbullying is much more difficult to avoid, as bullying messages can be sent continuously to the victim, be reposted by others, and can also reappear, making the victim feel helpless (Campbell, 2005; Li, 2006).

One of the most noteworthy examples of the impact of cyberbullying on youth depression and behavior is the experience of Ghyslain Raza, also known as the **"Star Wars Kid."** The 15-year-old Raza, a high school student in Trois-Rivieres, Quebec, Canada, made a video of himself swinging a golf ball retriever (Wei, 2010). His movements were similar to the style of Darth Maul, the dual-lightsaber-wielding Sith Lord from *Star Wars: Episode 1*. Raza had set up a camcorder to make a tape of himself for a school project in the fall of 2002 and filmed himself with no intention of others seeing his "lightsaber" strikes. However, one of his classmates found the tape in April 2003 and showed it to a friend, who then converted the tape to a digital format (Wei, 2010). The two boys then distributed the video via email to friends, and it began to spread across the student body. One student even posted the video to a peer-to-peer file sharing site with the title Jackass_star-wars_funny.wmv, where it became a viral phenomena.

The mental anguish young Raza experienced was quite severe because so many people saw the video and constantly made fun of him for his activities. He became severely depressed, dropped out of school, and was institutionalized for psychological treatment by the end of 2003 (Wei, 2010). Raza's family sued the families of four of the boys who discovered the video and posted it online for damages and emotional harm, which led to an out-of-court settlement for an undisclosed amount. The video, however, has been seen over 1 billion times on various online media outlets since it was first posted. Thus, the global spread of hurtful content can have substantial impact on a victim's emotional well-being.

In addition to school absences and emotional harm, some victims of cyberbullying report having suicidal thoughts, or suicidal ideation, as a result of their experiences (Hinduja and Patchin, 2008; Klomek *et al.*, 2008; Li, 2006). Individuals who experience suicidal ideation often have negative attitudes generally, which may be a long-term consequence of bullying experiences on and offline (Arseneault *et al.*, 2006; Beran and Li, 2007; Nansel *et al.*, 2001). Over the last few years, there has been a substantial amount of media attention around cyberbullying and suicide. Much of this stems from the seminal Megan Meier case discussed earlier and the multiple incidents of cyberbullying victimization leading to suicides around the world, causing some to question if suicidal ideation is a distinct problem or just an extreme and unusual circumstance (see Text Box 7.3 for details on the Audrie Pott suicide case). Thus, the connection between virtual and real experiences must be considered further.

Text Box 7.3: The unfortunate suicides resulting from bullying

http://usnews.nbcnews.com/_news/2013/04/14/17747411-california-case-another-three-part-tragedy-of-rape-cyber-bullying-and-suicide?lite
California case another three-part tragedy of rape, cyberbullying and suicide

> Three boys accused of sexually assaulting a 15-year-old California girl who took her own life after pictures of the attack were posted online are due in court this week, as authorities ramp up their investigation into the latest case involving rape and cyber bullying.

This article provides an overview of the harm that can result from cyberbullying incidents, as evident in the case of a young girl who committed suicide after being assaulted and having pictures of the incident posted online and shared by others.

Victims of cyberstalking and online harassment may report similar experiences to those of bullying because of the persistent messages and threats they receive. In particular, victims typically report feeling powerless, shamed, and socially isolated from others (Ashcroft, 2001; Blauuw *et al.*, 2002). Anxiety and depression may also be a common outcome due to concerns about actualizations of threats or the worry over receiving more messages.

Some victims of bullying, stalking, and harassment may begin to change their behaviors as a response to their victimization, deciding to either take steps to defend themselves or reduce their risk of further victimization. For instance, evidence from the NCVS supplemental study on bullying (Catalano, 2012) found that those who were cyberbullied were more likely to carry a knife, gun, or other defensive weapon to school. A comparative analysis by Sheridan and Grant (2007) found no differences in the behavioral patterns of victims of either traditional or cyberstalking. Victims of traditional stalking report changing their behavior patterns in order to reduce the risk of victimization. Some also change their address, phone number, or email address in order to help reduce their ability to be identified (Baum, Catalano, Rand, and Rose, 2009; Nobles, Reyns, Fox, and Fisher, 2012). A small proportion of victims also begin to carry a defense weapon, like pepper spray (Wilcox, Jordan, and Pritchard, 2007; Nobles *et al.*, 2012). Approximately 10 to 15 percent of victims either stop spending time around friends or family in order to minimize their risk of exposure, or they begin to stay with loved ones in order to increase their feelings of personal safety and protection (Nobles *et al.*, 2012). Victims who felt higher degrees of fear were more likely to engage in a higher number of these self-protective behaviors (Nobles *et al.*, 2012).

Reporting online bullying, harassment, and stalking

Though there are substantive psychological and behavioral consequences for victims of bullying, harassment, and stalking, it appears that very few report these incidents to agencies or individuals who can help them. While many researchers examine the prevalence of cyberbullying or traditional bullying, few have considered how often these behaviors are reported. One of the only studies to look at reporting with a nationally representative sample suggests that approximately 75 percent of kids harassed told someone about the incident, though they primarily told friends rather than parents (Priebe, Mitchell, and Finkelhor, 2013). Similarly, the NCVS supplemental survey on bullying (Catalano, 2012) found that 31 percent of youths contacted a teacher or school official about their experience. Those who did not report the incident made this decision because they felt that it was either not serious enough or was so common that no one would take them seriously (Priebe *et al.*, 2013).

The lack of reporting to parents or authority figures may be a consequence of concerns among youth that they may lose access to the technology that enables cyberbullying (Hinduja and Patchin, 2009; Marcum, 2010). In fact, youth who experience cyberbullying were likely to have had a conversation with their parent(s) about harassment and the risks associated with online communication, though it did not affect their likelihood of reporting the incident (Priebe *et al.*, 2013). A logical parental response may be to take away their child's cell phone or perhaps limit the amount of time that they can spend online. Such a response may be undesirable, especially for a teenager who only recently acquired a cell phone or is used to having unrestricted access to technology.

Instead, many youths who are cyberbullied tend to simply delete the messages they receive, ignore it when possible, or block the sender in order to reduce their exposure (Parris, Varjas, Meyers, and Cutts, 2012; Priebe *et al.*, 2013). In fact, most youth only report the incident if they feel it is severe (Holtfeld and Grabe, 2012; Slonje, Smith, and Frisen, 2013), such as if it lasts for several days or produces a severe emotional response (Priebe *et al.*, 2013). Limited research on the topic suggests that reporting cyberbullying experiences to parents decreases as youths age (McQuade, Colt, and Meyer, 2009; Slonje *et al.*, 2013). Instead, teens are more likely to report cyberbullying experiences to their peers as a coping strategy. In addition, parents do not appear to report instances of cyberbullying to police due to perceptions that they will not be able to handle the case due to limited laws (Hinduja and Patchin, 2009; McQuade *et al.*, 2009). Similarly, there is some evidence that school administrators may not want to contact police due to concerns over how the incident will impact the school's reputation (McQuade *et al.*, 2009).

Similar issues are evident in the number of cyberstalking or harassment cases reported to law enforcement agencies. Statistics on victim-reporting from the NCVS suggest that approximately 42 percent of female stalking victims and 14 percent of female harassment victims contacted police (Catalano, 2012). The data reported for this study were amended recently due to errors in the way in which some acts of stalking and harassment were coded. As a result, it is not clear how many cases were actually made known to police (Catalano, 2012). Using information from a nationally representative sample of female college students, Fisher and her colleagues (2000) found that less than four percent of women sought a restraining order against their stalker and less than two percent filed criminal charges. Though there is less information available on cyberstalking and harassment victim-reporting internationally, evidence from the Canadian Uniform Crime Reporting (UCR) Survey found that the majority (70 percent) of victims reporting intimidation or harassment online were female (Perreault, 2013).

The lack of reporting for stalking and harassment cases may be due to a perception among victims that their case will not be taken seriously by law enforcement (Nobles *et al.*, 2012). Victims of crimes like sexual assault or domestic violence often feel that their experience is not serious enough to report to police or will not be viewed as real by officers. In much the same way, victims of stalking and harassment cases, online or offline, may assume that officers will not be inclined to make a report or investigate. As a result, victims may feel abandoned by the criminal justice system and may proactively change behaviors that are perceived to put them at risk for further harassment. In fact, research suggests that victims who feel greater levels of fear because of the incident and perceive that they are being stalked are more likely to engage in multiple self-protective behaviors (Nobles *et al.*, 2012).

Regulating online bullying, harassment, and stalking

The prevalence of these various person-based online crimes requires substantive criminal laws in order to prosecute individuals who choose to engage in these behaviors. The amounts of legislative effort placed on these crimes, however, are mixed, depending on the offense. For instance, there are no federal statutes in the United States concerning bullying or cyberbullying. This is not a substantial issue given that most instances of cyberbullying involve people living in close physical proximity to one another. Some advocates called for the development of new federal laws after the death of Megan Meier and the subsequent failure to successfully prosecute this case. Specifically, Lori Drew, one of the two women responsible for the creation of the false MySpace page and comments that led to Meier's suicide, was charged in federal court for violations of the Computer Fraud and Abuse Act (Steinhauer, 2008; see Text Box 7.4 for detail on the applicability of these statutes). She was charged with three felony counts of computer fraud and one conspiracy count under the assumption that she violated MySpace's terms of service, which included the stipulation that users could not create fictitious accounts. The jury found Drew guilty on these three charges, though they were reduced to misdemeanor counts, and the conspiracy charge was thrown out (Steinhauer, 2008). The three charges of computer fraud, however, were also thrown out and Drew was fully acquitted in July 2009 after the judge argued against the use of this statute, which is normally reserved to prosecute computer hackers and data thieves (see Chapters 2 and 5 for details on the statutes; Zetter, 2009).

Text Box 7.4: The Computer Fraud and Abuse Act applied to Megan Meier's death

www.ecommercetimes.com/story/65424.html
    The Computer Fraud Act: Bending a Law to Fit a Notorious Case

> Officials were determined to punish Lori Drew for something – the suicide of young Megan Meier seemed a direct consequence of her actions ... Drew ultimately was convicted of three misdemeanors, but prosecutors had to stretch a law beyond its original intent in order to win that outcome.

This article explains how Lori Drew was prosecuted under CFA statutes in the US, and why the case was fraught with difficulty. The case demonstrates why cybercrime law must be developed with flexibility and prospective application as technologies change.

---

cyberbullying, online harassment, cyberstalking

In the wake of the failed prosecution and debate over the utility of existing legislation, the Meier family began to pursue the creation of new laws to protect victims and seek justice against offenders at the federal level. This led to the development of US HR1966, called the **Megan Meier Cyberbullying Prevention Act,** which was proposed in 2009. This legislation would have made it illegal for anyone to use CMC "to coerce, intimidate, harass or cause substantial emotional distress to a person," or use electronic resources to "support severe, repeated, and hostile behavior" (Hinduja and Patchin, 2013: 17). The proposed legislation would have allowed for either fines or a two-year prison sentence. This resolution was not successfully passed into law (see Text Box 7.5 for details on the failure of this legislation).

Text Box 7.5: The failure of the Megan Meier bullying legislation

www.wired.com/threatlevel/2009/09/cyberbullyingbill/
Cyberbullying Bill Gets Chilly Reception

> Proposed legislation demanding up to two years in prison for electronic speech meant to "coerce, intimidate, harass or cause substantial emotional distress to a person" was met with little enthusiasm by a House subcommittee on Wednesday.

This article provides an overview of the failures in creating legislation to outlaw cyberbullying at the federal level in the US. The political and legal challenges that affect the adoption of legislation are both interesting and divisive and are further elaborated in this work.

Though the lack of federal legislation on bullying is bothersome, 49 states (with Montana as the sole hold-out) and the District of Columbia have laws in place concerning bullying and require that schools have policies in place concerning bullying behaviors (Hinduja and Patchin, 2013: 1). In addition, 16 states have language incorporating the phrase "cyberbullying," and 47 states also include language concerning electronic harassment. However, only 12 states (Arkansas, Idaho, Kentucky, Louisiana, Mississippi, Missouri, Montana, Nevada, North Carolina, North Dakota, Tennessee, and Wisconsin) and the District of Columbia provide criminal sanctions for bullying behaviors (Hinduja and Patchin, 2013: 1). Virtually all states (43) require schools to provide some sort of punishment for bullying so as to affect the behaviors of the bully and give some retribution for victims. Ten states and the District of Columbia also include language indicating that bullying can occur off-campus and can still be sanctioned (Hinduja and Patchin, 2013: 1). Some argue that it may be inappropriate to extend school jurisdictions past the school grounds, as parents should be responsible for managing youth behavior. Given the impact that bullying victimization can have on students' academic performance, attendance, and mental health generally, some argue it is necessary for schools to extend protection to students and sanction bullies who engage in harmful communications while off-campus.

The complexities inherent in legislating against bullying are also evident around the world. For instance, there is no current legislation in Canada to deal with cyberbullying (Southey, 2013). Recently, legislators proposed **Bill C-13** that would make it a crime to share an intimate image without the consent of the subject of the image, punishable by up to five years in prison. The legislation also substantively expands police powers to investigate cybercrimes, which has led to public debate over the utility and rationale of the proposed bill (Southey, 2013). Similarly, there is no law specifically designed to deal with cyberbullying in the UK, the European Union, or Australia (Cybersmile, 2013). These offenses may be prosecuted under other existing laws, though nations may choose to develop cyberbullying-specific legislation in the near future as public outcry increases.

Harassment and stalking

Unlike cyberbullying, many nations have statutes that may be applied to instances of threatening or harassing communications. Under Title 47 of the US Criminal Code, Section 223(A) defines six acts involving a telecommunications device in interstate or foreign communications as illegal, including:

1) Making, creating, soliciting, or initiating, the transmission of requests or proposals that are obscene or involve child pornography with the intent to annoy, threaten, abuse, or harass;
2) Doing these same activities knowing that the recipient is under the age of 18;
3) Using a telecommunications device without disclosing your identity with the intent to annoy, abuse, threaten, or harass an individual at the called number;
4) Causing another person's phone to ring continuously to harass or annoy that person;
5) Making repeated calls designed solely to harass that person;
6) Knowingly permitting a telecommunications device or facility to be used for any of these activities.

While some of these behaviors may not seem criminal, it is important to recognize that a stalker or harasser can easily automate the process of calling a phone number over and over again in order to annoy the recipient. As a result, the outcome of the contact is just as pertinent as the behavior itself.

In addition, the phrase "telecommunications device" can be applied to a cellular phone or even voice over IP (VOIP) telephony. Thus, this law does not pertain solely to land-line phones. The punishment for these activities includes fines and/or imprisonment for up to two years.

In addition, Section 875 of Title 18 of federal code makes it a crime to transmit any of the following four communications via interstate or foreign commerce methods, including postal mail, telephone, or the Internet:

1) a demand for a ransom for the release of a kidnapped person
2) a message with the intent to extort money
3) a threat to injure a person
4) a threat to damage property.

The punishments for these offenses vary, including a fine and two years in prison for threats to property or extortion, as well as up to 20 years in prison for threats of kidnapping and physical injury.

Additionally, Code 18 Section 2261A of the federal law makes it illegal for any person to use an interactive computer service or any facility of interstate or foreign commerce in order to engage in activities that cause a person to feel substantial emotional distress or place that person in reasonable fear of death or serious bodily injury to themselves or their family (Brenner, 2011). In addition, this statute makes it illegal to travel across state lines with the intent to kill, injure, harass, or intimidate another person and place them or their family in fear of death or serious bodily injury (Brenner, 2011).

The penalties for these behaviors involve a fine and/or five years in prison if the individual simply makes the threat. If serious bodily injury resulted from the offender using a weapon, they may receive up to ten years in prison (Brenner, 2011). Should a victim be permanently disfigured or receive a life-threatening injury, then the offender may receive up to 20 years in prison. Finally, should the victim die as a result of the offender's actions in relation to threats made, they may receive up to a life sentence for their actions (Brenner, 2011).

It is important to note that these two statues require that a *credible threat* is made to either a person or property. The need for a so-called "true threat" stems from the case of **United States v. Alkhabaz**, involving a student at the University of Michigan named Abraham Jacob Alkhabaz, or Jake Baker (Brenner, 2011). He wrote graphic stories describing acts of rape, torture, and murder and posted them to a Usenet group starting in October 1994. In one of these stories, he described performing acts of rape and eventually killing a woman who had the same name as one of his female classmates. His posts led the subject of the story to complain to the University of Michigan police, who investigated and brought in the FBI due to the interstate nature of online communications (Brenner, 2011). Baker was arrested on six counts of communicating threats to kidnap or injure a person, though only one of those counts involved the woman who was the subject of the story. The case was dismissed by the judge due to a lack of evidence that Baker would actually act out the fantasies described in his writings (Brenner, 2011). The government appealed the case to a higher court, but the decision was upheld as the lack of evidence that Baker would act on the threat demonstrated a lack of a "**true threat**" to any individual (Brenner, 2011). Thus, this case established the need for the communications to generate actual fear or concern for safety.

For more on the Alkhabaz case, go online to: www.casebriefs.com/blog/law/criminal-law/criminal-law-keyed-to-dressler/inchoate-offenses/united-states-v-alkhabaz/

At the state level, virtually all states have legislation pertaining to either cyberstalking or harassment. There is some variation as to the type of laws in place, as 27 states have legislation against both offenses (Brenner, 2011). With regard to individual forms of offending, 37 states have established cyberstalking laws, usually recognizing that the offender uses electronic communications to stalk or engage in a pattern of threatening behaviors. All of these statutes incorporate language pertaining to a credible threat of harm to the victim (Brenner, 2011). In addition, 40 states have harassment statutes which do not necessarily require credible threats posed to victims or their families (Brenner, 2011). The statutes recognize the use of CMCs to annoy, harass, or torment the victim and are differentially located with state criminal codes. For instance, Arizona, Utah, and Virginia place online harassment under its own statute, while Delaware and New York incorporate these crimes under existing harassment legislation (Brenner, 2011). The punishments for both cyberstalking and harassing communications range from misdemeanors to felonies, depending on the severity of the offense.

It is important to note that most nations do not technically define cyberstalking in their actual legislation. In fact, there is no language in the European Convention of Cybercrime pertaining to stalking or harassment (Brenner, 2011). Instead, cyberstalking behaviors are subsumed under existing legislation regarding stalking generally. Australia, for instance, criminalized cyberstalking through the Stalking Amendment Act of 1999 (Bocij, 2004). This statute recognizes that contacting a person in any way, including phone, fax, email, or "through the use of any technology," to cause the victim apprehension or fear to their detriment constitutes unlawful stalking. Canadian law allows for prosecutions under section 264 of the Criminal Code for stalking offenses involving repeated communications directly or indirectly with the victim or anyone that they know and/or engaging in threatening conduct toward their victim or family members (Department of Justice Canada, 2012). The punishment for such a violation is up to ten years in prison if convicted.

Similarly, England and Wales have multiple laws related to stalking and harassing communications that can all be extended to online environments. First is the **Protection from Harassment Act 1997 (c40)**, which criminalized stalking and bullying in professional settings. This act prohibits conduct that constitutes harassment of others, assuming that a reasonable person would believe the behavior to be harassing (Crown Prosecution Service, 2013). Violations of this statute can be punishable by up to six months of incarceration and fines when considered appropriate by a judge.

Section 4 of the Act criminalizes the act of putting others in fear of violence, defined as any course of conduct that would cause "another to fear, on at least two occasions, that violence will be used against him is guilty of an offence if he knows or ought to know that his course of conduct will cause the other so to fear on each of those occasions" (Crown Prosecution Service, 2013). In addition, the offender must know that their actions will cause their prospective victim to fear that they will experience violence (Crown Prosecution Service, 2013). Thus, the offender must know that they are actively affecting the behavior and demeanor of their victim. Anyone found guilty of such an act could receive up to five years in prison and receive fines based on judicial discretion.

This Act was revised through the introduction of the **Protection of Freedoms Act 2012** to include language specifically related to stalking and incorporate aspects of technology into law (Crown Prosecution Service, 2013). Specifically, it added new language to Section 2 (regarding stalking to harass) and Section 4 (about stalking to cause fear). In Section 2, stalking is defined as harassment of a person or behaviors associated with stalking, including following a person, contacting them by any means, monitoring their victim through any form of electronic communications or the Internet, and publishing materials or statements about a person or claiming a comment originates from another person (Crown Prosecution Service, 2013). Anyone found guilty of such an offense can be imprisoned for no more than one year and/or receive a fine. Section 4 now defines stalking where the victim feels fear as any act that leads the target to fear they will be violently victimized or cause that person fear or distress that affects their day-to-day behaviors on at least two occasions (Crown Prosecution Service, 2013). Individuals found guilty of this activity can be imprisoned for up to five years and/or receive a fine.

In addition, the **Malicious Communications Act 1988** enables individuals to be prosecuted for sending messages to another person for the purpose of causing fear or anxiety (Crown Prosecution Service, 2013). This Act was revised in 2001 to include electronic communications of any kind that convey a threat, indecent or offensive content, or information that is false. Any violation of this Act is punishable by no more than six months imprisonment and a fine.

As noted earlier in the chapter, cases of cyberbullying, harassment, and stalking are not necessarily reported to law enforcement agencies either due to embarrassment on the part of victims or because the victim feels that the case may not be investigated or taken seriously by police. The lack of federal laws in the United States that can be used to pursue legal action means that the various federal agencies discussed throughout the book are not normally involved with these types of crime. The Federal Bureau of Investigation, however, may investigate cases of threats or stalking, but only if it involves a substantive threat that crosses state lines.

Instead, most incidents of bullying, stalking, and harassment in the US and elsewhere are handled by local or state law enforcement agencies due to the potential for offenders and victims to live in close proximity to one another. In fact, a sample of 358 state and local law enforcement agencies indicated that 71.8 percent of them investigated harassment cases (Holt, Bossler, and Fitzgerald, 2010). Despite the preference for local agencies to investigate, there are no immediate statistics available for the reported rates of cyberbullying, harassment, or stalking in official statistics provided by law enforcement agencies. This is largely the result of the fact that these items are not currently included in the existing reporting resources provided in the **Uniform Crime Report (UCR)**. Though there is some potential information available concerning the incidence of intimidation involving computers in the **National Incident-Based Reporting System (NIBRS)** (Addington, 2013), the data is limited due to the fact that only 31 states currently provide information to NIBRS, which is much lower than that of the UCR. As a result, it is unclear how frequently these offenses are reported to the police or cleared by arrest (Addington, 2013).

Though local law enforcement can serve as a critical investigative resource for the investigation of certain offenses, some victims may not choose to contact police because they are not sure if what they are experiencing may even be legally defined as stalking or harassment. To that end, there are several not-for-profit groups that operate to assist victims online. In the UK, the group **Cybersmile** is well known for its role in educating and assisting victims of cyberbullying. This charitable organization was founded in 2010 to educate the public on the harm caused by cyberbullying through service programs in schools and neighborhoods (Cybersmile, 2013). Cybersmile offers educational workshops for the public on cybersecurity and cyberbullying that are provided by community outreach workers affiliated with the group. In addition, they offer a helpline for bullying victims to help connect them with pertinent community services and counseling providers in their area (Cybersmile, 2013). The group funds research on bullying victimization in the UK, and advertises unique academic research publications related to cyberbullying victimization in order to communicate these issues to the public. Finally, Cybersmile organizes an annual Stop Cyberbullying Day designed to draw attention to the problem through community outreach events and fundraising to aid the organization (Cybersmile, 2013).

For more information on organizations that aid victims, go online to: 1) www.cybersmile.org/, and 2) www.haltabuse.org/

For cyberstalking victims, the group **Working to Halt Online Abuse (WHOA)** is a key resource to investigate cyberstalking and advocate on behalf of victims. This volunteer organization was created in 1997 in order to aid victims who are experiencing harassment or stalking around the world (WHOA, 2013). WHOA takes reports of cyberstalking incidents from victims who contact the group directly.

The group claims to receive an estimated 50 to 75 cases per week, though the actual number of cases reported by the agency handled each year is smaller than this due to the amount of information victims provide (WHOA, 2013). This affects the number of cases they report to the general public on a yearly basis. WHOA reported 220 cases in 2009, 349 in 2010, 305 in 2011, and 394 in 2012 (WHOA, 2013). This does not mean that there has been a substantive change in the incidence of cyberstalking. It may just reflect a larger number of respondents completely filling out the online reporting form from 2011 to 2012. Complaints made by prospective victims are then passed on to their staff of ten Internet Safety Advocates who work directly with victims in order to determine the source of harassing or stalking messages and contact web hosting services, ISPs, and law enforcement (WHOA, 2013). It is important to note that advocates cannot force any entity to remove content that may be harmful to a victim, but they may write and request that material be removed. WHOA is also not a law enforcement agency; thus, they cannot pursue an offender or bring charges against any entity involved in the hosting or facilitation of harassment (WHOA, 2013). The group's practical experience with stalking behaviors and technology, however, makes them well prepared to assist individuals who may experience cyberstalking.

As a result of the problems that law enforcement and non-profit organizations have in helping individuals after they have been victimized, researchers, advocacy groups, and even schools emphasize the need for individuals to take control of managing their personal safety as a key tool in reducing their risk of bullying, stalking, and harassment. This may be due to the overwhelming role of individual choice in online spaces. For instance, no one is required to have an account on a social networking site like Facebook or Twitter. Certainly, people are able to stay current with their friends and keep abreast of current events through these sites, but it is not a necessity. If they establish an account, they decide how much information to post about themselves and in what way they accept or maintain friends. Should that person feel dissatisfied with a post or an exchange with another person, they have the power to delete those messages. In fact, one of the top "tools" Facebook provides for users to maintain their security is the ability to unfriend someone, block individuals, and use the "Report" button on the page in order to bring that content to the attention of Facebook security. It is not clear how many reported incidents are investigated. Facebook notes (Facebook Tools, 2012):

> People you report won't know that they've been reported. After you submit a report, we'll investigate the issue and determine whether or not the content should be removed based on the Facebook Terms. We research each report to decide the appropriate course of action.

Since various tools are readily available, it makes sense to argue that personal responsibility and accountability for safety should be encouraged. The challenge lies in clearly communicating these issues to young people and those with less computer skill and online experience. An excellent example of security in action can be seen in the creation and use of email accounts. Various services provide free email accounts, such as Hotmail, Yahoo, and Gmail. When a person sets up their account, it is important to avoid using either their real name or a gendered term in the address. It may be easier to determine a person's identity if their email address or social media name is Janelovesmovies4419 than if it were something more neutral, like moviefan. Similarly, the use of sexual or explicit language in your email address or social networking profile may also increase the potential to receive unsolicited emails. Using something like hotpantzgirlie could bring unwanted attention and messages.

In order to curb instances of bullying and harassment among youth, many security experts recommend that parents place computers in public spaces within their home, like the kitchen or living room, and require kids to have some parental supervision while online. The ability to quickly observe the kinds of websites kids visit and periodically monitor their online activities could help to reduce the number of questionable websites to which they are exposed. However, cheap access to lightweight portable Internet-enabled devices, like iPods, iPads, Kindles, and laptops, makes it difficult to ensure that kids are using devices in close proximity to parents. Some also argue that parents should install filtering software to manage the kinds of websites their kids can visit. These devices can, however, be difficult for parents with little technological skill to set up or properly configure to ensure maximum effectiveness. Recent research suggests kids are able to easily circumvent these protective software programs or use other wireless Internet access points in order to avoid these devices altogether (Bossler et al., 2012; Jones et al., 2012). Even if a parent is able to properly configure software at home, it does not matter once their child goes to school or to a friend's house, where they have less control over their children's Internet activities and access.

Because of the inherent difficulty in managing the online experiences of young people, one of the most important steps that parents and schools can take is to begin a frank and honest conversation about Internet use (see Text Box 7.6 for Facebook's suggestions for parents). Understanding how and why young people are using technology is vital to keep pace with their changing online habits. Furthermore, it is important to recognize that adults can and should play a role in the socialization of youth into acceptable online behaviors. Parents and guardians teach kids what is right and wrong in the physical world, and that same experience must play out in online spaces. Admittedly, young people are exposed to millions of people around the world through the Internet, and not all of those people will be on their best behavior at all times. Thus, it is critical that someone be able to explain and give context to why certain activities may happen but should not be performed by their child. For instance, just because friends post their class schedule or where they will be at a specific time of day on Facebook does not mean that they have to do it as well.

Text Box 7.6: Facebook security suggestions for parents

www.facebook.com/safety/groups/parents/
Help your teens play it safe

> For years, teenagers spent much of their free time talking to friends on the phone. Today's teens aren't so different. They just have more ways to communicate … If you have a Facebook timeline, and have friended your child, try to respect the same boundaries you use offline.

This article provides Facebook's suggestions on how parents and teens should work together to be safe while online. Many of these ideas are not novel, but require a clear line of communication between adults and children and an ability to respect one another's privacy and responsibilities.

Summary

In reviewing our knowledge of bullying, harassment, and stalking, it is clear that this problem will not go away. Technology has made it incredibly easy for individuals to send hurtful or threatening communications online, and the perception that victims may not be able to report their experiences means that incidents may go unacknowledged. As a result, it is hard to combat this problem because of confusion over who has the appropriate jurisdiction to investigate the offense and whether or not it is a crime based on existing statutes. The increasing public attention drawn to the serious consequences of cyberbullying and stalking cases may, however, force a change in the policy and social response over the next five years. The attempts to develop national laws around cyberbullying are an excellent demonstration of the ways that society is attempting to respond to these acts. Thus, the way that we deal with bullying and stalking will no doubt change over the next ten years as perceptions of these behaviors change.

Key terms

Bill C-13
Catfishing
Cyberbullying
Cybersmile
Cyberstalking
Denigration
Exclusion
Flaming
Harassment
Impersonation
Lori Drew
Malicious Communications Act 1998
Megan Meier
Megan Meier Cyberbullying Prevention Act
National Centre for Cyberstalking Research
National Crime Victimization Survey-Supplemental Survey (NCVS-SS)
National Incident-Based Reporting System (NIBRS)
Online harassment
Outing
Protection from Harassment Act 1997 (c40)
Protection of Freedoms Act 2012
Stalking
Star Wars Kid
Trickery
Truant
True threat
Uniform Crime Report (UCR)

United States v. Alkhabaz

Working to Halt Online Abuse (WHOA)

Youth Internet Safety Survey (YISS)

Discussion questions

1) Should we define youth who make harassing or disparaging comments about their teachers in on-line spaces as engaging in cyberbullying, or is it harassment? Simply put, why should we define an act differently on the basis of the ages of the victim and offender?

2) How do we communicate what is acceptable on-line behavior to youth in a way that is accepted and clear? Furthermore, how do we limit the effects of "peer pressure" on technology use and acceptance, where friends post sensitive information about themselves or personal pictures that could be abused by others?

3) How easy is it to find the reporting tools and links for harassing language on the social networking sites you use most often? Look on the sites and see how long it takes you to find it on YouTube, Instagram, SnapChat, and Twitter. Are they easy to find? Are they in obvious places?

4) Should schools be able to punish students for on-line activities that take place outside of the campus and after or before school hours if it directly affects the behavior of other students? Why?

References

Addington, L. (2013). Reporting and clearance of cyberbullying incidents: Applying "offline" theories to online victims. *Journal of Contemporary Criminal Justice*, 3, 454–474.

Aftab, P. (2006). *Cyber bullying*. Wiredsaftey.net. [Online] Available at: www.wiredsafety.net

Arseneault, L., Walsh, E., Trzesniewski, K., Newcombe, R., Caspi, A., & Moffitt, T. E. (2006). Bullying victimization uniquely contributes to adjustment problems in young children: A nationally representative cohort study. *Pediatrics*, 118, 130–138.

Ashcroft, J. (2001). *Stalking and Domestic Violence*. NCJ 186157. Washington, DC: US Department of Justice.

Baum, K., Catalano, S., Rand, M., and Rose, K. (2009). *Stalking victimization in the United States*. Bureau of Justice Statistics, US Department of Justice. [Online] Available at: www.justice.gov/sites/default/files/ovw/legacy/2012/08/15/bjs-stalking-rpt.pdf

Beran, T., & Li Q. (2007). The relationship between cyberbullying and school bullying. *Journal of Student Wellbeing*, 1, 15–33.

Berson, I. R., Berson, M. J., & Ferron, J. M. (2002). Emerging risks of violence in the digital age: Lessons for educations from an online study of adolescent girls in the United States. *Journal of School Violence*, 1, 51–71.

Blauuw, E., Winkel, F. W., Arensman, E., Sheridan, L., & Freeve, A. (2002). The toll of stalking: The relationship between features of stalking and psychopathology of victims. *Journal of Interpersonal Violence*, 17, 50–63.

Bocij, P. (2004). *Cyberstalking: Harassment in the Internet Age and How to Protect your Family*. Westport, CT: Praeger Publishers.

Bocij, P., & McFarlane, L. (2002). Online harassment: Towards a definition of cyberstalking. *Prison Service Journal*, 39, 31–38.

Borg, M. G. (1999). The extent and nature of bullying among primary and secondary schoolchildren. *Educational Research*, 41, 137–153.

Bossler, A. M., Holt, T. J., & May, D. C. (2012). Predicting online harassment among a juvenile population. *Youth and Society*, 44, 500–523.

Boulton, M. J., & Underwood, K. (1992). Bully victim problems among middle school children. *British Journal of Educational Psychology of Addictive Behaviors*, 62, 73–87.

Brenner, S. (2011). Defining Cybercrime: A Review of Federal and State Law. In R. D. Clifford, *Cybercrime: The Investigation, Prosecution, and Defense of a Computer-Related Crime*, pp. 15–104. Raleigh, NC: Carolina Academic Press.

Camodeca, M., & Goossens, F. A. (2005). Aggression, social cognitions, anger and sadness in bullies and victims. *Journal of Child Psychology and Psychiatry*, 46, 186–197.

Campbell, M. A. (2005). Cyberbullying: An old problem in a new guise? *Australian Journal of Guidance and Counseling*, 15, 68–76.

Catalano, S. (2012). *Stalking Victims in the United States – Revised*. Washington, DC: US Department of Justice. [Online] Available at: www.bjs.gov/content/pub/pdf/svus_rev.pdf

Chamberlain, T., George, N., Golden, S., Walker, F., & Benton, T. (2010). *Tellus4 national report*. London: Department for Children, Schools and Families (DCSF).

Chen, E. (2011). *Girl, 16, fails to death in cyber-bully tragedy*. edVantage. [Online] Available at: www.edvantage.com.sg/content/girl-16-falls-death-cyber-bully-tragedy

Crown Prosecution Service. (2013). Stalking and Harassment. Crown Prosecution Service Prosecution Policy and Guidance. [Online] Available at: www.cps.gov.uk/legal/s_to_u/stalking_and_harassment/

Cybersmile. (2013). *FAQ*. [Online] Available at: http://cybersmile.org/who-we-are

Department for Children, Schools and Families. (2010). *Local authority measures for national indicators supported by the Tellus4 survey*. London: Department for Children, Schools and Families.

Department for Education. (2011). *The protection of children online: A brief scoping review to identify vulnerable groups*. London: Department for Education.

Department of Justice Canada. (2012). *A handbook for police and crown prosecutors on criminal harassment*. Department of Justice Canada. [Online] Available at: www.justice.gc.ca/eng/rp-pr/cj-jp/fv-vf/har/EN-CHH2.pdf

DeVoe, J. F., Bauer, L., & Hill, M. R. (2011). *Student Victimization in U.S. Schools: Results From the 2009 School Crime Supplement to the National Crime Victimization Survey*. Washington, DC: National Center for Educational Statistics. [Online] Available at: http://nces.ed.gov/pubs2012/2012314.pdf

Erdur-Baker, O. (2010). Cyberbullying and its correlation to traditional bullying, gender and frequent risky usage of Internet-mediated communication tools. *New Media Society*, 12, 109–125.

Facebook Tools (2012). *Safety*. [Online] Available at: www.facebook.com/safety/tools/

Finn, J. (2004). A survey of online harassment at a university campus. *Journal of Interpersonal Violence*, 19, 468–483.

Fisher, B., Cullen, F., & Turner, M. G. (2000). *The Sexual Victimization of College Women*. National Institute of Justice Publication No. NCJ 182369. Washington: Department of Justice.

Fricker, M. (2013). *Hannah Smith Suicide: Grieving dad sells home where cyber-bullying victim died*. Mirror, Oct 24, 2013. [Online] Available at: www.mirror.co.uk/news/uk-news/hannah-smith-suicide-grieving-dad-2485767#.Ut_h_bQo7IU

Haynie, D. L., Nansel, T., Eitel, P., Crump, A. D., Saylor, K, Yu, K., *et al*. (2001). Bullies, victims, and bully/victims: Distinct groups of at-risk youth. *Journal of Early Adolescence*, 21, 29–49.

Hinduja, S., & Patchin, J. (2008). Cyberbullying: An exploratory analysis of factors related to offending and victimization. *Deviant Behavior*, 29, 1–29.

Hinduja, S., & Patchin, J. W. (2009). *Bullying Beyond the Schoolyard: Preventing and Responding to Cyberbullying*. New York: Corwin Press.

Hinduja, S., & Patchin, J. W. (2012). *Summary of Cyberbullying Research From 2004–2012*. [Online] Available at: http://cyberbullying.us/summary-of-our-research/

Hinduja, S., & Patchin, J. (2013). *Description of State Cyberbullying Laws and Model Policies*. [Online] Available at: www.cyberbullying.us/Bullying_and_Cyberbullying_Laws.pdf

Hoey, D. (2012). Biddeford Man sentenced to five years for cyberstalking. *Portland Press Herald*, December 4, 2012. [Online] Available at: www.pressherald.com/news/Biddeford-man-sentenced-to-5-years-for-cyberstalking-.html

Holt, T. J., Chee, G., Ng, E., & Bossler, A. M. (2013). Exploring the consequences of bullying victimization in a sample of Singapore youth. *International Criminal Justice Review*, 23(1), 25–40.

Holt, T. J., & Bossler, A. M. (2009). Examining the applicability of Lifestyle-Routine Activities Theory for cybercrime victimization. *Deviant Behavior*, 30, 1–25.

Holt, T. J., Bossler, A. M., & Fitzgerald, S. (2010), Examining State and Local Law Enforcement Perceptions of Computer Crime. In Holt, T. J. (ed.), *Crime On-Line: Correlates, Causes, and Context* (pp. 221–246). Raleigh, NC: Carolina Academic Press.

Holt, T. J., Bossler, A. M., & May, D. C. (2012). Low self-control deviant peer associations and juvenile cyberdeviance. *American Journal of Criminal Justice*, 37(3), 378–395.

Holtfeld, B., & Grabe, M. (2012). Middle school students' perceptions of and responses to cyberbullying. *Journal of Educational Computing Research*, 46(4), 395–413.

Jones, L. M., Mitchell, K. J., & Finkelhor, D. (2012). Trends in youth Internet victimization: Findings from three youth Internet safety surveys 2000–2010. *Journal of Adolescent Health*, 50, 179–186.

Katzer, C., Fetchenhauer, D., & Belschak, F. (2009). Cyberbullying: Who are the victims? A comparison of victimization in internet chatrooms and victimization in school. *Journal of Media Psychology*, 21, 25–36.

Klomek, A. B., Sourander, A., Kumpulainen, K., Piha, J., Tamminen, T., Moilanen, I., Almqvist, F., & Gould, M. S. (2008). Childhood bullying as a risk for later depression and suicidal ideation among Finnish males. *Journal of Affective Disorders*, 109, 47–55.

Kowalski, R. M., Limber, S. P., & Agatston, P. W. (2008). *Cyberbullying: Bullying in the Digital Age*. Maldon, MA: Blackwell Publishing.

Kowalski, R. M., & Limber, P. (2007). Electronic bullying among middle school students. *Journal of Adolescent Health*, 41, 22–30.

Li, Q. (2006). Cyberbullying in schools. *School Psychology International*, 27(2), 157–170.

Li, Q. (2008). A cross-cultural comparison of adolescents' experience related to cyberbullying. *Educational Research*, 50(3), 223–234.

Marcum, C. D. (2010). Examining Cyberstalking and Bullying: Causes, Context, and Control. In T. J. Holt (ed.) *Crime On-Line: Correlates, Causes, and Context* (pp. 175–192). Raleigh, NC: Carolina Academic Press.

Marcum, C. D., Ricketts, M. L., and Higgins, G. E. (2010). Assessing sex experiences of online victimization: An examination of adolescent online behaviors utilizing Routine Activity Theory. *Criminal Justice Review*, 35(4), 412–437.

McQuade, S., Colt, J., & Meyer, N. (2009). *Cyber Bullying: Protecting Kids and Adults from Online Bullies*. ABC-CLIO: Santa Barbara, CA.

Mitchell, K. J., Finkelhor, D., & Becker-Blease, K. A. (2007). Linking youth internet and conventional problems: Findings from a clinical perspective. *Journal of Aggression, Maltreatment and Trauma*, 15, 39–58.

Morphy, E. (2008). The Computer Fraud Act: Bending a Law to Fit a Notorious Case. *E Commerce Times* December 9, 2008. [Online] Available at: www.ecommercetimes.com/story/65424.html

Nabuzoka, D. (2003). Experiences of bullying-related behaviours by English and Zambian pupils: A comparative study. *Educational Research*, 45(1), 95–109.

Nansel, T. R., Overpeck, M., Pilla, R. S., Ruan, W. J., Simmons-Morton, B., & Scheidt, P. (2001). Bullying behavior among U.S. youth: Prevalence and association with psychosocial adjustment. *Journal of the American Medical Association*, 285, 2094–2100.

National Centre for Cyberstalking Research. (2011). *Cyberstalking in the United Kingdom: An Analysis of the ECHO Pilot Survey 2011*. [Online] Available at: www.beds.ac.uk/__data/assets/pdf_file/0003/83109/ECHO_Pilot_Final.pdf

Nobles, M. R., Reyns, B. W., Fox, K. A., & Fisher, B. S. (2012). Protection against pursuit: A conceptual and empirical comparison of cyberstalking and stalking victimization among a national sample. *Justice Quarterly* DOI: 10.1080/07418825.2012.723030

Olweus, D. (1993). *Bullying at School: What We Know and What We Can Do*. Cambridge, MA: Blackwell.

Parris, L., Varjas, K., Meyers, J., & Cutts, H. (2012). High school students' perceptions of coping with cyberbullying. *Youth and Society*, 44, 284–306.

Perreault, S. (2013). *Self-reported Internet victimization in Canada, 2009*. [Online] Available at: www.statcan.gc.ca/pub/85-002-x/2011001/article/11530-eng.htm#n3

Peterson, H. (2013). "Catfishing:" The phenomenon of Internet scammers who fabricate online identities and entire social circles to trick people into romantic relationships. *Daily Mail Online*. January 17, 2013. [Online] Available at: www.dailymail. co.uk/news/article-2264053/Catfishing-The-phenomenon-Internet-scammers-fabricate-online-identities-entire-social-circles-trick-people-romantic-relationships.html

Priebe, G., Mitchell, K. J., & Finkelhor, D. (2013). To tell or not to tell? Youth's responses to unwanted Internet experiences. *Cyberpsychology: Journal of Psychosocial Research on Cyberspace*, 7.

Robers, S., Zhang, J., Truman, L., and Snyder, T. D. (2012). *Indicators of school crime and safety: 2011*. Bureau of Justice Statistics. [Online] Available at: http:// nces.ed.gov/programs/crimeindicators/crimeindicators2011/key.asp

Sbarbaro, V., & Smith, T. M. E. (2011). An exploratory study of bullying and cyberbullying behaviors among economically/educationally disadvantaged middle school students. *American Journal of Health Studies*, 26(3), 139–150.

Sheridan, L., & Grant, T. (2007). Is cyberstalking different? *Psychology, Crime & Law*, 13, 627–640.

Sinclair, H. C., & Frieze, I. H. (2000). Initial courtship behavior and stalking: How should we draw the line? *Violence and Participants*, 15, 23–40.

Slonje, R., Smith, P. K., & Frisen, A. (2013). The nature of cyberbullying, and the strategies for prevention. *Computers in Human Behavior*, 29, 26–32.

Smith, P. K., Mahdavi, J., Carvalho, M., Fisher, S., Russell, S., & Tippett, N. (2008). Cyberbullying: Its nature and impact in secondary school pupils. *Journal of Child Psychology and Psychiatry*, 49(4), 376–385.

Southey, T. (2013). Bill C-13 is about a lot more than cyberbullying. *The Globe and Mail* December 6, 2013. [Online] Available at: www.theglobeandmail.com/globe-debate/ columnists/maybe-one-day-revenge-porn-will-be-have-no-power/article15804000/

Spitzburg, B. H., & Hoobler, G. (2002). Cyberstalking and the technologies of interpersonal terrorism. *New Media & Society*, 4, 71–92.

Steinhauer, J. (2008). Verdict in MySpace Suicide Case. *New York Times* November 26, 2008. [Online] Available at: www.nytimes.com/2008/11/27/us/27myspace.html?_r=0

Tarapdar, S., & Kellett, M. (2011). *Young People's Voices on Cyber-bullying: What age Comparisons Tell Us?* London: The Diana Award.

Thorp, D. (2004). Cyberbullies on the prowl in the schoolyard. *The Australian*, 15 July. [Online] Retrieved from: www.australianit.news.com.au

Tokunaga, R. S. (2010). Following you home from school: A critical review and synthesis of research on cyberbullying victimization. *Computers in Human Behavior*, 26, 277–287.

Turmanis, S. A., & Brown, R. I. (2006). The stalking and harassment behavior scale: Measuring the incidence, nature, and severity of stalking and relational harassment and their psychological effects. *Psychology and Psychotherapy: Theory, Research and Practice* 79, 183–198.

Twyman, K., Saylor, C., Taylor, L. A., & Comeaux, C. (2010). Comparing children and adolescents engaged in cyberbullying to matched peers. *Cyberpsychology, Behavior, and Social Networking*, 13, 195–199.

Varjas, K., Henrich, C. C., & Meyers, J. (2009) Urban middle school students perceptions of bullying, cyberbullying, and school safety. *Journal of School Violence*, 8(2), 159–176.

Wang, J., Iannotti, R., & Nansel, T. (2009). Social bullying among adolescents in the United States; Physical, verbal, relational and cyber. *Journal of Adolescent Health*, 45(4), 368–375.

Wei, W. (2010). Where are they now? The 'Star Wars Kid' Sued the People Who Made Him Famous. *Business Insider.* May 12, 2010. [Online] Available at: www.businessinsider.com/where-are-they-now-the-star-wars-kid-2010-5

Wilcox, P., Jordan, C. E., & Pritchard, A. J. (2007). A multidimensional examination of campus safety: Victimization, perceptions of danger, worry about crime, and precautionary behavior among college women in the post-Clery era. *Crime and Delinquency*, 53, 219–254.

Willard, N. (2007). *Educator's guide to cyberbullying and cyberthreats.* [Online] Available at: www.accem.org/pdf/cbcteducator.pdf

Working to Halt Online Abuse. (2013). About WHOA. [Online] Available at: www.haltabuse.org

Ybarra, M. L., & Mitchell, J. K. (2004). Online aggressor/targets, aggressors, and targets: A comparison of associated youth characteristics. *Journal of Child Psychology and Psychiatry*, 45, 1308–1316.

Ybarra, M. L., Mitchell, K. J., Finkelhor, D., & Wolak, J. (2007). Internet prevention messages: Targeting the right online behaviors. *Archives of Pediatrics and Adolescent Medicine*, 161, 138–145.

Zetter, K. (2009). Judge acquits Lori Drew in Cyberbullying Case, Overrules Jury. *Wired* Threat Level. July 2, 2009. [Online] Available at: www.wired.com/threatlevel/2009/07/drew_court/

chapter 8

Online extremism, cyberterror, and cyber warfare

Introduction

Terror attacks have been a substantial problem around the world, driven in large part by regional interests and issues. For instance, members of various Irish Republican Army (IRA) groups engaged in terror attacks against English targets from the mid 1970s through the early 2000s. Similarly, domestic extremist groups within the United States have engaged in a number of attacks over the last few decades, such as Timothy McVeigh's

1995 bombing of a federal building in Oklahoma City, Oklahoma (Schmid and Jongman, 2005).

The terror attacks of September 11, 2001 in the United States, however, demonstrated the substantial threat posed by international terror groups who may operate in nations around the globe, though their agendas and interests may not be directly caused by their target (Schmid and Jongman, 2005). Major terror incidents have occurred worldwide, including attacks against commuter trains in Madrid, Spain in 2004, and the firebombing attack against Glasgow International Airport in Scotland in 2007. Though these incidents were perpetrated by radical Islamist extremists, various entities have attempted or succeeded in committing attacks of all sorts. As a consequence, physical security measures have been implemented in order to increase the successful identification and disruption of further attacks. For instance, the United States has radically changed their airport screening procedures to identify dangerous materials prior to entering flight terminals. Additionally, many governments have recalibrated their law enforcement and intelligence gathering agencies to focus on the prevention of terror and increased collaborative information-sharing programs.

Though the focus on real-world attacks is an obvious necessity due to the tremendous potential for civilian casualties and property damage, there has been less attention paid to the prospective threat of attacks through cyberspace. This is surprising, since virtually all industrialized nations are dependent on technology in order to engage in commerce and manage utilities, like water and power, as well as communications. A carefully targeted attack against any critical infrastructure resource could cause serious harm to the security of the network and potentially cause harm in the real world. Such a scenario has become increasingly popular in media and films, as in the movies *Live Free or Die Hard* and *Skyfall*, where groups of cyberterrorists compromise traffic control systems, government computers, utilities, and financial systems through a series of coordinated hacks.

The sensationalized appearance of cyberattacks in film has led to significant debate over the realities of virtual attacks against critical infrastructure. In the mid 1990s, when the World Wide Web and computer technologies were being rapidly adopted by industrialized nations, individuals in government and computer security theorized that such attacks were possible (Drogin 1999; Verton 2003). For instance, Deputy Secretary of Defense John Hamre and Richard Clark, an advisor on cybersecurity, used the term **electronic Pearl Harbor** to refer to a cyberattack against the United States that would take the nation by surprise and cause crippling harm (Verton, 2003). The lack of concrete evidence that such attacks were happening led some to dismiss these claims.

Their predictions, however, were surprisingly accurate, given the scope of attacks occurring around the world on a regular basis. There are now numerous examples of hackers gaining access to sensitive electrical grid networks and sewage control systems around the world. Perhaps most concerning is the emergence of military entities engaging in systematic attacks against corporations and government networks. In fact, the security firm Mandiant (2013) recently published a report linking multiple years of attacks to a single unit of the **People's Liberation Army of China (PLA)** that was previously unidentified. This group, designated Unit 61398 in the 3rd Department of the General Staff Department of the PLA, is thought to be staffed by dozens, if not hundreds, of workers with specialized knowledge of computer security and network attacks. The unit has actively compromised various targets for years, including attempts to gain access to companies managing electrical grids and pipelines for oil and gas. In addition, the attackers were able to stay inside of targeted systems for up to a year at a time and maintain backdoor access to systems. As a result, Mandiant refers to their attacks as Advanced Persistent Threat (APT) 1 due to their persistence and effectiveness. Such high-level attacks with direct connections to the military suggest that we may be in the middle of a new "cold war" that is otherwise unknown to the citizens of these nations.

For more on the APTI report, go online to: http://intelreport.mandiant.com/Mandiant_APT1_Report.pdf

These issues raise complex questions on the very nature of how these threats should be viewed and who has the responsibility to respond. For instance, when does an event move from being viewed as a crime to that of an act of war? Should cyberterror be defined or viewed differently from traditional acts of terror? This chapter will attempt to address these questions in a systematic fashion. First, we will define crime, terror, cyberterror, and war. In addition, the ways in which extremist groups and terror organizations utilize the Internet in order to support their activities or engage in attacks will be explored in detail. Finally, the legislative efforts in place to deal with terrorism as well as coordinate the response to cyberwar will be discussed in depth.

For more debate on the controversies of an electronic Pearl Harbor, go online to: 1) http://blog.radware.com/security/2013/12/electronic-pearl-harbor/, **2)** www.washingtonpost.com/blogs/innovations/post/digital-deterrents-preventing-a-pearl-harbor-of-cyberspace/2010/12/20/gIQASNKyoL_blog.html

Defining terror, hacktivism, and cyberterror

In order to understand the problem of terror, online or offline, we must first understand its relationship to crime. Both criminals and ideologically driven extremist or terror groups may use the same skills or behaviors in the course of an activity. Many nations charge terrorists under criminal statutes (Brenner, 2008). One way that we might be able to discern the differences between these behaviors is to consider both the motive of the actor and the number of people harmed. Criminals often target single individuals in order to increase their likelihood of success and are often driven by economic or emotional desires. For instance, an individual may assault another individual in order to get money in the course of a robbery or kill a person in retribution or cold blood. A terrorist or extremist group, however, tends to target large groups of people or physical locations that can cause massive collateral damage while at the same time drawing attention to a specific ideological, political, or religious agenda. In addition, many acts of terror are designed to target innocent people in order to cause general panic and fear among the larger populace, rather than simple economic gain (Brenner, 2008).

Recognizing the role of motivation is necessary to identify an act of terror. There are, however, a wide range of activities that people engage in that express their political or ideological beliefs. Thus, it is necessary to situate acts of terror within the spectrum of political behaviors on and offline, ranging from non-violent expression to serious physical violence (Holt and Kilger, 2012; Schmid, 1988, 2004). There are myriad forms of non-violent resistance that individuals engage in on a day-to-day basis. Prior to the emergence of the World Wide Web, individuals could express their dissent with political positions through letter-writing campaigns to print media outlets as well as their legislative representatives. Freedom of speech throughout the industrialized world also enables individuals to express their opinion in public settings, regardless of how negative they may be. The web has extended this capability, as individuals regularly post messages about their views on politics and social issues on Facebook, Twitter, and other social media (Martin, 2006; Schmid, 1988, 2004). In fact, individuals now contact politicians and representatives through the Internet at the same rate as postal mail and telephone (Best and Krueger, 2005).

The development of social media has had a substantive impact on the acceptance and growth of social movements across the globe. Individuals posting messages on Facebook, YouTube, or web forums can have their message viewed by others who share their point of view, or who may come to support their cause through convincing stories (Ayers, 1999; Chadwick, 2007; Jennings and Zeitner, 2003; Stepanova, 2011). The use of social media to develop networks of social support is crucial in the formation of a collective identity that can move into real spaces in order to effect social change. This was demonstrated in the recent protests of the Occupy movement in the United States and the Arab Spring protests across the Middle East. Social media was used as a means to promote protests and demonstrations in the real world (see Text Box 8.1 for details). In fact, social media allows for the formation of so-called **flash mobs**, where individuals coordinate organized activities, like dances or organized marches, through Facebook or Twitter which take others by surprise. In turn, videos and messages posted online about the events are able to generate additional attention to their causes. Thus, organized forms of non-violent expression can be enabled by virtual experiences and communication (Chadwick, 2007; Earl and Schussman, 2003; Jennings and Zeitner, 2003; Stepanova, 2011; Van Laer, 2010).

Text Box 8.1: Ultimatum For DDoS attacks against US banks

http://pastebin.com/EEWQhA0j

> Operation Ababil, AlQASSAM ULTIMATUM ... We, the Cyber Fighters of Izz ad-Din al-Qassam, had previously warned multiple times that, if the insulting movies not be removed from the Internet we will resume the Operation Ababil.

This story provides the details of the Cyber Fighters' campaign against various financial institutions in the US beginning in February 2013 as retaliation for the publication of a video on YouTube that insulted the image of the Prophet Mohammed. The announcement includes their future targets and their demands.

Political expression in the real world can also include the use of destruction or vandalism in order to express dissent (Brenner, 2008; Denning, 2010; Holt and Kilger, 2012). For instance, individuals may deface images of politicians or burn flags in order to express their dissent over a nation's positions toward an event. In virtual spaces, individuals may engage in similar forms of vandalism against websites or specific resources. For instance, individuals may engage in web defacements in order to express their disagreement with a policy or practice (Denning, 2010; Woo, Kim, and Dominick, 2004). One such example is a recent web defacement by an individual claiming to belong to the Animal Liberation Front (ALF) who defaced the website of a fur and leather retailer. The hacker also added the following message to the content of the site:

> To the owners of "The twisted pine fur and leather company" you have no excuse to sale [sic] the flesh, skin and fur of another creature. Your website lacks security. To the customers, you have no right to buy the flesh, skin or fur of another creature. You deserve this. You're lucky this is the only data we dumped. Exploiters, you've been warned. Expect us.
> | custFirst | custLast | custCity | custState | custZip |
> | -

These were just some of the vulnerable columns in the "customers" table of the "twistedp_db" database:

"custFirst" "custLast"
"custAdd1" "custAdd2" "custCity" "custState" "custZip" "custCountry"
"custEMail" "custPhone"
"cardType" "cardName" "cardExp" "cardCVS" "cardNumber"

Can you really put that much faith into the security of a company that sales [sic] the fur, skin and flesh of dead animals to make a profit?
We are Anonymous.
We are Legion.
We do not forgive.
We do not forget.
We are antisec.
We are operation liberate.
Expect us.

This simple image quickly expresses their point of view and disagreement with the company's practices.

This sort of attack is what some researchers refer to as **hacktivism**, in that the actors use hacking techniques to promote an activist agenda or express their opinion (Denning, 2010; Jordan and Taylor, 2004; Taylor, 1999). Such an attack may be illegal, but it does not create a high degree of fear or concern among the larger community (Jordan and Taylor, 2004). As a result, hacktivism provides a way to classify criminal acts of protest involving hacking techniques that are in some way analogous to offline political action (Denning, 2010). The use of this term does not, however, help to refine our understanding of cybercrime or terror as it is a more nebulous concept than anything else.

> **For more on hacktivism, go online to: 1)** http://opinionator.blogs.
> nytimes.com/2013/01/13/what-is-a-hacktivist/, **2)** www.thenation.com/
> article/154780/wikileaks-and-hacktivist-culture

At the most extreme end of political expression are planned acts of violence in support of a social agenda, typically referred to as **terror** (Schmid, 2004). This includes the use of explosives, such as the Oklahoma City bombings of the early 1990s in the United States, or the 9/11 attacks on the World Trade Center. These incidents can cause massive harm to both people and property and generate fear of future attacks (Martin, 2006; Schmid, 2004; Schmid and Jongman, 2005). Though there is no single agreed upon definition for what constitutes an act of physical terror, these elements are present in almost all of the existing frameworks used (Schmid and Jongman, 2005).

The definitional issues present for physical terror are exacerbated when attempting to define what constitutes **cyberterror**. In fact, the term cyberterror developed in the mid 1990s as technology was increasingly adopted by consumers and industry alike (Foltz, 2004). As increasing focus was placed on defining physical terror through the use of violence to promote fear; this challenged the notion of cyberterror since there have been few instances where individuals in the real world experience any physical harm from a cyber attack (Britz, 2010; Denning, 2010; Foltz, 2004; Martin, 2006; Pollitt, 1998).

An attack against the electronic infrastructure supporting financial institutions or power grids could, however, produce a catastrophic loss of service that results in economic harm or disruption of vital services (Brenner, 2008; Britz, 2010; Brodscky and Radvanovsky, 2010; Denning, 2010). For instance, if an attacker was able to knock out power to a major city, it could potentially result in significant dollar losses for corporations, and potentially lead to physical death if outages affected hospitals or medical services. The unexpected nature of such an attack would also, no doubt, generate panic over the prospect of future attacks occurring with almost no warning. Such fear and concern over cyber attacks may rival that of a physical terror incident (Britz, 2010; Denning, 2010; Kilger, 2010). As a result, physical harm may be less relevant in the definition of cyberterrorism compared to the fear that may stem from such an attack.

It is also important to recognize that some terror or extremist groups may not attempt to use the Internet as an attack vehicle. Instead, they may simply find value in using online communications in order to contact others, spread their message globally, and engage in fundraising activities to support their cause (Britz, 2010; Foltz, 2004). With that in mind, a truly expansive definition of cyberterror must recognize the variations that may be evident in the way an organization uses technology to further its agenda. Criminologist Marjie Britz (2010) has developed an inclusive definition for cyberterror that recognizes both of these issues:

> The premeditated, methodological, ideologically motivated dissemination of information, facilitation of communication, or attack against physical targets, digital information, computer systems, and/or computer programs which is intended to cause social, financial, physical, or psychological harm to noncombatant targets and audiences for the purpose of affecting ideological, political, or social change; or any utilization of digital communication or information which facilitates such actions directly or indirectly.
>
> (p. 197)

We will use this definition in order to frame the remainder of this chapter so as to recognize the various ways that extremists and terrorists use technology to further their agendas on and offline.

The role of nation-state vs. non-nation-state attacks

Since technology can be used to facilitate acts of crime or terror, we must consider the source of an attack and how this might relate to the actor's motivation and target. With that in mind, we must define a **nation-state** and contextualize how it might engage in an attack. Creveld (1999) argues that a nation-state has three characteristics: (1) sovereignty, (2) territoriality, and (3) is an abstract organization. Sovereignty involves the authority or power to rule, as well as make and enforce laws within a given area. Territoriality recognizes that a state or governing body exerts power within specific, recognized borders (Creveld, 1999). The idea of "abstract organization" involves the concept that each state has a distinct and independent persona which is separate from that of its people. Specifically, the state is a political entity, while the culture and/or ethnic composition of a place makes up its national identity (Creveld, 1999). For instance, the United States utilizes a democratic system of government, while its national identity is one that is a cultural mélange of various heritages and backgrounds based on the influx of immigrants over time.

Given their sovereignty and territorial control, nation-states have the capacity to exert influence over their citizens, as well as other nation-states, in order to further their interests. As a result, some nation-states may utilize their citizen populations to engage in illegal activities in order to gain either economic or political advantage over another nation. For instance, a nation-state might encourage individual citizens to engage in the theft of trade secrets or intellectual property in order to gain economic advantage over another country they must compete with in the open market. The originating nation may provide indirect economic support to actors in order to facilitate their activities, but it does not provide any overt recognition or direct orders that can be traced back to the government. Thus, the use of state-sponsored actors allows a government to perform illegal activities without directly engaging in the act (see Chapter 3).

The role of state sponsorship in cyberattacks that involve hacking and data theft has gained substantial attention over the last two decades. In fact, the computer security incident dubbed **Operation Aurora** by the security vendor McAfee provides some insight into this issue. In 2009, a group of very sophisticated Chinese hackers compromised multiple high-level targets including Google, Adobe, Juniper Networks, Yahoo, Symantec, Northrop Grumman, and Dow Chemical (Schmugar, 2010; Zetter, 2010). The attackers were able to gain access to these institutions through the use of a website hosting malware which would exploit a zero-day vulnerability in the Internet Explorer web browser. From there, the attackers appeared to use

online extremism, cyberterror, cyber warfare

these infected systems as launch points to identify and compromise source code repositories within these companies (Markoff and Barboza, 2010; Zetter, 2010). While it is possible that these attacks were driven by individual hackers without state support, the complexity of the attacks and the sophistication of the actors would have required a high degree of cooperation in order to be successful. Additionally, the targets of the attacks appear to be more in line with the interests of a corporate entity or government in order to achieve a competitive advantage in the market, without the need for research and development. Finally, the source of these attacks appears to come from two Chinese universities with links to both the Chinese search engine company Baidu and the Chinese government (Markoff and Barboza, 2010; Schmugar, 2010). All of these points provide circumstantial evidence that the attacks were the result of state-sponsored actors working on behalf of the Chinese government (Fritz, 2008).

The lack of concrete evidence to support the role of the state in sanctioning this activity makes it difficult to identify a clear policy response. It may be best to treat this incident as a crime due to the lack of substantial evidence that the Chinese government ordered this attack to take place. The totality of circumstances would suggest it is something greater than a crime, but the use of a military response may not be appropriate without more evidence. As such, the use of actors with no direct ties to a government entity makes it difficult to clearly define this incident as an act of crime, espionage, or war.

By contrast, individuals operating without state sponsorship, or **non-nation-state sponsored actors,** tend to have fewer resources at their disposal and may differentially target resources in order to affect the operational capabilities of a government or corporation, gain a direct profit from data theft, or cause fear among a population. Their attacks may not be as sophisticated as those used by nation-states, but they can still prove effective, depending on the target of an attack. Additionally, actors without state sponsorship do not have to operate within specific military hierarchies of command and may organize in any way necessary in order to succeed. That does not mean there are not leaders within groups; they may be driven by a small core of actors who come together and rally others to their cause. Often, this may be done through the use of web forums, IRC, instant messaging groups, and social networking sites that enable the rapid formation of groups. Thus, non-nation-state-sponsored actors can more quickly come together to complete attacks with a wide network of participants who can just as rapidly disband upon completion of the act because of the absence of chains of command or hierarchies.

One excellent example of non-nation-state-sponsored attacks based on loosely connected actors is a series of DDoS attacks against US financial institutions beginning in the fall of 2012 by the group Izz ad-Din al-Qassam Cyber Fighters (Gonsalves, 2013). The attacks themselves were directed at US Bankcorp, JP Morgan Chase & Co., Bank of America, PNC

Financial Services Group, SunTrust, and other institutions. The group utilized compromised web servers located in the US as a launch point and caused some interruptions of service for the banks. It is not clear how successful the attacks were, though one estimate suggests at least seven banks were taken down for minutes to hours, depending on the institution (Gonsalves, 2013).

The group indicated in posts on the website Pastebin that they were engaging in the attacks because of the treatment of the Islamic faith by the West and the US government's refusal to remove clips of a movie that disparages the prophet Mohammed from YouTube (see Text Box 8.2 for details). They claimed that they would engage in attacks against banks as retribution for these videos and base the duration of their attacks on the perceived damages that will result against these institutions relative to the number of times these videos have been viewed and the length of time they have been posted. While some of these institutions were able to use mitigation services to reduce the effectiveness of the DDoS attacks, it is likely the attacks will continue so long as the Cyber Fighters feel they are accomplishing some goal.

Text Box 8.2: The use of technology in the Arab Spring

www.huffingtonpost.com/andrew-lam/social-media-middle-east-protests-_b_1881827.html?view=print&comm_ref=false

From Arab Spring to autumn rage: The dark power of social media

> Mohamed Bouazizi ... set himself on ablaze protesting police corruption, became literally the torch that lit the Arab Spring revolution that spread quickly throughout the Middle East. Bouazzi achieved this in his very public death because many who had cell phones recorded his protest and the subsequent videos kick-started the uprising.

This article describes the Arab Spring uprising and how social media and cell phone technology engendered these events. The content provides a valuable example of how everyday technologies can be used to subvert the status quo in government and society as a whole.

Since the individual hackers engaging in these attacks appeared to be motivated entirely based on their religious backgrounds to target and affect business endeavors, it is reasonable to suggest that this is a crime. The religious component and the desire to change the attitudes and behaviors of the nation and the stance of those who posted the content may also lead some to call these attacks hacktivism. Regardless, it is important to consider how the role of state associations may affect both the activities of the attackers and the way an incident is defined.

The use of the Internet in the indoctrination and recruitment of extremist groups

Due to the prospective variations in the behavior and motives of actors, it is necessary to consider how technology may be used and to what ends. First and foremost, the Internet has tremendous value as a communications vehicle for extremists, terror entities, and nation-state actors. The easy and immediate access to technology, coupled with the anonymity and scale afforded by computers and the Internet, make email, forums, instant messaging, and virtually all other forms of CMC ideal for interpersonal communications. Almost every nation on earth now has some form of Internet connectivity, whether through cellular service providers, high-speed fiber optic connectivity, or even dial-up Internet access. Groups can maintain contact and reach out to others, no matter where they may be located, through plain text messages, email, or forums.

The ability to regularly communicate with others from diverse backgrounds ensures that individuals can be slowly, but steadily, introduced to the core principles of a movement (Gerstenfeld, Grant, and Chiang, 2003; Gruen, 2005; Weimann, 2005). Constant exposure and reinforcement of an ideology allows individuals to become accepting of an otherwise unusual perspective, and it may eventually enable the acceptance of an extremist ideology or identity (Gerstenfeld *et al.*, 2003). For example, the web forum Stormfront.org is extremely popular among the neo-Nazi movement to discuss all facets of this movement and even day-to-day activities through a white-power perspective (Castle, 2011; Gerstenfeld *et al.*, 2003; Weimann 2005). The site serves as a venue for individuals to engage in conversations and connect with others virtually and through the real world via localized subforums by nation, state, and city. There are also multiple sections devoted to politics, technology, philosophy, and entertainment. The global jihad movement has also leveraged a range of forums across the globe written in multiple languages to discuss justifications for the resistance of Western occupation of Iraq and the general lack of respect Western nations show to the Islamic value systems (Britz, 2010; Weimann, 2005).

> **For more information on Stormfront, go online to:** www.youtube.com/watch?v=CfUldhzPKC8

In addition to direct communications, the Internet also allows groups to directly communicate their beliefs and ideologies to the world without the need for mass-media marketing or news media coverage. Any terror or extremist group can post messages on blogs or websites in order to directly control the delivery of their message to the media and the public at large (Forest, 2009). For instance, members of the hacker group Anonymous regularly use Twitter, YouTube, and even written letters posted on websites in order to explain their actions or notify prospective targets that they may be attacked (see Text Box 8.3 for details).

Text Box 8.3: Anonymous open letter example

#Op TRUTH FORCE - April 6:day of civil disobedience against FB censorship

> It is time that Anonymous band together globally to prove that WE have the strength because we have the numbers. No one can stop free speech. No government, No corporation and especially not facebook. APRIL 6 - 1AM GMT it begins:#OP TRUTH FORCE

http://anonnews.org/press/item/2180/
This open letter posted by Anonymous details their rationale for a campaign of posting uncensored media content on Facebook and other social media. They even invite individuals to join and provide a link to their Facebook event page for the operation.

Computers and software suites for multimedia creation like Photoshop also allow groups to create and manipulate videos, photos, and stylized text. This enables extremist groups to develop more media-friendly materials or misrepresent facts in support of their own ideologies. In turn, they can promote their ideas and images to a larger audience in a subtle and convincing way that may instill anger and hostility toward groups that are perceived as oppressors or socially unacceptable (Forest, 2009; Gruen, 2005). The terrorist group Al Qaeda in the Arabian Peninsula (AQAP) operates an English-language magazine called *Inspire* which provides information on the perspectives of the group and the jihadist movement generally. An issue from March 2013 featured an article on the 11 public figures from the west who it feels should be wanted dead or alive for crimes against Islam (Watson, 2013). It also features regular details on techniques to engage in terrorism, ranging from simple bomb-making to how to handle firearms. The glossy magazine format allows the authors to promote their agenda in a way that is both attractive and appealing to readers. At the same time, the writing style may be more engaging and promote the jihadist agenda to those who may never have considered this point of view (Watson, 2013).

For more information on the magazine *Inspire* and its role in radical-ization, go online to: www.dailymail.co.uk/news/article-2287003/Al-Qaeda-releases-guide-torch-cars-make-bombs-naming-11-public-figures-wants-dead-alive-latest-edition-glossy-magazine.html

In much the same way, the extremist group Stormwatch operates a website about the civil rights leader, Dr Martin Luther King, Jr, which appears to discuss his role as an activist (martinlutherking.org, 2013). The content of the site, however, decries his role in the pursuit of equality and suggests he was actually a mouthpiece for Jews and Communists, in keeping with the perceptions of the White Supremacist movement generally (Weimann, 2005). It is written in a relatively persuasive fashion that may make an unsuspecting reader with little knowledge of King's role in social change believe the content to be factual. For instance, the writers argue King to be a fraud and not a religious man by taking facts and quotes out of context. In fact, they repeatedly argue he stole materials from other figures and claimed them as his own, stating:

> The first book that King wrote, "Stride Toward Freedom," – was plagiarized from numerous sources, all unattributed, according to documentation recently assembled by sympathetic King scholars Keith D. Miller, Ira G. Zepp, Jr., and David J. Garrow.
>
> And no less an authoritative source than the four senior editors of "The Papers of Martin Luther King, Jr." – (an official publication of the Martin Luther King Center for Nonviolent Social Change, Inc., whose staff includes King's widow Coretta), stated of King's writings at both Boston University and Crozer Theological Seminary: "Judged retroactively by the standards of academic scholarship, [his writings] are tragically flawed by numerous instances of plagiarism … Appropriated passages are particularly evident in his writings in his major field of graduate study, systematic theology.

This content derides the success of King and argues that there should be no national holiday or recognition for his work. In fact, they provide a link to downloadable flyers about these issues which reads "Bring the Dream to life in your town! Download flyers to pass out at your school." These are excellent examples of the way that multimedia content can be used by extremist groups to help indoctrinate individuals into their ideological or political worldview.

In addition, cell phone cameras and web cams allow individuals to create training videos and share these resources with others through video sharing sites like YouTube (Gruen, 2005). Posting videos and news stories through social media also provides a mechanism to publicly refute claims made by media and governments to ensure the group is presented in a positive light (Forest, 2009; Gruen, 2005). For instance, participants in the recent Arab Spring created videos on camera phones to show violent repression by government and police agencies, as it happened, to news agencies around the world (Stepanova, 2011). Such "on the ground" reporting allows individuals to provide evidence of their experiences.

This same capability, however, can be abused by extremist groups in support of their ideologies. One of the most extreme examples of such an act was a video posted by members of Al Qaeda in Pakistan on February 21, 2002. In the video, members of the group executed a journalist named Daniel Pearl, whom they kidnapped while he was traveling to conduct an interview (Levy, 2003). He stated his name for the camera, described his Jewish family heritage, and then condemned America's foreign policy strategies in the Middle East. Following these statements, his captors then slit his throat and cut off his head, ending the video with a statement demanding the release of all Guantanamo Bay detainees or otherwise more deaths would result (Levy, 2003). The gruesome video became a key piece of propaganda for the group and the jihadist movement generally, while inciting massive outrage in the United States. Such a chilling example demonstrates the value of interactive media and the Internet in the promotion of extremist movements generally.

In addition to video, social movements on the fringes of society have begun to utilize music and video games as a means to expose individuals to their perspectives in socially acceptable and engaging ways (Britz, 2010; Weimann, 2005). For instance, Resistance Records is a record label that produces and distributes music by bands that feature white power and right-wing extremist messages in a direct-downloadable format (Jipson, 2007). The label is owned and run by the National Alliance, a white power group, which gains a profit from album sales. Music allows what are otherwise extreme or socially unacceptable positions to be heard in ways that may appeal to younger generations or the general public.

Video games have also become a key resource for extremist groups to promote their beliefs in a socially acceptable, approachable, and extremely engaging way to younger audiences. The rewards and reinforcement individuals can receive through successfully completing the objectives of a game, coupled with the underlying themes of the content, can promote an extremist view in a very digestible format. One of the most well known of these games is called *Ethnic Cleansing* and was developed and released through Resistance Records using no-cost open-source software. This is a so-called "first person shooter," wherein the game is played from the point of view of a skinhead or Klansman who kills blacks, Jews, and Latinos in various urban ghetto and subway environments (Anti-Defamation League, 2002). This game, and its sequel "White Law," costs $14.99 and can be downloaded directly through the Resistance Records website (Anti-Defamation League, 2002). Similarly, Islamic extremists have released several video games that place the player in the role of a jihadist fighting against Jews, Westerners, and the US military (Gruen, 2005). The content utilizes pro-Islamic imagery, rap and popular music, as well as various images of and messages from Osama Bin Laden and the 9/11 terror attacks. The game has been posted and reposted across various websites online ensuring its spread to various interested groups (Weimann, 2005).

In addition to lifestyle publications and materials that encourage or support extremist ideologies, there are a number of training and support manuals that are distributed online. In fact, the open nature of the World Wide Web allows individuals to post information that could be used to engage in violence or cause physical harm in the real world. There are a number of training manuals and detailed tutorials for bomb-making, gunplay, and improvised weapons use on the Internet, many of which have been available online for years (Wall, 2001). This is because individuals can easily post a text file or word processor document and repost it in repositories, send via email, or share via social networks in different formats and languages. For example, the *Mujahadeen Poisons Handbook* from Hamas and the *Encyclopedia of Jihad* published by Al Qaeda are available in various online outlets (Weimann, 2005). Even the Earth Liberation Front and Animal Liberation Front have tutorials on how to engage in civil disobedience and protests against logging companies, construction sites, and animal testing facilities (Holt, 2012). These resources engender planning and tactical strategy development, regardless of the expertise of the individuals in a given area.

> **For an example of a tactical manual, go online to:** www.direkte-aktie. net/osh/

Electronic attacks by extremist groups

Though the communications capability afforded by the Internet is unparalleled, it is also important to consider how these technologies could serve as a target for attacks by extremists, terror groups, and even nation-states. The range of interconnected computer systems and sensitive data that could be compromised online presents a diverse range of high-value targets for attackers (Britz, 2010; Denning, 2010; Holt, 2012; Kilger, 2010). For instance, individuals could immediately target financial institutions in order to limit the functionality of online banking systems or harm databases of consumer information in order to cause chaos. Alternatively, attackers may target the computer systems that support the processes within nuclear power plants, hydroelectric dams, or sewage treatment plants. These systems, called **Supervisory Control and Data Acquisition (SCADA)** systems, are vital to the management and processing of critical infrastructure and are often connected to the Internet in some fashion (Brodsky and Radvanovsky, 2010). As a result, an attacker who can affect the functionality of these computers may cause substantial physical harm in the real world along with fear over future attacks (see Text Box 8.4 for details; Brenner, 2011; Denning, 2010).

Text Box 8.4: Examples of cyberattacks against SCADA systems in water treatment

www.infosecisland.com/blogview/18281-ICS-Cybersecurity-Water-Water-Everywhere.html

ICS Cybersecurity: Water, water everywhere

> Since then there have been numerous articles and events that have driven the public conversation about the security of the cyber systems at American water treatment facilities. The question at hand is whether this moment of attention will result in any improvements in cybersecurity of the nation's water supply.

This article provides a timeline of the cybersecurity incidents that have occurred over the last two decades that specifically target water management systems. The piece is invaluable in understanding the ways that systems have been compromised and what this may mean for the future.

The use of cyberattacks by extremist groups is infrequent, though they are facilitated in part by the nature of information sharing in the hacker subculture (see Chapter 2; Britz, 2010; Denning, 2010). Hackers regularly provide information on vulnerabilities present in the software and hardware of systems across the world (Taylor, 1999). This information can be leveraged by anyone with the time or inclination to identify systems with this vulnerability and attempt to attack them (Taylor, 1999). As a result, open disclosure may do more to facilitate attacks than to provide public awareness of weaknesses. In fact, hackers in support of Al Qaeda have posted various resources to facilitate cyberattacks, such as Youni Tsoulis, who published a hacker tutorial titled "The Encyclopedia of Hacking the Zionist and Crusader Websites" (Denning, 2010). This guide provided detailed information on vulnerabilities in US cyber infrastructure, as well as techniques to engage in data theft and malware infections. In addition, the ability to obtain free attack tools or malware and hacking resources through open markets (see Chapters 3 and 4) reduces the amount of resource development needed to successfully complete an attack. Thus, the modern hacker subculture facilitates both legitimate and illegitimate hacking behaviors, which can be used by any motivated actor.

One of the most common types of attack used in support of extremist or terror agendas is the denial of service attack (Denning, 2010; Kilger, 2010). These attacks may not cause significant system damage, though the fact that they keep users from accessing resources can cause massive dollar losses. In addition, they can be relatively easy to perform and are enabled in part by downloadable tools that will complete the attack at the click of a mouse. The history of downloadable DDoS tools stems from the hacker group, the Electronic Disturbance Theater (EDT; Denning, 2010). The group developed a program called **FloodNet** that could be downloaded directly from their website to be utilized by individuals who shared their perspectives on the use of the Internet as a space for social activism. It was first used in an attack against the Mexican government because of their treatment of Zapatista separatists who were fighting against what they perceived to be governmental repression (Denning, 2010). The EDT first used FloodNet against the Mexican President Zedillo's website, and then attacked US President Clinton's website because of his support of Mexico. A third, and even larger, attack was then launched against Zedillo, the Pentagon, and the Frankfurt Stock Exchange for its role in supporting globalization (Denning, 2010).

> **For more on the EDT, go online to:** www.youtube.com/watch?v=O-U-he8LN3k

The success of FloodNet led to its adoption by other activist groups to engage in DDoS attacks, such as an attack by animal rights protesters in Sweden and a British group called the Electrohippies Collective (Denning, 2010). In more recent years, additional DDoS tools have been developed by groups with diverse interests. For instance, a tool called Electronic Jihad was released through the Arabic language forum al-Jinan for use against various Western targets (Denning, 2010). Also, the group Anonymous uses a DDoS tool called the **Low Orbit Ion Cannon** in support of attacks against personal, industrial, and government targets around the world (Correll, 2010). This simple tool allows individuals to simply select a website to target and give parameters for the duration of the attack, then click the ready button. LOIC requires no technical knowledge to successfully complete an attack; the interest in targeting a specific entity is all that is necessary.

> **For more on LOIC, go online to:** http://sourceforge.net/projects/loic/

Another useful tool in the arsenal of hackers seeking to express their opinion are web defacements, where the normal HTML code of a webpage is replaced by images, text, and content of the attacker's choosing (see

Chapter 3; Denning, 2010; Woo *et al.*, 2004). Web defacements began as a vehicle for hackers to call out system administrators who used poor security protocols and generate a reputation in the hacker community for their actions (Woo *et al.*, 2004). As hackers increasingly recognized the value of web defacements as a means to express their political or ideological motives, the nature and targets for defacements began to change (Denning, 2010; Woo *et al.*, 2004). Specifically, web defacements increasingly appear to be triggered in response to real-world events. One of the first examples of such an incident occurred following the collision of a US EP-3 reconnaissance plane with a Chinese F-8 fighter jet over Chinese airspace in April 2001. The Chinese pilot died during the incident and the US flight crew was detained following an emergency landing (Henderson, 2007). As news of the story emerged in both nations, hackers began defacement campaigns against various websites to express their patriotism and support. These attacks gained prominence quickly, so much so that a group of US hackers called "Project China" began defacing Chinese websites in May of that year, affecting as many targets as possible. The defacements continued for some time by hacker groups and individuals with generally no evidence of state sponsorship (Denning, 2010). In fact, the Chinese government asked hackers to refrain from further attacks as the one year anniversary of the incident approached (Hess, 2002).

In light of the range of ways that the Internet may be used by ideologically driven groups in order to effect action or cause harm, we will now explore two different extremist group subcultures and their online activities: (1) the white power movement and (2) Al Qaeda and the e-jihad.

White power online

The term **white power** is often associated with white supremacist groups like the Ku Klux Klan, though it can actually be applied as an umbrella term to capture the collective of groups with overlapping perspectives, such as neo-Nazi groups, Aryan skinheads, and other Christian separatist movements. Though they have different individual views, they generally share a framework that the white race has been sublimated by non-white racial and ethnic groups, Jews, and Catholics. These groups operate around the world and take various forms. In fact, the Southern Poverty Law Center (2013) suggested that there were 1,007 active hate groups operating in the US in 2012. Though they are spread across the country, the white power movement is most prominent in the South, upper Midwest, and Southwestern United States. Similar groups are evident in Europe and Asia, including the National Socialist Movement, which has offshoots in England and the Philippines (National Socialist Movement, 2014).

The value of the Internet for the white power movement cannot be understated. Technology allows individuals from marginalized communities across the world to become indoctrinated into the culture and find

online extremism, cyberterror, cyber warfare

social support for their attitudes and beliefs over time. Donald Black, former KKK member and the founder of the website Stormfront, stated that "whereas we previously could only reach people with pamphlets and by sending out tabloid papers to a limited number of people or holding rallies with no more than a few hundred people – now we can reach potentially millions of people" (Faulk, 1997). Considering he made this statement in 1997, the white power movement has had a long history of Internet use.

Some of the most common tools used by the white power movement are websites, forums, chatrooms, blogs, and other forms of CMC. Individuals who find these sites may be first directed to them through Google searches or links through radical church websites (McNamee, Peterson, and Pena, 2010). Spending time reading the content and getting to know users may increase their willingness to accept the white power point of view. In fact, continuous involvement in these sites may help individuals to accept extremist perspectives, even if their peers or family do not agree with these positions. In addition, the ability to make multiple friends and associates online in addition to their real-world social relationships can help to insulate their perceptions (McNamee *et al.*, 2010).

It is important to note that CMCs used by the white power movement do not necessarily encourage violence. Some do and are overtly inflammatory in their language about the need to rise up in armed conflict or engage in a "race war" (McNamee *et al.*, 2010). Many sites and discussions simply revolve around the importance of the movement and the need to develop a strong white race. In fact, many users in forums and other sites communicate their interpretation of historical events, as in the discussion of Dr Martin Luther King, Jr mentioned earlier in this chapter (McNamee *et al.*, 2010). They may also promote the idea that the white race has been appointed by God or by natural right to dominate the world over other races and ethnic groups (McNamee *et al.*, 2010). Constant exposure to these messages will help to encourage an individual to believe them and be drawn into the movement as a whole.

At the same time, the Internet allows users to regularly access cultural currency related to the white power movement. For example, music became an important tool in the indoctrination of individuals through heavy metal bands and other musical styles in the mid 1990s (Simi and Futrell, 2006). Large concert venues became an important rallying point, drawing multiple acts to play at day-long festivals. The development of e-commerce sites and music sharing services aided the spread of white power music. In turn, the movement began to use music as a key resource to communicate the white power message through accessible media that may be more engaging to youth culture (Simi and Futrell, 2006).

The ability to access the Web has also enabled individuals to develop lifestyle-related content that incorporates their racial attitudes (Simi and Futrell, 2006). Images of tattoos, concerts, organized meetings, video games, music, and clothing are all easy identified via the Web. There are now even streaming-music services available for those interested in white power bands. In addition, the group "Women for Aryan Unity" (WAU) publishes a magazine called *Home Front* on parenting issues, home schooling, and ways to socialize children into the movement. There are also child-specific materials available to download, such as coloring pages, crosswords, and stories that are "age appropriate" (Simi and Futrell, 2006). They can also get positive reinforcement from peers and ask questions about how to stay loyal to the movement despite the problems that they may face from other parents. Thus, the web is a key resource in the communication of subcultural values within the white power movement as a whole.

Al Qaeda and the e-jihad

Over the last ten years, academic researchers and popular media have focused heavily on Al Qaeda and their role in global terror activities (Forest, 2009; Martin, 2006). Much of this work has helped inform our knowledge of the real-world threat that this group poses, though there has generally been little evidence demonstrating their role in successful cyberattacks (Denning, 2010; Ulph, 2006). There is, however, some evidence that loose associations of hacker groups are interested in and attempting to engage in cyber attacks against the West. This so-called **e-jihad** has ties to Al Qaeda and other Islamic extremist groups across the Middle East and Africa and depends on technology for communications infrastructure and as an attack platform (Denning, 2010; Ulph, 2006).

The use of the Internet as a platform for e-jihad has been supported by a variety of individuals tied to Muslim extremist groups. For instance, Mohammad Bin Ahmad As-Sālim wrote a book titled *39 Ways to Serve and Participate in Jihâd*, designed to promote discussion about the issue of war with the West and jihad generally (Denning, 2010; Leyden, 2003). The book discussed the issue of electronic jihad as the 34th principal way to engage in jihad. He identifies the need for both discussion forums for media campaigns and more specific applications of hacking techniques in order to harm the West. Specifically, he wrote: "He [anyone with knowledge of hacking] should concentrate his efforts on destroying any American websites, as well as any sites that are anti-*Jihâd* and *Mujâhidîn*, Jewish websites, modernist and secular websites" (As-Sālim, 2003). Thus, terror groups realize that Western nations' dependence on the Internet for both commerce and communications is a major vulnerability that can be exploited to cause economic harm and fear in the general populace.

To that end, the first hacker group that emerged with specific ties to Al Qaeda was the "al-Qaeda Alliance Online," an offshoot of the hacker group "GForce Pakistan." Members of the Alliance defaced a web server operated by the National Oceanic and Atmospheric Administration (NOAA) on October 17, 2001 (McWilliams, 2001). The defacement contained interesting, if not contradictory, information by condemning the September 11 attacks, stating: "bin Laden is a holy fighter, and whatever he says makes sense" (McWilliams, 2001). They went on to say that they would attack major websites in the US and Britain, though "we will not hurt any data as its [sic] unethical" (McWilliams 2001).

A subsequent defacement occurred ten days later on October 27th, though that was the last attack attributed to the group (Denning, 2010). It is not clear what happened to the Alliance, but it was replaced by a variety of forums and hacker groups actively engaged in the promotion of attacks against the West and others who disparaged the Islamic faith. For instance, the al-Farouq forum established a section encouraging electronic jihad, along with a downloadable library of tools and tutorials for engaging in attacks (Denning, 2010; Pool, 2005). Similarly, the al-Jinan forum created and offered a free download of a DoS tool called Electronic Jihad and gave awards and electronic medals to those who were the most effective attackers against sites that harmed Islam (Bakier, 2007).

One of the most well-known examples of information sharing was from a hacker named Youni Tsoulis, who used the handle Irhabi007. He developed multiple web forums and sites supporting Al Qaeda and even set up hidden links to propaganda websites on various forums (Corera, 2008). He also promoted hacking and gave multiple tutorials on hacker sites with substantial detail on methods of attack and tactics to compromise websites (Jamestown, 2008). Due to the degree to which he actively engaged and shared information about cyberattack techniques with others in the e-jihad movement, Tsouli came to the attention of law enforcement and military agencies around the world. In fact, his name was found on a laptop belonging to a member of an Al Qaeda cell in Bosnia who was arrested after making threatening videos against various European nations. Tsouli was arrested by the London Metropolitan Police during a raid in 2005 and was found guilty of charges under the Terrorism Act of 2000 (Corera, 2008). He received a 16-year sentence; he was 23 years old at the time.

Tsouli is one of the few examples of success in the e-jihad campaign against the West. For instance, individuals attempted to engage in a DoS attack against the Vatican website after Pope Benedict made comments about the Prophet Mohammad and Islam which were viewed as critical of their faith (Denning, 2010). In addition, individuals involved in the e-jihad planned a coordinated series of attacks against US financial institutions and the stock exchange in 2006. All of these attacks failed to materialize, calling into question the skill of the attackers relative to the preparations taken to defend against such attacks (Alshech, 2007; Denning, 2010; Gross and McMillan, 2006). This should not be taken as an indication that Al Qaeda and the e-jihad should not be taken seriously, but rather that they recognize the value of the Internet and are finding ways to leverage it toward effective attacks to cause harm.

Text Box 8.5: Questioning the reality of cyberterror (created by the authors)

This chapter provides substantive detail on the role of the Internet in facilitating communications, fundraising, and planning for terror groups. There is, however, scant evidence of actual cyberattacks performed by terrorist groups. Pundits and politicians have heralded this potential for almost two decades since the coining of the phrase "digital Pearl Harbor."

As a result, some scholars argue that the absence of actual evidence of attacks coupled with the expansion of the information collection and security apparatus of governments leads to a distinct conclusion: cyberterror is a social construction (Furedi, 2005; Yar, 2013). Specifically, the threat posed by terrorism is built up by media and seized upon by claims makers. The resulting public support can be used as a means to gain greater control over resources like the Internet and impose restrictions and surveillance on user activity. This position is supported by the recent revelations regarding the US National Security Agency's access to email and phone records, as well as a larger global surveillance mechanism (discussed later in this chapter).

This is a challenging position as the general public does not gain access to information on attacks against government systems and critical infrastructure. The classification of information makes it difficult to know the reality of terrorist group capabilities or their use of cyberattacks (Denning, 2010). At the same time, there has been a massive build-up in security spending and resource allocation to government agencies for what are otherwise extremely rare events (Yar, 2013). In the end, it is necessary to consider this position and ask what is the correct balance between national security and citizens' rights.

Cyberwar and the nation-state

As cyberspace plays an increasingly critical role in managing the everyday aspects of communication and critical infrastructure, governments and military agencies are increasingly attempting to establish their role in cyberspace. Many industrialized nations recognize the threat that cyberattacks can pose to military and governmental infrastructure. Some consider cyberspace to be a new warfare domain just like land, sea, air, and space (Andress and Winterfeld, 2011). As a consequence, it is necessary to consider how fighting a war in this domain may operate and what constitutes an act of **cyberwar**.

There is no single agreed-upon definition for warfare, even among the United Nations. The historical literature on war and warfare tactics, however, suggests that it can be viewed as an act of force or violence which compels the opponent to fulfill the will of the victor (Andress and Winterfeld, 2011; Brenner, 2008; Schwartau, 1996). When applied to cyberspace, the use of war tactics appears designed to control and affect the activities of an opposing force. Brenner (2008) defined cyberwarfare as nation-states' "use of military operations by virtual means ... to achieve essentially the same ends they pursue through the use of conventional military force" (p. 65). Thus, the domain of conflict for cyberwar is different from traditional conflicts in that the operations take place in a virtual space (Rid, 2013). The weapons of cyberwar are also different from those of traditional combat, in that actors may utilize malware and hacking techniques in order to affect system functionality, access to information, or critical infrastructure (Rid, 2013). The outcomes and goals of cyberwar, however, are similar to physical war in that fighters may attempt either targeted tactical strikes against a specific target or try to cause as much damage as possible to the operational capacity of a nation-state.

Though there has been some debate about the actual threat of cyberwarfare and the utility of this term generally (see Andress and Winterfeld, 2011; Rid, 2013), we must recognize why it may be a fruitful environment for attack. Nearly all critical systems in modern industrialized nations depend on the Internet for commercial or logistic support. For example, water and sewage treatment plants, nuclear, hydroelectric, and other power grids are dependent on the Internet for command and control. Virtually all facets of banking, stock exchanges, and economic systems are run through the Internet. Even aspects of the military and related defense contractors of the world are run through civilian or commercial telephony. Any attack that could effectively disrupt the communications capacity of the Internet could effectively cripple our society, which would have ripple effects throughout the real world. At the same time, the sensitive data maintained by government or military agencies could be compromised and/or stolen in order to gain an economic or defensive advantage (see the Operation Aurora story covered above). Thus, hacking sensitive systems would be an easy and immediate way to affect an enemy through cyberwarfare.

Over the last ten years, there have been an increasing number of incidents that might practically be viewed as cyberwar. A key example is the conflict between Russia and Estonia in 2007. A conflict developed between Russian and Estonian factions in April 2007 when the Estonian government removed a Russian war monument from a memorial garden in a national cemetery (Brenner, 2008; Jaffe 2006; Landler and Markoff, 2007). The statue, called The Bronze Soldier of Tallinn, was installed as a monument to the Russian involvement in World War II, and was viewed as a relic from Estonia's time as part of the former Soviet Union. Now that Estonia was its own independent nation, the government felt it appropriate to have the statue removed (Guadagno, Cialdini, and Evron, 2010). Russian citizens living in Estonia and elsewhere were enraged by this action, leading to protests and violence in the streets of both countries. Over 1,300 were arrested during protests in Estonia, many of whom were ethnic Russians living in the country.

The conflict quickly grew into online spaces, with hackers in both Estonia and Russia attempting to engage in different hacks and spam campaigns

(Brenner, 2008; Jaffe, 2006). Russian hackers also leveraged online forums and hacker sites in order to rally attackers together to increase the volume of their attacks and used huge botnets of compromised computers for DDoS attacks (Clover, 2009; Davis, 2007). The attacks incorporated many individuals who were interested in attacking Estonia out of their love and respect for their homeland, many of whom had little knowledge of computer hacking. As a consequence, Russian attacks were able to shut down critical components of Estonia's financial and government networks, causing significant economic harm to citizens and industry alike (Brenner, 2008; Landler and Markoff, 2007). The Estonian parliament and almost every governmental ministry website was affected. In addition, three of the six national news agencies and two of its largest banks also experienced problems (Clover, 2009). In fact, banks were knocked offline for hours and lost millions of dollars due to DDoS attacks (Landler and Markoff, 2007).

In the wake of this onslaught, the Estonian government accused the Russian government of supporting and encouraging these attacks. To date, there has been no concrete evidence provided to support Russian state sponsorship (Denning, 2010). Many observers, however, have argued this incident is a clear demonstration of how nation-states may engage in conflicts in the future. The actors involved may be driven by their own sense of duty to their country or by actual military doctrine. Regardless, the severity of the attacks demonstrates the need to identify how cyber-resources might be affected by conflicts in the real world.

A more recent example is the appearance of a piece of malicious software called **Stuxnet**. This computer worm was used in attacks against the Natanz uranium enrichment facility in Iran (Clayton, 2010; Kerr, Rollins, and Theohary, 2010). Stuxnet was designed to specifically compromise and harm computer systems in order to gain access to the SCADA systems and related programmable logic controllers (PLCs) inside of centrifuges in these plants (Clayton, 2010; Kerr *et al.*, 2010.) Specifically, the code would allow the PLC to be given commands remotely by the attacker, while shielding the actual behaviors of the centrifuges from the plant's SCADA control systems. As a result, attackers could surreptitiously disrupt the plant's ability to process uranium and cause confusion among operators and controllers. It is unknown how long the malware was able to operate inside of the facility, though estimates suggest it may have impacted 1,000 of the 5,000 centrifuges in the plant and delayed the overall functionality of the nuclear plant by months or years (Kerr *et al.*, 2010; Sanger, 2012).

For more information on Stuxnet, go online to: 1) www.youtube.com/watch?v=n7UVyVSDSxY, **and 2)** www.youtube.com/watch?v=863SNTqyYto

Recent evidence suggests that Stuxnet was developed by the United States under the Bush administration as evidence grew regarding the Iranian nuclear program aspirations. The program, called **Operation Olympic Games,** was proactively implemented by an executive order of President Obama because it was thought that this sort of attack would be more targeted, difficult to detect, and produce fewer civilian casualties or collateral damage than a physical strike (Sanger, 2012). In addition, the use of this code was thought to have reduced the likelihood of a conventional military strike by Israel which would have dangerous consequences for the region as a whole. The US has not acknowledged any of the claims made related to Stuxnet, though its release in the wild has given computer security professionals and hackers access to this extremely sophisticated malware. The program may serve as a basis for the development of tools in order to exploit or attack critical infrastructure across the globe (Brodscky and Radvanovsky, 2010; Clayton, 2010). The US Department of Homeland Security expressed substantial concern over the use of Stuxnet-like code in attacks against US power installations (Zetter, 2011). Thus, cyber attacks may be an increasingly common way for nation-states to engage one another to cause harm.

Legislating extremism and cyberterror

The Internet and CMCs clearly provide a mechanism for individuals to spread hurtful messages and ideas based on prejudice, racism, and other ideological and political stances. There is some tension in how to sanction hate speech, as nations like the US protect freedom of speech under the First Amendment to the Constitution. The only real way that speech is limited in this country is through the "imminent danger" test, where one's comments are unprotected if the speaker attempts to incite dangerous or illegal activities (Abrams, 2012). Recognizing that the Internet dramatically increases the risk of exposure to hurtful ideas and prospective radicalization of individuals toward violence, the Obama administration has begun to take steps to combat the problem of domestic and foreign terror and extremist groups without changing existing protections to free speech.

The White House released a policy and strategy document in August 2011 titled "Empowering Local Partners to Prevent Violent Extremism in the United States." This document details their desire to use a community-based approach to reduce the problem of extremist groups and violent behavior through the integration of law enforcement and public private partnerships with stakeholders in local communities (White House, 2011b). Religious leaders in mosques and Islamic centers of worship, as well as schools and community groups, should be brought together in order to foster trust between community residents, law enforcement, and the federal government. In fact, this strategy involves multiple federal agencies ranging from the Treasury, Department of Defense, Department of Justice, Department of Homeland Security, and the Federal Bureau of Investigation (White House, 2011b). The hope is that these inter-agency and community partnerships can better improve the scope of engagement with communities on issues that they are concerned about, and develop better partnerships that will make communities resilient to radicalization, whether from online groups or those in the real world.

The US is an isolate with regard to its equal protection of free speech, as many nations around the world have criminalized hate speech in some form. The UK's Public Order Act 1986 criminalized expressions of threats, abusive, or insulting behavior to any group of persons based on their race, color, ethnicity, nationality, or ethnic origin with a punishment of up to seven years in prison and/or a fine (Mendel, 2012). This law was amended in 2006 to include religious hatred and again in 2008 for protection of sexual orientations (Mendel, 2012). Similar legislation is present in Australia, Canada, Denmark, France, Germany, the Netherlands, Singapore, and South Africa (Mendel, 2012). Though these statutes do not primarily identify the Internet as a venue for the communication of hate speech, the laws can be extended to these environments.

The European Convention on Cybercrime also includes language criminalizing the use of the Internet in order to disseminate hate speech. Specifically, the CoC identifies "racist and xenophobic material," including writing, images, videos, and any other content that is designed to promote or encourage hate or discrimination against any group (Brenner, 2011). The distribution or posting of such material online is defined as criminal under the CoC, as is making online threats to any person on the basis of their racial, ethnic, or religious background, and the distribution of information that denies or otherwise attempts to misinform individuals regarding genocide and crimes against humanity (Brenner, 2011). This legislation has tremendous value in addressing the development and radicalization of individuals through the Internet, particularly white supremacist movements.

In addition to hate speech, many of the examples provided throughout this chapter reflect the use of hacking techniques in furtherance of terror or extremist group plots. As a result, several nations have extended their laws pertaining to computer hacking so that they can be applied to these offenses (see Chapter 2 for more detail). In fact, the Computer Fraud and Abuse Act in the United States was expanded following the 9/11 attacks through the introduction and passing of the **Uniting and Strengthening America by Providing Appropriate Tools Required to Intercept and Obstruct Terrorism (USA PATRIOT) Act** of 2001. This Act strengthened the existing CFAA laws to include any computer in the world so long as it is "used in a manner that affects interstate or foreign commerce or communications of the United States" (Brenner, 2011). This provision enables US law enforcement to engage in investigations in foreign countries, so long as the investigation is recognized as legitimate by that nation. In addition, the PATRIOT Act modified the law to also include any unauthorized access to a computer or network that:

1) modifies or impairs access to medical data;
2) causes physical injury to a person;
3) poses a threat to public health or safety; or
4) damages a computer used by a government entity in the administration of justice, national defense, or national security.

This expansion of the statute enabled greater latitude for federal law enforcement to pursue cybercriminals and more effectively prosecute those who would target either critical infrastructure or sensitive data sources that could cause significant harm in the real world.

In addition, the PATRIOT Act also relaxed the legal provisions needed for law enforcement agencies to engage in surveillance of electronic communications. For instance, the Act revised provisions of the **Electronic Communications Privacy Act** (ECPA) related to subpoenas of ISPs and cable companies. The Act enabled law enforcement to obtain the name and address of subscribers, along with their billing records, phone numbers called, duration of sessions while online, services used, communication device information, and other related data. The release of such information can enable law enforcement to more effectively trace the activities of a user to specific websites and content during a given session of Internet use. In addition, the ECPA now defines email that is stored on a third-party server for more than 180 days to be legally viewed as abandoned. As a result, law enforcement can request this data and the content of the email, whether opened or unopened, be turned over without the need for judicial review. Finally, the PATRIOT Act allowed ISPs to make emergency disclosures of information to law enforcement in instances of extreme physical or virtual threats to public safety. Such language allows for greater surreptitious surveillance of citizens with minimal government oversight or public awareness.

At the state level, there is generally little legislation that exists with regard to cyberterrorism. Arkansas, Connecticut, Georgia, Illinois, Indiana, and West Virginia all have statutes that directly or indirectly relate to cyberterrorism (Brenner, 2011). For example, Arkansas recognizes an act of terror as any act or series of two or more acts that attempt to disable or destroy data, computers, or computer networks used by industry, government, or contractors. Connecticut more narrowly defines an act of "computer crime furtherance of terrorist purposes" as an attempt to use computer crimes in order to intimidate or coerce either the government or civilian populations. Georgia has criminalized the use of a computer in order to disseminate information related to terrorist activities (Brenner, 2011). The lack of state-based legislation may stem from the recognition that an act of terror, whether virtual or real, will more immediately fall under the investigative responsibility of the federal government. At the same time, the presence of such legislation suggests these states are progressive in their thinking about these issues and may serve as models for other states across the country.

Other nations have adopted similar language to that of the US PATRIOT Act, such as Canada's Anti-terrorism Act of 2001, which changed standards for the interception of domestic communications of all kinds (Brenner, 2011). For instance, this law allows the Communications Security Establishment of Canada (an analog to the NSA) to intercept communications that either begin or end in Canada and involve a foreign source. Prior to this law, any domestic information acquired in the process of an international intercept would have been destroyed or ignored. Though there has been substantive public debate surrounding the legitimacy of these new laws, the Canadian government has not moved to strike them down. Similar legislation in Australia and New Zealand has, however, been repealed due to the perception that they are too extreme and degrade public trust in government (Rid, 2013).

Investigating and securing cyberspace from the threat of terror and war

Over the last decade, governments around the world have been making strides to improve their nation's cybersecurity posture. In the US, President Obama's **Comprehensive National Cybersecurity Initiative** (CNCI) was adopted in May 2009 in order to strengthen America's digital infrastructure (White House, 2011a). This involves three main goals to secure the US from cyberthreats:

1) Establish a front line of defense against immediate threats and a response capability through federal and local partnerships;
2) Defend against the full spectrum of threats;
3) Strengthen the future cybersecurity environment through education and research.

This plan involves long-range strategic planning and development in order to effectively develop an integrated response to cyberthreats. To that end, the CNCI has 12 major initiatives to achieve over the next decade (White House, 2011a):

1) Move towards managing a single federal enterprise network.
2) Deploy intrinsic detection systems.
3) Develop and deploy intrusion prevention tools.
4) Review and potentially redirect research and funding.
5) Connect current government cyber operations centers.
6) Develop a government-wide cyber intelligence plan.
7) Increase the security of classified networks.
8) Expand cyber education.
9) Define enduring leap-ahead technologies.

online extremism, cyberterror, cyber warfare

10) Define enduring deterrent technologies and programs.
11) Develop multi-pronged approaches to supply chain risk management.
12) Define the role of cyber security in private sector domains.

Some of these steps are more easily achieved than others (White House, 2011a). For instance, there is now a White House cybersecurity advisor who provides direct guidance to the President on cyberthreats and security issues. In addition, the government is developing an intrusion detection and prevention system referred to as "EINSTEIN" in order to help reduce the success of any attack against government systems.

Also, the **National Security Agency (NSA)** has begun to develop a massive data center in Utah in order to improve the cybersecurity response of the nation. This center, called the Community Comprehensive National Cybersecurity Initiative Data Center, is designed to process, aggregate, and verify threats across DoD and federal cyberspace (Fidel, 2011). As a result, there is some evidence that this plan is actually taking shape in the real world.

The scope of NSA data collection was recently and dramatically brought to light by the whistle-blowing efforts of a former contractor named Edward Snowden. He revealed the existence of multiple programs designed to capture and mine sensitive data from various electronic data sources around the world, including the **PRISM program** (Gidda, 2013). The NSA implemented this program in 2007 to collect email and other electronic communications data of all sorts, and it was carried out through cooperative relationships with various technology companies, including Apple, Facebook, Google, Microsoft, and Skype (Gidda, 2013). In turn, this data could be mined and queried for intelligence generation purposes to assess terror threats and networks of actors, as well as identify tactical and strategic information. News of this program drew tremendous outrage from various governments, particularly Germany and Brazil (Gidda, 2013). The United Kingdom, however, indicated that it received access to PRISM data and used this source in addition to its own surveillance and data collection programs (Gidda, 2013). It is unclear how such data collection programs will change or adapt with changing attitudes toward the Internet and data privacy generally, though it will continue to be a core issue for national security.

The Federal Bureau of Investigation

As noted earlier, the **Federal Bureau of Investigation** (FBI) plays a critical role in the investigation of both traditional and cybercrimes. In fact, the investigation of terror attacks and foreign intelligence operations are among the top priorities of the Bureau. The National Security Branch (NSB) of the FBI is designated with the task of gathering intelligence and coordinating investigative efforts to disrupt terrorist groups and foreign intelligence groups (FBI, 2013). The NSB was established in 2005 as a result of a presidential directive to combine the mission and resources of the counterterrorism, counterintelligence, and intelligence mission of the bureau under a single unit. This branch includes six divisions: (1) the Counterterrorism Division which addresses domestic and international threats; (2) the Counterintelligence Division to affect traditional and non-traditional espionage and intelligence gathering in the US; (3) the Directorate of Intelligence on various threats across the country; (4) the Weapons of Mass Destruction Directorate (WMDD) designed to reduce the threat and proliferation of nuclear, biological, and chemical weapons; (5) the Terrorist Screening Center, which generates actionable intelligence for state and local law enforcement agencies; and (6) the High-Value Detainee Interrogation Group that actively collects information from terror suspects in order to gain information to deter attacks against various targets (FBI, 2013). Thus, the NSB plays a critical role in both law enforcement, homeland security, and the intelligence community generally.

The Department of Energy

While most generally think of law enforcement agencies with regard to the investigation of crime and terror threats, other government agencies have an increasingly pertinent role in this space. For instance, the US **Department of Energy (DOE)** plays a critical role in the maintenance and protection of energy programs and production generally. As our energy infrastructure is becoming dependent on the Internet and computer technology for operation and management, the threat of external attacks and compromise has increased dramatically (Department of Energy, 2013). Thus the DOE operates the Office of Intelligence and Counterintelligence in order to generate intelligence on various threats to our energy infrastructure, as well as those of foreign governments and nations. In addition, the Office of the Chief Information Officer at DOE supports various resources to communicate information on cybersecurity threats to national security in general (Department of Energy, 2013). They support computer security protocols for DOE employees and techniques to secure various resources from external threats.

The DOE also operates an Incident Management Program, coordinated with US-CERT to respond to various cyberthreats. This includes reporting incidents, generating security bulletins for vulnerabilities in various desktop and SCADA systems, as well as incident response management and tracking (Department of Energy, 2013).

The Department of Homeland Security

The **Department of Homeland Security (DHS)** is a cabinet-level department which consolidated various federal agencies under a single department heading. Created in 2001 following the September 11 attacks, DHS handles

online extremism, cyberterror, cyber warfare

civilian infrastructure and populations within the borders of the United States (DHS, 2013). Their mission includes a variety of agencies focused on traditional physical resources, such as Customs and Border Patrol, though the cybersecurity role of DHS has expanded over the last decade. In fact, the National Cybersecurity and Communications Integration Center, which opened on October 30, 2009, serves to connect multiple government organizations together in order to protect computer systems and networked infrastructure in general.

> For more on the organizational structure of the US DHS, go online to: www.dhs.gov/xlibrary/assets/dhs-orgchart.pdf

This center also oversees the National Cyber Security Division (NCSD), which has two specific objectives: (1) build and maintain an effective national cyberspace response system, and (2) implement a cyber risk management program to protect critical infrastructure (DHS, 2013). This is achieved through the development of risk assessment mechanisms for private, government, and military networks through the National Cyber Incident Response Plan (NCIRP). The NCSD houses the US-Computer Emergency Readiness Team, or US-CERT, which serves as a response center and information clearing house for cyberthreats across the world (DHS, 2013). The CERT provides reporting mechanisms for vulnerabilities and threats to systems, as well security tools to help patch and protect systems from attack (DHS, 2013). The CERT can also serve to analyze and track threats as they evolve for virtually any branch of government and civilian networks, including threats to SCADA and industrial control systems. They act as a focal point for the coordination of information concerning cyberattacks that threaten civilian infrastructure through the National Cyber Awareness Center (NCSC; DHS 2013).

The NCSD also manages the National Vulnerability Database, which provides up-to-date information on vulnerabilities in various software and hardware (DHS, 2013). This data is informed by individuals in the general public who can report vulnerabilities, as well as those identified by the US-CERT and private industry. They also operate mechanisms to automate security processes and compliance to reduce the threat posed by various vulnerabilities and increase system security overall.

Operating in partnership with the DOD and DOF, the NCSD also manages the National Cyber Response Coordination Group (NCRCG), which is composed of 19 federal agencies that coordinate response efforts to recover from and combat cyber incidents (DHS, 2013). The NCRCG also operates nationwide exercises designed to simulate infrastructure attacks in order to identify response strategies to attacks in real time. Such training events demonstrate the procedures and response protocols in place within and across agencies and determine effective strategies to combat cyber attacks (DHS, 2013). Other nations utilize similar mechanisms to secure various infrastructure from cyberthreats. For instance, the **Centre for the Protection of National Infrastructure (CPNI)** in the UK exists to inform critical infrastructure owners of emerging threats and coordinate responses in the event of a compromise (CPNI, 2014).

Cyberwar and response

Though law enforcement has general oversight of cybercrimes and incidents of terror, the military has exclusive response to acts that might be defined as cyberwar, such as attempts to compromise DoD networks or those of related defense contractors. To that end, the Pentagon established the **US Cyber Command (USCYBERCOM)** in 2009 in order to manage the defense of US cyberspace and critical infrastructure against attacks (Andress and Winterfeld, 2011). The new Cyber Command is a sub-command of the United States Strategic Command (USSTRATCOM), which has responsibility over space, information operations, intelligence, nuclear arms, and combating weapons of mass destruction. This is sensible given the fact that cyberspace is an overarching environment that cuts across all branches of military service. This command focuses on DoD networks only, while all civilian aspects of cyberspace are managed by the Department of Homeland Security.

In addition, the Department of Defense is now placing a specific emphasis on the need for careful responses to theft of data, destructive attacks to degrade network functionality, and denial of service attacks, due to the direct threat they pose to the communications capabilities of the nation, as well as the maintenance of secrecy and intellectual property (Department of Defense, 2011). In order to reduce the risks posed by malicious actors and attacks, the report calls for improved relationships with private industry in order to develop an improved total government response and an expanded workforce focusing on cybersecurity.

In addition to the DoD, the NSA plays a critical role in the protection and investigation of attacks against sensitive military networks (NSA, 2013). The NSA serves as a key resource in both data encryption and protection of nearly all federal government computer networks. They also investigate attacks against computer networks from nation-state and non-nation-state actors alike (NSA, 2013). Finally, they play a critical role in intelligence gathering of foreign nations' cyber infrastructure in order to map vulnerabilities and develop offensive cyber strategies. The NSA combines agents with skills in computer science, engineering, mathematics, and linguistics in order to better investigate various issues related to cybersecurity threats. Similar agencies are present in various nations, such as Australia's Defence Signals Directorate (DSD), Canada's Communications Security Establishment (CSE), New Zealand's

Government Communications Security Bureau (GCSB), and the UK's Government Communications Headquarters (GCHQ).

The development of USCYBERCOM emerged around the same time as those of other similar command infrastructures across the world. For instance, Australia established the Cyber Security Operations Centre (CSOC) in 2009 as a coordinated response for cyberattacks against government systems. Canada, France, Japan, and the UK have established similar agencies in order to help defend against attacks. The Chinese government has established both offensive and defensive military organizations housed within so-called Information Warfare Militia Units, Technical Reconnaissance Bureaus (TRB), and the General Staff Department (GSD; Andress and Winterfeld, 2011). At the same time, these forces may be augmented by the larger population of active hackers operating within the bounds of the nation with or without state sponsorship. The Russian government also has some cyberwarfare capabilities which are housed within the Federal Security Service of the Russian Federation, the Federal Guard Service, and the General Staff (Andress and Winterfeld, 2011). There is even limited evidence that North Korea has established units in order to support cyberwar, though the lack of information about the nation makes it difficult to assess their true functionality (Andress and Winterfeld, 2011).

Summary

This chapter demonstrates the complex and very real threat that is posed by acts of online extremism and cyberterrorism, including the application of hacking techniques in furtherance of war between nation-states. These threats require a sophisticated response from law enforcement and military agencies alike in order to properly defend against attacks. At the same time, it may not be immediately clear when an attack is motivated by an extremist agenda or when it is simply criminal. Thus, the problem of cybercrime, hacktivism, and cyberterror will involve investigative resources and initiatives to determine the origins of an attack and the actors responsible. This issue will continue to evolve along with technology adoption and use across the globe. Hopefully, however, we will not experience an electronic Pearl Harbor incident in the years to come.

Key terms

Centre for the Protection of National Infrastructure (CPNI)
Comprehensive National Cybersecurity Initiative (CNCI)
Cyberterror
Cyberwar
Department of Energy (DOE)

online extremism, cyberterror, cyber warfare

Department of Homeland Security (DHS)

e-jihad

Electronic Communications Privacy Act (ECPA)

Electronic Pearl Harbor

Federal Bureau of Investigation (FBI)

Flash mob

FloodNet

Hacktivism

Low Orbit Ion Cannon (LOIC)

Nation-state

National Security Agency (NSA)

Non-nation-state-sponsored actor

Operation Aurora

Operation Olympic Games

People's Liberation Army of China (PLA)

PRISM program

Stuxnet

Supervisory Control and Acquisition System (SCADA)

Terror

USA PATRIOT Act

USCYBERCOM

White power

Discussion questions

1) How should we define or view the activities of Anonymous? They hack government targets, civilians, and industry. As such, should their actions be viewed as cybercrime, hacktivism, or cyberterror? Why?

2) What real-world events, whether political, military, or social, could trigger a cyberattack? For instance, why were there not more virtual sit-ins or DDoS attacks in response to the PRISM program?

3) Why do you think incidents like Operation Aurora did not lead to more substantial policy responses from the United States? Is it too difficult to find an appropriate response? What do you think would be acceptable?

4) The threat of nuclear war and the proliferation of WMD is deterred in part by the idea of mutually assured destruction, not only for the two nations but for the larger world. Given that nearly every nation has economic and critical infrastructure dependent on technology, if

online extremism, cyberterror, cyber warfare

a nation-state were to engage in cyberwar against a rival, it would demand a physical or cyber response. With that in mind, how can nation-states deter the use of cyber attacks against one another? How do we respond to attacks committed by hackers or nation-states who are not influenced by traditional deterrence methods?

References

Abrams, F. (2012). On American Hate Speech Law. In M. Herz & P. Molnar (eds), *The Content and Context of Hate Speech: Rethinking Regulation and Responses* (pp. 116–128). Cambridge: Cambridge University Press.

Alshech, E. (2007). Cyberspace as a combat zone: The phenomenon of electronic jihad. *MEMRI Inquiry and Analysis Series*, (329). The Middle East Media Research Institute, February 7.

Andress, J., & Winterfeld, S. (2011). *Cyber Warfare: Techniques, Tactics, and Tools for Security Practitioners*. Waltham MA: Syngress.

Anti-Defamation League. (2002). *Racist Groups Using Computer Gaming to Promote Violence Against Blacks, Latinos, and Jews*. New York, NY: Anti-Defamation League. [Online] Available at: www.adl.org/videogames/default.asp

As-Sālim, M. (2003). *39 Ways to Serve and Participate in Jihâd*. At-Tibyân Publications, [Online] Available at: www.archive.org/stream/39WaysToServeAnd Participate/39WaysToServeAndParticipateInJihad_djvu.txt

Ayers, J. M. (1999). From the streets to the Internet: The cyber-diffusion of contention. *The ANNALS of the American Academy of Political and Social Science*, 566, 132–143.

Bakier, A. H. (2007). Forum users improve electronic jihad technology. *Terrorism Focus*, 4(20), June 26.

Best, S. J., & Krueger, B. S. (2005). Analyzing the representativeness of internet political participation. *Political Behavior*, 27, 183–216.

Brenner, S. W. (2008). *Cyberthreats: The Emerging Fault Lines of the Nation State*. New York: Oxford University Press.

Brenner, S. W. (2011). Defining Cybercrime: A Review of Federal and State Law. In R. D. Clifford (ed.), *Cybercrime: The Investigation, Prosecution, and Defense of a Computer-Related Crime*, 3rd edition (pp.15–104). Raleigh, NC: Carolina Academic Press.

Britz, M. T. (2010). Terrorism and Technology: Operationalizing Cyberterrorism and Identifying Concepts. In T. J. Holt (ed.), *Crime On-Line: Correlates, Causes, and Context* (pp. 193–220). Raleigh, NC: Carolina Academic Press.

Brodscky, J., & Radvanovsky, R. (2010). Control Systems Security. In T. J. Holt & B. Schell (eds), *Corporate Hacking and Technology-Driven Crime: Social Dynamics and Implications* (pp. 187–204). Hershey, PA: IGI-Global.

Castle, T. (2011). The women of Stormfront: An examination of white nationalist discussion threads on the Internet. *Internet Journal of Criminology*. [Online] Available at: www. internetjournalofcriminology.com/Castle_Chevalier_The_Women_of_Stormfront_ An_Examination_of_White_Nationalist_Discussion_Threads.pdf

Chadwick, A. (2007). Digital network repertoires and organizational hybridity. *Political Communication*, 24, 283–301.

Clayton, M. (2010). Stuxnet malware is "weapon" out to destroy … Iran's Bushehr Nuclear Plant. *Christian Science Monitor*, September 21, 2010. [Online] Available at: www.csmonitor.com/USA/2010/0921/Stuxnet-malware-is-weapon-out-to-destroy-Iran-s-Bushehr-nuclear-plant

CPNI. (2014). CPNI: The policy context. [Online] Available at: www.cpni.gov.uk/about/context

Clover, C. (2009). Kremlin-backed group behind Estonia cyber blitz. *Financial Times*, March 11, 2009.

Corera, G. (2008). The world's most wanted cyber-jihadist. *BBC News*, January 16, 2008.

Correll, S. P. (2010). *An interview with Anonymous*. PandaLabs Blog. [Online] Available at: http://pandalabs.pandasecurity.com/an-interview-with-anonymous/

Creveld, M. V. (1999). *The Rise and Decline of the State*. Cambridge: Cambridge University Press.

Davis, J. (2007). Web war one. *Wired*, September, 2007, 162–169.

Denning, D. E. (2010). Cyber-Conflict as an Emergent Social Problem. In T. J. Holt & B. Schell (eds), *Corporate Hacking and Technology-Driven Crime: Social Dynamics and Implications* (pp. 170–186). Hershey, PA: IGI-Global.

Department of Defense. (2011). Department of Defense Strategy for Operating in Cyberspace. Washington DC. [Online] Available at: www.defense.gov/news/d20110714cyber.pdf

Department of Energy. (2013). *National Security and Safety*. [Online] Available at: http://energy.gov/public-services/national-security-safety

Department of Homeland Security. (2013). *U.S. Department of Homeland Security Department Components*. [Online] Available at: www.dhs.gov/department-components

Drogin, B. (1999). Russians seem to be hacking into Pentagon. *San Francisco Chronicle*, October 7.

Earl, J., & Schussman, A. (2003). The New Site of Activism: On-line Organizations, Movement Entrepreneurs and the Changing Location of Social Movement Decision-Making. In P. G. Coy (ed.), *Consensus Decision Making, Northern Ireland and Indigenous Movements* (pp. 155–187). London: JAI Press.

Faulk, K. (1997). White supremacist spreads views on net. *The Birmingham News*, October 19, 1997, 1. [Online] Available at: www.stormfront.org/dblack/press101997.htm

Federal Bureau of Investigation. (2013). *The National Security Branch of the Federal Bureau of Investigation*. [Online] Available at: www.fbi.gov/about-us/nsb/national-security-branch-brochure

Fidel, S. (2011). Utah's $1.5 billion cyber-security center underway. *Deseret News*, January 6, 2011. [Online] Available at: www.deseretnews.com/article/705363940/Utahs-15-billion-cyber-security-center-under-way.html?pg=all

Foltz, B. C. (2004). Cyberterrorism, computer crime, and reality. *Information Management & Computer Security*, 12, 154–166.

Forest, J. J. (2009). *Influence Warfare: How Terrorists and Governments Struggle to Shape Perceptions in a War of Ideas*. Westport, CT: Praeger.

Fritz, J. (2008). How China will use cyber warfare to leapfrog in military competitiveness. *Culture Mandala*, 8(1), October, 28–80. [Online] Available at: http://epublications.bond.edu.au/cm/vol8/iss1/2/

Furedi, F. (2005). *Politics of Fear: Beyond Left and Right*. London: Continuum Press.

Gerstenfeld, P. B., Grant, D. R., & Chiang, C. P. (2003). Hate online: A content analysis of extremist internet sites. *Analyses of Social Issues and Public Policy*, 3, 29–44.

Gidda, M. (2013). Edward Snowden and the NSA files – timeline. *The Guardian* 25 July 2013. [Online] Available at: www.theguardian.com/world/2013/jun/23/edward-snowden-nsa-files-timeline

Gonsalves, A. (2013). Islamic group promises to resume U.S. bank cyberattacks. *CSO Online* Febrary 28, 2013. [Online] Available at: www.csoonline.com/article/729598/islamic-group-promises-to-resume-u.s.-bank-cyberattacks?source=ctwartcso

Gross, G., & McMillan, R. (2006). Al-Qaeda "Battle of Guantanamo" cyberattack a no-show. *IDG News*, December 1.

Gruen, M. (2005). Innovative Recruitment and Indoctrination Tactics by Extremists: Video Games, Hip Hop, and the World Wide Web. In J. J. Forest (ed.) *The Making of a Terrorist*. Westport, CT: Praeger.

Guadagno, R. E., Cialdini, R. B., & Evron, G. (2010). Storming the servers: A social psychological analysis of the first Internet war. *Cyberpsychology, Behavior, and Social Networks*, 13, 447–453.

Henderson, S. J. (2007). *The Dark Visitor: Inside the World of Chinese Hackers*. Fort Leavenworth, KS: Foreign Military Studies Office.

Hess, P. (2002). China prevented repeat cyber attack on US, *UPI*, October 29.

Holt, T. J. (2012). Exploring the intersections of technology, crime and terror. *Terrorism and Political Violence*, 24, 337–354.

Holt, T., & Kilger, M. (2012). Examining willingness to attack critical infrastructure on and off-line. *Crime and Delinquency*, 58, 798–822.

Jaffe, G. (2006). Gates Urges NATO Ministers To Defend Against Cyber Attacks. *The Wall Street Journal On-line*. June 15, 2006. [Online] Available at: http://online.wsj.com/article/SB118190166163536578.html

Jamestown. (2008). Hacking manual by jailed jihadi appears on web. *Terrorism Focus*, 5(9). Jamestown Foundation, March 4.

Jennings, K. M., & Zeitner, V. (2003). Internet use and civic engagement: A longitudinal analysis. *Public Opinion Quarterly*, 67, 311–334.

Jipson, A. (2007). Influence of hate rock. *Popular Music and Society*, 30, 449–451.

Jordan, T., & Taylor, P. (2004). *Hacktivism and Cyber Wars*. London: Routledge.

Kerr,, P. K., Rollins, J., & Theohary, C. A. (2010). *The Stuxnet Computer Worm: Harbinger of an Emerging Warfare Capability*. Washington DC; Congressional Research Service.

Kilger, M. (2010). Social Dynamics and the Future of Technology-Driven Crime. In T. J. Holt & B. Schell (eds), *Corporate Hacking and Technology-Driven Crime: Social Dynamics and Implications* (pp. 205–227). Hershey, PA: IGI-Global.

Landler, M., and Markoff, J. (2007). Digital fears emerge after data siege in Estonia. *The New York Times*, May 29.

Levy, B. H. (2003). *Who Killed Daniel Pearl?* Brooklyn NY: Melville House.

Leyden, J. (2003). Al-Qaeda: The 39 principles of holy war. *Virtual Jerusalem*.

Mandiant. (2013). *APT1: Exposing one of china's cyber espionage units*. Mandiant. [Online] Available at: http://intelreport.mandiant.com/

Markoff, J., & Barboza, D. (2010). 2 China Schools Said to be Linked to Online Attacks. *The New York Times*. [Online] Available at: www.nytimes.com/2010/02/19/technology/19china.html

Martin, G. (2006). *Understanding Terrorism: Challenges, Perspectives, and Issues*, 2nd edition. Thousand Oaks, CA: Sage.

martinlutherking.org. (2013). *Martin Luther King Jr. – A true historical examination*. [Online] Available at: http://martinlutherking.org

McNamee, L. G., Peterson, B. L., & Pena, J. (2010). A call to educate, participate, invoke, and indict: Understanding the communication of online hate groups. *Communication Monographs*, 77(2), 257–280.

McWilliams, B. (2001). Pakistani hackers deface US site with ultimatum. *Newsbytes*, October 17.

Mendel, T. (2012). Does International Law Provide for Consistent Rules on Hate Speech. In M. Herz & P. Molnar (eds), *The Content and Context of Hate Speech: Rethinking Regulation and Responses* (pp. 417–429). Cambridge: Cambridge University Press.

National Security Agency. (2013). *Mission Statement*. www.nsa.gov/about/mission/index.shtml

National Socialist Movement. (2014). *National Socialist Movement FAQ*. [Online] Available at: www.nsm88.org/faqs/frequently%20asked%20questions%20about%20national%20socialism.pdf

Pollitt, M. M. (1998). Cyberterrorism – fact or fancy? *Computer Fraud & Security*, 2, 8–10.

Pool, J. (2005). *Technology and security discussions on the jihadist forums*. Jamestown Foundation, October 11.

Rid, T. (2013). *Cyber War Will Not Take Place*. London: Hurst & Company.

Sanger, D. E. (2012). *Confront and Conceal: Obama's Secret Wars and Surprising Use of American Power*. New York: Crown Publishing.

Schmid, A. P. (1988). *Political Terrorism*. Amsterdam: North Holland Press.

Schmid, A. P. (2004). Frameworks for conceptualising terrorism. *Terrorism and Political Violence*, 16, 197–221.

Schmid, A. P., & Jongman, A. J. (2005). *Political Terrorism: A New Guide to Actors, Authors, Concepts, Data Bases, Theories, and Literature*. New Brunswick, NJ: Transaction Publishers.

Schwartau, W. (1996). *Information Warfare*, 2nd ed. New York: Thunder's Mouth Press.

Schmugar, C. (2010). More Details on "Operation Aurora." *McAfee Security Blog*. [Online] Available at: http://blogs.mcafee.com/mcafee-labs/more-details-on-operation-aurora

Simi, P., & Futrell, R. (2006). White Power Cyberculture: Building a Movement. *The Public Eye Magazine Summer*, 69–72.

Southern Poverty Law Center. (2013). Hate Map. [Online] Available at: www.splcenter.org/get-informed/hate-map

Stepanova, E. (2011). The role of information communications technology in the "Arab Spring": Implications beyond the region. PONARS Eurasia Policy Memo No. 159. [Online] Available at: www.gwu.edu/~ieresgwu/assets/docs/ponars/pepm_159.pdf

Taylor, P. A. (1999). *Hackers: Crime in the Digital Sublime.* New York: Routledge.

Ulph, S. (2006). Internet mujahideen refine electronic warfare tactics. *Terrorism Focus*, 3(5). Jamestown Foundation, February 7.

Van Laer, J. (2010). Activists online and offline: The Internet as an information channel for protest demonstrations. *Mobilization: An International Journal*, 15, 347–366.

Verton, D. (2003). *Black Ice: The Invisible Threat of Cyber Terrorism.* New York: McGraw Hill.

Wall, D. S. (2001). Cybercrimes and the Internet. In D. S. Wall (ed.), *Crime and the Internet* (pp. 1–17). New York: Routledge.

Watson, L. (2013). Al Qaeda releases guide on how to torch cars and make bombs as it names 11 public figures it wants 'dead or alive' in latest edition of its glossy magazine. *Daily Mail*, March 4, 2013. www.dailymail.co.uk/news/article-2287003/Al-Qaedareleases-guide-torch-cars-make-bombs-naming-11-public-figures-wants-dead-alivelatest-edition-glossy-magazine.html

Weimann, G. (2005). How modern terrorism uses the Internet. *The Journal of International Security Affairs*, 8.

White House. (2011a). *The Comprehensive National Cybersecurity Initiative.* Washington DC. [Online] Available at: www.whitehouse.gov/cybersecurity/comprehensive-national-cybersecurity-initiative

White House. (2011b). *Empowering Local Partners to Prevent Violent Extremism in the United States.* Washington, DC. [Online] Available at: www.whitehouse.gov/sites/default/files/empowering_local_partners.pdf

Woo, H., Kim, Y., & Dominick, J. (2004). Hackers: militants or merry pranksters? A content analysis of defaced web pages. *Media Psychology*, 6, 63–82.

Yar, M. (2013). *Cybercrime and Society*, 2nd edition. London: Sage Publications.

Zetter, K. (2010). "Google" hackers had ability to alter source code. *Wired.* [Online] Available at: www.wired.com/threatlevel/2010/03/source-code-hacks/

Zetter, K. (2011). DHS fears a modified Stuxnet could attack US infrastructure. *Wired Threat Level*, 20. [Online] Available at: www.wired.com/threatlevel/2011/07/dhs-fears-stuxnet-attacks/

chapter 9

Cybercrime and criminological theories

Chapter goals

- Understand how traditional criminological theories can be applied to cybercrime offending and victimization
- Assess the usefulness of specific criminological theories, such as social learning theory and the general theory of crime, in explaining a variety of cybercrimes
- Compare a situational theory of victimization with an individual-level explanation to understand cybercrime victimization
- Explore a new cybercrime theory

Introduction

Over the last several decades, scholars have debated how cybercrime offending differs from traditional crime. The first eight chapters of this text discuss how the reasons or motivations for cybercrime offending are typically the same as those for traditional offending. Financial incentive is a substantial motive for some hackers, malware writers, and virtually all fraudsters. Individuals who download legal and illegal pornography enjoy the easy access to material that satisfies their sexual desires. Online harassment, similar to traditional bullying, allows someone to hurt others and therefore have power over them from a distance. There is also the thrill and rush associated with harassing others, downloading pornography, swindling others, and breaking into a computer system. Thus, Grabosky's (2001) comment seems apt:

> Computer crimes are driven by time-honoured motivations, the most obvious of which are greed, lust, power, revenge, adventure (p. 243),

and the desire to take "forbidden fruit." None of the above motivations is new. The element of novelty resides in the unprecedented capacity of technology to facilitate acting on these motivations.

(p. 244)

As a result, cybercrime could be viewed as "old wine in a new bottle" (Grabosky, 2001; Wall, 1998). If this is the case, traditional criminological theories should have no difficulty in explaining cybercrime if it is simply "old wine."

Chapters 2 through 8 also illustrated that there is something unique about cybercrime that separates it from traditional criminal activity. Although it might be the same "old wine," there are instances of "new wine," such as malware creation, that has little connection to the physical world. The second part of this analogy, the new bottle, is also pertinent in that virtual space is different than physical space. The Internet allows easy access to most people around the world, and provides an avenue for individuals to engage in cybercrime while feeling largely anonymous. The Internet also allows the offender, whether an individual, group, or nation-state, to avoid making physical contact with the victim or his/her property. Thus, cybercrime may not be viewed as "old wine in new bottles" or even "new wine in new bottles," but "rather many of its characteristics are so novel that the expression 'new wine, but no bottles!' becomes a more fitting description" (Wall, 1998: 202).

In addition, examining the uniqueness of cybercrime might allow us to not only understand more about these phenomena, but it might also provide brand new insights on traditional forms of crime as well. Discussions of new cyber-specific criminological theories might be a catalyst for additional theoretical creation and elaboration. Taken as a whole, this chapter will show that the future of cybercrime research is bright. Studies that elaborate complex associations that have been held in the traditional literature for decades will also provide new insights into the commission of crime – both traditional and cyber related.

Unlike traditional criminological textbooks that place theories into categories (e.g. classical, positivist, etc.), and then cover each theory in chronological order, our focus is on how criminological theories have been applied to cybercrime to help us better understand these phenomena. Thus, we focus on the theories that have been examined the most and have therefore provided the most insight into why individuals commit these offenses. Considering that a subcultural framework is used extensively through this text, this chapter first reminds the reader about information they read in the first eight chapters. The two strongest competing theories for explaining cybercrime based on empirical support – Ron Akers' (1998) social learning theory and Gottfredson and Hirschi's (1990) general theory of crime – will then be discussed. The chapter then progresses to cover theories that have recently been receiving more attention in the cybercrime literature, but still have not received the same level of focus as social learning theory and the general theory of crime – Agnew's general strain theory, techniques of neutralization, and deterrence theory. Two victimization theories that have been used to better understand cybercrime victimization – routine activity theory, a situational theory of victimization, and the general theory of crime, an individual-level theory – are then described and assessed. We finally conclude with a discussion of a new cybercrime theory – space transition theory.

Subcultural theories

Overview

Most criminological theories focus on offending as a consequence of individual-level factors that may be affected through properly targeted intervention strategies. These theories do not, however, explore the meaning that offending has for some individuals and the depth of their participation in peer networks that may facilitate criminal activity. Researchers who explore criminality through a subcultural lens, however, can provide substantive depth on the how and why of criminal behavior (Miller, 1958; Short, 1968).

Defined from a broad perspective, a **subculture** is any group having certain values, norms, traditions, and rituals that set them apart from the dominant culture (Kornblum, 1997; Brake, 1980). Subcultures form as a response to either a rejection of the dominant culture (Miller, 1958) or around a distinct phenomenon that may not be valued by the larger society (Quinn and Forsyth, 2005; Wolfgang and Ferracuti, 1967). This includes an emphasis on performing certain behaviors or developing skill sets (Maurer, 1981) and learning the rules or codes of conduct that structure how individuals view and interact with different groups (Foster, 1990). Subcultures also utilize special terms and slang, called an **argot**. They may also have some outward symbols of membership like tattoos or informal uniforms (Maurer, 1981). Thus, demonstrating such knowledge illustrates an individual's reputation, status, and adherence to a particular subculture.

In many ways, subcultural frameworks share common elements of social learning theory (Akers, 1998), since involvement in a subculture influences behavior by providing individuals with beliefs, goals, and values that approve of and justify particular types of activities, including crime (Herbert, 1998). In fact, the transmission of subcultural knowledge increases the likelihood of involvement in criminal behavior despite potential legal consequences for these actions (Miller, 1958; Short, 1968). As such, subcultural frameworks provide an important perspective to explain how the values and ideas espoused by members of a group affect the behavior of its members.

Subcultures and cybercrime

The development of the Internet and computer technology has had a dramatic impact on the formation of and participation in deviant or criminal subcultures (DiMarco and DiMarco, 2003; Quinn and Forsyth, 2005). The anonymity and distributed nature of the Internet enables individuals to connect to groups that share similar likes, dislikes, behaviors, opinions, and values, regardless of the participants' locations in the real world (DiMarco and DiMarco, 2003). Some individuals may not be able to discuss their interests or activities with others in the real world due to fear of legal reprisal or concerns that others around them may reject them because they do not share their interests.

Technology allows individuals to connect to others without these fears, and even provide information about a behavior or activity to improve their knowledge and minimize fear of detection (Blevins and Holt, 2009; Holt, 2007; Quinn and Forsyth, 2005). Individuals can readily communicate subcultural knowledge through email and other forms of CMC (Holt, Soles, and Leslie, 2008; Holt and Copes, 2010). In turn, this information can increase the likelihood of success when engaging in illicit behavior despite potential legal consequences. Thus, the value of the Internet and CMCs with individuals across the globe are pivotal in the pursuit of crime and deviance online and offline.

Throughout this textbook, we have used the subcultural framework extensively to describe the individuals that participate in a certain activity as well as the beliefs, structures, and interactions that provide support to them in opposition to community norms and standards that have defined them and their behavior in many cases as deviant or criminal. In Chapter 2, we explored the hacker subculture, devoid of Hollywood portrayals, and its primary norms of technology, the importance of knowledge and learning, and secrecy, regardless of the individual's involvement in malicious hacking. Chapter 3 described how the interests and beliefs of malware writers are generally congruent with those of the larger hacker subculture. In Chapter 6, we discussed how the Internet has allowed individuals with deviant sexual orientations to interact with one another, gain validation for their sexual desires, exchange both materials and beliefs, and be part of a community. Finally, Chapter 8 examined the ways the Internet provides a means for extremist groups to indoctrinate individuals in favor of their movement. Technology allows individuals to be introduced to core principles and norms of the group while allowing them to interact with members from a safe physical distance. Future cybercrime scholars will continue to find this framework fruitful in explaining how group dynamics affect individuals' belief systems and participation in cyber deviant acts.

Social learning theory and cybercrime

Overview

Over the last century of research, scholars have found that the most consistent predictor of future offending is whether an individual has committed an offense in the past. Arguably the second most important predictor is whether that person has friends or associates who engage in crime and delinquency. This link between peer behavior and offending has been the source of a substantial amount of both research and theory aimed at explaining this relationship.

In 1947, Edwin Sutherland presented in his book, *Principles of Criminology*, one of the first theories to explain the peer-offending relationship: differential association theory (Sutherland, 1947). Sutherland argued that criminal behavior was learned in a process involving interactions and communication with others, with the most important interactions stemming from intimate personal groups. During this process, an individual not only learned techniques on how to commit crimes, but also motives, rationalizations, and attitudes that supported the violation of the law. A person became more likely to commit delinquent or criminal acts when his or her "definitions," referring to rationalizations and attitudes, which supported the violation of the law exceeded those that were unfavorable to breaking the law. Criticisms over the years, however, have centered heavily on the theory's: (1) testability; and (2) lack of specificity on the learning process mechanisms responsible for the commission of deviant and criminal behavior (Kornhauser, 1978; Matseuda, 1988).

Since the 1960s, Ron Akers has reformulated differential association theory to specify the learning mechanisms through which criminal behavior is learned. In what has become known as **social learning theory**, Akers (1998) expanded upon Sutherland's original differential association theory by introducing principal components of operant conditioning, namely that behavior followed by rewards or reinforcements will be more likely to continue while acts followed by punishment will be less likely (Akers, 1998). Thus, Akers' (1998) social learning theory argued that the learning process of any behavior, including crime, includes four principal components: (1) **differential association**; (2) **definitions**; (3) **differential reinforcement**; and (4) **imitation**.

This dynamic learning process begins with associating with others, both deviants and non-deviants. Differential associations to deviants provide both models for deviant behavior and definitions, such as attitudes and norms, which may favor breaking the law or providing justifications that neutralize possible negative consequences of deviance. Following Sutherland's differential association theory, social learning theory holds that individuals who have a greater proportion of beliefs supportive of deviant behavior will be more likely to engage in those activities.

Although definitions supporting criminal activity are critical to the offender to justify their behavior, criminality will occur if it is reinforced through some means, whether social or financial. For example, an individual who perceives that he will receive praise from his friends for throwing a rock through a window will be more likely to throw the rock. If that praise comes, he will be more likely to continue this behavior in the future. Perceived or actual punishments, however, will decrease the likelihood of that behavior. The punishments can take the form of adding negative stimuli, such as spanking or arresting, or can be in the removal of positive stimuli, such as taking away television privileges. Finally, imitation plays a major role in the social learning process as individuals may engage in deviant behavior after watching someone else engage in the same behavior. Imitation plays a larger role in the earlier stages of the learning process. As the process continues, however, definitions and differential reinforcements become more important. Social learning theory has been one of the most commonly tested criminological theories and arguably has received the strongest empirical support to date in its favor for explaining a wide variety of behaviors (Akers and Jensen, 2006; Lee, Akers, and Borg, 2004; Pratt *et al.*, 2009).

Social learning theory and cybercrime

Given the support Akers' (1998) theory has in the larger research community, it is no surprise that scholars have seen its potential importance in explaining why individuals commit cybercrime. The complexities of computer programming make the connection between learning and cybercrime quite apparent. Depending on the specific cybercrime, individuals must "learn not only how to operate a highly technical piece of equipment but also specific procedures, programming, and techniques for using the computer illegally" (Skinner and Fream, 1997: 498). Even though computer technology has become more user friendly due to convenient interfaces, there is a need for a learning process in which the basic dynamics of computer use and abuse are learned from others.

Digital piracy (see Chapter 4) at first does not seem overly complex. Someone simply downloads a music or movie file without authorization. Social learning theory would hold that in order for individuals to commit digital piracy, they must participate in a social learning process. The individual must interact with fellow digital pirates, learn how and where to perform downloads, imitate what they have observed, learn definitions supportive of violation of intellectual property laws, and be rewarded either financially or socially for their efforts in order for the piracy to continue.

Virtually every study examining digital piracy finds that associating with pirating peers is the most significant correlate in predicting pirating behaviors (Higgins and Marcum, 2011; Hinduja and Ingram, 2008; Holt, Bossler, and May, 2012). Friends and intimate relationships can provide information on the methods required to engage in piracy and the location of materials on the Internet. Piracy requires some technological skill which can be garnered through direct associations with others. The continuous technological developments noted in this community also require peer associations in order to readily identify new mechanisms to download files. Individuals are then able to engage in simple forms of piracy through imitation (Hinduja, 2003; Holt and Copes, 2010; Holt, Burruss, and Bossler, 2010; Ingram and

Hinduja, 2008; Skinner and Fream, 1997). As pirating becomes easier for an individual, the need for these delinquent associations could decrease. Furthermore, positive reinforcement for participation in software piracy is evident through both financial (i.e. free movies and music) and social (i.e. praise for showing someone how to use torrent sharing software) rewards (Hinduja, 2003; Holt & Copes, 2010).

Studies have also shown that pirates have both definitions that favor the violation of intellectual property laws and techniques of neutralization that diminish their personal responsibility for their actions (Higgins and Marcum, 2011; Ingram and Hinduja, 2008; Skinner and Fream, 1997). Members of the piracy subculture espouse attitudes that minimize the impact of copyright law and the harms caused by pirating media. For instance, individuals who pirate materials commonly justify their actions by suggesting that downloading a few songs or media does not actually harm the property owners or artists (Higgins and Marcum, 2011; Ingram and Hinduja, 2008). Pirates also believe that their actions are not inherently wrong since there are no clear guidelines for ethical behavior in online environments (Higgins and Marcum, 2011; Ingram and Hinduja, 2008). These attitudes are often communicated between pirates and encourage further participation in piracy over time.

In much the same way, social learning theorists argue that individuals who engage in computer hacking would need to associate with individuals who hack. These relationships should increase their likelihood to imitate hacking activity early in their development as a hacker as well as be exposed to definitions favorable to using technology in this fashion. As they participate further in the hacker subculture, hacking would be socially reinforced, possibly even financially, and the behavior would continue.

Studies have shown that all four social learning components are empirically related to hacking behaviors (Bossler and Burruss, 2011; Skinner and Fream, 1997). The importance of peer associations in influencing hacking behavior is not only found in qualitative studies and anecdotal stories, but has been consistently found to be one of the most important predictors of hacking behavior in quantitative studies as well (Bossler and Burruss, 2011; Holt, Bossler, and May, 2012; Skinner and Fream, 1997). Morris and Blackburn (2009) found that college students who associate with delinquent youth had a larger impact on more serious forms of computer crime, such as attempting hacking, malicious file damage, or manipulation, than their attitudes. Delinquent peer associations have been empirically shown to be important in providing models to imitate (e.g. Morris and Blackburn, 2009) as well as in the introduction and acquisition of beliefs and excuses to justify computer attacks (Bossler and Burruss, 2011; Skinner and Fream, 1997). Similar to the arguments that the hacker subculture provides positive social encouragement and praise for successful and innovative hacks, scholars testing social learning hypotheses have found similar results (Bossler and Burruss, 2011; Skinner and Fream,

1997). Skinner and Fream (1997) found that teacher encouragement, as well as participation in electronic bulletin boards, increased the likelihood of students guessing passwords.

As discussed in Chapter 2, websites and chatrooms can play a large role in the social learning process of hackers. Text Box 9.1 displays an article that summarizes different websites where individuals can learn basic hacking skills. As the comments on the article indicated (not shown), many commenters posted negative and derisive comments, accusing the author of creating script kiddies. One commenter said, "You hack to learn; you don't learn to hack."

Text Box 9.1: Example of websites that provide information on hacking techniques

www.makeuseof.com/tag/top-5-websites-to-learn-how-to-hack-like-a-pro/

Top 5 websites to learn how to hack like a pro

> You might be surprised to learn just how many people want to learn how to hack. The stereotype is that of the young college guy … who spends his evenings and weekends writing up intricate hacking scripts to break into whatever computer system he can get his hands on.

This article provides an overview of five key websites that can help individuals learn to hack. There is inherent value in this article because it demonstrates that information on hacking can be acquired through virtual venues with a great deal of ease and engender the learning process in meaningful ways.

Although scholars have examined how the Internet has been used by terrorist groups, few have utilized criminological theory to understand why individuals join these groups or how they are influenced by them. A rare exception is Freiburger and Crane's (2011) study applying social learning theory to online extremism in which they argue that "by applying these four constructs [differential association, definitions, differential reinforcement, and imitation] to terrorists' uses of the Internet, researchers can better understand how the Internet is being used to enhance terrorist operations" (p. 128).

Terrorist groups have clearly been able to use the Internet to increase membership by gaining access to youth around the world (differential association) and communicating beliefs (definitions) that support terrorist activities. Freiburger and Crane (2011) argue that second-generation youth living in new countries are especially vulnerable since they are dealing with their lack of identity, unemployment, and feelings of isolation and discrimination. Within online support systems, however, they find and communicate with others who are in similar situations. The Internet has become more important for terrorist groups to find and indoctrinate members, making contact in physical space unnecessary.

The Internet is valuable in that it is accessible at any time and in most places. Depending on the severity of the individual's sense of isolation and lack of attachment to conforming groups, online associations with extremists and potential terror groups may provide a vital sense of meaning and connection for a disenfranchised youth. As their feelings intensify and they participate more often in online discussions, they will be more prone to accept the definitions favoring the particular ideological message promulgated on these websites. In addition, the Internet provides strong positive reinforcement in that it can make terrorists into instant celebrities, martyrs for the cause, and can glorify them long after they died. These reinforcements provide the perception to youth that the glory, not to mention increases in self-esteem and self-identity, stemming from violence and harm greatly outweigh the negative consequences. Finally, the information and videos posted online provide simple steps for someone to follow and imitate (Freiburger and Crane, 2011).

As the above paragraphs demonstrated, Akers' (1998) social learning theory is not just one of the most theoretically and empirically sound theories to account for traditional forms of crime, but it also applies equally as well to a wide variety of both simple and more complex forms of cybercrime.

General theory of crime

Overview

Unlike most traditional criminological theories that focus on examining why people commit crime, social control theories ask the opposite question: "What causes people to actually conform to the rules?" Control theories argue that individuals engage in crime as a function of our basic human nature, and the desire to obtain the rewards that crime can bring, whether economic or emotional. They argue that motivation is generally invariant among all individuals, meaning that no one person is any more motivated to commit a crime than another. What separates criminals from non-criminals then is the amount of control placed on the individual, whether by the law, society, school, family, friends, oneself, or other institutions and groups. Criminals simply have less control placed upon them, making them more free to pursue their pleasures through the most efficient means, which is quite often illegal.

cybercrime and criminological theories

Over the last two decades, the most popular, parsimonious, and highly tested social control theory developed has been Michael Gottfredson and Travis Hirschi's (1990) **general theory of crime**. The theorists argue that most crimes are relatively simple actions that provide immediate gratification. Based on the characteristics of most crimes, Gottfredson and Hirschi argue that offenders have certain behavioral and attitudinal characteristics, including being impulsive, insensitive, and giving little consideration to the future. Since they act on the spur of the moment, they give little thought to the consequences of their actions. The lack of forethought and other behavioral characteristics lead them to fail in school, have poor relationships with others, and engage in risky behaviors in which the long-term consequences outweigh the meager short-term benefits, such as smoking, drug use, and unprotected sex. Taken as a whole, Gottfredson and Hirschi (1990) argue that criminal behavior and other risky activities stem from one's level of **self-control**, or the ability to constrain their own behavior through internal regulation. Adequate levels of self-control are primarily formed in childhood through proper parental child-rearing techniques, including monitoring, recognizing inappropriate behavior, and punishing that inappropriate behavior. Although the theory might seem simplistic, low self-control is one of the strongest correlates of crime (Pratt and Cullen, 2000) and has been consistently linked to a wide range of crime and deviance.

The general theory of crime and cybercrime

The general theory of crime has frequently been applied to cybercrime since it is a general theory, meaning that it should be able to explain any form of crime. Self-control theorists argue that most forms of cybercrime are similar to that of traditional crime: they are simple in nature, can be performed with little to no skill, and will lead to long-term consequences greater than short-term benefits. Thus, the reason why people commit cybercrime is the same reason people steal, hit, rob, burglarize, and sell drugs – inadequate levels of self-control.

Empirical research consistently supports the argument that low self-control is a significant predictor in understanding why people commit a wide variety of cybercrimes and cyber deviance, including, but not limited to: online harassment (Holt *et al.*, 2012), downloading online pornography (Buzzell, Foss, and Middleton, 2006), digital piracy (Higgins and Marcum, 2011), and online economic crimes (Moon, McCluskey, and McCluskey, 2010). Individuals with low levels of self-control are more likely to harass, bully, or stalk others online due to both their inability to control their temper and their inclination to "solve" problems physically rather than mentally (Holt, Bossler, and May, 2012). Individuals who are impulsive and focus on easy and simple immediate gratification are more likely to view and download online pornography (Buzzell *et al.*, 2006; Holt *et al.*, 2012). Digital piracy, whether involving software, music, or movies, is considered a simple task that requires minimal skill, provides immediate gratification with almost no effort, and indicates little empathy for the owners of the intellectual property (Higgins and Marcum, 2011). In addition, individuals with low self-control are more likely to commit identity theft (Moon *et al.*, 2010), simply viewing online economic crime to be a simple and easy way to make quick cash to support immediate wants.

There is some potential that more complicated forms of cybercrime, such as computer hacking, may not be accounted for through the general theory of crime. Self-control theorists would argue that computer hacking is simplistic and that hackers are just taking advantage of easy opportunities. They would also expect hackers to have some of the same characteristics of "traditional" criminals, including impulsivity; lacking diligence; not focusing on long-term goals; not being cognitive; self-centered and non-empathetic; and easily becoming frustrated. Research provides some support for this idea, though there are some major inconsistencies as well (Bossler and Burruss, 2011). Both traditional criminals and computer hackers illustrate a lack of empathy for their victims (Turgeman-Goldschmidt, 2005). In addition, hackers often state that they engage in hacking activities because of the thrill or rush of the hack (Schell and Dodge, 2002). They also enjoy the adventure of exploring what new technology can do.

Much of what is known about sophisticated hacks and malware development, however, suggest hackers have higher levels of self-control. They can typically be cognitive and verbal, as demonstrated by their strong commitment to and mastery of technology (Holt, 2007; Schell and Dodge, 2002). Many hackers are also enrolled in high school/college or employed, sometimes in the security field, all indicating some interest in long-term goals (Bachmann, 2010; Holt, 2007; Schell and Dodge, 2002). The potential disparity between hackers and those who engage in "hacks" makes it difficult to apply the characteristics of low self-control to hacking in general. Hackers that can be considered "script kiddies" seem to have the characteristics of the traditional criminals to which Gottfredson and Hirschi (1990) refer (Holt, 2007). They fulfill their immediate gratification by using simple techniques, like downloading others' programs, shoulder surfing, brute-force attacks, and social engineering, that do not require any deep knowledge of technology or much time and effort (Holt and Kilger, 2012). More advanced forms of computer hacking, such as the creation of malicious software, require a much greater amount of technical proficiency as well as time and energy to perfect the program – concepts incongruent with low self-control (Bossler and Burruss, 2011; Holt and Kilger, 2012).

Empirical tests support the complex relationship between low self-control and computer hacking. Holt, Bossler, and May (2012) found that *low* self-control predicted computer hacking, specifically accessing another's computer account of files without his/her knowledge or permission, in a sample of youth. Holt and Kilger (2008), however, found that hackers "in the wild" had similar *higher* levels of self-control compared to a sample of college students in information security courses. Bossler and Burruss (2011) also found that in a college sample, youth who committed three types of hacking behaviors (guessing another person's password into his/her computer account or files; accessing another's computer account or files without his/her knowledge or permission to look at information; and adding, deleting, changing, or printing any information in another's files without permission) and did not partake in the social learning process needed higher levels of self-control in order to be able to figure out how to hack. Individuals with lower levels of self-control were more likely to be involved in a social learning process which connected them with peers who taught them methods of hacking and reinforced the value of these activities (Bossler and Burruss, 2011). Self-control had a larger influence on hacking via its indirect effect on hacking through the social learning process than its direct effect on hacking. In simpler terms, one can argue that lower levels of self-control were more related to computer hacking generally.

Bossler and Burruss (2011) considered this "partial support" at best for the general theory of crime's ability to explain computer hacking. The lack of general research on this issue, however, leads to a fundamental and basic question: Is computer hacking a simple activity that can be explained by one important concept such as low self-control or is it a more complex activity that requires being involved in a long-term social learning process that requires peers teaching and reinforcing behaviors? The current body of research suggests that both answers are correct. Simple hacking techniques, such as brute-force attacks (see Chapter 2) require little skill and can be explained by both low self-control and social learning, though the influence of the social learning process on hacking is always stronger than the effect of low self-control. At the same time, more complex forms of hacking require advanced skills that are acquired through a social learning process and/or on their own due to their higher levels of self-control.

In the end, there is no denying the importance of low self-control in understanding the commission of cybercrime. These studies indicate that self-control may predict crime in the cyberworld as well as it does in the terrestrial world. In addition, research also shows that the influence of delinquent peer associations is a stronger predictor of cybercrime than levels of self-control (Holt and Bossler, 2014). Thus, the general theory of crime and social learning must be discussed together in some respects rather than treated separately.

Agnew's general strain theory

Overview

Robert Agnew's (1992, 2006) **general strain theory** is an individual-level theory developed as an expansion of Robert Merton's (1938) classic strain theory. Merton's original version of strain theory posited that being unable to achieve the goal of economic achievement leads to a sense of frustration. To deal with this strain, individuals need to find other ways to satisfy their needs which could include criminal activity. In Agnew's version, he discusses the role of frustrations leading to negative emotions, such as anger, frustration, and depression, which if not addressed appropriately, can lead individuals to engage in crime as a response.

Agnew (1992) identified three primary categories of strains that can have a substantive impact on emotional states: (1) the threatened or actual failure to achieve positively valued goals; (2) threatened or actual removal of positively valued stimuli; and (3) threatened or actual presentation of noxious stimuli. In simpler terms, not achieving a goal (e.g. not landing the job that you wanted, failing a test), having something positive taken away (e.g. loss of a parent or loved one), or experiencing something bad (e.g. bullying, family conflict) can all lead to negative emotions such as frustration or anger. These central arguments have received sound empirical support since the theory's inception. Life strains significantly influence involvement in delinquency (Agnew and White, 1992; Broidy, 2001; Paternoster and Mazerolle, 1994), though this relationship is mediated by increased levels of negative emotions, particularly anger and frustration (Brezina, 1998; Mazerolle and Piquero, 1997). Those who experience greater negative emotions are more likely to respond to strain with delinquency and crime.

General strain theory and cybercrime

Almost all scholars who have applied general strain theory to cybercrime have chosen to examine cyberbullying. This is sensible, given that the virtual environment allows individuals to immediately and easily vent frustration and anger at others in a detached way that does not require direct interaction with their victim (see Chapter 6). Thus, it would make sense for it to also apply well to explaining why some individuals choose to cyberbully others. Another reason is that in Agnew's (2001) significant elaboration of general strain theory, he identified bullying as a strain that was particularly relevant for explaining delinquency. He specifically provided four conditions that bullying satisfies to cause strain: (1) the victim will perceive the bullying as unjust; (2) it will be perceived as being high in magnitude or importance because of the vitality of peer relationships for youth; (3) the bullying will be occurring away from traditional forms of social control such as parents or teachers; and (4) the victim will be exposed to aggressive behavior to model his or her own future behavior.

The empirical research to date has supported this application of general strain theory (see Text Box 9.2). Young people, who are more likely to experience a wide variety of strains, including poor school performance, perceived unfair sanctions from teachers or parents for conduct, and the experience of negative life events, are more likely to participate in bullying behaviors on and offline (Moon, Hwang, and McCluskey, 2011; Patchin and Hinduja, 2011).

Text Box 9.2: Understanding the consequences of cyberbullying

www.cyberbullying.us/cyberbullying_emotional_consequences.pdf
   This link demonstrates the substantive emotional harms that individuals can experience as a result of cyberbullying. The impact of this experience can be wide-ranging and may be sufficient to lead an individual to feel anger and frustration over a long period of time, which ties in to Agnew's general strain theory.

Cyberbullying victimization, however, can also be viewed as a strain on its own that may lead to delinquent behavior (Hinduja and Patchin, 2007). In Hay, Meldrum, and Mann's (2010) study consisting of middle and high school students, they found that both traditional and cyberbullying victimization significantly increased future offending as well as self-harm and suicidal ideation. In fact, cyberbullying had modestly larger effects than physical bullying on future offending. The victims were more likely, however, to self-harm or to have suicidal thoughts than engage in harm against others. Wright and Li (2013) found that both peer rejection and cyberbullying victimization predicted future online aggression even when controlling for past acts of cyber aggression. In addition, being cyberbullied led to more aggression when coupled with peer rejection (Wright and Li, 2013) and physical bullying (Wright and Li, 2012).

General strain theory has shown itself to be a relevant theory for explaining traditional forms of crime as well as cyberbullying, although the extent that it will apply to other forms of cybercrime has yet to be examined. Although its propositions are not strongly connected to property-driven cybercrime, such as digital piracy, its tenets marry well with the often predatory nature of computer hacking. General strain theory provides interesting propositions on why individuals would commit computer hacks. For instance, there may be certain life events, whether being fired, failing in school, or losing a boyfriend or girlfriend, that may lead individuals to experience negative emotions. Experiencing anger, resentment, frustration, or possibly depression may all be pertinent triggers that could lead someone to lash out and attempt to harm others by attacking their systems (for examples, see Rege, 2013). More advanced examinations of general strain theory could consider whether involvement in political or ideologically driven hacks, like those of Anonymous (see Chapter 13) could stem from individual perceptions of how technology and information is used in our society, coupled with anger or frustration, affects involvement in illegal computer intrusions to address their perception of the problem. Only future research can address how general strain theory can apply to forms of cybercrime other than cyberbullying.

Techniques of neutralization

Overview

Gresham Sykes and David Matza's (1957) **techniques of neutralization** focus on how beliefs affect the process of deciding to commit a delinquent or criminal act. This theory assumes that most people hold conforming beliefs, but may still engage in criminal behavior occasionally. Delinquents and criminals develop rationalizations or neutralizations prior to committing the act to justify why the behavior was acceptable and not in conflict with their general belief system. This allows them to **drift** between criminality and conformity without accepting a deviant or criminal identity (Matza, 1964). Unlike social learning theory, which would argue that the criminal offender had more beliefs supporting breaking the law than conforming beliefs, techniques of neutralization argue that the offender maintains a conventional belief system and can justify deviant behavior.

Sykes and Matza (1957) developed five basic techniques that allow individuals to break from conformity: (1) **denial of responsibility**: someone else, event, or situation will be directly responsible for the offense and should be blamed; (2) **denial of an injury**: no one or thing will get hurt or damaged; (3) **denial of a victim**: there is no discernible victim (e.g. large corporation) or the "victim" deserved it; (4) **condemnation of the condemners**: those who would condemn their actions are hypocritical and doing so out of personal spite; and (5) **appeal to higher loyalties**: the offense is for the greater good of the group. One can summarize these five techniques with the following statements: (1) "It wasn't my fault;" (2) "No big deal. Nothing really happened;" (3) "They deserved it;" (4) "You would have done the same thing;" and (5) "My friends needed my help."

Techniques of neutralization and cybercrime

Scholars have applied the techniques of neutralization to a range of cybercrimes in order to understand how these behaviors can be justified by individuals who primarily live conforming lifestyles and have value systems congruent with that of traditional society. Most of the research focus has been on digital piracy, particularly in college samples, arguing that students hold justifications that allow them to download music or media without believing themselves to be criminals. Quantitative analyses of piracy have found weak (Hinduja, 2007) to moderate support (Higgins, Wolfe, and Marcum, 2008; Ingram and Hinduja, 2008; Marcum, Higgins, Wolfe, and Ricketts, 2011;

Morris and Higgins, 2009) for the acceptance of various beliefs that justify this behavior. Scholars who have interviewed digital pirates have found stronger support for techniques of neutralization (Holt and Copes, 2010), which may be due to the nature of interviews allowing the respondents to express their feelings clearly, rather than giving pre-selected responses to a given question. Holt and Copes (2010), for example, found that persistent pirates do not see themselves as part of some piracy subculture, but simply that they have beliefs that justify these actions.

Ulsperger, Hodges, and Paul (2010) performed one of the most intensive qualitative examinations of music piracy using a sample of youth born in "Generation Y" between 1982 and 1992. The authors found that the most prevalent technique supported among this group was denial of responsibility, at 36 percent of all sampled. Individuals in the sample placed the blame for their pirating behaviors on the mere existence of the Internet, time constraints to go to the store, economic disadvantage, being underage and not being allowed to purchase the music, and the simplicity of downloading music. The second most common technique was condemning the condemners, with students focusing their attention on the fact that it seems that everyone does it, governmental apathy in addressing downloading music, and the record industry's need to refocus its energies to something else. Fifteen percent denied that there was a victim and thought that the music industry was greedy, CDs were too expensive, and corporations were exploiting customers. Another 15 percent denied that an injury even occurred. They argued that there was no moral harm, music is not a tangible product, they were previewing it for later purchase, and that they were informally promoting the artist. Finally, they also appealed to higher loyalties than the law and the music industry, including their friendships, freedom, God's gift of music, free trade, and environmental concerns.

Scholars have also found that hackers use a variety of techniques as well to justify their actions, as documented in Chapter 2 (see also Text Box 9.3). Many hackers deny any injury occurred by arguing that their computer exploits do not actually cause any harm (Gordon and Ma, 2003). Others blame victims for having inadequate computer skills or computer systems to prevent the victimization (Jordan and Taylor, 1998; Turgeman-Goldschmidt, 2005). They may also argue that the victim had it coming or that large corporations are greedy and do not really need the additional profits that their hacking prevented. In Morris's (2011) insightful study examining the justifications that hackers frequently use, he found that neutralizations help us understand password guessing and illegal access to a computer system specifically, but not for file manipulation. He also found that associating with delinquent peers was a significant predictor of computer hacking over and above individual beliefs and agreement with techniques of neutralization. He therefore summarized that the techniques of neutralization are complementary to other theories, but not necessarily a standalone theory.

Text Box 9.3: Justifications for hacking

http://debatewise.org/debates/3452-hacking-can-be-justified/

> With the possibility of cyber warfare and concerns over hacks that result in huge amounts of information being stolen getting more widespread white hat hackers are becoming more necessary to ensure security. Can such attacks be justified?

> This article provides a robust and informed debate on the ways that hackers may be able to justify their involvement in serious attacks. The article provides good insights from both the perspective of hackers and of infrastructure owners and governments that may be harmed.

Finally, Copes and Vieraitis's (2009) study on how traditional identity thieves use techniques of neutralization is insightful for understanding online economic crime, even if their sample did not include online identity thieves. The identity thieves stated that they would not engage in just any type of crime; they would not physically hurt others for money as this was perceived to be morally wrong. They most frequently used: (1) denial of injury; (2) denial of victim; (3) appeal to higher loyalties; and (4) denial of responsibility when justifying their actions. The most common justification used by the identity thieves is that their actions did not cause any real harm to actual individuals. Most loss was minor and victims resolved the problems with a few quick calls. If the thief acknowledged that a victim existed, they thought of large organizations that deserve victimization because of their unethical business practices. Thus, they not only denied these organizations victim status, but also "condemned the condemners" (Sykes and Matza, 1957).

The identity thieves also justified their crimes by stating that they were trying to help others (i.e. appeal to higher loyalties) by obtaining money. Their efforts could provide a better life for their children or give confidential information or government documents to family members and friends. In these cases, they did not normally think their actions were ethical, but that the needs of their families and friends were more important in the decision-making process. Finally, many of the identity thieves who worked within organizations claimed that they only played a minimal role in the crime, received little reward, and their supervisors in the organizational hierarchy had greater responsibility for the offense.

In summary, Sykes and Matza's (1957) techniques of neutralization provide scholars with a framework to understand various forms of cybercrime, particularly digital piracy, computer hacking, and identity theft. Although quantitative analyses usually only provide modest support for the theory's

cybercrime and criminological theories

propositions, in-depth qualitative interviews provide much stronger evidence. As a result, neutralization theory research will likely continue in the future as scholars attempt to identify rationalizations that allow usually conforming individuals to drift temporarily into online criminal behavior.

Deterrence theory

Overview

The Classical school of criminology, which dates back to the mid-eighteenth century, was the product of the intellectual beliefs of the Enlightenment era. They viewed humans as hedonistic, rational, and calculating. As a result, crime was the result of free will and rational decision-making by individuals. People weighed the benefits and costs of a possible decision and chose whichever increased pleasure and decreased pain. They were not compelled to do so by any internal (e.g. biological) or external (e.g. demons) forces beyond their control. In order to minimize the possibility of crime, society needed structures to convince individuals that crime was neither a profitable nor pleasurable choice. To do this, governments needed to clearly codify laws on what was inappropriate, set punishments that were equal to the pleasure of the crime so no incentive would exist, apprehend criminals when they broke the law, and punish them swiftly (Paternoster, 1987).

The principles of **deterrence theory**, generated by Cesare Beccaria, are a direct reflection of the ideas of the Classical school. This perspective argues that humans will be deterred from choosing to commit crime if they believe that punishments will be certain, swift, and proportionately severe. The **certainty** of the punishment refers to how likely it is that the individual will be caught and punished for the offense. Swiftness, or **celerity**, of the punishment refers to how quickly the punishment follows the criminal act, not the apprehension of the offender. Finally, the **severity** of the punishment involves the intensity of the punishment relative to the harm caused by the crime.

Scholarly research has shown modest support for deterrence theory propositions using a wide variety of methods, including retrospective accounts, perceptual surveys, and longitudinal assessments (Paternoster, 1987; Pratt et al., 2006; Yu and Liska, 1993). Studies have shown that certainty, not severity, is the most important deterrence component. Increasing the perceived probability of getting caught is more important than increasing the severity of the punishments (e.g. more years in prisons, larger fines) associated with the crime.

Deterrence and cybercrime

Based on Chapters 2 through 8 of this text, it is clear that most Western nations based their government structures and criminal justice systems on the tenets of the Classical school. Each chapter has ended with a discussion of the legislation that nations have passed to criminalize certain computer-related behaviors, the specific punishments associated with each offense, and the agencies that enforce violations of these laws. These structures should provide an easily communicated framework to deter would-be cybercriminals based on the certainty of getting caught and receiving appropriate punishments.

Research applying deterrence theory to cybercrime offending is not, however, as robust as that of other theories discussed thus far. For example, if digital pirates perceive there to be an increased chance of getting caught and receiving swift and harsh justice, they would theoretically be less likely to take the chance to pirate software, music, or movies. Bachmann (2007) found a temporary reduction in piracy rates after an anti-piracy campaign was enforced by the RIAA, illustrating that individuals were deterred for a short period of time. The rate of piracy, however, began to trend back up after several months. As a result, researchers have tried to identify what specific elements of deterrence appear to have an influence on behavior. Higgins, Wilson, and Fell (2005) found that certainty of punishment, not severity, reduced the likelihood of piracy, supporting deterrence research on traditional criminal offending.

Wolfe, Higgins, and Marcum (2008) examined whether intent to commit digital piracy was influenced by self-imposed guilt, the perception of whether family and friends might find out about the piracy, and the fear of getting a virus through pirated materials. Their results showed that guilt, an informal source of punishment, was one of the strongest factors preventing individuals from downloading music illegally. The fear of a malware infection was not, however, significant. Thus, it may be that informal levels of social control, such as guilt and embarrassment, might prove more useful in decreasing digital piracy than legal actions.

Scholars have also examined whether computer hackers can be deterred. In a sample of college students, Skinner and Fream (1997) found that the severity of punishment associated with computer intrusions decreased their occurrence. The certainty of detection, by either administrators or students, was not significantly related to hacking behavior. Extending this study, Maimon and associates (2014) conducted an experiment to study whether displayed warning banners affected the progression, frequency, and duration of computer intrusions or trespassing. Using a set of live computers connected to the Internet that are designed to be attacked, called honeypots, the authors found that the warning banners did not affect immediate termination of computer intrusion (Maimon et al., 2014). Individuals who saw the warning banner were no more likely to leave within the first five seconds than those who were not presented with the banner. In addition, the warning banners did not reduce the volume of repeated trespassing incidents. The warning banners did, however, shorten the duration of the trespassing incidents. Thus there is no immediate evidence that hackers can be readily deterred through traditional mechanisms.

cybercrime and criminological theories

Since the Internet allows individuals to attack both end users and government targets, researchers have presented arguments as to how deterrence can be used to prevent cyber attacks or cyber terrorism (e.g. Blank, 2001; Brenner, 2007; Geers, 2012). For example, Guitton (2012) argued that actor attribution (determining the source of an attack) can act as a deterrent, but only when the individual had a good knowledge of the attribution process, acted rationally, and was concerned about the costs of punishment. Attribution will not, however, be effective for irrational actors who do not fear punishments, possibly because the praise received from a successful cyber attack requiring skill is considered more important to these individuals. If deterrence only appears to be influential for rational actors, how should nation-states protect themselves from hackers who are more concerned about the perceived benefits of the cyber attack and to make a political statement regardless of the costs to him or his country? This assumes that a nation can actually identify the source of an intrusion in the first place, which is not always possible (Brenner, 2007).

Clearly, more research needs to be conducted on the benefits of a deterrence framework to understand various forms of cybercrime. In some instances, the lack of deterrence research regarding cybercrimes appears to have to do more with its testability and measurement issues than the logic of its theoretical arguments. Thus, future researchers might move away from conducting surveys which have had difficulty assessing the theory to more experimental designs.

Theories of cybercrime victimization

Criminologists have not only used traditional criminological theories to better understand why some individuals are more likely to commit various forms of cybercrime, but also what factors place individuals at risk for cybercrime victimization. The two most common theories used to assess the likelihood of cybercrime victimization are Lawrence Cohen and Marcus Felson's (1979) **routine activity theory** and Michael Gottfredson and Travis Hirschi's (1990) general theory of crime.

Routine activity theory

Cohen and Felson (1979) argued that direct-contact predatory victimization occurs with the convergence in both space and time of three primary components: (1) a **motivated offender**; (2) a **suitable target**; and (3) the **absence of a capable guardian**. If one component is missing, crime will not occur making this an ideal theory to examine how offender and victim interactions may be artificially affected to reduce crime. Motivated offenders constitute any individuals or groups who have both the inclination and ability to commit crime. Cohen and Felson assumed that there would always be an ample supply of motivated offenders. Thus, they were more interested in how social (e.g. more women joining the work force) and technological (e.g. lighter electronics) changes affected changes in national crime rates.

A target, whether referring to a person or object, is viewed as suitable based on how attractive it is to the offender on a wide range of factors, including monetary value, ease of access, and other intrinsic values. Finally, capable guardians exist to protect the target from harm. Guardianship can be expressed in various ways, including physical (e.g. security cameras, lighting, alarm systems, locks, etc.), social (e.g. friends), and personal (e.g. knowing martial arts, carrying pepper spray) forms.

Scholars who use routine activity theory are particularly interested in how daily behavioral routines increase a target's proximity to motivated offenders while also affecting both capable guardianship and target suitability. Understanding routine activities is important in that they normally separate individuals from the safety of their homes, people they trust, and their possessions. Scholars have found this theory to be very successful in predicting a wide variety of both property crime victimization, such as burglary (Cohen and Felson, 1979; Couple and Blake, 2006) and larceny (Mustaine and Tewksbury, 1998), as well as violence, such as physical assault (Stewart, Elifson, and Sterk, 2004) and robbery (Spano and Nagy, 2005).

Routine activity theory and cybercrime victimization

Routine activity theory was identified by early cybercrime scholarship as a key theory to better understand cybercrime (Grabosky and Smith, 2001; Newman and Clarke, 2003). Scholars have argued that each component of this theory – motivated offenders, suitable targets, and the absence of a capable guardian – are present in cyberspace. As the previous chapters have indicated, there is an abundance of individuals who have the inclination and ability to harass others, download child pornography, hack into computers, or try to commit online fraud. In keeping with the spirit of routine activity theory, cybercrime scholars do not assess motives but rather focus on the factors affecting victimization risk.

The suitability or attractiveness of a target in cyberspace varies substantially based on the interests of the offender. The target may be a computer system or network, sensitive data, or an individual. For the crime of computer intrusion, a hacker may want to compromise a system because he wants access to specific information or files. On the other hand, he may simply want to see whether the system can be penetrated (Holt, 2007). In incidents of harassment, an individual may be targeted for various reasons, whether because of a perceived slight, a failed relationship, or because of perceived weakness and social isolation (see Chapter 6 for detail).

Finally, there are guardians in cyberspace equivalent to the ones we use to protect ourselves in the physical world. Computers have various forms of physical guardianship, equivalent to locking our houses, such as antivirus software and password-protected screens. Antivirus and similar programs

cybercrime and criminological theories

are designed expressly to reduce harm from hackers and other cybercriminals who might want access to your sensitive information (see Chapter 3). Social guardianship can play a large role in the cyberworld as well since our friends can protect us from harassment and other forms of victimization or they can be the ones that harass us, unintentionally send us corrupted files via email, or teach risky activities such as how to commit digital piracy. Finally, personal guardianship in cyberspace could include developing an understanding of computer technology, updating software, changing passwords, and not providing sensitive personal information (see Text Box 9.4 for example).

Text Box 9.4: Self protection while online

www.us-cert.gov/ncas/tips/ST06-003

Security tip (ST06-003)

Staying safe on social network sites

> While the majority of people using these sites do not pose a threat, malicious people may be drawn to them because of the accessibility and amount of personal information that's available. The more information malicious people have about you, the easier it is for them to take advantage of you.

This security bulletin from the US-CERT provides practical information on the ways that individuals can protect themselves and their personal information in social media sites like Facebook. The article also demonstrates the inherent benefits of self protection in online environments.

Although the components of routine activity theory easily apply to all forms of cybercrime victimization, Majid Yar (2005) expressed concern regarding the applicability of the theory as a whole. He notes that routine activity theory:

> requires that targets, offenders and guardians be located in particular places, that measurable relations of spatial proximity and distance pertain between those targets and potential offenders, and that social activities be temporally ordered according to rhythms such that each of these agents is either typically present or absent at particular times. Consequently, the transposability of RAT to virtual environments requires that cyberspace exhibit a *spatio-temporal ontology* [emphasis in original] congruent with that of the "physical world," i.e. that place,

proximity, distance and temporal order be identifiable features of cyber-space. (p. 414)

In essence, cyberspace does not meet these criteria because virtual environments are spatially and temporally disconnected, disorganized, active at all times, and web pages are born and die in relatively short amounts of time. Most scholars, however, view the interaction of the offender and victim in cyberspace through the web or email as analogous to physical interactions (Bossler and Holt, 2009). Reyns, Henson, and Fisher (2011) addressed this concern theoretically with their cyberlifestyle-routine activities theory which connects motivated offenders and victims through networked systems. The network between victim and offender allows for both a conduit to exist in cyberspace between the two groups and an eventual overlap in time for the interaction to occur.

A large body of scholarship has developed which empirically tests the applicability of routine activity theory to cybercrime. Most of this research has focused on its ability to predict online harassment and cyberstalking victimization. The findings provide limited evidence that routine technology use affects risk of online harassment or cyberstalking victimization, including spending time in chatrooms, social networking sites, and email (e.g. Bossler, Holt, and May, 2012; Hinduja and Patchin, 2009; Holt and Bossler, 2009; Moore, Guntupalli, and Lee, 2010; Ngo and Paternoster, 2011; Reyns et al., 2011; Ybarra, Mitchell, Finkelhor, and Wolak, 2007; see Hinduja and Patchin, 2008 for an exception).

Individual involvement in various forms of cybercrime increases the risk of victimization. Specifically, engaging in bullying, harassment, computer hacking, digital piracy, and other forms of cybercrime appears to increase the risk associated with harassment and bullying (Holt and Bossler 2009; Holt et al., 2012; Hinduja and Patchin, 2009; Ngo and Paternoster, 2011; Reyns et al., 2011; Ybarra et al., 2007). The activities of a person's friends also increase the risk of victimization as this directly increases exposure to motivated offenders while also decreasing guardianship (Bossler et al., 2012; Hinduja and Patchin, 2008; Holt and Bossler, 2009; Reyns et al., 2011).

The use of protective software programs, such as parental filtering software and antivirus programs, appears to do little to reduce the risk of online harassment victimization (Holt and Bossler, 2009; Marcum, 2010; Ngo and Paternoster, 2011). Moore et al. (2010) found that parental regulation of Internet use also had no significant influence on the risk of victimization. Individual technical skills, a form of personal guardianship, have a mixed influence on the risk of online harassment victimization (Bossler et al., 2012; Holt and Bossler 2009). In some instances, those with greater computer proficiency may have an increased risk of victimization, which may stem from the potential to recognize when they are exposed to harmful behaviors or by being in spaces that increase their

cybercrime and criminological theories

risk of victimization (Bocij and McFarlane, 2002; Hinduja and Patchin, 2008; Holt and Bossler, 2009).

The importance of online routine behaviors in understanding online economic crime victimization is also dependent on the type of victimization examined. In Ngo and Paternoster's (2011) examination of phishing victimization in a college sample, they found little evidence to support the argument that knowing respondent online routine behaviors would help predict who is more likely to be a victim of phishing. The only significant behavior that increased victimization was whether the respondent committed various forms of computer deviance. They did not find that measures of exposure to motivated offenders (e.g. spending more time on the Internet, writing emails, being in chatrooms, etc.), target suitability (e.g. communicating with strangers, providing personal information, demographics, etc.), and capable guardianship (e.g. security software, computer skill, etc.) were related to phishing victimization. Van Wilsem (2013), however, found in the Dutch general population that buying products online and participating in web forums increases the likelihood of being a victim of online fraud. These behaviors both increase victim visibility online and make them more accessible by motivated offenders, which differentially increases risk of victimization.

In a recent study that specifically examined online forms of identity theft, Holt and Turner (2012) examined the protective factors that made certain individuals more resilient in high-risk online environments where sensitive information must be transmitted to complete an economic transaction or communicate generally. Within their sample of students, faculty, and staff at a large university, they found that only 2.3 percent of individuals who reported no risk factors (defined in their study as the commission or victimization of different forms of online deviance) had someone obtain their financial information electronically without their knowledge or permission within the last 12 months. Almost 15 percent of individuals who reported at least five of these risk factors reported being victims of online identity theft. Within this group of high-risk individuals, they found that that individuals who updated their protective software, such as antivirus, spybot, and ad-aware, were less likely to be victimized. They did not find, however, that having firewall protection or higher levels of computer skills decreased victimization within this group.

In another recent study examining how online routines affected identity theft victimization, Reyns (2013) used data from the 2008 and 2009 British Crime Survey and found that individuals that do their banking online or spend more time emailing are almost 50 percent more likely than others to be victims of identity theft. Online shopping and downloading items from the Internet increased identity theft victimization by roughly 30 percent. It also appears that males, older persons, and individuals with higher income are viewed as more suitable targets or participate in online activities that increase their chances of identity theft victimization. In summary, routine activity theory has shown itself to be the most empirically sound theory in explaining both traditional and cyber victimization.

General theory of crime and victimization

Another theory used by scholars to account for cybercrime victimization is whether the individual characteristics of the victim somehow influenced the odds of their victimization. The most common individual theoretical trait that researchers have examined in relation to victimization is the individual's level of self-control. Although Gottfredson and Hirschi (1990) consider self-control theory to be a *general theory of crime*, and not technically a theory of victimization, they argue that the high correlation between offending and victimization is because both are a result of inadequate levels of self-control (pp. 92–94).

The characteristics of low self-control (i.e. short-sighted, insensitive, impatient, risk-taking) that increase the odds of offending also theoretically increase the likelihood of victimization through various mechanisms (Schreck, 1999). Individuals with lower levels of self-control do not accurately consider and perceive the consequences of their actions, both increasing the probability of crime and victimization. They put themselves in risky situations and act inappropriately, increasing opportunities to offend, while at the same time placing themselves in close proximity to offenders who may prey upon them.

Research over the last decade has shown that Gottfredson and Hirschi's concept of low self-control is a consistent but modest predictor of why certain individuals are more likely to be victimized (Pratt, Turnanovic, Fox, and Wright, 2014). Its effect, however, is stronger for non-contact forms of victimization (e.g. fraud) than direct contact victimization, and decreases when controlling for risky behaviors that could possibly mediate the relationship (Pratt *et al.*, 2014).

Low self-control and cybercrime victimization

The link between low self-control and traditional victimization appears to apply to cybercrime victimization in a variety of ways. First, individuals with low self-control favor short-term immediate gratification with little regard to long-term consequences (Gottfredson and Hirschi, 1990). Their enjoyment of risk-taking and thrill-seeking decreases the safety of themselves and their property, increasing **vulnerability** to victimization (Schreck, 1999). In online environments, individuals with low self-control engage in risky behaviors which opens them up to malicious software infection and other forms of victimization (Holt and Bossler, 2009). They may also interact with strangers in chatrooms and other virtual environments and provide them with sensitive information that could lead to online harassment or cyberstalking.

cybercrime and criminological theories

Second, individuals with low self-control have little empathy for others. This makes it difficult for them to relate to others, create stronger social ties, and understand other people's intentions (Gottfredson and Hirschi, 1990; Schreck, 1999), all increasing their vulnerability. If individuals have challenges interacting with others face to face, their problems are probably compounded in a virtual environment. Third, their low tolerance means they are more likely to want to resolve issues physically rather than mentally and may get easily angered or frustrated. Individuals who may get easily frustrated or provoked when dealing with others online may simply escalate situations and increase the changes of harassment, bullying, or threatening online interactions.

Finally, individuals with low tolerance may increase their vulnerability when they become easily frustrated with complex security devices and stop using them or not use them correctly (Schreck, 1999). Unfortunately, computer security programs can be quite complex and are not necessarily intuitive. They are, however, necessary to protect a computer, its data, and the security of the user. In addition, computer owners must be diligent and regularly update protective software. Individuals with low self-control are generally not diligent and will not consistently make the effort to protect their computer and themselves.

Empirical research generally finds that self-control is associated with cybercrime victimization. The type of cybercrime victimization is, however, an important factor in assessing the size of the relationship. Low self-control might help understand cybercrime victimization where the person is the target (e.g. having password changed; harassment) and not computers in general (e.g. large phishing attempts; Bossler and Holt, 2010; Pratt *et al.*, 2014). When the effect of low self-control is statistically significant, its impact is small.

For example, Bossler and Holt (2010) examined the effect of low self-control on five cybercrime victimization types in a college sample. They found that having lower levels of self-control increased the risk of one's passwords being obtained to access computer accounts and files, someone adding, deleting, or changing information in one's computer files without the owner's knowledge or permission, and being harassed online. Ngo and Paternoster (2011) also found that low self-control increased college students' odds of online harassment by both strangers and non-strangers.

The literature on the relationship between low self-control and economic crime victimization is mixed as it depends on the type of victimization studied and the sample utilized. Low self-control has not been found to be significantly related to electronic credit card theft (Bossler and Holt, 2010) and phishing attacks (Ngo and Paternoster, 2011) in college samples. Van Wilsem (2013), however, found that low self-control increased the risk of consumer fraud victimization in a large-scale victimization study of the Dutch general population.

In summary, Gottfredson and Hirschi's (1990) general theory of crime provides an interesting perspective of how an individual's characteristics increase the risk of victimization. The inability of individuals with low self-control to prevent themselves from committing acts that have long-term negative consequences may also increase their odds of victimization by placing them in risky situations with the wrong people (Schreck, 1999). Although the major arguments logically apply to cybercrime victimization as well, empirical studies show that low self-control is a weak predictor of person-based cybervictimization types, such as online harassment and hacking victimization.

It may be that this relationship stems from the fact that individuals with low self-control are more likely to associate with delinquent peers who are more likely to victimize those who are in close proximity to themselves. For instance, Bossler and Holt (2010) found that low self-control's effect on hacking and harassment victimization became non-significant when controlling for peer offending. This meant that low self-control did not directly cause these victimizations because of impulsivity or carelessness, but that low self-control increased their likelihood of associating with delinquent peers who were probably more likely to victimize the respondent. Thus this relationship should be further explored to refine our understanding of the relationship between self-control and victimization generally.

Need for new cyberspace theories?

Though there are a number of traditional criminological theories that have been applied to cybercrimes, a few researchers have called for new theoretical paradigms that may more accurately account for these offenses. For instance, K. Jaishankar (2008) proposed a theory he called space transition theory, which argues that people behave differently while online than they otherwise would in physical space. In turn, individual behavioral patterns are different online than they are in physical space. This theory has seven basic postulates about both human behavior and offending generally:

1) Persons with repressed criminal behavior (in the physical space) have a propensity to commit crime in cyberspace, which, otherwise they would not commit in physical space, due to their status and position.
2) Identity flexibility, dissociative anonymity, and lack of deterrence factor in that cyberspace provides the offenders the choice to commit cyber crime.
3) Criminal behavior of offenders in cyberspace is likely to be imported to physical space; that in physical space may be exported to cyberspace as well.
4) Intermittent ventures of offenders in cyberspace and the dynamic spatio-temporal nature of cyberspace provide the chance to escape.

5) (a) Strangers are likely to unite together in cyberspace to commit crime in physical space; and (b) associates in physical space are likely to unite to commit crime in cyberspace.
6) Persons from closed society are more likely to commit crimes in cyberspace than persons from open society.
7) The conflict of norms and values of physical space with the norms and values of cyberspace may lead to cybercrimes.

The utility of this theory has yet to be identified as few have empirically investigated these hypothesized relationships. Some of these concepts are variants of concepts from previously discussed theories, such as social learning theory. Other propositions, however, appear incongruent with some of the information presented throughout this book. For instance, there is clear evidence that data thieves may not know one another offline but regularly interact in virtual spaces to buy and sell personal information (see Chapter 5). Furthermore, the rates of participation in cybercrimes like cyberbullying are somewhat consistent across place, regardless of the political landscape of the nation (see Chapter 6). Thus, it is possible that his insights apply better to some forms of cybercrime than others. Regardless, space transition theory is one of the few theories created specifically to address cybercrime. Only future empirical testing of his theory will be able to assess these propositions. In addition, his theory may inspire other scholars to create cybercrime-specific theories.

Another possible step for criminologists to better understand cybercrime offending and victimization is to look at scholarly work from other fields, including, but not limited to: computer science, information technology, psychology, and political science. Criminologists primarily examine the behavioral aspects of cybercrime offending and victimization from a sociological perspective. They do not have the expertise and backgrounds needed to properly examine how the brain operates, how global dynamics influence individual behavior, and how to improve computer security safeguards. Drawing from the expertise of these relevant fields could greatly improve our understanding of cybercrime and identify alternative strategies to address involvement in cybercrime offenses (see Text Box 9.5 for examples of psychological theories of cybercrime).

Text Box 9.5: Psychological theories of cybercrime

Needs analysis surveys for computer crime investigations indicated the ability to obtain reliable and valid offender profiles were pressing issues in law enforcement (Rogers and Seigfried, 2004). In addition, Loch and Conger (1996) concluded, "individual characteristics all appear to be important in determining ethical computing decisions" (p. 82). Thus, research should not only focus on information assurance and security, but it should also focus on the personality and cognitive characteristics associated with computer criminality. This Text Box briefly summarizes three psychological theories which have been applied to various cyberdeviance: theory of moral development, theory of planned behavior, and theory of reciprocal determinism.

Theory of moral development (Kohlberg, 1976)

According to Kohlberg (1976), moral reasoning transforms and develops through three levels, with two stages within each level. In the **preconventional level (I)**, morality is "external," meaning children view a behavior as "good" or "bad" due to perceived rewards and consequences. In **Stage 1**, children engage in behavior because of hedonistic rewards and praise that follow and refrain from engaging in certain behaviors to avoid possible negative consequences. In **Stage 2**, the child continues to make decisions that satisfy their own needs while occasionally satisfying the needs of others. A sense of reciprocity and the motto, "you scratch my back, and I will scratch yours" begins. In the **conventional level (II)**, the individual begins to recognize and be influenced by social order. In order to move into Stage 3, the child must be able to recognize the viewpoints of others. In **Stage 3**, moral behavior is reflected in the labels assigned to the child by his/her family, peers, and other social groups. The child recognizes that there are good and bad behaviors and it is important to be viewed by others as either a "good girl or good boy." **Stage 4** refers to the "law and order" orientation, meaning the child feels bound by the need to follow rules in order to maintain social order. Acting morally means conforming to authoritative figures and obeying social rules. In the final level, **post-conventional (III)**, morality is ultimately internalized, and the individual begins to define morality apart from formal (laws, social rules) and informal social controls (peer groups, family). In **Stage 5**, the individual recognizes the welfare of others and the fact that moral decisions are made for "the greater good." There is a **utilitarian** approach to moral decision-making, meaning decisions should be made to maximize happiness and reduce suffering. Finally, **Stage 6** is the highest stage of moral development known as the "universal ethical-principle orientation." In this stage, an individual has abstract moral principles guided by a sense of basic human rights, objectivity, and equal respect for all.

Research has compared the stages of moral development with ethical computer decisions. For example, Gordon (1994) compared the moral stages of development in a sample of virus writers classified as adolescent, young adult, professional adult, or ex-virus writers. Results suggested the adolescent and young adult virus writers were within normal ranges for moral development when compared to their non-virus writer age mates. The adult virus writers, however, were in lower stages of moral development compared to their non-virus writer age mates (Gordon, 1994). Rogers (2010) believed script kiddies, the least technical hacker, were only at Stage 2 of moral development due to their immaturity and attention-seeking behavior. As for cyber-punks and identity thieves, their disregard for authority and selfish tendencies also place them into a similar stage of moral development as script kiddies. The heterogeneity of virus writers makes it difficult to assign a specific stage of moral development, as virus writers can range anywhere from Stage 2 to Stage 5 of moral development. Finally, Rogers (2010) suggests the professionals (i.e. an elite group of hackers) rank in one of the higher categories of moral development, Stage 5, because of their flexibility of moral character, since professionals may be either white-, gray-, or black-hat hackers, depending on which hacker code they follow.

Theory of planned behavior (Ajzen, 1985, 1991)

The **theory of planned behavior** (Ajzen, 1985) argues that whether a person intends to engage in certain behaviors is determined by: attitude toward the behavior, subjective norm, and perceived behavioral control. First, this theory suggests that beliefs create attitudes. **Behavioral beliefs**, which are the expected outcomes for engaging in a particular behavior, influence our **attitude toward the behavior**. For example, we are more likely to have a positive attitude toward eating apples if we have positive beliefs about apples, such as "an apple a day keeps the doctor away." In predicting someone's behavior, we also need to examine their concern over "what others might think," referred to as **subjective norms**, as well as how other people will react to that particular behavior, or **normative beliefs**. Returning to the example of the apple, we might be more motivated to eat an apple rather than French fries if we want to be perceived as healthy by our peers. Finally, our opinions of **perceived control**, whether we are capable of engaging in the particular behavior, also affect whether we are likely to engage in certain behaviors. Perceived control is influenced by our **control beliefs**, which are beliefs about the presence of factors that may help or hurt our ability to engage in a particular behavior. If your favorite fast-food chain was closing, you might need to decide between being perceived as healthy by your friends or eating your favorite unhealthy food at the restaurant that is closing. Overall, all of these beliefs – behavioral, normative, and control – guide the creation of behavioral intentions, and these beliefs will be weighted differently based on their importance to a particular behavior.

Only a few studies have applied the theory of planned behavior (Ajzen, 1985, 1991) to unethical computer behaviors. Chang (1998) found that perceived behavioral control was the most significant predictor of people's intentions to pirate software. Regardless of a person's intentions, the appropriate resources or opportunities must be present in order for that person to engage in the unethical computer behavior. Rennie and Shore (2007) suggested six controls to curb a person's intentions to engage in computer hacking: (1) computer security legislation; (2) reducing vulnerability of computer systems; (3) parental controls; (4) reducing peer pressure; (5) cyber policing; and (6) reducing access to hacking tools. These controls relate directly to Ajzen's (1985) perceived control, subjective norms, and attitude toward the behavior. For example, encouraging parents to talk to their children about computer ethics, as well as reducing the impact of peer pressure, may deter an individual from computer hacking due to changes in subjective norms. In addition, strengthening computer and information security, as well as making it difficult to obtain computer hacking tools, will increase the perceived controls over one's ability to engage in computer hacking. Finally, through computer security legislation and cyber policing, an individual will more likely view computer hacking in a negative light due to the possible negative outcomes (i.e. prosecution).

Theory of reciprocal determinism (Bandura, 1977)

When we try to understand "why" people behave in a certain way, we tend to argue for either nature or nurture explanations. Bandura's (1977) theory of reciprocal determinism combined the classic "nature versus nurture" attitude into a social cognitive theory that acknowledges both the external and internal factors related to human behavior. The **theory of reciprocal determinism** states psychological, biological, and cognitive (**personal internal factors = P**) and environmental (**external factors = E**) factors all interact and exert bidirectional influences on human nature (**behavior = B**). These factors intermingle and affect one another in multiple directions; however, reciprocity does not imply equality in the amount of influence that one factor has over another (Bandura, 1977, 1978, 1994). Overall, determinism reflects an interaction between multiple variables in multiple directions rather than an independent relationship resulting in unidirectional cause and effect. In addition, the variables in the tripartite model differ in regards to their strength or magnitude of influence on human nature. According to Bandura (1986), "when situational constraints are weak, personal factors serve as the predominant influence in the regulatory system" (p. 35). If environmental constraints are "weak," then there are ineffective barriers keeping an individual from engaging in a particular behavior.

For example, the globalization of technology has created an environment where Internet child pornography is readily available, accessible, and affordable (**Triple-A Engine**, see Cooper, 1998). Essentially, viewing child pornography is both easy to commit and not get caught. There are other external factors, unique in some aspects to cyberspace, which may influence whether an individual engages in computer deviance. According to Campbell and Kennedy (2009), "characteristics inherent to the electronic environment may contribute to antinormative behaviors" (p. 18), specifically anonymity (Lipson, 2002), reduced social cues (Kiesler and Sproull, 1992), and deindividuation (Zimbardo, 1969). As stated by Morahan-Martin and Schumacher (2000), "Social contact over the Internet does not involve face-to-face communication and can even be anonymous, which can lessen social risk and lower inhibitions" (p. 25). Internet users are able to try out new roles, identities, and self-presentations,

cybercrime and criminological theories

which is facilitated by the perceived anonymity or "cloak of safety" provided by the Internet. For example, anonymizers, steganography, and encryption are considered hacker "tools of the trade," which provide some level of anonymity and secrecy online (Holt, 2010).

Overall, Bandura's theory of reciprocal determinism incorporates both the environmental and personal factors associated with human behavior. Preliminary research suggests this theory may explain why some people are more likely to engage in cybercrime, specifically Internet child pornography, when others do not. Future research is needed to determine if this theory is applicable to other forms of cybercrime.

What similarities do you see between these three psychological theories and the criminological theories covered in this chapter?

Summary

Criminological theory has much to offer to our understanding of both cybercrime offending and victimization. Although the criminological theories discussed in this chapter have important insights on why certain individuals are more likely to offend or be victimized, empirical studies have provided more support for certain theories overall. For example, Ron Akers' (1998) social learning theory is currently the best theoretical framework that we have to understand both traditional and cybercrime offending. Cohen and Felson's (1979) routine activity theory is the most utilized and supported theory to explain traditional and cyber victimization. Other theories have shown moderate support and need more scrutiny to determine their validity for cybercrime.

Most assessments involve some form of digital piracy offending and harassment victimization. An increased amount of work is occurring explaining the correlates and causes of computer hacking and identity theft, but scant research has been conducted on more complex forms of cybercrime such as malicious software distribution and cyberterrorism. In addition, it is possible that cybercrime with all of its unique characteristics will prompt new theories to be created like Jaishankar's (2008) space transition theory. The creation of new theories to explain crime in the virtual world might not only help provide a better understanding of cybercrime, but may possibly lead to new insights about crime in the physical world as well.

Key Terms

Absence of a capable guardian
Appeal to higher loyalties
Argot
Celerity

Certainty

Condemnation of the condemners

Definitions

Denial of a victim

Denial of an injury

Denial of responsibility

Deterrence theory

Differential association

Differential reinforcement

Drift

General strain theory

General theory of crime

Imitation

Motivated offender

Routine activity theory

Self-control

Severity

Social learning theory

Space transition theory

Subculture

Suitable target

Techniques of neutralization

Vulnerability

Discussion Questions

1) Do you agree that cybercrime is "old wine in a new bottle?"

2) Which theory applies to most forms of cybercrimes?

3) Which theory made the most sense to you in explaining crimes in a virtual world? Why?

4) Think of a recent news event involving cybercrime. Which theory helps you understand better why that individual committed that crime?

5) Does the idea of a low-self-control hacker make sense to you? Why or why not?

6) What risky activities do you partake in when you are online? How do those actions relate to routine activity theory?

7) Do we need cybercrime-specific theories or are traditional criminological theories adequate?

References

Agnew, R. (1992). Foundation for a general strain theory of crime and delinquency. *Criminology*, 30, 47–87.

Agnew, R. (2001). Building on the foundation of general strain theory: Specifying the types of strain most likely to lead to crime and delinquency. *Journal of Research in Crime and Delinquency*, 38, 319–361.

Agnew, R. (2006). General Strain Theory: Current Status and Directions for Further Research. In Cullen, F. T., Wright, J. P., and Blevins, K. R. (eds), *Taking Stock: The Status of Criminological Theory*, Advances in Criminological Theory Vol. 15. (pp. 101–123). New Brunswick: Transaction.

Agnew, R., & White, H. R. (1992). An empirical test of general strain theory. *Criminology*, 30(4), 475–499.

Ajzen, I. (1985). From Intentions to Actions: A Theory of Planned Behavior. In J. Kuhl & J. Beckman (eds), *Action-Control: From Cognition to Behavior* (pp. 11–39). Heidelberg, Germany: Springer.

Ajzen, I. (1991). The theory of planned behavior. *Organizational Behavioral and Human Decision Processes*, 50, 179–211.

Akers, R. L. (1998). *Social Learning and Social Structure: A General Theory of Crime and Deviance*. Boston: Northeastern University Press.

Akers, R. L., & Jensen, G. F. (2006). The Empirical Status of Social Learning Theory of Crime and Deviance: The Past, Present, and Future. In F. T. Cullen, J. P. Wright, and K. R. Blevins (eds), *Taking Stock: The Status of Criminological Theory*. New Brunswick, NJ: Transaction Publishers.

Bachmann, M. (2007). "Lesson spurned? Reactions of online music pirates to legal prosecutions by the RIAA." *International Journal of Cyber Criminology* 2(1): 213–227.

Bachmann, M. (2010). The risk propensity and rationality of computer hackers. *International Journal of Cyber Criminology*, 4, 643–656.

Bandura, A. (1977). *Social Learning Theory*. Englewood Cliffs, New Jersey: Prentice Hall.

Bandura, A. (1978). The self system in reciprocal determinism. *American Psychologist*, 33, 344–358.

Bandura, A. (1986). *Social Foundations of Thought and Action: A Social Cognitive*. Englewood Cliffs, New Jersey: Prentice-Hall.

Bandura, A. (1994). Social Cognitive Theory of Mass Communication. In J. Bryant & D. Zillmann, *Media Effects: Advances in Theory and Research* (pp. 61–90). Hillsdale, New Jersey: Erlbaum.

Blank, S. (2001). Can Information Warfare be Deterred? In Alberts, D. S. and Papp, D. S. (eds), *Information Age Anthology, Volume III: The Information Age Military*. Washington, DC: Command and Control Research Program.

Blevins, K., & Holt, T. J. (2009). Examining the virtual subculture of johns. *Journal of Contemporary Ethnography*, 38, 619–648.

Bocij, P., & McFarlane, L. (2002). Online harassment: Towards a definition of cyberstalking. *Prison Service Journal*, 39, 31–38.

Bossler, A. M., & Burruss, G. W. (2011). The General Theory of Crime and Computer Hacking: Low Self-Control Hackers? In T. J. Holt & B. H. Schell (eds), *Corporate Hacking and Technology-Driven Crime: Social Dynamics and Implications*, pp. 38–67. ISI Global: Hershey, PA.

Bossler, A. M., & Holt, T. J. (2009). On-line activities, guardianship, and malware infection: An examination of routine activities theory. *International Journal of Cyber Criminology*, 3, 400–420.

Bossler, A.M., & Holt, T. J. (2010). The effect of self-control on victimization in the cyberworld. *Journal of Criminal Justice*, 38(3), 227–236.

Bossler, A. M., Holt, T. J., & May, D. C. (2012). Predicting online harassment among a juvenile population. *Youth and Society*, 44, 500–523.

Brake, M. (1980). *The Sociology of Youth Cultures and Youth Subcultures*. London: Routledge and Kegan Paul.

Brenner, S. W. (2007). "At light speed": Attribution and response to cybercrime/terrorism/warfare. *The Journal of Criminal Law and Criminology*, 97(2), 379–475.

Brezina, T. (1998). Adolescent maltreatment and delinquency: The question of intervening processes. *Journal of Research in Crime and Delinquency*, 35, 71–99.

Broidy, L. (2001). A test of general strain theory. *Criminology*, 39, 9–36.

Buzzell, T., Foss, D., & Middleton, Z. (2006). Explaining use of online pornography: A test of self-control theory and opportunities for deviance. *Journal of Criminal Justice and Popular Culture*, 13, 96–116.

Campbell, Q., and Kennedy, D. (2009). The Psychology of Computer Criminals. In S. Bosworth & M. E. Kabay (eds), *Computer Security Handbook*, 4th ed. (pp. 140–160). New York: John Wiley & Sons, Inc.

Chang, M. K. (1998). Predicting unethical behavior: A comparison of the theory of reasoned action and the theory of planned behavior. *Journal of Business Ethics*, 17(16), 1825–1834.

Cohen, L. E., & Felson, M. (1979). Social change and crime rates trends: A routine activity approach. *American Sociological Review*, 44, 588–608.

Cooper, A. (1998). Sexuality and the internet: Surfing into the new millennium. *CyberPsychology & Behavior*, 1, 181–187.

Copes, H., & Vieraitis, L. M. (2009). Bounded rationality of identity thieves: Using offender-based research to inform policy. *Criminology & Public Policy*, 8(2), 237–262.

Couple, T., & Blake, L. (2006). Daylight and darkness targeting strategies and the risks of being seen at residential burglaries. *Criminology*, 44, 431–464.

DiMarco, A. D., and DiMarco, H. (2003). Investigating Cybersociety: A Consideration of the Ethical and Practical Issues Surrounding Online Research in Chat Rooms. In Y. Jewkes (ed.) *Dot.cons: Crime, Deviance and Identity on the Internet*. Portland, OR: Willan Publishing.

Foster, J. (1990). *Villains: Crime and Community in the Inner City*. London: Routledge.

Freiburger, T., & Crane, J. S. (2011). The Internet as a terrorist's tool: A social learning perspective. In K. Jaishankar (ed.), *Cyber Criminology: Exploring Internet Crimes and Criminal Behavior* (pp. 127–138). Boca Raton, FL: CRC Press.

Geers, K. (2012). The challenge of cyber attack deterrence. *Computer Law and Security Review*, 26(3), 298–303.

Gordon, S. (1994, September). *The generic virus writer*. Presented at the 4th International Virus Bulletin Conference, Jersey, UK. Retrieved from http://vxheavens.com/lib/asg03.html

Gordon, S., & Ma, Q. (2003). *Convergence of Virus Writers and Hackers: Factor or Fantasy*. Cupertino, CA: Symantec Security White paper.

Gottfredson, M. R., & Hirschi, T. (1990). *A General Theory of Crime*. Stanford, CA: Stanford University Press.

Grabosky, P. N. (2001). Virtual criminality: Old wine in new bottles? *Social & Legal Studies*, 10(2), 243–249.

Grabosky, P. N., and Smith, R. (2001). Telecommunication Fraud in the Digital Age: The Convergence of Technologies. In Wall, D. (ed.), *Crime and the Internet* (pp. 29–43). New York: Routledge.

Guitton, C. (2012). Criminals and cyber attacks: The missing link between attribution and deterrence. *International Journal of Cyber Criminology*, 6(2), 1030–1043.

Hay, C., Meldrum, R., & Mann, K. (2010). Traditional bullying, cyber bullying, and deviance: A general strain theory approach. *Journal of Contemporary Criminal Justice*, 26(2), 130–147.

Herbert, S. (1998). Police subculture reconsidered. *Criminology*, 36, 343–369.

Higgins, G. E., & Marcum, C. D. (2011). *Digital Piracy: An Integrated Theoretical Approach*. Durham, NC: Carolina Academic Press.

Higgins, G. E., Wilson, A. L., & Fell, B. D. (2005). An application of deterrence theory to software piracy. *Journal of Criminal Justice and Popular Culture*, 12(3), 166–184.

Higgins, G. E., Wolfe, S. E., & Marcum, C. D. (2008). Music piracy and neutralization: A preliminary trajectory analysis from short-term longitudinal data. *International Journal of Cyber Criminology*, 2(2), 324–336.

Hinduja, S. (2003). Trends and patterns among online software pirates. *Ethics and Information Technology*, 5, 49–61.

Hinduja, S. (2007). Neutralization theory and online software piracy: An empirical analysis. *Ethics and Information Technology*, 9(3), 187–204.

Hinduja, S., & Ingram, J. R. (2008). Self-control and ethical beliefs on the social learning of intellectual property theft. *Western Criminology Review*, 9, 52–72.

Hinduja, S., & Patchin, J.W. (2007). Offline consequences of online victimization: School violence and delinquency. *Journal of School Violence*, 6(3), 89–112.

Hinduja, S., & Patchin, J.W. (2008). Cyberbullying: An exploratory analysis of factors related to offending and victimization. *Deviant Behavior*, 29(2), 129–156.

Hinduja, S., & Patchin, J. W. (2009). *Bullying Beyond the Schoolyard: Preventing and Responding to Cyberbullying*. New York: Corwin Press.

Holt, T. (ed.) (2010). *Crime On-Line: Correlates, Causes, and Context*. Durham, NC: Carolina Academic Press.

Holt, T. J. (2007). Subcultural evolution? Examining the influence of on- and off-line experiences on deviant subcultures. *Deviant Behavior*, 28, 171–198.

Holt, T. J., & Bossler, A. M. (2009). Examining the applicability of lifestyle-routine activities theory for cybercrime victimization. *Deviant Behavior*, 30, 1–25.

Holt, T. J., & Bossler, A. M. (2014). An assessment of the current state of cybercrime scholarship. *Deviant Behavior*, 35, 20–40.

Holt, T. J., Bossler, A. M., & May, D. C. (2012). Low self-control, deviant peer associations, and juvenile cyberdeviance. *American Journal of Criminal Justice*, 37(3), 378–395.

Holt, T. J., Burruss, G. W., & Bossler, A. M. (2010). Social learning and cyber deviance: Examining the importance of a full social learning model in the virtual world. *Journal of Crime and Justice*, 33, 15–30.

Holt, T. J., & Copes, H. (2010). Transferring subcultural knowledge on-line: Practices and beliefs of persistent digital pirates. *Deviant Behavior*, 31(7), 625–654.

Holt, T. J., & Kilger, M. (2008). Techcrafters and makecrafters: A comparison of two populations of hackers. 2008 WOMBAT Workshop on Information Security Threats Data Collection and Sharing, pp. 67–78.

Holt, T. J., & Kilger, M. (2012). Examining willingness to attack critical infrastructure on and off-line. *Crime and Delinquency*, 58(5), 798–822.

Holt, T. J., Soles, J., & Leslie, L. (2008). Characterizing malware writers and computer attackers in their own words. Paper presented at the 3rd International Conference on Information Warfare and Security, April 24–25, in Omaha, Nebraska.

Holt, T. J., & Turner, M. G. (2012). Examining risks and protective factors of on-line identity theft. *Deviant Behavior*, 33, 308–323.

Ingram, J. R., & Hinduja, S. (2008). Neutralizing music piracy: An empirical examination. *Deviant Behavior*, 29(4), 334–365.

Jaishankar, K. (2008). Space Transition Theory of Cyber Crimes. In F. Schmalleger & M. Pittaro (eds), *Crimes of the Internet* (pp. 283–301). Upper Saddle River, NJ: Prentice Hall.

Jordan, T., & Taylor, P. (1998). A sociology of hackers. *The Sociological Review*, 46, 757–780.

Kiesler, S., & Sproull, L. (1992). Group decision making and communication technology. *Organizational Behavior and Human Decision Processes*, 52, 96–123.

Kohlberg, L. (1976). Moral stages and moralization: The cognitive-developmental approach. *Moral Development and Behavior: Theory, Research, and Social Issues*, 31–53.

Kornblum, W. (1997). *Sociology in a Changing World*, 4th edition. Fort Worth, TX: Harcourt Brace and Company.

Kornhauser, R. R. (1978). *Social Sources of Delinquency*. Chicago: University of Chicago Press.

Lee, G., Akers, R. L., & Borg, M. J. (2004). Social learning and structural factors in adolescent substance use. *Western Criminology Review*, 5, 17–34.

Lipson, H. (2002, November). *Tracking and tracing cyber-attacks: Technical challenges and global policy issues*. Retrieved from Carnegie Mellon Software Engineering Institute: http://resources.sei.cmu.edu/library/asset-view.cfm?assetid=5831

Loch, K. D., & Conger, S. (1996). Evaluating ethical decision making and computer use. *Communications of the ACM*, 39(7), 74–83.

Maimon, D., Alper, M., Sobesto, B., & Culkier, M. (2014). Restrictive deterrent effects of a warning banner in an attacked computer system. *Criminology*, 52(1), 33–59.

Marcum, C. D. (2010). Examining Cyberstalking and Bullying: Causes, Context, and Control. In Holt, T. J. (ed.), *Crime On-Line: Correlates, Causes, and Context*, (pp. 175–192). Raleigh, NC: Carolina Academic Press.

Marcum, C. D., Higgins, G. E., Wolfe, S. E., & Ricketts, M. L. (2011). Examining the intersection of self-control, peer association and neutralization in explaining digital piracy. *Western Criminology Review*, 12(3), 60–74.

Matsueda, R. L. (1988). The current state of differential association theory. *Crime and Delinquency*, 34, 277–306.

Matza, D. (1964). *Delinquency and Drift*. Hoboken: John Wiley & Sons.

Maurer, D. W. (1981). *Language of the Underworld*. Louisville, KY: University of Kentucky Press.

Mazerolle, P., & Piquero, A. (1997). Violent responses to strain: An examination of conditioning influences. *Violence and Victims*, 12, 323–343.

Merton, R. K. (1938). Social structure and anomie. *American Sociological Review*, 3, 672–682.

Miller, W. B. (1958). Lower class culture as a generating milieu of gang delinquency. *Journal of Social Issues*, 14(3), 5–19.

Moon, B., Hwang, H. W., & McCluskey, J. D. (2011). Causes of school bullying: Empirical test of a general theory of crime, differential association theory, and general strain theory. *Crime & Delinquency*, 57(6), 849–877.

Moon, B., McCluskey, J. D., & McCluskey, C. P. (2010). A general theory of crime and computer crime: An empirical test. *Journal of Criminal Justice*, 38, 767–772.

Moore, R., Guntupalli, N. T., & Lee, T. (2010). Parental regulation and online activities: Examining factors that influence a youth's potential to become a victim of online harassment. *International Journal of Cyber Criminology*, 4, 685–698.

Morahan-Martin, J. & Schumacher, P. (2000). Incidence and correlates of pathological Internet use among college students. *Computers in Human Behavior*, 16, 13–29.

Morris, R. G. (2011). Computer Hacking and the Techniques of Neutralization: An Empirical Assessment. In Holt, T. J. and Schell, B. H. (eds), *Corporate Hacking and Technology-Driven Crime: Social Dynamics and Implications* (pp. 1–17). Hershey: IGI Global.

Morris, R. G., & Blackburn, A. G. (2009). Cracking the code: An empirical exploration of social learning theory and computer crime. *Journal of Crime and Justice*, 32, 1–32.

Morris, R. G., & Higgins, G. E. (2009). Neutralizing potential and self-reported digital piracy: A multitheoretical exploration among college undergraduates. *Criminal Justice Review*, 34(2), 173–195.

Mustaine, E. E., & Tewksbury, R. (1998). Predicting risk of larceny theft victimization: A routine activity analysis using refined lifestyle measures. *Criminology*, 36, 829–857.

Newman, G., & Clarke, R. (2003). *Superhighway Robbery: Preventing E-commerce Crime*. Cullompton, NJ: Willan Press.

Ngo, F. T., & Paternoster, R. (2011). Cybercrime victimization: An examination of individual and situational level factors. *International Journal of Cyber Criminology*, 5, 773–793.

Patchin, J. W., & Hinduja, S. (2011). Traditional and nontraditional bullying among youth: A test of general strain theory. *Youth and Society*, 43(2), 727–751.

Paternoster, R. (1987). The deterrent effect of the perceived certainty and severity of punishment: A review of the evidence and issues. *Justice Quarterly*, 4, 173–217.

Paternoster, R., & Mazerolle, P. (1994). General strain theory and delinquency: A replication and extension. *Journal of Research in Crime and Delinquency*, 31, 235–263.

Pratt, T. C., & Cullen, F. T. (2000). The empirical status of Gottfredson and Hirschi's general theory of crime: A meta-analysis. *Criminology*, 38, 931–964.

Pratt, T. C., Cullen, F. T., Blevins, K. R., Daigle, L. E., & Madensen, T. D. (2006). The Empirical Status of Deterrence Theory: A Meta-Analysis. In Cullen, F. T., Wright, J. P., and Blevins, K. R. (eds), *Taking Stock: The Status of Criminological Theory*. New Brunswick, NJ: Transaction.

Pratt, T. C., Cullen, F. T., Sellers, C. S., Winfree, T., Madensen, T. D., Daigle, L. E., Fearn, N. E., & Gau, J. M. (2009). The empirical status of social learning theory: A meta-analysis. *Justice Quarterly*, 27, 765–802.

Pratt, T. C., Turnanovic, J. J., Fox, K. A., & Wright, K. A. (2014). Self-control and victimization: A meta-analysis. *Criminology*, 52(1), 87–116.

Quinn, J. F., & Forsyth, C. J. (2005). Describing sexual behavior in the era of the Internet: A typology for empirical research. *Deviant Behavior*, 26, 191–207.

Rege, A. (2013). Industrial Control Systems and Cybercrime. In T. J. Holt (ed.), *Crime On-line: Causes, Correlates, and Context*, 2nd edition (pp. 191–218). Raleigh, NC: Carolina Academic Press.

Rennie, L., & Shore, M. (2007). An advanced model of hacking. *Security Journal*, 20, 236–251.

Reyns, B. W. (2013). Online routines and identity theft victimization: Further expanding routine activity theory beyond direct-contact offenses. *Journal of Research in Crime and Delinquency*, 50, 216–238.

Reyns, B. W., Henson, B., & Fisher, B. S. (2011). Being pursued online: Applying cyberlifestyle-routine activities theory to cyberstalking victimization. *Criminal Justice and Behavior*, 38(11), 1149–1169.

Rogers, M. (2010). The Psyche of Cybercriminals: A Psycho-Social Perspective. In S. Ghosh & E. Turrini (eds), *Cybercrimes: A Multidimensional Analysis* (pp. 217–235). Geidelberg, Germany: Springer-Verlag.

Rogers, M., & Seigfried, K. (2004). The future of computer forensics: A needs analysis survey. *Computers & Security*, 23, 12–16.

Schell, B. H., & Dodge, J. L. (2002). *The Hacking of America: Who's Doing it, Why, and How*. Westport, CT: Quorum Books.

Schreck, C. J. (1999). Criminal victimization and self control: An extension and test of a general theory of crime. *Justice Quarterly*, 16, 633–654.

Short, J. F. (1968). *Gang Delinquency and Delinquent Subcultures*. Oxford: Harper & Row.

Skinner, W. F., & Fream, A. M. (1997). A social learning theory analysis of computer crime among college students. *Journal of Research in Crime and Delinquency*, 34, 495–518.

Spano, R., & Nagy, S. (2005). Social guardianship and social isolation: An application and extension of lifestyle/routine activities theory to rural adolescents. *Rural Sociology*, 70, 414–437.

Stewart, E. A., Elifson, K. W., & Sterk, C. E. (2004). Integrating the general theory of crime into an explanation of violent victimization among female offenders. *Justice Quarterly*, 21, 159–181.

Sutherland, E. (1947). *Principles of Criminology*, 4th edition. Philadelphia: Lippincott.

Sykes, G. M., & Matza, D. (1957). Techniques of neutralization: A theory of delinquency. *American Sociological Review*, 22(6), 664–670.

Turgeman-Goldschmidt, O. (2005). Hacker's accounts: Hacking as a social entertainment. *Social Science Computer Review*, 23, 8–23.

Ulsperger, J. S., Hodges, S. H., & Paul, J. (2010). Pirates on the plank: Neutralization theory and the criminal downloading of music among Generation Y in the era of late modernity. *Journal of Criminal Justice and Popular Culture*, 17(1), 124–151.

van Wilsem, J. (2013). "Bought it, but never got it": Assessing risk factors for online consumer fraud victimization. *Eur Sociol Rev*, 29, 168–178.

Wall, D. S. (1998). Catching cybercriminals: Policing the Internet. *International Review of Law, Computers & Technology*, 12(2), 201–218.

Wolfe, S. E., Higgins, G. E., & Marcum, C. D. (2008). Deterrence and digital piracy: A preliminary examination of the role of viruses. *Social Science Computer Review*, 26(3), 317–333.

Wolfgang, M. E., & Ferracuti, F. (1967). *The Subculture of Violence: Toward an Integrated Theory in Criminology*. Tavistock Publications.

Wright, M. F., & Li, Y. (2012). Kicking the digital dog: A longitudinal investigation of young adults' victimization and cyber-displaced. *Cyberpsychology, Behavior, and Social Networking*, 15(9), 448–454.

Wright, M. F., & Li, Y. (2013). The association between cyber victimization and subsequent cyber aggression: the moderating effect of peer rejection. *Journal of Youth and Adolescence*, 42(5), 662–674.

Yar, M. (2005). The novelty of "cybercrime": An assessment in light of routine activity theory. *European Journal of Criminology*, 2(4), 407–427.

Ybarra, M. L., Mitchell, K. J., Finkelhor, D., & Wolak, J. (2007). Internet prevention messages: Targeting the right online behaviors. *Archives of Pediatrics and Adolescent Medicine*, 161, 138–145.

Yu, J., & Liska, A. (1993). The certainty of punishment: A reference group effect and its functional form. *Criminology*, 31, 447–464.

Zimbardo, P. G. (1969). The Human Choice: Individuation, Reason, and Order versus Deindividuation, Impulse, and Chaos. In W. J. Arnold & D. Levine (eds), *Nebraska Symposium on Motivation* (pp. 237–309). Lincoln, Nebraska: University of Nebraska Press.

chapter 10

Evolution of digital forensics

Chapter goals

- Differentiate between computer forensics and digital forensics
- Explain the *ad hoc*, structured, and enterprise phases of digital forensics
- Identity potential sources of digital evidence
- Understand the differences between closed source and open source software
- Describe the four stages in a digital forensic investigation
- Examine the role of digital evidence in criminal and civil court cases
- Understand the importance of evidence integrity to digital forensic investigations and the court of law

Introduction

In March 2010, 18-year-old Kimberly Proctor was brutally raped and murdered in the small town of Langford in British Columbia, Canada, by two teenage boys, Kruse Hendrik Wellwood, 16, and Cameron Alexander Moffat, 17 (CBC News, 2010). Kimberly was lured to Wellwood's home where she was beaten, tortured, and sexually assaulted for several hours, her legs and arms were bound with duct tape, and her head was covered with a plastic bag. Kimberly was stuffed into a freezer then left overnight, and according to court documents, she died of asphyxiation. The medical examiner, however, was unable to determine if she was deceased prior to or after being placed in the freezer. In the morning, her body was driven to a secluded area under a bridge where the teenage boys set her on fire.

This crime was solved thanks to a digital trail of evidence left behind by the two teenage boys. According to Roberts (2011), "police investigating this case ... gathered the digital equivalent of 1.4 billion pages of paper evidence, including Facebook and MSN messages, text messages and chat histories" (para. 7). For example, while chatting on *World of Warcraft*, Wellwood confessed to the murder of Kimberly Proctor to his online gamer girlfriend (Zetter, 2011). In 2011, both teenage boys pleaded guilty to first-degree murder and indignity to human remains and were sentenced as adults to life imprisonment with no possibility of parole for ten years. The murder of Kimberly Proctor was solved through the use of digital forensics.

Before we discuss the evolution of digital forensics, it is important to understand what we mean by the term forensic science. **Forensic science** is the application of science to the law, meaning the scientific process of gathering and examining information to be used by the criminal justice system (see Saferstein, 2010). When compared to the other fields of forensic science, digital forensics is in its infancy. Consider the field of forensic entomology. Forensic entomology is the study of insects in death investigations, and its first recorded use was in a homicide investigation in thirteenth-century China (McKnight, 1981). The case involved a homicide where the weapon was determined to be a sickle. All of the men in the village laid their sickles down on the ground, and although they all appeared to be "clean" to the naked eye, the murderer's sickle became covered with flies due to the small traces of blood and tissue that remained on the sickle – the murderer then confessed to the crime (McKnight, 1981). So, you might be asking yourself, what does forensic entomology have to do with the history of digital forensics? Think about all of the changes that have occurred over the years in the different branches of forensic science – the advancements with technology in DNA analysis or the ability to obtain latent fingerprints. It only makes sense that digital forensics is a new branch of forensic science – it could not exist without the advent of computer technology.

A central theme throughout this chapter is the fact that technology has been the driving force behind the field of computer forensics. The field of computer forensics evolved into the field of digital forensics as technology continued to influence law enforcement investigations.

Digital forensics may be the youngest of the forensic sciences, but that does not mean it is the least important. By the end of this chapter, you will appreciate how almost every criminal investigation now involves some form of digital evidence. In addition, you will understand the difficulty law enforcement faces when trying to identify and recover evidence from the ever-changing and developing digital world. Finally, we will explore the importance of evidence integrity and forensic soundness since digital evidence is only admissible if its authenticity can be verified in a court of law.

From computer forensics to digital forensics

The need for computer forensics developed with the onset of the **Information Age** or **Digital Age**; this digital revolution was marked by the increased production, transmission, and consumption of, and reliance on, information. Modern computers began to emerge in the mid-twentieth century and were mostly owned and operated by large corporations, such as universities and government agencies. At this time, traditional computer crime investigations were theft of computers or computer components. However, the Information Age changed the meaning of the word computer crime. As personal computers surfaced in the mid 1970s, old crimes with new tricks emerged as well, and computer crimes were no longer limited to only theft of components. Computers were now being used to commit *old crimes* using *new tricks*, specifically referring to financial crimes (fraud, embezzlement), the majority of which were committed by insiders (Clifford, 2006). For example, individuals employed at financial institutions embezzled money by writing computer programs that would transfer a tenth of a cent into their account (Fernandez, Smith, Garcia, and Kar, 2005). This type of fraud is referred to as *salami slicing* because only small amounts of money are taken from each account, but the dividends add up to a tremendous sum (Kabay, 2002). With computers being used as *the means* for criminal activity, such as computer fraud or embezzlement, there was a growing concern of how best to combat these "old crimes with new tricks."

By the late 1970s, there was an increasing recognition that computer criminality was growing on a national and international scale. In 1976, the Council of Europe Conference on Criminological Aspects of Economic Crime was held in Strasbourg, France. This conference identified several categories of computer crime, including fraud (Schjolberg and Tingrett, 2004). In the United States, the first federal cybercrime legislation was introduced, the Federal Computer Systems Protection Act of 1977, by Senator Ribikoff. This Act would make "the use, for fraudulent or other illegal purposes, of any computer owned or operated by the United States, certain financial institutions, and entitles affecting interstate commerce" a federal crime. Although this act was not passed, Senator Ribikoff is credited for raising awareness of the need for cybercrime legislation (Clifford, 2006).

Shortly thereafter, Florida became the first state to enact a cybercrime law, the **Florida Computer Crimes Act of 1978**. This legislation was in response to a scandal at the Flagler Dog Track in Miami, Florida, where employees used a computer to print fraudulent tickets (see Text Box 10.1; Hochman, 1986). The Florida Computer Crimes Act (1978) cited offenses against intellectual property, offenses against computer equipment or supplies, and offenses against computer users. In other words, it was a felony to access another's computer or modify, delete, or copy files without authorization, and it became a misdemeanor to modify or damage computer equipment without authorization. In the United States, a *felony* is considered to be a more serious criminal act that is usually punishable by one year or more in prison, whereas a *misdemeanor* is considered a less serious offense that is usually punishable up to one year in jail (see Kamisar, LaFave, Israel, King and Kerr, 2008). It was not until 1986 that the United States passed its first federal law criminalizing the unauthorized access of a computer, the **Computer Fraud and Abuse Act** (see Chapters 2 and 3 for more detail of the revised statutes).

Text Box 10.1: The Flaggler Dog Track incident

Win, place ... and sting

www.si.com/vault/1979/07/23/823826/win-place-and-sting-the-computerized-betting-setup-seemed-foolproof-until-jacques-found-a-flaw-for-a-scam-so-slick-its-victims-didnt-even-know-they-had-been-stung
John Underwood
July 23, 1979

> [Jacques Lavigne] knew he was going to make a potful of money ... He could do it quickly enough to avoid suspicion. And ... right under the noses of the men the state paid to stand watch – because they knew zilch about computers.

This article describes one of the first instances of computer crime, which became a seminal case in the development of legislation for the United States. Readers will gain an understanding for how technology was viewed at the time, and how it has dramatically changed over the last few decades.

In 1979, Interpol, the world's largest police agency, was the first international organization to address the growing concern of computer fraud: "The nature of computer crime is international, because of the steadily increasing communications, ... between the different countries. International organizations, like Interpol, should give this aspect more attention" (Interpol, 1979; Schjolberg and Tingrett, 2004). It was not until 1983 that an *ad hoc* committee sponsored by the OECD assessed the need for an international response to cybercrime. The OECD is an intergovernmental organization comprised of 29 countries, including the United States, which promotes policy-making among member and non-member states and the United Nations (Clifford, 2006). The final report recommended a "harmonization of criminal laws" that penalized computer fraud, computer forgery, damage to computer data, copyright infringement, and unauthorized computer access (Schjolberg, 2008).

Image 10.1 Floppy disks
The 8 inch floppy disk was created by IBM's Alan Shugart in 1971.
http://commons.wikimedia.org/wiki/File:8%60%60_floppy_disk.jpg

By the 1980s, more and more computer crimes were being committed during the Information Age, and law enforcement officers found themselves collecting digital evidence, specifically computers and floppy disks from financial and computer fraud investigations. However, law enforcement needed a way to convert computer evidence into "physical" evidence. For example, holding an 8 inch floppy disk (see Image 10.1) in front of the jury does not give them a sense of its evidentiary value – the jury must be able to *see* the contents of the floppy disk.

The ability to convert computer evidence into "physical" evidence fueled the need for computer forensics, which is the examination of powered-down computer components, also known as **dead-box forensics. Computer forensics,** a branch of the forensic sciences, refers to the investigation and analysis of media originating from digital sources in an effort to uncover evidence to present in a court of law (Britz, 2009). However, only government agencies, such as the Internal Review Service (IRS), were developing computer forensic tools at this time, and these tools were not made available to other law enforcement agencies or industry. This all changed when Norton Utilities released to the public the UnErase tool, which was capable of recovering lost or deleted files (Fernandez *et al.*, 2005; Nelson, Phillips, Enfinger, and Steuart, 2004). Norton did not intend to create a forensic tool, but this

326   evolution of digital forensics

product's ability to recover **latent,** or hidden, evidence made an important contribution to the computer forensics field.

> **For more information on the utility and processes of UnErase, go online to:** www.symantec.com/press/1999/n990623d.html

Although there was some progress being made with computer evidence, Charters (2009) states that the early 1980s should be considered **pre-forensics** because there was a lack of formal structure, protocols, training, and adequate tools. This pre-forensics stage is also known as the *Ad Hoc* phase and is considered to be the first stage of evolution for computer forensics. The term *"ad hoc"* refers to something that has been created because of an immediate need, and because of this immediate need, the approach is usually unmethodical or unprincipled (i.e. not theory-driven). According to Charters (2009), it was during the *Ad Hoc* phase that corporations began to collect evidence that their computer systems were being "inappropriately" used by employees. According to Shaw, Ruby, and Post (1998), "staff employees pose perhaps the greatest risk in terms of access and potential damage to critical information systems" because they are viewed as trusted members of the organization (p. 3). However, during the *Ad Hoc* phase, upper management lacked specific company policies defining "appropriate vs. inappropriate computer usage" as well as procedures for due process. Therefore, when these inappropriate use cases did make it to trial, the courts raised questions about the chain-of-custody procedures and accuracy of the computer forensic tools.

In addition, during the *Ad Hoc* phase, law enforcement officers were analyzing the *original* evidence – rather than a duplicate or backup copy – so any modifications or errors during the computer forensic examination directly affected the accuracy of the evidence. **Accuracy** refers to the integrity of the data, such as whether or not the evidence remains unchanged or has been altered by the computer forensics tool. In addition, the courts were concerned with **chain of custody**, which refers to the chronological documentation of evidence as it is processed during the investigation (i.e. seizure, custody, transfer, and analysis; Britz, 2009). This was one of the most unfortunate things about the *Ad Hoc* phase – the fact that cases were lost due to the lack of policies and standardized tools in this new field of forensic science (Charters, 2009).

For example, an employee was fired for violating the company's appropriate use policy when he was caught searching through private personnel files. The employee claimed that he accidentally came across the personnel files, and that just so happened to be the moment his boss walked into the office. After being fired, the employee sued the company for wrongful termination, claiming that law enforcement officers did not follow procedures for collecting and analyzing the computer evidence. For instance, who was in possession of the evidence during transfer and how was the computer evidence stored? Of course, in the 1980s, there were no guidelines or protocols for computer evidence collection. In addition, the attorney argued that there was no proof of the computer forensic tool's accuracy and it was possible that this tool had tampered with the computer evidence. Due to the lack of structure in the *Ad Hoc* phase, cases like this proved difficult to prosecute.

In response to the problems associated with the *Ad Hoc* phase, computer forensics progressed into the **Structured phase** during the mid 1980s. The Structured phase is specifically characterized by the harmonization between computer forensic procedure/policy and computer crime legislation. First, several federal statues criminalized various forms of hacking (see Chapter 2) and **wire fraud** (i.e. fraud committed through the use of electronic communication; Clifford, 2006). In addition, companies drafted appropriate use policies for their employees as well as due process procedures for investigating violations of these new policies. Finally, the courts pushed the field of computer forensics to develop tools that could withstand courtroom challenges, along with standards for evidence collection (Charters, 2009). During the beginning of the structured phase, most of the computer forensic examinations were confined to a single computer component and suspect. Few law enforcement officers were "trained" in computer forensics (i.e. they were self-declared experts), and the forensic tools were expensive, so the collection and examination of computer evidence was either inaccessible or unaffordable for most law enforcement agencies.

However, more and more people began owning a personal computer, cell phone, or other digital device, so more and more crimes were being committed that involved some form of digital evidence. The way people used technology was continuously changing as well. For example, cell phones had limited functionality during the early 1990s (e.g. they could not send text messages or connect to the Web) until the development of the Blackberry and related devices in the late 1990s. Therefore, technological change forced changes in how law enforcement viewed computer evidence. In response to technological change, a number of professional organizations emerged, such as the Scientific Working Group on Digital Evidence (SWGDE; Whitcomb, 2002). At the inaugural meeting of SWGDE in 1998, Federal Bureau of Investigation and Postal Inspection Service officers created the first definition of digital evidence: "any information of probative value that is stored or transmitted in a binary form" (Whitcomb, 2007: 7). It may seem counterintuitive for the PIS to have such an influential role in digital forensics; however, this agency investigates more than just mail fraud. Shortly thereafter, the first forensic science section on digital evidence was held at the International Association for Forensic Science conference in 1999 (IAFS; Whitcomb, 2007). In addition, the first peer-reviewed journal dedicated to digital evidence, the *International Journal of Digital Evidence*, debuted in 2002. As evidenced, the field of computer forensics became more structured and organized as industry, practitioners, and academia pursued the science behind digital investigations.

evolution of digital forensics

Toward the end of the Structured phase, computer forensics evolved into what we now understand to be the field of digital forensics. Computer forensics was no longer a term that accurately represented the various forms of digital evidence. After all, computer forensic examinations extend beyond the traditional forms of computer hardware to include other forms of **digital evidence**, defined as information that is either transferred or stored via a computer (Casey, 2011). Digital evidence may be found on mobile phones, GPS devices, cameras, and networks, to name a few. Recognizing this growth in digital evidence, an umbrella term was created, digital forensics. **Digital forensics** refers to the analysis of digital evidence, which includes network forensics (Internet traffic), computer forensics, mobile-device forensics (e.g. cell phone), and malware forensics (e.g. viruses; see Chapter 3; Casey, 2011). Overall, digital forensics included a whole array of digital devices, and in most cases, the development of new technology (e.g. Xbox, PlayStation 2) required new forensic tools. For example, many gaming consoles, such as Xbox and PlayStation 2, have similar properties to other digital devices in that users can surf the web or use the gaming consoles as storage devices for media. What these technological advances meant for law enforcement was the fact that the same criminal activities afforded to more "traditional" digital devices (e.g. mobile phones) were now being committed on less-traditional digital devices (e.g. Xbox). This assortment of digital technology meant law enforcement needed more forensic tools to conduct their investigations. Thus, this surge in forensic tools moves us into the final phase of digital forensics – the Enterprise phase.

According to Charters (2009), the **Enterprise phase** of digital forensics – also known as the **Golden Age** (Garfinkel, 2010) – began in the early 2000s. The courts were becoming more and more familiar with the process of collecting and examining digital forensic evidence, and the forensic industry began to develop tools that allowed for the examination of computer evidence. In response to demands by law enforcement, commercial tools were created that allowed for the examination of evidence on-site, that is to say, at the scene rather than back in the laboratory. During this time, **open source** digital forensic tools debuted, which are software programs that can be freely used, modified, and shared with anyone (see Altheide and Carvey, 2011). There is a lot of controversy surrounding open source digital forensic tools because, as part of the distribution terms, the source code must be made available, without discrimination, to the general public (Open Source Initiative, n.d.). In other words, computer criminals and law enforcement (and anyone else) will have access to the source code for open source digital forensic tools.

> **For more information on the Open Source Initiative, go online to:**
> https://joinup.ec.europa.eu/elibrary/case/netherlands-forensic-institute-develops-and-publishes-open-source-software-0

The *source code* is simply the human-readable instructions written by the programmer for how the software works (e.g. Java); this code is then translated into object code so the computer can execute the instructions (Zanero and Huebner, 2010). For **closed source** or **proprietary software**, usually the source code is not made available to the general public; only the **object code**, which restricts the ability of users to modify and share the software due to copyright infringement, is publicly shared (Zanero and Huebner, 2010). The benefits of open source digital forensic tools are the ability to identify and fix bugs within the software, and the opportunity to learn more about how the tool works (Altheide and Carvey, 2011; Zanero and Huebner, 2010). There is an inherent transparency with open source software compared to the black box of proprietary software, which some argue makes it easier for open source tools to be admissible in court (Carrier, 2002). Both open source and closed source tools will continue to play an important role in digital forensics, especially since crimes increasingly involve at least one digital element (Clifford, 2006; Maras, 2012).

Think about your own technological devices. You may own a laptop or tablet, and possibly a smart phone, but what about your MP3 player, gaming system, or Wi-Fi-enabled television? It is possible that all of these devices would need to be collected and examined for potential evidence during a digital forensic investigation, and with the globalization of technology and the Internet, there will continue to be an increase in the abundance of digital data that needs to be analyzed for potential evidence. In addition, not only are there more devices, the sizes of the storage systems have increased as well. Thus, the sheer amount of data that needs to be examined is daunting for law enforcement as well as the cost associated with training, certification, and the forensic equipment. For these reasons, Garfinkel (2010) argues the Golden Age of digital forensics will be coming to an end, and the future of digital forensics will rely on advancements in scientific research, standards for education and certification, and diversity of forensic tools to handle the ever-changing world of technology and digital evidence.

Stages of digital forensic investigation

In an attempt to standardize the steps for conducting a digital forensic investigation, **process models** were developed which provided practical guidelines and general procedures to conducting a digital forensic investigation (Casey, 2011). Standardizing the investigation process generates consistency in how digital evidence is handled by law enforcement personnel. However, what is interesting is the fact that there is no standard process model used to describe the stages of a digital forensic investigation (see Casey, 2011). Although the terminology is different, there are four common stages in the digital forensic investigation: survey/identification, collection/acquisition, examination/analysis, and report/presentation.

evolution of digital forensics

Survey/identification is the initial step of a digital forensic investigation. During this stage, law enforcement personnel and digital forensic technicians survey the physical (e.g. home office) and digital crime scenes (e.g. Internet) to identity potential sources of digital evidence. This step is often the most difficult because technology is constantly changing and evolving, and less "obvious" digital devices (e.g. PlayStation vs. desktop computer) may be overlooked for their potential evidentiary value. For example, the Xbox gaming system can be modified to run a different operating system, thereby making it possible to function as a traditional personal computer (e.g. store files, surf the web; see Burke and Craiger, 2007; Bolt, 2011). In 2010, 20-year-old Timothy Hammerstone was arrested for soliciting sexually explicit photos of a 10-year-old boy through his Xbox (see Text Box 10.2).

Text Box 10.2: Video game systems and digital evidence

http://archive.news10.net/news/local/story.aspx?storyid=92886&catid=243

Folsom boy, 10, victimized through Xbox; Florida man arrested

12:06 PM, Aug 28, 2010

> Timothy Wayne Hammerstone, 22, was arrested for obtaining sexually explicit photos of a young boy through his Xbox. [Police] advise parents to be aware that internet-connected gaming systems such as Xbox and PlayStation pose the same threats as an internet-connected computer or telephone.

This article provides an excellent example of the ways that the Xbox gaming system can be abused by cybercriminals. In this case, an individual was able to use the gaming system to acquire sexual images of a minor, and demonstrates why all technology can play a role in cybercrime in some fashion.

Along with non-traditional digital devices, some sources of potential evidence may be hidden or disguised as non-digital devices, such as the concealed camera in the ballpoint pen or lighter. There are also websites that provide helpful hints for concealing Universal Serial Bus (USB) flash drives in everyday household items (see Image 10.2). Finally, surveying the digital crime scene may be difficult because specific cybercrimes, such as hacking and malware, are often committed thousands of miles away from their targeted devices (Britz, 2009). Once the physical and digital crime scenes are surveyed, and potential sources of digital evidence are identified, the digital

Images 10.2a and 10.2b Hiding flash drives
There are websites that provide advice on how to disguise your USB flash drive.

http://commons.wikimedia.org/wiki/File:USB_Flash_Drive_Chapped.jpg

http://commons.wikimedia.org/wiki/File:USB_Flash_Drive_Lighter.jpg

evolution of digital forensics

devices must be searched and seized. This stage of the digital forensic investigation is known as the collection or acquisition phase.

The **collection/acquisition phase** of the digital forensic investigation is concerned with the retrieval and preservation of digital evidence (ISO/IEC, 2012). First, digital forensic technicians must document how the digital evidence was retrieved from the digital source (e.g. mobile phone) – that is to say, how the mobile phone was searched and how the digital evidence was seized. For example, during computer forensic investigations, technicians must determine whether to conduct an on-site or off-site search; in other words, whether to seize the digital device and search it on-site or off-site at a forensic laboratory (Maras, 2012). It is important for law enforcement to maintain detailed notes and documentation of the search and seizure process of the digital forensic investigation. In addition, for any crime scene, whether traditional or digital, the evidence must be collected in a manner that is forensically sound and preserves the evidence's integrity. Evidence retrieved from a digital device must be authenticated in order for it to meet admissibility standards for evidence in a court of law (see Chapter 12). The goal of evidence **preservation** is to make a copy of the original data files for examination in a way that minimizes the possibility of any changes being made to the original data files (International Organization for Standardization and the International Electrotechnical Commission; ISO/IEC, 2012). The process of preserving digital evidence will be discussed further in the next chapter.

Once a copy of the original data is verified, the **examination/analysis stage** refers to data recovery/extraction and analysis of digital data. First, manual and automated programs should be used to uncover digital evidence, that is to say, recover and restore hidden files, manipulated, and deleted files. Once the data has been restored, the digital forensic technician must analyze the digital data to determine its relevance to the investigation (e.g. Rule 401 of the US Federal Rules of Evidence; see Chapter 12). By the end of the examination/analysis phase, the digital forensic technician has reconstructed the digital crime scene. This stage will be discussed further in Chapter 11. After this reconstruction, the digital forensic investigation enters its final stage – the report/presentation stage.

The final phase in the digital forensic investigation is the **report/presentation stage**. Here, the findings that are determined relevant to the investigation are finalized in a report. How evidence is determined to be relevant to an investigation will be discussed further in Chapter 12. In addition, this report should reflect complete transparency, meaning each step described in detail so as to leave no mystery in the digital forensics process. Specifically, the digital forensic technicians should be prepared to testify in court regarding the survey/identification (e.g. chain of custody), collection/acquisition (preservation, forensic tools), and examination/analysis (data recovery and reduction) stages of the digital forensic investigation. The report/presentation stage will be discussed further in Chapter 11.

In a perfect world, these four stages would be conducted by a trained digital forensic technician who is responsible for identifying, preserving, analyzing, and reporting the findings of the digital forensic investigation. However, digital forensic training and certification is expensive, and many law enforcement departments do not have the funding or resources available to purchase the necessary forensic equipment. For most law enforcement agencies, it is not plausible to always have a certified digital forensic technician at the scene, just as it is equally implausible for a law enforcement officer to collect all potential sources of digital evidence to be sent to an external forensic laboratory for examination (Cohen, 2007). For each tier, there are specially trained law enforcement officers who are knowledgeable, to various extents, in the digital forensic process. Since all law enforcement personnel (e.g. patrol officer, detective) have the potential to come into contact with digital evidence, "each officer has a role to play in the safeguarding and examination of that material" (Cohen, 2007: 3).

The Role of Digital Evidence

In this Digital Age, technology is inescapable in our daily lives; and those who commit crimes use technology to their advantage. For a crime to be labeled a "computer crime," the computer must be either the **target** or **tool** for committing the crime. In other words, a hacker may target and take down a specific website whereas child pornography consumers use the Internet as a tool for downloading child sex abuse images. However, the computer may also be an **incidental** to a crime, meaning the computer is either involved in the commission of a crime, or the computer is being used merely as a storage device (Maras, 2012). With the globalization of technology and the Internet, there will continue to be an increase in the abundance of digital devices that need to be analyzed for potential digital evidence. Digital evidence is information that is either transferred or stored in a binary form that is relevant to the crime under investigation (Casey, 2011).

According to Locard's Principle of Exchange, when there is contact between two items, there is an exchange of material (Locard, 1934). That is to say, there is an exchange of evidence between the offender and the crime scene – the offender will leave something at the scene of the crime (i.e. fingerprints) as well as take something away from the scene of the crime (e.g. victim's DNA). Locard's Principle of Exchange is important because one of the reasons evidence is sought after is to *link* the people, places, and objects involved in the crime. In addition, it is important to obtain evidence in order to provide additional leads, eliminate potential suspects, identify the suspect, corroborate or refute testimony, and, most importantly, prove that a crime has been committed, otherwise known as **corpus delicti** (see Girard, 2011). Digital evidence may be the "link" between the victim and the offender, just like traditional trace evidence (e.g. hair, fibers, blood) in the other forensic sciences. For example, Philip Markoff, otherwise known as the craigslist killer, was arrested after investigators were able to link the IP address used to send an email to the murder victim to Markoff's home address (see Hansen, 2013).

We are trying to tell a story – the who, what, when, where, why, and how of a criminal or civil offense. In general, a **criminal offense** (state and federal) is the violation of a law in which a crime (e.g. murder, rape) is committed against the state, society as a whole, or a member of society. In criminal cases, the plaintiff is either the state or federal government since the state is representing not only the victim but also society as a whole. A **civil offense** is a non-criminal offense, usually a dispute, between private parties (e.g. individuals, organizations, or businesses). In addition, the punishment in civil cases usually consists of monetary damages as compensation, as opposed to incarceration, which can only be imposed by criminal law violations (see Allen, Kuhns, Swift, Schwartz, and Pardo, 2011). Digital evidence may play a role in both criminal and civil cases.

Let's first look at the role of digital evidence in a criminal case – *State of Florida* v. *Casey Marie Anthony*. In 2008, Casey Anthony was charged with the murder of her daughter, Caylee Anthony. At the trial, the prosecutor argued that Casey Anthony had used chloroform on her daughter before duct-taping her mouth; a computer forensic examiner testified that someone had conducted Internet searches using the keyword "chloroform" on the home computer (Hayes, 2011). This digital artifact was determined to be relevant to the case, therefore admissible as evidence, since it made the prosecutor's argument that Casey Anthony had used chloroform on her daughter more probable. On the stand, Casey Anthony's mother claimed that she was the one who had searched for "chloroform," and that it was an accident – she had meant to search for "chlorophyll." In a controversial verdict, Casey Anthony was acquitted of first-degree murder. After the trial, the Orange County Sheriff's department admitted to overlooking evidence of a Google search for "fool-proof suffocation" methods the day the daughter was last seen alive (see Associated Press, 2012). We will never know how this uncaptured digital evidence would have influenced the Casey Anthony trial.

In a cannibalism trial in Germany, the digital forensic evidence suggested the victim of a murder was actually a willing participant in his own death (see Davis, 2008; King, 2013). In 2001, 41-year-old Armin Meiwes posted an Internet ad on the Cannibal Café forum for a "well-built 18 to 30-year old to be slaughtered and then consumed" – this ad was answered by 43-year-old Bernd-Jurgen Brandes. Searches of Meiwes' computer reviewed chat logs between the two men before they set their in-person meeting on March 9, 2001. In one of these chat logs, Meiwes stated, "I would rather kill only those who want to be killed" (King, 2013). Meiwes videotaped the encounter with Brandes. This video suggested Brandes was a "voluntary victim." After killing Brandes, Meiwes consumed his flesh for ten months until police were contacted by a college student who saw advertisements for more victims on the Internet, including details about the killing. According to the police, Meiwes was involved in several cannibal forums and had been in contact with over 400 people from these Internet forums. In addition, Meiwes had received emails from over 200 people who wanted to be killed and eaten. After a re-trial, Meiwes was convicted of murder and sentenced to life. Although this was not a traditional cybercrime case, digital evidence revealed a timeline between when the Cannibal Café ad was posted, the chat logs between Meiwes and Brandes, and the additional Internet postings that eventually led police to the Rotenburg Cannibal (Davis, 2008; King, 2013).

For more information on the Rotenburg Cannibal, go online to: www.crimelibrary.com/blog/2013/11/18/armin-meiwes-the-rotenburg-cannibal/index.html

Next, consider the role of digital evidence in the civil case *Berryman-Dages* v. *City of Gainesville*. In 2011, Kim Berryman-Dages (the plaintiff) sued the City of Gainesville, Florida (defendant), claiming she was adversely treated and demoted at work (Gainsville Fire Rescue service) due to her gender and sexual orientation. In 2011, Berryman-Dages subpoenaed the computer of a non-party to the case, Ms Thayer, because Ms Thayer admitted (although later denied) to sending an anonymous letter to the plaintiff criticizing her sexual orientation. Ms Thayer was married to the Gainesville Fire Rescue Chief at the time this letter was written and at the time of the demotion. The court ruled that Ms Thayer must comply with the subpoena and allow a computer forensics expert to search her personal computer for digital evidence of the letter in question (see *Berryman-Dages* v. *City of Gainesville*, 2011).

Overall, as evidenced by these cases, the cyberworld is not that different from the physical world – digital evidence is just as important as physical evidence in criminal and civil cases. However, before law enforcement can examine the digital evidence, they must be able to identify which digital devices at a crime scene may contain evidentiary information. Since the advent of the personal computer, the number of people who own computers has increased; according to the United States Census Bureau (2014), only 8.2 percent of all households had a computer in the home in 1982, compared to 78.9 percent in 2012. Unlike the early years of digital forensics, identifying electronic evidence has become more complicated for law enforcement officers due to the advancement and increased use of technology in our everyday lives.

Types of hardware, peripherals, and electronic evidence

In 2008, the National Institute of Justice released a report entitled *Electronic Crime Scene Investigation: A Guide for First Responders*, which

evolution of digital forensics

Image 10.3 An older model computer
A photo of an old IBM Personal Computer XT released in 1983.
http://commons.wikimedia.org/wiki/File:Museum-Enter-6094770.
JPG?uselang=en-gb

was intended to assist law enforcement with the recognition and collection of electronic evidence. Traditionally, the most common form of digital evidence is the computer system, which consists of hardware, software, and peripheral devices to either input (introduce information to the computer), analyze (process), or output (produce/display information processed by the computer) data (Britz, 2009). **Hardware** is considered the tangible or physical parts of a computer system (e.g. motherboard). **Software** consists of programs that include instructions which tell computers what to do (e.g. operating systems). **Peripheral devices** are externally connected components that are not considered essential parts of a computer system, such as scanners, printers, and modems. As shown in Image 10.3, the size and look of computers have changed dramatically over the years, from large, desktop computers (e.g. a legacy system) to personal tablets, including the Apple iPad mini, which weighs only 0.75 pounds (341 grams).

These outdated computer systems, devices, or software are often referred to as **legacy systems** (see Seacord, Plakosh, and Lewis, 2003). For example, mainframes are considered the legacy system for the personal desktop computer. Since technology is constantly changing and developing, it may be

Image 10.4 The evolution of removable storage devices
http://commons.wikimedia.org/wiki/File:Storage_size_comparison.jpg

traditionally easier for law enforcement to identify legacy systems (e.g. desktop computers) compared to their newer counterparts (e.g. tablets). Therefore, it is important that law enforcement remain vigilant of the trends in technology in order to identify both legacy systems and more current technology.

Along with computer systems, law enforcement officers must be able to identify the various forms of storage device, which include hard drives and removable media (Allen *et al.*, 2011). First, **hard drives** are data storage devices used for storing and retrieving data. **Internal hard drives** are installed inside the computer whereas **external hard drives** are portable storage devices located outside of the computer and are usually connected via a USB port. Internal or external hard drives do not need to be connected to a computer in order for them to have evidentiary value. For example, Ryan Loskarn, ex-chief of staff to Senator Lamar Alexander of Tennessee, was charged with possession and distribution of child pornography after the PIS located an external hard drive hidden on the roof of Loskarn's home (Marimow, 2013). According to court documents, investigators saw Mr Loskarn leaning out of a window from the second floor of his home during the raid. Upon further inspection, investigators found an external Toshiba hard drive on the roof (Marimow, 2013).

evolution of digital forensics

Image 10.5 The evolving state of mobile phones
The handheld mobile phone has evolved immensely in size and function.

http://commons.wikimedia.org/wiki/File:Mobile_phone_evolution.jpg

Another form of storage device is the removable media device, which is used to store and share digital information. As shown in Image 10.4, removable storage devices have evolved over the years and include floppy disks, zip disks, compact disks (CDs), CompactFlash card, smart media (SM) cards, and USB flash drives, to name just a few.

USB flash drives, or **thumb drives**, are one of the most common removable storage devices. They are small, lightweight, and can easily be transported and concealed. In addition, memory cards, such as the CompactFlash card or SM card, are small data storage devices that are commonly associated with digital camera, mobile phones, video game consoles, and other handheld devices (Allen *et al.*, 2011). Overall, data storage devices may contain a plethora of electronic evidence, but they may also be more difficult to identify due to their small size and portability.

Handheld devices are another source of potential electronic information and include mobile phones, digital multimedia devices (e.g. iPod), digital cameras, and GPS, to name just a few (see Image 10.5).

According to the PEW Internet Project (Brenner, 2013), 91 percent of Americans over the age of 18 years have a mobile phone. According to the International Telecommunication Union (ITU, 2013) report, there were as many mobile cellular subscriptions as people in the world. Handheld devices are capable of providing communication (e.g. texting), photography (e.g. built-in camera), navigation (e.g. maps), entertainment (e.g. music) and data storage (e.g. word processing documents, contacts). Many of these devices were initially intended to perform a certain function; for example, Apple released the first iPod in 2001 as a portable music storage device. Unless the crime involved copyright infringement, a basic first responder may not necessarily consider an iPod as a storage device for electronic evidence other than music. However, law enforcement and computer forensic technicians should not be fooled by how these tools may be "traditionally" used – criminals have found other ways to use these handheld digital devices. For example, in 2004, the ringleader of a car theft gang in London was arrested due to the incriminating evidence found on his iPod (see Text Box 10.3).

Text Box 10.3: Digital evidence and real-world crime

iPod car theft ringleader jailed

http://news.bbc.co.uk/2/hi/uk_news/england/london/3932847.stm

> The gang "hijacked" identities to drive off Jaguars, Mercedes, BMWs and a Porsche, before selling them. The Vehicle Fraud Unit raided the estate and found a mass of incriminating evidence stored on an iPod.

This article provides an in-depth overview of the ways that digital evidence can demonstrate criminal activity of any sort, whether online or offline. Readers will gather an appreciation for the ways that digital devices provide a record of individual activity in multiple environments and can be invaluable for investigators of all crimes.

Another popular feature of mobile phones and tablet computers is the **app**, which is a software application typically downloaded by the user that performs a certain function, such as gaming, sharing information (pictures), communicating, or providing entertainment. According to Bushney (2013), the top five most popular free iPhone apps of 2013 were: *Candy Crush Saga, YouTube, Temple Run 2, Vine,* and *Google Maps.* Although many of these apps were designed for a specific purpose, law enforcement has seen many of these apps being used nefariously. For example, *Words with Friends* is an app that allows you to play word games with your friends by connecting via Facebook or inviting them to play. This game, however, also allows you to play with complete strangers by selecting the "random opponent" option. In addition, this app, and others like it, allows you to chat with the person you are playing against. In a 2012 Zynga poll surveying more than 118,000 users, 1 out of 10 players admitted to "hooking up" with someone as a direct result of the game *Words with Friends* (Lynley, 2012). This chatting feature, however, has become a tool for online predators targeting minors (personal communication, Lt Dennis McMillian, February 4, 2014). *Words with Friends* is a great example of how a gaming app, which on the surface may not seem relevant to a case, in actuality may provide important information during a digital forensic investigation, such as proof of a prior relationship or chat history.

Not only do some apps have chat features (e.g. *Words with Friends*), but research shows people, in general, are moving away from traditional text messaging to the use of mobile messaging apps specifically designed for chatting, such as *Viber* and *WhatsApp*. These mobile messaging applications replace the short message service (SMS), which is the traditional method of sending short messages or "texts" between mobile devices through your cell phone provider. Mobile messaging applications allow you to send and receive pictures or text messages without paying for SMS. Some of these mobile apps are considered anonymous and provide privacy online by masking users' identities and having messages that "self-destruct," meaning they are only visible for a short period of time (e.g. *Snapchat*, *Whisper*, and *Backchat*). Overall, these messenger apps are becoming more popular because of the growing concerns over wiretapping and surveillance (i.e. recording phone conversations or reading text messages; Vincent, 2014). Law enforcement and security experts are well aware that these mobile apps are well suited for criminal behaviors, and retrieving digital information during an investigation will prove to be difficult (Mengle, 2013).

> **For more information on the ways that offenders are using mobile apps, go online to:** http://archive.indianexpress.com/news/mumbai-police-worried-as-more-criminals-take-to-chat-apps/1144802/

As previously discussed, crimes increasingly involve at least one digital element (Clifford, 2006), and any digital device, regardless of its primary function, may be of evidentiary value. For example, a digital device may store digital information (emails) that is relevant to an investigation or be a source of fingerprints or trace evidence. Digital evidence comes in many shapes and sizes and is no longer limited to traditional desktop computers. Instead, storage devices, handheld devices, video game consoles, and computer network devices should be identified for their *potential* evidentiary value during any criminal investigation. As we have seen, the identification of digital devices may be a complicated task for law enforcement as technology continues to become smaller, more compact, and in some cases, disguised.

Evidence integrity

We have discussed the first step of the digital forensic investigation – the survey/identification of potential sources of digital evidence. Next, the importance of evidence integrity will be discussed with regards to forensic soundness and authentication. For any crime scene, whether traditional or digital, the evidence must be collected in a manner that is forensically sound and preserves the evidence's integrity. **Forensic soundness** refers to the validity of the method for collecting and preserving evidence. In digital forensics, evidence is forensically sound when it is collected in a way where the data is unaltered, the copied data is an exact duplicate of the original, and the examiner documents every part of the acquisition process (see Vacca and Rudolph, 2010).

Complete **transparency** is important in the acquisition of evidence. The digital forensic technician is responsible for documenting which tools were used during the forensic examination as well as the date and time of evidence preservation. When the examiner is transparent, it is easier for the courts to determine the **validity** of the process, meaning whether the evidence was collected and preserved in a manner so that an accurate conclusion can be drawn (Slay, Lin, Turnbull, Beckett, and Lin, 2009). The validity of digital forensics is assessed by whether or not the evidence is admissible in a court of law. The process by which a digital forensics examiner preserves and validates the evidence will be discussed in greater detail in Chapter 11, and the admissibility standards for evidence in a court of law will be discussed in greater detail in Chapter 12. For now, remember that it is not the job of a digital forensic examiner to "prove" a suspect's guilt or innocence. Instead, the number one priority of the digital forensic examiner is to maintain **evidence integrity**, which is the reliability and truthfulness of the evidence.

Summary

Overall, virtually every crime will involve some form of digital evidence, and it is up to law enforcement to be able to identify the possible sources thereof. However, digital evidence may be collected from not-so-obvious devices, such as flash drives disguised as a teddy bear or Barbie doll (see Image 10.6).

With digital devices increasingly being used to target, act as a tool, or provide support for criminal activities, it is important for law enforcement to understand the crime scene in the Digital Age. There is no doubt that technology will continue to evolve, meaning law enforcement must be able to quickly react to the new and different ways technology may be used for nefarious acts. However, one thing will always stay the same – the importance of evidence integrity. Regardless of whether it is a computer, mobile phone, or USB flash drive, digital evidence will only be admissible in a court of law if it is collected in a forensically sound manner. The importance of being forensically sound cannot be reiterated enough, for it can be the deciding factor in any court case, especially in our current, Digital Age.

(a)

(b)

Images 10.6a and 10.6b Hidden media examples
During a search and seizure, law enforcement may not recognize a teddy
bear keychain or bracelet as a USB flash drive.

10.6a
http://upload.wikimedia.org/wikipedia/commons/b/be/Teddy_
USBear_%281a%29.jpg

10.6b
http://www.shutterstock.com/pic-119772592/stock-ph
oto-usb-flash-drive-bracelet-on-a-white-background.html?sr
c=0gJGHsG2jXkyrz0BhAnqWQ-1-2
Courtesy of www.Shutterstock.com

Key terms

Accuracy

Ad Hoc phase

App

Chain of custody

Civil offense

Closed source software

Collection/acquisition phase

Computer as a target

Computer as a tool

Computer as incidental

Computer forensics

Computer Fraud and Abuse Act

Corpus delicti

Criminal offense

Dead-box forensics

Digital Age

Digital evidence

Digital forensics

Enterprise phase

Evidence integrity

Examination/analysis stage

External hard drives

Florida Computer Crimes Act of 1978

Forensic science

Forensic soundness

Golden Age

Handheld devices

Hard drives

Hardware

Information Age

Internal hard drives

Latent

Legacy systems

Object code

Open source software

Peripheral device

Pre-forensics

Preservation

Proprietary software

Process models

Report/presentation stage

Software

Structured phase

Survey/identification stage

Transparency

Thumb drives

USB flash drives

Validity

Wire fraud

Discussion questions

1) If technology is constantly evolving, will law enforcement and judicial legislation always be "one step behind" the criminal? Are there any crimes that do not leave behind digital evidence?

2) What are some of the problems law enforcement investigators face when collecting digital evidence from a crime scene?

3) Garfinkel (2010) argues that the Golden Age of digital forensics is nearing its end – what do you think is the next stage or era of digital forensics?

4) Maintaining evidence integrity is one of the most important steps in the digital forensic investigation. Provide some examples of how the integrity of evidence can be discredited during a digital forensic investigation. What are some ways that law enforcement can ensure that evidence integrity is maintained during a digital forensic investigation?

References

Allen, R. J., Kuhns, R. B., Swift, E., Schwartz, D. S., & Pardo, M. S. (2011). *Evidence: Text, Cases, and Problems*, 5th ed. New York, NY: Aspen Publishers.

Altheide, C., & Carvey, H. (2011). *Digital Forensics with Open Source Tools*. Waltham, MA: Syngress.

Associated Press. (2012, November 25). *Casey Anthony detectives overlooked "fool-proof suffocation" Google search*. Retrieved from www.newsday.com

Berryman-Dages vs. City of Gainsville, 2011, US Dist. LEXIS 78849 (N.D. Fla. July 20, 2011).

Bolt, S. (2011). *Xbox360 Forensics: A Digital Forensics Guide to Examining Artifacts*. Burlington, MA: Syngress.

Brenner, J. (2013). *Pew internet: Mobile*. Retrieved from www.pewinternet.org

Britz, M. T. (2009). *Computer forensics and cyber crime*, 2nd ed. Upper Saddle River, NJ: Prentice Hall.

Burke, K. P., & Craiger, P. (2007). Xbox forensics. *Journal of Digital Forensic Practice*, 1, 1–8.

Bushney, R. (2013, December 17). *The 15 most popular free iPhone apps of 2013*. Retrieved from www.businessinsider.com

Carrier, B. (2002, October). *Open source digital forensics tools: The legal argument*. @stake, Inc. Retrieved from www.atstake.com

Casey, E. (2011). *Digital Evidence and Computer Crime: Forensic Science, Computers, and the internet*, 3rd ed. Waltham, MA: Academic Press.

CBC News. (2010, October 27). *Teen boys admit to murder of Victoria girl*. Retrieved from www.cbc.ca

Charters, I. (2009). *Digital forensics: Civilizing the cyber frontier*. Retrieved from www.guerilla-ciso.com

Clifford, R. D. (ed.) (2006). *Cybercrime: The Investigation, Prosecution, and Defense of a Computer-Related Crime*, 2nd ed. Durham, NC: Carolina Academic Press.

Cohen, C. L. (2007, March). Growing challenge of computer forensics. *The Police Chief*, 74(3), 1–4.

Davis, R. (2008) You Are What You Eat: Cannibalism, Autophagy and the Case of Armin Meiwes. In N. Billias (ed.). *Territories of Evil* (pp. 152–169). Amsterdam, Netherlands: Rodopi.

Federal Computer Systems Protection Act. Congressional Records, 95th Congress, Vol. 123, No. 111, June 27, 1977. Retrieved from http://thomas.loc.gov

Fernandez, J. D., Smith, S., Garcia, M., & Kar, D. (2005). Computer forensics – A critical need in computer science programs. *Journal of Computing in Small Colleges*, 20(4), 315–322.

Florida v. Casey Marie Anthony, No. 48-2008-CF-015606-O (9th Cir. Ct).

Florida Computer Crimes Act (1978). *Fla. Stat. 815.01-07*. Retrieved from www.leg.state.fl.us

Garfinkel, S. (2010). Digital forensics research: The next 10 years. *Digital Investigation*, 7, S64–S73.

Girard, J. E. (2011). *Criminalistics: Forensic Science, Crime, and Terrorism*, 2nd ed. Boston, MA: Jones & Barlett Learning.

Hansen, M. (2013, April 8). Connecting the digital dots to catch the "Craigslist Killer". *ABA Journal*. Retrieved from www.abajournal.com

Hayes, A. (2011, June 8). *Anthony trial: "Chloroform" searched on computer*. Retrieved from www.cnn.com

Hochman, M. (1986, Summer). The Flagler dog track case. *Computer/Law Journal* 117, 7(1), 177–127.

International Telecommunication Union. (2013, February). *The world in 2013: ICT facts and figures*. www.itu.int

Interpol. The Third Interpol Symposium on International Fraud, Saint-Cloud, Paris, France, December 11–13, 1979.

evolution of digital forensics

ISO/IEC (2012). 27037: *Guidelines for identification, collection, acquisition, and preservation of digital evidence*. Retrieved from www.iso.org

Kabay, M. E. (2002). Salami fraud. *Network World*. Retrieved February 21, 2014 from www.networkworld.com

Kamisar, Y., LaFave, W. R., Israel, J. H., King, N. J., Kerr, O. S. (2008). *Basic Criminal Procedure: Cases, Comments and Questions*, 8th ed. Eagan, MN: West.

King, G. (2013, November 18). *Armin Meiwes, The Rotenburg Cannibal*. Retrieved from http://crimelibrary.com

Locard, E. (1934). *Manuel de technique policière: Les constats, les empreintes digitales* [Manual Police Technique: Criminal Investigation], 2nd ed. Paris: Payot.

Lynley, M. (2012, February 14). *Your chances of hooking up go up if you play Words with Friends*. Retrieved from www.businessinsider.com

Maras, M. (2012). *Computer Forensics: Cybercriminals, Laws, and Evidence*. Sudbury, MA: Jones and Bartlett Learning.

Marimow, A. E. (2013, December 12). *Child porn found on computer hard drive of senator's fired chief of staff, court papers say*. Retrieved from washingtonpost. com

McKnight, B. E. (trans.) (1981). *The Washing Away of Wrongs: Forensic Medicine in Thirteenth-Century China by Sung Tz'u*. The University of Michigan: Center for Chinese Studies.

Mengle, G. S. (2013, July 22). Mumbai police worried as more criminals take to chat apps. *The Indian Express*. Retrieved from http://indianexpress.com

Nelson, B., Phillips, A., Enfinger, F., & Steuart, C. (2004). *Guide to Computer Forensics and Investigations*. Boston, MA: Couse Technologies.

Open Source Initiative. n.d. *The Open Source Definition*. Retrieved from http:// opensource.org

Roberts, H. (2011, November 9). *Teenage killer who tortured and suffocated classmate, 18, had left digital trail of sick plot and confessed on World of Warcraft*. Retrieved from www.dailymail.co.uk

Saferstein, R. (2010). *Criminalistics: An Introduction to Forensic Science*, 10th ed. Upper Saddle River, NJ: Prentice Hall.

Schjolberg, S. (2008, December). *The history of global harmonization on cybercrime legislation – The road to Geneva*. Retrieved from http://cybercrimelaw.net

Schjolberg, S., & Tingrett, M. (2004). *Computer-related offences*. Presentation at the Octopus Interface 2004 Conference on the Challenge of Cybercrime, September, 15–17 2004, Council of Europe, Strasbourg, France.

Seacord, R. C., Plakosh, D., & Lewis, G. A. (2003). *Modernizing Legacy Systems: Software Technologies, Engineering Processes, and Business Practices*. Boston: Addison-Wesley Professional.

Shaw E., Ruby K., & Post, J. (1988). The insider threat to information systems: The psychology of the dangerous insider. *Security Awareness Bulletin*, 2, 1–10.

Slay, J., Lin, Y., Turnbull, B., Beckett, J., & Lin, P. (2009). Towards a Formalization of Digital Forensics. In G. Peterson & S. Shenoi (eds), *Advances in Digital Forensics V* (pp. 37–49). Berlin, Germany: Springer.

United States Census Bureau. (2014). *Measuring American: Computer and internet trends in America*. US Department of Commerce. Retrieved from www.census.gov

Vacca, J. R., & Rudolph, K. (2010). *Systems Forensics, Investigation, and Response*. Sudbury, MA: Jones & Barlett Learning.

Vincent, J. (2014, January 13). C u l8r SMS: Text messages decline in the UK for the first time as WhatsApp, Snapchat rise. *The Independent*. Retrieved from www.independent.co.uk

Whitcomb, C. (2002). An historical perspective of digital evidence: A forensic scientist's view. *International Journal of Digital Evidence*, 1(1), 1–9.

Whitcomb, C. (2007). The evolution of digital evidence in forensic science laboratories. *The Police Chief*, 74(11).

Zanero, S., & Huebner, E. (2010). The Case for Open Source Software in Digital Forensics. In E. Huebner & S. Zanero (eds), *Open Source Software for Digital Forensics* (pp. 3–8). New York, NY: Springer Science+Business Media, LLC.

Zetter, K. (2011, November 3). *Teen Murderer Undone by World of Warcraft Confession and Trail of Digital Evidence*. Retrieved from wired.com

chapter 11

Acquisition and examination of forensic evidence

Chapter goals

- Explain the two steps in the data preservation process
- Identify and describe two digital forensic imaging tools
- Understand the differences between physical and logical extraction
- Understand the importance of repeatability and reproducibility as standards for imaging tools
- Differentiate between allocated, unallocated, slack, and free space
- Understand the importance of report objectivity and reducing confirmation bias
- Identify different data files as potential sources of evidence

Introduction

In 1992, the Colorado-based company Gates Rubber filed a lawsuit against Bando Chemical Industries, accusing them of stealing trade secret information, specifically two computer programs (*Gates Rubber Co. v. Bando Chemical Industry*, 1996). Both companies were competing against one another in the industrial belts market, and Bando Chemical Industries hired several former employees of Gates in 1988. Gates believed that two computer programs were stolen and copied by the former employees, who were now using the computer programs under a different name. Gates sued for copyright infringement, embezzlement of trade secrets, and breach of contract (*Gates Rubber Co. v. Bando Chemical Industry*, 1996).

In 1992, the judge granted Gates's computer forensics expert, Voorhees, access to the defendant's computer in order to examine whether or not the defendant had maliciously deleted files in an attempt to destroy evidence. However, the defendant's computer forensics expert, Wedig, presented testimony that Voorhees failed to maintain the authenticity of the computer evidence. Wedig stated that Voorhees inappropriately copied a computer program (Norton's Unerase) directly onto the defendant's computer, which "obliterated, at random, seven to eight percent of the information which would otherwise have been available [and] no one can ever know what items were overwritten" (*Gates Rubber Co.* v. *Bando Chemical Industry*, 1996). Wedig argued that by not making an image copy of the hard drive, Voorhees failed to preserve evidence – and the court agreed. In the ruling, the US District Court of Colorado stated, "a party has a duty to utilize the method which would yield the most complete and accurate results" (*Gates Rubber Co.* v. *Bando Chemical Industry*, 1996). Essentially, the court mandated that all litigants be required to obtain competent computer forensic examiners in order to preserve and authenticate the integrity of the digital evidence.

It is clear from the *Gates Rubber Company* v. *Bando Chemical Industry* (1996) case that some small portion of potential evidence was lost because the plaintiff's computer forensic examiner failed to acquire and examine the defendant's computer hard drive accurately. As a result of faulty procedures, no one will ever know what seven to eight percent of potential evidence was overwritten. By the end of this chapter, you will understand the process by which a digital forensics examiner preserves and authenticates digital evidence. In addition, you will understand how examiners utilize forensic tools to assist in the preservation and extraction of digital evidence. We will explore in detail the examination/analysis phase of the digital forensics process by describing how and where potential evidence may be uncovered from a digital device, including the ability to recover deleted files. Finally, we will conclude this chapter with a discussion of report objectivity and forensic confirmation bias; after all, the integrity of the report is just as important as the integrity of the evidence itself.

Data preservation

Data preservation is the first step in uncovering digital evidence and occurs during the collection/acquisition phase of the digital forensic investigation (see Chapter 10). The goal of evidence **preservation** in digital forensics is to make a copy of the original data files for examination in a way that minimizes the possibility of any changes being made to the original data files (ISO/IEC, 2012). Just as in any forensic science (i.e. entomology, pathology), it is important to protect the crime scene in order to preserve the integrity of the evidence. Digital evidence needs to be preserved just like other traditional forms of physical evidence, such as blood or hair (see Saferstein, 2010). However, what makes digital forensics unique is the fact that preservation specifically refers to the ability to make a *duplicate* copy of the original digital evidence.

acquisition, examination of forensic evidence

Consider the murder of 30-year-old David Guy of southern England. On July 3, 2012, the torso of David Guy, which was wrapped in a pink shower curtain and stuffed in a plastic bin, was found by a group of students on vacation at Portsmouth beach (BBC News, 2013). On July 8, 2012, David Hilder was charged with the murder and dismemberment of David Guy. The prosecutor's key evidence was DNA samples taken from Hilder's cat, Tinker. The pink shower curtain that wrapped Guy's torso was covered in cat hair, and the police were able to extract DNA from the cat hair follicles. Tinker's DNA was then compared to two cat DNA databases at the Veterinary Genetics Laboratory at the University of California in the United States and Leicester University's Department of Genetics in the United Kingdom. It was determined that Tinker had an uncommon DNA type, and this case became the first time that cat DNA was used during a criminal trial in the United Kingdom (Bond, 2013). Hilder was sentenced to life in prison on July 30, 2013.

In this example, the crime scene technicians preserved the cat hairs from the pink shower curtain, which ultimately resulted in cat DNA evidence linking Hilder to the murder. However, the word *preserve* in this example does not mean that the crime scene technicians, or even the veterinary geneticists, were able to make a *duplicate copy* of the cat hairs. Instead, the crime scene technicians and geneticists must alter (thereby damaging) the original cat hairs collected at the crime scene in order to test for DNA evidence. Overall, preservation has a different connotation depending on whether you are referring to physical or digital evidence. Digital forensics is unique in some ways when compared to the other forensic sciences since the forensic examination is not limited to the original digital device. Instead, there are forensic tools that are capable of making a duplicate, thereby preserving the original source of digital evidence. This process is known as imaging.

Imaging

Imaging is the initial step in the preservation process of digital evidence. **Imaging** is the process of making an exact copy (bit-by-bit) of the original drive onto a new digital storage device (Casey, 2011; Maras, 2012; Britz, 2009). This new digital storage device should be clean, meaning there is no digital data present or left over which could contaminate the imaging process (Johnson, 2006). The process of cleaning a digital storage device to ensure that there are no remnants of data present is known as **wiping** (Wiles, 2007). When imaging a drive, the digital forensics tool must be forensically sound. To be **forensically sound**, the digital forensics tool must eliminate the possibility of making any changes to the original data source (Casey, 2011). To ensure that no changes are made to the original data source, a write blocker is used. A **write blocker** is a device that allows read-only access to all accessible data on a drive, as well as preventing anything from being written to the original drive, which would alter or modify the original evidence

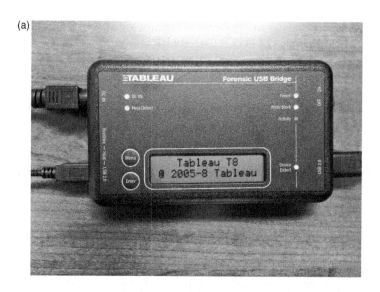

Images 11.1a and 11.1b Write blockers

A write blocker is device that allows read-only access to all accessible data on a drive, as well as preventing anything from being written to the original drive, which would alter or modify the original evidence. Figure 11.1a shows an example of a hardware-based write blocker, Tableau T8.

In Figure 11.1b, a suspect's hard drive is connected to a hardware-based write blocker, which is then connected to the examiner's laptop.

Photos courtesy of Lt Dennis McMillian, the University of Alabama Police Department

acquisition, examination of forensic evidence

(NIST, 2004; see Image 11.1). Essentially, the imaging system is sending **read-only** commands to the drive and not **write** or modify commands (NIST, 2004). There are a number of hardware (external) and software (internal) write blockers on the market (see www.cftt.nist.gov); although, hardware write blockers are often preferred because it is argued that they have a lower failure rate (see Falayleh and Al-Karaki, 2013). Hardware write blockers are also known as **bridges** since the digital evidence is connected to the examiner's computer through the write blocker (see Image 11.1; Wiles, 2007). Once the original data device is imaged, the next step is for the digital forensic examiner to determine whether or not the original and duplicate copies are in fact one and the same.

Verification

Verification is the last step in the preservation process of digital evidence. **Verification** establishes the integrity of the digital evidence by proving that the duplicate is **authentic,** meaning a true and unaltered copy of the original data source (Casey, 2011). Digital forensic investigators verify the duplicate copies by comparing **hash algorithm** values (e.g. MD5, SHA). A hash algorithm is a set of calculations that takes any amount of data (input) and creates a fixed-length value (output), known as a **hash,** which acts as a unique reference number for the original data (Liu, 2011). Hash values are fixed in length and made up of a unique combination of hexadecimal digits (which can be the numbers 0–9 or the letters a–f). These hash values act as digital fingerprints since they are unique to the original data they reference (Liu, 2011). Hash values play an integral part in the verification of digital evidence because they are extremely sensitive to any changes in the original data, even if changing only one bit. The process of creating a hash value from a variable amount of data is known as **hashing.**

In order to verify that the original data was preserved during imaging, a hash value is created for the original drive and its image. If the hash values match, the investigator has *verified* that the original and duplicate copies are one and the same. In other words, the digital forensic examiner can now search the duplicate copy for digital evidence as if searching the original digital device (e.g. cell phone). If during the imaging process any changes occur to the original drive, the hash values will be different indicating that the image is *not* an exact copy of the original drive. Hash values act as a digital fingerprint for both electronic files (e.g. images, documents) and storage media (e.g. hard drive). For example, the National Center for Missing and Exploited Children (NCMEC) established the Hash Value Sharing initiative in 2008, which is a constantly updated list of hash values for known child sex abuse images/videos (Larence, 2011). This list of known hash values is distributed to law enforcement who can cross-check the known hash values with the hash values from their child pornography cases to determine if there are any "new" instances of child sex abuse (i.e. not currently listed by NCMEC).

Currently, the two most common hash algorithms are MD5 and SHA (Casey, 2011). **MD5 (Message Digest Version 5)** is a type of hashing algorithm that takes a large amount of data of arbitrary length (input) and calculates a unique "fingerprint" of this data (known as hashing) expressed as a unique combination of digits and letters of a specified length (output). In this case, an MD5 hash algorithm produces a 128-bit hash value represented in text as a unique string of 32 digits and letters (Casey, 2011; Marcella and Menendez, 2008; Rivest, 1992; see Text Box 11.1).

Text Box 11.1: An example of how the MD5 algorithm works (created by the authors)

An example of how the MD5 algorithm works:

1) First, the MD5 hash for the original file is calculated.
   You will receive payment after you murder my brother.
   6b605a8f218ac7923e173c8082c52845
2) Any exact copies of the file will produce the same MD5 value.
   Copy 1: 6b605a8f218ac7923e173c8082c52845
   Copy 2: 6b605a8f218ac7923e173c8082c52845
3) Should any data in the file change, the MD5 value will change as well. For example:
   Copy 1: You will receive payment after you murder my brother.
   6b605a8f218ac7923e173c8082c52845
   Copy 2: You will receive payment after you murder my mother.
   21502c8d206b36391a029a7372e87777

Another common hashing algorithm is the **SHA** or **Secure Hash Algorithm,** originally created by the National Security Agency in 1993. Using a different algorithm, SHA follows the same basic principles as MD5 in that an arbitrary amount of information can be uniquely represented by a combination of hexadecimal digits, resulting in a "digital fingerprint." The original version of SHA, known as SHA-0, was a 160-bit unique value (Eastlake and Jones, 2001). However, the original SHA algorithm was revised to SHA-1 due to unspecified cryptographic flaws (see Biham and Chen, 2004), but there are still concerns about the vulnerability of SHA-1 to collision attacks (see Polk, Chen, Turner, and Hoffman, 2011; Wang, Yin, and Yu, 2005).

In the hashing world, when two different sets of data (input) result in the same hash value (output), a **collision** has occurred (Wang, 2012). For example, a digital forensics examiner collects two different computers from a crime scene (computers X and Y). Before analyzing the evidence, the

acquisition, examination of forensic evidence

examiner images each computer to create a copy (X-copy and Y-copy). The hash values for X and X-copy should match, just as the hash values for Y and Y-copy. However, a collision occurs when hashing a hard drive does not result in a unique "digital fingerprint," but instead, the same hash value is produced (e.g. X-copy and Y-copy have the same hash value). If a collision occurs, then the digital forensics examiner is unable to verify and authenticate the imaged drive. Research suggests it is theoretically possible for a collision to occur with MD5 and SHA-1 (see Polk *et al.*, 2011; Wang *et al.*, 2005; Xie and Liu, 2013). However, these collisions are theoretical and have yet to occur in the real world, making the MD5 and SHA-1 hash algorithms still secure for digital evidence authentication (Forte, 2009; Schmitt and Jordaan, 2013; Thompson, 2005; Wang, 2012). In response to these collision concerns, several additional hash algorithms were created and have been approved for use in the digital verification process by NIST alongside MD5 and SHA-1 (i.e. SHA-224, SHA-256, SHA-384, and SHA-512; Wang, 2012).

Several court cases have verified the use of hash algorithms in digital forensic investigations. For example, in *XPEL Technologies Corporation* v. *American Filter Film Distributors* (2008), the judge ordered that all of the images made from the seized digital devices "be authenticated by generating an MD5 hash value verification for comparison to the original hard drive." In addition, the Third Circuit described the SHA-1 hash value as "more unique to a data file than DNA is to the human body" (*United States* v. *Beatty*, 2011). The courts have also ruled on the degree of accuracy for the use of hash algorithms in digital forensics. Specifically, in *United States* v. *Cartier* (2008), the Eighth Circuit ruled that a "theoretical possibility" of a collision is not grounds for excluding digital evidence authenticated with hash values:

> In arguing that the hash values do not establish probable cause for a search warrant, Cartier asserts that it is possible for two digital files to have hash values that collide or overlap. The district court heard the factual evidence presented on the issue of hash values at the suppression hearing. Cartier's expert testified that hash values could collide and that in laboratory settings these values had done just that. However, the government's expert witness testified that no two dissimilar files will have the same hash value. After hearing all of the evidence presented by both parties, the district court settled the factual dispute about hash values in favor of the view offered by the government.
>
> (p. 5)

Overall, the imaging and verification process of data preservation is extremely important in order to maintain the integrity of digital evidence. Hash values will continue to be used as a means for verifying the authenticity of an imaged drive. However, the data preservation process relies on the use of digital forensic tools, many of which are dual purposed in that they both image and hash hard drives (e.g. EnCase, FTK). Therefore, data preservation and evidence integrity relies heavily on the validity and reliability of digital forensic tools.

Digital forensic imaging tools

During the *pre-forensics* era of the early 1980s, few forensic tools were available. In fact, only government agencies were developing computer forensic tools at this time, and these tools were not made available to other law enforcement agencies or industry (see Chapter 10). In addition, the courts were concerned with the accuracy of the computer forensics tools. During the 1980s, there were few law enforcement officers "trained" in computer forensics (i.e. most were self-declared experts), and the forensic tools that were available were expensive, making the collection and examination of computer evidence either inaccessible or unaffordable for most law enforcement agencies. However, by the early 2000s, the forensic industry began to develop tools that allowed for the examination of computer evidence. This surge in forensic tools became known as the Golden Age of digital forensics (Garfinkel, 2010).

During this Golden Age, it became even more important for law enforcement to verify that the digital forensic tools were producing reliable evidence in order to meet admissibility standards in a court of law (Garfinkel, 2010; National Research Council, 2009; see Chapter 12). In response, NIST, an agency of the United States Department of Commerce, launched the **Computer Forensic Tool Testing project (CFTT)**. According to NIST, there are approximately 150 different digital forensic tools currently being used by law enforcement worldwide (NIST, n.d.). The purpose of the CFTT project is to "provide unbiased, open, and objective means for manufacturers, law enforcement, and the legal community to assess the validity of tools used in computer forensics" (NIST, n.d.). In addition, these test results must be repeatable and reproducible, both of which are needed to assess "trueness and precision" (NIST, 2001: 4).

According to NIST (2001), **repeatability** is "where independent test results are obtained with the same method, on identical test items, in the same laboratory, by the same operator, using the same equipment within short intervals of time" (p. 4). In other words, the digital forensics tool replicates the *same* results when using the exact *same* methodology (i.e. exact duplicate of the testing process). On the other hand, **reproducibility** is "where test results are obtained with the same method on identical test items in different laboratories with different operators using different equipment" (NIST, 2001: 5). Thus, the digital forensic tool produces the same results even in a *different* testing environment. Both are necessary in order for the tool's results to be admissible as evidence in a court of law. With over 150 digital forensic tools available, it is important that law enforcement choose those tools which have been tested for repeatability and reproducibility by NIST as well as accepted by the court.

acquisition, examination of forensic evidence

There are a number of both *commercial* (e.g. EnCase, FTK, WinHex) and *open source* tools (see http://opensourceforensics.org) available for digital forensic investigations (see Chapter 10). However, without a doubt, the two most commonly used digital forensic tools are EnCase and FTK. The general acceptance of EnCase and FTK by the scientific community was even noted in the court case *United States* v. *Gaynor* (2008). In *United States* v. *Gaynor* (2008), the defendant was charged with possession and distribution of child pornography. The defendant requested that mirror copies of the seized computer hard drives be made available to his computer forensics examiner. The Adam Walsh Child Protection and Safety Act (2006; see Text Box 11.2), however, prohibited the defense from obtaining copies of the child pornography evidence, in order to limit distribution of said illicit materials, so long as the defense has an ample opportunity to examine the evidence at a government facility (*United States* v. *Gaynor*, 2008).

Text Box 11.2: The Adam Walsh Act

Excerpt from the Adam Walsh Act (2006) – Discovery in child pornography cases. The importance of protecting children from repeat exploitation in child pornography:

(A) The vast majority of child pornography prosecutions today involve images contained on computer hard drives, computer disks, and related media.
(B) Child pornography is not entitled to protection under the First Amendment and thus may be prohibited.
(C) The government has a compelling State interest in protecting children from those who sexually exploit them, and this interest extends to stamping out the vice of child pornography at all levels in the distribution chain.
(D) Every instance of viewing images of child pornography represents a renewed violation of the privacy of the victims and a repetition of their abuse.
(E) Child pornography constitutes prima facie contraband, and as such should not be distributed to, or copied by, child pornography defendants or their attorneys.
(F) It is imperative to prohibit the reproduction of child pornography in criminal cases so as to avoid repeated violation and abuse of victims, so long as the government makes reasonable accommodations for the inspection, viewing, and examination of such material for the purposes of mounting a criminal defense.

SEC. 504. PREVENTION OF DISTRIBUTION OF CHILD PORNOGRAPHY USED AS EVIDENCE IN PROSECUTIONS.
Section 3509 of title 18, United States Code, is amended by adding at the end the following: "PROHIBITION ON REPRODUCTION OF CHILD PORNOGRAPHY."

(1) In any criminal proceeding, any property or material that constitutes child pornography shall remain in the care, custody, and control of either the Government or the court.

(2) (A) Notwithstanding Rule 16 of the Federal Rules of Criminal Procedure, a court shall deny, in any criminal proceeding, any request by the defendant to copy, photograph, duplicate, or otherwise reproduce any property or material that constitutes child pornography, so long as the Government makes the property or material reasonably available to the defendant.

(B) For the purposes of subparagraph (A), property or material shall be deemed to be reasonably available to the defendant if the Government provides ample opportunity for inspection, viewing, and examination at a Government facility of the property or material by the defendant, his or her attorney, and any individual the defendant may seek to qualify to furnish expert testimony at trial.

The defendant argued that the Adam Walsh Act violated his "right to adequately prepare his defense, his right to effective assistance of counsel, and his right to a fair trial" (*United States* v. *Gaynor*, 2008). The court ruled against Gaynor citing that the government had offered to provide a computer that met the minimum system requirements to run both FTK® and EnCase®. The court cited that EnCase and FTK are the most commonly used digital forensic tools (*United States* v. *Gaynor*, 2008; Leehealey, Lee and Fountain, 2012).

EnCase®

EnCase® is a digital forensics tool created by Guidance Software in 1997 (Ambhire and Meshram, 2012). Guidance Software is considered a world leader in digital forensics, with clients including government agencies (e.g. United States Department of Justice), law enforcement (e.g. Korean National Police, London Metropolitan Police), and industry (e.g. Microsoft, Boeing; Guidance Software, n.d.). According to Guidance Software's website, more than 65 percent of Fortune 100 and 40 percent of Fortune 500 companies (i.e. the largest US companies ranked on gross revenue by *Fortune* magazine) use EnCase for their digital forensic investigations (Guidance Software, n.d.).

Encase is capable of acquiring data from a variety of digital devices, including smartphones, hard drives, and removable media (e.g. thumb drives). This automated tool can image the drive, without altering its contents, and then verify that the image is an exact copy of the original drive. EnCase is capable of searching the unallocated space as well as locating hidden data

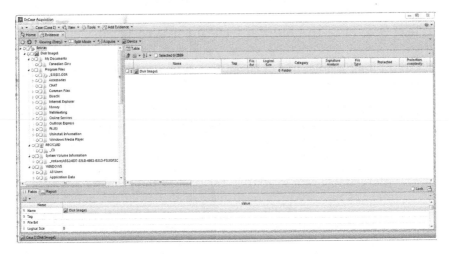

Image 11.2 Screenshot of EnCase created by Guidance Software

Screenshot courtesy of Eric Katz, Law Enforcement Coordinator and Instructor for Purdue University's Cyber Forensics Laboratory

and deleted files (Maras, 2012). As shown in Image 11.2, EnCase displays a user-friendly Windows interface (Garber, 2001).

In the United States, the first court case specifically addressing the validity of EnCase was *State (Ohio)* v. *Cook* (2002; Guidance Software, 2003). The defendant, Brian Cook, was found guilty of child pornography possession after his brother-in-law, Brian Brown, stumbled across a folder on Cook's computer that contained sexualized images of children. After notifying the Kettering Police Department, a search warrant was executed and the police seized several hard drives, diskettes, and computer peripheral devices from the Cook's residence (*State* v. *Cook*, 2002). According to court documents, a Detective Driscoll identified over 14,000 pornographic images from a forensic copy of Cook's hard drive that was created using the digital forensics tool, EnCase.

At trial, the defendant challenged the "admission of any materials connected with the mirror image on the basis that the state did not establish the reliability of the mirror image" (*State* v. *Cook*, 2002: 8). The Ohio appellate court upheld the validity of the EnCase software since Detective Driscoll was trained to use EnCase, and he described the process of imaging and verifying the duplicate copy. The Ohio appellate court stated, "there is no doubt that the mirror image was an authentic copy of what was present on the computer's hard drive" (*State* v. *Cook*, 2002: 9). International courts, including Singapore, Australia, and Canada, have also upheld the validity of digital evidence retrieved by EnCase (Guidance Software, 2003; see Text Box 11.3).

acquisition, examination of forensic evidence

Text Box 11.3: The murder trial of Ler Wee Teang

Excerpt from: Murder trial of Public Prosecutor v. Anthony Ler Wee Teang (Singapore)

Retrieved from Attorney-General's Chambers Annual Report 2001–2002
https://app.agc.gov.sg/DATA/0/docs/Who%20We%20Are/AGC_Annual_
Report_2001-2002.pdf

> The trial of *PP v Anthony Ler Wee Teang* was perhaps the most unforgettable case in 2001 ... Ler claimed the evidence retrieved from EnCase, which included deleted files from the defendant's computer, was unreliable ... [but] the Court of Appeal in Singapore cited that the evidence retrieved by EnCase was forensically sound.

EnCase has been involved in a number of high-profile cases. In 2002, San Diego computer forensic examiners uncovered child pornography after examining 50-year-old David Westerfield's computer and removable media files using EnCase (McKay, 2002). The child pornography evidence was presented as a possible motive during the trial (Congressional Record, 2005), and in 2003 David Westerfield was sentenced to death for the murder and kidnapping of 7-year-old Danielle Van Dam. In the Richard Reid case, also known as the "Shoe Bomber," EnCase uncovered a farewell email that was sent from the Al-Qaeda Shoe Bomber to his mother two days before he attempted to blow up United Airlines Flight 63, which was carrying 197 passengers and crew, departing from Paris to Miami (McKay, 2002; Shannon, 2002).

> For more information on how EnCase was used in the Shoe Bomber case, go online to: http://content.time.com/time/nation/article/0,8599,249418,00.html

Forensic Toolkit® (FTK®)

Forensic Toolkit® (FTK®) is another commercial software application commonly used in digital forensic investigations, and was created by AccessData. AccessData was founded in 1987 and is considered a pioneer in digital forensics and cybersecurity (AccessData, n.d.a). Currently, there are more than 130,000 FTK users in law enforcement, government, and industry worldwide (AccessData, n.d.a). For example, FTK is the standard computer forensics tool used by the United States Federal Bureau of Investigation (FBI) and the United Kingdom's Royal Military Police Cyber Crime Centre of the British Army (Leehealey *et al.*, 2012; AccessData, 2013). Like other

acquisition, examination of forensic evidence

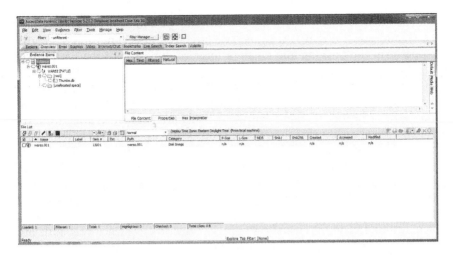

Image 11.3 Screenshot of Forensic Toolkit (FTK) created by AccessData
Screenshot courtesy of Eric Katz, Law Enforcement Coordinator and Instructor for Purdue University's Cyber Forensics Laboratory

digital forensic software, FTK is capable of imaging a hard drive, scanning slack space, and identifying steganography; however, it is also capable of cracking passwords and decrypting files (Maras, 2012).

In its current version, FTK 5 has new capabilities, including a data visualization tool that creates a timeline and visual depiction of the social interactions (e.g. emails) of the person under investigation (AccessData, n.d.b; see Image 11.3). In addition, FTK 5 includes Explicit Image Detection (EID) which sorts through the images on a digital device and flags the ones that are more likely to be child pornography by using algorithms that search for flesh tones, certain shapes, and orientations (AccessData, n.d.b). This feature speeds up the investigation process by allowing computer forensic examiners to identify illicit images more quickly. For example, a one terabyte (1TB) external hard drive is capable of holding up to a million high-quality photos (the exact number depends on the camera's specifications), which is a lot of images to search through during a digital forensic investigation.

The first court case to establish the validity of Forensic Toolkit was the civil lawsuit *Gutman* v. *Klein* (2008). During a five-year discovery period, the judge ordered the defendant, Zalman Klein, to assist the opposing counsel with locating all of his personal computers. According to court documents, prior to the date that he was to surrender all of his computers to the opposing counsel's computer forensic examiner, Klein attempted to alter and destroy digital evidence on his laptop. Klein finally turned over his computer to the plaintiff's computer forensic expert, Douglas Vitale, who noticed that the laptop was "hot to touch and a screw was missing from the hard drive enclosure" (*Gutman* v. *Klein*, 2008). Vitale forensically imaged the defendant's computer, using the current version of FTK at that time (2.2), and testified that it was an "accepted tool under industry standards to perform the imaging and create a forensic duplicate of the hard drive" (Leehealey *et al.*, 2012: 10).

The forensic analysis revealed a number of large-scale modifications to the Klein laptop, including deleted files and altered time/date stamps. In addition, the browser history revealed that the defendant downloaded a file from the Internet that was meant to overwrite space and erase data. However, during the forensic examination, Vitale's computer battery malfunctioned and saved the imaged hard drive as occurring on January 1, 2000 instead of the actual date, December 8, 2005. In *Gutman v. Klein* (2008), the defense argued that the inconsistent date suggested that the examiner had failed to authenticate the evidence; however, the court ruled that since the hashes used by FTK matched and chain of custody was maintained, the evidence was authentic despite the inconsistent dates (Leehealey *et al.*, 2012). Since the defendant destroyed and altered evidence, the judge recommended a default judgment, which is an automatic ruling in favour of the plaintiff (*Gutman* v. *Klein*, 2008).

For more on this case, go online to: www.kramerlevin.com

EnCase and FTK are both examples of digital forensic imaging tools, meaning the tools are designed to make an exact copy of the entire hard drive (bit for bit) so the investigator can examine the duplicate rather than the original evidence. To ensure reliability, NIST established specific criteria, as recommendations, for imaging tools used in digital investigations:

1) the tool shall make a bit-stream duplicate or an image of an original disk or partition,
2) the tool shall not alter the original disk,
3) the tool shall be able to verify the integrity of a disk image file,
4) the tool shall log I/O errors, *and*
5) the tool's documentation shall be correct

(NIST, 2001: 4; see Lyle, 2003).

In general, the digital imaging tool must be able to make an *exact copy* (without altering the original) and *verify* that the duplicate and original copy are exactly the same (e.g. compare hash values). Although not required, NIST recommends that two duplicate copies be made so that one is left undisturbed while the other is considered a "working copy" which is examined during the digital forensic investigation.

However, sometimes the hash values for the duplicate and original copy will not match, which is why it is important for the tool to keep an I/O error log. *I/O errors* mean input/output errors, and these errors are often

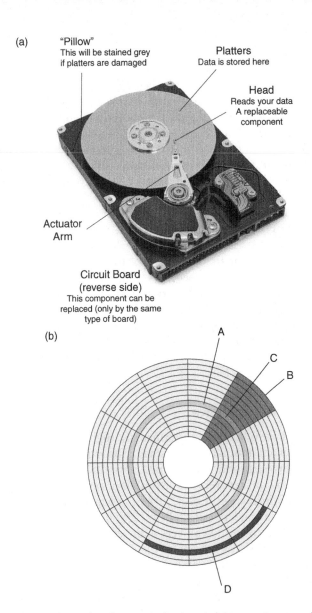

Images 11.4a and 11.4b Diagram of a hard drive, sectors, and clusters
The hard disk platter is divided into sectors, which is where the data is stored. The data can be read on good sectors (010101), but the data on a bad sector cannot be read.

http://commons.wikimedia.org/wiki/File:Open_hard-drive.jpg

http://commons.wikimedia.org/wiki/File:Disk-structure.svg

A) Data is stored on circular *tracks*
B) A disk is divided into pie-shaped *sectors*
C) A sector of a track
D) The part of a track that contains two or more adjacent sectors form a *cluster*

acquisition, examination of forensic evidence   363

the result of a bad sector on the hard drive. A **sector** is the smallest physical storage unit on a computer disk drive and is almost always 512 bytes (Marcella and Menendez, 2008). Data files are assigned to the different sectors by the file system. **File systems** are simply the way in which data is organized and retrieved on a computer drive, and each piece of data is called a **file** (Bunting, 2008). So, if there is a damaged sector, then the imaging tool will not be able to read the data stored in that sector. If the imaging tool is unable to read the sector, then it is not possible to copy bit for bit all of the information on the hard drive (see Image 11.4). Therefore, bad sectors will result in mismatching hash values.

However, if the imaging tool maintains an error log identifying the bad sectors, it will be possible for the examiner to verify that the original and duplicate copy are in fact the same despite the mismatching hash values. Finally, it is important for the imaging tool to document the examination process (e.g. time, action performed). Overall, both EnCase and FTK meet the NIST requirements for imaging tools and both have undergone scrutiny in a court of law. However, digital forensics tools are not infallible, so the examiner should always proceed with caution and verify any spurious results. For example, it may be necessary for one digital forensics examiner to repeat the analyses of another examiner in order to verify the findings independently (Casey, 2011).

Uncovering digital evidence

Once the digital drive is imaged and verified, the digital forensic investigation moves into the **examination/analysis stage**. The examination phase of the digital forensic investigation is concerned with the recovery or extraction of digital data. **Data recovery** or **extraction** refers to the process of salvaging digital information (Casey, 2011). In general, there are two types of extraction: logical and physical (Britz, 2009; NIJ, 2004). The **physical extraction** phase identifies and recovers data across the entire physical drive regardless of the file systems present on the drive (NIJ, 2004). As mentioned previously, **file systems** are the way in which data is stored and retrieved on a computer drive, and each piece of data is called a **file** (Bunting, 2008). In other words, the file system dictates how the computer manages and keeps track of the name and location of every file on a computer (Maras, 2012). For example, FAT and NTFS are the file systems used by certain Microsoft Windows operating systems (e.g. Windows 98, Windows XP). Overall, a physical extraction pulls all of the digital data from a computer hard drive but does not take into account how the data was stored on the drive. On the other hand, **logical extraction** refers to the process of identifying and recovering data based on the file systems present on the computer hard drive (NIJ, 2004). Each extraction phase involves different methods for acquiring potential digital evidence.

Image 11.5 Keyword searching through forensic software

Example of keyword search for the last name "Bennett" using the digital forensics software WinHex

Screenshot courtesy of Lt Dennis McMillian, the University of Alabama Police Department

Physical extraction

According to the NIJ (2004), there are three methods of physical extraction: keyword searching, file carving, and extraction of the partition table and unused space on the physical drive. When performing a **keyword search,** the digital forensic examiner is able to look for a word or series of words (i.e. phrase) in the entire physical drive regardless of the file systems. For example, the examiner may be able to search for a specific name (e.g. "Donna Smith") to determine if there is any evidence that the suspect contacted this person. In addition, the digital forensics examiner can conduct a **nested search,** which is a "search within a search" (see Brown, 2003). In this case, once all of the data that contains the name "Donna Smith" is located, the examiner can conduct an additional keyword search (e.g. "murder for hire") within that data, which further narrows the results. There are several digital forensics tools and software packages available on

acquisition, examination of forensic evidence   365

Hex Signature	File Extension	Description
FF D8 FF	jpg, jpeg	JPEG
4D 5A	exe	DOS executable file format
25 50 44 46	pdf	PDF document
52 49 46 46 nn nn nn nn 57 41 56 45	wav	Waveform Audio File Format
D0 CF 11 E0	doc	Microsoft Office documents

Figure 11.1 Common file signatures

the market for conducting a keyword search (e.g. Sleuth Kit, Autopsy, FTK; Mishra, 2007; see Image 11.5).

File carving is another physical extraction method for data recovery (NIJ, 2004). According to Casey (2011), **file carving** is the "process of searching for a certain file signature and attempting to extract the associated data" without regard for the file systems (p. 445). Essentially, this means extracting pieces of information from a larger dataset without taking into consideration how the files were stored on the computer. File carving is a great method for recovering files when the file allocation table is corrupt or a file has been deleted, because in both cases, there will no longer be an entry in the directory for that file's location (Beek, 2011). Instead of relying on the file system to locate the file, the forensic examiner searches for fragments of the file according to its file signature. A **file signature** is used to identify the content of a file, which in this case describes common file headers. File signatures can be used to locate and salvage deleted files (Casey, 2011). A **header** is the first few bytes that mark the beginning of a file, whereas the **footer**, also known as the **trailer**, is the last few bytes that mark the end of the file. All files, whether they are Word documents or JPEGs, contain a header and usually a footer (see Sammes and Jenkinson, 2000). Figure 11.1 contains a list of common file signatures, also known as **magic numbers**, which can vary greatly in value and length.

> **For more information on common file signatures, go online to:** www. garykessler.net/library/file_sigs.html

In the file carving process, the digital forensics examiner will first identify a particular header of interest (e.g. FF D8 FF E0) then locate the footer (e.g. 00 3B) in order to extract the information in between. By extracting the information in the middle, you are *carving* out a block of data (i.e. a file) from a larger set of raw data. In the example shown in Image 11.6, the examiner was using the forensics software tool WinHex to search for JPEG headers.

acquisition, examination of forensic evidence

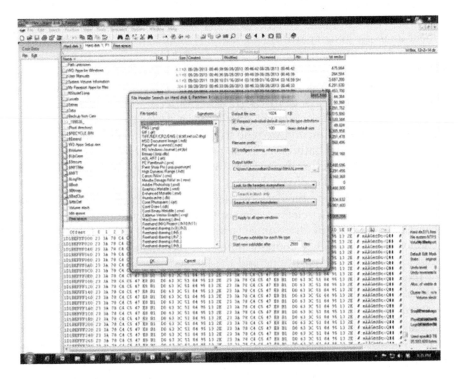

Image 11.6 File carving

Example of file carving using a file header search for "JPEG" with the digital forensics software WinHex

Screenshot courtesy of Lt Dennis McMillian, the University of Alabama Police Department

Common digital forensics tools that are capable of file carving include EnCase, FTK, Scalpel, and Foremost (Shaw, 2013).

The last method of physical extraction is known as **partition recovery**, which is the process of evaluating the partition table and the unused space on the physical drive (NIJ, 2004). Evaluating the partition tables is considered a physical extraction method because all partition tables conform to a standard layout regardless of the operating system. First, when a hard drive is installed in a computer, you must partition the drive before you can use it. As discussed in Chapter 10, a **hard drive** is simply a data storage device for storing and retrieving data. However, before you can begin to store information on a hard drive, you must organize the drive into **partitions**, which act similar to storage bins in the real world. Partitioning determines how much space is allocated to each storage bin, or partition. Thus, the process of dividing up the hard drive into separate storage spaces, known as partitions, is referred to as **partitioning** (Marcella and Guillossou, 2012).

acquisition, examination of forensic evidence

The process of partitioning may be explained by using a house or apartment analogy. Your apartment or house is similar to a hard drive in that there is a certain amount of space that is available for storage. In your house or apartment, you can divide up the square footage to create separate rooms that vary in size – you are essentially *partitioning* your house. Now, these separate rooms can then be made to "store" different things, so they act like *partitions*. For example, a house usually has a designated room/space for a kitchen and bathroom, and we tend to store cooking utensils in the kitchen and toiletries in the bathroom. Thus, partitioning is really just the process of creating individual or designated storage space (i.e. partitions) within a larger storage unit (i.e. physical drive).

At the beginning of the data on each disk is a partition table. The **partition table** acts as a reference description for how the operating system has divided the hard drive into partitions (Casey, 2011; Marcella and Guillossou, 2012). They contain important information, such as the sizes and locations of the partitions and the file systems operating within each of these partitions on the hard drive. These partition tables can reveal to a digital forensics examiner whether or not space on the hard drive is hidden or contains leftover data from prior partitioning. For example, **free space** is that portion of the hard drive that has yet to be assigned to a partition (Mandia and Prosise, 2003). Therefore, partitions contain both *allocated* space (i.e. written to) and **unallocated space** (i.e. not written to) on a hard drive, and any non-partitioned space on the hard drive is free space. Many of the digital forensics software tools available today automatically identity partitions, which simplifies the partition recovery process for investigators (e.g. EnCase, FTK, NTFS Recovery, Partition Table Doctor).

> **For more information, go online to:** www.symantec.com/connect/
> articles/maintaining-system-integrity-during-forensics

Logical extraction

As discussed previously, logical extraction refers to the process of identifying and recovering data based on the file systems present on the computer hard drive (NIJ, 2004). Unlike the physical extraction method, logical extraction takes into consideration the operating system (e.g. Windows XP) and file systems (e.g. NTFS) installed on the drive. During logical extraction, data may be retrieved from a variety of sources, such as active files, deleted files, file slack, and unallocated file space (NIJ, 2004). In addition, logical extraction may recover digital evidence from hidden files, password-protected files, encrypted files, and steganography.

Active files are existing files that are currently available on a hard drive, meaning they have not been deleted. On the other hand, a **deleted file** is a file whose entry has been removed from the computer's file system (e.g. FAT) so that this space is now marked as usable again. As we recall from Image 11.4, a **sector** is the smallest physical storage unit on a computer disk drive, and a **cluster** is two or more consecutive sectors. It is the job of the computer's file system to allocate space (i.e. sectors) to store information (see Text Box 11.4).

Text Box 11.4: Example of partition recovery (created by the authors)

Ryan Jaye is a child pornography user who stores all of his images and videos on his computer hard drive. In an attempt to conceal his crimes, Ryan Jaye created two partitions on his 80 GB hard drive so that his day-to-day non-criminal activity would be separate from his child pornography activity. The hard drive was partitioned so that 60 GB were dedicated to non-criminal activities whereas 20 GB were dedicated to his child pornography collection. Unfortunately for Ryan, law enforcement was well aware of his criminal activity. When Ryan Jaye became suspicious that he had been discovered, he decided to delete the second partition that contained all of the child pornography. By deleting the second partition, this space was no longer accounted for by the partition table, and Ryan believed that he had concealed his crimes.

With an authorized warrant in hand, law enforcement seized Ryan Jaye's computer in order to conduct a digital forensic investigation. The digital forensics investigator, Chat Stellar, examined the imaged hard drive using digital forensics software to identity the partition table. However, the partition table revealed only one partition (60 GB), leaving 20 GB of the hard drive unaccounted for. Luckily for law enforcement, when a partition is deleted, the data within that partition remains until it is overwritten. Therefore, since Chat Stellar was able to identity space on the hard drive which was unaccounted for, it is likely that further forensic analysis would be able to recover the deleted partition.

Overall, understanding how a partition table can reveal information about the layout of a suspect's hard drive is extremely important as a physical extraction method for uncovering digital evidence.

The space allocated to these clusters is fixed in length depending on the operating system, but the files saved to these clusters rarely equal the same size of the allocated space. Consider a file that is 800 bytes in size. As previously discussed, a sector usually stores 512 bytes of data. So, we would need two sectors in order to store an 800 byte file. If two consecutive sectors are not available, then the file system must allocate the data to another sector on the drive. A file that is stored in nonconsecutive sectors is considered to be **fragmented** (Marcella and Menendez, 2008). As with the example, the 800 byte file is smaller than the two sectors allocated to store its data (512 bytes + 512 bytes = 1024 bytes). Therefore, this leftover space between the end of the file and the end of the last storage unit for that file is known as **file slack** or **slack space** (Scientific Working Groups on Digital Evidence and Imaging Technology, 2011). In other words, file slack or slack space is the leftover area not used between the current allocated file and the end of the last cluster in which the file is stored. Therefore, our current example would have 224 bytes of slack space.

We also discussed how the file systems dictate how the computer manages and keeps track of the name and location of every file on a disk. For example, **FAT32 (File Allocation Table)** is the type of file system used in older versions of Windows operating systems (e.g. Windows 98, Windows ME), whereas **NTFS (New Technology File System)** is the later file system for the Windows NT operating systems (e.g. Windows NT 3.1, Windows XP; Marcella and Menendez, 2008). FAT32 identifies where on the hard drive a particular file is stored, that is to say, which clusters have been allocated to that file. Compared to the older versions (e.g. FAT12, FAT16), FAT32 manages the space on a hard drive more efficiently by using smaller cluster sizes, which reduces slack space (Britz, 2009). In contrast, NTFS offers better security since it can restrict access to specific partitions or files on a hard drive, making it more difficult to recover files (Marcella and Menendez, 2008). However, NTFS creates a **Master File Table (MFT)**, which contains information about all of the files and folders on a drive. The MFT can provide valuable information to a forensic examiner, including file type, size, and the data/time of creation and modification (see Carrier, 2005).

To better understand sectors, clusters, and file slack, consider the two-car garage analogy. A two-car garage can be considered a cluster that is made up of two separate garages (sectors). In this two-car garage, we can fit different models of vehicle, all of which vary in size. In fact, we can choose to store one or two larger vehicles or several smaller vehicles, such as motorcycles or dirt bikes. However, the space allocated to the two-car garage remains the same; the only thing that changes is what is being stored in the garage. So, if we can only afford to buy one car, then we will have leftover space in the two-car garage – this leftover space is the "file slack" or "slack space" for our two-car garage analogy.

Intuitively, it makes sense why a digital forensics examiner would be interested in the active files and deleted files on a hard drive. However, you might be wondering why a digital forensic examiner would be interested in this *leftover* space on a hard drive? Well, the file slack can be a rich source of information because this leftover space does not remain *unused*. In fact, the computer's operating system wants to use all available space in a cluster, so it will either write random bits of data (known as padding) or store whatever bits of old data remain in the unused sectors. In general, file slack can be broken down into either RAM slack or drive slack (Barrios and Signori, 2010).

If there is unused space between the end of the last file and the end of the sector, then the operating system will store bits of information from its **Random Access Memory (RAM)**. The RAM is considered "working memory" because it stores that part of the data that is currently being used by the computer. In addition, RAM is considered **volatile** in nature, meaning the data disappears when the computer is powered off (Maras, 2012; see Text Box 11.5). When randomly selected data from RAM is stored in the file slack, it is known as **RAM slack** (Barrios and Signori, 2010). In contrast to RAM, RAM slack is not volatile since these random bits of data are written to the hard drive. Therefore, it is possible for RAM slack to contain important information, such as network login names and passwords.

Text Box 11.5: Data sectors

In this example, the cluster contains four sectors. Each sector is able to hold 512 bytes of data. So, if the file system assigns a data file that is larger than 512 bytes of data, the file will be stored in the consecutive sectors.

Cluster			
Sector 1 (512 bytes)	Sector 2 (512 bytes)	Sector 3 (512 bytes)	Sector 4 (512 bytes)

If there is any unused space between the start of the next sector and the end of the cluster, then the operating system uses this space as **drive slack** by storing old information that was once available on the storage device (Barrios and Signori, 2010). In other words, the operating system does not write any new information to that space, so instead, old information that was once stored there will remain until those sectors are filled with new file data. For example, the drive slack could contain fragments of deleted word processing documents or old emails. Overall, file slack is a gold mine of information in digital forensics because it contains either randomly dumped information from the computer's memory (i.e. RAM slack) or remnants of previously deleted files (i.e. drive slack; see Text Box 11.6).

Text Box 11.6: Slack space

As shown in this example, a data file was stored in Sector 1 and in part of Sector 2. The unused space from the end of the data file to the end of the cluster is known as slack space or file slack. There are two types of slack space: RAM slack and drive slack. The remaining space between the end of the data file and the end of Sector 2 is called RAM slack, and from the beginning of the next sector to the end of the last sector is known as drive slack (see Barrios and Signori, 2010).

Cluster

Slack Space

		RAM Slack	Drive Slack	Drive Slack
Data File				

| Sector 1 | Sector 2 | Sector 3 | Sector 4 |

Data may also be retrieved from unallocated space in the partitioned hard drive during a logical extraction. **Unallocated space** is the unused portion of the hard drive that the operating system can write to (Casey, 2011; Mandia and Prosise, 2003), and may best be thought of as unallocated clusters (Mallery, 2007). Essentially, unallocated space is that part of the hard drive that is not currently storing any files, but unallocated space is not empty per se. Instead, when a file is deleted, the entry in the file system that used to reference the now deleted file is removed so that the operating system is aware that this space is now unallocated. During this process though, the actual file is not deleted, just the entry in the file system. The "deleted" file, or parts of it, will remain in the unallocated space until it is completely written over by a new file. Therefore, it may be possible to extract information from deleted files that have yet to be overwritten in the unallocated space of a hard drive (Mallery, 2007). There are several forensic tools available for logical extraction of the unallocated space of a hard drive, such as WinHex, EnCase, FTK, and DataLifter.

For more information, go online to: www.sans.org/reading-room/whitepapers/incident/secure-file-deletion-fact-fiction-631

acquisition, examination of forensic evidence

Logical extraction may also recover digital evidence from hidden files, password-protected files, encrypted files, and steganography. **Hidden files** are files that have been manipulated in such a way as to conceal the contents of the original file (Britz, 2009). For example, an individual attempting to hide a file might try to alter the file extension. **File extensions** are that part of the file's name that tells the operating system what program to use when you want to open it (Savage and Vogel, 2009). Common file extensions are .doc (Microsoft Word documents), .pdf (Adobe portable document format), and .mp3 (MP3 audio file). Therefore, one easy way to conceal or hide a file is to change the file extension so that the operating system will use the wrong program to open the file, resulting in an error. So, if you want to conceal a Microsoft Word document (.doc), then you could alter the file extension to .mp3 (MP3 audio file). Now, if someone double-clicks on the file to open it, the operating system will fail to open the file because it treated it as an audio file rather than a Word document. However, as you may recall, files also contain a file header or signature that is placed at the beginning of the file, which identifies the file type to the operating system. So, luckily for digital forensic examiners, these file headers can be identified and compared to the file extensions using basic digital forensics tools. Any files that have mismatched headers and extensions are then flagged for further analysis.

According to Casey (2011), two of the greatest obstacles for digital forensics examiners are password-protected and encrypted files. **Password-protected files** are locked files that require a password to gain access, which prevents other people from opening or modifying these files (Britz, 2009). For password-protected files, digital forensics examiners use specialized cracking dictionaries and software in order to circumvent the protection, such as AccessData's Distributed Network Attack (DNA) and Password Recovery Toolkit (PRTK; Casey 2011; Wiles, 2007). However, it is a time-consuming process to crack passwords.

Similar to password-protected files are encrypted files in that both are concerned with privacy. **Encryption** is the process of transforming information (plaintext) so that it is no longer legible (ciphertext) by using a mathematical algorithm (Casey, 2011; Kessler, 2000; Sammons, 2012). In other words, **plaintext** (i.e. the legible message) is transformed into **ciphertext** (an illegible message) by using a **cipher,** which is a mathematical formula (algorithm) that uses a set of rules for transforming the message (Kessler, 2000). Most encryption programs require an **access key,** which is essentially a password that unlocks the file so that the same algorithm that encrypted the information is now used to decrypt it (see Text Box 11.7). In other words, by entering the access key, the same algorithm used to encrypt the illegible message (ciphertext) now decrypts it back into the original legible message (plaintext). Using encryption is not uncommon; in fact, it is commonly used by businesses (e.g. banks) and government agencies (e.g. NSA), both of which have vested interests in protecting privacy. The strength of encryption programs varies, and sometimes digital forensics examiners can use specialized programs to break encryption. However, there are encryption programs that have proven resilient and remain unbreakable, leading some countries to consider whether a suspect can be compelled by a court of law to provide the encryption key (see Chapter 12).

Text Box 11.7: An example of encryption

The plaintext message (original) states, "Hello! Pretty Good Privacy (PGP) is the most widely used non-proprietary email encryption program." However, once the plaintext message is encrypted, it is illegible (ciphertext). Notice the subject line is not encrypted. In order to decrypt the message, you will need to enter the access key to unlock the decryption.

(a)

(b)

----BEGIN PGP MESSAGE----
Version: GnuPG/MacGPG2 v2.0.17 (Darwin)

hQEMA08wFQpWGKaXAQf/Soe2pdhb0oeTvhsP4tw9SFZSPJ/BmzQXgKNKBNCKU5Y7
KZsv9zJwWp2qjr/YwMTlwOIEZlmQB4SU1+qf7FVEhr8P8ktUPaZb8/6QdJBytd35
5IUHGkVzt4tx2rarxPOq1Uy6OTCr0oeY4jLMb4sU/0KdOnGZNtLtfuszYD5jqhQ+
ilc1iQm70o6J1iu1u3zhSXJSZ+5b3cOwg47kFBUSOq2+1iEPdEMaaV05yzphiK2P
ZucQQNrlH5igqHPV/N1Z2gtJvRZScWGt3DSgqrMYi26JFfSHnMQpF8Cl+tgrtgVl
xNBgLVI1cJ//UbdBmjaF0yYChJccTUzK3/DYbhVZzYUBDANxpkhSlhF/GwElAMis
H9LzcxiZdGaswJO2VOlLLVCyoQnJ1UPTpbONMNzClrU1V6e398X44AGJR56mlV8P
XKtQYtht0Ade+0YBbqg0sf4p6vkyXkx+pD2bOKwv921qAr/68JDx9GOgt/9LbGWg
s4YBoWWfMzdBy3LeWUvuM8k8nuVdvKxTOGFdlDgyo8f72ElZ/vQ0uHMwS+IujEDB
bHu8WSvpmOk7StGjJnMStJ0VqN/Uau15L0BSAh6aCmH+ifQhJjJp53FKGLsXVxot
0fS1bE30x7OF+OdRjXw36JoeUpjv1b/C6ATmNdwN/LRZ34dESjrixkE9WBzfNsVk
dA6p0m5UOviBARZIlYvS6wEr+LlhY5qUtjEPYQ77LhTZgGLhRLWdQWvQrkz7fjcH
9lzU1ACLiPg4KxJa7Z5dZ6gHyCHkEtk+solMKlY7CSYJUUsLBjsbTp3BUQCjtFGR
STgo7cjJKIoZXjUiglUq0ld7zlcc0v7oudPQOgWP9+h+o1SRpBVR6ByG4ccdzpvY
H3dyQPIHLXP62JYQKCXy3oBk0rlUq6A/zivymVtTpcgA00vD853Swr4jGWJrvcqP
GuteRvO7ViT5bn73dV+WiYOKpquDXl2agA+pP/aYrOrlXAlil1MePb2wZal0OzUv
c8PLYrWLdMpFXbRP+FOA48hMl26oqiU7QqzAqa1AEQwaBdecNv2uCN9yjsAvF5gY
onvm8Fzuw3DPSxv18c3eVFhhyOBtaPRvM55uDPglxywyaHNoLdH+r0Zz+1Ph0lBU
YBlgzfs2miDEW7B8kTNtq2ghaGSbB5Qw/cJTwxKi/gO1Z9klt/lmjknagga0UlEo
hcMTuZ59B+HegXWFF8Hlkih+ByjF77Y6/llwo0pjzlxTsKwVlVvtznTslLw19gRU

----END PGP MESSAGE----

Finally, **steganography** is the practice of hiding information in such a way that others are not aware that a hidden message exists (Kessler, 2004). Steganography is different from encryption because the goal of steganography is *secrecy* rather than *privacy* (i.e. hidden data vs. illegible data). In other words, the purpose of steganography is to hide a secret message within a transport medium (e.g. image, video). This transport medium is known as a **carrier** (Kessler, 2004). The process of steganography involves replacing bits of useless or unused data in a file with bits of different, invisible data. Once the carrier medium has the secret message embedded it becomes the **steganography medium,** and only those individuals with the appropriate knowledge and software can reveal the secret message hidden within the carrier. There are a number of software programs available for creating steganography (see Johnson, n.d.), and there are even mobile phone apps available too.

acquisition, examination of forensic evidence   375

Steganography can be used to conceal a variety of criminal activities, such as stolen credit card information, child sex abuse images, or terrorist plots. For example, a child pornography user may covertly send child sex abuse images via email by embedding the illicit images within neutral images, such as images of a cat. In this example, the neutral image of the cat is the carrier, and once the child pornography image is embedded within the carrier, it becomes steganography. Luckily, there are a number of digital forensics tools available for detecting steganography, including ILook Investigator, Stegdetect, Xsteg, and Foundstone (see Richer, 2003).

For more on the use of steganography, go online to: www.washington-post.com/wp-dyn/content/article/2010/06/30/AR2010063003108_pf.html

Overall, uncovering digital evidence is a time-consuming process to ensure that all possible data is recovered using both physical and logical extraction methods. Not including active files, there is a mountain of data that can be extracted from the allocated, unallocated, and free space of a hard drive. Digital forensics examiners not only extract data from active files, but they recover data from deleted partitions, hidden files, encrypted files, and file slack. Now that the data has been recovered, the digital forensics examiner must be able to reconstruct the digital crime scene. The process of reconstructing the digital crime scene leads us to the analysis phase.

Data analysis

The analysis phase of the investigation refers to the interpretation and reconstruction the digital crime scene (Casey, 2011; NIJ, 2004); however, this process is not an easy task due to the large amounts of data uncovered during a digital forensic investigation. For example, consider a **1 terabyte (1 TB)** hard drive. A 1 TB hard drive is essentially one trillion bytes; as discussed in Chapter 10, a byte is a unit of digital information. Since a computer traditionally uses one byte of space to represent a single character (e.g. a single letter such as "a"), and if we assume a single word processing document holds 5,000 characters per page, then a 1 TB hard drive could hold 220 million pages of text (Baier, 2011/2012)! In addition, if we could print 20 sheets per minute, it would take approximately 21 years to print all of the documents on a 1 TB hard drive, and if we stacked up all of these printed pages, it would be over 13 miles tall (Baier, 2011/2012). Currently, a 1 TB hard drive costs less than $100, and companies are even manufacturing 1 TB USB flash drives as well as 6 TB hard drives. With so much data, one of the most important steps in the analysis phase of the digital forensic investigation is the filtering and reduction of evidence.

Data reduction and filtering

After recovering the data during the examination phase, the next step is data reduction and filtering which occurs during the analysis phase. By reducing the dataset, the digital forensics examiner only interprets those files relevant to the investigation. Filtering may involve removing duplicate files, searching for keywords, or grouping data based on file types (Casey, 2009). For example, a digital forensics examiner may search for and group together image file types (e.g. JPEG, GIF, BMP) when investigating a child pornography case. In addition, file hashes can be used to eliminate duplicate data (Pollitt and Whitledge, 2006). As discussed previously, a hash value is a number generated by an algorithm to substantiate the integrity of digital evidence (Scientific Working Groups on Digital Evidence and Imaging Technology, 2011). However, a hash value can also be used to identify unique or duplicate files. A hash value can be created for every file, and is a unique number similar to a digital fingerprint. If two files have the same hash value, then they are duplicates or exact copies of one another, which can be filtered out as nuisance data.

Hash values can also be compared to datasets that contain known hash values for specific files, such as illicit materials (e.g. child pornography), steganography, or proprietary software. For example, HashKeeper, Maresware, and the National Software Reference Library are datasets designed to exclude "known to be good" hash values (Kessler, 2004). Specifically, the **National Software Reference Library (NSRL)** is supported by the DHS and NIST (NSRL, n.d.). According to NSRL, a typical desktop computer may contain between 10,000 and 100,000 files, so by using a repository of known hash values, a forensic examiner can reduce the number of files that need to be manually examined. The process of filtering the dataset and removing non-user-created files (e.g. operating system, program files) is sometimes referred to as **de-NISTing**. The term de-NISTing comes from the fact that the known hash values for these noise files are maintained and published by NIST's NSRL (see Waxse, 2013). Overall, filtering the dataset for known hash values not only reduces the number of files that need to be examined but also increases the efficiency of the investigation (NSRL, n.d.).

The ultimate goal of data reduction and filtering is creating the smallest dataset with the highest potential of containing relevant digital evidence (Casey, 2011). However, the criteria for including and excluding data is extremely important otherwise potential digital evidence may be discarded or overlooked during the filtering process. The final result of the examination/analysis phase is a reconstruction of the digital crime scene, so any disregarded evidence could significantly impact the findings of an investigation.

Reporting of findings

The final stage in the digital forensic investigation is the report/presentation phase. In the **report/presentation stage**, the findings that are determined to be relevant to the investigation are finalized in a report. How evidence is determined to be relevant to an investigation will be discussed further in Chapter 12; however, it essentially refers to evidence that pertains directly to the facts of a case. Therefore, only relevant evidence should be included in the final report, rather than hypothetical or theoretical evidence (see Beebe and Clark, 2005). In addition, this report should reflect complete transparency, meaning each step described in detail so as to leave no mystery in the digital forensics process. Specifically, the digital forensic technicians should be prepared to testify in court regarding the survey/identification (e.g. chain of custody), collection/acquisition (preservation, forensic tools), and examination/analysis (data recovery and reduction) stages of the digital forensic investigation.

Along with transparency, the digital forensic examiner should remain objective when drawing conclusions from the digital evidence. According to the Association of Chief Police Officers of England, Wales, and Northern Ireland, "a digital forensic practitioner must be aware of their duty of impartiality and that they must communicate both the extent and the limitations of the digital forensic evidence" (Williams, 2012: 12). Thus, all conclusions made by the examiner should be supported by objective evidence to limit confirmation bias. **Confirmation bias** is the tendency to accept information that confirms our beliefs while rejecting information that contradicts those beliefs (Goodwin, 2009). That is to say, we are naturally drawn to information that matches our belief system and we tend to ignore conflicting information. So, if a digital forensics examiner believes that a suspect is guilty, prior to examining the evidence, it is plausible that potential evidence exonerating a suspect may be overlooked or evidence may be labeled as incriminating even when it is not.

> **For more information on issues of evidence, go online to:** www.huffing-tonpost.com/jeff-kukucka/forensic-evidence_b_3178848.html

Kassin, Dror, and Kukucka (2013) use the term **forensic confirmation bias** to "summarize the class of effects through which an individual's pre-existing beliefs, expectations, motives, and situational context influence the collection, perception, and interpretation of evidence during the course of a criminal case" (p. 45). The authors make a number of proposed reforms for reducing bias in the forensic laboratory and in the courtroom. For example, forensic examiners should not receive irrelevant information that may taint their evaluation of the evidence – a digital forensics examiner does not need to know that the suspect confessed to downloading Internet child pornography; the fact that the suspect confessed should have no bearing on whether evidence is present or absent on a hard drive. In addition, Kassin *et al.* (2013) recommend that an independent forensics examiner verify the

acquisition, examination of forensic evidence

findings of the initial examination. This independent forensic examiner should also be completely unaware, or **blind,** to the conclusions reached by the initial examiner. Finally, the authors conclude that any forensic science education or certification should include training in basic psychology and, more specifically, the influence of confirmation bias (Kassin *et al.*, 2013). Overall, the final report should reflect not only the integrity of the evidence but also the integrity of the forensic examiner.

Summary

We saw in the beginning of this chapter with the case of *Gates Rubber Company* v. *Bando Chemical Industry* (1996) the importance of data preservation. A small error, such as forgetting to use a write blocker or create a duplicate image, could result in a loss of potential evidence. In addition, the Casey Anthony case is a perfect example of how uncaptured data (e.g. Google search for "fool-proof suffocation" methods) may have influenced the outcome of the trial. Casey Anthony was charged with the murder of her daughter, Caylee Anthony; in a controversial verdict, she was acquitted of first-degree murder. After the trial, the Orange County Sheriff's department admitted to overlooking evidence of a Google search for "fool-proof suffocation" methods the day the daughter was last seen alive (see Associated Press, 2012). Thus, we may never know how this uncaptured digital evidence influenced the Casey Anthony trial. There are a number of mistakes that can be made during the perseveration and acquisition phases; however, we also need to be worried about objectivity and forensic confirmation bias. If the court questions the integrity of the examiner or the forensic laboratory, evidence may be deemed inadmissible in a court of law. The digital forensic investigation is constantly under scrutiny, and the validity of digital forensics is assessed by whether or not the evidence is admissible in a court of law.

Key terms

1 terabyte (1 TB)
Access key
Active files
Authentic
Blind
Bridges
Carrier
Cipher
Ciphertext

Cluster

Collision

Computer Forensic Tool Testing project (CFTT)

Confirmation bias

Data recovery

Deleted files

De-NISTing

Drive slack

EnCase®

Encryption

Examination/analysis stage

Extraction

File

File allocation table (FAT)

File carving

File extensions

File signature

File slack

File systems

Footer

Forensic confirmation bias

Forensic Toolkit® (FTK)

Forensically sound

Fragmented

Free space

Hard drive

Hash

Hash algorithm

Hashing

Header

Hidden files

Imaging

Keyword search

Logical extraction

Magic numbers

Master file table (MFT)

Message Digest Version 5 (MD5)

National Software Reference Library (NSRL)

acquisition, examination of forensic evidence

Nested search

New Technology File System (NTFS)

Partition recovery

Partition table

Partitions

Partitioning

Password-protected files

Physical extraction

Plaintext

Preservation

RAM slack

Random access memory (RAM)

Read-only

Repeatability

Report/presentation stage

Reproducibility

Sector

Secure Hash Algorithm (SHA)

Slack space

Steganography

Steganography medium

Trailer

Unallocated space

Verification

Volatile

Wiping

Write

Write blocker

Discussion questions

1) The data preservation stage of the collection/acquisition phase of the digital forensic process involves careful planning on the part of the examiner. Identify five ways in which the digital evidence can be tainted during the data preservation process.

2) A fellow classmate is confused about the following terms: slack space, clusters, and sectors. The book provided the analogy of a two-car garage to assist readers with these different terms. Create a different analogy to explain these different terms to your classmate.

3) It is extremely important that digital forensic examiners are able to verify the authenticity of the digital evidence. Explain whether the courts should be concerned with the use of hash algorithms for verifying the authenticity of digital evidence.

4) Provide two examples of how confirmation bias could influence the integrity of a case. What are some ways we can limit the influence of forensic confirmation bias?

References

AccessData. (n.d.a). *AccessData Group Overview*. Retrieved from http://www.accessdata.com/about/company

AccessData. (n.d.b) *What's new in FTK 5?* Retrieved from http://marketing.accessdata.com

AccessData. (2013). *Case study: Royal Military Police seeks out AccessData for digital forensics*. Retrieved from http://marketing.accessdata.com

Adam Walsh Child Protection and Safety Act. Pub. L. No. 109–248, *codified at* 42 U.S.C. §16911 *et seq.* (July 27, 2006).

Ambhire, V. R., & Meshram, B. B. (2012, March). Digital forensic tools. *IOSR Journal of Engineering*, 2(3), 392–398.

Associated Press. (2012, November 25). *Casey Anthony detectives overlooked Google search*. Retrieved March 19, 2014 from www.bigstory.ap.org

Baier, H. (2011/2012). *On the use of hash functions in computer forensics*. Retrieved from https://www.fbi.h-da.de

Barrios, R. M., & Signori, Y. (2010). RAM and File Systems Investigations. In J. Bayuk (ed.), *CyberForensics: Understanding Information Security Investigations* (pp. 103–116). New York, NY: Springer.

BBC News. (2013, July 30). *David Guy dismemberment: David Hilder guilty of manslaughter*. Retrieved from www.bbc.com/news

Beebe, N. L., & Clark, J. G. (2005, June). A hierarchical, objectives-based framework for the digital investigations process. *Digital Investigation*, 2(2), 147–167.

Beek, C. (2011). *Introduction to file carving*. Retrieved March 12, 2014 from www.mcafee.com

Biham, E., & Chen, R. (2004, August). New Results on SHA-0 and SHA-1. In V. Shoup (series ed.), *Lecture Notes of the Institute for Computer sciences, Advances in Cryptography – Crypto 2004* (pp. 290–305).

Bond, A. (2013, August 14). *DNA from a cat snares killer after its hair was found on victim's dismembered body*. Retrieved from www.dailymail.co.uk

Britz, M. T. (2009). *Computer Forensics and Cyber Crime*, 2nd ed. Upper Saddle River, NJ: Prentice Hall.

Brown, C. (2003). *The art of key word searching*. Technology Pathways. Retrieved from http://techpathways.com

Bunting, S. (2008). *EnCE – The Official EnCase Certified Examiner Study Guide*, 2nd ed. Indianapolis, IN: Wiley Publishing, Inc.

Carrier, B. (2005). *File System Forensic Analysis*. Boston: Addison-Wesley.

Casey, E. (2009). *Handbook of Digital Forensics and Investigation*. Burlington, MA: Elsevier Academic Press.

Casey, E. (2011). *Digital Evidence and Computer Crime: Forensic Science, Computers, and the Internet*, 3rd ed. Waltham, MA: Academic Press.

Congressional Record. (2005). *Proceedings and debates of the 109th Congress, September 8 to September 22, 2005*, Vol. 151(Part 15), 19737–21176. Washington, DC: United States Government Printing Office.

Eastlake, D., & Jones, P. (2001, September). US Secure Hash Algorithm 1 (SHA1). IETF. Retrieved from http://tools.ietf.org

Falayleh, M. A., & Al-Karaki, J. N. (2013). *On the selection of write blockers for disk acquisition: A comparative practical study*. The Society of Digital Information and Wireless Communications (SDIWC). Retrieved from http://sdiwc.net

Forte, D. (2009, February). The death of MD5. *Network Security*, 2009(2), 18–20.

Garber, L. (2001, January). EnCase: A case study in computer-forensic technology. *IEEE Computer Magazine*.

Garfinkel, S. L. (2010). Digital forensics research: The next 10 years. *Digital Investigation*, 7, S64–S73.

Gates Rubber Company v. Bando Chemical Industry, Limited. 167 F.R.D. 90 (D.C. Col., 1996).

Goodwin, C. J. (2009). *Research in Psychology: Methods and Design*, 6th ed. New York, NY: John Wiley & Sons, Inc.

Guidance Software, Inc. (n.d.). *EnCase®: Digital Forensics*. Retrieved from www.guidancesoftware.com

Guidance Software, Inc. (2003, December). *EnCase® legal journal*. Retrieved from http://isis.poly.edu

Gutman v. Klein. US Dist. LEXIS 92398 (E.D.N.Y. Oct. 15, 2008).

ISO/IEC (2012). 27037: *Guidelines for identification, collection, acquisition, and preservation of digital evidence*. Retrieved from www.iso.org

Johnson, N. F. (n.d.). *Steganography software*. Retrieved from www.jjtc.com

Johnson, T. A. (2006). *Forensic Computer Crime Investigation*. Boca Raton, FL: CRC Press.

Kassin, S. M., Dror, I. E., & Kukucka, J. (2013, March). The forensic confirmation bias: Problems, perspectives, and proposed solutions. *Journal of Applied Research in Memory and Cognition*, 2(1), 42–52.

Kessler, G. C. (2000). An Overview of Cryptographic Methods. In J. P. Slone (ed.), *Local Area Network Handbook*, 6th edition (pp. 73–84). Boca Raton, FL: CRC Press LLC.

Kessler, G. C. (2004, July). An overview of steganography for the computer forensics examiner. *Forensic Science Communications*, 6(3).

Larence, E. R. (2011, March). *Combating Child Pornography: Steps are needed to ensure that tips to law enforcement are useful and forensic examinations are cost effective*. Darby, PA: DIANE Publishing.

Leehealey, T., Lee, E., & Fountain, W. (2012). *The rules of digital evidence and AccessData technology*. AccessData. Retrieved from https://www.accessdata.com

Liu, D. (2011). *Next Generation SSH2 Implementation: Securing Data in Motion*. Burlington, MA: Syngress.

Lyle, J. R. (2003, Winter). NIST CFTT: Testing disk imaging tools. *International Journal of Digital Evidence*, 1(4), 1–10.

Mallery, J. R. (2007). *Secure file deletion: Fact or fiction?* SANS *Institute.* Retrieved from www.sans.org

Mandia, K., & Prosise, C. (2003). *Incident Response and Computer Forensics,* 2nd ed. New York, NY: McGraw-Hill Osborne Media.

Maras, M. (2012). *Computer Forensics: Cybercriminals, Laws, and Evidence.* Sudbury, MA: Jones and Bartlett Learning.

Marcella, A. J., & Guillossou, F. (2012). *Cyber Forensics: From Data to Digital Evidence.* Hoboken, NJ: John Wiley & Sons, Inc.

Marcella, A. J., & Menendez, D. (2008). *Cyber Forensics: A Field Manual for Collecting, Examining, and Preserving Evidence of Computer Crime,* 2nd ed. Boca Raton, FL: Taylor & Francis Group, LLC.

McKay, J. (2002, August 13). *Encase helps finger murder suspect.* Retrieved from www.govtech.com/security

Mishra, S. (2007). *Keyword indexing and searching for large forensics targets using distributed computing.* Unpublished Master's thesis, University of New Orleans, New Orleans, LA.

Morris, J. (2010, November 2). *Maintaining system integrity during forensics.* Security Focus. Retrieved from www.securityfocus.com

National Institute of Justice. (2004, April). *Forensic Examination of Digital Evidence: A Guide for Law Enforcement.* Washington, DC: US Department of Justice.

National Institute of Standards and Technology. (n.d.). *Computer forensics tool testing program – Overview.* Retrieved from www.cftt.nist.gov/project_overview.htm

National Institute of Standards and Technology. (2001, November 7). *General test methodology for computer forensics tools.* US Department of Commerce.

National Institute of Standards and Technology. (2004, May 19). *Hardware Write Blocker Device (HWB) Specification* (Version 2.0). US Department of Commerce.

National Research Council. (2009, August). *Strengthening Forensic Science in the United States: A Path Forward.* Washington, DC: The National Academic Press.

National Software Reference Library (n.d.). *Introduction to the NSRL.* Retrieved from www.nsrl.nist.gov/

Polk, T., Chen, L., Turner, S., & Hoffman, P. (2011, March). *Security Considerations for the SHA-0 and SHA-1 Message-Digest Algorithms.* Internet Engineering Task Force (REF #6194). Retrieved from http://tools.ietf.org

Pollitt, M., & Whitledge, A. (2006). Exploring Big Haystacks: Data Mining and Knowledge Management. In M. Olivier & S. Shenoi (eds.), *Advances in Digital Forensics II* (pp. 67–76). Boston, MA: Springer.

Richer, P. (2003). *Steganalysis: Detecting hidden information with computer forensics analysis.* SANS Institute. Retrieved from www.sans.org/reading-room

Rivest, R. (1992). *The md5 message-digest algorithm.* IETF. Retrieved from www.ietf.org

Saferstein, R. (2010). *Criminalistics: An Introduction to Forensic Science,* 10th ed. Upper Saddle River, NJ: Prentice Hall.

Sammes, A., & Jenkinson, B. (2000). *Forensic Computing: A Practitioner's Guide.* Great Britain: Springer-Verlag London Limited.

Sammons, J. (2012). *The Basics of Digital Forensics: The Primer for Getting Started in Digital Forensics.* Waltham, MA: Syngress.

Savage, T. M., & Vogel, K. E. (2009). *Digital Multimedia*. Sudbury, MA: Jones and Bartlett Publishers.

Schmitt, V., & Jordaan, J. (2013, April). Establishing the validity of MD5 and SHA-1 hashing in digital forensic practice in light of recent research demonstrating cryptographic weaknesses in these algorithms. *International Journal of Computer Applications*, 68(23), 40–43.

Scientific Working Groups on Digital Evidence and Imaging Technology. (2011, January 14). *SWGDE/SWGIT Digital & Multimedia Evidence Glossary (Version 2.4)*. Retrieved from www.crime-scene-investigator.net/swgde_swgit_glossary_v2-4.pdf

Shannon, E. (2002, May 23). Did Richard Reid let mom know? *Time*. Retrieved from http://content.time.com/

Shaw, R. (2013, October 4). *File carving*. Infosec Institute. Retrieved from http://resources.infosecinstitute.com/file-carving/

State v. Cook. 149 Ohio App.3d 422, 2002-Ohio-4812.

Thompson, E. (2005). MD5 collisions and the impact on computer forensics. *Digital Investigation*, 2(1), 36–40.

United States v. Beatty. 437 Fed.Appx. 185 (3rd Cir. 2011 No. 10–3634).

United States v. Cartier, 543 F.3d 442, 446 (8th Cir. 2008).

United States v. Gaynor. WL 113653 (D.Conn., January 4, 2008).

Wang, Q. (2012, August). *Recommendation for applications using approved hash algorithms*. NIST Special Publication 800-107, Revision 1. Retrieved from www.cftt.nist.gov

Wang, Z., Yin, Y. L., & Yu, H. (2005, August). Finding Collisions in the Full SHA-1. In V. Shoup (series eds.). *Lecture Notes of the Institute for Computer sciences, Vol. 3621, Crypto 2005*, pp. 17–36.

Waxse, D. J. (2013). Advancing the goals of a "just, speedy, and inexpensive" determination of every action: The recent changes to the district of Kansas guidelines for cases involving electronically stored information. *Regent University Law Review*, 26, 111–142.

Wiles, J. (2007). *Techno Security's Guide to E-discovery and Digital Forensics*. Burlington, MA: Syngress Publishing, Inc.

Williams, J. (2012). *ACPO good practice guide for digital evidence*. Association of Chief Police Officers of England, Wales and Northern Ireland. Retrieved from www.acpo.police.uk

Xie, T., & Liu, F. (2013). *Fast collision attack on MD5*. International Association for Cryptologic Research. Retrieved from www.iacr.org

XPEL Technologies Corporation v. American Filter Film Distributors. WL 744837 (W.D. Tex. Mar. 17, 2008).

chapter 12

Legal challenges in digital forensic investigations

Introduction

In April 1991, Kevin Poulsen was arrested and charged with several computer hacking crimes, including telecommunications and computer fraud (*United States* v. *Poulsen*, 1994). Additional espionage charges for illegal possession of classified government secrets were filed after computer tapes were found in a storage locker rented by Poulsen. However, he claimed the computer tapes were illegally obtained, and therefore could not be used as evidence in the espionage case (*United States* v. *Poulsen*, 1994). According to court documents, Poulsen rented a storage locker from the Menlo-Atherton Storage Facility in April 1987. Poulsen was 71 days behind in rent and owed the company $155.50 for the storage locker. In January

1988, Menlo mailed a notice to Poulsen (who provided a false address and name on the rental agreement) stating that if the rent were not paid in full within 14 days, Menlo would terminate Poulsen's right to the storage unit. In February 1988, after not receiving rental payment in full, the manager of Menlo removed the contents of Poulsen's locker but noticed "a large amount of telecommunications equipment and manuals that apparently belonged to PacBell" (*United States* v. *Poulsen*, 1994, para 7). Since the manager of the storage facility believed the telecommunications equipment was stolen, he contacted the police department and gave the detectives permission to seize all of the contents of Poulsen's locker.

When PacBell investigators examined the computer tapes, they contained classified military secrets including "air tasking orders, which list targets that the United States Air Force will attack in the event of hostilities" (*United States* v. *Poulsen*, 1994, para 16). Poulsen filed a motion in 1993 to suppress the computer evidence retrieved from the storage unit. He claimed that seizing evidence from his storage locker violated his Fourth Amendment right to privacy and unlawful search and seizure. The US government argued that the "renter does not have a legitimate expectation of privacy in the contents of a rental unit if the rent is not paid" (*United States* v. *Poulsen*, 1994, paras 29–30).

In 1994, the Ninth Circuit Court for California ruled that the computer evidence tapes were admissible and Poulsen did not have an expectation of privacy regarding the contents of his storage locker. Specifically, the court agreed that Poulsen's expectation of privacy to the storage unit was terminated when he failed to pay the full amount of his rent as stated in the signed rental agreement (*United States* v. *Poulsen*, 1994). In 1996, Poulsen's espionage indictment was dropped, but he served five years in prison for the other crimes he committed. Kevin Poulsen is currently the investigations editor for *Wired*, an American magazine that reports on current and future trends in technology.

The court's ruling in the *United States* v. *Poulsen* (1994) case was important since the computer tapes were the sole evidence for the espionage charges. If this evidence were not admitted, then it would have substantially hindered the ability of the government to bring charges against Poulsen. As a result, the admissibility of digital evidence has the ability to significantly impact the outcome of a trial. By the end of this chapter, you will understand a variety of legal issues surrounding digital forensic evidence in the courtroom. We will begin this chapter by exploring two constitutional rights in the United States often challenged in cases involving digital forensic evidence: right to privacy (Fourth Amendment) and the right against self-incrimination (Fifth Amendment). Next, we will explore the standards for admissibility of digital evidence in criminal cases in the United States. In addition, there will be a brief discussion of some international responses (e.g. UK, Ireland, Canada, and the Philippines) to issues similar to those facing the United States, including key disclosure laws and assessing the reliability of expert witness testimony. Finally, we will conclude with a discussion of the admissibility and reliability standards for digital forensic examiners providing expert testimony in the courtroom.

Constitutional issues in digital investigations

The **United States Constitution** was adopted on September 17, 1787 (Levy, 2001), and is the highest form of law within the nation. It mandates that all state judges must follow federal law when a conflict arises between state and federal law. The first ten amendments of the US Constitution are known as the **Bill of Rights** and were ratified on December 15, 1791 (Levy, 2001). For an **amendment**, meaning an addition or alteration, to be made to the United States Constitution, two-thirds of the members from both the House of Representatives and the Senate must approve it and three-fourths of the states must ratify it.

With that in mind, the Fourth Amendment and Fifth Amendment are arguably the most influential to cases involving digital forensics, yet these amendments were written during a time without concern for the influence of digital technology on the law. As discussed in Chapter 10, almost every criminal investigation now involves some form of digital evidence. Therefore, the Constitution is constantly being reinterpreted and challenged in this Digital Age of technology. The following section will discuss the legal issues surrounding the Fourth Amendment and Fifth Amendment as they relate to cases involving digital evidence.

The Fourth Amendment

The **Fourth Amendment** is often summarized as the **right to privacy**; yet, there is no explicitly stated "right to privacy" in the United States Constitution or Bill of Rights (del Carmen, 2014). Instead, the Fourth Amendment limits the government's ability to search and seize evidence without a **warrant**. In other words, it prohibits unlawful search and seizure but only applies to law enforcement officers, and not private individuals so long as they are not acting as an agent of the government (James and Nordby, 2009). Overall, the Fourth Amendment may be viewed as a *narrow* rather than *general* right to privacy (see del Carmen, 2014). The amendment reads:

> The right of the people to be secure in their persons, houses, papers, and effects, against unreasonable searches and seizures, shall not be violated, and no Warrants shall issue, but upon probable cause, supported by Oath or affirmation, and particularly describing the place to be searched, and the persons or things to be seized.

Thus, the Fourth Amendment begins with a clause protecting your body, home, and other belongings from unlawful search and seizure by any government agency. It also indicates that probable cause is required in order to issue a warrant. However, the Fourth Amendment does not explicitly define what constitutes unlawful search and seizure, probable cause, or one's "effects" or belongings. For example, an estimated 375 million people used paid or free cloud storage services in 2012 (Lardinois, 2012). **Cloud storage** is like a virtual warehouse where people can store data on a network (e.g. Dropbox, iCloud, and Google Drive). So, is the data stored "in the cloud" (e.g. pictures stored in Dropbox) considered private and/or protected under the Fourth Amendment? These are the types of questions facing the courts, which must determine how to interpret and apply the Fourth Amendment in this Digital Age.

Privacy

Since the right to privacy is not overtly outlined in the Constitution, the courts were left to decide when privacy was protected under the Constitution. One of the most influential cases that defined one's right to privacy was *Katz v. United States* (1967). In 1965, Charles Katz was convicted of conducting illegal gambling operations across state lines. Agents from the FBI placed a warrantless wiretap on the public phone booth that Katz was using to conduct his gambling operations, which allowed them to listen only to Katz's conversations that related to the illegal gambling operations. Evidence from the warrantless wiretap was used to convict Katz of illegal gambling (see Image 12.1).

Katz appealed his conviction, arguing that the public telephone booth was a constitutionally protected area so the warrantless wiretap violated his Fourth Amendment right to unreasonable search and seizure (*Katz v. United States*, 1967). Therefore, any evidence obtained from the warrantless wiretap should be inadmissible in court. In contrast, the federal agents argued that the evidence was admissible since they did not need a warrant to wiretap a public telephone booth. In 1967, the United States Supreme Court ruled that the warrantless wiretap did violate Katz's Fourth Amendment right to unlawful search and seizure, so any evidence obtained because of the wiretap was inadmissible in court. Most importantly, the US Supreme Court ruled that Katz had a constitutionally protected reasonable expectation of privacy (*Katz v. United States*, 1967). As stated in the opinion:

> What [Katz] sought to exclude when he entered the booth ... was the uninvited ear. One who occupies [a telephone booth], shuts the door behind him, and pays the toll that permits him to place a call is surely entitled to assume that his conversation is not being intercepted.

In the concurring opinion, Justice Harlan outlined two criteria for when there is a **reasonable expectation of privacy**: the person must have exhibited an actual expectation of privacy, *and* the expectation must be one that

Image 12.1 A pay phone booth
An example of an old pay phone. Although this pay phone is "public,"
Katz v. *United States* (1967) ruled that a person who enters a phone
booth, and closes the door, has a reasonable expectation of privacy, so a
warrantless wiretap would violate the Fourth Amendment.

http://www.shutterstock.com/pic.mhtml?id=13525399&src=e709roJo
BBPLRODOiYV6IQ-1–29

Image courtesy of www.Shutterstock.com

society is prepared to recognize as reasonable (*Katz* v. *United States*, 1967).
In addition, the Fourth Amendment protects people and not places, so the
question was not if the public phone booth was constitutionally protected
but whether the person making the phone call had a reasonable expectation
of privacy (*Katz* v. *United States*, 1967). For example, if you are talking on
your cell phone while in a university classroom waiting for the beginning of
your class, you would not be protected by the Fourth Amendment because
it would be *unreasonable* to assume that you have an *expectation of privacy* if you have a conversation in the open where it can easily be overheard
by the other students. Based on the *Katz* v. *United States* (1967) ruling, the
first part of the Fourth Amendment is often referred to as the **reasonableness**

clause, meaning a search is constitutional if it does not violate a person's *reasonable* and *legitimate* expectation of privacy (Neubauer and Fradella, 2014).

Search and seizure

As discussed previously, the second clause of the Fourth Amendment restricts the government's ability to search and seize evidence without probable cause to issue a warrant. The second clause of the Fourth Amendment is often referred to as the **warrants clause,** indicating a **warrant** or signed document issued by a judge or magistrate authorizes a specific course of action. The Fourth Amendment specifically refers to a **search warrant,** which is a signed document by a judge or magistrate authorizing law enforcement to conduct a search (Neubauer and Fradella, 2014).

A search warrant is different from an **arrest warrant,** which is a signed document by a judge or magistrate authorizing law enforcement to take the person into custody (Neubauer and Fradella, 2014). A **search** is specifically defined as the "exploration or examination of an individual's home, premises, or person to discover things or items that may be used by the government as evidence in a criminal proceeding," and **seizure** is defined as "the exercise of control by the government over a person or thing because of a violation of the law" (del Carmen, 2014: 195). Therefore, when law enforcement officers conduct a **search and seizure,** they are identifying and collecting potential evidence to be used in the court of law.

In *United States* v. *Jacobsen* (1984), the Supreme Court defined the meaning of search and seizure. This case involved a damaged cardboard box that exposed several bags containing a white powdery substance. After seeing the contents of the box, the employees of the freight company contacted the Drug Enforcement Administration (DEA) to investigate. When an agent arrived, he tested the white powdery substance onsite and determined it was cocaine. Based on the results of the field test, the DEA agent then obtained a warrant to search the address where the box was being shipped. After a sting operation on the shipping destination, Bradley and Donna Jacobsen were convicted of possession with intent to distribute cocaine (*United States* v. *Jacobsen,* 1982). They appealed their conviction, arguing that the Fourth Amendment required the DEA agent to obtain a search warrant *before* testing the white powder. The Supreme Court disagreed and held that the defendants' Fourth Amendment rights were not violated because the initial invasion of privacy occurred as a result of private action rather than governmental action.

In addition, the United States Supreme Court stated that a search occurs when an "expectation of privacy that society is prepared to consider reasonable is infringed," and a seizure of property occurs when there is "some meaningful interference with an individual's possessory interests in that property" (*United States* v. *Jacobsen,* 1984). In this case, the search and seizure was reasonable and did not violate the defendant's expectation of privacy since the unsealed, damaged box was compromised. The employees of the freight company also opened the damaged, unsealed box and discovered the suspicious white powder and then invited the DEA to inspect the contents of the box. Therefore, the warrantless search and seizure was legal since there was no expectation of privacy. The conduct of the agent was reasonable given the prior knowledge, shared by a private third party, that the box contained a suspicious white powder (*United States* v. *Jacobsen*, 1984). That is to say, the agents can reenact the original private search without violating any expectation of privacy, so long as they do not exceed the scope of the private search (*United States* v. *Jacobsen*, 1984).

There are three basic requirements for a warrant (see Text Box 12.1; Bloom, 2003; del Carmen, 2014; Neubauer and Fradella, 2014). First, a warrant must be signed by a neutral and impartial judge or magistrate who does not have a vested interest in whether the search warrant should be issued. Second, the Fourth Amendment specifically requires that there must be probable cause, supported by oath and affirmation, to issue a warrant. **Probable cause** means there must be adequate reasons or justifications, rather than mere suspicion, to conduct a search. According to *Brinegar* v. *United States* (1949), "probable cause deals with probabilities. These are not technical; they are the factual and practice considerations of everyday life on which reasonable and prudent men, not legal technicians, act" (175). In general, to issue a warrant, there must be probable cause to support the belief that both a crime has been committed and that evidence of a crime will be found (see *Brinegar* v. *United States,* 1949).

Text Box 12.1: A fictional sample search warrant (created by the authors)

Sample search warrant template from the University of Alabama Police Department

> **SEARCH WARRANT**
> **THE DISTRICT COURT OF FICTICIOUS COUNTY, MY CITY, MY STATE**
> STATE OF "_____" & COUNTY OF "_____"
> WARRANT NUMBER_____
> To Any Law Enforcement Officer Within The State of _____:
> Affidavit having been made before me by <u>I.M. ACOP</u> in support of application for a search warrant, and as I am satisfied that grounds for the issuance exist or that there is probable cause to believe that they exist, under Section <u>LIST CRIMINAL CODES</u>, Code of MY STATE, 1975, pursuant to Rule 3.8, MY STATE Rules of Criminal Procedure, you are hereby ordered and authorized to forthwith search:

legal challenges in digital forensics

THE FOLLOWING PERSON(S), TO-WIT:
Marlena Roar
W/F
DOB: 01/01/1901
SSN# 123456789
THE FOLLOWING PLACE(S) AND/OR VEHICLE(S), TO-WIT:
Item must be "described to a particularity".
Location:
1234 Anystreet Ln.
Anytown, STATE
12345
or
Purple 4-door, model car
STATE tag #123456
Or
Brand 17" laptop computer
Grey in color w/ black skull sticker affixed to screen top
Serial # 987654321
DIRECTIONS:
Directions to the location of the item(s) to be searched. Describe in detail. Use a beginning point such as the police department or the courthouse and describe the route to the end point where the item is located.
FOR, AND IF FOUND SEIZE, THE FOLLOWING PROPERTY, TO-WIT:
1. Any and all stored, downloaded, transmitted or created data (images, still photos and/or videos regardless of format, any emails or correspondence, any computer logs and/or computer files) pertaining to or containing images of minor children engaged in sexual or obscene acts.

and make return of this warrant and an inventory of all property seized there under before me within ten (10) days as required by law.
THIS WARRANT MAY ONLY BE EXECUTED
_____ in the daytime.
_____ controlled substance, at any time in day or night.
_____ at any time in day or night, as I find positive cause
 to believe that a nighttime search is necessary.
ISSUED TO: _____for execution, at
_____o'clock, _____.M., this _____day of _____,
19____.

      _____
      JUDGE/MAGISTRATE
Sample search warrant courtesy of Lt Dennis McMillian, the University of Alabama Police Department

Probable cause may be viewed as a **standard of proof** on a continuum of probability ranging from mere suspicion to almost complete certainty (del Carmen, 2014). For example, in a criminal case, the prosecution must show the jury and/or judge there is proof **beyond all reasonable doubt** that the person on trial committed the crime. In other words, believing that the defendant *probably* committed the crime or is *most likely* guilty is not the same thing as being almost 100 percent certain, or in other words, beyond a reasonable doubt. This high standard of proof makes it less likely that an innocent person will be convicted. In contrast, a civil case requires only a **preponderance of the evidence** standard of proof. Essentially, it must be more likely than not that the accused committed whatever acts to which they are charged.

As previously discussed, the Fourth Amendment requires probable cause in order to obtain a search warrant. The probable cause is usually presented as an **affidavit**, which is a written, or occasionally verbal, statement to which the law enforcement officer has sworn an oath to the magistrate that the information is true and factual (del Carmen, 2014; Neubauer and Fradella, 2014). Finally, the warrant must explicitly state what crime was committed, the location to be searched, and the specific items that are to be seized (Bloom, 2003). Essentially, warrants should be carefully constructed and detailed so that the law enforcement officers executing the warrant can "identify the items with reasonable certainty, and are left with no discretion as to which property is to be taken" (Neubauer and Fradella, 2014: 290). However, there are a number of exceptions to the rule, meaning not all searches and seizures require a warrant.

Exceptions to the rule

In general, the United States Supreme Court has ruled that a warrant is only required if the search violates a person's reasonable expectation of privacy (*Illinois* v. *Andreas*, 1983). In addition, a warrantless search may be constitutional even if it does violate a person's reasonable expectation of privacy, so long as it falls within an established exception to the rule (*Illinois* v. *Rodriguez*, 1990). There are a number of exceptions to the warrant requirement of a search and seizure: search incident to arrest, consent searches, motor vehicle searches, border searches, open fields, plain view, and third-party disclosure, to name a few (see Neubauer and Fradella, 2014).

For example, a person may be searched and any evidence seized once they have been arrested. The process of searching a person who has been arrested for a crime is known as a **search incident to arrest**. In *United States* v. *Robinson* (1973), the court ruled that a search incident to arrest is not only an exception to the warrant requirement, but is also viewed as a reasonable search under the Fourth Amendment. Searches incidental to arrest protect officers by allowing them to search for weapons or instruments to escape on the arrested person as well as ensure that potential evidence is not going to be destroyed (see *United States* v. *Robinson*, 1973).

In *United States* v. *Finley* (2007), the defendant appealed his conviction on possession and intent to distribute methamphetamine arguing that his Fourth Amendment rights were violated since law enforcement conducted a warrantless, post-arrest search of his cell phone, which was retrieved from his pants pocket. The search revealed text messages and call records related to narcotics use and trafficking, which were presented as evidence during his trial. The Fifth Circuit court ruled that searching the cell phone did not violate Finley's Fourth Amendment rights since it occurred post-arrest and the cell phone was retrieved from his pants pocket (i.e. search incident to arrest).

Since cell phone data can be altered or changed, the officers were searching for potential evidence in order to prevent its destruction (*United States* v. *Finley*, 2007). In contrast, *State* v. *Smith* (2009) ruled that the warrantless search of a cell phone seized incident to arrest violates the Fourth Amendment when the "search is unnecessary for the safety of law enforcement officers and there are no exigent circumstances" (line 171). **Exigent circumstances** refer to emergency situations that allow law enforcement officers to conduct a warrantless search when they believe people are in danger or potential evidence will be destroyed (see McInnis, 2009).

The United States Supreme Court, however, recently unanimously ruled in *Riley* v. *California* (2014) that police will not be allowed to search cellular devices without a warrant after a person has been arrested (Bekiempis, 2014). Prior to this decision, there were no specific standards for cell phone seizure. In fact, law enforcement officers were seizing cell phones and imaging them during traffic stops in some states. There are digital forensic tools available that are portable and allow law enforcement to extract cell phone data (see Image 12.2). For example, in 2012, Noe Wuences was pulled over by an Oklahoma City police officer because the license plate tag was improperly displayed (*United States* v. *Zaavedra*, 2013). The driver consented to a search of the vehicle and 9.5 pounds of methamphetamine was found hidden inside. Also located inside the car were two cell phones. The officer proceeded to conduct a warrantless search of the cell phones using a Cellebrite device, which extracted information including contacts, phone history, text messages, and pictures. During trial, Wuences submitted a motion to suppress any evidence retrieved from the cell phones because the search violated his Fourth Amendment rights (*United States* v. *Zaavedra*, 2013). Since prior courts ruled that law enforcement may search a cell phone seized during a **traffic stop** so long as there is probable cause to believe the phone contains evidence of a crime (see *United States* v. *Garcia-Aleman*, 2010), and are recognized tools of the drug trade (see *United States* v. *Oliver*, 2004), the Northern District of Oklahoma court ruled that Wuences's Fourth Amendment rights were not violated.

legal challenges in digital forensics

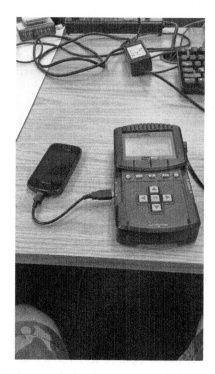

Image 12.2 Cellebrite devices

Cellebrite Universal Forensic Extraction Device (UFED) is a portable device used for forensically extracting data from cell phones.

See www.cellebrite.com

According to the Cellebrite brochure, the Cellebrite UFED allows for the "complete extraction of existing, hidden, and deleted phone data, including call history, text messages, contacts, images, and geotags."

Photo courtesy of Eric Katz, Law Enforcement Coordinator and Instructor for Purdue University's Cyber Forensics Laboratory

For more on cell phone seizure issues, go online to: 1) http://blogs.findlaw.com/blotter/2014/04/supreme-ct-debates-cell-phone-searches-upon-arrest.html#more **2)** www.nytimes.com/interactive/2014/06/25/us/annotated-supreme-court-cellphone-privacy-decision.html?_r=0

This new ruling by the Supreme Court in *Riley*, however, demonstrates that the opinion regarding cell phones has changed (Bekiempis, 2014). Previously, the courts traditionally viewed cell phones as an electronic version of a phone book, which contained only contact information (phone numbers, addresses). Now, cell phones are essentially mini-computers that contain a lot more information than mere phone numbers and addresses. For example, the iPhone 5 is capable of storing over 8,000 pictures or 800 million words of text (Totenberg, 2014).

As discussed in Chapter 10, smart phones function similarly to computers in that they allow web browsing, emailing, video conferencing, and a variety of apps for data entry and editing. According to Professor Kerr of George Washington University: "It's misleading to even think of them as phones; they are 'general purpose computers' that have a bunch of apps, one of which is a telephone function" (Totenberg, 2014, para 8). As a consequence, the court stipulated in its ruling that cell phones "with all they contain and all they may reveal, they hold for many Americans the privacies of life" (Bekiempis, 2014). Thus, police must obtain appropriate warrants prior to conducting a search of a cell phone seized incident to an arrest.

The Canadian Supreme Court concurred with this argument when they ruled that during a search of any premises, additional court authorization is needed to search any computers or cell phones found onsite (R v. Vu, 2013). Thus, law enforcement officers may seize computers or cell-phones during a search, but must obtain additional court authorization to search the electric devices. In that respect, the Canadian Supreme Court argued that a cell phone or computer was not the same thing as a dresser drawer or filing cabinet. If conducting a legal search of physical property, law enforcement are allowed to search inside dresser drawers and filing cabinets, even if the drawers are closed. Computers and cell phones are different than filing cabinets; for instance, they may be connected to a network whose data is not technically part of the premises being searched (R v. Vu, 2013). As a result, perceptions on the status of cell phones and legal searches is evolving, and will continue to evolve over the next few decades (see Image 12.3).

Other exceptions to the warrant requirement are the search of open fields and the plain view doctrine. **Open field searches** do not require a warrant since an open field (i.e. property not adjacent to one's home, such as fields or water) cannot be considered "persons, houses, papers, or effects" as stated by the Fourth Amendment (see United States v. Hester, 1924). The **plain view doctrine** allows law enforcement officers to conduct a search and seizure for evidence that may not be in the search warrant but is in plain view and its incriminating nature is immediately apparent. For example, in Horton v. California (1990), law enforcement executed a warrant for stolen property in the home of Terry Horton, who was suspected of armed robbery. Although the warrant only authorized the search and seizure of stolen property, the law enforcement officer discovered, in plain view, then seized the weapons, as potential evidence related to the armed robberies. The judge ruled that a warrantless seizure of evidence (e.g. weapons), while executing a legal search warrant (e.g. stolen property), does not violate the

Image 12.3 Map of the USA showing which states allow the police to search your phone without a warrant

Image courtesy of www.Shutterstock.com. Image adapted from original

Fourth Amendment since the discovery of said evidence was in plain view (see *Horton* v. *California*, 1990).

There is a current exception to the plain view doctrine. In *United States* v. *Carey* (1999), the defendant argued that his Fourth Amendment rights were violated after a detective searched for evidence on a computer that was outside the scope of the original warrant. Patrick Carey was being investigated for possible sale and possession of cocaine. After providing consent, the defendant's computers were taken to the police station and a warrant was obtained by the officers allowing them to search the files on the computers for "names, telephone numbers, ledger receipts, addresses, and other documentary evidence pertaining to the sale and distribution of controlled substances" (*United States* v. *Carey*, 1999, 1265–1267). While searching the computer, the detective identified a JPEG file that constituted an image of child pornography. After finding this image, the detective admitted in court that he abandoned his search for drug trafficking evidence in pursuit of evidence related to child pornography. The detective spent approximately five hours downloading over 200 files in search of child pornography (*United States* v. *Carey*, 1999). Since the Fourth Amendment requires that a search warrant specify the location and items to be seized, the defendant argued that the original warrant was transformed into a "general warrant." However, the government argued that the child pornography images fell within the plain view doctrine.

legal challenges in digital forensics

The Tenth Circuit court rejected the government's argument citing the *Coolidge* v. *New Hampshire* (1971) ruling that "the plain view doctrine may not be used to extend a general exploratory search from one object to another until something incriminating at last emerges" (line 466). In addition, the detective was not seizing the files themselves, but the content *within* the files. In this case, the content was not in plain view. The court ruled that the discovery of the first child pornography image was admissible (the initial discovery), while all subsequent images discovered were beyond the scope of the original warrant. As a result, the contents of a computer file are not considered in "plain view" since they must be opened in order to view them. This case established that when evidence is discovered (e.g. child pornography JPEG) related to a different crime (e.g. child pornography possession) outside the scope of the original warrant (searching for evidence related to drug trafficking), the investigator must stop the search entirely and obtain a new warrant based on the newly discovered evidence.

Finally, the role of consent is one of the most relevant exceptions to the warrant requirement. Fourth Amendment rights may be voluntarily waived, meaning a search without probable cause or a warrant may occur if a person who has authority over the place or items to be searched provides consent (Neubauer and Fradella, 2014). A *consent search* is made when an individual gives permission, voluntarily and without deceit, to law enforcement to conduct a search. Problems arise when the person providing the consent is not the same person who is being searched.

Courts in the US have ruled that law enforcement may obtain permission from third-party members so long as they share a common authority over the place or property being searched (see *Illinois* v. *Rodriquez*, 1990). In addition, the Supreme Court ruled that a warrantless search of a premise does not violate the Fourth Amendment if it occurred under the **apparent authority principle** (del Carmen, 2014) which states that if the police obtain consent to search a premises from someone whom they *reasonably believe* shares a common authority over said premises, it does not violate the Fourth Amendment even if the third-party member did not actually have the authority to give consent.

A number of cases have challenged the exception to the warrant requirement as a result of third-party consent to search another person's computer or electronic devices. For instance, in **United States v. Smith** (1998), the defendant, David Smith, was convicted of possession and distribution of child pornography. The case began when Cindy Ushman contacted police and alleged that the computer contained child pornography images. The police received consent from Cindy Ushman to enter the premises to search for and seize the defendant's computer.

The child pornography evidence was retrieved from a computer that was located in the bedroom of his house, which he shared with Cindy

Ushman and her two daughters. The defendant argued that the evidence was inadmissible since the search of the computer was conducted illegally because the consent given by Cindy Ushman did not extend to the bedroom which is where the computer was kept. Cindy Ushman, however, testified that the computer was not password protected, was used by the entire family, and was kept in a common area accessible to other family members. Based on this information, the Supreme Court ruled that a roommate has the legal authority to provide consent to a search and seizure of items and spaces that are shared with the defendant (*United States v. Smith*, 1998).

So in a hypothetical example, even though Kathy shares the same dormitory room as Noel, she would only be able to provide consent to law enforcement if she also has access to and uses Noel's computer as well. In other words, if Kathy has joint access to Noel's computer, then Kathy also has a shared common authority over said computer. However, if Kathy uses a password to protect her computer, or locks it away in a desk drawer, and Kathy does not know the password or have a copy of the key, then she no longer shares a common authority over the computer. In this case, Kathy would be unable to provide legal consent for law enforcement to search for and seize Noel's computer since it is secured.

In general, the courts have ruled that roommates, apartment managers, spouses, and employees/employers may provide consent to law enforcement if they have a shared authority over the space or objects to be searched (see del Carmen, 2014). Parents can give consent to search a child's computer so long as the child is dependent on the parents, meaning the child is a minor and is not paying rent. If the child is a legal adult (over the age of 18 years in the United States), parents are not able to provide legal consent to search the child's room without a warrant so long as the child is paying rent to the parents (see *United States v. Rith*, 1999; *United States v. Whitfield*, 1991). So, the next time you go home during summer break to live with your parents, you might want to consider paying your parents rent if you want to limit their ability to provide consent to a warrantless search.

The Fifth Amendment

As discussed in Chapter 11, two of the greatest obstacles for digital forensics examiners are password-protected and encrypted files (Casey, 2011). **Password-protected files** are locked files that require a password to gain access, which prevents other people from opening or modifying these files (Britz, 2009). **Encryption** is the process of transforming text, such as an email, through the use of mathematical algorithms so that it is no longer legible to others (Casey, 2011; Kessler, 2000; Sammons, 2012). Most encryption programs require an **access key**, which is essentially a password that unlocks the file so that the same algorithm that encrypted the information

legal challenges in digital forensics

is now used to decrypt it. Digital forensics examiners can use specialized programs to break encryption and crack passwords. There are, however, some encryption and password-protected files that have proven resilient and unbreakable. Therefore, many countries are considering whether a suspect can be compelled by a court of law to provide an encryption key or password.

In the United States, this specifically becomes a Fifth Amendment issue. The **Fifth Amendment** of the United States constitution reads:

> No person shall be held to answer for a capital, or otherwise infamous crime, unless on a presentment or indictment of a Grand Jury, except in cases arising in the land or naval forces, or in the Militia, when in actual service in time of War or public danger; nor shall any person be subject for the same offense to be twice put in jeopardy of life or limb; nor shall be compelled in any criminal case to be a witness against himself, nor be deprived of life, liberty, or property, without due process of law; nor shall private property be taken for public use, without just compensation.

In general, the Fifth Amendment lists specific constitutional rights protected within the criminal justice system (Garcia, 2002). First, a person accused of a crime must be indicted by a **grand jury**, who are a group of people that determine whether or not there is enough evidence to formally charge the individual with a crime. Second, the **double jeopardy clause** states that an individual is protected from being prosecuted or punished twice for the same crime. For example, in 1995, OJ Simpson was found not guilty of murdering his ex-wife Nicole Brown Simpson and her friend Ron Goldman. Even if evidence resurfaced that proved OJ Simpson was guilty, the Fifth Amendment states that that he could not be charged and prosecuted twice for the same crime due to the double jeopardy clause (see Text Box 12.2).

Text Box 12.2: Double jeopardy

Double jeopardy: Getting away with murder

Vermont case reignites debate on justice, constitutional rights in America
Aug. 4, 2011
By ANN MARIE DORNING
Retrieved from: http://abcnews.go.com/US/double-jeopardy-murder/story?id=14230469&singlePage=true

> OJ Simpson may be the most famous name associated with double jeopardy. In 1995, Simpson was acquitted in the killing of his ex-wife Nicole Brown Simpson and her friend Ron Goldman. 11 years later

---

> ... Simpson was writing a book tentatively titled "If I did it" ... which left people wondering why Simpson could not be re-tried for the murders if he confessed or if new details came to light.

Next, the Fifth Amendment protects criminal defendants from self-incrimination, meaning giving a statement that might expose oneself to punishment for a crime (Garcia, 2002). This section of the Fifth Amendment is known as the self-incrimination clause. During a trial, the defendant may "plead the Fifth" so he/she does not have to answer any questions or provide testimony that might be self-incriminating. As a result of *Miranda v. Arizona* (1966), the Fifth Amendment was extended to not only include trial testimony but also statements made while in police custody. In the United States, the police are required to read the suspect his/her *Miranda* rights before questioning:

> You have the right to remain silent. Anything you say can and will be used against you in the court of law. You have the right to talk to a lawyer and have him or her present with you while you are being questioned. If you cannot afford to hire a lawyer, one will be appointed to represent you before any questioning, if you wish.
>
> (*Miranda* v. *Arizona*, 1966)

If a suspect waives his/her Miranda rights, then any statements made to the police by the suspect may be used as evidence in a court of law. However, *Griffin* v. *California* (1965) ruled that exercising Fifth Amendment rights to not testify should not be used as evidence of guilt. Essentially, if you decide to "plea the Fifth" and not testify or answer any questions, your silence cannot be used against you as evidence of your guilt.

Fourth, the due process clause states that the government cannot deprive someone of "life, liberty, or property" without due process, meaning the government must follow rules and procedures for conducting legal procedures to limit arbitrary decisions (see Garcia, 2002; Wasserman, 2004). Finally, the last section of the Fifth Amendment is referred to as the just compensation clause, and states that any property taken by the government must be for public use and the owner must be fully reimbursed its market value (see Schultz, 2009). Overall, the Fifth Amendment provides several different protections against the federal government. However, the most relevant clause to our discussion of legal issues surrounding digital investigations is the right against self-incrimination.

Protection against self-incrimination

In order for your statements to be protected under the Fifth Amendment, they must be compelled, testimonial, and incriminating in nature (*Fisher*

v. *United States*, 1976). In other words, any statements made voluntarily (i.e. not compelled) are not protected under the Fifth Amendment. In addition, the statement must be testimonial, meaning oral or written communication, rather than physical evidence (e.g. blood samples, fingerprints; see *Doe* v. *United States*, 1988). Finally, the Fifth Amendment protects individuals from making statements that are incriminating, meaning statements that imply one's guilt or provide evidence that can be used against them in a court of law. Overall, this clause becomes extremely important when a suspect is compelled to provide the encryption key or password to an electronic device that may contain incriminating files.

For example, in 2007, Sebastien Boucher crossed the Canadian border into the United States and the officers found a laptop computer in the back seat of his car (*In re Boucher*, 2007). The officer searched the computer and found approximately 40,000 files that contained child pornography. After arresting Boucher, the examiner identified a hard drive that was protected by the encryption software, Pretty Good Privacy (PGP), which requires an encryption key or password to unlock the drive (see Chapter 11; *In re Boucher*, 2007). In addition, a computer forensics expert from the United States Secret Service claimed it would take approximately two years to break the PGP encryption. Therefore, the grand jury subpoenaed Boucher for the encryption key to unlock the computer drive. A **subpoena** is a court order requiring a person to appear before a grand jury or produce documents (Neubauer and Fradella, 2014).

Boucher argued that providing the encryption key violated his Fifth Amendment right against self-incrimination. The United States District Court of Vermont had to determine if Fifth Amendment privilege applied to this case. First, the court agreed that the act of requesting a subpoena involved *compulsion* since it requires compliance. In addition, the court agreed that providing the password would be *incriminating* since the government argued that the computer contained child pornography.

The last requirement was the most difficult to determine – whether the communication was considered testimonial. As discussed previously, testimonial refers to non-physical evidence, so the court acknowledged that the contents (e.g. files) of the laptop computer were not privileged under the Fifth Amendment. In addition, the prosecutor acknowledged that if Boucher provided the encryption key to the grand jury it would be testimonial (*In re Boucher*, 2007). Instead of providing the password, the prosecutor argued that Boucher could simply enter the password into the computer while no one was observing or recording said password, which would still allow access to the hard drive without violating Boucher's Fifth Amendment rights (*In re Boucher*, 2007).

However, the Court ruled in favor of Boucher, stating that the act of entering a password or encryption key is testimonial (*In re Boucher*, 2007):

Entering a password into a computer implicitly communicates facts. By entering the password Boucher would be disclosing the fact that he knows the password and has control over the files. (p. 9)

Essentially, the password is not a physical form of evidence. Therefore, by compelling Boucher to provide his encryption key, the grand jury was requiring Boucher to "display the contents of his mind to incriminate himself" (*In re Boucher*, 2007: 16).

The government appealed and revised the original subpoena in *In re Boucher* (2009) stating that they were not specifically seeking the password for the encrypted hard drive. Instead, they simply wanted Boucher to provide an unencrypted version of the hard drive to the grand jury. This time, the Court ruled in favor of the prosecutor since the law enforcement officer already knew that there was child pornography on the computer after Boucher initially opened the hard drive and showed him. They argued that since the government already knows that the drive exists, and the type of files that are on the drive, Boucher's Fifth Amendment rights cannot be violated when he produces an unencrypted version of the hard drive (*In re Boucher*, 2009).

Similar cases have led to contradictory conclusions. For instance, Ramona Fricosu was compelled to provide the encryption key to her Toshiba laptop so that law enforcement could execute a previously authorized search warrant (*United States* v. *Fricosu*, 2012). During the investigation, the defendant acknowledged that she was the sole owner of the computer and that the computer possibly contained information the authorities were searching for. Based on this evidence, the Court ruled that producing an unencrypted version of the laptop did not violate Fricosu's Fifth Amendment rights since she acknowledged to law enforcement that the computer was hers and that it might contain incriminating information (*United States* v. *Fricosu*, 2012). However, in *In re Doe* (2012) the Eleventh Circuit Court ruled that the government wrongly charged John Doe with contempt of court when he refused to comply with a subpoena compelling him to provide the encryption key to his computer. In this case, the court lacked independent evidence that the encrypted hard drives contained incriminating evidence. Therefore, charging John Doe with contempt of court for refusing to provide his encryption key violated his Fifth Amendment rights to protection against self-incrimination (*In re Doe*, 2012).

For more on how the Fifth Amendment applies to encryption in the US, go online to: http://arstechnica.com/tech-policy/2012/02/appeals-court-fifth-amendment-protections-can-apply-to-encrypted-hard-drives/

Key disclosure law

Based on the current court cases in the United States, a person may be compelled to provide the encryption key or password for an electronic device so long as the government has independent evidence, not just mere suspicion, that the encrypted drive contains incriminating evidence. There is not, however, any specific key disclosure law in the United States. A **key disclosure law** is legislation that mandates a person to provide encryption keys or passwords to law enforcement for digital forensic investigations (see Westby, 2004). There are several countries that have specific key disclosure laws that require a suspect to provide all encryption keys and passwords during a digital investigation (see Koops, 2013; Madsen and Banisar, 2000), such as the United Kingdom's **Regulation of Investigatory Powers Act (RIPA)**. This law mandates key disclosure so long as law enforcement obtains signed authorization from a high-ranking official (e.g. judge, chief of police) using a specialized form known as a **Section 49 request** (Madsen and Banisar, 2000).

> **For more on Section 49 requests, go online to:** www.washingtonpost.com/wp-dyn/content/article/2007/10/01/AR2007100100511.html

In addition, the Australian **Cybercrime Act 2001** inserted a new section into the Crimes Act 1914 giving law enforcement the ability to compel a person to provide all encryption keys or passwords when investigating a computer-related crime (James, 2004). Failure to comply with this law may result in a six month jail sentence. In Malaysia, the **Communications and Multimedia Act 1998** allows law enforcement conducting a search to compel a suspect to provide all encryption keys or passwords in order to search the computerized data (The Commissioner of Law Revision, 2006). Similar to Australian law, a person in Malaysia who refuses to provide the encryption keys could be fined and/or imprisoned for six months. Although a few countries have implemented key disclosure mandates, there are many more that have no policies at all regarding lawful access to encrypted or password-protected electronic devices (e.g. Argentina, Czech Republic, Greece; see Koops, 2013).

Overall, there are no consistent guidelines on how the law should balance one's privilege against self-incrimination and diminishing obstruction of justice for cases involving encrypted or password-protected digital devices. With the rise in encryption use, there is no doubt that law enforcement will continue to face the challenge of overcoming encryption and password-protected devices (see Chapter 11). However, even if a suspect is compelled to provide the encryption key or password, the evidence derived must still be admissible in a court of law.

As discussed in Chapter 11, it is important for law enforcement to verify that the digital forensic tools are producing reliable evidence in order to meet admissibility standards in a court of law (Garfinkel, 2013; National Research Council, 2009). Digital forensics tools must be able to replicate the same results when using the exact same methodology (i.e. repeatability) as well as the same results even in a different testing environment (i.e. reproducibility; see NIST, 2003). Both are necessary in order for the digital evidence to be admissible in the court of law. In addition, the digital forensic technician is responsible for documenting which tools were used during the forensic examination as well as the date and time of evidence preservation.

Digital forensic technicians should be prepared to testify in court regarding all stages of the digital forensic investigation (see Chapter 11). If the examiner lacks transparency, all of these stages could be scrutinized in a court of law. Thus, transparency of the digital forensics process makes it easier for the courts to determine the validity of the process, and by extension easier to determine whether the digital evidence is admissible in a court of law. **Admissibility** is the process of determining whether evidence will assist the fact finders (e.g. judge) through their decision-making process. The judge determines whether the digital evidence is admissible in court based on different standards for evaluating the relevance and reliability of the evidence. Evidence is considered **relevant** when it can make the fact presented in a case more or less probable, and evidence that does not tend to prove or disprove a presented fact in a case is deemed irrelevant, therefore inadmissible (Federal Rules of Evidence 2010, 401–402; Neubauer and Fradella, 2014). **Reliability** refers to the accuracy of the evidence deemed relevant to a case.

In the United States, the case of *Lorraine* v. *Markel American Insurance Company* (2007) established guidelines for assessing the admissibility of digital evidence. In this civil case, Jack Lorraine and Beverly Mack were suing Markel American Insurance Company for damages that were covered by the insurance policy after their yacht was struck by lightning. After electronic evidence (emails) was ruled inadmissible, the judge highlighted five evidentiary issues when assessing the admissibility of electronic evidence: relevance, authenticity, not hearsay or admissible hearsay, original writing rule, and not duly prejudicial (*Lorraine* v. *Markel American Insurance Company*, 2007). These issues are addressed individually by the **Federal Rules of Evidence (FRE)**, which govern the admissibility of evidence in federal court proceedings in the United States.

First, **FRE 401** defines **relevance** as the tendency to make the fact being presented in a case more or less probable. Second, **authenticity** refers to the ability to prove that the evidence is genuine. According to **FRE 901**, "the proponent must produce evidence sufficient to support a finding that the item is what the proponent claims it is." In cases involving digital evidence (e.g.

emails, web postings, digital photographs), authenticity is often challenged since electronic evidence can easily be deleted, corrupted, or modified (see *Lorraine v. Markel American Insurance Company*, 2007). Third, **hearsay** is considered second-hand evidence, meaning it is testimony not based on a first-hand or personal knowledge (**FRE 801**). Testimony that is hearsay is inadmissible because there is no way to validate its truthfulness.

The fourth consideration is referred to as the original writing rule. According to FRE 1001–1008, the **original writing rule** states that the original evidence, rather than a duplicate, is generally required unless the duplicate can be authenticated and proven that its contents are the same as the original. The original writing rule is sometimes referred to as the **best evidence rule** (see Chapter 11). Lastly, FRE 403 states that evidence is not admissible, even if it is relevant, if it could unfairly bias, confuse, or mislead the fact finders (i.e. **unfair prejudice**; see Text Box 12.3).

Text Box 12.3: An excerpt from the US Federal Rules of Evidence

United States Federal Rules of Evidence 401–403

ARTICLE IV. RELEVANCY AND ITS LIMITS

Rule 401. Definition of "Relevant Evidence"
"Relevant evidence" means evidence having any tendency to make the existence of any fact that is of consequence to the determination of the action more probable or less probable than it would be without the evidence.

Rule 402. Relevant Evidence Generally Admissible; Irrelevant Evidence Inadmissible
All relevant evidence is admissible, except as otherwise provided by the Constitution of the United States, by Act of Congress, by these rules, or by other rules prescribed by the Supreme Court pursuant to statutory authority. Evidence which is not relevant is not admissible.

Rule 403. Exclusion of Relevant Evidence on Grounds of Prejudice, Confusion, or Waste of Time
Although relevant, evidence may be excluded if its probative value is substantially outweighed by the danger of unfair prejudice, confusion of the issues, or misleading the jury, or by considerations of undue delay, waste of time, or needless presentation of cumulative evidence.

Overall, *Lorraine v. Markel American Insurance Company* (2007) outlined the importance of several legal issues when determining the admissibility of electronic evidence in the United States. Other countries have

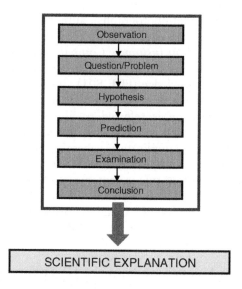

Figure 12.1 The scientific method
Following the scientific method in a digital forensic investigation will increase the likelihood of the examiner coming to an objective, valid conclusion as to whether the relevant findings refute or support the original hypothesis, such as whether a crime was committed.

developed admissibility standards for electronic or digital evidence (e.g. Canada, Germany, UK, Philippines; see Bidgoli, 2006; Xue-Guang, 2011). For example, in 2002, the Supreme Court of the Philippines amended the **Philippine Rules of Electronic Evidence (PREE)** to both criminal and civil court cases (Supreme Court Resolution, 2002). The PREE specifically outline the admissibility rules for electronic evidence compared to the Philippine Rules of Evidence (PRE), which is a separate standard for non-electronic evidence. The PREE has similar criteria to the United States Federal Rules of Evidence for assessing the admissibility of electronic evidence, including the best evidence rule and an authenticity standard.

Along with these general admissibility criteria, there are specific standards set for the admissibility of scientific evidence in the United States. **Scientific evidence** is information derived from the scientific method that is relevant to the facts of a case. The **scientific method** is a "process that uses strict guidelines to ensure careful and systemic collection, organization, and analysis of information" (Saferstein, 2010: 15). The scientific method occurs in the following stages: observation, hypothesis, prediction, experimentation, and conclusion (Casey, 2011; see Figure 12.1).

First, the scientific method begins with an **observation** followed by a question worth investigating. For example, consider the hypothetic case of Jai Max who is suspected of being a child pornography user after his wife overheard a conversation about viewing illicit images on the Internet.

legal challenges in digital forensics

Law enforcement officers execute a legal search warrant and seize his laptop computer. Based on the facts of the case, the digital forensic examiner may ask whether or not there is evidence of Internet child pornography on the laptop. Next, a **hypothesis** is generated, which is a reasonable explanation as to what might have occurred or why. In this case, the examiner may hypothesize that Jai Max was surfing the Internet and downloaded child pornography images.

Based on the hypothesis, a **prediction** is a specific statement as to how you will determine if your hypothesis is true. For example, the digital forensic examiner may predict that Internet artifacts (e.g. browser history) and image files (e.g. JPEG) will be found on the suspect's hard drive. Based on these predictions, the examiner will test the hypothesis by conducting a digital forensic **examination** and analysis of the imaged hard drive in search of evidence that will either support or refute the hypothesis (see Chapter 11). This stage is meticulously constructed in order to limit any bias or distortion of the evidence (see Saferstein, 2010). The final stage of the scientific method is drawing a **conclusion**, which is an overall summary of the findings derived from the examination. This conclusion will either support or refute the original hypothesis and should be objective and transparent (see Chapter 10). In the hypothetical case of Jai Max, the digital forensic examiner will conclude whether or not there is evidence of child pornography use on the suspect's hard drive.

In the United States, there are traditionally three standards for assessing the admissibility of scientific evidence from expert testimony: *Frye*, *Daubert*, and *Federal Rules of Evidence 702*. Each of these standards will be discussed in greater detail as it pertains to scientific evidence derived from digital forensic investigations.

The Frye *standard*

In *Frye* v. *United States* (1923), the defendant, James Alphonso Frye, appealed his conviction of second-degree murder on the basis that the defense wanted to provide expert witness testimony on the results of a systolic blood pressure deception test (see Figure 12.1). In *Frye*, the technology in question was a precursor to what is commonly referred to as the polygraph or lie detector test. The theory was that the rise in blood pressure is evidence that the person is lying, concealing facts, or guilty of a crime (*Frye* v. *United States*, 1923). The defense also offered to conduct the lie detector test in the courtroom. However, the prosecution argued that:

> … while courts will go a long way in admitting expert testimony deduced from a well-recognized scientific principle or discovery, the thing from which the deduction is made must be sufficiently established to have gained general acceptance in the particular field in which it belongs.
>
> (*Frye* v. *United States*, 1923)

In its ruling, the District of Columbia Court of Appeals upheld the lower court's decision that the expert witness's testimony regarding the results of the lie detector test was not admissible. Therefore, the **Frye standard** states that scientific evidence is only admissible if it is generally accepted as reliable by the scientific community (*Frye v. United States*, 1923).

To determine if the evidence meets the *Frye* standard, the proponent of the evidence would have to present a collection of experts to testify on whether the technique or issue being presented is generally accepted by the relevant scientific community (Saferstein, 2010). Although quickly accepted as the standard for admitting expert testimony, legal scholars became concerned as to whether this standard was sufficient or flexible enough to recognize novel or controversial scientific breakthroughs that have not yet gained acceptance in the scientific community (see Smith and Bace, 2002). In other words, the evidence may be derived from a valid technique that has not gained *general* acceptance from the scientific community (see *United States v. Downing*, 1985; Watson and Jones, 2013). Despite these concerns, a few state court jurisdictions in the United States still adhere to the *Frye* standard of scientific evidence (e.g. Alabama, California, Illinois). However, Rule 702 of the Federal Rules of Evidence replaced the *Frye* standard in the federal and some state jurisdictions.

Federal Rules of Evidence 702

Created in 1975, Article VII of the Federal Rules of Evidence outlined specific guidelines for the admissibility of expert witnesses' testimony in Rule 702. The original version of **FRE 702** stated:

> ... if scientific, technical, or other specialized knowledge will assist the trier of fact to understand the evidence or to determine a fact in issue, a witness qualified as an expert by knowledge, skill, experience, training, or education, may testify thereto in the form of an opinion or otherwise (1975).

In the United States, Rule 702 superseded the *Frye* standard at the federal level (Marsico, 2005). Many state jurisdictions were confused as to whether this standard was an addition to or replacement of the *Frye* standard. In addition, the original FRE 702 standard was rather ambiguous as to how the court was to determine whether someone was *qualified* to be an expert witness. In 1993, the debate on the admissibility standard for scientific expert witness testimony all changed with the landmark case *Daubert v. Merrell Dow Pharmaceuticals*.

The Daubert *standard*

In 1993, the United States Supreme Court ruled on a case where the plaintiffs, two minors and their parents, sued Merrell Dow Pharmaceuticals claiming that the drug Benedictine caused the childrens' birth defects since it was ingested during pregnancy by the mothers (*Daubert* v. *Merrell Dow Pharmaceuticals*, 1993). The case was eventually heard by the United States Supreme Court. Both sides presented expert witness testimony. Merrell Dow Pharmaceuticals presented an expert's affidavit, which summarized the published scientific literature and concluded that the drug did not have a history of causing human birth defects. This expert witness testimony was ruled admissible by the court.

When the plaintiffs presented eight experts who testified that the drugs did in fact cause birth defects in animal research, the court ruled that this evidence was inadmissible because it did not meet the FRE 702 standards for admissibility. Specifically, the United States Supreme Court ruled, "general acceptance is not necessary precondition to the admissibility of scientific evidence under the Federal Rules of Evidence" (*Daubert* v. *Merrell Dow Pharmaceuticals*, 1993).

In addition, *Daubert* v. *Merrell Dow Pharmaceuticals* (1993) held that any scientific expert testimony presented in federal court must undergo a reliability test. This reliability test is an independent judicial assessment, which is determined by the trial judge, and is known as a *Daubert* hearing. The Supreme Court's intention through this test was to end the "battle of the experts." In addition, the US Supreme Court stated that the Federal Rules of Evidence imply that the judge acts as a **gatekeeper,** meaning the person responsible for assessing both the relevancy *and* reliability of the scientific evidence. In other words, "the responsibility of a judge in a Daubert hearing is to determine whether the underlying methodology and techniques that have been used to isolate the evidence are sound, and whether as a result, the evidence reliable" (Watson and Jones, 2013). By acting as a gatekeeper, the trial judge is responsible for keeping junk science out of the courtroom.

Daubert v. *Merrell Dow Pharmaceuticals* (1993) suggested four criteria for determining whether the *relevant* scientific evidence, theory, or study is reliable, therefore admissible, in court:

1. Testing: Has the theory or technique been empirically tested?
2. Publication: Has the theory or technique been subjected to peer review and publication?
3. Error Rate: What is the known or potential rate of error?
4. Acceptance: Has the theory or technique been generally accepted within the relevant scientific community?

These criteria for determining the reliability and admissibility of scientific evidence became known as the *Daubert* standard. In the *Daubert* v. *Merrell Dow Pharmaceuticals* (1993) ruling, the Supreme Court did not specify whether some or all of these criteria are required in order for the scientific evidence to be admissible in court. Instead, it is up to the trial judge to determine which criteria are applicable to the scientific technique, theory, or study being examined at the *Daubert* hearing.

Initially, the *Daubert* standard only applied to scientific evidence. However, in 1997, the court ruled in **General Electric Co. v. Joiner (1997)** that not only was the scientific evidence itself under review but the methodology and reliability of an expert's reasoning process are also vulnerable to scrutiny under *Daubert*. The court has judicial discretion when determining if "there is simply too great an analytical gap between the data and the opinion proffered" for it to be admissible as scientific evidence in court (*General Electric Co. v. Joiner*, 1997).

In 1999, the *Daubert* standard was extended to *all* expert testimony that involves scientific, technical, or other specialized knowledge in **Kumho Tire Co. v. Carmichael (1999)**. In this case, the judge stated that since Rule 702 of the Federal Rules of Evidence does not make a distinction between "scientific, technical, and other specialized knowledge," then the *Daubert* standard applies to each of these expert disciplines to assess reliability and admissibility. Overall, the current interpretation of the *Daubert* standard is really a summary of these three cases, *Daubert* v. *Merrell Dow Pharmaceuticals* (1993), *General Electric Co. v. Joiner* (1997), and *Kumho Tire Co. v. Carmichael* (1999), which are sometimes referred to as the **Daubert trilogy** (Berger, 2000).

In 2000, Rule 702 of the Federal Rules of Evidence was amended to include the *Daubert* standard for determining the reliability and admissibility of expert witness testimony. In its most recent version, amended in 2011, Rule 702 of the Federal Rules of Evidence now states that a witness who is qualified as an expert by knowledge, skill, experience, training, or education may testify in the form of an opinion or otherwise if:

(a) the expert's scientific, technical, or other specialized knowledge will help the trier of fact to understand the evidence or to determine a fact in issue;
(b) the testimony is based on sufficient facts or data;
(c) the testimony is the product of reliable principles and methods; and
(d) the expert has reliably applied the principles and methods to the facts of the case.

Overall, in the United States, the *Daubert* standard has had a significant impact on the way expert witness testimony is evaluated in the federal courtroom, as well as in most states. However, some states still apply the *Frye* standard or have adopted a standard of their own. Regardless, the field of digital forensics must be prepared to be scrutinized in the courtroom.

International response to Daubert *and* Frye

The *Daubert* and *Frye* standards have spurred international recognition for the need to keep junk science out of the courtroom. According to the **Law Reform Commission** of Ireland (2008), the legal reform in the United States

legal challenges in digital forensics

(i.e. *Frye* and *Daubert*) has been the "main catalyst for reform internationally ... for developing admissibility criteria based on the reliability of evidence" (pp. 104–105). The Law Reform Commission of Ireland is an independent statutory body established by the Law Reform Commission Act of 1975. The primary role of the Law Reform Commission is to review and conduct research to determine if the law needs to be revised or simplified, and, specifically, one of the Law Reform Commission's projects was to evaluate the standards and procedures for evaluating scientific evidence (Law Reform Commission, 2008).

In 2008, the *Consultation Paper on Expert Evidence* was released by the Law Reform Commission. In this report, the Commission summarized the case law from several countries that appeared to be moving toward a *Daubert*-like standard for assessing the reliability of expert witness testimony (e.g. Australia, England and Wales). In addition, the report weighed the advantages and disadvantages of implementing a reliability test for Irish courts similar to the *Daubert* standard in the United States. Overall, the Law Reform Commission recommended that Ireland also adopt a reliability test for assessing the admissibility of all expert testimony (see Law Reform Commission, 2008).

Admissibility of digital forensics as expert testimony

According to Casey (2011), the digital forensics tools and techniques have successfully withstood the courts' assessment of reliability and admissibility as scientific evidence. However, the ever-changing growth in technology makes it difficult to test and evaluate the variety of digital forensic tools in a quick and efficient manner. For example, as discussed in Chapter 11, NIST, an agency of the United States Department of Commerce, launched the Computer Forensic Tool Testing project (CFTT) to "provide unbiased, open, and objective means for manufacturers, law enforcement, and the legal community to assess the validity of tools used in computer forensics" (NIST, n.d.). In addition, CFTT determines whether the results of the tools are repeatable and reproducible, both of which are needed to assess "trueness and precision" (NIST, 2003: 4). According to NIST, there are approximately 150 different digital forensic tools currently being used by law enforcement worldwide (NIST, n.d.).

Although these goals clearly reflect the *Daubert* standards, the major weakness of the CFTT project is the *amount of time* required to conduct these empirical evaluations (Flandrin, Buchanan, Macfarlane, Ramsay, and Smales, 2014). Therefore, "by the time the results are publicly available, the version of the tested tool might be deprecated" (Flandrin *et al.*, 2014: 2). In addition, the time required to test the tools, as well as the fact many of these tools' source codes are proprietary, make it difficult to determine known error rates (Carrier, 2003; Meyers and Rogers, 2004). Still, the two most common digital forensics imaging tools, EnCase® and Forensic Toolkit®, along with others have met the *Daubert* standard for admissibility (see Chapter 11; Guidance Software, Inc., 2003; Leehealey, Lee, and Fountain, 2012). For example, the general acceptance of EnCase and FTK by the scientific community was noted in the court case *United States* v. *Gaynor* (2008). In addition, EnCase and FTK have been extensively tested by the CFTT project.

Finally, not only is the actual digital forensic evidence being reviewed, but the credentials of the digital forensic examiner or expert also fall within the *Daubert* reliability test. In other words, the digital forensic examiner's education, experience, and training (i.e. credentials) may also be considered by the courts. As discussed further in Chapter 13, this may be a problem in the field of digital forensics, which does not have a set standard for certifying digital forensic examiners (Meyers and Rogers, 2004). In fact, there is a wide variability of certifications available for digital forensic examiners. For example, there are currently a number of professional certifications available, both vendor neutral (e.g. GIAC Certified Forensic Analyst) and vendor specific (i.e. tool specific, such as EnCase® Forensic Training Series; Ryan and Ryan, 2014). In other words, there is no standardized list of certifications or qualifications required in the digital forensics discipline in order to be considered a digital forensics professional or expert.

Although the field of digital forensics is in its infancy, it has quickly gained recognition as a legitimate subdiscipline within the forensic sciences (see Chapter 10). For example, the American Academy of Forensic Science (AAFS) formally recognized the field of digital forensics in 2008 with the creation of the Digital and Multimedia Sciences section – the first section added to the AAFS in 28 years.

In addition, a number of peer-reviewed journals have emerged, including the *International Journal of Digital Evidence, Digital Investigation,* and the *International Journal of Digital Crime and Forensics.* Thus, the peer recognition and publication prong of the *Daubert* standard has clearly gained momentum within the past decade for the field of digital forensics.

Still, being well versed on the extensive body of case law and federal regulations pertaining to the role of digital evidence is a difficult task. In a recent study by Lovasiao, Adams, and Rogers (2006), state general jurisdiction judges from around the country were surveyed to gain insight as to exactly what they know about digital forensics. Lovasiao *et al.* (2006) found that the judges in the study admitted to a low level of understanding and training with digital evidence in the courtroom. However, these same judges displayed an eagerness to gain understanding through effective training methods. Since then, several government agencies and public–private partnerships have emerged around the country to address this gap in judicial experience. One of the most successful programs is the National Computer Forensics Institute (NCFI), a division of the United States Secret Service located in Hoover, Alabama. The NCFI is a training center operated by the United States Secret Service's Criminal investigative Division and the Alabama Office of Prosecution Services with the mission of providing high-quality, hands-on experience to law enforcement personnel around the country (see www.ncfi.usss.gov). State and local officials, prosecutors, and judges can enroll in any of the 12 courses offered at no cost. Overall, with the Internet's growth and the corresponding increase in computer-related crime, it is essential and inevitable that training and educational programs emerge for all members of the criminal justice system.

Summary

We saw in the beginning of this chapter with the case of *United States* v. *Poulsen* (1994) that the admissibility of digital evidence has the ability to significantly impact the outcome of a trial. In the United States, violating the Fourth or Fifth Amendments could mean the inadmissibility of a crucial piece of digital forensic evidence. This chapter also highlighted the inconsistencies between state and federal legislation in the United States, as well as a variety of international judicial systems. For example, both the United Kingdom and Australia have a key disclosure mandate for all encryption keys or passwords, whereas there are no specific key disclosure laws in the United States. In addition, there are different admissibility standards for expert testimony of scientific evidence at the federal and state levels in the United States as well as internationally. What remains consistent is the fact that the entire digital forensics process is under scrutiny, and the validity of digital forensics is assessed by whether or not the evidence is admissible in a court of law. Overall, technology is constantly changing so it is inevitable that national and international case law and federal regulations will change as well.

Key terms

Access key

Admissibility

Affidavit

Amendment

Apparent authority principle

Arrest warrant

Authenticity

Best evidence rule

Beyond a reasonable doubt

Bill of Rights

Cloud storage

Communications and Multimedia Act 1998

Discussion questions

1) There are a number of exceptions to the warrant requirement for a search and seizure. Identify five different exceptions to this rule and create a different scenario for each that would involve the search and seizure of electronic evidence.

2) Identify the four criteria for determining whether digital forensic expert testimony is admissible in court according to the *Daubert* standard. Assess each of these criteria and explain whether or not digital forensic evidence should be admissible in court.

3) There are inconsistencies between national and international laws on a variety of legal issues associated with digital forensic investigations. Describe two of these inconsistencies and discuss whether or not a universal, international law or policy is possible regarding the treatment of digital forensic evidence in court.

4) Create two different scenarios involving third-party consent to conduct a search and seizure. In the first scenario, the third-party member is not legally able to provide consent to law enforcement. In the second scenario, the third-party member is able to provide consent to law enforcement to conduct a search and seizure. Finally, do you agree with the current interpretation of the apparent authority principle? Explain.

References

Bekiempis, V. (2014). US Supreme Court's Cellphone Ruling is a Major Victory For Privacy. *Newsweek* June 25, 2014. Retrieved from: www.newsweek.com/us-supreme-courts-cell-phone-ruling-major-victory-privacy-256328

Berger, M. A. (2000). The Supreme Court's Trilogy on the Admissibility of Expert Testimony. In *Reference Manual on Scientific Evidence*, 2nd ed. Washington, DC: Federal Judicial Center.

Bidgoli, H. (2006). *Handbook of Information Security Vol. 2: Information Warfare, Social, Legal, and International Issues and Security Foundations*. Hoboken, NJ: John Wiley & Sons, Inc.

Bloom, R. M. (2003). *Searches, Seizures, and Warrants: A Reference Guide to the United States Constitution*. Westport, CT: Praeger Publishers.

Brinegar v. United States, 338 U.S. 160 (1949).

Britz, M. T. (2009). *Computer Forensics and Cyber Crime*, 2nd ed. Upper Saddle River, NJ: Prentice Hall.

Carrier, B. (2003). *Open source digital forensics tools: The legal argument*. (Original was published in 2002; the 2003 version is updated.) Retrieved from www.digital-evidence.org

Casey, E. (2011). *Digital Evidence and Computer Crime: Forensic Science, Computers, and the Internet*, 3rd ed. Waltham, MA: Academic Press.

Coolidge v. New Hampshire, 403 U.S. 443 (1971).

Daubert v. Merrell Dow Pharmaceuticals, Inc., 113 S.Ct. 2786 (1993).

del Carmen, R. V. (2014). *Criminal Procedures: Law and Practice*, 9th ed. Belmont, CA: Wadsworth, Cengage Learning.

Doe v. United States, 487 U.S. 201 (1988).

Federal Rules of Evidence. (2010, December 1). Retrieved from www.uscourts.gov/

Fisher v. United States, 425 U.S. 391 (1976).

Flandrin, F., Buchanan, W., Macfarlane, R., Ramsay, B., & Smales, A. (2014). *Evaluating digital forensic tools (DFTs)*. Presented at the 7th International Conference: Cybercrime Forensics Education and Training (CFET 2014). Canterbury, UK.

Frye v. United States, 293 F. 1013 (D.C. Cir 1923).

Garcia, A. (2002). *The Fifth Amendment: A Comprehensive Approach*. Greenwood Publishing Group, Incorporated. Westport, CT: Praeger.

Garfinkel, S. L. (2013). Digital Forensics. *American Scientist*, 101(5), 370.

General Electric v. Joiner, 522 U.S. 136 (1997).

Griffin v. California, 380 U.S. 690(1965).

Guidance Software, Inc. (2003, December). *EnCase® legal journal*. Retrieved from http://isis.poly.edu

Horton v. California, 496 U.S. 128 (1990).

Illinois v. Andreas, 463 U.S. 765 (1983).

Illinois v. Rodriguez, 497 U.S. 177 (1990).

In re Boucher, 2007 WL 4246473 (D. Vt. Nov. 29, 2007).

In re Boucher, 2009 WL 424718 (D. Vt. Feb. 19, 2009).

In re Doe, 2012 WL 579433 (11th Cir. FL Feb. 23, 2012).

James, N. J. (2004). Handing over the keys: Contingency, power, and resistance in the context of section 3LA of the Australian Crimes Act 1914. *University of Queensland Law Journal*, 23, 7–21.

James, S. H., & Nordby, J. J. (eds). (2009). *Forensic Science: An Introduction to Scientific and Investigative Techniques*, 3rd ed. Boca Raton, FL: CRC Press.

Katz v. United States, 389 U.S. 347 (1967).

Kessler, G. C. (2000). An Overview of Cryptographic Methods. In J. P. Slone (ed.), *Local Area Network Handbook*, 6th edition (pp. 73–84). Boca Raton, FL: CRC Press LLC.

Koops, B. J. (2013, February). *Crypto Law Survey Version 27.0: Overview per country*. Retrieved from www.cryptolaw.org

Kumho Tire Co. v. Carmichael, 526 U.S. 137 (1999).

Lardinois, F. (2012, October 15). *Report: Cloud storage services now have over 375M users, could reach 500M by year-end*. Retrieved from http://techcrunch.com

Law Reform Commission. (2008, December). *Consultation paper: Expert Evidence*. Retrieved May 2, 2014 from www.lawreform.ie

Leehealey, T., Lee, E., & Fountain, W. (2012). *The rules of digital evidence and AccessData technology*. AccessData. Retrieved from https://www.accessdata.com

Levy, L. W. (2001). *Origins of the Bill of Rights*. Harrisonburg, VA: Yale University Press.

Lorraine v. Markel American Ins. Co., 241 F.R.D. 534 (D. Md. 2007).

Lovasio, M., Adams, J., & Rogers, M. (2006). Gap analysis: Judicial experience and perception of electronic evidence. *Journal of Digital Forensic Practice*, 1, 13–17.

Madsen, W., & Banisar, D. (2000). *Cryptography and Liberty 2000: An International Survey of Encryption Policy*. Washington, DC: Electronic Privacy Information Center.

Marsico, C. V. (2005). *Computer evidence v. Daubert: The coming conflict*. (CERIAS Tech Report 2005–17). Retrieved from www.cerias.purdue.edu

McInnis, T. N. (2009). *The Evolution of the Fourth Amendment*. Lanham, MD: Lexington Books.

Meyers, M., & Rogers, M. (2004). Computer forensics: The need for standardization and certification. *International Journal of Digital Evidence*, 3(2).

Miranda v. Arizona, 384 U.S. 436 (1966).

National Institute of Standards and Technology. (n.d.). *Computer forensics tool testing program – Overview*. Retrieved from www.cftt.nist.gov/project_overview.htm

National Institute of Standards and Technology. (2003). *General test methodology for computer forensic tools*. Retrieved February 10, 2014 from www.cftt.nist.gov

National Research Council. (2009, August). *Strengthening Forensic Science in the United States: A Path Forward*. Washington, DC: The National Academic Press.

Neubauer, D. W., & Fradella, H. F. (2014). *America's Courts and the Criminal Justice System*, 11th ed. Belmont, CA: Wadsworth, Cengage Learning.

R v. Vu, 2013 SCC 60.

Riley v. California, 134 S. Ct. 2473 (2014).

Ryan, J., & Ryan, D. (2014, February). *Credentialing the digital and multimedia forensics professional*. Presented at the 66th Annual Scientific Meeting of the American Academy of Forensic Sciences, Seattle, WA.

Saferstein, R. (2010). *Criminalistics: An Introduction to Forensic Science*, 10th ed. Upper Saddle River, NJ: Prentice Hall.

Sammons, J. (2012). *The Basics of Digital Forensics: The Primer for Getting Started in Digital Forensics*. Waltham, MA: Syngress.

Schultz, D. (2009). *Encyclopedia of the United States Constitution*. New York, NY: Facts on File, Inc.

Smith, F. C., & Bace, R. (2002). *A Guide to Forensic Testimony: The Art and Practice of Presenting Testimony as an Expert Technical Witness*, 1st ed. Boston, MA: Addison-Wesley Professional.

State v. Smith, 124 Ohio St. 3d 163 (2009).

Supreme Court Resolution, No. 01-7-01-SC (2002) (Philippines).

The Commissioner of Law Revision (2006). *Communications and Multimedia Act 1998*. Retrieved from www.agc.gov.my

Totenberg, N. (2014, April 29). *Weighing the risks of warrantless phone searches during arrest*. National Public Radio. Retrieved from http://npr.org

United States v. Carey, 172 F. 3d 1268 (1999).

United States v. Downing, 753 F.2d. 1224 (1985).

United States v. Finley, 477 F. 3d 250 (2007).

United States v. Fricosu, 841 F. Supp. 2d 1232 (2012).

United States v. Garcia-Aleman, 2010 WL 2635071 (E.D. Tex., June 9, 2010).

United States v. Gaynor, 472 F.2d 899 (2nd Cir. 2008).

United States v. Hester, 265 U.S. 57 (1924).

United States v. Jacobsen, 683 F. 2d 296 (8th Cir. 1982).

United States v. Jacobsen, 466 U.S. 109, 113 (1984).

United States v. Oliver, 363 F. 3d 1061, 1068 (10th Cir. 2004).

United States v. Poulsen, 41 F.3d 1330 (9th Cir. 1994).

United States v. Rith, 164 F.3d 1323 (10th Cir. 1999).

United States v. Robinson, 414 U.S. 218 (1973).

United States v. Smith, 156 F. 3d 1046 (10th Cir. 1998).

United States v. Whitfield, 939 F. 2d 1071 (D.C. Cir. 1991).

US v. Zaavedra, 73 F.4a 156 (10th Cir. 2013).

Wasserman, R. (2004). *Procedural Due Process: A Reference Guide to the United States Constitution*. Westport, CT: Praeger Publishers.

Watson, D., & Jones, A. (2013). *Digital Forensics Processing and Procedures: Meeting the Requirements of ISO 17020, ISO 17025, ISO 27001 and Best Practice Requirements*. Waltham, MA: Syngress.

Westby, J. R. (ed.) (2004). *International Guide to Cyber Security*. Chicago, IL: American Bar Association.

Xue-Guang, W. (2011). *Research on Relevant Problems of Computer Crime Forensics*. In L. Jiang (ed.), *International Conference on ICCE2011, AISC 112* (pp. 169–173). Berlin: Springer-Verlag.

chapter 13

The future of cybercrime, terror, and policy

Chapter goals

- Identify future trends in cybercrime offending and victimization
- Recognize the prospective impact that new technologies will have on human behavior
- Understand the ways that leaderless networks like Anonymous may affect the nature of social movements worldwide
- Assess the ways that criminological theory can be improved with respect to cybercrime
- Understand the ways that law enforcement strategies may need to adapt to online spaces
- Recognize how digital forensics will evolve with technology generally

Introduction

The range of cybercrimes discussed throughout this book illustrates the complexity of these offenses and the unique ways that technology is being used by criminals to hide themselves, make it easier to engage in crime, and connect with others. Since technology is constantly changing, it is difficult to know when or how offenders will adopt a new mode of offending based on access to the Internet. Even more real-world oriented crimes can have an online component, as evident in recent news regarding the sale of illicit narcotics like cocaine and methamphetamine. A number of online markets have developed enabling individuals to buy and sell narcotics through various mechanisms internationally. One of these, called the **Silk Road**, garnered the greatest attention from both researchers and the popular media due in part to the fact that transactions were paid using **bitcoins,** a relatively anonymous form of electronic currency (Franklin, 2013). The Silk Road began in 2011 operating through websites running on the encrypted and anonymous **Tor** network (Franklin, 2013). The site was created to enable individuals to buy various materials ranging from computer equipment to clothing, though sellers offered various narcotics internationally through a variety of mechanims. In fact, its name was a reference to the trade routes used to transport goods between Europe, India, and Asia throughout history (Franklin, 2013).

As the Silk Road gained prominence as a venue for the sale of various narcotics, law enforcement agencies in both the US and Australia conducted sting operations against buyers. In fact, since it opened in 2011 the Silk Road enabled over one million transactions worth an estimated $1.2 billion in revenue (Barratt, 2012). An FBI investigation into the site administrator, who used the handle **Dread Pirate Roberts,** led to the arrest of Ross William Ulbricht in San Francisco, California on October 2, 2013 (Gibbs, 2013). Ulbricht was charged with drug trafficking, soliciting murder, enabling computer hacking and money laundering, and had several million dollars worth of bitcoins seized.

> **For more information on the arrest of Dread Pirate Roberts, go online to:** http://arstechnica.com/tech-policy/2013/10/how-the-feds-took-down-the-dread-pirate-roberts/

The rather unprecedented nature of the Silk Road demonstrates the difficulty that is present in forecasting the future of cybercrime. There are a range of factors that will influence any trends in cybercrime, including the popularity of a given technology, the recognition among offenders of how to use these devices, and the ability for law enforcement to investigate these offenses. This chapter will attempt to consider all of these issues in order to provide some context for the future of cybercrime from the standpoint of offenses, researchers, and policing. We will also discuss the challenges inherent in legislating against cybercrimes in an increasingly borderless world.

Considering the future of cybercrime

It is extremely difficult to forecast the future of cybercrime due to the inherent changes in technology use and implementation both nationally and internationally. As one type of product gains a large market share, hackers and cybercriminals will find ways to exploit it to their advantage (see Chapters 2 and 3). For instance, hackers and malware writers slowly began to target smartphones as these devices garnered a larger proportion of the mobile phone market. Today, the small proportion of malware writers targeting mobile platforms is exploiting a target that gives them the greatest ease of access: Android phone users (Panda Security, 2013). The Android application market is largely unregulated and can easily serve as a vehicle to distribute malicious software under the guise of a legitimate application (see Chapter 3 for details). Hackers who are able to exploit this platform as a venue to capture sensitive information and generate a profit will increase their activities in order to become more effective and efficient. In fact, McAfee predicts that mobile malware will be the key form of malware to explode in terms of both quantity and popularity among hackers over the next decade (McAfee Labs, 2014). This pattern will no doubt continue until such time as mobile phone users recognize the threat they face and take steps to secure their systems through antivirus software and regular updates.

The increased use of cloud storage, where files and documents are stored remotely on web servers that can be accessed via the Internet rather than stored on individual devices, also creates a novel attack point for hackers (Mulazzani, Schrittwieser, Leithner, Huber, and Weippl, 2011). Individuals and corporations are increasingly turning to **cloud storage** providers like Google and Dropbox to provide both easy remote access to files to enable working in groups from any location and simple backups for data in the event of loss. In fact, estimates suggest that Dropbox has over 200 million users around the world, making them one of the largest cloud storage providers to date (Constine, 2013). While this sort of storage provides an invaluable mechanism to share files securely, individuals may place files that contain sensitive information on these servers, including personally identifiable information or intellectual property that could be stolen (Mulazzani *et al.*, 2011). In addition, there are multiple ways that hackers could compromise user accounts to capture shared files, from stealing a username and password to more complex methods involving the use of tools to capture data while in transit (Mulazzani *et al.*, 2011). Given the tremendous popularity of these services, it is likely that this will become a valuable resource for hackers to identify sensitive information and affect individuals and corporations worldwide.

> For more information on threats to cloud storage, go online to: www.globalscape.com/news/2014/2/5/dangerous.filesharing.practices.put.sensitive.corporate.data.at.risk

An additional trend that is likely to occur is the continuous increase in fraud and data theft over the next five years (see Chapter 5). The substantial quantity of information acquired through mass data breaches of major retailers suggests this problem will continue throughout the next decade (McAfee, 2014). In addition, the number of stolen data markets that emerged to sell data to others means this sort of fraud will continue at the global level (Holt, 2013). It is likely that spam-related frauds may trend down as the Internet-using population is comprised of a larger proportion of digital natives who are able to identify fraud schemes and not respond (McAfee, 2014). Well-crafted and targeted spam messages that target one person or a small group, called **spear phishing**, should continue on as the scammers can increase their likelihood of a successful campaign (see Text Box 13.1 for details).

Text Box 13.1: Spear phishing threats in 2014

http://blogs.wsj.com/cio/2014/04/08/mining-manufacturing-at-highest-risk-for-spear-phishing-symantec/

Mining, manufacturing at highest risk for spear phishing: Symantec

> The results of the research revealed that one in 2.7 mining companies were subject to targeted email-based cyberattacks in 2013 known as spear phishing. In the finance, insurance and real estate sectors, that ratio was one in 4.8.

This article provides a summary of a recent research report on the problem of targeted phishing campaigns by the computer security vendor Symantec. It demonstrates the way that various industries are targeted by cybercriminals and provides a forecast for this activity over time.

It is also likely that person-based cybercrimes such as bullying and harassment will continue to increase over the next decade (see Chapter 7). As digital natives continue to utilize various forms of social networking through mobile phones and tablets, the opportunities for individuals to be targeted by bullies and stalkers will increase. Applications such as SnapChat, Vine, Twitter, and Instagram easily allow anyone to post personal information about where they are, who they are with, and preferences for activities. In turn, individuals can easily single someone out and use social media to post hurtful messages that may embarrass or shame them directly to their target or to a wider audience. In addition, the easy use of digital media can allow youth to share sexual images with others. As a result, sexting behaviors can be expected to persist, and perhaps intensify, over time.

How technicways will shift with new technologies

As evident throughout this book, human beings readily adapt their social habits and methods of engaging with the world to fit with available technologies. This process of behavioral changes based on technological changes is referred to as technicways, and can lead to large-scale institutional changes based on evolutions in behavior (see Chapter 1; Odum, 1937). For instance, individuals now use email and electronic communications to connect with others rather than traditional hand-delivered mail through a postal service. How technicways will continue to lead to behavioral change is not immediately apparent, though it will most likely stem from the success or failure of several new technologies that are becoming available to consumers over the next few years.

For instance, there is a range of Internet-enabled **wearable devices** that are being introduced to more completely integrate technology into our daily lives. The creation of Google's new **Google Glass** technology may have a substantial impact on the way that we record our lives and interact with the Internet (Torbert, 2013). These thin glasses come with a wearable computer featuring a heads-up display that is voice-activated and -controlled. Users can do a variety of things while wearing Glass, including taking photos and videos, searching the Internet, checking email, and several other activities that are evolving through the creation of new applications (Torbert, 2013). As a result, Google Glass users could easily record events from their perspective, such as medical procedures. In fact, Dr Rafael Grossman was the first person to stream a surgical procedure using Google Glass. In turn, a number of individuals in the medical field are adopting this technology for educational purposes and consultations with experts (Nosta, 2013).

Such an innovation, if popular, could greatly extend our technological use beyond how we currently use mobile phones and tablet/laptop computers. We will no longer have to open and turn on a device in order to get online and engage in basic online activities. This may promote further miniaturization of technology and integration into wearable forms. At the same time, this may lead people to record and stream all facets of their day-to-day lives with others to social media. The impact that this could have on both privacy and security is hard to tell, as it may further degrade our sense of personal privacy or space.

For more on the applications designed specifically for Google Glass that may change our relationships to technology and one another, go online to: www.huffingtonpost.com/2014/01/21/google-glass-sex_n_4637741.html?view=print&comm_ref=false

In much the same way, companies and utilities providers are encouraging consumers in the US and UK to adopt thermostats and home security systems that can be accessed and controlled via wireless Internet connections (Curtis,

2013). These devices allow consumers to easily manage their energy use and view goings-on in their home with great ease. Some of these devices can even be controlled through applications on smartphones or web browsers, creating what some refer to as the **Internet of Things**, or all non-computing devices connected together via the Internet (Curtis, 2013). The convenience afforded by these technologies cannot be understated, though the implications that they have for our personal security are significant. For instance, running an app on your phone that allows you to access and control home security settings in effect turns the device into a set of keys (Curtis, 2013). If you were to lose your phone, then an individual who picks it up could be able to remotely control the security of your home. Similarly, controlling the heating and cooling system of your home through a wireless device means that hackers could potentially access these systems remotely. Thus, we should give careful consideration to the impact that our rather immediate adoption of technologies can have on our lives before we take the equipment out of the box.

For more on the threats to smart homes and devices, go online to: www. forbes.com/sites/kashmirhill/2013/07/26/smart-homes-hack/

Social movements, technology, and social change

While technology will no doubt force subtle shifts in patterns of human behavior, it will also be at the forefront of rapid social changes in political and government structures. The Internet and CMCs provide individuals with an outlet to express dissent with policies and practices of their own government or those of foreign nations (see Chapter 8; DiMaggio, Hargittai, Neuman, and Robinson, 2001; Van Laer, 2010). These technologies also allow nation-states' most vulnerable and critical systems to be attacked with greater secrecy and fewer resources than might otherwise be required offline (Brodscky & Radvanovsky, 2010). Now that attack techniques like Stuxnet have made cyberattacks against critical infrastructure a reality rather than a theoretical potential, we can expect this to become increasingly problematic.

As discussed in Chapters 2 and 8, an increasing number of hackers target government and industry resources based on their individual political, nationalistic, and religious motives (Holt, 2009; Kilger, 2011). In fact, web defacements by politically motivated hacker groups are common following political events in the real world (Denning, 2010; Kilger, 2011; Woo, Kim, and Dominick, 2004). Denial of service attacks have also become a common tactic to disrupt the electronic resources of a nation-state when physical conflicts emerge, as evident in the Russia–Estonia conflict. As a result, we can expect these sorts of attacks to increase over the next decade as more countries gain consistent Internet access and become technologically sophisticated (McAfee, 2013).

The source of ideologically driven cyberattacks will also change over the next decade as technology increasingly allows individuals who are not citizens of a certain place, or physically present in a country, to engage in attacks (Kilger, 2011). In fact, there have been a substantial number of attacks by hackers around the world who belong to the collective **Anonymous**. The origins of Anonymous stem from the image board 4chan, where people upload and share images with one another without revealing any personal information about themselves (Olson, 2012). Individuals continuously posting pictures without identifying themselves led to the popularity of the idea of Anonymous as a real person. This crystallized in 2004 when one of the 4chan administrators implemented a "Forced_Anon" protocol signing all posts to Anonymous (Olson, 2012). As a result, this led to the acceptance of a collective identity of Anonymous centering on the idea that the Internet is an outlet that has no limits or boundaries.

The group encourages awareness and recognition of individuals who are engaging in either illicit activities or unacceptable actions that harm society. There is no way to identify a member of Anonymous; instead they are a collection of individuals who support an idea or goal without the need for individual recognition (Olson, 2012). In most of their online communications, they utilize the following language as an expression of these values: "We are Anonymous. We are Legion. We do not forgive. We do not forget. Expect us." The group also utilizes Guy Fawkes masks and a body wearing a black suit with a question mark for a head in representation of the anonymous nature of the group. There is also no necessary leadership of Anonymous.

They are often perceived as hacktivists in the general media, as they utilize DDoS attacks, group-based research, email hacking, and other techniques in order to affect a target. For instance, one of the first targets of the group was a white supremacist radio show host named Hal Turner. Members of Anonymous DDoSed his site offline causing thousands of dollars in losses (Olson, 2012). A subsequent attack by individuals associated with Anonymous targeted the Support Online Hip Hop (SOHH) website and its forums. Individuals in the SOHH forum made disparaging comments against Anonymous in June 2008. Their website was then attacked in two stages. The first attack utilized DDoS tools to knock out access followed by a series of web defacements adding Nazi images and racial language to change the site content (Reid, 2008). Shortly thereafter, Anonymous accessed and shared personal information for a teenage boy who ran the site "No Cussing Club" (Olson, 2012). The boy's family was harassed by individuals associated with the group, including hate mail and obscene phone calls.

After these attacks, the focus of Anonymous turned toward social activism in support of free access to information. For instance, the group engaged in a DDoS attack against multiple targets in both the music and private industries in a campaign called "Operation Payback." The

the future of cybercrime, terror, and policy

attacks began in September 2010 as retaliation against anti-piracy initiatives started by media companies in order to reduce access to copyrighted materials online. The attacks expanded to include Sony and their PlayStation Network in 2011. The company began to crack down on attempts to pirate games and media, such as their lawsuit against a hacker who released information on techniques to download PlayStation 2 video games (Olson, 2012). Anonymous members used the Low Orbit Ion Cannon attack tool to engage in a DDoS campaign that took down the PlayStation Network for hours and days at a time. They also accessed and released personal information of PlayStation users obtained by hacking (Olson, 2012).

Shortly after these attacks began, Anonymous also engaged in a series of attacks against PayPal, MasterCard, and Visa in response to their removal of financial support for the website WikiLeaks (Olson, 2012). The site WikiLeaks published a series of 250,000 diplomatic cables acquired through the theft of information by an Army Private named Bradley Manning. Anonymous supported the activities of WikiLeaks because of their role in the free distribution of information (Olson, 2012). The Anonymous attacks used a DDoS campaign in order to successfully take down these groups for hours at a time.

Their involvement in a variety of attacks and hacktivist operations continued throughout 2011 and 2012, including engaging in DDoS attacks against the governments of various Middle Eastern governments during the Arab Spring (Rifai, 2011). Similarly, they attacked the company HBGary Federal after the company attempted to identify the leaders of Anonymous in order to support federal investigations against the group (Leyden, 2011). They also attacked various government and industry targets involved in the attempt to take out a file-sharing service called Megaupload in 2012. Finally, they aided in the Occupy protests through the use of social media to organize and promote various events (Kazmi, 2011).

Despite their prominent role in recent social events, several members of Anonymous have been arrested by federal law enforcement in the US, Spain, and UK on violations of various cybercrime statutes. This has led to some decrease in the frequency of posts and calls to action from members of the collective, though they are still active in certain parts of the world. Thus, Anonymous is an excellent example of how political and ideologically driven attacks will occur in the next decade in an attempt to create change in real-world policies.

Need for new cyber criminological theories?

Chapters 2 through 8 illustrated the various ways in which technology has influenced the commission of many forms of crime. In most instances, "newer" forms of crime were not born from technology. Instead, criminals were able to use the Internet and various devices to commit traditional forms of crime and deviance in more effective and efficient ways. Thus, the notion that cybercrime can be viewed as "old wine in a new bottle" (Grabosky, 2001: Wall, 1998; see Chapter 9) has strong merit. In fact, the current body of criminological research on cybercrime as discussed in Chapter 9 demonstrates that traditional theories of offending apply well to cybercrimes that have substantively similar counterparts in the physical world, such as theft, harassment, bullying, and pornography. In addition, traditional criminological theories have also provided considerable insight to the more complex cybercrimes of malware creation/distribution and unauthorized access to computer systems. For example, one of the strongest predictors of cybercrime offending is the same as that of traditional crime – associating with delinquent or criminal peers (Holt and Bossler, 2014). Having friends who engage in various forms of cybercrime increases the likelihood that the individual will engage in these same offenses as well. Also, definitions (e.g. values, norms, statements, etc.) that support involvement in cybercrimes are also associated with an individual's willingness to engage in cybercrime, as is their acceptance of techniques of neutralization that justify offending behavior. In the social control literature, low self-control has been repeatedly found to be a substantive predictor of almost all types of crime, including various forms of cybercrime (Holt and Bossler, 2014).

Given the support that these theories have in the larger literature, one of the most critical steps researchers can take to move the discipline forward is to elaborate on these existing theories. For instance, though it is clear that deviant peer relationships directly increase the risk of cybercrime offending, few have identified whether virtual peer networks or those in the real world have a greater impact on activity (Higgins, 2005; Holt, Burruss, and Bossler, 2010). It may be that having friends in the real world who engage in cybercrime is more pertinent to the introduction of these activities. They can serve as sources of imitation for cybercrime offenses and may make it easier for individuals to understand why a person may pirate music, media, or engage in simple forms of hacking like password guessing. The role of virtual peers may become more significant after their initial offending, as individuals have to learn new techniques to offend and ways to justify their actions (Holt et al., 2010). Until such time as researchers examine these relationships more specifically, we will be unable to disentangle this relationship.

There is also a need for research considering how certain demographic factors affect the likelihood of engaging in or becoming a victim of cybercrime in some way. In criminological research on real-world offenses, there is a significant relationship between living in poverty and the risk of offending and victimization (see Bradshaw, Sawyer, and O'Brennan, 2009; Bursik and Grasmick 1993). There is minimal research on the ways that an individual's socio-economic background affects the risk of both cybercrime victimization and offending. While technology use has become more ubiquitous, even for those living in low-income communities, it is possible that the degree to which individuals use these devices on a daily basis may significantly affect the risk of cybercrime victimization. Individuals living in poverty generally may have little disposable income for Internet connectivity or online shopping and may be less inclined to own their own computer. Instead, they may use computers in local libraries or other publicly accessible locations, which may reduce their risk of malware infections or computer hacking (Smith, 2013). The same individual may be more likely to use a mobile phone in order to access social media and email, which may increase their risk of cyberbullying and harassment (Smith, 2013). Research that can measure and assess the relationship between socio-economic status and cybercrime could prove invaluable to better document the predictors of risk for both victimization and offending.

At the same time, this book has demonstrated that there is something unique about cybercrime offending that separates it from traditional crime. There are some instances of "new wine," such as malware creation, that has little connection to either the physical world or the second part of the analogy – the new bottle. In this case, examining the uniqueness of cybercrime might allow us to not only understand more about these phenomena, but it might also provide brand new insights on traditional forms of crime as well. Considering that criminological theory development has slowed over the last few decades, discussions of new cyber-specific criminological theories might be the catalyst that rejuvenates this field. Taken as a whole, the future of cybercrime research is bright. The field will help elaborate complex associations that have been held in the traditional literature for decades while also providing new insights into the commission of crime – both traditional and cyber-related.

Shifting enforcement strategies in the age of the Internet

As noted throughout this text, law enforcement agencies across the world are engaged in the investigation of cybercrime. The capabilities of these agencies to investigate cybercrimes range greatly based on both the specific agency in question as well as the type of cybercrime being investigated. Governments have provided substantive resources to fund policing agencies to pursue child exploitation crimes and child pornography as individual units and in connection with one another (see Chapter 6). Few mechanisms, however, exist to help connect the investigative capabilities of local, state, federal, and international agencies in their investigations of malicious software utilization and data theft.

In order to move beyond the limits posed by limited inter-agency cooperation, some degree of innovation is required in order for police agencies to disrupt and deter some forms of cybercrime. For instance, US law enforcement agencies have begun to target the online payment systems used by data thieves and hackers to pay for malware and information (see Chapters 3 and

5 for details). Using money laundering statutes, the Department of Justice was able to prosecute the payment service e-Gold due to its use by data thieves in the early 2000s (Holt and Lampke, 2010; Peretti, 2009; Surowiecki, 2013). The service provided a digital gold-backed currency system that members of the carding group, the Shadow Crew, used to send and receive payments for data and services (Peretti, 2009). The prosecution forced the company to close, and made market actors move to other payment systems, thereby disrupting the practices of hackers and flow of money between actors (see Text Box 13.2 for details). Similarly, the payment processor **Liberty Reserve** is being prosecuted in the US for its role in money laundering for various forms of crime (Surowiecki, 2013). This technique therefore provides an indirect method to disrupt the practices of cybercriminals.

Text Box 13.2: Investigating Tor users

www.techweekeurope.co.uk/news/tor-anonymisation-nccu-cyber-crime-129249

New UK cyber police chief: We need skills to de-anonymise Tor crooks

The National Cyber Crime Unit (NCCU), launched alongside the National Crime Agency earlier this week, has continued an ongoing project to break the anonymisation of Tor users where it believes illegal activity is taking place, NCCU chief Andy Archibald told *TechWeek* this morning, during a discussion hosted by Symantec.

This article provides an important example of the ways that law enforcement agencies are attempting to diminish the available resources cybercriminals have at their disposal to hide their identity. The discussion also demonstrates the difficulty that agencies have in terms of hiring the right people with the right skills to combat cybercrime.

In addition to taking out payment systems, law enforcement agencies are beginning to adopt strategies to weaken the utility of anonymization tools like Tor that help to shield the identity and location of computer users (Dredge, 2013). Tor is a widely popular and relatively secure service that individuals download and install on their system. Once downloaded and activated, Tor encrypts an individual's web traffic and routes it through a network of other Tor users' systems that is randomized, making it difficult to locate the actual source of any user's computer (Dredge, 2013). Because of the security that Tor affords, a wide range of cybercriminals use this service to conceal their activities, including child pornography trading, drug markets (as noted above), and sensitive information exchanges. As a result, the FBI, NSA, and GCHQ in the UK have begun to develop rather sophisticated resources to help identify vulnerabilities in Tor's infrastructure that can give them information on individual users (see Text Box 13.3 for details; Brewster, 2013). Such efforts are extremely labor intensive and do not guarantee that Tor and other services like it can be rendered useless, but demonstrate that law enforcement recognize the need to better identify offenders and disrupt the most practical resources they have to hide their identities online.

Text Box 13.3: Pursuing online payment systems

www.reuters.com/article/2013/08/09/net-us-cybercrime-digital-currency-idUSBRE9780GM20130809

Hackers switch to new digital currency after Liberty Reserve

> Three months after a team of international law enforcement officials raided the digital currency firm Liberty Reserve, cyber experts say criminals are increasingly turning to another online currency called Perfect Money ... some online scam artists and thieves are using Perfect Money's digital currency to launder money and conceal profits.

> This article provides a robust discussion of the ways that cybercriminals change their practices after law enforcement investigations. In this case, the author describes cybercriminals' transition from the use of the online payment system Liberty Reserve to Perfect Money after the former was closed by law enforcement. The article demonstrates the value in alternative strategies to affect cybercrime activities.

Considering the future of forensics

The globalization of technology has vastly changed the field of digital forensics. Traditional computer forensics focused only on dead-box forensics involving cases of inappropriate use policies or unauthorized computer access. Today, almost every criminal investigation will involve at least one form of digital evidence due to the increased use of technology in our daily lives (see Chapter 10 for discussion). Approximately 39 percent of the world's population will have Internet access by the end of 2013 (International Telecommunication Union, 2013), which is up from 20 percent in 2006. In addition, there are almost as many mobile phone subscriptions (6.8 billion) as there are people in the world (7.1 billion), and 22 percent of the world's population owns a smartphone (Heggestuen, 2013).

This continued increase guarantees that the criminal justice system (e.g. law enforcement, prosecutors, judges) will need to become more familiar with the basic, if not more advanced, forms of digital forensic investigation. In addition, the digital forensics investigator will need to sort through a variety of digital devices as well as filter out irrelevant digital information from massive volumes of data (e.g. 6 TB hard drive). As a result, this will likely force changes in the ability of criminal justice personnel to become more adept at recognizing technological devices and their role in offending. In addition, this understanding of basic digital evidence collection will have to take place at crime scenes themselves to ensure a successful prosecution.

The expansion of technology also has implications for the forensic sciences generally. For example, The National Research Council (NRC, 2009) recently issued a report on the status of forensic science in the United States that recognized the field of digital and multimedia analysis as a new subfield within the larger discipline of forensic science (NRC, 2009: 178–185). Although the NRC acknowledged that the digital forensics discipline "has undergone a rapid maturation process" (p. 181), the report noted that several challenges still remain if digital forensics is to be a rigorous, forensic science discipline: (1) lack of an agreed-upon certification program or list of qualifications for digital forensic examiners; (2) clarifying whether the examination of digital evidence is an investigative or a forensic activity, and (3) wide variability in, and a degree of uncertainty about, the education, experience, and training of digital forensics professionals (p. 181). To that end, there are currently a number of professional certifications available, both vendor neutral (e.g. GIAC Certified Forensic Analyst) and vendor specific (i.e. tool specific, such as EnCase® Forensic Training Series; Ryan and Ryan, 2014). No standardized list of certifications or qualifications required in the digital forensics discipline in order to be considered a digital forensics professional or expert exists, however.

Overall, the future of digital forensics relies on the discipline's ability to conquer each of the concerns highlighted by the NRC. The discipline needs to establish a standard of accreditation for digital forensic laboratories as well as a standard for training and continued education for digital forensic examiners. In addition, the digital forensics community needs to create a standardized protocol for the process of conducting a digital forensics investigation that focuses on the forensic scientific method (Casey, 2011). By following a scientific method, the examiner is less likely to overlook potential digital evidence or report erroneous findings. According to Casey (2011), a protocol that focuses on the scientific method will encourage digital forensics examiners to follow procedures that are "generally accepted, reliable, and repeatable" as well as more likely to lead to "logical, well-documented conclusions of high integrity" (p. 224).

The challenge to policy-makers globally

The trends identified in this chapter all demonstrate that technological innovations create myriad opportunities for crime and deviance. One of the most common ways that policy-makers, particularly in government and private industry, discuss how we may combat these problems is through the cultivation of better cybersecurity principles that can be employed by the common person every day. Every time an individual uses their antivirus software or carefully reviews an email message before responding, they are taking basic steps to secure their computer or device from compromise. As digital natives age, their use of and appreciation for technology may provide them with an even greater degree of computer security awareness than that of the digital immigrants of older generations. This may create a slight improvement in the general security posture of society as a whole.

Any benefits provided by improvements in security awareness may, however, be diminished by vulnerabilities and flaws in the computer systems and servers managed by ISPs and industry. When a new vulnerability in an otherwise secure product is identified and weaponized by hackers, this directly threatens the security of all computer users through no fault of their own. The resources owned and operated by private and public entities that have a responsibility to protect personal information and resources should be secured through the best practices available. There is no guarantee that such protection may matter when large-scale vulnerabilities are found that directly impact the security of sensitive information. For instance, a vulnerability in the OpenSSL (Secure Socket Layer) library used to encrypt sensitive data as it moves between systems online, was identified on April 1, 2014 (Kaminsky, 2014). The vulnerability, called Heartbleed, would essentially allow an attacker to steal the encryption keys used by servers to secure sessions between users' computers and servers, allowing them to capture cookies and password data (Kaminsky, 2014). More than 17 percent of all secured servers online could be harmed as a result of the vulnerability, and several related incidents of the loss of personal information have been reported.

> **For more information on the Hearbleed vulnerability and its impact, go online to:** http://money.cnn.com/2014/04/24/technology/security/heartbleed-security/

The Heartbleed incident clearly demonstrates that cybersecurity extends beyond the individual, and cannot be easily guaranteed. While nothing can ever be guaranteed to be "hack proof," if developers are careful to identify as many bugs and flaws as possible during the design phase, it may help minimize the likelihood of attacks once a product is available on the open market. Such a model is not currently in use among software and hardware developers as it is viewed as too prohibitive and costly. Instead, vulnerabilities are often identified and patched once the product is adopted and in use in the field.

As a result, some government agencies have begun to push for standards of cybersecurity that promote the development of products that are more secure by design. For instance, the ISA Security Compliance Institute (ISCI) in the US has developed multiple testing and compliance specifications, along with a certification program for SCADA system hardware and software, that are used in various critical infrastructure (Andress and Winterfeld, 2013). By emphasizing and establishing basic guidelines, the hope is that these systems may be hardened against attacks and better designed generally. Similar entities exist throughout North and South America, Europe, and the UK to promote more secure products and create a degree of compliance that can be enforced by industrial regulatory bodies (Andress and Winterfeld, 2013). Though these entities cannot guarantee that a product will be completely hardened to compromise, the creation of standards and guidelines provides a measurable standard that can be considered by regulators and policy-makers when attempting to improve cyber security practices among private industry.

In addition to the development of regulatory and industrial standards, lawmakers must create legislation that is both broad and flexible enough to be applied to a range of technological misuse while at the same time having substantive legal sanctions to deter individual offenders. Such a task is extremely difficult as there is no way to know how a new device or application will be adopted by offenders for nefarious purposes. For example, the failure to successfully prosecute Lori Drew for misuse of the web site MySpace under the CFA laws (Chapter 7) suggests that there is a potential need to develop legislation against extreme outcomes resulting from cyberbullying. At the same time, legislative overreach can have negative outcomes as well. For instance, some local prosecutors have applied child pornography creation laws to individuals who send or receive sexting images (see Text Box 13.4 for an example).

Text Box 13.4: Sexting prosecutions of child pornography

http://edition.cnn.com/2009/CRIME/04/07/sexting.busts/index.html#cnnSTCText

"Sexting" lands teen on sex offender list

Phillip Alpert ... had just turned 18 when he sent a naked photo of his 16-year-old girlfriend ... to dozens of her friends and family after an argument ... Alpert was arrested and charged with sending child pornography ... He was sentenced to five years probation and required ... to register as a sex offender.

This article demonstrates the substantive difficulties prosecutors and legislators face when dealing with new forms of cybercrime. There is no necessary agreement as to whether child pornography laws are appropriate to use when dealing with materials sent between minors. As a result, this article is a pertinent example for readers on the challenges posed by cybercrime.

There are no easy ways to facilitate the creation of appropriate legislation, and many attempts to regulate online spaces have been struck down. Most recently, the US Congress attempted to pass a bill called the **Stop Online Piracy Act (SOPA)** in 2012. The legislation was designed to expand the capabilities of law enforcement to combat both digital piracy and online counterfeiting and would have enabled courts to order that websites be blocked in the event that they hosted or were in some way involved with either piracy or counterfeiting activities (Chozick, 2012). The legislation drew tremendous criticism from privacy advocates and some websites such as Wikipedia, while proponents argued that it would have been tremendously helpful to protect intellectual property (Chozick, 2012). The legislation eventually failed after numerous online "blackouts" organized by Wikipedia and other websites in protest against the Act, along with multiple DDoS attacks performed by Anonymous members against the RIAA and other pro-SOPA entities (Chozick, 2012). This example clearly demonstrates the challenges that legislators face in attempting to bring about legislative changes to deal with cybercrimes.

At a global level, there is also a need for improved international mechanisms to help combat serious financial and hacking-related cybercrimes. As noted in Chapter 6, there are a number of working groups that exist to coordinate transnational responses to child exploitation crimes. There are few similar entities to pursue hacking and fraud-related crimes, making it difficult to effectively sanction and deter offenders. In fact, the lack of resources may account for the continuing number of mass data breaches that also foster the global market for stolen data (Peretti, 2009).

One way to expand the response to cybercrime is through the integration of corporations and private industry that either own or control sensitive systems and networks (Wall, 2007). In fact, corporations like Microsoft have formed working groups to combat cybercrimes through the creation of their new **Digital Crimes Unit** (Adhikari, 2013). This unit recently worked with law enforcement agencies in the US and Europe to track the addresses of computers infected with the ZeroAccess botnet malware and push security updates to those systems to disrupt the size of the network. This effort was combined with a civil lawsuit filed by Microsoft against the botnet operator, which was eventually dropped after the company was able to work with law enforcement to directly identify infected systems (Adhikari, 2013). Such a strategy is interesting as it means that victim systems can be cleaned and repaired without the need to directly arrest the botnet operator. At the same time, this technique actually harmed legitimate computer users whose systems were not infected but were associated with the infected nodes (Adhikari, 2013). In addition, there are substantive questions concerning the impact of corporate entities playing a major role in the investigation of cybercrimes and how this may diminish the perceived ability of law enforcement.

> **For more on the Microsoft Digital Crimes Unit, go online to:** http://blogs.microsoft.com/blog/2013/12/19/zeroaccess-criminals-wave-white-flag-the-impact-of-partnerships-on-cybercrime/

An additional strategy that some have proposed to aid in the investigation and prosecution of cybercrimes internationally is to develop an **international criminal tribunal** for cyberspace that can sanction offenders (Schjolberg, 2012). The formation of a truly international court that could represent the victim nations and offenders could be a valuable tool to pursue cases where multiple nations were affected by a group of actors. There is also a precedent for the use of tribunals at the international level, such as the International Criminal Court, to provide a venue for prosecution (Schjolberg, 2012). There are substantive concerns among nations that such a strategy could obviate justice mechanisms within their own nation and directly hinder the investigation of cybercrimes within nations. Furthermore, there is no guarantee that all nations would be willing to participate in a tribunal because of the perceived legitimacy of such a body. Thus, it is not clear if such a strategy can ever truly be implemented in the real world.

Summary

Computers and the Internet have radically changed how we communicate, engage in business, and interact with the larger world in a very short amount of time. The benefits of these technologies are substantial, though they also create a range of threats to personal safety and national security. As a result, we have to continuously identify these threats and the ways that technologies are being abused by offenders to facilitate criminal behaviors. Only then can we improve our understanding of the influence of technology on the nature of crime and deviance in the twenty-first century and better protect ourselves.

Discussion questions

1) Can you think of any distinct technologies that you use that could be exploited by hackers? In what way could they be harmed? What information could be gathered from their compromise?

2) How could innovations like unmanned aerial vehicles (UAVs) or drones be used by cybercriminals to effectively collect information or offend? How could law enforcement agencies around the world use these devices to disrupt cybercriminals generally?

3) Based on everything you read throughout this book, what do you think the future of cybercrime offending and offenders will look like?

4) What other solutions can you think of to better prepare law enforcement to investigate cybercrimes? How can we improve the overall response?

References

Adhikari, R. (2013). Microsoft's ZeroAccess Botnet Takedown No 'Mission Accomplished'. *TechNewsWorld* December 9, 2013. [Online] Available at: www.technewsworld.com/story/79586.html

Andress, J., & Winterfeld, S. (2013). *Cyber Warfare: Techniques, Tactics, and Tools for Security Practitioners*, 2nd edition. Waltham MA: Syngress.

Barratt, M. J. (2012). Silk Road: Ebay for drugs. *Addiction*, 107, 683.

Brewster, T. (2013). New UK Cyber Police Chief: We need skills to de-anonymise Tor crooks. *Tech Week Europe* October 10, 2013. [Online] Available at: www.techweekeurope.co.uk/news/tor-anonymisation-nccu-cyber-crime-129249

Brodscky, J., & Radvanovsky, R. (2010). Control Systems Security. In T. J. Holt & B. Schell (eds), *Corporate Hacking and Technology-Driven Crime: Social Dynamics and Implications* (pp. 187–204). Hershey, PA: IGI-Global.

Bradshaw, C. P., Sawyer, A. L., & O'Brennan, L. M. (2009). A social disorganization perspective on bullying-related attitudes and behaviors: The influence of school context. *American Journal of Community Psychology*, 43, 204–220.

Bursik, R. J., & Grasmick, H. G. (1993). *Neighborhoods and Crime: The Dimensions of Effective Community Control*. New York, NY: Macmillan.

Casey, E. (2011). *Digital Evidence and Computer Crime: Forensic Science, Computers, and the Internet*, 3rd ed. Waltham, MA: Academic Press.

Chozick, A. (2012). Tech and media elite are likely to debate piracy. *New York Times* July 10, 2012. [Online] Available at: www.nytimes.com/2012/07/10/business/media/tech-and-media-elite-are-likely-to-debate-piracy.html?_r=0

Constine, J. 2013. Dropbox hits 200m users, unveils new "for business" client combining work and personal files. *TechCrunch* November 13, 2013. [Online] Available at: http://techcrunch.com/2013/11/13/dropbox-hits-200-million-users-and-announces-new-products-for-businesses/

Curtis, S. (2013). Home invasion 2.0: How criminals could hack your house. *The Telegraph* August 2, 2013. [Online] Available at: www.telegraph.co.uk/technology/internet-security/10218824/Home-invasion-2.0-how-criminals-could-hack-your-house.html

Denning, D. E. (2010). Cyber-Conflict as an Emergent Social Problem. In T. J. Holt & B. Schell (eds), *Corporate Hacking and Technology-Driven Crime: Social Dynamics and Implications* (pp. 170–186). Hershey, PA: IGI-Global.

DiMaggio, P., Hargittai, E., Neuman, W. R., and Robinson, J. P. (2001). Social implications of the Internet. *Annual Review of Sociology*, 27, 307–336.

Dredge, S. (2013). What is Tor? A beginner's guide to the privacy tool. *The Guardian* November 5, 2013. [Online] Available at: www.theguardian.com/technology/2013/nov/05/tor-beginners-guide-nsa-browser

Franklin, O. (2013). Unravelling the dark web. *British GQ*. [Online] Available at: www.gq-magazine.co.uk/comment/articles/2013-02/07/silk-road-online-drugs-guns-black-market/viewall

Gibbs, S. (2013). Silk Road underground market closed – but others will replace it. *The Guardian*, October 3, 2013. [Online] Available at: www.theguardian.com/technology/2013/oct/03/silk-road-underground-market-closed-bitcoin

Grabosky, P. N. (2001). Virtual criminality: Old wine in new bottles? *Social Legal Studies*, 10, 243–249.

Heggestuen, J. (2013, December 15). *One In Every 5 People In The World Own A Smartphone, One In Every 17 Own A Tablet*. Business Insider. [Online] Available at: www.businessinsider.com

Higgins, G. E. (2005). Can low self-control help with the understanding of the software piracy problem? *Deviant Behavior*, 26, 1–24.

Holt, T. J. (2009). The Attack Dynamics of Political and Religiously Motivated Hackers. In T. Saadawi & L. Jordan (eds) *Cyber Infrastructure Protection* (pp. 161–182). New York: Strategic Studies Institute.

Holt, T. J. (2013). Examining the forces shaping cybercrime markets online. *Social Science Computer Review*, 31, 165–177.

Holt, T. J., & Bossler, A. M. (2014). An assessment of the current state of cybercrime scholarship. *Deviant Behavior*, 35, 20–40.

Holt, T. J., Burruss, G. W., & Bossler, A. M. (2010). Social learning and cyber deviance: Examining the importance of a full social learning model in the virtual world. *Journal of Crime and Justice*, 33, 15–30.

Holt, T. J., & Lampke, E. (2010). Exploring stolen data markets on-line: Products and market forces. *Criminal Justice Studies*, 23: 33–50.

International Telecommunication Union. 2013. *The world in 2013: Facts and figures*. [Online] Available at: www.itu.int/ict

Kaminsky, D. (2014). Be Still My Breaking Heart. *Dan Kaminsky's Blog*, 10 April, 2014. [Online] Available at: http://dankaminsky.com/2014/04/10/heartbleed/

Kazmi, A. (2011). How Anonymous emerged to Occupy Wall Street. *The Guardian*. September 26, 2011. [Online] Available at: www.guardian.co.uk/commentisfree/cifamerica/2011/sep/27/occupy-wall-street-anonymous

Kilger, M. (2011). Social Dynamics and the Future of Technology-Driven Crime. In T. J. Holt & B. Schell (eds), *Corporate Hacking and Technology-Driven Crime: Social Dynamics and Implications* (pp. 205–227). Hershey, PA: IGI-Global.

Leyden, J. (2011). Anonymous security firm hack used every trick in book. *The Register* February 18, 2011. [Online] Available at: www.theregister.co.uk/2011/02/17/hbgary_hack_redux/

McAfee Labs. (2013). *2013 Threat Predictions*. [Online] Available at: www.mcafee.com/us/resources/reports/rp-threat-predictions-2013.pdf

McAfee Labs. (2014). *McAfee Labs 2014 Threat Prediction*. [Online] Available at: www.mcafee.com/us/resources/reports/rp-threats-predictions-2014.pdf

Mulazzani, M., Schrittwieser, S., Leithner, M., Huber, M., & Weippl, E. (2011, August). Dark Clouds on the Horizon: Using Cloud Storage as Attack Vector and Online Slack Space. In *USENIX Security Symposium*.

National Research Council (2009). *Strengthening Forensic Science in the United States: A Path Forward*. Washington, DC: US Department of Justice.

Nosta, J. (2013). Inside the operating room with Google Glass. *Forbes*, June 21, 2013. [Online] Available at: www.forbes.com/sites/johnnosta/2013/06/21/google-glass-in-the-operating-room/

Odum, H. (1937). Notes on technicways in contemporary society. *American Sociological Review*, 2, 336–346.

Olson, P. (2012). *We are Anonymous: Inside the Hacker World of LulzSec, Anonymous, and the Global Cyber Insurgency*. New York: Little, Brown, and Company.

Panda Security. (2013). *Annual Report Pandalabs 2013 Summary*. [Online] Available at: http://press.pandasecurity.com/wp-content/uploads/2010/05/Annual-Report-PandaLabs-2013.pdf

Peretti, K. K. (2009). Data breaches: What the underground world of "carding" reveals. *Santa Clara Computer and High Technology Law Journal*, 25, 375–413.

Reid, S. (2008). Hip-hop sites hacked by apparent hate group: SOHH, AllHipHop Temporarily Suspect Access. *MTV*. [Online] Available at: www.mtv.com/news/articles/1590117/hip-hop-sites-hacked-by-apparent-hate-group.jhtml

Rifai, R. (2011). Timeline: Tunisia's Uprising. *Al Jazeera*, Jan 23, 2011. www.aljazeera.com/indepth/spotlight/tunisia/2011/01/201114142223827361.html

Ryan, J., & Ryan, D. (2014, February). *Credentialing the digital and multimedia forensics professional*. Presented at the 66th Annual Scientific Meeting of the American Academy of Forensic Sciences, Seattle, WA.

Schjolberg, J. (2012). Recommendations for potential new global legal mechanisms against global cyberattacks and other global cybercrimes. EastWest Institute (EWI) Cybercrime Legal Working Group. [Online] Available at: www.cybercrimelaw.net/documents/ICTC.pdf

Smith, A. (2013). *Technology adoption by lower income populations*. Pew Internet and American Life Project. [Online] Available at: www.pewinternet.org/Presentations/2013/Oct/Technology-Adoption-by-Lower-Income-Populations.aspx

Surowiecki, J. (2013). Why did criminals trust Liberty Reserve? *The New Yorker*, May 31, 2013. [Online] Available at: www.newyorker.com/online/blogs/newsdesk/2013/05/why-did-criminals-trust-liberty-reserve.html

Torbert, S. (2013). Google Glass Teardown. *TechRadar* June 12, 2013. [Online] Available at: www.catwig.com/google-glass-teardown/

Van Laer, J. (2010). Activists online and offline: The Internet as an information channel for protest demonstrations. *Mobilization: An International Journal*, 15, 347–366.

Wall, D. S. (1998). Catching cybercriminals: Policing the Internet. *International Review of Law, Computers, & Technology*, 12: 201–218.

Wall, D. S. (2007). *Cybercrime: The Transformation of Crime in the Information Age*. Cambridge: Polity Press.

Woo, H., Kim, Y., & Dominick, J. (2004). Hackers: Militants or merry pranksters? A content analysis of defaced web pages. *Media Psychology*, 6, 63–82.

Glossary

.xxx domain	A web domain address that provides a voluntary option for individuals to host pornographic content online.
1 terabyte (1 TB)	One trillion bytes.
419 scams	Another term for advance fee email schemes. The name references the Nigerian legal statutes that are used to prosecute fraud.
Absence of a capable guardian	Variable in routine activity theory that references the lack of physical, personal, or social protection that can minimize harm to a target.
Access key	The password used by encryption programs that unlocks a file using the same algorithm that encrypted the information in order to decrypt it.
Accuracy	The integrity of the data.
Action Fraud	The UK national agency that handles complaints of Internet-based fraud and theft.
Active files	Existing files that are currently available on a hard drive, meaning they have not been deleted.
Ad Hoc phase	A term used to describe the pre-forensics age of computer forensic technologies.
Adam Walsh Child Protection and Safety Act	US law that, among other protections, prohibited the defense from obtaining copies of child pornography evidence, in order to limit distribution of said illicit materials, so long as the defense has an ample opportunity to examine the evidence at a government facility.
Admissibility	The process of determining whether evidence will assist the fact finders (e.g. judge) through their decision-making process.
Advance fee email schemes	A scheme where a spam mail sender requests a small amount of money up front from the recipient in order to share a larger sum of money later.
Affidavit	A written, or occasionally verbal, statement to which the law enforcement officer has sworn an oath to the magistrate that the information is true and factual.

Age Verification Services (AVS)	A web-based service that, upon entry into a website, verifies the age of an individual via either a valid credit card or a driver's license.
Amendment	An addition or alteration to the US Constitution.
Anonymous	A group that stemmed from the image board 4chan that engages in a number of hacks and attacks against targets around the world.
Anti-Malware Testing Standards Organization (AMTSO)	An organization that exists to provide a forum to improve the process of malware identification and product testing across the global security industry.
Anti-Phishing Working Group (APWG)	A not-for-profit global consortium of researchers, computer security professionals, financial industry members, and law enforcement designed to document the scope of phishing attacks and provide policy recommendations to government and industry groups worldwide.
App	A software application typically downloaded by the user that performs a certain function.
Apparent authority principle	US legal standard that states that if police obtain consent to search premises from someone who they reasonably believe shares a common authority over the premises then it does not violate Fourth Amendment rights even if the individual did not have the authority to give consent.
Appeal to higher loyalties	One of the five basic techniques Sykes and Matza developed that allows individuals to break from conformity, operating on the basis that an offense is for the greater good of the group.
Argot	Special language utilized by subcultures to refer to individuals in and out of the group and demonstrate connection to the subculture.
Arrest warrant	A signed document by a judge or magistrate authorizing law enforcement to take the person into custody.
Australian Federation Against Copyright Theft (AFACT)	A non-governmental federation that targets pirates in Australia and Oceania generally.
Authentic	A true and unaltered copy of the original data source.
Authenticity	The ability to prove that the evidence is genuine in a court of law.
BackOrifice 2000 (BO2K)	A piece of malware written by members of Cult of the Dead Cow which infected Microsoft BackOffice server programs.
Berne Convention for the Protection of Literary and Artistic Works	A legal framework created in 1986 to provide a common framework for intellectual property rights.
Best evidence rule	See *original writing rule*.
Bestiality	Experiencing sexual arousal from sex with animals.

Beyond a reasonable doubt	Term used to refer to the standard of proof needed in US criminal courts to show that a person on trial committed a crime.
BigDoggie	A website that enables individuals to access and post reviews of escort services.
Bill C-13	Proposed legislation that would make it a crime to share an intimate image without the consent of the subject of the image, punishable by up to five years in prison.
Bill of Rights	The first ten Amendments of the US Constitution.
Bitcoin	A relatively anonymous form of electronic currency used by a range of actors to pay for goods.
Black-hat hacker	Uses techniques and vulnerabilities in order to gain access to information or harm systems.
Blended threat	Any form of malware that combines aspects of viruses, worms, and trojan horses together in a single tool.
Blind	Term used to refer to the idea that an independent forensic examiner should be completely unaware of the conclusions reached by the initial examiner.
Boot sector	A region of any sort of storage media or the hard disk of a computer that can hold code and be loaded into the computer's memory by its firmware.
Boot sector virus	A form of malware that operates by attempting to install code into the boot sector of either a form of storage media like a flash drive or the hard disk of the targeted computer.
Botnet	A form of malware that combines aspects of trojan horse programs and viruses and allows an infected computer to receive commands and be controlled by another user through Internet Relay Chat channels or the web via HTTP protocols.
Bridges	A hardware write blocker.
Bulletin board system (BBS)	A form of asynchronous computer-mediated communication used heavily during the 1980s.
Bureau of Customs and Border Patrol (CBP)	The US federal agency responsible for policing and managing the borders of the country and the movement of products in and out of the nation.
Cam whores	Performers who engage in text-based conversations with individuals viewing them on streaming-video feeds and take requests for specific behaviors or sexual acts.
Canadian Anti-Fraud Centre (CAFC)	A joint effort between the RCMP, Ontario Provincial Police, and the Competition Bureau, that collects reports on various forms of fraud that take place online and offline.
Canadian National Child Exploitation Coordination Center (NCECC)	The Canadian agency that serves as a focal point of contact for online exploitation cases that cross jurisdictional boundaries within Canada or internationally.

Capture the Flag	Competitions where hackers compete against each other individually or in teams to hack one another, while at the same time defending their resources from others.
Carding	When an individual sells personally identifiable information acquired in some fashion via markets operating online, most often involving the use and abuse of credit and debit card details.
Carding markets	Markets that enable individuals to efficiently engage in credit card fraud and identity theft with minimal effort and limited technical knowledge or skill.
Carnegie Mellon Report	A report published by a student at Carnegie Mellon University which suggested that over 80 percent of images on the Internet involved sexually explicit content. The findings were subsequently debunked.
Carrier	The transport medium for digital information.
Catfishing	The creation and development of relationships through social media predicated on false information.
Celerity	Swiftness, in the context of deterrence theory.
Centre for the Protection of National Infrastructure (CPNI)	The Center designed to protect UK critical infrastructure owners from emerging threats and coordinate responses in the event of a physical or cyber-based compromise.
Certainty	Refers to how likely it is that an individual will be caught and punished for an offense within deterrence theory.
Chain of custody	The chronological documentation of evidence as it is processed during an investigation.
Chaos Communication Congress (CCC)	One of the oldest and largest computer hacking and security conferences held in Europe.
Child Exploitation and Online Protection (CEOP) Command	The FBI-operated agency that takes reports of exploitation, abuse, and missing youth and will directly investigate threats and coordinate responses, depending on the scope of harm across multiple areas.
Child Exploitation Task Forces (CETF)	This FBI-operated task force provides a reactive and proactive response to online sexual exploitation cases and sex tourism practices.
Child love	A term used by pedophiles to describe their sexual attraction to youth.
Child pornography	The real or simulated depiction of sexual or sexualized physical abuse of children under 16 years of age, or who appear to be less than 16, that would offend a reasonable adult.
Child Pornography Protection Act of 1996	This US Act extended existing laws regarding child pornography by establishing a new definition for this term, amending the criminal code under Title 18 to define child porn as "any visual depiction, including any photograph, film, video, picture, or computer or computer-generated image or picture of sexually explicit conduct."

Child Protections Operations (CPO) Teams	The Australian Federal Police team that investigates and coordinates the response to child exploitation cases both domestically and internationally.
Child Victim Identification Program (CVIP)	A US FBI-led program that examines images of child pornography in order to determine the identity and location of child victims.
Children's Internet Protection Act (CIPA)	This US federal act requires the implementation of filters in all schools that teach students from kindergarten through 12th grade.
Cipher	A mathematical formula (algorithm) that uses a set of rules for transforming a message.
Ciphertext	An illegible message.
Civil offense	A noncriminal offense, usually a dispute between private parties.
Closed source software	Software where the source code is not made available to the general public; only the object code, which restricts the ability of users to modify and share the software due to copyright infringement, is publicly shared.
Cloud storage	A virtual warehouse where people can store data on a network.
Cluster	Two or more consecutive sectors on a hard drive.
Code-Red Worm	A form of malware activated online on July 13, 2001 that infected any web server using Microsoft's IIS web server software.
Collection/acquisition phase	Phase of the digital evidence collection process concerned with the retrieval and preservation of digital evidence.
Collision	When hashing a hard drive does not result in a unique digital fingerprint for an item, but instead the same hash value is produced.
Commodity	The way that the clients of sex workers describe prostitutes in online forums.
Communications and Multimedia Act 1998	Malaysian act that allows law enforcement to conduct a search to compel a suspect to provide all encryption keys or passwords in order to search computerized data.
Compelled	Being forced to give information in the context of a police investigation or criminal court proceeding.
Comprehensive National Cybersecurity Initiative (CNCI)	The Presidential strategy adopted in May 2009 to strengthen America's digital infrastructure from various cyberthreats.
Computer-mediated communication (CMC)	Communications technologies that utilize the Internet to connect individuals, such as email, Instant Messaging Systems, and Facebook.
Computer as a target	When the computer or network is the aim of the attack.
Computer as a tool	When the computer itself is used as an instrument to commit a crime.
Computer as incidental	When the computer is either involved in the commission of a crime but has a smaller role, or the computer is being used merely as a storage device.

Computer contaminants	A term for a virus or malware designed to damage, destroy, or transmit information within a system without the permission of the owner.
Computer crime	Crime in which the perpetrator uses special knowledge about computer technology to commit the offense.
Computer Crime and Intellectual Property Section (CCIPS)	The sub-section of the US Department of Justice that prosecutes computer hacking cases at the federal level.
Computer Emergency Response Team (CERT)	An agency that serves as a coordinating point for responses to major network emergencies.
Computer Forensic Tool Testing project (CFTT)	Provides unbiased, open, and objective means for manufacturers, law enforcement, and the legal community to assess the validity of tools used in computer forensics.
Computer forensics	The investigation and analysis of media originating from digital sources in an effort to uncover evidence to present in a court of law.
Computer Fraud and Abuse Act (CFAA)	The first US federal law which made it illegal to engage in various forms of computer hacking and fraud.
Computer Security Incident Response Teams (CSIRT)	A different name for Computer Emergency Response Team.
Con	A computer hacking or computer security conference.
Concept virus	A form of malware that demonstrated the potential use of macro programming languages as a method of compromise.
Conclusion	An overall summary of the findings derived from the examination.
Condemnation of the condemners	One of the five basic techniques Sykes and Matza developed that allows individuals to break from conformity, operating on the basis that those who would condemn their actions are hypocritical and doing so out of personal spite.
Confirmation bias	The tendency to accept information that confirms our beliefs while rejecting information that contradicts them.
Convention on Cybercrime (CoC)	The first international treaty designed to address cybercrime and synchronize national laws on these offenses.
Copyright	A legal form of protection for intellectual property that provides exclusive use of an idea or design to a specific person or company, the right to control how it may be used, and legal entitlement to payment for its use for a limited period of time.
Copyright Act of 1976	The US federal law that removed the power to prosecute copyright infringement cases from state courts in 1976.
Copyright laws	Laws designed to protect the creators of intellectual property.

Coroners and Justice Act	This UK act extended the PCA to include all sexual images depicting youth under the age of 18, whether real or created.
Corpus delicti	Refers to the principle that a crime must be proven to have been committed.
Crack	A term that emerged within the hacker subculture to recognize and separate malicious hacks from those supported by the hacker ethic.
Cracker	A negative term referring to those who engage in deviant or criminal applications of hacking.
Crimeware	Malware that can be used as a stable platform for cybercrime, such as botnets.
Criminal Justice and Administration Act 2008	This UK law criminalized the possession of extreme pornography.
Criminal Justice and Public Order Act	This UK act extended the PCA to include images that appear to be photos, so-called pseudo-photographs.
Criminal offense	The violation of a law in which a crime is committed against the state, society as a whole, or a member of society.
Cryptolocker	A form of malware that spreads via attachments in emails or as downloadable malware online that encrypts data on any hard drives attached to the infected system using a very strong encryption protocol and holds the user's system hostage until payment is received.
Cult of the Dead Cow (cDc)	A well-known hacker group in the 1990s that developed the BO2K malware.
Cyber trespass	The act of crossing boundaries of ownership in online environments.
Cybercrime	Crime in which the perpetrator uses special knowledge of cyberspace.
Cybercrime Act 2001	Inserted a new section into the Crimes Act 1914 giving law enforcement the ability to compel a person to provide all encryption keys or passwords when investigating a computer-related crime.
Cyber-deception and theft	All the ways that individuals may illegally acquire information or resources online.
Cyberdeviance	Any activity facilitated by technology that may not be illegal, but is not socially accepted by the majority of groups in a local area.
Cyber-porn	The range of sexually expressive content online.
Cybersmile	A charitable organization, founded in 2010, to educate the public on the harm caused by cyberbullying through service programs in schools and neighborhoods.
Cyberstalking	Online communication that may lead a victim to feel fear for their personal safety and/or experience emotional distress.
Cyberterror	The premeditated, methodological, and ideologically motivated dissemination of information, facilitation of communication, or attack against physical targets,

digital information, computer systems, and/or computer programs which is intended to cause social, financial, physical, or psychological harm to noncombatant targets and audiences for the purpose of affecting ideological, political, or social change; or any utilization of digital communication or information which facilitates such actions directly or indirectly.

Cyberterrorism   The use of digital technology or computer-mediated communications to cause harm and force social change based on ideological or political beliefs.

CyberTipline   An electronic resource operated by the US National Center for Missing and Exploited Children that provides a way for individuals to report suspected incidents of child abuse, child pornography, and sexual exploitation online.

Cyber-violence   The ability to send or access injurious, hurtful, or dangerous materials online.

Cyberwar   Term used to describe the use of cyberattacks in support of conflict between nation-states.

Data breaches   The illegal acquisition of mass quantities of information through hacking techniques.

Data recovery   Process of salvaging digital information.

Daubert hearing   A hearing in US courts to determine whether a piece of scientific evidence, a theory, or study is reliable and therefore admissible in court.

Daubert standard   The four criteria for determining whether the relevant scientific evidence, theory, or study is reliable, and therefore admissible in US courts, based on testing, publication, error rates, and acceptance of the theory or technique.

Daubert trilogy   The three cases that helped to establish the current interpretation of the *Daubert* standard. These cases are *Daubert* v. *Merrell Dow Pharmaceuticals* (1993), *General Electric Co.* v. *Joiner* (1997), and *Kumho Tire Co.* v. *Carmichael* (1999).

Daubert v. *Merrell Dow Pharmaceuticals* (1993)   US court case which held that any scientific expert testimony presented in federal court must undergo a reliability test.

Dead-box forensics   The examination of powered-down computer components.

DefCon   An annual computer security and hacking conference held each year in Las Vegas, Nevada.

Definitions   One of the four principal components of Akers's social learning theory, suggesting that the way an individual views a behavior will affect their willingness to engage in that activity.

Deleted files   A file whose entry has been removed from the computer's file system so that this space is now marked as usable again.

Denial of a victim	One of the five basic techniques Sykes and Matza developed that allows individuals to break from conformity, operating on the basis that there is no discernible victim (e.g. large corporation) or the "victim" deserved it.
Denial of an injury	One of the five basic techniques Sykes and Matza developed that allows individuals to break from conformity, operating on the basis that no one or thing will get hurt or damaged.
Denial of responsibility	One of the five basic techniques Sykes and Matza developed that allows individuals to break from conformity, operating on the basis that some other person, event, or situation will be directly responsible for the offense and should be blamed.
Denial of service	A form of cyberattack where a service or resource supported by the Internet is overloaded with requests, keeping legitimate users from access.
Denigration	A form of cyberbullying involving making comments about individuals' characters or behaviors that are designed to harm their reputation, friendships, or social positions.
De-NISTing	The process of filtering the dataset and removing non-user-created files.
Department of Defense Cyber Crime Center	A specialized agency run by the Air Force to perform forensic analyses and training for attacks against DoD computers and defense contractors.
Department of Energy	The US federal agency which oversees the production and safety of power grids and energy production.
Department of Homeland Security	The US federal department which houses multiple law enforcement entities and coordinates responses to cyberthreats and attacks.
Deterrence theory	This perspective argues that humans will be deterred from choosing to commit crime if they believe that punishments will be certain, swift, and proportionately severe.
Deviance	A behavior that may not be illegal, though it is outside of the formal and informal norms or beliefs of the prevailing culture.
Differential association	One of the four principal components of Akers's social learning theory, arguing that who we associate with influences our willingness to engage in crime and our exposure to definitions supporting offending.
Differential reinforcement	One of the four principal components of Akers's social learning theory, arguing that the punishments or positive reinforcement we receive after engaging in crime will influence our willingness to perform that act again.
Digital Age	The era of digital technologies.
Digital evidence	Information that is either transferred or stored in a binary form.

Digital forensics	The analysis of digital evidence, which includes network, computer, mobile device, and malware forensics.
Digital immigrant	Those born before the creation of the Internet and digital technologies.
Digital Millennium Copyright Act (DMCA)	US law designed to directly affect media piracy online through further revisions to the Copyright Act by extending protection to various music and performances that have been recorded in some fashion.
Digital native	Youths that were brought into a world that was already digital, spend large amounts of time in digital environments, and utilize technological resources in their day-to-day lives.
Digital piracy	A form of cybercrime encompassing the illegal copying of digital media such as computer software, digital sound recordings, and digital video recordings without the explicit permission of the copyright holder.
Distributed denial of service (DDoS) attack	When individuals send multiple requests to servers that house online content to the point where these servers become overloaded and are unable to be used by others.
Double jeopardy clause	US legal clause that states that an individual is protected from being prosecuted or punished twice for the same crime.
Dread Pirate Roberts	The handle for Ross William Ulbricht. Ulbricht was the site administrator for the Silk Road.
Drift	Term used by David Matza to refer to the transition between criminality and conformity without accepting a deviant or criminal identity.
Drive slack	When the operating system does not overwrite old information that was once available on the storage device between the start of the next sector and the end of the cluster.
Due process clause	US legal clause which states that the government cannot deprive someone of "life, liberty, or property" without due process, meaning the government must follow rules and procedures for conducting legal procedures to limit arbitrary decisions.
e-jihad	Term used to describe the use of the Internet as a venue for indoctrination and cyberattack by Islamic extremist groups.
Electronic Communications Privacy Act (ECPA)	The US law that enabled law enforcement to obtain the name and address of ISP subscribers, along with personal details and sensitive data.
Electronic Pearl Harbor	Term used to refer to an unexpected and catastrophic cyberattack against the United States.
Elk Cloner	An early form of malware, designed to infect Apple II computers via a floppy disk, that did not cause any actual harm but was difficult to remove.
EnCase®	A forensics tool created by Guidance Software in 1997. This automated tool can image a drive, without altering

	its contents, and then verify that the image is an exact copy of the original drive.
Encryption	The process of transforming text, such as an email, through the use of mathematical algorithms so that it is no longer legible to others.
Endangered Child Alert Program (ECAP)	A US FBI-led program that seeks to identify the adults featured in some child exploitation content so they may be brought to justice.
Enterprise Phase	The period of digital forensic technologies in the early 2000s marked by familiarity with digital evidence handling and the creation of tools specifically designed for digital forensic analysis.
Escort	A type of sex worker who operates behind closed doors and typically makes appointments with clients rather than soliciting publicly.
European Union Directive 2001/29/EC	Also known as the Copyright Directive, this European Union statute establishes guidelines concerning the adequate legal protection of copyrighted materials through technological means.
European Union Directive 91/250/EEC/ 2009/24/EC	A European Union statute that provides legal protection for computer programs and harmonized copyright protection across the EU.
Evidence integrity	The reliability and truthfulness of the evidence.
Examination/analysis stage	The stage of digital forensic investigation involving data recovery/extraction and analysis of digital data.
Exclusion	A form of cyberbullying involving intentionally keeping others from joining an online group, such as a network on Facebook or some other site online.
Exigent circumstance	Refers to emergency situations that allow law enforcement officers to conduct a warrantless search when they believe people are in danger or potential evidence will be destroyed.
Exploit	A program that can take advantage of vulnerabilities to give the attacker deeper access to a system or network.
Exploit packs	A form of malware that can infect web browsers and thereby enable remote takeovers of computer systems.
External hard drives	Portable storage devices located outside of the computer and are usually connected via a USB port.
Extraction	See *data recovery*.
Extreme pornography	UK-centric definition for materials produced for the purpose of sexual arousal which depicts acts that "threaten a person's life; acts which result in or are likely to result in serious injury to a person's anus, breasts or genitals; bestiality; or necrophilia."
Fair and Accurate Credit Transactions Act of 2003	The US law that provides multiple protections to help reduce the risk of identity theft and assist victims in repairing their credit in the event of identity theft.

Federal Bureau of Investigation (FBI)	A prominent US federal law enforcement agency that can be involved in the investigation of most forms of cybercrime, particularly hacking, financial crimes, and cyberterrorism.
Federal Bureau of Investigation's Violent Crimes Against Children (VCAC)	This US-based law enforcement agency investigates a range of sexual offenses and criminal activities that affect youth, ranging from child pornography to sex trafficking to kidnapping.
Federal Rules of Evidence (FRE)	Governs the admissibility of evidence in federal court proceedings in the United States.
Federal Trade Commission (FTC)	An independent watchdog agency within the US federal government responsible for consumer protection and monitoring the business community.
Federation Against Copyright Theft (FACT)	The primary trade organization in the UK dedicated to the protection and management of intellectual property, notably that of film and television producers.
Fifth Amendment	The Fifth Amendment to the US Constitution that protects an individual from self-incrimination, double jeopardy, and deprivation of liberty without due process.
File	A piece of computer-based data.
File Allocation Table (FAT)	The type of file system used in older versions of the Windows operating systems.
File carving	The process of searching for a certain file signature in a hard drive and attempting to extract the associated data without regard for the file system.
File extension	The part of the file's name that tells the operating system what program to use to open it.
File sharing	The process of electronically exchanging intellectual property over the Internet without the permission of the original copyright holder.
File signature	An identifying value for the content of a computer file.
File slack	The leftover space between the end of the file and the end of the last storage unit for that file.
File system	The way in which data is organized and retrieved on a computer hard drive.
Financial Coalition Against Child Pornography (FCACP)	A coalition that is comprised of 39 financial institutions and Internet service providers who are jointly operating to take complaints of child pornography and disrupt the businesses that are engaged in the sale of or profit generation from this content.
Fisher v. United States (1976)	US court case which demonstrated that statements given voluntarily to police and criminal justice system actors are not protected by the Fifth Amendment.
Flaming	A form of cyberbullying involving engaging in online fighting where users directly target one another with angry or irritated messages, often featuring vulgar language.

Flash mob	Mass organizations of people who organize quickly and move rapidly through the use of online media without alerting local citizens or law enforcement.
FloodNet	The DDoS tool that was developed by the Electronic Disturbance Theater. The program could be downloaded directly from their website to be utilized by individuals who shared their perspectives on the use of the Internet as a space for social activism.
Florida Computer Crimes Act of 1978	The US state law which was the first codified state statute regarding computer crime, involving offenses against intellectual property, offenses against computer equipment or supplies, and offenses against computer users.
Footer	The last few bytes that mark the end of a file.
Forensic confirmation bias	Term referencing the class of effects through which an individual's preexisting beliefs, expectations, motives, and situational context influence the collection, perception, and interpretation of evidence during the course of a criminal case.
Forensic science	The application of science to the law, meaning the scientific process of gathering and examining information to be used by the criminal justice system.
Forensic soundness	The validity of the method for collecting and preserving evidence.
Forensic Toolkit® (FTK)	Commercial software commonly used in digital forensic investigations that was created by AccessData. It is capable of imaging a hard drive, scanning slack space, and identifying steganography; however, it is also capable of cracking passwords and decrypting files.
Forum for Incident Response and Security Teams (FIRST)	A global organization that serves to coordinate information sharing and connections between all teams worldwide.
Fourth Amendment	Limits the US government's ability to search and seize evidence without a warrant.
Fragmented	A file that is stored in nonconsecutive sectors on a computer hard drive.
Fraud	Wrongful or criminal deception intended to result in financial or personal gain.
FRE Rule 401	Defines relevance as the tendency to make the fact being presented in a case more or less probable. It also defines authenticity as the ability to prove that the evidence is genuine.
FRE Rule 702	States that if scientific, technical, or other specialized knowledge will assist the trier of fact to understand the evidence or to determine a fact in issue, a witness qualified as an expert by knowledge, skill, experience, training, or education may testify thereto in the form of an opinion or otherwise.

FRE Rule 801	States that hearsay is considered second-hand evidence, meaning it is testimony not based on first-hand or personal knowledge.
FRE Rule 901	States "the proponent must produce evidence sufficient to support a finding that the item is what the proponent claims it is."
Free space	The portion of the hard drive that has yet to be assigned to a partition.
French postcards	Images of nudes printed on postcard stock and sent through the mail to others.
Frye standard	States that scientific evidence is only admissible if it is generally accepted as reliable by the scientific community.
Frye v. *United States* (1923)	US court case which led to the development of the *Frye* standard for the presentation of scientific evidence.
Gatekeeper	A term used to refer to a judge in the context of assessing both the relevance and reliability of scientific evidence.
General Electric Co. v. *Joiner* (1997)	A US Court case that demonstrated that not only was scientific evidence under review, but so was the methodology and reliability of an expert's reasoning process.
General strain theory	An individual-level theory developed by Robert Agnew that discusses the role of frustrations leading to negative emotions which, if not addressed appropriately, can lead individuals to engage in crime as a response.
General theory of crime	Gottfredson and Hirshi's theory which argues that crime stems from low self-control and opportunities to offend.
Girlfriend Experience (GFE)	A term used by the customers of prostitutes to refer to a sexual experience meant to feel like a consensual relationship with no money involved.
Golden Age	See *Enterprise phase*.
Google Glass	A form of wearable technology created by the company Google. These thin glasses come with a wearable computer featuring a heads-up display that is voice activated and controlled. Users can do a variety of things while wearing Glass, including taking photos and videos, searching the Internet, checking email, and several other activities that are evolving through the creation of new applications.
Grand jury	A group of people that determine whether or not there is enough evidence to formally charge the individual with a crime.
Gray-hat hacker	A group of hackers that falls between black- and white-hat hackers who have shifting or changing ethics depending on the specific situation.
Grooming	The misuse of the Internet by using it to engage in inappropriate communication with children.

Hack	The modification or alteration of computer hardware or software to enable technology to be used in a new way, whether for legitimate or illegitimate purposes.
Hacker	An individual who modifies or alters computer hardware or software to enable technology to be used in a new way.
Hacker space	A physical location where individuals can converge to discuss technology and learn from one another.
Hacktivism	Using hacking techniques to promote an activist agenda or express their opinion.
Handheld devices	A source of potential electronic information that includes mobile phones, digital multimedia devices (e.g. iPod), digital cameras, and global positioning systems (GPS).
Handle	The nicknames used by individuals in on and offline environments.
Harassment	The repeated distribution of cruel or mean messages to a person in order to embarrass or annoy them.
Hard drives	Data storage devices used for storing and retrieving data.
Hardware	The tangible or physical parts of a computer system.
Hash	A fixed value (output) – see also *hashing*.
Hash algorithm	A set of calculations that takes an arbitrary amount of data (input) and creates a fixed value (output) which acts as a unique reference number for the original data.
Hashing	The process of creating a hash value from a variable amount of data.
Header	The first few bytes that mark the beginning of a file.
Hearsay	Term used to refer to second-hand evidence, or information obtained on a first-hand or personal knowledge basis.
Hidden files	Files that have been manipulated in such a way that the contents of the original file are concealed.
Hypothesis	A reasonable explanation as to what might have occurred or why.
I/O error	Input/output errors that are often the result of a bad sector on a hard drive.
Identification document	A document made or issued by or under the authority of a government with information concerning a particular individual intended to serve as a form of identification.
Identity fraud	Within the UK, this term refers to the illegal misuse of a document made or issued by or under the authority of the government.
Identity theft	Within the US, this term refers to the unlawful use or possession of a means of identification of another person with the intent to commit, aid, or abet illegal activity.
Identity Theft and Assumption Deterrence Act of 1998	This US law made it a federal crime to possess, transfer, or use a means of identification of another person without authorization with the intent to commit or aid in the commission of illegal activity at the local, state, or federal level.

Identity Theft Enforcement and Restitution Act of 2008	This US federal act allows offenders to be ordered to pay restitution as a penalty to victims of identity theft and enhanced existing laws regarding cybercrime.
Identity Theft Penalty Enhancement Act of 2003	This US act added two years to any prison sentence for individuals convicted of a felony who knowingly possessed, used, or transferred identity documents of another person.
Imaging	The process of making an exact copy (bit by bit) of the original drive onto a new digital storage device.
Imitation	One of the four principal components of Akers's social learning theory, suggesting that an individual's first act of deviance or criminality is an attempt to model the behavior of their peers and intimate others.
Immigration and Customs Enforcement (ICE)	The US federal agency which manages the processing and prosecution of illegal immigrants and the movement of materials through the borders of the nation.
Impersonation	A form of cyberbullying involving falsely posting as other people to harm their reputation or social status by logging into their existing accounts to post messages or by creating fake accounts to masquerade as that person.
In re Boucher (2007)	US Court case which led to Fifth Amendment challenges to encryption protocols.
Incidental	When the computer is either involved in the commission of a crime in a smaller accompanying role or is being used merely as a storage device.
Incriminating	Information which implicates an individual in a criminal incident or wrongdoing.
Information Age	Period of time marked by the increased production, transmission, consumption of, and reliance on information.
InfraGard	A non-profit public–private partnership designed to facilitate information sharing between academics, industry, and law enforcement.
Intellectual property	Any work or artistic endeavor created by an individual which has been fixed in some form, such as being written down.
Internal hard drives	Hard drives that are installed inside a computer or device.
International Center for Missing and Exploited Children (ICMEC)	A non-profit agency with a similar mission to the NCMEC, though it is focused on building partnerships in a global context to better investigate child exploitation cases and build the legal capacity of nations so that there is consistency in laws to prosecute these offenses.
International Criminal Tribunal	The formation of a truly international court that could represent the victim nations and offenders could be a valuable tool to pursue cases where multiple nations were affected by a group of actors.

Internet Corporation for Assigned Names and Numbers (ICANN)	International organization that is responsible for the coordination and stability of the Internet over time.
Internet Crime Complaint Center (IC3)	A collaborative effort of the National White Collar Crime Center (NW3C) and the FBI operating for crime victims, consumers, and researchers to understand the scope of various forms of online fraud. Victims can contact the agency through an online reporting mechanism that accepts complaints for a range of offenses.
Internet Crimes Against Children (ICAC)	US-based local task forces that provide a mechanism for coordination between local, state, and federal law enforcement, as well as prosecutors, to combat child sex offenses.
Internet of Things	All non-computing devices connected together via the Internet, including thermostats, refrigerators, and other appliances.
Internet Watch Foundation (IWF)	A UK-based charitable organization that is focused on reducing the amount of child pornography and exploitation materials hosted worldwide, along with criminally obscene adult content.
Johns	A term used to refer to the customers of prostitutes.
Just compensation clause	States that any property taken by the government must be for public use and the owner must be fully reimbursed its market value.
Katz v. *United States* (1967)	Key US court case which defined an individual's right to privacy in public spaces.
Key disclosure law	Legislation that mandates a person to provide encryption keys or passwords to law enforcement for digital forensic investigations.
Keyword search	The process of using a word or series of words to conduct a search in the entire physical drive of a computer regardless of the file systems.
Kumho Tire Co. v. *Carmichael* (1999)	US court case which helped inform the *Daubert* standard of evidence.
Lamer	A term used by hackers to refer to individuals with limited capacity and/or skills.
Latent	Another term for hidden.
Law Enforcement and CSIRT Cooperation (LECC-BoF)	A sub-group of FIRST designed to provide a venue for police and response teams to work together and create trusted relationships between these communities.
Law Reform Commission	Irish body of law which helped inform standards of evidence.
Legacy systems	Outdated computer systems, devices, or software.
Liberty Reserve	An electronic payment processor who is being prosecuted in the US for its role in money laundering for various forms of crime.
Logical extraction	The process of identifying and recovering data based on the file systems present on the computer hard drive.

Lori Drew	A woman alleged to have created a fictitious MySpace profile in order to harass a 13-year-old girl named Megan Meier, who eventually committed suicide as a result of contact with Drew's profile.
Low Orbit Ion Cannon (LOIC)	The DDoS tool that is used by the group Anonymous to support attacks against personal, industrial, and government targets around the world.
Macro virus	A popular way to infect systems by using a common weakness in a variety of popular programs like Excel, Word, and PDFs.
Macro programming language	A programming language common to Microsoft Office products that was used by virus writers to compromise user systems.
Magic numbers	See *file signatures*.
Malicious Communications Act 1998	Enables individuals to be prosecuted for sending messages to another person for the purpose of causing fear or anxiety. Revised in 2001 to include electronic communications of any kind that convey a threat, indecent or offensive content, or information that is false.
Massage parlor	A business that operates as a supposedly legitimate massage clinic but actually provides sexual services to clients.
Master File Table (MFT)	Contains information about all of the files, folders, and directories on a drive.
Megan Meier	A young woman who committed suicide after receiving bullying messages from a fake MySpace profile, alleged to have been created by Lori Drew, the mother of one of Megan's friends.
Megan Meier Cyberbullying Prevention Act	Proposed US federal legislation would have made it illegal for anyone to use CMC "to coerce, intimidate, harass or cause substantial emotional distress to a person," or use electronic resources to "support severe, repeated, and hostile behavior." This resolution was not successfully passed into law.
Melissa virus	A well-known virus that spread throughout the globe in the 1990s.
Message Digest Version 5 (MD5)	A type of hashing algorithm that takes a large amount of data of arbitrary length (input) and calculates a unique "fingerprint" of this data expressed as a unique combination of hexadecimal digits of a specified length (output).
Metropolitan Police Central e-crime Unit (PCeU)	The London, England police agency that responds to serious forms of cybercrime affecting citizens.
Microsoft Digital Crimes Unit	A working group created by the Microsoft corporation to combat cybercrime in conjunction with law enforcement.

Mileage	Term used by the customers of prostitutes in web forums to refer to the appearance of sex workers and their deterioration in appearance over time in the sex trade.
Miller v. *California*	US court case which established the definition of obscene content that is still in use today.
Morris worm	The first worm created by Robert Morris that caused substantial harm to the Internet in the 1980s.
Motion Picture Association of America (MPAA)	The US association that operates to protect the intellectual property of their artists and creative producers.
Motivated offender	Variable within routine activity theory that constitutes any individual or group who has both the inclination and ability to commit crime.
MP3 format	A software standard designed to compress audio files.
MuTation Engine (MtE)	A polymorphic generator that not only encrypts a virus but randomizes the routine used so that it varies with each replication.
Napster	A popular file sharing program developed in 1999 that allowed a larger population of Internet users to engage in piracy.
Nation-state actor	Hackers who engage in attacks at the behest of or in cooperation with a government or military entity.
National Centre for Cyberstalking Research	A UK-based research center designed to address the problem of cyberstalking.
National Center for Missing and Exploited Children (NCMEC)	One of the key non-profit organizations in the US that deals with missing children and child exploitation. It performs multiple roles to facilitate the investigation of crimes against children.
National Crime Agency (NCA)	UK national criminal justice agency that has both national and international reach and works in partnership with law enforcment organizations to particularly focus on serious and organized crime.
National Crime Victimization Survey-Supplemental Survey (NCVS-SS)	A US-based survey with a nationally representative sample of respondents that demonstrates the prevalence and incidence of cyberstalking.
National Fraud Authority (NFA)	This UK agency was formed in 2008 in order to increase cooperation between the public and private sectors to investigate fraud.
National Fraud Intelligence Bureau (NFIB)	The NFIB collects information on various forms of fraud and aggregates this data along with reports from business and industry sources into a large database called the NFIB Know Fraud system. It is operated by the City of London police.
National Incident-Based Reporting System (NIBRS)	The US-based incident reporting system used by law enforcement agencies to collect and report data on crime.

National Security Agency (NSA)	The US agency which supports offensive and defensive operations in support of US military and civilian networks.
National Software Reference Library (NSRL)	The US NIST-supported reference library that maintains details on various software programs.
Nation-state	A nation-state is any sovereign nation with a defined territory and a governmental organizational structure.
Necrophilia	Experiencing sexual arousal from sex with the dead.
Neighborhood Children's Internet Protection Act (NCIPA)	This US law requires Internet filtering technology in public libraries to block young people from accessing harmful content, including pornographic and obscene materials.
Nested search	A search within a search.
Networking	A way in which those who have sexual attraction to children may misuse the Internet to communicate and share ideas with like-minded persons.
New Technology File System (NTFS)	The current file system for Windows NT operating systems.
No Electronic Theft (NET) Act of 1997	A US federal law designed to increase the penalties for the duplication of copyrighted materials.
Non-nation-state-sponsored actor	An individual who acts without any sort of state or military backing.
Noob	An individuals new to hacking and with minimal knowledge of technology.
Object code	Code that restricts the ability of users to modify and share the software due to copyright infringement.
Obscene Publications Act (OPA) 1959	Law applicable in England and Wales that indicates any article may be obscene if its effect on the audience member who reads, views, or hears it is to "deprave and corrupt."
Obscene Publications Act 1857	This UK act made it illegal to sell, possess, or publish obscene material, which was not clearly defined in the law.
Obscenity	Term used to refer to content that may be indecent, lewd, or vulgar, which varies based on the legal standards of a given nation.
Observation	The first stage of the scientific method.
Online harassment	The repeated distribution of cruel or mean online messages to a person in order to embarrass or annoy them.
Open-field searches	A form of legal search that can be conducted by law enforcement without a warrant in any open field or large area that cannot be considered persons, houses, papers, or effects.
Open source software	Software programs that can be freely used, modified, and shared with anyone.
Operation Aurora	The name given to a series of cyberattacks against various major corporations to steal sensitive intellectual property information, which appeared to originate in China.

Operation Olympic Games	The name of a classified US military operation to disrupt the Iranian nuclear program.
Operation Predator	This US ICE-led program is designed to facilitate the investigation of child exploitation in the US and abroad.
Operation Rescue Me	This US FBI-led program has been in operation since 2008 to identify victims of child exploitation based on their appearance in images or video of child pornography.
Operation Spade	Name given to a multinational investigation of a child pornography ring operating out of multiple nations to produce content.
Operation: Bot Roast	An investigation conducted by the US FBI targeting botnet operators.
Original writing rule	States that the original evidence, rather than a duplicate, is generally required unless the duplicate can be authenticated and it can be proven that its contents are the same as the original.
Outing	A form of cyberbullying involving the posting of real personal information about individuals to embarrass them, such as sending images of them in states of undress, posting who they are attracted to, or information about homosexual preferences which may not be known to the general public.
Partition recovery	The process of evaluating the partition table and the unused space on the physical hard drive of a computer.
Partition table	Computer-based reference description for how the operating system has divided the hard drive into partitions.
Partitioning	The process of dividing up a computer hard drive into separate storage spaces.
Partitions	Separate storage spaces in a computer hard drive that determines how much space is allocated to each storage bin, or partition.
Password-protected files	Locked files that require a password to gain access.
Patent	See *Copyright*.
Payload	The changes that a piece of malware causes to a computer system upon activation.
Pedophile	An individual with a sexual attraction to individuals under the age of 18.
Peer-to-peer (P2P) file sharing protocols	Protocols that enable direct file sharing between two computer systems over the Internet.
People's Liberation Army of China (PLA)	The name of the Chinese military.
Peripheral device	Externally connected components that are not considered essential parts of a computer system, such as scanners, printers, and modems.
Personal Identification Number (PIN)	The four-digit number used as a password to secure access to bank accounts at ATMs.
Personally identifiable information (PII)	Information that is unique to an individual that can be used on its own or with other information to identify, locate, or contact a single individual.

Philippine Rules of Electronic Evidence (PREE)	This specifically outlines the admissibility rules for electronic evidence compared to the Philippine Rules of Evidence (PRE), which is a separate standard for non-electronic evidence.
Phishing	Using email messages to try to acquire bank account information or other valuable information from victims.
Phreak	An individual interested in using hacking techniques to exploit vulnerabilities within telephony.
Phreaking	The act of using hacking techniques to exploit vulnerabilities within telephony.
Physical extraction	The process of salvaging digital information.
Pirate Bay	A well-known group that enables piracy.
Plain view doctrine	Allows law enforcement officers to conduct a search and seizure for evidence that may not be in the search warrant but is in plain view and its incriminating nature is immediately apparent.
Plaintext	A legible message or piece of content.
Police and Justice Act 2006	The UK law that enhanced sentences for computer hacking cases.
Police Intellectual Property Crime Unit (PIPCU)	A unit in the London Police that investigates and handles various forms of piracy.
Pornography	The representation of sexual situations and content for the purposes of sexual arousal and stimulation.
Prediction	A specific statement as to how you will determine if your hypothesis is true.
Pre-forensics	A term used to refer to the 1980s regarding digital forensic technologies, characterized by the lack of formal structure, protocols, training, and adequate tools.
Preponderance of evidence	Means it must be more likely than not that the accused in fact committed whatever acts they are accused of.
Preservation	Making a copy of the original data files for examination in a way that minimizes the possibility of any changes being made to the original data files.
PRISM program	An NSA-implemented program beginning in 2007 to collect email and other electronic communications data of all sorts, carried out through cooperative relationships with various technology companies, including Apple, Facebook, Google, Microsoft, and Skype.
Probable cause	Means there must be adequate reasons or justifications, rather than mere suspicion, to conduct a search.
Process models	Techniques and strategies designed to provide practical guidelines and procedures for conducting a digital forensic investigation.
Proprietary software	See *closed source*.

Prosecutorial Remedies and Other Tools to end the Exploitation of Children Today Act (or PROTECT Act) of 2003	This US law criminalized virtual child pornography and extended the legal definition to include "a digital image, computer image, or computer-generated image that is, or is indistinguishable from, that of a minor engaged in sexually explicit conduct."
Prostitution	The practice of paying for sex, which may or may not be illegal depending on place.
Protection from Harassment Act 1997 (c40)	This UK law criminalized stalking and bullying in professional settings. Section 4 of the Act criminalizes the act of putting others in fear of violence, defined as any course of conduct that would cause "another to fear, on at least two occasions, that violence will be used against him," where the offender "is guilty of an offence if he knows or ought to know that his course of conduct will cause the other so to fear on each of those occasions."
Protection of Children Against Sexual Exploitation Act	This US law made it illegal for anyone under the age of 16 to participate in the visual production of sexually explicit materials, though this was revised to the age of 18 in 1986.
Protection of Freedoms Act 2012	Revised the Protection from Harassment Act 1997 to include language specifically related to stalking and incorporate aspects of technology into law.
Proxy server	A server that can be used to hide a computer's location by acting as an intermediary between a computer and the servers and systems it connects to through the Internet.
Pump and dump messages	A form of spam-enabled fraud that attempts to manipulate the value of corporate stocks.
Punternet	A UK-based website designed for individuals to post reviews of escorts and sex workers.
RAM slack	When randomly selected data from RAM is stored in the file slack.
Random Access Memory (RAM)	Type of computer-based memory that stores that part of the data that is currently being used by the computer.
Ransomware	Malware that demands the operator of the infected system pay in order to have their system's functionality restored.
Read-only	Term referencing the ability of a device to only view accessible data on a drive but not alter it in any way.
Reasonable expectation of privacy	The person must have exhibited an actual expectation of privacy, and the expectation must be one that society is prepared to recognize as reasonable.
Reasonableness clause	A search is constitutional if it does not violate a person's reasonable and legitimate expectation of privacy.

Recording Industry Association of America (RIAA)	A trade organization that supports the recording industry and those businesses that create, manufacture, or distribute legally sold and recorded music within the US.
Regulation of Investigatory Powers (RIPA)	This law mandates key disclosure so long as law enforcement obtains signed authorization from a high-ranking official.
Relevant	When evidence can make the facts presented in a case more or less probable; evidence that does not tend to prove or disprove a presented fact in a case is deemed irrelevant, and therefore inadmissible.
Reliability	The accuracy of the evidence deemed relevant to a case.
Repeatability	Where independent test results are obtained with the same method, on identical test items, in the same laboratory, by the same operator, using the same equipment within short intervals of time.
Report/presentation stage	The final step in the process of digital forensic investigation where the findings that are determined relevant to the investigation are finalized in a report.
Reproducibility	Where test results are obtained with the same method on identical test items in different laboratories with different operators using different equipment.
Revenge porn	Websites explicitly for individuals to post sexual images and videos they received or acquired for others to see without the consent of the creator.
Right to privacy	See *Fourth Amendment*.
Ripper	A seller in carding markets who does not provide data after being paid, is slow to respond to customers, or sells bad data and does not offer to replace their products.
Routine activity theory	Cohen and Felson (1979) argued that direct-contact predatory victimization occurs with the convergence in both space and time of three primary components: (1) a motivated offender; (2) a suitable target; and (3) the absence of a capable guardian.
Rule 34	Online meme which states that "if it exists, there is pornographic content of it."
Scareware	See *Ransomware*.
Scientific evidence	Information derived from the scientific method that is relevant to the facts of a case.
Scientific method	A process that uses strict guidelines to ensure careful and systematic collection, organization, and analysis of information.
Script kiddie	A derogatory term meant to shame individuals by recognizing their use of pre-made scripts or tools, their lack of skill, and the concurrent harm that they may cause.
Search	The exploration or examination of an individual's home, premises, or person to discover things or items that may be used by the government as evidence in a criminal proceeding.

Search and seizure	When law enforcement officers are identifying and collecting potential evidence to be used in the court of law.
Search incident to arrest	The process of searching a person who has been arrested for a crime.
Search warrant	A document signed by a judge or magistrate authorizing law enforcement to conduct a search.
Secret shopper schemes	A form of spam-enabled fraud where sellers pretend to operate legitimate businesses that are seeking employees who can cash checks and purchase goods with the proceeds.
Section 49 request	In the UK, a law enforcement mandate which requires encryption key disclosure so long as law enforcement obtains signed authorization from a high-ranking official using a specialized Section 49 form.
Sector	The smallest physical storage unit on a computer disk drive, which is almost always 512 bytes.
Secure Hash Algorithm (SHA)	A common hashing algorithm created by the US National Security Agency that creates a 160-bit value for an item using a unique combination of hexadecimal digits.
Seizure	The exercise of control by the government over a person or thing because of a violation of the law.
Self-control	The ability to constrain one's own behavior through internal regulation.
Self-incrimination	Giving a statement that might expose oneself to punishment for a crime.
Self-incrimination clause	In the US, a Fifth Amendment rule that provides defendants with protection from self-incrimination.
Severity	Involves the intensity of the punishment relative to the harm caused by the crime in the context of deterrence theory.
Sexting	The practice of sending photos or videos of individuals in provocative outfits or engaging in sexually suggestive activities through text messaging.
Sexual fetishes	The experience of sexual arousal or enhancement of a romantic encounter based on the integration of physical objects or certain situations.
Shoulder surfing	The act of stealing someone's passwords for email accounts or access to a system by looking over their shoulder and watching their keystrokes.
Silk Road	An online market developed to enable individuals to buy and sell narcotics through various mechanisms internationally. It garnered great attention from both researchers and the popular media due in part to the fact that transactions were paid using bitcoins.
Slack space	See *file slack*.
Social engineering	The use of tactics that try to fool or convince people to provide information that can be used to access different resources.

Social learning theory	Criminological theory created by Akers which argues that the learning process of any behavior, including crime, includes four principal components: (1) differential association; (2) definitions; (3) differential reinforcement; and (4) imitation.
Software	Consists of programs that include instructions which tell computers what to do.
Space transition theory	This theory created by K. Jaishankar argues that people behave differently while online than they otherwise would in physical space.
Spam	Unsolicited emails sent to large groups.
Spear phishing	Well-crafted and targeted spam messages that target one person or a small group.
Special Interest Group for Vendors (SIG Vendors)	A subgroup of FIRST that links respondents with software, hardware, and security vendors in order to handle emergent threats and mitigation techniques.
Stalking	The use of repeated and intense harassing messages that involve threats or cause the recipient to feel fear for their personal safety.
Standard of proof	A continuum of probability used to assess suspicions of an individual's guilt based on the evidence presented.
Star Wars Kid	The name given to a video featuring a young boy flailing a stick around a room in a similar fashion to a lightsaber, which was released to the Internet by classmates without his permission and went on to become a key example of cyberbullying behavior.
Steganography	The practice of hiding information in such a way that others are not aware that a hidden message exists.
Steganography medium	The type of digital media containing a steganographic message, typically in video or picture files.
Stop Online Piracy Act (SOPA)	This legislation was designed to expand the capabilities of law enforcement to combat both digital piracy and online counterfeiting and would have enabled courts to order that websites be blocked in the event that they hosted or were in some way involved with either piracy or counterfeiting activities.
Street prostitution	Prostitutes who solicit individuals on the street.
Streetwalker (SW)	A term used to reference a street-walking prostitute in online forums.
Structured phase	A term given for the mid 1980s to describe the state of digital forensic technology, characterized by the harmonization between computer forensic procedure/policy and computer crime legislation.
Stuxnet	A computer worm that was used in attacks against the Natanz uranium enrichment facility in Iran.
Subculture	Any group having differentiating values, norms, traditions, and rituals that set them apart from the dominant culture.

Subpoena	A court order requiring a person to appear before a grand jury or produce documents.
Suitable target	A variable in routine activity theory referring to a person or object that has traits making him/her attractive to the offender on a wide range of factors.
Supervisory Control and Acquisition System (SCADA)	Computer systems that support the processes within industrial systems such as nuclear power plants, hydroelectric dams, or sewage treatment plants.
Survey/identification stage	The initial step of a digital forensic investigation. During this stage, law enforcement personnel and digital forensic technicians survey the physical and digital crime scene to identity potential sources of digital evidence.
Technicways	Term referring to the ways that behavior patterns change in response to, or as a consequence of, technological innovations.
Techniques of neutralization	Theory created by Sykes and Matza that focuses on how beliefs affect the process of deciding to commit a delinquent or criminal act. This theory assumes that most people hold conforming beliefs, but may still engage in criminal behavior occasionally through the application of definitions that justify their actions.
Terror	Planned acts of violence designed to promote fear or cause harm in a general population in support of a social agenda.
Testimonial	A statement made to law enforcement.
The Hacker Ethic	A series of values developed by hackers in the 1960s that espouse their beliefs about the use of technology.
The Hacker Manifesto	An article published in the magazine Phrack written by "The Mentor" that details his perceptions of hacking and rationalizing involvement in illegal hacks.
The Protection of Children Act 1978 (PCA)	The first UK legislation that made it illegal to obtain, make, distribute, or possess an indecent image of someone under the age of 18.
ThinkUKnow	A UK-based program designed to educate children and adults about threats to youth safety.
Thumb drives	See *USB flash drives*.
Tor	An anonymous and encrypted network used by individuals to hide their physical location.
Torrent	A form of file sharing that enables easy and distributed access to various intellectual property and online content, commonly used to pirate materials.
Trademark	See *Copyright*.
Traders	The misuse of the Internet by individuals who traffic in child pornography.
Traffic stop	Occurs when the driver of the vehicle is stopped because there is suspicion that a traffic violation has occurred or a crime is being committed.
Trailer	See *Footer*.

Transparency	Term used to describe the reporting of forensic evidence analysis findings that are detailed in such a way as to leave no mystery in the digital forensics process.
Travelers	The misuse of the internet by individuals who attempt to find children to molest through computer-mediated communications.
Tricking	A form of cyberbullying that involves convincing individuals to provide personal information about themselves in what they think is a personal conversation, which is then revealed to the general public.
Tricks	A term used by sex workers to describe their clients or customers.
Trojan	A form of malware that appears to be a downloadable file or attachment that people would be inclined to open, that when opened executes some portion of its code and delivers its payload on the system.
Truant	An individual who routinely skips school.
True threat	Term used in US law to identify statements where the speaker means to communicate a serious expression of intent to commit an act of violence against another person or group.
Truth in Domain Names Act of 2003	A US law that makes it illegal for individuals to create domain names that are misleading or designed to directly expose individuals to pornographic content without their knowledge.
UK Computer Misuse Act	UK law developed in the 1990s that enabled the prosecution of computer hacking cases.
Unallocated space	Space on a hard drive to which data has not yet been written.
Unfair prejudice	A form of prejudice that could bias or confuse fact finders.
Uniform Crime Report (UCR)	The primary US reporting mechanism used by law enforcement agencies to collect and report data on crimes made known to the police.
United States Constitution	Legal document in the US that was adopted on September 17, 1787 that mandates all state judges to follow federal law in the event that conflicts arise between state and federal law.
United States Department of Justice (US DOJ)	The US federal department that has the responsibility to "enforce the law and defend the interests of the United States according to the law."
United States Secret Service (USSS)	The US federal law enforcement agency which provides protection for the President and foreign dignitaries and investigates hacking and financial crime cases.
United States v. Alkhabaz	A major US federal court case that established the concept of true threats in the prosecution of stalking cases.
United States v. Fricosu (2012)	US court case that involved a woman's right to protection from self-incrimination on the basis of encrypted data on a laptop.

United States v. *Smith* (1998)	US court case that ruled that the warrantless search of a cell phone seized incident to arrest violates the Fourth Amendment.
Unverified seller	A seller in carding markets who has not provided a sample of data to a forum moderator or administrator, or alternatively offering malware or other services to be reviewed.
US Postal Inspection Service	The US federal agency that investigates child pornography and other crimes facilitated through the US mail.
USA PATRIOT Act	A US law, the Provide Appropriate Tools Required to Intercept and Obstruct Terrorism (PATRIOT) Act was passed in 2001 to support law enforcement investigations of terrorism.
USB flash drives	The most common removable storage device for digital media that are small, lightweight, and can easily be transported and concealed.
USCYBERCOM	Created in 2009 by the Pentagon in order to manage the defense of US cyberspace and critical infrastructure against attacks.
Validity	Term used to describe whether forensic evidence was collected and preserved in a manner so that an accurate conclusion can be drawn.
Verification	Establishes the integrity of the digital evidence by proving that the duplicate is authentic.
Verified seller	A seller in carding markets who has provided a sample of data to a forum moderator or administrator, or alternatively offering malware or other services to be reviewed.
Video cassette	A form of media utilizing magnetic tape that could record and store visual and audio content.
Video cassette recorders (VCRs)	A form of technology that allows individuals to watch and record media using magnetic cassette tapes.
Violent Crimes Against Children International Task Force (VCACITF)	The largest global task force in the world that investigates child exploitation cases.
Virtual Global Taskforce (VGT)	Established in 2003, an alliance of agencies and private industry that work together in order to identify, investigate, and respond to incidents of child exploitation.
Virus	One of the oldest forms of malware that cannot be activated or execute its payload without some user intervention, such as opening a file or clicking on an attachment.
Volatile	Term referring to the potential for data loss when a computer is powered off.
Vulnerability	Flaws in computer software, hardware, or people (in the case of social engineering or committing risky activities which open oneself to victimization).

Wannabe	A reference to noobs or script kiddies, referencing their limited capacity and skills.
Warez	Pirated software and intellectual property which was commonly used by hackers in the 1980s.
Warez doodz	Individuals who posted and shared programs.
Warrant	A signed document issued by a judge or magistrate that authorizes a specific course of action for law enforcement.
Warrants clause	The second clause of the Fourth Amendment indicating that a warrant or signed document issued by a judge or magistrate authorizes a specific course of action.
Wearable devices	Any sort of Internet-enabled device that can be worn by a person, such as a watch or pair of glasses.
Web defacement	An act of online vandalism wherein an individual replaces the existing HTML code for a web page with an image and message that they create.
White-hat hacker	A type of hacker with some skill who works to find errors in computer systems and programs to benefit general computer security.
White power	A term often associated with white supremacist groups like the Ku Klux Klan and other religious or ideologically based groups with an emphasis on the purity and separation of the white race.
Wiping	The process of cleaning a digital storage device to ensure that there are no remnants of data present.
Wire fraud	Fraud committed through the use of electronic communication.
Work-at-home schemes	A form of spam-enabled fraud where the seller promises recipients substantial earnings for just a few hours of work per day.
World Intellectual Property Organization (WIPO)	An international agency designed to support intellectual property rights.
Worms	A unique form of malware that can spread autonomously, though it does not necessarily have a payload.
Write	The process of altering or modifying data on a hard drive.
Write blocker	A device that allows read-only access to all accessible data on a drive, as well as prevents anything from being written to the original drive, which would alter or modify the original evidence.
Zeus Trojan	A form of malware that targets Microsoft Windows systems and is often sent through spam messages and phishing campaigns.

Index